Also in the Variorum Collected Studies Series:

R.B. SERJEANT
Customary Lawand Shari'ah Law in Arabian Society

R.B. SERJEANT
Studies in Arabian History and Civilization

R.B SERJEANT
Farmers and Fishermen in Arabia

C.E. BOSWORTH
The Arabs, Byzantium and Iran
Studies in Early Islamic History and Culture

SAMIR KHALIL SAMIR
Foi et culture en Irak au XIe siècle
Elie de Nisibe et l'Islam

GÉRARD TROUPEAU
Etudes sur le Christianisme arabe au Moyen Age

SIDNEY H. GRIFFITH
Arabic Christianity in the Monasteries of 9th-Century Palestine

M.J. KISTER
Society and Religion from Jāhiliyya to Islam

WILFERD MADELUNG
Religious and Ethnic Movements in Medieval Islam

FRANZ ROSENTHAL
Muslim Intellectual and Social History

SHAUL SHAKED
From Zorastrian Iran to Islam
Studies in Religious History and Intercultural Contacts

ETAN KOHLBERG
Belief and Law in Imāmī Shī 'ism

AMNON SHILOAH
The Dimension of Music in Islamic and Jewish Culture

COLLECTED STUDIES SERIES

Society and Trade in South Arabia

Professor R.B. Serjeant

R. B. Serjeant

Society and Trade in South Arabia

Edited by G. Rex Smith

VARIORUM
1996

Published by VARIORUM
Ashgate Publishing Limited
Gower House, Croft Road,
Aldershot, Hampshire GU11 3HR
Great Britain

Ashgate Publishing Company
Old Post Road,
Brookfield, Vermont 05036
USA

ISBN 0–86078–603–X

British Library CIP Data
Serjeant, R.B. (Robert Bertram).
Society and Trade in South Arabia.
(Variorum Collected Studies Series; CS552).
1. Arabia, Southern–History. 2. Arabia, Southern–Social conditions.
3. Arabia, Southern–Commerce.
I. Title. II. Smith, G.R. (Gerald Rex), 1938– .
953'. 05

US Library of Congress CIP Data
Smith, G. Rex (Gerald Rex).
Society and Trade in South Arabia/ R.B. Serjeant; edited by G. Rex Smith.
p. cm. – (Collected Studies Series; CS552).
Includes index (cloth: alk. paper).
1. Arabia, Southern. I. Smith, G. Rex (Gerald Rex). II. Title.
DS247. A14A37 1996 96–20174
953–dc20 CIP

The paper used in this publication meets the minimum requirements of the American National Standard for Information Sciences – Permanance of Paper for Printed Library Materials, ANSI Z39.48–1984. ∞ ™

Printed by Galliard (Printers) Ltd, Great Yarmouth, Norfolk, Great Britain

COLLECTED STUDIES SERIES C552

CONTENTS

This volume contains xii + 350 pages

PUBLISHER'S NOTE

The articles in this volume, as in all others in the Collected Studies Series, have not been given a new continuous pagination. In order to avoid confusion, and to facilitate their use where these same studies have been referred to elsewhere, the original pagination has been maintained wherever possible.

Each article has been given a Roman number in order of appearance, as listed in the Contents. This number is repeated on each page and is quoted in the index entries.

INTRODUCTION

This volume of articles is dedicated to memory of their author, Professor R.B. Serjeant. After a long, distinguished career as an Arabist, culminating in his appointment as Sir Thomas Adams's Professor of Arabic in the University of Cambridge, he died suddenly in Denhead near St Andrews in April, 1993.

Bob Serjeant was born in 1915 and read Arabic and Hebrew at the University of Edinburgh where he came under the early influence of the late Richard Bell, a Quran scholar of some note. From Edinburgh, he travelled to Trinity College, Cambridge, where, supervised by Professor C.A. Storey, he gained a PhD degree about the time of the outbreak of the Second World War. Though clearly influenced by both, Serjeant always attributed his precision and meticulousness of scholarship to Storey. The years of the War saw Serjeant in the Aden Protectorate, a period which marked the beginning of his major scholarly effort in Arabian Studies, and working back in Britain with the BBC, editing the Arabic Listener. Academic posts at the School of Oriental and African Studies followed with periods of fieldwork in Arabia, mostly southern Arabia. In 1964, he returned to Cambridge where he became Director of the Middle East Centre and in 1970 he was appointed to the Sir Thomas Adams's chair of Arabic which he held until he retired in 1981. He and Marion, his wife, went to Denhead near St Andrews and there Bob Serjeant continued his academic work until his death.

The fruits of his labours were many. A comprehensive Serjeant bibliography can be found to the year 1983 by J.D. Pearson, 'Published works of Robert Bertram Serjeant' in Robin Bidwell and G. Rex Smith (eds.), *Arabian and Islamic Studies* (London & New York 1983), 268–79. This has been updated in *New Arabian Studies* 3 (1995), 69–78, where a 1983–93 supplementary bibliography has appeared. Among the books were *The Portuguese off the South Arabian Coast* (Oxford, 1963), *Ṣanʿāʾ, an Arabian Islamic City* (London, 1983), which he edited with Ronald Lewcock and a great deal of which he wrote himself. Some of his articles have already formed volumes of the Variorum series: thirteen were published as *Studies in Arabian History and Civilisation* (1981), eighteen as *Customary and Shariʿah Law in Arabian Society* (1991), eleven as *Farmers and Fishermen in Arabia* (1995). This present volume of eighteen articles is the fourth.

***

Trade and maritime affairs are the subjects of articles I–IV, before customary law takes over (articles V–VII, VII being right up to date and published posthumously), these topics perhaps reflecting best Serjeant's unique scholarly output. There follow eleven articles less easily pigeon-holed, but all reflecting his enormous range of interest and some of which can be highlighted here: VIII – a new and invaluable, not to say unbiased, account of the history and ideas of the Fāṭimī-Ṭayyibī *daʿwah* and the Bohrah community; IX – a masterly survey of government and society in South Arabia; X – a review article of Dresch's recent study of the Zaydī tribes of the Yemen; XI – a relatively early, though still important, study of quarters and wards in South-West Arabia; XII – a recent study of the unusual (certainly in the Islamic context) sexual practices found in the area; XIII – an important study of recent Zaydī politics accompanies the study of a polemical poem; and XVII – finally, after a long wait, we have here reproduced Serjeant's illuminating account of the coastal population of the island of Socotra, the fieldwork for which was carried out in 1967. Once again in all these articles without exception we are treated to an object lesson in joining together information discovered in the field with the vast array of Arabic literature found in the library.

The articles were written between the years 1958–95. As with *Farmer and Fishermen*, little interference has been necessary on my part and I have added only one or two cross-references and a few observations of my own. Printing and other typographical errors have been corrected. As always in such collections, different house rules in different journals and other publications have resulted in inconsistencies of spelling and may thus have caused some difficulties; I have tried to overcome these difficulties by judicious cross-referencing and other means in the Index.

***

Once again my sincere thanks are due to Mrs Marion Serjeant who has done all in her power to assist in the publication of this collection of her late husband's articles. She and I are both grateful to all those individuals and publishers who have given permission for the inclusion of the articles of this volume. Their names are recorded in detail in the Acknowledgements. We are grateful also to Dr John Smedley and Ruth Peters and to their staff for all the help and advice they have so readily and courteously given us, as well as for all the hard work necessary in putting this volume together. Finally, our thanks are due to my wife, Cerries, who has given enormous help during the preparation of the volume.

G. REX SMITH

Department of Middle Eastern Studies
University of Manchester
March 1996

ACKNOWLEDGEMENTS

Grateful acknowledgement is made to the following persons, editors, publishers, institutions and journals for their kind permission to reprint the articles included in this volume: Denys Lombard and the Ecole des Hautes Etudes en Sciences Sociales, Paris (for articles I & II); Scorpion Publishing Ltd., Essex (III); Rika Gyselen Director of *Res Orientales* (IV); the Secretary General of the Société Jean Bodin (V); Poul Lindegård Hjorth on behalf of The Royal Danish Academy of Sciences and Letters, Copenhagen (VII); Dominique Chevallier on behalf of the Université de Paris-Sorbonne (VIII); E.J. Brill, Leiden (IX); Oxford University Press (X, XV, XVIII); Peter Lang GmbH (XII); Harper Collins, London (XIV); Alan Jones (XVI); Brian Doe and Immel Publishing, London (XVII).

I

Yemeni Merchants and Trade in Yemen 13th-16th Centuries

"Muslims know that Exalted God's elect, His most sincere worshipper, the one entrusted with His revelation, was a member of a merchant house."
(Al-Jāḥiẓ, *In Praise of Merchants*)

"Concerning merchants, the gaining of pence sets up an obstacle between them and manly virtue and interposes a barrier for them from all connected with chivalrous qualities."
(Al-Tawḥīdī, *al-Ṣadāqah wa-'l-ṣadīq*)

Before the steamship era the pattern of trade movement along the south-western Arabian coast, i.e. Ẓafār in the South-East to Jeddah in the North-West, was mainly determined by the monsoons. Shipping from India made its landfalls at Ẓafār, al-Shiḥr, Aden, chief of these ports; it might touch at Mocha, al-Buqʻah or Fāzah, the two ports of Zabīd, and other lesser coastal ports before Jeddah. Western Arabia was intimately linked to the African coast, Zaylaʻ especially, with Mogadisho and the coast even so far South as Sufālah in Mozambique. The pre-Islamic trade cycle, merchants starting at Dūmat al-Jandal (Wādī Sirḥān), moving to the Gulf, Dibā (in the United Arab Emirates), Oman, al-Shiḥr, Aden Ṣanʻā', and ʻUkāẓ in the Hijaz moved with the South-East monsoon. The famous summer and winter journeys of Quraysh, to which the Qur'ān alludes, would have been timed to coincide with the arrival of the India trade fleet in the South—we do not know at which points, or even whether the Quraysh caravan route ran along the Tihāmah coast or by the interior, East of the mountains. Goods travelling such distances overland would surely be light in weight, high in value, to ensure a profit; tribal insecurity or piracy at sea could affect the commercial viability of land or sea routes.

The Yemeni Merchants

Yemeni history in the first two or three Islamic centuries is somewhat obscure. If Abū Makhramah[1] is to be credited, Aden itself was an island from which goods had to be transported in skiffs to al-Maksar —the flat sandy shore of the mainland upon which the waves dash *(kasara)*—where they were met by camels and beasts of burden. Before Islam the Persians had built a bridge there; it was eventually rebuilt by a certain Tilimsānī, but Aden only seems to have begun to flourish again under the Zuray'ids in the 3rd and 4th Centuries H. Earlier, shipping by-passed it, going on to al-Ahwāb and Ghulāfiqah. In the first half of the 6th/12th Century a tariff of port dues *('ushūr)*[2] was drawn up by a Jew of Persian descent, Khalaf al-Nahāwandī. A semi-legendary hagiology[3] tells of a Jew to whom a sultan of the Yemen who is un-named gave control of the monies *(amwāl)* of Aden and he unjustly introduced taxes exacted from the merchants on their monies/properties—*aḥdatha 'l-ḍarā'ib* (text *ḍ rāb*) *min al-tujjār bi-amwā li-him*—, so Sufyān b. 'Abdullāh, a Ṣufī, for this and other reasons murdered him. Adjustments were of course made to the tariff under new rulers from time to time and that which is set out in the *Mulakhkhaṣ al-fiṭan*[4] (1411-1412) is an interesting comprehensive document.

Yemeni monarchs, whether ruling from the Southern capital Ta'izz, or Ṣan'ā', or other temporary capitals in the North, could only maintain themselves in power by employing the port revenues to defray the costs of supporting armies and the civil service, and to subsidise tribes, especially in the North. Ḥaḍramawt, conquered once by the Rasūlids and some centuries later by the Zaydīs, soon threw off the control which Yemeni monarchs found it too costly and impractical to continue, but the ports al-Shiḥr, Ẓafār, and more recently al-Mukallā, though ruled by local tribal sultans, could be overlorded by a strong power in Aden with command of the sea. So al-Shiḥr and Ẓafār had perforce to pay tax to the Rasūlids. The commercial capital of the Wādī Ḥaḍramawt is Shibām.

Since the Aden port dues (1 470 000 *dīnārs* in 1411)[5] were vitally important to the Rasūlids they were careful to protect merchants and keep on amicable even respectful terms with them—though their officials often treated traders with some severity and extorted extra dues from them. Their predecessors, the Ayyūbids, on the contrary seem to have forced the merchants to make them payments. The conduct of al-Malik al-Mas'ūd[6] when departing for Egypt in 625 or 626 H. was outrageously unscrupulous. He issued a proclamation in all the *bandars* that any merchants wishing to travel with him to Egypt should join him. From all quarters many came with their goods to meet him at Aden where he proposed they sell him their goods to avoid the tithes/customs *('ushūr)*. This they did and, after receiving them, "he wrote down the prices of the goods to the Yemen and gave them credit notes on others *(aḥāla la-hum ḥawālāt)* on all parts". They were loud in their protestations but he paid no attention and most of them received nothing.

Yet it was the Ayyūbid Ṭughtakīn who was persuaded to set galleys *(shawānī)* lying at Aden to protect merchant shipping against pirates, by way of legalizing the *ʿushūr* exacted from them.[7] These were at first 10% of the receipts from this taxation, but later al-Malik al-Masʿūd made the *shawānī*, galley tax, additional to the *ʿushūr*, and so this tax figures in the *Mulakhkhaṣ al-fiṭan* (1411-1412). The galleys were stationed at the "head of the landfalls (reading *al-manādikh*)".[8] I am persuaded however that even in those days a system of convoy would have been in existence, on the lines of the *sanjarah* (Persian *zinjīr*) which I have described elsewhere,[9] intended to protect vessels against ill weather as well as pirates.

In much of the territory of Southern Arabia, particularly when the central government was weak, caravans would have had to travel under tribal protection, paying *siyārah/khafārah* levies for the privilege, though such classes as Sayyids and lords of *ḥawṭahs* would usually, though not invariably, be exempt from such dues. The sources seem to show that under the Rasūlids Manṣabs of the Mashāyikh class would be exempt from certain forms of taxation. In the Yemen, in the Zaydī North in particular, I have often come across *samsarahs* built to accommodate travellers, consisting most often of a square court surrounded by individual chambers. In Ṣanʿāʾ the *samsarahs* are many; we have described and planned them in *Ṣanʿāʾ : an Arabian Islamic City*. Ibn Rustah,[10] in the latter half of the 3rd/9th Century H., calls them *khāns*.

The *khān*, *qayṣariyyah* and other terms, in the view of André Raymond[11] are more or less synonymous. The earliest epigraphic evidence for the *khān* being 612/1213, and for the *qayṣariyyah* 594/1198, according to his statement. The *samsarah* seems a purely Yemeni word, replacing *khān*, possibly no older than the first Ottoman occupation of the Yemen. Between 571-579/1175-1183 the Ayyūbid *nāʾib* of Aden, ʿUthmān b. ʿAlī al-Zinjīlī, a Damascene, constructed the well-known harbour *(furḍah)* in which he built a *qayṣariyyah*, markets, and shops *(dakākīn)*. Under the Banū Ayyūb dynasty many people settled there to form a community *(jamāʿah)*, coming from all sides.[12] In this context Abū Makhramah stated that Ibn al-Zinjīlī "has a mosque in Aden and made a *waqf* to it the *khān* which is in Aden". A freed slave, Jawhar al-Ṣūfī,[13] was a cloth dealer *(bazzāz)* in the *khān* of Aden with a well-known shop *(dukkān)*—those who dealt with it prospered!

Perhaps Jawhar traded with Abyssinia for he died there in 590/1194. The Ayyūbid, Ṭughtakīn, who followed al-Zinjīlī, made a new "block of houses", all of which was shops at al-Bāb and al-Qufl (Bāb al-Qufl?) for the *ʿaṭṭārūn* (in Ṣanʿāʾ[14] today rather more than simply "perfumers"), a new *qayṣāriyyah.*[15] "Ṭughtakīn built for the *'aṭṭārūn* a new *qayṣāriyyah*, all of it shops, with a gate *(bāb)* locked at night." It was rebuilt in the reign and in the name of al-Malik al-Mas'ūd.

At Zabīd, al-Mujāhid (721-764/1321-1362) founded *al-khān al-mujāhidī al-jadīd.*[16] It seems to have had its share of troubles—in 795-796/1392-1393 fire reached the *khān* of Zabīd and their Sūq al-Ma'āṣir (Oil-Press Market).[17] The *Qurrat al-'Uyūn*[18] records that in 843/1439 the Qurashiyyūn (of Wādī Rima') attacked the village al-Mimlāḥ (the Salt Market) beyond *(fī ẓāhir)* Zabīd and plundered the Qayṣariyyah.

This latter must have been on the coast for Zabīd itself is some miles inland. It is probably not to be identified with the *khān* of Zabīd, for in 890/1485 earthquakes made people leave the Zabīd Sūq al-Khān in such haste that they went out barefoot without their shoulder-cloths *(ardiyah).*[19] Ibn al-Dayba' alludes[20] to the shops *(dakākīn)* of the Ibn al-Wajīh in the 9th/15th Century. I think they must be the forbears of the wealthy Wajīh merchant family of Zabīd today, several of whom I know personally; I even have an old ledger in Arabic showing their transactions with local people.

It was probably the *qayṣāriyyah* at al-Mimlāḥ that figures in a *fatwā* delivered by the Yemeni *faqīh* Ibn Ja'mān[21] (d. 1034/1624-25) who flourished during the Ottoman occupation: "*Question* about a man who inspects *(yufattish)* al-Qayṣariyyah—the custom of the merchants in Zabīd being that he comes to the baskets *(zanābīl)* and recognizes their owners and he allows the testimony of witnesses to them (the baskets: *yumḍī 'alay-hā shahādat al-shuhūd*) and gives each one of the merchants an official note *(tadhkirah)*; then the inspector goes out to al-Zaydiyyah (North of Zabīd in the Tihāmah) and takes the 'official note' from them. Now were the 'official note' of one of the merchants to go missing and the inspector were to demand it and were he (the merchant) to tell him it had gone missing, but he would not accept (this) from him and withholds a basket of silk *(ḥarīr)* from him, only releasing it in return for about seventy *kabīrs*[22] *(dirhams)* for himself—and were the merchant to prove this against him and that this had not been a custom *('ādah)*, should he return him the seventy *kabīrs* or not? *Response:* Yes. He will make a claim against the inspector for restitution of the money he paid him, as on the written side." The last phrase seems to indicate that the *muftī* simply endorsed the petitioner's question on the back of the sheet. Although the text makes no reference to a tax or duty payable by the merchant the very presence of the inspector implies that he was there to collect some sort of customs or market tax.

Of the organisation of the ports of Aden and al-Shiḥr I have already written.[23] The arrival and departure dates of vessels from various quarters were well-known and recorded in almanacs; though these are of uncertain date they were obviously used in the Rasūlid era.

Arrivals of the Mogadishan, Ẓafārī, Egyptian, Indian, Qaysī, Hurmuzī, B. Kāriyyah (whoever they were), al-Kārim, Barbarī, Qalhātī, Ceylonese, Somali, are all given according to the Rūmī months, as are their departures. Vessels arriving at the port of Aden produced a manifest and list of merchants written out by the clerk *(karrānī)* on the vessel. This was taken to the governor. Merchants landing brought their baggage with them and three days later the goods *(qumāsh)* and merchandise were landed and examined bale by bale and cloth by cloth *(thawb)*. Ibn al-Mujāwir[24] speaks of the agonies undergone by merchants when their goods were watched and examined. Passengers were also subjected to a strict body search, even women being searched by women employed for this purpose.

As Ibn Faḍl Allāh al-ʿUmarī[25] says of Aden: "The bulk of its wealth is from the waves of merchants arriving from India, Egypt and Abyssinia." During the Rasūlid period the revenues of Aden were taken with great panache and a heavy escort up to their capital Taʿizz four times a year, often accompanied by some of the notable merchants.[26] In 817/1414, to take a case in point, the treasure chest *(al-khizānah al-saʿīdah)* arrived from Aden accompanied by the Mashāyikh, the secretaries, and notables of the merchants *(aʿyān al-tujjār)* with gold, silver and commodities valued at more than ten lacs. Again in 834/1431[27] the chest was accompanied by the chief minister and a group of merchants and ships' captains *(nawākhīdh)* who brought a present to the sultan. The chest included an interesting list of commodities, among which were Egyptian, Shīrāzī, Iraqi cloth and china-ware; this chest was valued at 5 lacs.[28]

When the Rasūlid sultans in their turn visited Aden they paid considerable attention to the merchant group. When sultan al-Mu'ayyad succeeded in taking Aden which he had been besieging, the governor, the inspector *(nāẓir)*, this latter an important official concerned with the port and its revenues, the notables of the town and the principal merchants *(ṣudūr al-tujjār)* came out to meet him,[29] and again at his visit in 698/1299 "the merchants resident in the port *(thaghr)* presented precious gifts *(taqādīm)* according to the customs (with) kings and the sultan returned them and gave orders for the bestowal upon them of robes of honour *(khilaʿ, tashārīf)* and mounts —select mules complete with harness, gilded saddles and horse-cloths *(zanānīr)* of several colours. He (also) assigned (allowances?) to the ships' captains of India *(nawākhīdh al-Hind)* according to their custom. He commanded that the ships' captains and the merchants who ply to and fro to the preserved port (Aden) be entertained, and he commanded that the farming of the House of Vinegar *(ḍamān Bayt al-Khall)* be abolished. Through his bounty he established a (trading) season *(mawsim)* of justice. He attended the horse season *(mawsim al-khayl)* from al-Ṭawīlah Gate. So the ships' captains and Kārimiyyah merchants went off spreading the banner of his justice in their countries *(amṣār).*"[30] The historians not infrequently refer to actions of the sultans taken to abolish dues arbitrarily imposed by their officials. The "House of Vinegar" must, I think, be a euphemism for the making of wine or other spirituous liquors. The export of horses from Arabia to India is noted in the *Mulakhkhaṣ al-fiṭan*[31] and other Arabic sources. At an earlier period when sultan al-Muẓaffar visited Aden he questioned the merchants about the *qāḍī* (al-Junayd) and when they praised him the sultan increased his stipend.[32] It does appear therefore that merchants were consulted or at least heard in certain matters of policy.

In the year 816/1413-14 it is recorded that a certain *qāḍī*, Mufliḥ al-Turkī, arrived in the Yemen with property which the Sharīf of Mecca had taken from the Yemeni *qāḍī* Wajīh al-Dīn.[33] He was accompanied by merchants and all were well received by the sultan who excused these merchants payment of *'ushūr* that year. "The sultan commanded those in control of the *bandars* and coasts to extend justice and benevolence *(rifq)* to all merchants and retailers *(mutasabbibūn).*"

References to "the notables of the merchants" *(a'yān al-tujjār)* are fairly common, they being distinct from the retailers and *mudakkins*, and of greatly superior standing. Even in Najāḥid times for example, when the inhabitants of Zabīd came out to greet the Qā'id Surūr, the merchants were next in order of precedence to the ulema of the three schools, the Qā'id dismounting to greet the ulema although he did not extend this courtesy to the merchants![34] Abū Makhramah[35] alludes to a certain Idrīs al-Sarrāj as a notable of the merchants (early 7th/13th Century) and in the following century al-Sakhāwī[36] speaks of a notable, Ibn 'Afīf, at Aden, as moving to Jeddah. Merchants organized themselves, whether formally or informally, under a headman—the *mashāyikh al-tujjār* of Wuṣāb—in 827/1424, after a rebellion, came to seek the sultan's protection and were well received.[37] There died, in 706/1306, a certain Ahmad al-Ṣa'dī al-'Adanī, chief of the Yemen merchants *(ra'īs tujjār al-Yaman)*[38] at the early age of twenty-five—al-Maqrīzī met him in Cairo. Was the post perhaps then hereditary? This person enjoyed much respect and influence *(tamakkun)* with sultan al-Ashraf Ismā'īl. In the first half of the 9th/15th Century, Mūsā b. 'Alī...al-Ṣan'ānī al-'Adanī followed his father's footsteps in the office of headship *(waẓīfat riyāsah)* of the merchants and al-Matjar al-Sulṭānī, the sultan's trading establishment.[39]

It was the Fāṭimids in Cairo who first instituted this state trading organization,[40] but the earliest evidence for its existence in the Yemen so far known to me is when al-Malik al-Ashraf Ismā'īl commanded the building of the Zabīd *matjar* in Rabī' I 798/December-January 1395-96.[41] Strangely this *matjar* does not figure in the *Mulakhkhaṣ al-fiṭan* compiled only some years later, though it provides a complete list of officials at the Aden *matjar*. The latter might even have been founded in the reign of al-Mujāhid (about mid-8th/14th Century) who is credited by the author of the *Mulakhkhaṣ* with a larger administrative establishment than in his own day. Perhaps the vessel of al-Ashraf at al-Ahwāb in 790/1388 may have been attached to the *matjar*, perhaps not.[42]

Ibn Ḥaddād of Taʿizz who in the early 9th/15th Century used to travel to and fro to Mecca for trading, once went there on behalf of sultan al-Nāṣir al-Ashraf—who then changed and turned against him—this merchant may have been an employee of the *matjar*.[43] An obviously unsatisfactory official was al-Tawrīzī, called al-Qāhirī al-Tājir, born in Gīlān, who came from Mecca to Aden and was put in authority *(taḥadduth)* over al-Matjar al-Sulṭānī, but returned, dismissed, to Mecca whence he went to Cairo but left it in 824/1421 because of debts he owed there.[44] An Arab in 835/1431, a native of the South, the qāḍī Nūr al-Dīn al-Ḥimyarī, took over permanent charge of what are described as the two *wakālahs*, al-Matjar and al-Sāḥil (lit. the Coast).[45] I am inclined to understand *wakālah* here in its Egyptian sense of warehouse, hostelry, inn, since the *Mulakhkhaṣ* alludes only to an *ʿāmil* of the Matjar and the Bāb al-Sāḥil.

Next in the official hierarchy to the governor in Aden was the *nāẓir*, inspector (there was also a *nāẓir* in Zabīd) who dealt with administrative matters at the port which would include the customs among other duties. Foreigners, if men of ability, readily found employment in the administration of the port and its revenues. A case in point is that of a Persian[46] recommended by the merchant body because of his skill in *kitābah*—secretaryship, more than mere clerking. He was appointed in charge of the Dīwān al-Naẓar. He used every day to maintain an open table *(simāṭ)* attended by the merchants and *fuqarāʾ* (here meaning men of religion). He turned out to be oppressive in his handling of the inspectorate, so people complained to the sultan. He was tortured and thirty thousand *dīnārs* wrung out of him, then he was beaten again and this resulted in his death after the year 660/1262. An Egyptian merchant, al-Khuṭabāʾ, was known to Abū Makhramah[47] as having settled in Aden; another of the Egyptian merchants was appointed *nāẓir* in the reign of al-Afḍal (last quarter of the 8th/14th Century). A Yemeni, Ibn Hilīs, from al-Mahjam (one of the Rasūlid mint cities of which today only a single tower remains), one of the notable merchants, was appointed to the Aden inspectorate (d. 802/1400).[48] A Yemeni also, a Shāfiʿī from near al-Ḥajar, was established by the Ṭāhirid sultan ʿAlī b. Ṭāhir in the inspectorate of Aden port "as his agent *(bi-ḥukm al-wakālah)*" and also over its dependencies *(aʿmāl)*; for a short time he was also inspector of the *waqf* of Taʿizz (third quarter 9th/15th Century).[49]

At this point may be mentioned the appointment during the first Ottoman occupation of an Ahdalī Sayyid to be head of al-Ḥudaydah *(riyāsat al-Ḥudaydah)*.[50] I am ignorant of what his function there was, but the Ahādilah/Mahādilah, of al-Marāwiʿah, played an important part in the Tihāmah and East Africa and I seem to recall that they were active as merchants. In this paper I do not attempt to cover the Ottoman period, but for the merchant community the significant change they effected was by their exactions at Aden to divert most shipping to the port of Mocha.[51]

* Discussing Aden's multi-racial population round about 1500, Abū Makhramah's description[52] has it that "most of the inhabitants of the town are a conglomeration from Alexandria, Cairo (Miṣr) and the countryside [of South Arabia?], Africans, *('Ajam)*, Persians, Ḥaḍramīs, Mogadishans, Jibālīs (?),[53] the people of Dhubḥān (modern Ḥujariyyah), Zaylaʿīs, Barābir (my reading, probably the modern Somali coast), Abyssinians, and they have assimilated to them from every land and place and become wealthy and prosperous". But he adds that the majority are Abyssinians and Barābir. Elsewhere[54] he speaks of Syrians and North Africans (Sha'miyyūn wa-Maghāribah) in Aden. In my own time Syrians used to sell cloth in Aden's Sūq al-Zaʿfarān. Presumably the races Abū Makhramah mentions were Muslims, for he does not include either the Jewish community or the Bāniyāns. In passing[55] he alludes to three wells in Aden owned by Dāwūd b. Maḍmūn al-Yahūdī, probably a son of Goitein's Maḍmūn.[56]

This paper cannot include a discussion of Jewish merchants in Southern Arabia, in part because this has been already done in *Ṣanʿā'* and my *Portuguese*, in part because Goitein's *A Mediterranean Society* (I) leaves little scope for any new observations and there are already other studies by Jewish writers in some abundance. Hunter however remarks[57] that they and the Bāniyāns lend out on interest but of course Muslims have their devices for receiving interest without infringing the *sharīʿah*. In fact Hunter's *Account* gives a very full picture of 19th-century commerce in Aden.

The Merchants of the Kārim

The Kārimī merchants have been sufficiently studied for their organisation to be familiar to historians of mediaeval Islam. In the 12th Century, says Goitein,[58] the Kārim does not appear as a company handling goods, but rather as a convoy or group of *nākhudhāhs* or ship-owners in whose ships merchants travelled and goods were transported. In my *Portuguese*[59] I have given some indication as to how a sailing was notified and contracts entered into for the carriage of goods and persons. On board ship Ibn Mājid,[60] towards the end of the 15th Century, lays down a code for conduct with merchants. "The pilot should listen to their complaints, not anger them over regulations but not tolerate disobedience in navigational matters. He should not complain of one man before another or wrong one on behalf of another and so on. Most important of all, he should size them up as soon as

* The description of Aden is rather that of Ibn al-Mujāwir than of Abū Makhramah. It is therefore the Aden of the early 7th/13th century.

possible, preferably before the ship sails. If he knows what to expect of them at the beginning, it will make things easier in the midst of a storm when his time is taken up with other things."

Goitein is of the opinion[61] that the overwhelming importance reached by the Kārim by Ayyūbid and Mamlūk times may have had its roots in the Fāṭimid period, and the Fāṭimid navy stationed at ʿAydhāb provided powerful protection against piracy which according to his Genizah documents was rampant. "Maḍmūn the representative of the merchants in Aden (not al-Kārim only)... had agreements with 'the rulers of the seas and deserts', in order to protect ships and caravans owned or supervised by him."

The first Kārimī merchant so far known to me from Arabic sources to have come to the Yemen was a certain ʿAbdullāh al-Umawī al-ʿUthmānī, an Alexandrian, a cloth merchant, *al-tājir al-bazzāz al-Kārimī*, also a transmitter of Islamic Tradition *(ḥadīth)*, a man with a religious inclination or interest, like so many other merchants. He was active about the latter half of the 11th Century.[62] At this time merchants, the Kārimīs included, seem to have been far less influential than they later became, to judge at least by the high-handed treatment they received from the first Rasūlid sultan, when he visited Aden in 624/1227, at the time when madder was being purchased for export to India near the change in monsoon, and forced everyone to buy it at an enormously inflated price. The next year he impounded all the pepper at a price doubtless set by himself and made a forced sale of it to the Ahl al-Kārim at a profit of 50%— likewise he took brass *(ṣufr)* from the Kārimīs and sold it to others at a profit of 33 1/3rd %. He went even further, insisting that when he bought he received a *buhār* (usually 300 lbs.) and a quarter but when he sold he gave a *buhār* less a quarter, each being reckoned a full *buhār*.[63] The steelyard *(qabbān)* was farmed out at twenty thousand *dīnārs* per annum, an enormously inflated figure, which of course the weigh-man had to recover, undoubtedly by dishonest means, from his clients. Additionally goods coming to the port had to pay tithes, *shawānī* (galley-tax), Dār al-Wakālah, Dār al-Zakāt, and brokerage *(dilālah)*.

Another case of 'squeeze' of the wealthy merchant is recorded by al-Khazrajī[64] towards the end of the 7th/13th Century. A magnate of the China trade, ʿAbd al-ʿAzīz b. Manṣūr al-Kūlamī (of Quilon?) al-Kārimī, who had been born in Aleppo, whence he migrated to Baghdad then crossed to India via the islands of Kīsh and Hurmuz and reached China, entered and left that country five times. Then he returned from India to Aden and the Lord of the Yemen in 703/1303-4 took a quantity of his property, of Chinese *objets de vertu* and china-ware which he had brought with him—going beyond the established limits with him; he also had silk, musk and jade vessels inlaid with gold. Not unnaturally the magnate went off to Egypt the following year.

Perhaps however the case was out of the ordinary to judge by a

Meccan Sharīf quoted by al-Qalqashandī[65] who averred that the Imām of the Zaydiyyah at Ṣanʻā' and the then Zaydī Ashrāf of Mecca were cautious of the (Rasūlid) Lord of the Yemen because of his wheedling of those Kārimis arriving *(wāṣil al-Kārimī)* (at Aden) and the customs of making gifts *(rusūm al-inʻām)*, the latter presumably meaning gifts to the Holy Cities. This statement was made about the first half of the 8th/11th Century and it may have been true that concessions were made to the Kārimīs about this time, for the *Mulakhkhaṣ al-fiṭan*, compiled in 1411-1412, but embodying earlier practice also, registers that the rebate of the Kārimīs *(ḥaṭīṭ al-Kārim)*[66] on pepper was 20 *raṭls* or pounds in the *faṣlah* (?) of 420 pounds, presumably meaning that nothing was charged on this quantity. Brazilwood *(buqqam)* and *maḥlab* (kernel of the wild cherry) also attracted a rebate.

The career of another Kārimī merchant, Nūr al-Dīn al-Fāriqī,[67] is dramatic in his rise and fall. He came from Egypt to the Yemen in the reign of al-Mujāhid with whom he found favour, receiving promotion in the Sultanic services little by little until he reached the office of *mushidd* of the Dīwāns, the ministries as one would say today. He was beloved by the *raʻiyyah* but hated by the *nā'ibs* and secretaries of the Government because of his scrupulously careful auditing—nor did the sultan's mamlūks *(ghilmān)* and those who consumed the property of the *Dīwān* like him either. So they spoke to the sultan, telling him what was true and what was not true about him, and al-Mujāhid ordered him to be arrested. Al-Fāriqī fled to Zabīd then Bayt al-Faqīh to take sanctuary at the shrine there[68]—which seemed to the sultan to confirm what his enemies said. He was arrested and died under torture in 747/1347. Abū Makhramah comments: "It appears he came from Egypt to Aden because the merchants of al-Kārim come to Aden only." This is probably to be understood as meaning they did not touch at other ports.[69] It was this sultan, al-Mujāhid, who was taken prisoner by the Egyptian at the *ḥajj* in 751/1351 and sent to Cairo, but eventually got back to the Yemen—his mother was in touch with him through certain Kārimī merchants and thus able to supply him with money.

In 770/1368-9 we hear of the Rasūlid al-Afḍal at Dumluwah fortress with the treasure-chest *(khizānah)* from Aden and presents from the merchants of al-Kārim.[70] Again in 776/1375—it would be a little after the end of the South-East monsoon—al-Afḍal came to Aden "and dispensed unaccustomed justice and made an investiture of the *nākhudhāhs*, abolishing also much of what the government officials *(ʻummāl)* had innovated—and the merchants began to tell to every part on land or sea of his good conduct and his great liberality".[71] The innovations are of course new taxes—the type of illegal imposts that unscrupulous governors would introduce may be seen in the list of those abolished by the great Zaydī Imām al-Mutawakkil some three centuries later, of whom al-Muḥibbī[72] remarks: "From every town *(balad)* over which he gained control he lifted the *mukūs* (market-taxes, customs, etc.) and extortions/injustices *(maẓālim)*,'' but, he comments cynically: ''When he ordered injustices to be lifted (abolished) and sent someone to see about this, they would outwardly obey his order, but when his commissioner *(ma'mūr)* had left, they would go back to the very injustice they had been practising.''

Two Kārimī merchants with the name al-Maḥallī[73] brought huge presents in Ramaḍān 789/1387 and Ramaḍān 790/1388 for the sultan, the latter including, *inter alia*, comestibles, drink, clothing, musk, hunting dogs and birds. Again their arrival would be about the time of the change in monsoons in spring.

Other Kārimīs in Aden about this time were a certain Khiḍr al-Rūmī[74] (d. 820/1417-1418), who went to Mecca and rented a *waqf* there, but returned to Cairo because of vexations he suffered from the Dawlah, an Egyptian, Ibn Hilīs,[75] who arrived in the Yemen in 800/1397-98 and stayed in the Tihāmah centre al-Mahjam but, after nearly forty years, also returned to Egypt. Al-Sakhāwī mentions even a lady known as Sitt al-Tujjār,[76] daughter of an Egyptian Kārimī merchant interested in *ḥadīth*, or Islamic Tradition; she does not appear to have had any known connection with western Arabia. She died in 848/1444. The celebrated pilot, Aḥmad b. Mājid,[77] about the close of the 15th Century speaks of the Kārimī merchants still travelling to India, and he alludes to their old *Rahnāmaj* or pilot-book. Their organisation cannot have survived the Portuguese blockade of the Red Sea.

The Bāniyāns and the Trade with India

Though one would think that Hindu merchants are likely to have been settled in Aden from early times, the earliest reference I have discovered so far is to the *Ḥāfat al-Bāniyān*, the ward or quarter of these Indian traders already established by 786/1384. ''In the commercial sphere Ibn Ja'mān alludes to a man purchasing cloth from the infidel Hindus, al-Bāniyān al-Kuffār, then as now, probably, the principal commodity in which they dealt. There is a case of a man borrowing on interest from a Bāniyān, of a debt owed by a Muslim to a Bāniyān, of a man being imprisoned for a debt to one, and the vexed question of the Bāniyān's oath in a debt case where a Muslim is involved.''[78]

They became engaged in the coffee trade and with tobacco but probably mainly through Mocha. When La Roque arrived at Aden the principal Bāniyāns who are the ''Brokers of Arabia'' came to pay him a visit and offer their services. Their headman he calls ''the Captain of the Banyans'' and adds that it is by their assistance that all the trade in Arabia is managed. La Roque noted that the Arabs much dislike the Bāniyāns, but in the century previous to his visit the Zaydī prince al-

Ṣafiyy acted with them in the same way as the Rasūlid monarchs had done with the foreign merchants coming into the port.[79]

The important issue of security for the Indian shipping using Yemeni ports may be appreciated from measures taken by al-Ṣafiyy subsequent to Hubert Hugo's assault in 1078/1662 on vessels at Mocha as recounted in my *Portuguese*[80]. In this the Omanis were not involved.

"When al-Ṣafiyy arrived in Aden the merchants of India came to him and he treated them with friendliness, giving them places of honour and precious gifts. During the two months he stayed in Aden two vessels put in there, one called al-Sawākinjī (margin: Kunḥ sawā ī), and the other al-Markab al-Ṣāḥibī, i.e. the Queen of Bijapur, Baṛī Ṣāḥibah's vessel. These were the largest that ever put in to Aden—each with a cargo of four hundred bales *(bandalah)* and one thousand and five hundred persons. So large was each bale that the Gate of the Harbour (Bāb al-Furḍah) was not wide enough to admit its passage and they could only be brought in by the Coast Gate (Bāb al-Sāḥil). The Indians prepared a feast for Ṣafiyy al-Islām and his entourage the like of which they had never experienced, but on discovering to their dismay that it was prepared by the Bāniyāns, the Barāhimah, they vomited it up! When the ʿĪd arrived Ṣafiyy gave a splendid and varied banquet to his chiefs, to which the notables of the Indians were also invited. He inspected the port *(al-bandar al-saʿīd)* and found much of it in poor state, so he collected builders *(ʿammār)* from Yāfiʿ, the Yemen and Ṣanʿāʾ, and rebuilt the walls. When this was completed he sent for the chief men of the Indians to whom he made presents, "for each *nākhūdhah* a horse, and he wrote to the sultan, the Lord of India, and sent one of his men along with them with five noble Arab horses, and their trappings, gear ornamented with silver, and a gift similar to this to the ministers. Then he sent to the Lord of Barr al-ʿAjam (the African coast), the Lord of Ẓafār, the Amharī and the Lord of Ḥaḍramawt, and established regulations *(qawāʿid)* for the people of those countries to which they assented, and (confirmed?) demands which they named."

In Aden at the British conquest the six hundred inhabitants included two hundred and fifty Jews and fifty Bāniyāns; they took refuge in the mosque with a flag of truce flying. A Hindu place of worship in Crater is mentioned; so, in practice, there was a large measure of tolerance of them by the Arab community.[81]

In Zaydī Yemen there were Bāniyāns in Shahārah; in the 18th Century they had a *khān* at Bīr al-ʿAzab, the suburb of Ṣanʿāʾ and in Ṣanʿāʾ itself they appear to have been numerous. Because of the security on land and at sea during the reign of the Zaydī Imām al-Mutawakkil Ismāʿīl it was rare for a town or market not to have some Bāniyāns, and people not only traded with them but would borrow from them. They incurred the enmity of the Yemeni merchants by their success in business and they tried to have their activities curbed. The

Imām protected the Bāniyāns but eventually he issued an order that they should pay poll-tax of a *qirsh* per mensem. They had been many thousands in the Yemen, but some refused to submit to this and returned to India. The fanatical Sayyid al-Maḥaṭwarī at the end of the 17th Century massacred many Bāniyāns and Jews or forcibly circumcized them, but was himself suppressed and Yemeni society would certainly not have approved of his actions. A *khān* of the Bāniyān in Ibb was sacked by Yāfiʻī tribesmen at the beginning of the 18th Century when they raided the city. Their numbers in Ṣanʻā' dropped to about three during the anarchy of the 19th Century, but the Yemen still had many Bāniyāns till World War I after which their numbers diminished. However Crown Prince Aḥmad, during his journey to the Tihāmah in the days of his father Imām Yaḥyā, encountered many Bāniyāns and Bohrah in Hodeidah.

The Bāniyāns were obviously a closed community, returning to India when they wished to marry, and little is known of how they conducted their business, but John Jourdain writes[82] that in 1609 "the trade of this cittye (Ṣanʻā') is cheiflie with the Benaianes of Guzaratt... (who) lye here as factours for the Banians of Aden, Moucha, Zida, to whom they yield there accompts: for in each of those places before mentioned there is one cheife Banane as Consull or such like, which doth all the buysines in each place."

In the second half of the 11th/17th Century al-Jarmūzī reckoned that at the Ḥaḍramī port al-Shiḥr, or along its coast, there were about three hundred Bāniyāns, *Barāhimah*, and he speaks of a tax on Bāniyāns at al-Shiḥr. The jurist Bin Jaʻmān reports a *fatwā* on a case where a man has deposited a trust *(amānah)*, perhaps some object (?) with a Bāniyān and takes a piece of merchandise in its place. A curious custom was that if a Bāniyān went bankrupt he would light lamps in daytime and his creditors would come and divide out such assets as he had.[83]

In the heyday of the Rasūlid sultans merchants would arrive from various Indian ports bringing with them gifts; sometimes these were from Indian rulers. The gifts were on occasion of interest in themselves, e.g. when rare plants were sent for the sultanic gardens, but were naturally intended to keep the sultan sweet. Calicut (Kālīqūṭ) is chronicled as the source of a present on several occasions, but, in 776/1374-75, a letter came with the *qāḍī* of Calicut to al-Malik al-Ashraf from the merchants resident there—some of their names reveal their diverse countries of origin (Ghassānī, Ardabīlī, Rūmī)—seeking his consent to make the address *(khuṭbah)* at the Friday prayer in his name—the form of acknowledgement of sovereignty in Islam. This body of noble merchants declared they had not introduced the name of any monarch of the Yemen or Egypt into the address, though the Lord of Delhi and the Lord of Hurmuz had, at an earlier time, gained control over them so they had made the address in both of their names together. The sultan accepted their submission, sending them gifts and making a royal investiture. The motive of the merchants was to gain prestige with others, but the incident is curious.[84]

Relations with Calicut come to the fore again in 836/1433 when the *nākhūdhah* Kirwah—the name looks foreign—accompanied the treasure-chest *(khizānah)* up to the sultan in Ta'izz. It looks as if he had gone to complain of the Aden officials at the port, for the high ordinance *(al-marsūm al-'ālī)* was issued commanding that the *'ushūr* only should be taken from the Calicut merchants, and the sultan also relaxed the regulations *(qawā'id)*, these doubtless also involving dues and taxes. He made an investiture of the *nākhūdhah* and absolved him of some of the *'ushūr*.[85] This naturally made an excellent impression of his leniency and justice on the merchants.

Gifts from Bengal *(al-Banjālah)* in 783/1381-82 and 793/1391, and from the Lord of Kanbāyah (Cambay) in 827/1424, mainly textiles, are recorded.[86] A *nākhūdhah*, perhaps an Indian, Nāṣah (?), accompanied this gift to the sultan who was at a fort in the North.

Chinese Naval Expeditions and South Arabia in the 15th Century

Despite the lively traffic in Chinese commodities to the Middle East over many centuries, Chinese shipping rarely seems to have come to the Arabian coasts. That the Chinese did, at times, manifest some interest in events on the Arabian coast is suggested when we find that, after the combined land and naval expedition of the Rasūlid monarch, al-Muẓaffar, who captured Ẓafār in 678/1279-80, gifts arrived from the "Lords of Oman and China".[87] Or could "China" be more of a figure of speech that is not to be taken in a strictly literal sense?

The exploratory naval expeditions of Cheng Ho, grand eunuch of the Ming Emperor between 1405 and 1433, are novel in bringing China into direct contact with the Islamic West; trade and commerce with the countries of the Indian Ocean was obviously of great interest to the expeditions. Aden was visited by the Chinese on the fifth, sixth and seventh expeditions, and La-sa (Laḥsā'/al-Aḥsā)[88] near al-Mukallā, Ẓafār, Hurmuz and the East African ports, as far as Malindi, on some of the voyages. It is curious that al-Shiḥr is not mentioned. The account of Cheng Ho's Muslim interpreter, Ma Huan, has been well studied by J. V. G. Mills[89] but, to the best of my knowledge, Ma Huan's narrative has not been compared with the Arab historians' notices of the Chinese visitors to their shores.

The anonymous Rasūlid chronicler records[90] in 821/1419 "the arrival (January) of the vessels of the junk *(marākib al-z n k)* at the 'protected port' (Aden), accompanied by a messenger from the Lord of

China with a magnificent gift for our Lord the sultan al-Malik al-Nāṣir". The sultan at the time was at al-Janad and, about mid-March 822/1419, "the present of the Lord of China was conducted to him in procession. It was a splendid present consisting of all manner of rareties *(tuḥaf)*, splendid Chinese silk cloth woven with gold *(al-thiyāb al-kamkhāt al-mudhahhabah)*, top quality musk, storax *(al-ʿūd al-raṭb)* and many kinds of china-ware vessels, the present being valued at twenty thousand *mithqāls*." The spelling *z n k* for junk may be compared with Ibn Baṭūṭah's *j n k* (plur., *junūk*).[91] This is the fifth Chinese expedition; it also went to Mogadisho, Brava and Malindi.[92]

Ibn al-Daybaʿ[93] and other historians report a visit of the envoy *(qāṣid)* of the Lord of China to the sultan (probably at Zabīd) in 823/1420; he came with three great vessels containing precious gifts, the value of which was twenty lacs of gold. "He had an audience with al-Malik al-Nāṣir without kissing the ground in front of him, and said: 'Your Master (Sayyid) the Lord of China greets you and counsels you to act justly to your subjects.' And he (al-Malik al-Nāṣir) said to him: '*Marḥaban*, and how nice of you to have come!' And he entertained him and settled him in the guesthouse. Then al-Nāṣir wrote a letter to the Lord of China: 'Yours it is to command and (my) country is your country.' He despatched to him wild animals and splendid sultanic robes, an abundant quantity, and ordered him to be escorted to the city of Aden." The *Qurrat al-ʿUyūn*[94] comments adversely on the Lord of China's arrogance!

This would tally with the Chinese account[95] of the visit of the eunuch Chou with three treasure-ships. "When the king heard of his arrival, he led his major and minor chiefs to the sea-shore, and welcomed the imperial edict and the bestowal of gifts. At the king's palace they rendered a ceremonial salutation with great reverence and humility." The Chinese were able "to buy" items listed, including leopards, ostriches, lions, zebras and white pigeons. The date however does not tally with that reported by Mills which is 1421.[96]

A brief notice is accorded by the anonymous chronicler[97] to the seventh voyage of Cheng Ho under the year 835/1432. At the end of February "the captain of the junk *(nākhūdhuh al-z n k)*, the servant of the Lord of China, arrived with gifts for our Lord the Sultan... to Lahej and accompanying him arrived our Lord the Chief Minister". The Arabic sources give no indication of any developments resulting from Cheng Ho's expeditions and as Mills concludes: "The Ming court failed to grasp the possibilities of sea-power and lost interest in maritime expansion; so the great expeditions were not followed up."[98]

*

Additional Note
on dallāl, wadīʿah *and* qirāḍ

The *dallāl*, "courtier", plays an essential role at all levels of commerce and trading, but the popular proverb, "the *dallāl* is the dog of the *sūq*," precisely conveys how society regards him. In the Yemen *Qānūn Ṣanʿā'*[99] shows him to be a sort of commission agent and fixes standard fees *(dilālah)* for him. There it is the *muṣliḥ*, literally "conciliator", who acts as dealer or middleman. In Shibām, commercial capital of Wādī Ḥaḍramawt, however, his function is much less sophisticated for there the *dallāl* acts as intermediary for the tribesman, buying and selling on his behalf. From the headman of the Shibām *dallāls* I learned that goodwill in an individual tribe can be bought or sold, but the profession itself is hereditary in certain families. It is a skilled trade for the *dallāl* must know the different weights and measures for each district and keep his wits about him—*dallāls* employ a "cant" language to conceal what they are doing from their clients. In the present century Ḥaḍramī *dallāls* were responsible for seeing that the market tax on a range of items was paid to the Dawlah, the sultanic government.

At Zabīd in the Rasūlid period a *dallāl* is recorded as dealing with the headman *(naqīb)* of the used goods vendors;[100] a *dallāl* in books is an unusual case but Zabīd was also a city of learned men. A Ẓafārī settled in Mecca was a *dallāl* in slaves, and would be either of Yemeni or Ḥaḍramī origin.[101] There were other Yemeni *dallāls* in Mecca perhaps to deal with south Arabians.[102] *Dallāls* were probably organised everywhere in groups like other professions, to judge at least by a *muʿallim* of them at Jeddah, not a Yemeni, a man of humble origin for he had been a *mawlā* of the Nā'ib who had purchased him from the people of the Mint there.[103]

My impression is that *dallāls* rarely rose to high office or position and could not aspire to join the ranks of the *tujjār*. But Goitein states[104] that "a *dallāl* could be a wealthy person, participating with a large sum in an overseas undertaking, or a miserable broker earning a few dirhems a day."

For tribesfolk the *dallāl*, being inferior, can act as a go-between in tribal disputes, and in tribal *manʿah* law the testimony of the tax-collector *(jabbā)*[105] and *tājir* is inadmissible, as indeed is that of any *dhū mihrah daniyyah*, person engaged in what Brunschwig calls "les métiers vils." In the cities however circumstances might presumably demand his testimony be considered. ʿAfīf, the *qāḍī* of Zaylaʿ is cited in the *Fatāwā* collection of Bā Makhramah[106] (mid 10th/16th Century) as asking for an opinion as to whether the testimony of the *dallāl* and *makkās* (collector of octroi, market dues, etc.) is admissible, and who was it of the forbears *(salaf)* who declared their testimony inadmissible?

Bā Makhramah's reply was: "The testimony of the *makkās*, by consensus of the community *(ummah)*, is inadmissible because of his moral depravity. As for the *dallāl*, broking *(dilālah)*, i.e. mediation in buying and selling for example, in itself, does not render testimony inadmissible when it does not detract from the person engaged in it nor impair his honour. Yes indeed, if with it there be combined lying, giving rise to deception of the vendor or purchaser, or fraud and concealment of the statutory *(shar'ī)* defects and suchlike prohibited things—as in this age predominates with many—testimony is rejected thereby."

Ibn Ja'mān replies[107] to the question of the *dallāl*'s testimony on similar lines: it is admissible, provided there is no *shar'ī* witness who attacks it. Another question[108] concerns a *dallāl* whose father stands surety for him to the *kaykhyā* (Turkish *kyahya*) of the *dallāls*, the term clearly corresponding to some such word as *naqīb*, "the standing surety of the *dallāls*, one on behalf of the other, being a well-known matter among them."

There were *dallāls* in all the ports even in our own time—I found one who was of some local importance even in the tiny port of Qalansiyyah on Socotra island. Ibn Baṭūṭah,[109] though he does not use the term *dallāl*, met them in the port of Mogadisho.

In legal literature and indeed in historical narrative in general one comes across references to the *wadī'ah*, the article deposited or left in trust with another person. To go back to the Prophet himself, Ibn Isḥāq/Hishām states[110] that the Prophet ordered 'Alī to remain in Mecca when he made his *hijrah* to Yathrib "to pay back/deliver over, on behalf of the Apostle of God, the *wadā'i'* of the people which were with him, for there was no one in Mecca who had something about which he feared (the loss) but he deposited it with him." The Prophet was known for his trustworthiness *(amānah)*. In the biographical collections of later periods, from time to time, it is noted that a certain man of religion would have deposits placed with him. For example the house of a learned *faqīh* was plundered by Zaydī soldiers in 793/1391—much property belonging to people *(amwāl jammah mūda'ah)* was taken. Many other cases could be quoted.[111]

While the motive of the depositers was primarily to find a safe place for their property, the question arises as to whether the *faqīh* or *'ālim* whom the authorities held in respect and even in fear, received some fee in return. Secondly, when a holy man, or even a merchant without pretensions to sanctity, had large sums deposited with him *in specie* did he make this money work for him by using it as a sort of working capital? I am led to speculate on this issue because in the Samsarah of Muḥammad b. al-Ḥasan in Ṣan'ā' there was, until 1948, a sort of "bank" the *amīn* of which was al-Ḥājj 'Abdullāh b. Sinhūb with whom the tribesman would deposit his money. To the *amīn* a service-fee *(fā'idah)* used to be paid, a known percentage, a quarter *qirsh Faranṣī* in one hundred. When Ṣan'ā' was besieged by Imām Aḥmad's soldiers, some people thought the Samsarah would be spared, but it was looted and some wealthy families lost a great deal of their property there including the wealthy Sinaydār house, a member of which in Ottoman times had been accounted "the greatest of the Ṣan'ā' merchants."[112]

It would be by consultation of the many books on *fatāwā*, i.e. legal opinions on cases brought to a recognised authority on Islamic law, that the practice of merchants could be reconstructed in detail and compared with Goitein's *Economic Foundations*. The literature however does give some indications of how business was transacted. One form was *qirāḍ*, entrusting property to a person to traffic with it on the basis that the profit is divided between the parties and the loss falls upon the property. Abū Makhramah speaks[113] of a *faqīh* of Jiblah who used to enter into this type of contract with persons in easy circumstances there and take their goods to Aden. He was reckoned to be of the people of religion and trust *(al-dīn wa-'l-amānah)* and was active till about 682/1283. Again, in the 7th-8th/13th-14th century he cites an Abyanī,[114] a *qāḍī*, who undertook ventures to India with *qirāḍ* contracts with merchants, and met his death on a voyage to that country.

There are some interesting illustrations of the method of conducting business in Aden in F. M. Hunter's *Account of the British Settlement...*, published in 1877, which *mutatis mutandis* would doubtless also be true of earlier centuries. Ibn Ja'mān has a short section on *wadā'i'*, including what looks like a *qirāḍ* case.

BIBLIOGRAPHY

Abū Bakr b. Aḥmad al-Khaṭīb al-Anṣārī al-Tarīmī (d. 1356 H.), *al-Fatāwā al-nāfi'ah*, ed. Salīm b. Ḥāfiẓ... b. al-Shaykh Abū Bakr b. Salim al-'Alawi, Cairo, 1379/1960.

Abū Makhramah, ed. O. Löfgren, *Texte zur Kenntnis der Stadt Aden im Mittelalter*, Uppsala, 1936-1950.

Goitein, S. D., *Studies in Islamic History and Institutions*, Leiden, 1966.

— *A Mediterranean Society*, I : *Economic Foundations*, Berkeley-Los Angeles, 1967.

Ibn al-Dayba', 'Abd al-Raḥmān b. 'Alī, *Qurrat al-'Uyūn*, ed. Muḥammad b. 'Alī al-Akwa', Cairo, 1391-98/1971/77.

— *Bughyat al-mustafīd fi tārīkh Madīnat Zabīd*, ed. 'Abdullāh al-Ḥabshī, Ṣan'ā', 1979.

Ibn al-Mujāwir, ed. O. Löfgren, *Tārīkh al-Mustabṣir : Descriptio Arabiae Meridionalis*, Uppsala, 1951-1954.

Ibn Ja'mān (Ibrāhīm b. Muḥammad), *Fatāwā*, ms. in writer's possession.

Ingrams, W. H., *Report on the Social, Economic and Political Condition of the Hadhramaut*, H. M. S. Colonial Series 123, London, 1937.

al-Jarmūzī, al-Ḥasan b. al-Muṭahhar, *al-Sīrat al-Mutawakkiliyyah*, photocopy from al-Maktabat al-Sulṭāniyyah, al-Mukallā.

al-Khazrajī, 'Alī b. al-Ḥasan, *al-'Uqūd al-lu'lu'iyyah*, ed. Muḥammad 'Asal, GMS, 2 vol., Leiden-London, 1906-1908. A second edition has been published by Muḥammad al-Akwa'.

al-Muḥibbī, *Khulāṣat al-athar*, Cairo, 1284/1867.

Rabie Hassanein, *The Financial System of Egypt A.H., 564-741/1169-1341*, Oxford, 1972.

Raymond, A., *Artisans et commerçants au Caire au 18e siècle*, Damas, 1974, 2 vol.

al-Sakhāwī, *al-Ḍaw' al-lāmi'*, Cairo, 1353/1934.

Serjeant, R. B., *The Saiyids of Ḥaḍramawt*, London, 1957.

— *The Portuguese off the South Arabian Coast*, Oxford, 1963; reprint Beirut, 1974.

— «Maritime Customary Law off the Arabian Coasts», in : M. Mollat, ed., *Sociétés et Compagnies de commerce en Orient et dans l'Océan Indien*, Actes du VIIIe colloque international d'Histoire Maritime, Paris, 1970, p. 195-207.

— «The Ports of Aden and Shiḥr», in : *Les grandes escales*, Recueil de la Société Jean Bodin, XXXII, Bruxelles, 1974.

— «Notes on Some Business Practices in Aden», in : *Al-Bahit : Festschrift Joseph Henniger*, Studia Instituti Anthropos, Bonn-Fribourg, 1976.

— «South Arabia», in : C. A. O. Niewenhuijze, ed., *Commoners, Climbers and Notables : a Sampler of Studies on Social Life in the Middle East*, Leiden, 1977.

— «Wards and Quarters of Towns in South West Arabia», in : *Storia della città*, VII, Roma, 1978.

— *The Islamic City : Selected Papers from the Colloquium Held in the M E C, Faculty of Oriental Studies, Cambridge*, Paris, 1980, I : *Social Stratification in Arabia.*

— *Studies in Arabian History and Civilisation*, Variorum reprints, London, 1981.

Serjeant, R. B., and R. B. Lewcock, *Ṣan'ā' : an Arabian Islamic City*, London, 1983.

al-Sharjī, *Ṭabaqāt al-khawāṣṣ*, Cairo, 1321/1903.

Wagner, E., «Eine Liste der Heiligen um Harar», *Zeitschrift der Deutschen Morgenländischen Gesellschaft* (Wiesbaden), 123, 1973 (for some South Arabian family names).

Yajima, Hikoichi, *A Chronicle of the Rasūlid Dynasty of the Yemen*, Tokyo, 1974.

NOTES

1. Abū Makhramah, 1936-1950, I, p. 8 sq.
2. *Ibid.*, I, p. 58.
3. al-Sharjī, 1321/1903, p. 56 sq.
4. Text in preparation; see C. Cahen and R. B. Serjeant, «A Fiscal Survey of the Mediaeval Yemen», *Arabica*, 4, 1957, p. 1.
5. *Mulakhkhaṣ al-fiṭan*, f° 17 r.
6. al-Sharjī, 1321/1903, p. 68.
7. Abū Makhramah, 1936-1950, I, p. 61.
8. *al-manādiḥ*, according to Löfgren, which is not a locality. See Serjeant, 1963, p. 192, with variant *manālikh*.
9. Serjeant, 1970, p. 199.
10. Serjeant and Lewcock, 1983, p. 128 b.
11. Raymond, 1974, I, p. 252.
12. Abū Makhramah, 1936-1950, I, p. 10 and II, p. 131.
13. *Ibid.*, II, p. 39. A poet is cited (see I, p. 66) as speaking of al-Khān al-Ḥasan (a proper name perhaps?) in the first half of the 7th/13th Century.
14. Serjeant and Lewcock, 1983, p. 185 a.
15. Abū Makhramah, 1936-1950, I, p. 49 and II, p. 223.
16. al-Khazrajī, 1906-1908, I, p. 363.

17. *Ibid.*, II, p. 2.
18. Ibn al-Daybaʿ, 1979, p. 174.
19. Ibn al-Daybaʿ, 1391-1398/1971-1977, II, p. 137, and 1979, p. 113.
20. *Ibid.*, p. 165.
21. Ibn Jaʿmān (Ibrāhīm b. Muḥammad), *Fatāwā*, ms. in writer's possession. He was a Shāfiʿi mufti.
22. On the *dirham kabīr*, see Serjeant, 1963.
23. Serjeant, 1974.
24. Ibn al-Mujāwir, 1951-1954, p. 139.
25. Ayman Fuʿad Sayyid, *Bāb al-Yaman min kitāb Masālik al-abṣār fi mamālik al-amsār*, Cairo, s.d., p. 49.
26. Cf. Yajima, 1974; see *Khizanah* in index. See also Serjeant and R. Lewcock, 1983, p. 68 a, *passim*.
27. Yajima, 1974, p. 63.
28. *Ibid.*, p. 142.
29. al-Khazrajī, 1906-1908, I, p. 285.
30. *Ibid.*, I, p. 320 sq. About the end of the 6th/12th Century, Abū Makhramah (1936-1950, I, p. 51) records that Sunqur the *atābak*, the *mawlā* of the Ayyūbid, al-Muʿizz Ismaʿil, was so pleased with *nabīdh* made at Aden from the water of the Zaʿfaraḥ well there that this water began to be taken to al Janad, Taʿizz, Ṣanʿa' and Zabid to make *nabīdh*. The same author (II, p. 249) also reports an incident that took place in the time of the Rasūlid al-Muẓaffar, in the latter half of the 7th/13th Century. Near the mosque of a certain *faqīh*, in Aden, were houses in which intoxicants *(muskir)* were made, to the great annoyance of the *faqīh*'s companions. So he ordered them to assemble with sticks and led them to these houses and smashed the containers of the intoxicants. The people of the houses however, as they paid a large amount to the Diwan to be allowed to carry on their work, hastened to the governor and he ordered a body of government *(ghulmān)* to punish the *faqīh* and his companions. In the *Mulakhkhaṣ al-fiṭan* (about the first decade of the 9th/15th Century) a tax on *dādhī* figures — this might well be an euphemism for *nabīdh*, since *dādhī*, hypericum, was infused in it.
31. See note 4.
32. al-Khazrajī, 1906-1908, I, p. 252.
33. Yajima, 1974, p. 90, 102.
34. *ʿUmārah*, in : H. Cassels Kay, *Yaman : its Early Mediaeval History*, London, 1892, p. 120.
35. Abū Makhramah, 1936-1950, I, p. 16, II, p. 22.
36. al-Sakhāwī, 1353/1934, I, p. 367.
37. Yajima, 1974, p. 117.
38. al-Sakhāwī, 1353/1934, II, p. 45.
39. *Ibid.*, X, 183, no. 783. He was skilled in administration and writing *(kitābah)*.
40. Rabie, 1972, p. 92.
41. Ibn al-Daybaʿ, 1979, p. 100.
42. Yajima, 1974, p. 46. The vessel came from Aden with all sorts of rareties and gifts.
43. al-Sakhāwī, 1353/1934, VI, 74, and V, p. 249.
44. *Ibid.*, X, p. 10, no. 14.
45. Yajima, 1974, p. 144. al-Sakhāwī, VI, p. 50, no. 138, speaks of a certain ʿAlī b. Yaḥā al-Ṣaʿdī called Ibn Jumaʿy, of northern Yemeni origin, who was one of the *aʿyān al-tujjār* in the Yemen. The Rasūlid monarch al-Ashraf, before 845/1441, put him in charge of the Matjar at Aden and «deputed to him all its [Aden's] affairs and the Amīr and Nāẓir were under his command. He was beloved by the foreigners/strangers *(ghurabā')* and immoderately good to them and beloved by the (sultan's) subjects *(raʿiyyah)*, a Zaydī by belief, but he used to keep this hidden.» By *gharīb* (pl. *ghurabā'*) non-Adenese merchants are probably meant, not only actual foreigners — cf. Serjeant and Lewcock, 1983, glossary, 578 b.
46. Abū Makhramah, 1936-1950, II, p. 221.

47. *Ibid.*, I, p. 10.
48. al-Sakhāwī, 1353/1934, VI, p. 154, no. 489.
49. *Ibid.*, IV, p. 208, no. 529. I am not quite certain of the meaning of the text here.
50. al-Muḥibbī, 1284/1867, IV, p. 9.
51. R. B. Serjeant, «The Yemeni Coast in 1005/1579 : an Anonymous Note on the Flyleaf of Ibn al-Mujāwir's *Tārīkh al-Mustabṣir*», in : *Arabian Studies*, London-Cambridge, 1985, p. 187-191. See article III below.
52. Abū Makhramah, 1936-1950, I, p. 54.
53. These must presumably be simply «mountain men», not the Jibbālīs of Oman.
54. Abū Makhramah, 1936-1950, I, p. 23.
55. *Ibid.*, I, p. 49.
56. Goitein, 1966, p. 336 and *passim*.
57. F. M. Hunter, *An Account of the British Settlement of Aden in Arabia*, Edinburgh, 1877, p. 36 sq.
58. Goitein, 1966, p. 358.
59. Serjeant, 1963, p. 34 sq.
60. G. R. Tibbetts, *Arab Navigation in the Indian Ocean before the Coming of the Portuguese*, London, 1971, p. 388, p. 61 sq.
61. Goitein, 1966, p. 359.
62. Abū Makhramah, 1936-1950, II, p. 115.
63. *Ibid.*, I, p. 68 sq. The text here is a little faulty — for *al-burr bahār*, read *al-barbahār*, spices, and possibly for *ḥ ff*, Goitein's *khaff*, light baggage. al-Sakhāwī (1353/1934, V, p. 318, no. 1050) notes a Meccan called al-Barbahārī.
64. R. B. Serjeant, «Pottery and Glass Fragments from the Aden Littoral», in : 1981, XI, p. 113.
65. *Ṣubḥ al-aʿshā*, Cairo, 1331-1338/1913-1919, XIII, p. 277.
66. *Ibid.*; cf. f° 26 v. The *faṣlah*, assuming the reading is correct, is unknown to me.
67. Abū Makhramah, 1936-1950, II, p. 137 sq.
68. His intention in fleeing to this small town or large village was to take sanctuary *(tajawwar)* there at the tomb of the celebrated saint Ibn ʿUjayl.
69. S. D. Goitein (1966, p. 358) says : «The [Kārimī] convoy sometimes touched Aden on its way out from India and at other times passed it by.» However, he also observes (p. 349) : «Each ship or convoy had its own port of destination and was labelled accordingly 'the one bound for Broach' or Tana, or Kulam, etc.»
70. Yajima, 1974, p. 31.
71. *Ibid.*, p. 34.
72. al-Muḥibbī, 1284/1867, III, p. 396.
73. al-Khazrajī, II, 1906-1908, p. 193, 198.
74. al-Sakhāwī, III, 1353/1934, p. 78, no. 694.
75. *Ibid.*, XI, p. 19, no. 51.
76. *Ibid.*, XII, p. 16, no. 84.
77. *Instructions nautiques*, ed. G. Ferrand, Paris, 1921-1928, I, p. 60 r, *rahmānaj*. Cf. G. R. Tibbetts, *Arab Navigation in the Indian Ocean before the Coming of the Portuguese*, London, 1971, p. 527.
78. Serjeant, 1963, p. 32-33. See also Serjeant and Lewcock, 1983, p. 432-435.
79. «Omani Naval Activities off the southern Arabian Coast in the late 11th/17th Century Yemeni Chronicles», *Journal of Oman Studies*, Bristol-Muscat, VI, I, 1983, p. 86 b-87 a.
80. Serjeant, 1963, p. 122 sq.
81. J. Kirkman and B. Doe, «The First Days of British Aden», in : *Arabian Studies*, II, 1975, p. 187.
82. Serjeant and Lewcock, 1983, p. 245 b.
83. *Ibid.*, p. 435 a. For comparison see C. H. Allen, «The Indian Merchant Community of Masqat», *Bulletin of the School of Oriental and African Studies*, 44, 1, 1981, p. 39-53.

84. Yajima, 1974, p. 160.
85. *Ibid.*, p. 40.
86. *Ibid.*, p. 117.
87. al-Khazrajī, 1906-1908, I, p. 213.
88. J. V. G. Mills (*Ying-yai Sheng-lan : the Overall Survey of the Ocean's Shores, 1433*, Hakluyt Society extra series, Cambridge, 1970, XLII, p. 347) discusses its location.
89. *Ibid.*, p. 151 sq.
90. Yajima, 1974, p. 105-106.
91. For «junk» in its various spellings, see Hobson-Jobson, *A Glossary of Anglo-Indian Words and Phrases*, London, 1886, p. 472.
92. Mills, 1970, preface, p. 13.
93. Ibn al-Dayba', 1979, p. 164. Cf. Yahyā b. al-Ḥusayn b. al-Qāsim, *Ghāyat al-amānī fi'l-quṭr al-Yamānī*, ed. S. A. F. 'Āshūr et al., Cairo, 1388/1968, II, p. 565.
94. Ibn al-Dayba', 1391-1398/1971-1977, p. 123-124.
95. Mills, 1970, p. 154 sq.
96. *Ibid.*, p. 14.
97. Yajima, 1974, p. 145.
98. Mills, 1970, p. 34.
99. Serjeant and Lewcock, 1983, p. 183 sq.
100. Abū Makhramah, 1936-1950, II, p. 197.
101. al-Sakhāwī, 1353/1934, V, p. 124, no. 440.
102. *Ibid.*, V, p. 70, no. 255.
103. *Ibid.*, III, p. 210, no. 788, and III, p. 107, no. 407, notes of a Yemeni *dallāl* (d. 866/1462) that he was a *ḥāfiẓ al-Qur'ān* and knew the Qur'ān by heart.
104. Goitein, 1967, p. 161.
105. Ibn Ja'mān (f° 385 b) supports tribal law in his *fatwā* that the testimony of the *dīwānī, al-mu'arraf bi-'l-nās*, the government official (doubtless involved in taxation) with whom the people are acquainted, is not admissible. Perhaps *mu'arraf* should be understood as «notorious».
106. Abū Makhramah, *Fatāwā*, Ms. seen in Dathīnah from which I transcribed extracts, this coming under the heading *shahādat al-dallāl*. The author flourished ca. mid-10th/16th Century (cf. Serjeant, 1963, p. 28, 168).
107. Ibn Ja'mān, f° 384 b.
108. *Ibid.*, f° 155 a.
109. Discussed in Serjeant, 1970, p. 203.
110. *al-Sīrat al-Nabawiyyah*, ed. al-Saqqā et al., Cairo 1375/1955, I, p. 485; trans. A. Guillaume, Oxford-London, 1955, p. 224.
111. Al-Khazrajī, 1906-1908, II, p. 221. For a somewhat legendary tale about articles deposited with a man who died before he could return them, see Abū Makhramah, 1936-1950, I, p. 4; Islamic *ḥadīth* insists that the deceased may not receive blessing until his debts be paid and this reflects or continues the attitude of the pre-Islamic age — the pre-Islamic inscriptions of southern Arabia sometimes state that such and such a deceased person's debts have been discharged.
112. Serjeant and Lewcock, 1983, p. 278.
113. Abū Makhramah, p. 132.
114. *Ibid.*, p. 192.

II

The Ḥaḍramī Network

Although we read in al-Jumaḥī's *Ṭabaqāt al-shuʿarā'*[1] that the Āl al-Ḥaḍramī were allies of ʿAbd al-Shams in pre-Islamic Mecca and he cites also a poet of the Umayyad period as speaking of "the way in which merchants *(tijār)* in Ḥaḍramawt fold striped woollen clothes *(burūd)*", virtually nothing, to the best of my knowledge, is known of Ḥaḍramī merchants or emigrations until, say, the Rasūlid period, and even then there seem only to be scattered references to them. Ḥaḍramīs of course did move out and settle elsewhere—I have hazarded the suggestion that the once heavily cultivated area West of Qabr Hūd, now only visited by a few shepherds, may have begun to suffer from erosion at the time when the Islamic conquests drew so many people from it that there was insufficient labour to maintain the barrages. East Africa was an outlet for Ḥaḍramīs and when I visited the Kazimkazi Mosque[2] in Zanzibar, built in 500/1107, I found it was associated with the names of Ḥaḍramī Sayyids though I am uncertain quite when they arrived there.

There is a curious passage in al-Jāḥiẓ' *al-Ḥayawān*[3] relating to al-Sufālah which might indicate that it was the Persians who in the first Islamic centuries dominated the sea routes. "The sea-folk *(al-baḥriyyūn)* maintain that in *Bilād al-Sufālah* there are two birds, one of which appears before ships (from the shore?) come up with them and before the sea makes it possible for them to land at their trading places *(matājir)* and the bird says: '*Qurb āmad*, Approach.' So they realize that the time is nigh and the possibility (of making the landfall?) is close at hand. And they say: 'And at (that time) another bird of a different form comes, and it says: *Samārū*.' This is at the time of the return of those of them who have been away. They call those two species Qurb and Samārū." *Samārūk* in Persian means pigeon.

Al-Hamdānī remarks[4] that the Ḥaḍramī port al-Shiḥr is, like China, proverbial as a remote place. It no doubt appeared outlandish to the Mashāyikh al-Furḍah, the port officials of the Ayyūbid Ṭughtakīn in the late 6th/12th Century, when they asked for the names of merchants arriving in vessels from al-Sḥihr and Ḥaḍramawt and were given such vulgar or obscene titles as Abā Ḥajr, Abā Fiswah, etc. These they refused to enter in the *dafātir al-Sulṭān* and the Ḥaḍramīs' goods remained trodden underfoot till they appealed to the Sultan who told the Mashāyikh that if they refused to write down their names he could not take customs-duties *(ʿushūr)* from them![5] That this was a practical joke must be discounted, for al-Sakhāwī speaks of a Yemeni family called Banū Zibr after an ancestor so nick-named, and Khazrajī tells of a man called Kharyah who used to serve in the *qayṣariyyah* at Mecca.

The Rasūlid almanac, quoted above, reports the arrival and departure at fixed seasons of Ḥaḍramī and Ẓafārī vessels. They traded in shark *(lukham)* which the *Mulakhkhaṣ* says was imported to Aden from al-Rayḍah, Ẓafār and Ḥaḍramawt as it is today. *Lubān* incense is also listed. When in control of al-Shiḥr the Rasūlids put in a *nāẓir* with doubtless the same functions as at Aden—a merchant notable of Aden, Ibn al-ʿAsqalānī, is recorded[6] by Abū Makhramah as appointed to this office by the sultan. A famous merchant, Bā Rāshid, resident at Aden about the 6th/12th Century, obviously a Ḥaḍramī, built a *sabīl* at Mecca.[7]

At Ẓafār an enterprising Ḥaḍramī from Ḥabūẓah, just outside Saywūn, formerly in charge of agriculture and *tijārah* under the Badawī Manjūwī ruler, succeeded the Manjūwīs about 600/1203 and was in charge of revenue collection *(jibāyah)* after the Ghuzz (Rasūlids) conquered Ḥaḍramawt.[8]

Two merchants of the Ḥaḍramī house Bā Ḥannān[9] (probably of Dawʿan—one of this family a few years ago displayed strong anti-Sayyid tendencies) flourished under the first sultan of the Ṭāhirids, successors of the Rasūlids. One of the two, Muḥammad al-Ḥaḍramī al-Kindī, a merchant at Aden port, never imprisoned a debtor nor raised a man before the *ḥākim* (judge). A reckoning of his goods *(qumāsh)* in Abyssinia alone came to 230 000 *dīnārs*. Though extremely wealthy he was a modest man wearing simple white cotton while his servants wore fine clothes! That he did not go to law in debt cases is of interest in view of the present day practice of Ḥaḍramīs—discussed below—of settling their disputes within their own group without reference to the courts.

A relative of this al-Kindī, Muḥammad b. Ibrāhīm al-Ṣadr (d. 865/1460/61), was resident in bandar Zaylaʿ then removed to Aden. He too was extremely wealthy and when he knew he was about to die he made a bequest of a third of his property to the Ḥaramayn, 1 000 *ūqiyahs* (ounces) of gold. As trustee for his sons he appointed the sultan of the Yemen, ʿĀmir b. Ṭāhir, who in turn put it in charge of one of the *faqīhs* residing in Aden, and this latter consigned it to the charge of a third—"and it was lost in the quickest possible time—may God grant them pardon!"[10]

Al-Sakhāwī's massive encyclopaedia of biographies of the 9th/15th Century ulema shows that many Ḥaḍramīs had settled in the Yemen and Aden; there is, for example, a Ḥaḍramī Zabīdī, and I have myself stayed in the house of a Zabīdī family known as al-Ḥaḍramī. He includes a certain Bā Ṣuhayy and a family of this name were merchants in Aden—I visited them in 1948—; al-Sakhāwī calls[11] this merchant al-Shibāmī, from Shibām the busy merchant city of interior Ḥaḍramawt, and he was also al-Kindī al-Ashʿarī al-Shāfiʿī—he went to Mecca from the Yemen about 893/1488.

In the 7th/13th Century al-Khazrajī speaks[12] of the tax exemptions of the *faqīhs (musāmaḥāt al-fuqahā')* and the *"arbāb al-manāṣib"* like the Banu 'l-Ḥaḍramī. I suppose the second term must refer to what is nowadays called a *manṣab*, i.e. the lord of a *ḥawṭah* or sacred enclave. There are lists of these exemptions in a Ms. of the writings of the Rasūlid sultan al-Afḍal, as yet unpublished.

The arrival of the Portuguese and their domination of the Indian Ocean, the Turkish conquest of the Yemen and the rise of the Zaydī imāms introduced new economic and social factors which affected the maritime and merchant communities all over the area. Ṣanʿā' became the capital of the Yemen and as the chroniclers tell us, merchants flocked to it from every quarter. It is about the 11th/17th Century that the biographical collections seem to reveal the great expansion of the influence of the Ḥaḍramī Sayyids—we find them in the Holy Cities, Africa and India. The India connection with Ḥaḍramawt had always been close and the Sayyids are said to have first gone to India in 617/1220.

As Sayyids and ulema largely wrote the histories and biographies upon which we must rely, the danger of over-emphasis on and distortion of their role is clearly apparent but nevertheless they undoubtedly prospered and gained high social prestige through their special religious status and effort to spread the faith of Islam and eliminate pagan practices.

The migrations to India from the Middle Ages onwards led the Sayyids to settle in important commercial, cultural and political centres like Bijapur and Surat where their descendants are said still to live, Aḥmadābād, Broach, Ḥaydarābād, Gujerat, Delhi, Baroda, Calicut (a centre for Arab merchants), Malabar and Bengal. The greatest migrations of all however were to Java, Sumatra, Aceh and Malaya; Malacca was one of the most ancient settlements of the Arabs and Ḥaḍramīs. The ʿAlawī Sayyids arrived some time before the Dutch. At one time the coastal trade of the Dutch East Indies was largely in the hands of Ḥaḍramī sailing vessels. Dr Andaya (Auckland University) writes: "Local accounts in Palembang (South Sumatra) which became the main stream of Ḥaḍramī settlements in South Sumatra suggest that 'Arabs' first reached there around 1700... Particular encouragement was given them around 1770 by one ruler, and by the 1780s there was a commercial network linking Aceh, Penang, Jambi, Palembang, Batavia and the North coast ports of Java." Dr Andaya has collected shipping lists that indicate the commercial dominance of this relatively small but highly influential group. In 1699 an Arab dynasty was installed in Aceh (Ashī). The reasons for this emigration on so much larger a scale are still obscure.

Sayyid writers aver that the great migrations to Africa took place in the 8th/14th and 9th/15th Centuries. Ḥaḍramīs in East Africa are known as Shiḥrīs, doubtless because their port of embarcation was al-Shiḥr, and earlier Asiatic emigrants are called Shīrāzīs, a mediaeval appellation which today applies to the mixed Afro-Asian population. In the 11th/17th Century the merchants of the Muslims and Ashrāf of Ḥaḍramawt known as Banū Abī 'Alawī mixed with *S ḥrl* of Abyssinia, the Lord of the town of Mombasa whom they converted to Islam, and he married a Bā 'Alawī woman.[13]

About the beginning of the 19th Century a Sayyid of Tarīm, a merchant, Sayyid Ḥusayn b. Sahl, attained to a position of great wealth, but, characteristic of the insecurity of the age, he was kidnapped by one of the Yāfi'ī tribal rulers of Tarīm. He threatened the chief Yāfi'ī chief in the city that he would leave for the coast unless the latter took his former captor's castle—which was achieved by an assault on it from towers constructed of bags of dates, at obviously fantastic expense. The Bin Sahl house actually introduced a coinage of its own —presumably minted abroad—; I have seen a copper piece known as *sayf wa-mīzān*, sword and balance, because these emblems are stamped on it, but no other denominations are known to survive. Bin Sahl left a manuscript library in Tarīm which I used to use in 1947.

More recently the great Sayyid merchant house was the Āl Kāf, Ḥaḍramī Sayyids of Tarīm, whose ancestor migrated to Singapore. I have even seen in 1954 the draft of a book, *Dawr Āl Kāf*, covering one hundred and thirty years of their activities and influence. Their fortune in Singapore must once have been considerable and in the fifties some three hundred persons were living on the *muwāṣalāt*, remittances from it in Ḥaḍramawt, and as many more, it is said, in Malaysia. They owned a department store in Singapore which I visited in 1962 and some members of the family were living in *Arab Street* there.[14] The Āl Kāf also minted a coinage of their own, a set of which was recently given me in Jeddah. This was in current use in the Wādī or parts of it till about the thirties. It was the readiness of Sayyid Sir Bū Bakr Āl Kāf to expend the bulk of his fortune on welfare and the promotion of peace in the country that largely aided the British Political Resident,

W. H. Ingrams, to pacify much of the country in the thirties, as also the benefit of his wise counsel. Though many of the younger members of the Āl Kāf house dabbled in business, their influence had already much declined by the time of the British withdrawal. The prominent merchants of the coastal ports of al-Mukallā and al-Shiḥr known to me, Bā Raḥīm and Bā Ḥakīm, were not Sayyids, but mainly hailed from Wādī Daw'an, emigrants from which have been successful in business in many countries abroad. In 1948 I was entertained by the leading merchant in Asmara, Bā Khashab, who has substantial interests in Sa'udi Arabia and who, in 1967, provided the young sultan Ghālib b. 'Awaḍ with a vessel to sail to al-Mukallā, to try to recover his throne from the communist faction that had taken over the port in his absence—unfortunately he did not succeed.

As Sa'udi Arabia developed into a petro-economy state, it attracted a flood of Ḥaḍramī emigrants; two Ḥaḍramī multi-millionaires were known everywhere, Bin Maḥfūẓ and Bin Lādin. I recall and I actually met the latter once in the British Residency, a small unpretentious man; all hail from Wādī Daw'an. Bin Maḥfūẓ, a tribesman, to raise the passage-money on a dhow to Jeddah, is said to have pledged his dagger, the token of a tribesman's honour, or so the story goes. His rise from pennilessness to wealth, his many interests including banking and lending money to the Sa'udi Government would be a tale worth the telling. I recall that as early as 1954 the names above the shops in al-Khubar were largely Ḥaḍramī Bā Fulān or Sayyid Fulān. Ḥaḍramī merchants in the Hijaz are of course no new phenomenon. Snouck Hurgronje remarks[15] that the poorest Ḥaḍramī when he finds a job puts money aside to lay out at interest, even getting 100% and he adds that the Ḥaḍramī "has a certain cult for the place where he hides his money from strange eyes and he takes nothing from the receptacle in the ground or the wall until he moves the whole for some business purpose —replacing the money as soon as he can with a *ḥaqq al-qahwah* in addition!" I have myself heard it said that the Ḥaḍramī in East Africa puts away each shilling with the words: "*Mā bā tashūf al-shams illā wa-ant fī Ḥaḍramūt*, You aren't going to see the sun till you're in Ḥaḍramawt." His parsimony has not made the Ḥaḍramī liked and I recall in conversation with an Arab when flying to Bahrain his remark: "*Al-Ḥaḍramī wa-law taḥallā amarr min al-ṣabir al-Suquṭrī*, The Ḥaḍramī, even if he should act sweetly, is bitterer than Socotran aloes!" My own experience of Ḥaḍramīs has been far more favourable. Remittances *(muwāṣalāt)* from abroad have had a not inconsiderable impact on the country's economy.

Wādī Daw'an Ḥaḍramīs go to Aden, India, Sawākin (where I listed the names of three Ḥaḍramī families, Bā Zar'ah, Bā 'Abbūd and Bā Ḥaydar about 1962) or Cairo; those of the coast seem to prefer Malabar and Ḥaydarābād. In Abyssinia the numbers of Ḥaḍramīs had much diminished as I learned in Harar in 1966 when talking to probably the only Ḥaḍramī merchant and shopkeeper left there, because of the unfavourable attitude of the government at that time.

Ḥaḍramī merchants, says Ingrams,[16] are dealers in *batik*; this was notably the chief import to Ḥaḍramawt after World War II, when they could not transfer money from Indonesia. They export also sandalwood, incense, crockery and brassware to Ḥaḍramawt. From their native land they export ghee, the famous Daw'an honey, *lubān*-incense, some local medicines, rosaries and (probably Yāfi'ī) coffee.

L. W. C. Van Den Berg, as long ago as 1886, compiled an excellent survey unlikely ever to be surpassed, of the Ḥaḍramīs in the Dutch East Indies. There the Sayyids were recognised by all as the highest ranking element in Islamic society, the affluent merchant of humble degree not being accorded the respect paid to them. Their position was later assailed by what grew into the Irshādī group and a bitter dispute between Irshādīs and 'Alawīs ran on till the early 1930s. In Ḥaḍramawt itself the Sayyid Lords of *ḥawṭahs*, sacred enclaves, claimed exemption from all taxation and produced documents from the sultans in support of this privilege—this included the customs duties at the ports. Exemptions were granted from time to time by the Qu'ayṭī sultans, but sultan Ghālib informs me that it was only the Manṣab house of 'Īnāt whom the Qu'ayṭīs regarded as entitled to these exemptions.

While the Arabs had relatively limited capital compared with the Europeans or Chinese, Van Den Berg adds: "Il est rare de rencontrer, dans l'Archipel indien, des Arabes qui ne soient pas plus ou moins intéressés dans le commerce."[17] Van Den Berg's study deals at some length with the economic side of Ḥaḍramī activity and he points out that although usury is a major sin in Islam there can be few Arab capitalists who have not lent for usury.[18] This usually takes the form of sale with possible repurchase at an exorbitant price, with additional stipulations of pledges *(nantissement)* and guarantees of security *(caution)*. The conditions are such that a native debtor can scarcely free himself from his creditor; but the Ḥaḍramīs also lent to those who were not poor, such as chiefs and merchants. I should stress however that these devices to conceal usury are common all over the Islamic world, including Ḥaḍramawt itself. Many Ḥaḍramīs had left their native land after pledging their palm groves under the device known as *'uhdah*,[19] a sale with the possibility of repayment and recovery of the property.

A fair picture of Ḥaḍramī business spanning the communities between the Far East and their homeland may be formed from the cases set forth in *al-Fatāwā al-nāfi'ah fī masā'il al-aḥwāl al-wāqi'ah* (Cairo, 1379/1960) of the *faqīh* Abū Bakr b. Aḥmad al-Khaṭīb al-Tarīmī (d. 1356/1937). It has incidentally a reference to Bin Sahl coins guaranteed in Java to a person in the Ḥaḍramawt town of Tarīm. Perhaps the cases that follow will be sufficient illustration of the complicated nature of their business. How is the fee *(khidmah/ʿamūlah)* to be calculated for making out a draft, cashing it, the cost of pen and ink, etc., in the case of a certain money-changer with a branch in Sourabaya and another in Singapore? One rupee per hundred is suggested. In another case drafts are sent from Singapore, Java, etc., to Ḥaḍramawt for which a merchant in exchange for the rupees or Būrūm (?) *riyāls* of the draft pays out part in Maria Theresa dollars and part in goods, but he puts up the price of the goods. Yet again a Ḥaḍramī in Singapore makes a bequest in *"riyālāt"* without specifying whether they are "Farānṣah" or "Būrūm", there being a difference in the exchange for these two coinages—the case being complicated because of minors and absentees.

On the Ḥaḍramī merchants in Aden, let me quote my friend, Dr ʿAbdullāh Maqṭarī,[20] whose father was in Aden a leading merchant of great wealth until the British withdrawal in 1967. "There are however two communities among the merchants of Aden whose members are known never to go to the courts unless they are involved with outsiders—these are the Ḥaḍramī Dawʿanīs (Ahl Dawʿan) and the Ḥabbānīs (Ahl Ḥabbān)—; the Dawʿanīs are particularly well known as merchants both in Ḥaḍramawt and abroad. A member of the former community, a Bā Zarʿah man, told me that he has never known a Dawʿanī merchant to take another Dawʿanī to the ordinary courts of justice. He stated that some Dawʿanīs even wait for years until they go back home, and then file their cases against their fellow countrymen in front of their elders. Muḥammad Aḥmad Bā Junayd (pronounced Gunayd), a Dawʿanī, a well known merchant in Aden who was previously established in Asmara confirmed this, and told me of several persons in Asmara who waited for periods of over six years before they were able to go home and settle their disputes. He added that Dawʿanīs considered it an *ʿayb*, a shaming act, to disclose their disputes to strangers." In an agreement made at al-Mukallā in 1290/1873[21] it is interesting to see that "if any quarrel should arise among the sea-faring men, they are to be sent to those of their own class. In all cases relating to law, justice to be done according to the Muhammadan law. All mercantile classes to be sent to the merchants for trial. Khayrullāh, the slave of the Naqīb Ṣalaḥ, is to do all the work relating to the Bazaar."

At this point I might add that Yemeni merchants in Aden, probably jealous of the influential and wealthy merchant ʿAlī al-Jabalī, who acted on behalf of Imām Aḥmad, helped support financially movements against the Ḥamīd al-Dīn régime of Ṣanʿāʾ and Taʿizz. As far as I know, all these merchants were Shāfiʿīs from the Lower Yemen or Tihāmah.

NOTES

See bibliography, *supra*, p. 78-79.

1. J. Hell, ed., *Die Klassen der Dichter*, Leiden, 1916, p. 8.
2. S. Flury, «The Kufic Inscriptions of Kisimkazi Mosque, Zanzibar, 500 H (A.D. 1107)», *JRAS*, 1922, p. 257-318, mentioning a certain Abū Musā b. al-Ḥasan b. Muḥammad, Abū ʿImrān.
3. ʿAbd al-Salām Hārūn ed., Cairo, 1356-1364/1938-1945, III, p. 5 — or perhaps Persian was the *lingua franca*?
4. *Ṣifah*, ed. D. H. Müller, Leiden, 1884-1891, p. 203.
5. Ibn al-Mujāwir, 1951-1954, p. 254.
6. al-Sakhāwī, 1353/1934, VIII, p. 288, no. 798, and II, p. 226, no. 630.
7. *Ibid.*, II, p. 108.
8. Abū Makhramah, 1936-1950, II, p. 195.
9. al-Sakhāwī, 1353/1934, VII, p. 125, no. 273.
10. *Ibid.*, VI, p. 283, no. 944.
11. *Ibid.*, VI, p. 37, no. 16.
12. al-Khazrajī, 1906-1908, II, p. 36.
13. Serjeant, 1957, p. 23.
14. I am informed that the buildings in this street are now demolished or in the process of demolition.
15. *Mekka in the Latter Part of the 19th Century*, trans. J. H. Monahan, Leiden, 1931, p. 5, 96-97.
16. Ingrams, 1937, p. 150 sq.
17. *Le Hadhramout et les colonies arabes dans l'Archipel Indien*, Batavia, 1886, p. 134.
18. *Ibid.*, p. 136 sq.
19. For *ʿuhdah* see R. B. Serjeant, «Materials for South Arabian History, II», *Bulletin of the School of Oriental and African Studies*, 13, 3, 1950, p. 591 sq. I now have copies of several mss. on *ʿuhdah*.
20. Quoted in : Serjeant, 1976, p. 314.
21. Serjeant, 1977, p. 242, quoting Ismail Hakki Tevfik, *Güney Arabistan meselesi*, I, Hadramut, Filibe, 1935, p. 42.

Since writing this article two new sources have been brought to my attention, namely: ʿAbd al-Raḥmān b. Muḥammad b. Ḥusayn al-Mashhūr, Shams al-ẓahīrah fī ansāb ahl al-bayt min Banī ʿAlawī, *edited with copious notes by Muḥammad Ḍiyāʾ Shihāb, Jeddah, 1984, 2 vols, of which I had only a ms. copy: these notes show the distribution of Ḥaḍramī Sayyids, the majority probably merchants, in the Far East and East Africa; and Hikoichi Yajima,* The Islamic History of the Maldive Islands, *Tokyo, 1984, 2 vols, showing Ḥaḍramī and other Arab links with the Maldives. I gratefully acknowledge gifts of these volumes from Ḥusayn Hādī ʿAwaḍ (now at Abu Dhabi) and Hikoichi Yajima respectively.*

III

The Yemeni Coast in 1005/1597; An Anonymous Note on the Flyleaf of Ibn al-Mujāwir's *Tārīkh al-Mustabṣir*

Immediately following the Aya Sofia text of Ibn al-Mujāwir's *Tārīkh al-mustabṣir* (fol. 119a)[1] comes a note which I copied in Istanbul in 1963. I am indebted to Professor O. Löfgren both for permission to publish the text with translation of this note and for supplying me with his own copy and draft notes certain of which I have incorporated in my own. The note is written in semi-colloquial Arabic, by a man not unacquainted with writing but certainly no grammarian, although for that matter Ibn al-Mujāwir himself, to judge by the Ms. text before us was not impeccable in this respect either. No attempt has been made to force the Arabic of the note into a classical mould, but it is simply left as it is.

اخبرني الخواجا الاجل الاكرم اتكير[1] زخيم بن المعلم احمد زخيم
وكان رجلًا ممن مضت عليه التجارب وكان ابوه المعلم احمد يسافر
في المراكب معلم الحقّه وكان صاحب دنيا واسعه اخبرني الخواجا
ايكر[1] زخيم ليلة الإثنين عشرين شهر ذي الحجة سنة ١٠٠٥
وكان قد ناهض من العمر ثلاثه وستين سنه وكان رجلًا صادقًا
مِمَّن يُثَقْ[2] به وكنا واصلين من المجبا محبات[3] بندر المخا فجرا
بيننا كلام فسألتُهُ متى صارت المراكب تدخل بندر المخا فذكر
لي ان بعد خراب بندر عدن اي بطل الموسم وقلّ دُخول المراكب
اليها مثل ما ذكر بن مُجَاوِر في تاريخه انه كان يدخلها اول نحو
المائة من المراكب بل اريد فلما حدث فيها الظلم انتقل الموسم
الى بندر جدّه وبندر الخور والجزيره ايضا بين سماد وبين القصيري[4]
من (اعمال)[5] بندر الحُدَيْده واما الان الجزيره خراب وقد شاهدت
انا الجزيرة بعيني سنه ١٠٠٣ لان كان سبب رواحي الى هذاك
المكان لانه خرج بَتَّان حوت طوله اربعه وثلاثين ذراع وعرضه

اربعه عشر ذراع وعرض كل عين اى دورتها ثلاثه عشر شبر وكنت انا والنقيب محمد والقاضى عبد الوهاب ويوسف تابع الجناب الحاج ياقوت فلما وصلنا الى هذاك المكان راينا البتان قد عرى[6] ما بين جزر هناك وبين البر الذى نحن فيه اى شَمَاد فقال اصحابنا ارجعوا بنا[7] البتان قد عَرِى والبلاد بها لانى كنت ذاك الأوان حاكمها فما سمعت كلامهم وتغدينا ورقدنا فما قمت الا والبتان قد خرج البر لان اول عند وصولنا كان البحر عارى لاجل ذالك عرى الحوت فلما أمتَلَا البحر اخرجه الموج الى البر فقمت أريق الما فرأيت البتان قد خرج فرحنا الى عنده نتفرج. فلما رجعنا الى البلاد ذكر لى النقيب محمد ان هذه الجزيره كان فيها قوم ومعهم جلاب تدخل الهند واهل الخور كذلك كان معهم جلاب تدخل الهند وتاتيهم[8] من القماش مثل الدوتى واللاتى[9] والكَندكى والعطب وغيره الى ان حدث الظلم فى البلاد وراح الجسم وبقى الاسم فصارت المراكب تدخل بندر جده وكانة[10] الدولة الاشرفيه الملك الاشرف ابوا مطهر وكان تختهم مدينة تعز. فصار يدخل المراكب والمراكبين[11] الى بندر المخا الى ان صار يدخل الأربعين والسبعين وكانت المخا هذاك الأوان اعنى ضمانها حسبه[12]... ١٥٠٠ الى ان وصلت فى زماننا هذا .بماية وعشرين الف ذهب وما بقى يدخلها الا سبعه عشر الى عشرين لا زايد واما الخور وهذيك الجزيره الذى ذكرناها قد فنيوا[13] اهلها ومدفونين قبال الجزيره فى مكان معروف بالجبانه وهو محل معروف يتعدى عليها المسافر الى الزيديه والى الضحى وطريق ساحليه الى الصليف والى اللحيه وقد سلكتها انا مرارا لله الحمد من قبل ومن بعد واما المخا فهى قديمه هكذا اخبرنى الفدر الاجل ابكر زعيم فى التاريخ المذكور والله اعلم فى ٢٠ شهر ذى الحجه سنه ١٠٠٥.

Marginal note 2

واما عدن فبقى يدخلها فى زماننا هذا نحو المركب والمركبين مثل التواهى مراكب صغار مليباريه فقط والبلد خراب فاذا غضب على احدًا[14] جعلوه فيها والرهاين وغيرهم نعوذ بالله ...

Notes to text

1 Löfgren corrects to Iykur.
2 Properly *yūthaq*.
3 Löfgren reads *majbāt*.
4 Löfgren reads Quṣayr.
5 *A'māl* is written over the line.
6 Qāḍī Ismā'īl al-Akwa' read *'arrā*.
7 Though unlikely, *nabā* might be read – 'the news is that'.
8 The text seems to have *nātbhm* but tā'tī-him is clearly correct.
9 *Al-lāfī* may be read here, but *al-lātī* seems correct.
10 A not uncommon spelling error for *kānat*.
11 Löfgren reads *markabayn*.
12 *Ḥasanah is written over the figure*.
13 *Faniyū* = *fanū*, a common colloquial form.
14 Sic.

There told me the honourable the noble Khawājā Iykur Zikhkhīm[2] son of the Pilot Aḥmad Zikhkhīm, a man of those who have passed through [many] experiences. His father the Pilot Aḥmad used to voyage in vessels as the compass pilot (*mu'allim al-ḥuqqah*) and was possessed of ample world(ly wealth). The Khawājā Iykur Zikhkhīm told me on the night of Monday the 20th of the month of Dhu 'l-Ḥijjah of the year 1005 (4 August, 1597), he having come up to[3] 63 years of age, a truthful man – one of those who can be trusted, when we were coming from [collecting] the duty, the duties of Mocha bandar[4]. We fell into conversation and I asked him when vessels started to put into Mocha bandar and he mentioned to me that after the ruination of Aden bandar, i.e. the stopping of the trading fleet (*mūsim* [5]) and the paucity of vessels putting in to it – as Ibn Mujāwir remarks in his *History*[6], a hundred vessels used formerly to put into it, nay, more – but when the oppression[7] took place there the trading fleet transferred to Jeddah bandar and bandar al-Khawr and al-Jazīrah[8] also, between Sumād and al-Qaṣīrī/Quṣayrī[9] of the Ḥudaydah bandar districts, but nowadays al-Jazīrah is ruinous. I have seen al-Jazīrah myself with my own eyes in the year 1003/1594-5, because the reason for my going to that place was because a whale (*battān*[10]), a whale/fish[11] came in (to the shore), the length of which was 34 cubits, its breadth 14 cubits, and the width of each eye, i.e. its circumference (?[12]), was 13 spans (*shibr*[13]). I was with the *naqīb*[14] Muḥammad, the *qāḍī* 'Abd al-Wahhāb and Yūsuf, the follower of his worship al-Ḥājj Yāqūt, and when we reached that place we saw the whale stranded[15] between the islands there and the land where we were, i.e. Sumād. So my companions said: 'Let us go back; the whale is stranded and the village is poorly provided[16]', because at that time I was the governor (*ḥākim*) of it. But I did not listen[17] to what they were saying and we lunched and slept. No sooner did I get up but the whale had come in to the land for when we first arrived the tide was down[18] – because of that the whale got stranded – then when the tide was full the waves brought it in to the land. So I got up to pass water and saw the whale had come in so we went up to it to have a look. When we returned to the village the *naqīb* Muḥammad remarked to me that in this al-Jazīrah there used to be people with *jalabah*-dhows[19] entering India, and the people of al-Khawr likewise had *jalabah*-dhows entering India and bringing them cloth (*qumāsh*) like *dūtī*, *lātī*, *kandakī*[20] and cotton, etcetera, until oppression fell upon the village and the body departed but the name remained – so vessels began to put in to Jeddah bandar. It was the Ashrafī dawlah, al-Malik al-Ashraf Abū Muṭahhar, their seat/capital (*takht*) being the city of Ta'izz[21]. So ships and sailors (*murākibīn*) began to put in to Mocha bandar till forty and seventy would put in there. Mocha at that time – I mean its tax farmed return (*ḍamān*) – was 15,000 good (gold pieces[22]) until, in this time of ours, it reached as many as 120,000 gold pieces (*dhahab*) though only 17 to 20 (vessels), no more, still put in to it. As for al-Khawr and that al-Jazīrah (Island) I have mentioned their inhabitants have passed away and are buried facing al-Jazīrah in a place known as al-Jabbānah (the Cemetery[23]), a well known place by which one passes when travelling to al-Zaydiyyah and al-Ḍaḥī and a coastal road to al-Ṣalīf and al-Luḥayyah – I have travelled it myself a number of times, praise God, before and since. As for Mocha it is ancient – so the illustrious Iykur Zikhkhīm told me, but God is most knowing, on the 20th of the month of Dhu 'l-Ḥijjah of the year 1005 (August 4th, 1597).

There are further, two marginal notes to the above account. The first says of Khawājā Iykur, 'As for his father Aḥmad he died in the year 1(000)/1591-2'. The second note is interesting:

> As for Aden in this time of ours, a vessel or two still puts in to it, (to such as al-Tawwāhī[24]), only small Malabarī vessels, and the town is ruinous. When anger is felt against a certain person[25] they post him there – and the hostages[26] and others – we take refuge in God [several only semi-legible words follow of a pious nature].

Comment

This note was penned during the first Ottoman occupation of the Yemen when Ottoman power seemed at its height, just one year before the Imām al-Qāsim al-Kabīr opened his *da'wah* or call, in the north, and during the governorship of Ḥasan Bāshā al-Wazīr (988-1013/1580-1604).

Mocha rose as Aden fell, owing to the exactions and mismanagement of the Ottoman officials, and this is repeated up to a point today for since 1967 Aden as a port has declined while Mocha and Ḥudaydah have increased in importance, though the fall of Aden is on a scale proportionately far less than during the first Ottoman occupation. Mocha is not mentioned by name in the Red Sea ports by the *Mulakhkhaṣ al-fiṭan* of 1411-12, and its revenues must have been relatively trivial. The same authority does not seem to refer either to the textiles from India imported to al-Khawr and al-Jazīrah.

It is curious that while the tax farming brought in to Mocha at this date no less than eight times its former revenue, the number of vessels had dropped to not more than 20. The revenues would be drawn mainly from customs and other port charges. The writer of the note mentions 15,000 gold pieces as the former revenue of Mocha – this might be compared with the list of expenditure of Sultanic affairs (*mühimme*) dated 990/1582 at Mocha, 16,439 gold pieces, out of a principal of 32,731[27], and the 120,000 gold pieces mentioned by our author. It would be interesting to see how these figures tally with the Ottoman archives.

Notes

1 Ed. Oscar Löfgren, *Descriptio Arabiae Meridionalis*, Leiden, 1951-54.
2 Löfgren cites Steingass, *Persian-English dict. aygar* (Greek '*akoron*, sweet cane; Dozy, *Supplément*, *iykur*; Berggren, 826, *Acorus*, *Calamus off.*; and Dozy, *zikhkhīm*, *fort* (*odeur*) – the name then meaning 'strong-smelling sweet cane'. This is not like Yemeni names, and perhaps the family was of Indian or Persian extraction. This seems superior to my reading *Atkyr*/*A.kr*, and makes sense, though strange.
3 Lexicons consulted are not very helpful with *nāhaḍa*, and this rendering is semi-conjectural.
4 Cf. *Ṣan'ā': an Arabian Islamic city*, ed. R.B.Serjeant & Ronald Lewcock, London, 1983, Glossary, *majbā* (pl. *majābī*), impost, tax, duty. Löfgren reads *majbāt* for my *ḥ j bāt* and I have followed this reading though this plural is not so far attested. In the Yemen *djaḥab* means 'to beach, draw up on the beach' (*The Portuguese off the South Arabian coast*, Oxford, 1963/Beirut, 1974, 188) which I thought would be the correct reading in the sense of 'beaching places', with *majbā*/*mijbā* perhaps in the sense of customs post.
5 Cf. *The Portuguese*, *mūsim*/*mawsim*, 194.
6 *Tārīkh al-mustabṣir*, I, 144, says 70 to 80 ships used to anchor annually under Jabal Ṣīrah.
7 The writer means oppression during the reign of the Zaydī Imām Sharaf al-Dīn (ob. 965/1558) mentioned below.
8 Al-Khawr, the lagoon or bay, at al-Ḥudaydah seems to have also been the name of a little port there. Al-Jazīrah, the Island, it is clear from the remark that it faces al-Jabbānah (infra), is the island marked there on the maps and charts.
9 Sumād and al-Qaṣīrī are unknown to the standard sources consulted, but of course might be names still known to the local inhabitants.
10 From my draft list of fish names from the Aden Protectorate coasts I find the *battān* is known off the Ḥadramī coast. Muḥammad 'Abduh Ghanem calls it a huge fish of the shark variety. Cf. G. Ferrand, *Instructions nautiques*, II, Paris, 1925, 85b (Sulaymān al-Mahrī); A. Jahn, *Die Mehri-Sprache in Südarabien*, Wien, 1902, 269. Ibn al-Mujāwir, op. cit., II, 282 & 284, describes a sperm whale (*battān al-'anbar*) brought in to shore at Qalhāt.
11 *Ḥūt* is the ordinary south Arabian word for 'fish'.
12 *Dawrah* is not found in this sense in the standard lexicons.
13 The hand span is from the little finger to the thumb of the extended hand – this seems impossibly large; perhaps 'three' only should be read.
14 The *naqīb* may be a military officer or a tribal chief.
15 Qāḍī Ismā'īl al-Akwa' reads this verb as '*arrā*, but '*arī* was mentioned to me elsewhere. *Al-baḥr 'ārī*, infra, means that the tide was down and the shore uncovered.
16 If *bahā* is to be read here it could be the *maṣdar* of *bahiya*, *bahan*, to be completely without utensils, of a tent (Lane), but I am not at all certain of the sense here.
17 The writer of the note does not express himself clearly here, but when he states that he is governor, he probably means of al-Ḥudaydah. It is suggested that, being in authority, he did not listen but over-ruled his companions.
18 See fn. 15.
19 *Jalabah*, dhows of planks sewn together with coir (*The Portuguese*, 134).
20 *Dūtī* is clearly the same as dhoty, for which see H. Yule & A.C. Burnell, *Glossary of Anglo-Indian colloquial words and phrases*, reprint London, 1968, 314, dhootie being known in 1609, and, in 1614, dutties, such as may be fit for making and mending sails, a corge (*kawrajah*), i.e. a score, of dutties is mentioned. Maḥmūd Qārī of Yazd, *Dīwān-i albisah*, Istanbul, 1303 H., 20C, mentions *dūtū*, cloth made of cotton, double, about the third quarter of the 9th/15th century. For *kandakī*, a coarse muslin, see early references in my *Islamic textiles* , Beirut, 1972. For *lāṭī* imported to Mocha, see *Ṣan'ā'*, 75.
21 Though not well expressed the writer seems to mean that it was the Zaydī government of the Imām Sharaf al-Dīn which oppressed al-Jazīrah; his son Muṭahhar was a warrior of renown who resisted the Ottoman invaders. He had taken Ta'izz in 941/1534-5 but the Ottomans took it in 952/1545-6.
22 *Ḥasanah* stands for *sikkah ḥasanah* = *dhahab*, gold coin in the context (the Ottomans minted much bad coinage in the Yemen). See *Ṣan'ā'*, 75 seq.
23 This word is discussed in *The Portuguese*, glossary, *Ṣan'ā'*, glossary.
24 *Tawwāhī*, the mooring place, from *tawwah*, to moor (*Portuguese*, 42).
25 Presumably by the Ottoman administration.
26 Hostages were taken from the tribes as surety of their good behaviour by the Rasūlids, the Zaydī Imāms and Sultans of the Aden Protectorates. In my experience their legs were fettered but otherwise they were not restricted.
27 *Ṣan'ā'*, 75.

IV

FIFTEENTH CENTURY 'INTERLOPERS' ON THE COAST OF RASŪLID YEMEN

Intrigued by a reference to merchants described as *mujawwirūn* by the anonymous *Chronicle of the Rasūlid Dynasty of Yemen*, I followed up de Sacy's [1] citation of a passage from al-Maqrīzī [2] concerning a merchant who *jawwara ilā Juddah* and later *jawwara ᶜan ᶜAdan*. The classical lexicons are unhelpful over the sense of *jawwara* as used by these authors, but Sayyid Ḥasan Ṣāliḥ Shihāb of Aden, author of a number of studies on Arab navigation [3] was able to inform me that *jawwara* means 'to smuggle', a sense also found in Landberg [4] *faire la contrebande*, and Stace.[5] While the sense of smuggling may be said to be implicit in the above passage from al-Maqrīzī, Stace assigns it also the sense of 'to evade' which is clearly the basic sense of *jawwara*, and this is how al-Maqrīzī uses it. I have preferred to render *mujawwir* by the 17th century Anglo-Indian term 'interloper' rather than 'smuggler'.[6]

My 'Yemeni merchants and trade in the Yemen, 13th-16th centuries' [7] provides a general picture of the situation there into which the intrusion of the 'interlopers' may be fitted.

'INTERLOPER' ACTIVITIES IN THE CHRONICLES

Al-Maqrīzī, al-Mawā'iẓ [8]

ᶜAydhāb... When the vessels of India and the Yemen stopped putting in there, Aden of the land of Yemen became the great(est) anchorage (*marsā* [9]) until the eight hundred and twenties (1418-25) when Jeddah became the greatest anchorage of the world, and Hurmuz also, for it is an important anchorage.

---

[1] Silvestre de Sacy, *Chrestomathie arabe*, Paris, 1826, II, 55-56.

[2] *Al-Sulūk ilā maᶜrifat duwal al-mulūk*, ed. Saᶜīd...ᶜĀshūr, Cairo, 1975, IV, II, 680-81.

[3] *Aḏwā' ᶜalā tārīkh al-Yaman al-baḥrī*, Beirut, 2nd ed. 1981 ; *Furjat al-humūm wa-'l-ghumūm fī'l-ᶜalāmāt wa-'l-masāfat wa-'l-nujūm, li-baḥḥār majhūl*, Kuwait, 1404/1984 : *ᶜUlūm al-ᶜArab al-baḥriyyah*, Kuwait, 1404/1984 ; *Qawāᶜid ᶜilm al-baḥr*, Kuwait, 1406/1986 : *al-Marākib al-ᶜArabiyyah*, Kuwait, 1987.

[4] *Glossaire daṯînois*, 310.

[5] E.V. Stace, *English-Arabic Vocabulary*, London, 1893, 58, 159.

[6] Gerald Tibbetts, *Arab navigation in the Indian Ocean before the coming of the Portuguese*, London, 1971, 519, draws attention to two passages in the sailing directions (*al-Fawā'id*) of Ibn Mājid in which the verb *jāwara/ jāwaza* figures, the former from the same root as *jawwara*. One passage (14v, 16) reads : *al-mawsim al-kabīr li-'l-mujāwiz*, the major (wind) season for the *mujāwiz*. The other (84v, 3) reads : Asmā is an islet (*ẓahrah*) and anchorage from the north wind (*shimāl*) and between the two (i.e. Asmā and Sāsū island) and Masnad (island) is closed (*mughallaq*) to *al-marākib al-mujawwirah* but not to light (*al-khifāf*) vessels. Ḥasan Ṣāliḥ Shihāb writes categorically that the correct reading comes from the verb *jāwaza*, to pass along/ voyage on the high seas (*fī ᶜurḍ al-baḥr*). So both passages would refer to deep sea vessels. Tibbetts tentatively suggests the reading *mujāwirah* may be linked with the terms *ḥiml jā'ir* and *shiḥnah jā'irah*, a heavy load/ cargo — I have myself noted in north Yemen : *jawr ᶜalayk*, it is too heavy for you. The weakness in this suggestion is that morphologically *jwr* could hardly convey such a sense. However since a deep sea vessel's draught is obviously greater than that of light craft and it could not pass through the shallows between the islets the reading *yujāwiz* would seem to settle the question.

[7] In *Marchands et hommes d'affaires asiatiques*, ed. Jean Aubin & Denys Lombard, Paris, 1987, 61-82. See article I above.

[8] Būlāq, 1270 H., Beirut reprint, I, 203.

[9] *Marsā* is translated in its original sense of anchorage, mooring place, but is used loosely in the sense of harbour, haven. ᶜAydhāb lost its importance after 760/1359.

Al-Maqrīzī, al-Sulūk [10]

On the seventh (of Rabī^c I, 828/ February 26, 1425) the Amīr Arim Bughā [11], an amīr of the tens [12], went on a expedition to Mecca accompanied by a hundred mamlūks ; and Sa^cd al-Dīn Ibrāhīm al-Murrah, one of the secretaries (*kuttāb*) set out to receive the customs-duties (*mukūs*) of the vessels arriving at Jeddah from India. From of old the custom was that the vessels of the India merchants would put into Aden and it was never known for them to by-pass Aden *bandar.* However when the year (8)25/ December 6th, 1421) came, a *nākhudhāh* from the city of Kālīkūt called Ibrāhīm, put to sea (*kharaja*) and when he passed by Bāb al-Mandab he took an evading route (*jawwara ilā*) to Jeddah in an open skiff (*ṭarrādah* [13]), in anger at the Lord of the Yemen [14] because of his ill treatment of the merchants. The Sharīf Ḥasan b. ᶜAjlān [15] took possession of the goods he had with him and forced them on (*ṭaraḥa-hā ᶜalā* [16]) the merchants at Mecca at an exorbitant price. In the year (8)26/ December 15th, 1422 - December 5th, 1423 the said Ibrāhīm arrived at Bāb al-Mandab without passing through Aden, by-passed Ḥaly [17] and anchored at the town of Sawākin [18] then Dahlak island, the Lords [19] of which treated him exceedingly badly. In the year (8)27/ December 5th, 1423 - November 22nd, 1424 he returned, avoiding (*jawwara ᶜan*) Aden, and by-passed Jeddah, making for Yanbuᶜ. The amīr Qurqmāṣ was in Mecca and he kept on cajoling Ibrāhīm until he anchored off (*ᶜalā*) Jeddah with a couple of vessels, and he treated him so courteously that [20] his hopeful wish [for a good reception there] was reinforced and he departed grateful and full of praise (*thāniy-an*). In the year (8)28/ November 23rd, 1424 - November 12th, 1425 he returned with fourteen vessels laden with goods. News of him reached the sultan (of Egypt, al-Ashraf Barsbāy) and, (as) he wanted to appropriate (Jeddah's) customs-duties to himself, he despatched Ibn al-Murrah for that (purpose). From that time henceforth Jeddah became a great *bandar* while Aden *bandar* fell into disuse, all but a little. Jeddah had only been an anchorage from the year 26 of the *hijrah*, for ᶜUthmān, Allah be pleased with him, developed it (*iᶜtamara fī-hā*) and his clients spoke to him to transfer the commercial entrepot (*sāḥil* [21]) to Jeddah, it having been at al-Shuᶜaybah during the Jāhiliyyah era [22]. So he transferred it to Jeddah.

Al-Maqrīzī, al-Sulūk [23]

During it (Muḥarram, 829/ November, 1425) a fresh injustice which had not been encountered before was perpetrated on the pilgrims — namely on the days of the (pilgrimage) season (*mawsim*) the merchants were prevented from setting out from Mecca for the land of Syria with the sorts (*aṣnāf* [24]) of merchandise of India they had purchased and were compelled to go along with the (pilgrim) caravan to

---

10 IV, II, 680.

11 De Sacy, *op.cit.*, II, 156 reads the name thus, but *al-Sulūk*, IV, II, 715 & al-Sakhāwī, *al-Ḍaw' al-lāmiᶜ*, Cairo, 1353, II, 269, no. 840, read Urunbughā and no. 842 is the person intended here. He was a *muqaddam* of the Sultanic Mamlūks.

12 David Ayalon, *Studies on the Mamluks of Egypt*, London, 1977, I, 462, VIII, 46, the third rank of Mamlūk officers, entitled to keep in their service between 10 to twenty horsemen.

13 Defined in *The Portuguese off the south Arabian coast*, reprint, Oxford-Beirut, 1974, 136-137.

14 Al-Malik al-Nāṣir Ṣalāḥ al-Dīn Aḥmad b. Ismāᶜīl, the Rasūlid.

15 *Al-Ḍaw' al-lāmiᶜ*, III, 103 seq. 'He governed the affairs at Jeddah with the merchants until their arrival there and after their leaving it'. Since his son Barakāt who succeeded him undertook 'not to interfere/ intervene in the tithes taken at Jeddah on the goods of merchants arriving from India and elsewhere' (*al-Sulūk*, IV, II, 723) the Mamlūk officials evidently took over during the period the India merchants spent there. Each year according to al-Maqrīzī (*loc.cit.*) and *al-Ḍaw'* (III; 105), Barakāt agreed to pay the Mamlūk sultan 10,000 dinars 'along with the current custom that the Jeddah customs duties (*maks*) should go to him (Barakāt) and such (dues) as had newly begun to be taken on the India vessels should be the perquisite of the sultan'. ᶜAjlān died in 829/1426 shortly after the events described here.

16 So Dozy, *Supplément*.

17 ᶜĀshūr reads 'Jeddah' which a glance at the map shows must be incorrect and one Ms. reads جدى obviously a mistake for Ḥaly (b. Yaᶜqūb) south of Sawākin on the Tihāmah coast.

18 *Sākin* means a village in parts of south Arabia, plural *sawākin*.

19 Presents and money are noted by the *Mulakhkhaṣ* as coming from Dahlak to the Rasūlids. This suggests that Dahlak was subject in some degree to them, as was Ḥaly. See also Anon, *Chronicle* ed. Yajima (fn 32), 56, 131; al-Daybaᶜ, *Qurrat al-ᶜuyūn*, ed. Muḥammad al-Akwaᶜ, Cairo, 1971-77, II, 182. Sawākin also sent presents (Yajima, 49).

20 Reading *ḥattā* for *ḥatama*.

21 Dozy defines *sāḥil* as *un entrepôt de commerce qui a des communications faciles avec la mer, un port*, but sometimes it simply means coast.

22 As in Yāqūt, *Muᶜjam*.

23 IV, II, 707.

24 *Aṣnāf* is also a term for 'spices'.

Egypt so that customs duties on what was with them could be taken from them. When the pilgrims dismounted at Birkat al-Ḥājj [25] the pilgrim commissioners (*mubāshirū al-ḥājj*) and their assistants came out and treated all merchants and pilgrims arriving with great severity, exerting themselves to the utmost in searching their saddle-boxes (*maḥāyir* [26]) and loads. They brought out all the presents they had with them and took the customs-duties on them, even a duty of ten dirhams in copper coins (*fulūs*) on a poor woman's leather mat. As for the merchants, in the past year one of the new Coptish converts to Islam (*musālimah*) had been produced to them, as previously mentioned, and he arrived at Mecca, went on to Jeddah accompanied by his assistants, recorded those sorts of goods [27] in the vessels which came from the land of India and Hurmuz, taking the tithes (*ᶜushūr*) on them. This year over forty vessels with cargoes of various goods arrived among the Indian vessels putting in to Jeddah. That was because at Jeddah the merchants found relief contrary to what they were experiencing at Aden. So they abandoned Aden and adopted Jeddah *bandar* instead of it. So Jeddah *bandar* continued important while, because of this, the circumstances of Aden were reduced to nothing and the state of the ruler of the Yemen turned weak. The inspectorate of Jeddah turned into a sultanic office (*waẓīfah*) conferred upon the revenue collector of it and every year at the times when the vessels of India put into Jeddah he would betake himself to Mecca and collect what the merchants were due to pay and present himself to Cairo with it. What was brought of this to the Treasury amounted to more than seventy thousand dinars, apart from what was not brought (to it).

Al-Maqrīzī comments that this was quite a different state of affairs from what obtained in the past when monarchs sent money to Mecca. Now it was taken from Mecca and the Ashrāf of Mecca were forced to provide the transport of it and merchants could not move freely to do business but were compelled to go to Cairo so that customs-duty could be collected on their property.

Ibid., *Year 829/1425-26* [28]

In it the amīr Urunbughā came, setting out by sea to Mecca. With him he had a present for the Lord of the Yemen. Then he went on with it from Jeddah by sea, accompanied by a person called Altunbughā Firanjī — he was at times in charge of Damietta — they being escorted by fifty men of the Sulṭanic mamlūks. [Some] person had recommended the seizure of the Yemen with this [body of] troops to the sultan. Firanjī stayed behind with the mamlūks in a vessel off the coast of Ḥaly Banī Yaᶜqūb [29] while Urunbughā escorted by five men of them set out with the present and the [accompanying] letter,[30] containing a request for money to assist in performing the *jihād* against the Franks. So the ruler of the Yemen began to assemble the present [in return]. Then news reached him that Firanjī had plundered one of the villages/ properties (*ḍiyāᶜ*) and killed four men. The Lord of the Yemen disliked this affair of theirs and became alerted to them, and said to Urunbughā: 'This is n't nice news ! The custom is that a single person comes in charge of a present that is being brought (*risālah* [31]) but you have come at the head of fifty men and of these of you, only you with five men have presented yourselves to me while the rest of you stayed behind and killed four of my men'. He expelled him from his presence without preparing a present or giving him anything. So he and these accompanying him escaped with their persons and all returned to Mecca, Urunbughā returning with little baggage.

Anonymous Rasūlid Chronicle [32]

News reached our lord, the sultan al-Malik al-Ẓāhir, Allah render him victorious, at the time when he was at the auspicious Dār al-Marsā (Anchorage Building) on the sea, that two of the vessels of the interlopers (*mujawwirūn*) had foundered at (*inṣalaḥū ᶜalā*) [33] Jabal al-Zuqar.[34] So our lord the sultan, Allah

---

[25] Richard F. Burton, *A Personal narrative of a pilgrimage to al-Madinah and Meccah*, London, 1893, II, 136, calls it simply al-Birkat, about 23 miles from the *mīqāt*, al-Zarībah.

[26] A. Barthélemy, *Dictionnaire Arabe-Français*, Paris 1935-54, 778, *maḥārah*, pl. *āt* (*maḥāyir* is another pl.), *couple de caisses, cacolet de bois qu'on fixe sur le dos d'une bête de somme.*

[27] This seems the most logical rendering of *aṣnāf al-matjar* as also of *aṣnāf* in the sentence following.

[28] IV, II, 715.

[29] Text (Ḥaly) Banī Yaᶜqūb.

[30] The letter has not previously been mentioned.

[31] Dozy, *risālah, présent que l'on porte à quelqu'un.*

[32] *A Chronicle of the Rasūlid dynasty of Yemen*, ed. Hikoichi Yajima, Tokyo, 1974, 122.

[33] Al-Khazrajī, *al-ᶜUqūd al-lu'lu'iyyah*, ed. Muḥammad ᶜAsal, *GMS*, Cambridge-Cairo, 1914-18, V, 101, records a

render him victorious, despatched the amir Zayn al-Dīn Shukr al-ᶜAdanī, accompanied by the inspector (*nāẓir*), the superintendants (*mubāshirūn*) and a company of the ever-victorious troops. They went to the site of the wreck (*mawḍiᶜ al-mukassar*) and stopped two days, then returned to our lord the sultan with such of the cargo as was showing.[35] Then subsequently it happened that some of the passengers (*rakabah*) that were in the vessels arrived — who confirmed that some of the cargo and specie (*naqd*) were still left. So our lord the sultan, Allah render him victorious, sent them back for it and they stopped two more days and brought back what was left. What they brought back in the way of stuffs (*qumāsh*), saffron, broadcloth (*jūkh*) and specie amounted to over a hundred thousand dinars' (worth). Our lord the sultan, Allah render him victorious, conferred the whole lot on the troops, the amīrs and the captains (*muqaddam* [36]). So on the day the dhows (*jilāb*) arrived from the wreck there was much pleasure and rejoicing, thronging and processions (*mawākib*) as outdid the pleasure at feasts and *subūt*.[37] They paraded the prisoners, over fifty individuals, for the inspection of our lord the sultan al-Malik al-Ẓāhir, Allah render him victorious, then he pardoned them and set them free... This took place in the month of Dhu 'l-Qaᶜdah al-Ḥarām, 25th of the year 832/ August 26th, 1429.

Ibid., *Year 833/1429* [38]

It happened that news arrived that the interlopers' vessels (*marākib al-mujawwirīn*) had reached Mocha *bandar* and that they petitioned our lord, the sultan, Allah render him victorious, for guarantees of protection and security (*al-dhimmah wa-'l-amānah*), and when our lord the sultan, Allah render him victorious, learned of this he kindly bestowed upon them solicitude and the guarantee of protection. The qāḍī Jamāl al-Dīn Muḥammad al-Ṭayyib b. Mukāwish [39] accompanied by the qāḍī Raḍiyy al-Dīn Abū Bakr b. Sālim came bringing them the honourable guarantee of protection. It chanced that a favourable breeze befell one of the two vessels so it went ahead intending to enter (*shā yadkhul*) the protected port (*al-thaghr al-maḥrūs* [40]) while the other vessel stayed until the mamlūks (*ghilmān* [41]) of our lord the sultan, Allah render him victorious, came up with it. So they gave in of free will, surrendering such precious articles (*tuḥaf*) as they had with them.[42] They came to the honourable court (*al-bāb al-sharīf*) in Zabīd the protected and our lord the sultan, Allah render him victorious, received them with every kindness, ignoring,[43] Allah render him victorious, their disgraceful action, may his practices (*ᶜawā'id*) con-

---

shipwreck at a reef (*shiᶜb*) at Jabal Zuqar in 755/1354 in December when a craft (*qiṭᶜah*) and all in it perished. Lane - *inṣalaḥa*, to become broken up, and (*ibid.*, 1536) *tashaᶜᶜāba*, citing *inṣalaḥa* as meaning 'it became cracked in several places... it became rendered unsound, impaired'.

[34] When visiting al-Fāzzah I noted that Zuqar is an island in front of it. In 822/1419 al-Nāṣir went down to Zabīd and ordered the new mooring place/ harbour to be constructed at al-Fāzzah (al-Daybaᶜ, *Qurrat al-ᶜuyūn*, ed. Akwaᶜ, II, 132 ; *al-Faḍl al-mazīd* (see fn. 59), 107. I have described it as I last saw it in 'Tihāmah notes', *Arabicus Felix: Luminosus Britannicus: Essays in Honour of A.F.L. Beeston on his eightieth birthday*, ed. Alan Jones, Oxford, 1991, 55-6, and was told that there was an old pier (*dakkah*) about a fathom below the sea surface. Al-Malik al-Nāṣir would have been at the Dār al-Marsā here. See article XVI below.

[35] *Mā ẓuhira* (sic); the passive seems incorrect. The probable sense is 'what showed above water' or 'what showed in the wreck'.

[36] A *muqaddam* can also mean a tribal chief.

[37] *Bughyat al-fallāḥīn*, 20a, states: 'The first of the Saturdays of the palms (*subūt al-nakhl*) at Zabīd is always on the first Saturday of Ayyār'. Allusion is often made in Yemeni writings to the festival *Sabt al-Subūt*. In 1974 I was reliably informed that it fell at the end of Ramaḍān, i.e. October 12th. In that year the first of the *subūt al-nakhl* would have fallen nearly at mid-May. I think it must be derived from the sense of *insabatat al-ruṭabah*, the ripe dates became soft (*Tāj al-ᶜarūs*, Kuwait, 1387/1968, IV, 540). Moshe Piamenta, *Dictionary of post-classical Yemeni Arabic*, Leiden, 1990-91, I, 212a, however makes it equivalent to Yom Kippur, Day of Atonement. Al-Khazrajī, IV, 219 & *Qurrat al-ᶜuyūn*, II, 53, note that in 696/1269 the sultan *sabata sabt-an* at *Zabīd*. In 747/1346, says al-Khazrajī, V, 79, he *tafarraja fī Zabīd ᶜala 'l-subūt* & (V. 261) at Zabīd he spent the first and second *sabts* on Rajab 1st & 8th, 796 (May 2nd & 9th, 1394), and (*ibid.*, V, 273) the first *sabt* is Rajab 3rd, 797 (April 24th, 1395). *Chronicle*/ Jajima, 92, shows that in 817/1414 the second of the *subūt al-nakhl* would fall in the last week in May or first in June, and in 834/1421 the first of them fell on Ramaḍān 28th/ June 9th. The *Qurrat al-ᶜuyūn*, II, 135, says that al-Malik al-Zāhir (821-42/1418-39) revived the *subūt* and days of the palms at Zabīd with great concourses and festivity (*faraḥ*) comprising kinds (of celebration) with which the people of religion were not pleased.

[38] Anonymous *Chronicle of the Rasūlid dynasty*, 124.

[39] *Kāwasha*, to abuse, to slang (*Gloss. dat.*) but this sense seems unlikely here.

[40] The vessel travelling in October would be proceeding to the north, so the *thaghr maḥrūs* would be the port of Zabīd. *Maḥrūs* is commonly applied to cities.

[41] Probably Kurds or Ghuzz, as distinct from Yemeni Arabs. They may not have been slaves.

[42] As gifts or to pay duty?

[43] Reading *taghaṭṭā* for *taᶜaṭṭā*.

tinue ever noble and his mercies vast, Allah render him victorious. This took place in the month of al-Muḥarram al-Ḥarām of the year 833/ October, 1429.

Ibid., *Year 833/1429* [44]

News reached our lord the sultan al-Malik al-Ẓāhir, Allah render him victorious, that a collection of open skiffs (*ṭarārīd*) from the vessels of the interloper merchants (*min al-tujjār al-mujawwirīn*) had approached the auspicious anchorage petitioning for the guarantee of protection from our lord the sultan al-Malik al-Ẓāhir and [to be permitted] to come to the honourable court. So our lord the sultan al-Malik al-Ẓāhir despatched the qāḍī Jamāl al-Dīn Muḥammad al-Ṭayyib b. Mukāwish with the honourable guarantee and they arrived in his company at the noble court.[45]

The writer lauds al-Malik al-Ẓāhir whom Allah has supported against all who disobeyed him after his dispensing of justice and his reputation for this had spread abroad to all regions. He continues:

So when the interlopers (*al-mujawwirīn* [46]) disobeyed his order Allah chastised them for their disobedience to him, scattered them (*shattata aḥwāla-hum*) and tore them utterly to pieces in the desolate wastes and deserts — after which no alternative lay before them but to enter under submission to him, Allah render him victorious, since he is one of the monarchs concerning whom the Tradition [47] has come down from the Apostle of Allah, Allah bless and honour him, that he said: 'The sultan is the shadow of Allah on His Earth with whom any person oppressed may find refuge' ... This took place in Ṣafar of year 833/ November, 1429.

Ibid., *Year 833, Jumādā II, 21 /1430, March 17th* [48]

On that very day messengers arrived with the good news that the vessel of the Dīwān [49] posted at Bāb al-Mandab had overcome the Sumatra vessel, one of the interlopers' vessels, and arrested it. They took the merchants on board it and sent them in custody to the protected port.[50] This took place in year 833/1429.

Ibid., *Year 833/1430*

On Rajab 3rd, 833/ March 28th, 1430, the sultan goes from Mawzaᶜ to Bāb al-Mandab with an escort of soldiers to superintend the vessels of the Dīwān and post soldiers in them (*mubāsharat al-marākib* [51] *wa-tartīb al-ᶜaskar fī-him*), leaving the rest of the baggage (*rakht*) [52] at Mawzaᶜ. The author [53] continues:

It so happened, by the decree and predestination of Allah, that one of the interlopers' vessels arrived at Bāb al-Mandab, and one of the vessels with the amīr Sayf al-Dīn Sunqur aboard it and a number of dhows came alongside it. Then another of the interlopers' vessels arrived and the naqīb [54] Shujāᶜ al-Dīn ᶜUmar b. Masᶜūd, he being in the vessel al-Nāṣirī,[55] with a number of light skiffs (*ṭarārīd*) came alongside of it. They overcame the vessel, slew the *nākhūdhah* and a number of the merchants of the vessel, taking the rest of them prisoner. Some of the merchants left went into their cabins (*bilālanij* [56]) and started to shoot arrows at the soldiers. So a body of the soldiers put to sea (*kharajū*). The naqīb ᶜUmar b. Masᶜūd became enraged [57] at this and ordered the vessel to be set on fire. But they advised him not to fire (it) because the two vessels had got locked together (*murtabiṭayn*) so if one of them were set on fire the other could hardly be saved. But he would not accept their advice on this and threatened to kill the Greek-fire thrower (*al-nafaṭī*) if he did not do that. When the Greek-fire thrower launched the naphta against them the fire spread over to the other vessel so the soldiers moved over [58] to the other side and it foundered. The other vessel foundered (also) and most of the people

---

44 P. 125.

45 The sultan was at Taᶜizz at this time.

46 Read *al-mujawwirūn*.

47 This *ḥadīth* does not figure in Wensinck.

48 P. 129.

49 The Rasūlid administration, as detailed in *Mulakhkhaṣ al-fiṭan*.

50 At Zabid ?

51 *Rattaba*, to garrison, *rutbah*, a garrison.

52 *Rakht*, goods & chattels, Dozy, *meubles*; a Persian word used in Mamlūk Egypt.

53 P. 129.

54 *Naqīb* usually a tribal chief but probably a military rank here.

55 Doubtless named after the Rasūlid sultan al-Malik al-Nāṣir (ob. 827/1424).

56 Reading this with Yajima following Buzurg b. Shahriyār, *ᶜAjā'ib al-Hind*.

57 Reading *ightāẓa* for *iᶜtāḍa*.

58 Reading *taᶜaddat* for *baᶜudat*.

perished in the sea, the naqīb ᶜUmar b. Masᶜūd perishing [along with them] by drowning in the sea. Then the vessel with the amīr Sunqur in it was unsuccessful in overcoming the vessel with which it had come alongside and he resolved to return to Mocha, but he chanced on another of the interlopers' vessels, grappled with it and overcame it. His letters dealing with the incident reached our lord al-Malik al-Ẓāhir, Allah render him victorious, and our lord the sultan commanded that they send the vessel to the auspicious anchorage at the sea of al-Ahwāb [59] and the qāḍī ᶜAfīf al-Dīn b. ᶜUmar al-Qubāṭī proceeded to Mocha for that purpose. This happened on Sunday, the 16th of the month of Rajab, 833/ April 10th, 1430.

Ibid., *Year 837/1434* [60]

Of what Allah decreed it so happened that the north monsoon wind (*al-shimāl*) deflected all the interloper vessels and drove them back from the vicinity of Jeddah to the territory (*ḥadd*) of the protected port (Zabīd? or perhaps Aden?) and they petitioned our lord the sultan, Allah render him victorious for guarantee of protection and (permission) to enter the protected port in security and tranquillity. His honourable command came to the qāḍī Raḍiyy al-Dīn Abū Bakr, son of the late ᶜAbd al-Qādir, inspector of the protected port, to allow them a reduction of a fifth [of the customary tithes [61]], and our lord the sultan, Allah render him victorious, pardoned them for all of the offence they had committed, Allah render him victorious, out of his graciousness and munificence.

Ibid., *Year 838/1435* [62]

It so happened that the officials (? *aṣḥāb*) of al-Ḥudaydah seized one [63] of the vessels of the interlopers and apprized our lord the sultan, Allah render him victorious, of this. So he, Allah render him victorious, commanded the amīr Jamāl al-Dīn Najīb al-Jamdār,[64] the qāḍī Shujāᶜ al-Dīn Umar b. Ibrāhīm al-Ṣanᶜānī and the qāḍī Jamāl al-Dīn al-Ṭāhir al-Miṣrī to proceed with the soldiers to al-Ḥudaydah on this account. Then the inspector proceeded from Zabīd. When they arrived there they put aside what was inside the vessel and went with what was light to convey (*bi-'l-khiff*) to the honourable court of al-Mahjam [65] the protected, accompanied by mamlūks, servants, the merchants from the vessel, the pilot (*muᶜallim*), the merchants all in shackles (*taḥt al-asr* [66]), to the honourable court. Their entry took place on Tuesday the 8th of Shaᶜbān al-Karīm of the year 838/ March 9th, 1435. The contents of the vessel, comprising various kinds of spice (*bahār*), top quality Yazdī cloth, silk, *bayram* (pl. *bayārim*) cloth [67], muslins (*shāshāt*), et cetera, were valued at over a hundred thousand dinars — this through the auspicious fortune of our lord the sultan, Allah render him victorious. He, Allah render him victorious, commanded the vessel with the cargo it contained should proceed to the new *bandar* [68] at Zabīd the protected in the year 838/1435.

Al-Maqrīzī, al-Sulūk, *Year 838/1435* [69]

On the 13th [of Ṣafar]/ 18th September he (sultan Barsbāy) wrote... that the *ᶜushr* only, is to be charged

---

[59] The *Mulakhkhaṣ al-fiṭan* describes both *bandars* al-Ahwāb and al-Buqᶜah as of Zabīd al-maḥrūs. Al-Ahwāb is south (*ᶜAdanī*) of Zabīd. Ibn al-Daybaᶜ, *Bughyat al-mustafīd fī akhbār madīnat Zabīd*, ed. ᶜAbdullah al-Ḥabshī, Ṣanᶜā', 1979, 36 & *ibid.*, *al-Faḍl al-mazīd ᶜalā Bughyat al-mustafīd*, ed. Yūsuf Shulhud, Beirut, 1983, 107, writing before 944/1537, states that Ghulāfiqah of the sea coast was the *bandar* of Zabīd and the *bandar* was transferred to al-Ahwāb village which today is called al-Buqᶜah. Al-Khazrajī is cited by Cassels Kay, *Yemen its early mediaeval history*, London, 1892, 221 to the same effect. As he died in 812/1409 al-Fāzzah founded in 822/1419 would have come to take pride of place over al-Ahwāb/ al-Buqᶜah later. See fn. 26.

[60] P. 167.

[61] *Al-Mulakhkhaṣ*, 26v, has a heading "The rebate (*ḥaṭīṭ*) of al-Kārim, the Kārimī merchants". Grammatically here the text reads 'the customary fifth of the tithes' — which might be the correct sense indeed.

[62] P. 175.

[63] Reading *markab-an* with the Ms. for *marākib-an*.

[64] An honorary title for the keeper of the wardrobe (Steingass). The office is described by Qalqashandī, *Ṣubḥ al-aᶜshā*, Cairo, 1913 ff., V, 459.

[65] Al-Mahjam was a Rasūlid resort in the winter and a mint city. When I visited it in 1974 I found only a ruined minaret and a vast quantity of potsherds.

[66] The text is not explicit here; perhaps the pilot was also in shackles.

[67] Yajima's proposed reading, *bahram*, bastard saffron, for an unclear text, is improbable; *bayram* cloth should be read. Cf. *al-Sulūk*, IV, II, 977, *thiyāb bayram*; it also figures in *al-Mulakhkhaṣ* and other writers. The interloper vessel should have come from the Gulf of India. *Bayram*, *shāshāt*, etc. also figure in the *Dīwān-i-albisah* of Maḥmūd Qārī of Yazd, Constantinople, 1303, about contemporary with these events.

[68] Al-Fāzzah.

[69] IV, II, 929.

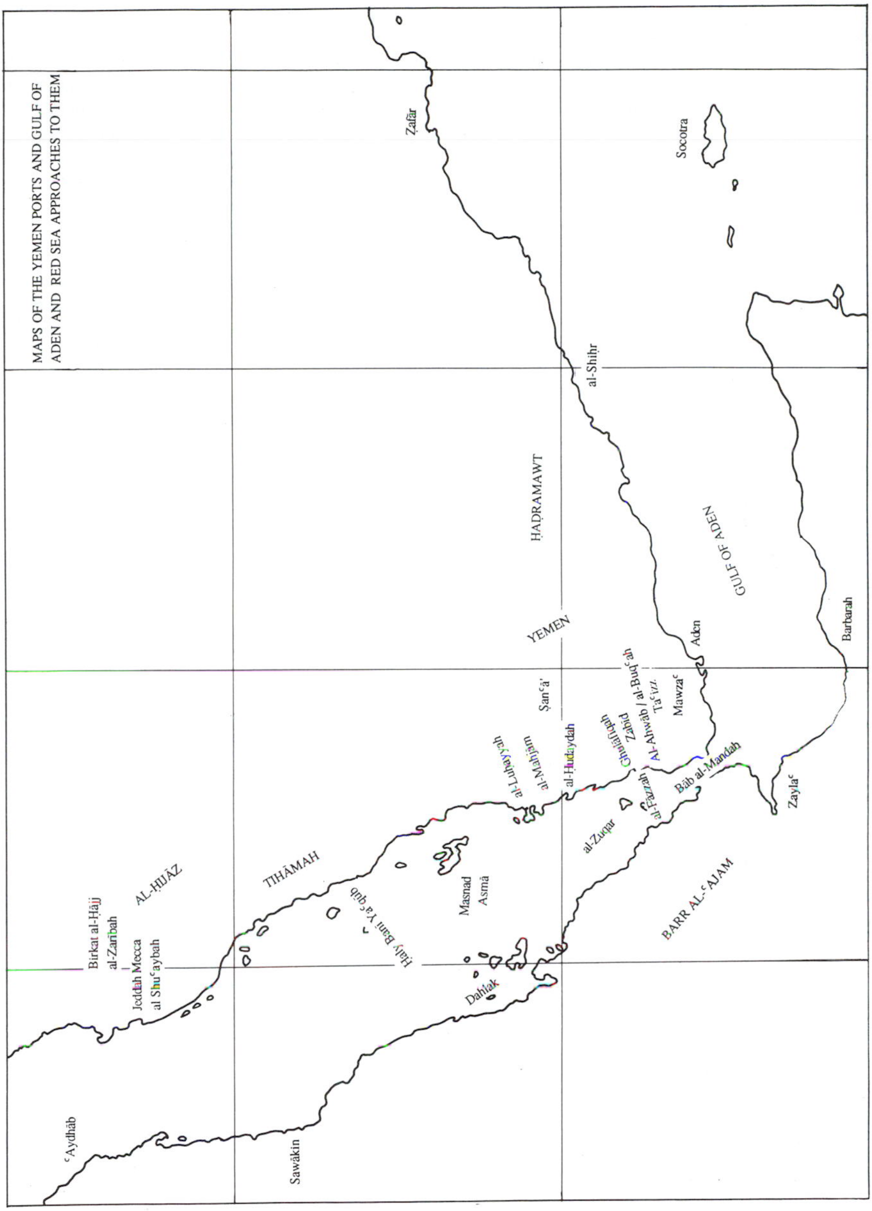
MAPS OF THE YEMEN PORTS AND GULF OF ADEN AND RED SEA APPROACHES TO THEM
Ẓafār
Socotra
al-Shiḥr
ḤAḌRAMAWT
GULF OF ADEN
Barbarah
YEMEN
Aden
Ṣanʿāʾ
Mawzaʿ
Taʿizz
Al-Aḥwāb / al-Buqʿah
Zabīd
Ghulāfiqah
al-Ḥudaydah
al-Mahjam
al-Luḥayyah
Bāb al-Mandab
Zaylaʿ
al-Fāzzah
al-Zuqar
BARR AL-ʿAJAM
TIHĀMAH
Masnad
Asmā
Ḥaly Banī Yaʿqūb
AL-ḤIJĀZ
Birkat al-Ḥājj
al-Zarībah
Jeddah
Mecca
al Shuʿaybah
Dahlak
ʿAydhāb
Sawākin

on the merchants of the Indians putting into Jeddah but that two *ᶜushrs* are to be charged on the Shāmī and Egyptian (Miṣrī) merchants when they put into Jeddah with goods of the Yemen and that any of the Yemeni merchants putting into Jeddah with merchandise, all of his goods should be seized for the sultan (of Egypt) without a price being paid for them. The reason for this is that of latter years the merchants of India, when they pass by Bāb al-Mandab, have begun to evade Aden [70] *bandar* so as to anchor at the entrepôt (*sāḥil*) of Jeddah, as previously remarked.[71] Thus Aden was deserted by merchants and the king of the Yemen became reduced in circumstances because of the diminution of his revenue while Jeddah has become the *bandar* of the merchants and the sultan of Egypt obtains such money from the tithes (*ᶜushūr*) on the merchants. The inspectorate (*naẓar*) of Jeddah [customs] has become a sultanic office (*waẓīfah*) and the tithes on their goods are received from the merchants from India putting in there along with fixed charges (*rusūm*) imposed for the inspector (*nāẓir*), the *shādd*,[72] the intendants of the large scales (*qabbān*), the cashier (*ṣayrafī* [73]) and so on, customs officers [74] and others. On behalf of the sultan of Egypt there began to be transported coral, copper etc., of the kinds (of goods) transported to the land of India and (this) was forced on (*yuṭraḥ ᶜalā*) the merchants.[75] In this more than one of the officials of the state (*ahl al-dawlah*) copied him. The merchants were grievously oppressed by this, and in the previous year (p. 88) a group of them disembarked at Aden. The sultan in Egypt was annoyed at them because of his loss of the *ᶜushūr* chargeable on them. So he inflicted as a punishment upon them that anyone who bought an item of merchandise from Aden and took it to Jeddah should have the *ᶜushr* charged him doubled to two *ᶜushūr* if he were of the Shāmīs or Egyptians and that his merchandise, were he of the people of Yemen should be impounded altogether. However by the grace of Allah upon his servants he did not put any of this innovation into practice, but these written orders were read out in front of the Black Stone and Sharīf Barakāt b. ᶜAjlān petitioned the amīr of Mecca to get the sultan to rescind the order till he pardoned the merchants and cancelled the order he had made.

*

* *

Before taking up the question of the 'interlopers' one has to dispose of Subhi Labib's contention [76] that in the Yemen the Rasūlids ruled 'theoretically as representative of the Mamlūk sultans'. Ibn al-Daybaᶜ states categorically that the first Rasūlid monarch, ᶜUmar b. ᶜAlī who ruled from Ḥaḍramawt to Mecca, when he became independent (*istaqalla*) had his name pronounced in the khuṭbah and struck on the coinage.[77] The Rasūlids were not breakaway rulers from Mamlūk Egypt, omitting to pay tribute, though pressures were put on sultan al-Mujāhid taken prisoner by the Egyptians at the *ḥajj* in 751/1351 to send a gift and money each year to the Mamlūk Sultan instead of a ransom.

If merchants were maltreated and exploited at Aden as Labib affirms with some justice, the treatment they received at the hands of Mamlūk customs officials, as can be seen from al-Maqrīzī's *al-Sulūk*, was also severe. Certainly Ibn al-Mujāwir [78] (ob. 690/1291) does describe the strict body search and * indignities to which voyagers were subjected at Aden — there is no evidence that these had been relaxed when the Kālīkūt merchant Ibrāhīm was disgusted by his treatment there. Nevertheless as I have remarked [79]: 'The [Yemeni] historians not infrequently refer to actions of the sultans taken to abolish dues arbitrarily imposed by their officials. The sultans spent the winter season in the Tihāmah coinciding with the S.E. monsoon (Azyab) spending much of it about Zabīd, but when their backs were turned rapacious officials apparently reverted to their malpractices. If the Kārimī merchants complained of the

70 Reading *yujawwirūn* for *yajūzūn*.

71 P. 84 supra.

72 The *shādd al-dawāwīn* in Mamlūk Egypt appears to have been a soldier member of the tax-collecting team, collecting arrears and punishing tax evaders. Hassanein Rabie, *The Financial system of Egypt*, London-Oxford, 1972, 150-51 passim. Dozy — *officier pour presser le payement de douane et autres contributions.*

73 Rabie, *op.cit.*, 159.

74 Dozy, *Aᶜwān al-zakāt*, douaniers.

75 Dozy, *ṭaraḥa*, *imposer une denrée à un homme, le forcer de l'acquérir à un prix excessif que l'on a fixé soi-même.*

76 'Egyptian commercial policy in the Middle Ages' in M.A. Cook, *Studies in the economic history of the Middle East*, London-Oxford, 1970, 68.

77 *Al-Faḍl al-mazīd*, 89.

78 Cited in my 'Yemeni merchants...', 65. See article I above.

79 *Ibid.*, 66.

* Ibn al-Mujāwir undoubtedly flourished in the early 7th/13th century and this date of death is too late.

'illegitimate tax demands of the Yemenite ruler' in 704-5/1304 [80] they continued to have close links with Aden and in the 9th/15th century Abū Makhramah [81] can write that 'the merchants of al-Kārim come to Aden only' ; this probably means they did not call at other ports in the Red Sea and Gulf of Aden. In the time of al-Mujāhid they owned various kinds of merchandise (*aṣnāf al-matjar*), perhaps in depots, at Aden, Zabīd and Taᶜizz.[82] In the early 9th/15th century too the *Mulakhkhaṣ* registers that there was a rebate (*ḥaṭīṭ*) for the Kārim on pepper, brazilwood and *maḥlab* (kernel of the wild cherry).

The sultan's trading establishment (*al-matjar al-sulṭānī* [83]) may have been felt to be oppressive in its activities. Its officials seem to have had a priority in the selection of at least certain commodities of which they could chose the best. The Fāṭimids set up a *matjar* and possibly the Ayyūbids may have founded one in Aden along with other Egyptian administrative practices which they introduced, or it might be a Rasūlid innovation. The *matjar* at Zabīd was founded only in 798/1395.[84]

The Ayyubids had employed galleys (*shawānī*) lying at Aden to protect merchant shipping from pirates and about the second decade of the 7th/13th century al-Malik al-Masᶜūd had the tax to maintain the *shawānī* added to the *ᶜushūr* charged on merchandise; the *shawānī* still figure in *al-Mulakhkhaṣ* (22v). Under the Ayyūbids these galleys were posted 'at the head of the landfalls'. The Rasūlids possessed vessels and the Dīwān at Aden numbered among its officials an *ᶜāmil*, *mushārif* and *nā'ib* in charge of the inspectorate (*naẓar*) of ship-building (*inshā'*) at the port.[85] I have not ascertained whether this inspectorate had also to do with vessels constructed by private enterprise. An Ashrafī ship [86] laden with many various sorts of gifts and presents (*tuḥaf wa-hadāyā* [87]) in 790/1388 arrived from Aden at al-Ahwāb where al-Malik al-Ashraf was staying. It remained there for a time and al-Ashraf used to go on pleasure cruises in it with those drinking companions (*ḥurafā'*) and amīrs he liked. The vessel al-Nāṣirī, doubtless so called after al-Malik al-Nāṣir was used in action against interlopers (p. 87).

The historians do no commit themselves as to whether the Rasūlid naval vessels continued to protect merchant shipping from pirates, for which purpose the continuing *shawānī* tax should have been expended; it certainly would have been in the interest of the sultanic government to do so. In March 833/1430 government ships with complements of soldiers were posted at Bāb al-Mandab to intercept interlopers and actual engagements with them took place as seen above. It looks as if the Rasūlid authorities has resorted to action by force to compel 'interlopers' to call at a Yemeni port and that they were already concerned at the loss of revenue because shipping bound for Jeddah was by-passing Aden. From the silence of the historians and some more positive indications it would seem that the Kārimī vessels did not attempt to 'interlope'. Interloper vessels at least mostly seem to have been coming from the Far East, no doubt with more valuable cargos than coming from the Mediterrean. The vessel that foundered off al-Zuqar in August 1429 was evidently travelling in the period closed to shipping (*taghlīq al-baḥr*); from the nature of its cargo it seems to have been eastward bound.

Did interloping ships engage in smuggling into the Yemen? It seems to me that possibly local craft might put out to accost a passing vessel, but in any anchorage of importance there is likely to have been a government official, and merchants bound for the Mediterranean states and large profits would be disinclined to look for casual trading with the coastal people.

Within about thirty years of the démarche by Ibrāhīm of Kālīkūt and Jeddah's supplanting Aden as a premier entrepôt the Rasūlids lost control of the Yemen to the Ṭāhirids. A cogent factor in their decline — as in that of the Zaydī imāms of the early ninteenth century — was in all likelihood, a heavy fall in the lucrative customs revenues listed in a wealth of detail by the *Mulakhkhaṣ al-fiṭan*.

---

80 Labid, *loc.cit.*

81 In *Arabische Texte zur Kenntnis der Stadt Aden im Mittelalter*, ed. O. Löfgren, Uppsala, 1936-50, II, 138.

82 Al-Maqrīzī, *al-Sulūk*, II, II, 852. To compel the *tujjār al-Kārim* to help her release her son from captivity in Egypt, his mother sealed (*khatamat*) their property in these cities.

83 For the institution of *matjar* in general see Rabie, 92-4.

84 *Al-Faḍl al-mazīd*, 104, al-Malik al-Ashraf commanded *ᶜimārat al-matjar bi-Zabīd*.

85 The Ṭāhirids possessed shipping for *al-Faḍl al-mazīd*, 318, records that in 915/1509-10 'the vessels of the sultan al-Malik al-Ẓāhir arriving from India were lost and only one vessel and two *ṭalīᶜahs* of them were safe'. A *ṭalīᶜah* is a 'swift sambook or *sāᶜī* (dhow)' (my *Portuguese*, 136).

86 Anon. Chronicle, 46.

87 *Hadiyyah*, according to Dozy, can mean *provisions de voyage* in another context. *Tuḥaf* are rare objects etc.

V

THE CUSTOMARY LAW OF SOUTH-WEST ARABIA AND BEDOUIN JUSTICE IN JORDAN

Customary law first caught my attention towards the end of 1940 when I accompanied the Political Officer to 'Awdhali territory in the West Aden Protectorate when he went to settle a dispute there. The 'Awdhali Sultan, Salih, produced a short tribal code called *shar'*[1], the ordinary term for such customary law, which is *not* Islamic *shari'ah*. Pursuing this subject when Colonial Research Fellow in Hadramawt in 1947 I purchased a Ms. composed in the early 14th century at Bayt al-Faqih in the Yemen Tihamah which gives a systematic exposition of that branch of customary law known as *man'ah*[2]. At the same time, unbeknown to me, the late Professor Ettore Rossi[3] published extracts from a small corpus of parallel tribal law treatises he acquired in the Yemen in 1935. When we met some years later in Rome, aware he had not long to live, he permitted me to publish all his materials (and make photographic copies of them) with my own edited text. All these I have correlated but his documents present many difficulties of language and interpretation. On my travels in Royalist Yemen in 1964 I found ordinary tribesmen could help me little with them – while the shaykhs were too busy with the war to have time for matters academic. Meanwhile I have collected many further customary law documents while in southern Arabia.

---

1 Summarized in Naval Intelligence Division, *Western Arabia and the Red Sea*, B.R. 527, Oxford, June, 1946, 587 seq.

2 *Kitab al-Adab wa-'l-lawazim fi ahkam al-man'ah*, see my «Materials for south Arabian history», II, *Bulletin of the School of Oriental and African Studies*, London, 1950, XIII, iii, 589 seq.

3 «Il Diritto consuetudinario delle tribù arabe del Yemen», *Rivista degli studi orientali*, Roma, 1948, XXIII.

It became increasingly evident to me that the study of Arabian tribal law, its intrinsic interest apart, would throw light on the bases of Islamic *shari'ah*, and the work of Colonel 'Uwaydi with me at Cambridge, on tribal judicial processes in Jordan[4], and that of Dr Muhammad al-Zulfah on 'Asir helped to confirm this.

Shari'ah, theoretically, is mainly based on the Prophet's *sunnah*, his way, custom, even precedent. Muhammad, a member of a holy house of arbiters associated with the Meccan Temple, is one of a series of arbiters, a giver of law insofar as his decisions, most probably within the existing framework of customary law, themselves became law. Nor did *sunnah* precedents stop with Muhammad for his successors, Abu Bakr, 'Umar, 'Uthman, 'Ali, all had *sunnahs* – the principle of evolving new precedents survives in the power of the Imams of the Shi'ah to exercise their opinions – the function called *ijtihad*[5].

My Mss. deal with *man'ah*, competence to defend oneself and protect others – that branch of customary law covering not only maintenance of security in inter-tribal anarchy, but the closely allied business of personal honour. Muhammad had *sharaf*, honour, and this *man'ah*. He was not *naqis al-hasab*, lacking in status, as the poet A'sha Maymun calls it. Of this *man'ah* law the 13th century Ibn al-Mujawir[6] tells us, «All the Arabs ['Arab] of these regions [south-western Arabia], mountain and Tihamah plain up to the Hijaz borders – not one of them accepts judgement by the *shari'ah* (*hukm al-shar'*), for they accept judgement only of man'. There is no doubt», he adds, «that it is the judgement of the pagan era to which they would resort by referring their law-suits to the *kahins*». These *kahins*, priestly arbiters, claimed supernatural powers, the *kahin* of paganism often being identified with the *taghut*, said to be «interpreters of idols».

The author of my treatise on *man'ah*[7], a Shafi'i, a little later than Ibn al-Mujawir, explicitly avers, «Judgement by *man'* does not infringe judgement by *shar'* (= *shari'ah*) – on the contrary in it lies support for restraining those who create disorder – and its roots are firmly planted in the Book of the Lord of the Universe and word of His Prophet».

These passages demonstrate that over this wide territory ancient tribal customary law continued, without reference to Islamic *shari'ah* evolved in the cities of Iraq, Syria or Persia, though as both stem from one source the divergence is less than might be expected. However a recent Hadrami author, Ba Sabrayn, returning from the Hijaz about a century ago, penned a polemic against 74 practices current in Hadramawt which he indignantly stigmatises as against *shari'ah*. Judgement based on causes

---

4 Ahmad Oweidi Abbadi, *Bedouin justice in Jordan*, Cambridge Ph. D. thesis, 1982, XXX. Cf. his «Muqaddimah li-dirasat al-'asha'ir al-Urdunniyyah», *Man hum al-badw ?*, Series, 'Amman, 1404/1984.

5 See my exposition in *Cambridge History of Arabic Literature*, I, Cambridge, 1983, 122, 132 seq.

6 «Tarikh al-mustabsir», ed. O. Löfgren, *Descriptio Arabiae meridionalis*, Leiden, 1951, 99.

7 See note 2.

8 Transcription in writer's possession, a work composed in 1294/1877. See my «Materials...», II, 593. There is a passing reference to Ba Sabrayn in C. Brockelmann, *GAL*, Sup., II, 604.

stemming from agriculture, commerce, tribalism (*qabwalah*) and the crafts, though contrary to *shari'ah*, are believed in Hadramawt, nonetheless, he says, to be branching from *shari'ah* (*hukm al-far'*). This attitude he totally rejects, asserting that what is contrary to *shari'ah* is invalid and judgement by the *Taghut*.

Taghut is a term still applied today to law outside the *shari'ah* in parts of Arabia but in no pejorative sense by those following it. Philby reported it from several places; I heard it on the lips of Kuwait tribesmen in 1953, with the comment that the Shaykh had abolished it, and in Hadramawt. Yemeni commentators on verses of the celebrated poet al-Anisi praise an Imam for slaying the head of the *Taghut*[9], a tribal chief following customary law while the famous scholar al-Amir al-San'ani[10], a few centuries ago, alludes to tribes repairing to the north Yemen town, Huth, to seek judgement of the *Taghut*.

In certain Qur'anic passages *Taghut* must be understood as arbiter, notably *Surat al-Nisa'*[11] which accuses Medinans in treaty relation with Muhammad of desiring to go to the *Taghut* for arbitration, not to what God revealed or to God's Apostle who is elsewhere named the *maradd* or final arbiter[12]. The Prophet's policy was to concentrate this central function in himself – the same *Surah* says the Believers must obey the Apostle and those in authority over them – their *naqibs*, tribal chiefs. They were not to go to outside arbiters, whether families of hereditary judges or the *Taghut*. Supernatural means to uncover a culprit practised by *kahins* or *Taghut* may have been such as *al-mandal*, still used in Hadramawt – for example a child sees a thief in the act of stealing as he gazes into a saucer made shiny with lamp-black mixed with oil. Then there is trial by ordeal, known today in north and south Arabia as *bish'ah*[13] – I know of only two classical Arabic references to it.

The maxim, *al-amr bi-'l-ma'ruf wa-'l-nahy 'ani 'l-munkar*, enforcing what is customary and prohibiting what is unknown, may be both pre-Islamic and Islamic. It is important that in the major Islamic document establishing the *Ummah* confederation in Medina, Muhammad accepted that its tribes settle blood-money according to custom (*ma'ruf*). However, while much Islamic *shari'ah* is founded on ancient Arabian custom, parts of this have been subtly modified, even rejected by the ulema in the conquered countries, often Jewish or Christian converts – they seem to have tried to eliminate certain Arabian custom as unpalatable to them. There is clear evidence that the Shu'ubiyyah, the anti-Arabian ulema of the conquered lands, introduced an egalitarian element into Islam by the manipulation of Traditions – native Arabian society was not egalitarian.

---

9 'Abd al-Rahman AL-ANISI, *Tarji' al-atyar bi-murqis al-ash'ar*, ed. Cairo, 1369/1950, 252.

10 *Diwan al-Amir al-San'ani*, ed. al-Sayyid AL-SABAH AL-MADANI, Cairo, 1384/1964, 168. *Taghut* is also discussed in the *Cambridge History of Arabic Literature* with further references.

11 *Surah* IV.

12 See my reprint volume, *Studies in Arabian History and Civilisation*, London, 1981, «The Constitution of Medina» (*Islamic quarterley*, London, 1964, «The Sunnah Jami'ah... the Documents comprised in the so-called 'Constitution of Medina'» (*BSOAS*, London, 1978).

13 See my note in M. LOEWE & Carmen BLACKER, *Divination and oracles*, London, 1981, 220. See article XIV below.

Islamic legal literature differs much on *qasamah*, the multiple oath of innocence of a crime, taken corporately by a tribe or most of its adult males. A judge today might say, *'Fi 'l-qatil arba'in hallafah*, i.e., the tribe accused of murder must produce 40 men to swear to the innocence of its members. This is still practised by the Nakha'iyyin[14], east of Aden, the tribe of al-Ashtar al-Nakha'i the supporter of the Caliph 'Ali b. Abi Talib. I took notes from the customary court there on this multiple oath. In the formative centuries of Islam *qasamah* was clearly disliked as the arguments against it in the literature show. In tribal districts it is effective – in urban areas probably not.

The fundamental law of Arabian society is, however, that of *man'ah* involving the physical security from violence of the individual and group. This is primarily the concern of the noble arms – bearing tribes – as the security of all other groups, even the religious aristocracy when unarmed, is, one way or another, guaranteed by them, all other law is secondary to the question of maintaining security. I refer of course to tribes that have not been subjected to the forceful rule of a centralised authority like the theocratic rule of Muhammad or the Imams of the Yemen, or the secular rule of colonial powers and rulers of the type now predominating in the Arab world, all of them by their nature opposed to tribalism. Arabia has always alternated between centralisation, secular or theocratic, and that de-centralisation so often conceived of as tribal anarchy. Thus it is no accident that, when a centralised government gains control of a province, it immediately assumes the responsibility for blood, and writes off previous blood-feuds. When centralisation of power breaks down, the one remaining sanction against lawlessness is the fear of initiating a blood-feud with all the attendant loss and expense. To the outside world it may seem strange to speak of the care of tribes to maintain security when, to all appearances, they seem to be perpetually at war, but it is fear of the consequences that leads tribal headmen to restrain the impetuosity and military ardour of the young hotheads of the tribe.

For maintenance of security the Arabians evolved their collective system – the tribe is responsible for the protection of each of its members and for their misdemeanours. In such a society the tribeless unprotected person cannot survive, so an elaborate structure for protection developed, similar, in many respects to that of feudal Europe. Any group, or individual, unable to protect itself must have a lord or other tribal group to guarantee it protection – for this protection, one way or another, payment must be made. Injuries done to the lowest in the social scale, or to such as the Jews, not even Muslims, touch the protector's honour, and compensation must be exacted by him.

---

14 See my «The 'White Dune' at Abyan : an ancient place of pilgrimage in southern Arabia», *Journal of Semitic Studies*, Manchester, 1971, XVI, i, 83 : C. de Landberg, «Notes sur quelques serments et pratiques chez les Bédouins de l'Arabie», *Arabica*, V, Leiden, 1898, 124 seq. and my paper at the Mahmoud Ghul Memorial Conference at Yarmouk University, 1984, entitled 'Dawlah, tribal shaykhs, the Mansab of the Waliyyah Sacidah, qasamah, in the Fadli Sultanate, South Arabian Federation's. This has now appeared in *Arabian studies in honour of Mahmoud Ghul*, ed. M.M. Ibrahim, Wiesbaden, 1989.

Some of the principles of tribal law as laid down in the Ms. I found in Hadramawt in 1947 will now be surveyed.

First then comes the common responsibility of the tribe for actions by individual members of it and for actions committed against them. But a tribe can proclaim in a frequented market – the proclamation called in the Yemen *zahirah*[15] – made by a herald who beats a drum to summon those present to attention, that it dissociates itself entirely from a certain member or group of the tribe. This makes them/him an outlaw – but such drastic measures are taken only when a tribesman has proved impossible to restrain or has commited heinous offences within the tribal circle. The outlaw at once seeks to affiliate himself for protection to another tribe – the former Aden Protectorate Sultans had, attached to them, men called *'asakir al-Sultan*, the soldiers of the Sultan, often men outlawed from other tribes. The Prophet himself indeed had followers of this category. Sometimes entire tribes seek affiliation to another confederation, breaking away from their own Hence any one Arabian confederation contains mixed ethnic elements. I recall the case in the 'Awdhali Sultanate where, on account of a grudge, a tribesman admitted armed foes into his castle – but even his closest relations repudiated him and the tribe declared his blood to be «blood of a snake (*dam al-hanash*)» – i.e., anyone might slay him with impunity. The principle of collective security used to govern the relations between the tribes and the Aden Government. If the tribesman has a grievance against the Government he may take action – in plain words, to shoot – any one of its representatives, from the highest official down to Arab soldiers in its pay. The Government, if a tribesman kills one of its men, would be acting correctly in taking retaliatory measures against any adult male of the tribe, or against its property.

Elaborate rules govern the extension of tribal protection to groups or individuals. A protector may guarantee total protection – though to do so he must be a very powerful man – or he may guarantee protection within certain boundaries. Protection may be for all time or for a specified time – it may be heritable, so that one's heirs assume one's responsibilities. You may take protection (*jiwar*) to have an injustice done you righted – in some cases you can oblige a tribe or tribesman to act on your behalf. Among the 'Awadhil, if robbed of a sheep you kill another sheep for the Sultan and he must replace your loss, but he reovers it fourfold from the thief. Somestimes the request for assistance is made by an *'aqirah*, i.e., hocking or slaughtering a bull in front of, for example, an Imam. Naturally mostly only those too weak (*da'if*) to obtain restitution or avenge themselves resort to this means, and, as I have indicated, a tribesman's social status is determined by his capability to defend himself and his dependants. It is absolutely obligatory on the tribal protector to rise and fight on behalf of his protégé, however humble the latter may be, and to take action against the murderer's tribe, though of course, if the injured party assents, money may be accepted in lieu of blood. Hadrami tribesmen nevertheless sometimes refuse to accept blood money for a relative with the words, «We will not eat our brother's blood

15 Cf. R.B. Serjeant & Ronald Lewcock, *San'a' : an Arabian Islamic City*, London, 1983, 598 b.

(*Ma ba nakul dam akhu-na*)». Sould the protector intentionally kill his protégé this is termed «the black shame (*al-'ayb al-aswad*)» and tribal honour is only cleansed, or «whitened», as they say, through the slaying of the murderer by his tribe, it is said, by the hand of his nearest relative. It is also a black shame not to avenge your protégé. Should a protector who has defaulted in this fashion visit any house he will be entertained, but everything brought him will be black – he will be set on black rugs reversed, his food will come in black pots, and so on; then all will be burned in his presence so that they can never be used again. By not avenging his protégé he and his tribe have blackened their faces so, in turn, their faces are blackened by this insulting behaviour. My manuscript describes this and, over 40 years ago, the late Lord Belhaven actually witnessed such a procedure[16]. If you should wish to terminate your responsibility for your protégé, or if he has committed some misdemeanour against you, then he must be given suitable notice to remove himself and his goods from your jurisdiction – then you may take whatever action possible to you against him if you are able to do so.

Another type of protection is escort, called by the Aden Protectorate tribes *siyarah*, classical *khafarah*. The Zaydi tribes call one's escort *khubara'*, and to pass through the Republican village of Kuhlan in 1966 I was provided with *khubara'* by a Royalist shaykh who took me through it, though with some speed, and stayed with me until we were safely in Royalist territory again – usually however it was one of the Zaydi princes who provided tribal troops as escort in uncertain territories. The escort must take the person escorted safely to his destinaticn or to the limit of the area controlled by his tribe. After that he may take another escort from the tribe whose territory he is entering – often in Arabia this is linked with hiring camels in the first district which must be exchanged for camels belonging to the tribe in the next district which is providing the new escort. Often an escort fee (*siyarah*) is also payable. It is reckoned a dastardly crime to kill the person escorted – it too is the «black shame». The escort is bound to acquaint the person escorted with the limits of the protection he accords him. In this connection may be quoted the proverb – do not take a barber (*muzayyin*) or a Jew as your companion of the road (*rafiq*) – because, neither being an armed tribesman, will be able to partake in the defence of the party. Technically they are called *da'if*, weak. It is axiomatic that the members of a caravan are responsible for their joint defence during the journey.

There is an elaborate system of calculation of blood money – actual figures vary from place to place, but in principle a woman is reckoned at half a man's blood money, and so likewise a Jew; a slave is counted only as his value as a chattel – incidentally there were slaves in both the Yemens till at least a few years ago. But the circumstances of the slaying are taken into account, though damages are incurred for an accidental as well as for an intentional killing. If a woman is killed such charges

---

16 R.A.B. Hamilton, «The social organisation of the tribes of the Aden Protectorate», *Royal Central Asian Journal*, London, 1942, XXIX, iii & iv, 244, though he does not mention the blackening. Cf. *Ahkam al-man'ah* (note 2), 9a; *Jahiz 'al-Hayawan*, Cairo, 1359/1940, IV, 473, *nar al-musafir*, the fire burned after the guest or visitor whose return is not desired.

as «*lawm*, blame money»[17], which far exceed the blood wit, must be paid in order to compensate the tribe for the damage done its honour by slaying one of its womenfolk. For other offences touching honour, «respect money, *hasham*» must be paid in addition to compensation, while many mediaeval or modern documents lay down doubling or quadrupling of blood money or compensation for a whole range of offences. Offences touching the honour of a free woman, attacking or insulting a woman were mentioned to me by the Wahidi Sultan in the unsettled conditions of 1947. If, he said, his wife were to go visiting relations unaccompanied and she encountered a hostile tribesman on the road, he might cut off a lock of her hair as an insult to the Sultan. Tribesmen of course do not molest women. Insulting of persons of standing is always punished by heavier fines, Sayyids, chiefs and others, and a sultan's blood money was at least double that of a tribesman.

Theft of all categories has its set fines. A favourite trick of a tribesman was to put a ban on the cultivation of a field by firing a shot in the air and refusing to let the cultivator work by threats or by stabbing his oxen in the belly; or he might ban a shopkeeper from buying and selling by slashing his sword across his scales and cutting their chains[18]. All these incur known fines. A tribe can be charged and fined for making a hostile approach to a village, or simply for threatening. A man can be penalised for such actions as throwing a stone at or shooting birds on another man's roof. I have even come across in Mss. allusions to a mock attack made at weddings – probably a relic of marriage by capture which was still known in the 'Awlaqi Shaykhdom where a woman might boast to another, «*Khadhaw-na bi-' l-barut ya bint al-masajid*, They took me by gun-powder, you daughter of the mosques» ! The mock attack is however regulated, so that if it goes beyond the limits of place and time recognised, it becomes an offence.

Everyone knows the supreme Arab virtue is *karam*, or hospitality – it is a right, an honour and a genuine pleasure for an Arab to entertain his guest – but there are many rules about who has the right first to entertain the guest and even how many sheep must be slaughtered, normally one sheep for ten guests. In Bayhan in days bygone a sheep would be slaughtered for each horseman in a party. The heart is placed on top of the meat in Upper 'Awlaqi country – if it is not there when the meat is brought in the whole sheep is sent back. Meat is divided in accordance with the guests' social standing, by an elder man of rank. In Wahidi country the hosts leave the guests to eat alone shutting the door on them to emphasize that the meat is a gift to them, but some is kept aside for them by the chief guest.

---

17 About 1953 troubles with the Rabiz tribe were accerbated when Aden Government Arab soldiers accidentally shot and killed a woman. The political staff agreed the sum of blood-money to be paid in restitution, but the Governor of the time, ignorant of tribal customary law, refused to pay the *lawm*, a sum of about £ 50 at that time, as Government, he maintained, should not be said to be «blamed». The tribe refused to accept a truce on these terms and many months of fighting followed this unjust decision.

18 See my «Two tribal law cases», I, *Journal of the Royal Asiatic Society*, April 1951, 41-2.

Tribal law is not deemed applicable by women, children, mental defectives or slaves, but protection guaranteed by any one of these persons seems to be binding on the whole tribe.

In tribal country where there is no power to compel any party to accept a decision by an arbiter it is necessary to have some assurance that the parties to a suit are prepared to take the matter seriously and also to accept the judge's decision. So each side deposits some article of value and/or significance like a dagger or rifle with a pledge-holder who is often also the judge-arbiter, in earnest of their willingness to proceed to justice. An arbiter arbitrates in accordance with tribal law and he may also fix damages payable according to a recognized scale or tariff. Often he requires the accused to take the oath following the ancient maxim I have quoted. Trial by ordeal (*bish'ah*), when the accused has his tongue flicked with a red-hot knife, may well now have disappeared from the Peninsula – the Islamic ulema are opposed to it, but if this is so it is quite recent.

In fact, identical procedures, or nearly so, are followed by every community in judging disputes, such as the wards of towns, the fishermen, and many others. In the pre-Islamic temple litigants took the oath at a special place for swearing called *maqsamah*[19] – in Islam they seem to swear at the *minbar* (pulpit), but in San'a', I found they swear at two pillars in the Jami' Mosque, the Zubayri oath. There is real fear of the consequences of a false oath at a saint's shrine-tomb for which the dead saint would punish the perjured. The Zubayri oath goes back to the time of the Caliph Harun al-Rashid.

Occasionally one of the parties to a tribal lawsuit refuses to accept the verdict and accuses the judge-arbiter of partiality or of having issued an incorrect decision. This creates a fresh suit between the dissatisfied tribesman and the judge. The plea, the defence and the arbitration which, let it be said, are often submitted in writing in what appears very archaic language, are then sent to a sort of appeal judge, often hundreds of miles away, such as the *manqads* of Qa'udah in Hadramawt or those of Jirdan. The appeal judges make their decision as to the correctness or otherwise of the original judgement award by scrutinising the written documents – and this decision is final.

Settlement of the blood-feud is, of all tribal issues, the most important. Inevitably the tribes tire of the feud and have then somehow to meet and discuss their differences. They must assemble then on neutral ground. I have discussed in several places how the lord of a sacred enclave will take the initiative of inviting the tribal chiefs to meet there under his aegis – the Haram of Mecca under divine protection

---

19 *Diwan Zuhayr b. Abi Sulma*, Cairo, 1384/1964. «Oaths from you and us are brought together at a *muqsamah/maqsamah* at which blood flows». The commentator explains this as two parties taking oaths together at «the place of taking an oath at idols» and the blood of sacrifical animals (*budun*) is meant. He adds that «Oaths are taken like the oaths taken at a slaying (lit., *dam*, blood), at the multiple oath (*qasamah*», in declaration of one's innocence of the crime of murder. See also R.B. SERJEANT & Ronald LEWCOCK, *San'a'*, *op.cit.*, 317 a.

was just such an enclave, as also is the *hawtah* in Hadramawt[20]. But tribes may assemble in a protected market where foe may meet foe without fear of either resorting to arms. Should there be an incident the aggressor would thereby be infringing the honour of the market's protectors and incur the heaviest of penalties – the same would be the case with violation of the sacred enclave. Any feud to be settled resolves itself eventually into a long catalogue of aggressions and counter-aggressions, murders and retaliations. The damages which these actions have made liable are totted up and the balance is paid over. Documents will be written recording the settlement at which the parties have arrived, not, let me say, without much wrangling, raised voices, throwing down of turbans, grasping of beards and other gestures. In pre-Islamic Arabia the protected market functioned the same way, for the poet al-Harith b. Hillizah for example, exhorts his listeners «to remember the treaty at Dhu 'l-Majaz (market) and the covenants and treaties produced thereat»[21]. The guarantor (*kafil*) is equivalent to the present day Yemeni *damin* or *shaykh al--daman* – these shaykhs meet, settle the case before them and pay over the damages – which they recover, I think, from the offending tribe. The *kafil*, guarantor, is always mentioned in the tribal documents in my collection. The lord protector of a market can exclude as well as admit – an outlaw can be banned from a market altogether – in this way recalcitrant individuals, indeed whole tribes can be brought to heel.

An institution peculiar to the Yemen is the *hijrah*[22] where persons under tribal protection (also known as *hijrah*) live. I have dealt with this elsewhere in detail. Let it suffice to say that I see evidence of the *hijrah*'s existence in some pre-Islamic inscriptions and I believe that Muhammad's *hijrah* (hegirah) is closely connected with it.

In the former Aden Protectorates the lord of a sacred enclave might even intervene in tribal battles, marching forth with the banner of the patron saint, the original founder of the enclave. Alternatively he might send the market brokers (*dallal*) to intervene, or the latter might intervene of their own accord. The *dallal* is in closely intimate relation with the tribes who, when they come to market, stay in his house and are fed by him while the broker sells their animals for them and purchases their requirements on, of course, a commission basis. Sometimes the lords of the sacred enclaves and the brokers are accused of stirring up trouble among the tribesmen, with whose law and custom they are well acquainted, for interests of their own; they know also how to play on the fiery sense of tribal honour which, to more sophisticated minds, has sometimes a little of the ridiculous about it.

Tribal customary law needs further exploration, but there are many other branches of custom besides – the law of irrigation alone is quite varied though it

20 «*Haram* and *hawtah* : the sacred Enclave in Arabia» (*Mélanges Taha Husain*, Cairo, 1962), reprint in *Studies in Arabian History...*, *op.cit.*, etc. Cf. my «*Haram, hawtah, hijrah*», in *Encyclopaedia of Religion*, MacMillan, New York.

21 *Mu'allaqat* ed. C.J. Lyall, *A Commentary on ten ancient Arabian Poems*, Calcutta, 1894, 133.

22 See *San'a'*, *op.cit.*, index, 579 a.

seems to follow certain basic principles and I know from the code of maritime and fishery law drafted by the former Mukalla Government under the Protectorate how complex Arabian sea-law is[23]. The market law of the Yemeni capital San'a' (*Qanun San'a'*) I have made available in translation[24]. What remained a puzzle to me was how customary law, based on a series of decisions on cases doubtless going far back into antiquity, equivalent to *sunnahs* before Islam and in Islamic *shari'ah*, is transmitted to arbiters and indeed to the community at large. It is immaterial whether the community be illiterate or the decisions be recorded in writing. How can these decisions and cases create a code of customary law ? Custom in Arabia is no random collection of cases but its founded on certain established concepts and principles.

It appears to me that Colonel 'Uwaydi's researches into Bedouin justice in Jordan[25] provide not only a solution to some of these problems but also, by analogy, show how customary law operated in ancient Arabia at the time when the Prophet Muhammad appeared on the scene. Incidentally, I do not consider Muhammad replaced existing law by a new code of law, though he made a number of modifications of it. Islamic *Shari'ah* as it evolved is the creation of centres outside the Peninsula, largely Iraq, though, as indicated, it does embody important elements of ancient Arabian law. 'Uwaydi says, «The Bedouin recognise two types of tribal law known to them as *shari'ah*, 1) the individual type of *shari'ah* which applies to one's own tribe, 2) the common *shari'ah* which applies to the Bedouin in general. This *Shari'ah* has synonyms *tariqat-na*, our way, *'awa'id* (plur. of *'adah*) custom(s)». This *shari'ah*, like the 'Awdhali *shar'*, is *not* the Islamic code which has the same name. I suggest that the term *shar'/shari'ah* has been used by tribesfolk for their law from remote times, even before Islam. In Sabaic it means 'right, due'.

'Uwaydi's survey of the judicial system (prior to the changes introduced firstly under the Mandate and later after independence) provides a clue as to how living customary law is maintained without recourse to writing. There are naturally exceptional cases where customary law is written down, or at least certain aspects of it – as in the *sijills*[26] of some Yemeni tribes stated in one case to be pre-Islamic by the Yemeni author al-Hamdani, and the *Seven Qanuns* of the Zaydi tribes of the north – this is apart from actual legal documents of which there is a plethora – they follow customary law and may even cite its maxims. In Jordan the law is maintained without the necessity of writing it down and it has a flexibility in the hands of the customary law judges which allows of modification to suit changed circumstances – it is in fact much more flexible than Islamic *shari'ah*.

---

23 See my «Customary law among the fisherman of al-Shihr», in B.C. Bloomfield, *Middle East Studies and Libraries. A felicitation volume for Professor J.D. Pearson*, London, 1980, 193-203, with further bibliographical material.

24 See *San'a'*, *op.cit., 179-232.*

25 See note 4.

26 Discussed in *CHAL* (note 5 above), 115.

To quote 'Uwaydi again, there are four major tribal offices (*sultah*) «Each office covers a certain area (*majalat*) of tribal power, and involves a particular role» (*dawr*), which is performed by certain parties or individuals. Each family has its own specialization in a certain office but may hold more than one of them. Within its own area of specialization and authority... each family aims at the preservation of the standard manners of tribal ethics. These offices are hereditary and elective with the exception of «spiritual authority (*al-sultat al-ruhiyyah*)» which is confined to families already in possession of it. He lists the families with spiritual authority to formulate legislation in accordance with the «line of acceptability» (by the community) and even to modify this «acceptability itself». All these families also hold other tribal offices. The judge/shaykh can initiate, amend or abrogate tribal laws if the matter in question lies within his legal competence and jurisdiction. Broadly speaking, judges in general come from families in which this function is hereditary, and a judge may have a specialization in one field only, exceptionally in all four. There is evidence in Arabic literature on pre-Islamic times which supports my view that this type of specialization existed then also. Observers are sent in Jordan to judicial/arbitratorial proceedings to watch the outcome, and when a judge of standing makes a modification of established custom he would make a statement in support of it. 'Uwaydi's researches reveal a highly complex organisation among the Jordanian Bedouin. It will be perceived that the Prophet Muhammad, himself coming of a family holding spiritual power at the Meccan sanctuary, may be regarded when acting as arbiter as functioning in a capacity similar to the Bedouin hereditary judges possessed of spiritual authority. Jordanian Bedouin consider their customs (*'awa'id*) and law as a part of their Islamic heritage, says 'Uwaydi, although, in fact, certain *'awa'id* practices and law are sometimes un-Islamic.

A constantly recurring theme of 'Uwaydi's survey is that «unlike civil and *shari'ah* judges, far stronger emphasis is laid by Bedouin judges on conciliation between parties to a dispute». He points out that the other courts take rigid attitudes on both procedure and culpability that are both foreign and distasteful to the Bedouin ethic. I have made a recent study[27] of the celebrated letter of the second Caliph 'Umar, supposedly written about 638 or 639 A.D., to his governor of Basrah, concerning procedure for the *qadi*, considered by western scholars and even a few mediaeval Muslim writers as pseudo-epigraphical (perhaps of the 8th century). The letter gives conciliation (*sulh*) a sanction, one might say, almost grudging. There are however two other letters, virtually identical in form and content, to 'Umar's governors in Syria and Iraq on procedure and I consider these genuine and that sent to Iraq the basis upon which the famous but «improved» version dealing with procedure for the *qadi* was constructed. The terse genuine letter requires witnesses and oaths to be produced as in the adage «the onus of the proof is on the plaintiff and the oath on him who denies

---

27 «The Caliph 'Umar's letters to Abu Musa al-Ash'ari and Mu'awiya», *JSS*, Manchester, 1984, XXIX, i, 65-79.

[the charge]» which latter is ancient pre-Islamic Arabian law. This letter says emphatically, «Take pains to arrive at conciliation so long as judgement [or 'a decisions' (*qada'*)] is not clear». There is no reference to a *qadi*.

Comparison of the shorter letters with the «improved» letter suggests that that *qadis* in the 2nd *hijrah* century were relegating conciliation to a second place in the settled urban community that was replacing tribal conditions. Perhaps one may draw a parallel with the situation in Jordan today and the alterations made to incorporate tribal in state justice. Yet in my personal experience of Arabia ordinary folk, be they tribesmen, peasants, fishermen, all normally resort to conciliation by a *muslih*[28]. When in Dathinah in 1954 I found the *qadi*'s court all but empty whereas the customary law court was clamorous with the «give and take», as they say, of disputing litigants. The proverb says, «*Al-sulh sayyid al-ahkam*», i.e., «Conciliation is the lord of [legal] decisions». It is preferred to the court of the *qadi*, regarded as more often corrupt than not, in most Muslim countries.

Additional bibliography

A.M.A. Maktari, *Water rights and irrigation practices in Lahj*, Cambridge, 1972.

R.B. Serjeant, Maritime customary law off the Arabian coast, *Actes du 8e Colloque international d'Histoire maritime, Beyrouth, 5-11 sept. 1966)*, présentés par Michel Mollat, Paris, 1970, 195-207.

Ahmad 'Uwaydi al-'Abbadi, al-Adillah al-qada'iyyah 'ind al-badw, *Man hum al-badw ?*, Series, n° 5, 'Amman, 1983, with a discussion (on Islamic lines) of 'Umar's letters to Abu Musa and Mu'awiyah.

Current research into tribal customary law is being carried out by Paul Dresch (Oxford Ph.D. thesis, 1982) and in southern Palestine by Clinton Bailey who has published a number of illuminating articles on the Bedu. Ahmad Oweidi's thesis contains a critical bibliography of earlier writings on the Jordanian Bedu. Current interest in customary law in Arabia has considerably developed and more recent writings may be found in the *Index Islamicus*.

Since the above was written there have appeared the following : Paul Dresch, *Tribes, government and history in Yemen*, Oxford, 1989; Clinton Bailey, *Bedouin poetry from Sinai and the Negev*, Oxford, 1991.

28 For the social structure of southern Arabia see my «South Arabia», in C.A.O. van Nieuwenhuijze, *Commoners, climbers and notables*, Leiden, 1977 (reprint in *Studies in Arabian History*, *op.cit.*).

VI

CUSTOMARY LAW DOCUMENTS AS A SOURCE OF HISTORY

The commonest form of history writing in Arabia as in other countries is the annual chronicle of outstanding events, ranging from political occurences such as raids, battles, murders, to natural calamities like famines, floods, plagues, the arrival of locusts, and natural phenomena like earthquakes and the appearance of meteors and strange stars. These are the substance, recorded without comment, except rarely, of a simple chronicler like the Ḥaḍramī historian Shanbal. A more developed type of chronicle with a sense of the continuity of historical narrative is the Yemeni *Ghāyat al-amānī*, though it has limitations in its choice of data; but the Yemen has had some exceptionally able historians, especially the biographers of some of the Zaydī *Imāms*. Al-Jarmūzī's *Sīrat al-Mutawakkil* succeeds in weaving accounts of campaigns, policies, the controversies of scholars, economics and their effect on the townsfolk and peasants into a true picture of life and conditions in the 11th/17th century, documented with a judicious selection of correspondence exchanged between the principal actors in the historical scene.

It must be confessed nevertheless that such historians are rare in the Peninsula, and most, naturally enough, concern themselves mainly with the exciting events of battle and intrigue, especially that which touched their own lives. They are rarely interested to tell us about what are to them the ordinary humdrum course of actual living, other than say current prices of comestibles, sometimes. It does not occur to them to describe society in the broadest sense of the word as they see it around them — this they take for granted — but those of us in later ages, knowing nothing of the society of these earlier times, are at a loss to understand the interplay of forces and currents behind the events that they record so starkly. We have therefore to try to re-constitute what is lacking in other ways.

Our interest lies in social history rather than in battles of long ago. Archaeology has of course done much to redress the balance, and if I were to take an example I should point to the vivid living picture of the Roman world that is revealed to us in Pompeii and in the Pompeii Exhibition in London.

How much the history of commerce is neglected by historians in general is revealed by the immense mass of documents preserved in the medieaval Cairo Genīza which contained actual Arabic documents, Arabic in Hebrew character, and of course Hebrew. But this collection is of prime value for social life in the mediaeval Islamic world, including the Arabian Peninsula.

The purpose of this paper however is to draw attention to an almost completely neglected source of information through which it is possible to supplement the writings of the historians of the Arabian Peninsula, and indeed to go further than this, and interpret obscurities in ancient pre-Islamic and Islamic history. This is by collecting the numerous agreements, often in colloquial Arabic, that are to be found with the various segments of Arabian society, and getting their owners to explain and comment on them. Most of such documents take the form of an agreement following upon a dispute which has been settled by some third party. A first observation one makes is that custom — *'urf* or *'āda* — is not a jumble of *ad hoc* rules, but a well established and logical law. In fact in much of south-west Arabia instead of these two terms, they use *shar'* as for example at Ṣa'da of the northern Yemen, but they mean customary law, not the Islamic *sharī'a*. Of course the two are probably only rarely inconsistent with each other.

The most important of the various types of document I have collected is, in my view, the corpus relating to the *ḥawṭa* which I discussed in a general fashion in my contribution, some years ago, to the Ṭaha Ḥusain Anniversary Volume. For those who do not know what a *ḥawṭa* is, may I say that in nearly every respect it resembles the pre-Islamic *ḥaram*, a sacred enclave, and is presided over by a *Manṣab*, traditionally an authority on *sharī'a* and *'urf*, but more often than not his function will be to give a decision in accordance with *'urf* when he is asked to make a judgement. The *Manṣab* will be of a family of the class known as *Mashāyikh*, or a Sayyid. The security of the *ḥawṭa* is guaranteed by the surrounding tribes with written guarantees of a pattern much the same basically in the case of every *ḥawṭa*, and the *Manṣab* acts as an arbiter between these tribes in their disputes. The tribes make an annual *ziyāra* to the tomb of the *Manṣab's* ancestor inside the area of the *ḥawṭa* and are entertained by him. The *Manṣab's* property inside and outside the *ḥawṭa* is exempt from taxation. This is obviously a very ancient institution and it will be recalled that in the Jāhiliyya, the Prophet's forbears exercised the function of *ḥakam*, 'Abd al-Muṭṭalib being specially famous in this office. Apart from the intrinsic interest of these documents for Ḥaḍramī history itself in showing the interplay of tribal organisation, the sultans, and the 'ulamā', they do help to understand how the pre-Islamic *ḥaram* worked.

If the *ḥawṭa* is considered to have something of a sacred quality like the *ḥaram* so friend and foe can alike meet there, the guaranteeing of the inviolability of the central market of tribes is a secular institution with some points in common. The *shar'* customary law of the 'Awdhillāh tribe says for instance "A foe may not enter the market (of Lawdar). If he be a peasant or a craftsman (he is of no account and may do so). If he has already entered (it) he may not be molested in the market on a Sunday, but must depart on the Monday evening."

واخصم ما يدخل شى امسوق . انكان امضعيف وامسكين ، وان قد دخل
ما ينتكر شى بسوق الاحد ، مروحه الاثنين .

The city of Ṣan'ā' is said to be *muḥajjara* by the seven great tribal confederations in its vicinity — if this inviolability is infringed the guilty party has to bring cattle to slaughter as *'aqīras* as a case in point would be when a tribesman robs or murders in the city. When discussing the *taḥjīr* with a Ṣan'ānī scholar he agreed that there must be tribal documents which give the rules for the preservation of the city's security and a list of penalties for infringing it. We know from the *Ta'rīkh al-Rāzī* that San'ā' was considered *maḥfūẓa* or *maḥmiyya* and the pre-Islamic Sabaean inscriptions show that it was regarded as a *maḥram* — so if such *taḥjīr* documents are to be found they could well throw light on the special protection accorded the city from the Jāhiliyya onwards — I intend to pursue this line of research.

Aḥmad al-Sayaghi has published in *Majallat al-makhṭūṭāt* an invaluable document, *Qānūn Ṣan'ā'*, though he does not say, unfortunately, where he found the MS original. This I have, with the aid of my friend, Qāḍī Ismā'īl al-Akwa', translated into English with many additional notes. It consists of regulations for the shopkeepers and craftsmen, the fixing of prices, etcetera, and except that it does not have anything about a *muḥtasib*, it resembles the rules of the *ḥisba* manuals. The *Qānūn* appears to be based upon or codified from regulations made by each craft for carrying on its particular trade. Many of such agreements seem to exist in San'ā' but do not figure in the *Qānūn*, such as one with the carpenters by Professor W. Dostal, which we expect to publish in our large volume on Ṣan'ā'. Obviously these would enable us to build up a picture of the city's economic and social life. Moreover, I can trace back earlier versions of the *Qānūn* at least to the first half of the 11th/17th century but oviously market regulations for Ṣan'ā' must have been in existence long before that.

Qānūn Ṣan'ā' is a fairly sophisticated document reflecting mediaeval market organisation, but in Shibām the commercial capital of Ḥaḍramawt al-Dākhil, well over twenty years ago, I was able to obtain through the good offices of one of its principal merchants, Ḥusayn La'jam, a series of documents from the chief of the *dallāls* there, which seemed to show an earlier stage of development than Ṣan'ā'. Whereas the tribeman coming into Ṣan'ā' stays in a *samsara* or *khān*, in Ḥaḍramawt he stays with the *dallāl* as his guest, while the latter sells his animals for him and buys what he needs — all this on a commission basis. At one time the *dallāls* in Shibām even used to collect the market tax for the sultan, being I suppose, informed about all transactions taking place. A curious feature is that the Shibām *dallāl* families regarded individual tribes as belonging to a certain house of *dallāls*, and they could buy and sell the good-will in a tribe between each other — some of the documents containing such transactions.

In Ḥaḍramawt the Quarters *(ḥāfāt/ḥuwayf)* of the little towns were highly organised, and here again I have a collection of some of their *wathā'iq*, one going back nearly two centuries and showing that in the orthodox Shāfi'ī city of Tarīm trial by *bish'a* was exercised by the tribal rulers, i.e. testing a mans's veracity by flicking his tongue with a red-hot knife. The Quarters provided a large range of what nowadays would be considered social and municipal services and organised dancing on ceremonial occasions *(afrāḥ)*. They kept the Quarter swept, looked after foundling children, guarded the Quarter boundaries and provided gear for washing the dead and even the bier - *al-ālat al-ḥadbā'* as the poet calls it. In Ṣan'ā' the Quarters have lost many such functions which have passed to the *Baladiyya* founded by the Ottomans at their second occupation, but perhaps their role had much diminished even before then. One feature of the Ḥaḍramī town Quarters I must not omit to mention is that they participated in organising the traditional ibex hunts which have a complicated set of laws and are in fact a relic of pre-Islamic ritual — for we know from the inscriptions that it was essential for a community to hunt the ibex from time to time to procure rain *(raḥma)*. This idea is still current in the hunting poems known as Banī Mighrāh in such verses as

اذا شيء قتل عند القبايل واهل كوشار
نشوفه في فرح كن عنده عيد لافطار
عسى رحمه بها ينجلي همى ولاكدار

In 1953 and 1963-64 I had begun to investigate through written agreements among fishermen, both the customary law on fishing and that on navigation — for the latter there was and is a sort of *'urfī* maritime law that existed long before international maritime law imposed by the west. I hope to correlate this with *fatāwā* cases that seem to involve a code of maritime law which the Arabic sources have ignored. I have tried to collect, in order to supplement my south Arabian documents, some material from the Gulf, and have in fact published an article on the fish-traps *(ḥaḍra)* of al-Baḥrayn, but there must be many documents on the pearl-fishing industry. On a recent visit to al-Baḥrayn I was delighted to see that documents of all sorts, including maritime industries of course, are being collected at the Museum. A curious example of what the regulations of ordinary folk can preserve in these papers is that in al-Mukalla they refer not to the port by that name, but by al-Khīṣa, meaning the Bay, the name by which al-Hamdānī knew it a thousand years ago.

There is a mass of customary law relating to irrigation, and some of this may be consulted in Dr. A.A. Maktarī's study on irrigation in Lahej, but in a report of Wādī Zabīd a facsimile of al-Jabartī's regulations for the division of water there has been published, belonging to the 9th/15th century — such documents should be rich in history. Share-cropping agreements one already finds in the *fatāwā* which deal with *'urfī* cases in general, and often the *su'āl* itself is in technical colloquial Arabic.

Tribal law is of great interest to the historian both the written cases and the mediaeval Yemeni Mss. of which I have copies. In the Yemen this is still called *Taghut* but I do not think it is invariably different from *sharī'a* — a study of it might well aid us towards better understanding of the pre-Islamic legal inscriptions, and I have come across practices existing today such as testing the *bish'a* judge's competence by making him guess what secret thing the contending parties have brought with them — just as they used to test the *kāhin* as you may read in the books of Ibn al-Ḥabīb.

In the former Aden Protectorates I have seen many documents lying about folded into tapers, and when the British Resident in 1948 was settling Kathīrī-Qu'ayṭī boundaries documents like this were produced by the sackful. In British files from British residencies in various parts of Arabia, now in Britain, there are more than a few Arabic documents often not easy to understand, which are of the types I have mentioned. It is advisable to study these now for dialect is being forgotten, and in Kuwait for example when I went with Miss Quṭāmī to see a famous *nawkhudha*, even she was not able to understand a number of his expressions.

There are many groups I should like to consult on their *wathā'iq* — the Tihāma peoples, ship-builders, the 'Uqaylīs who for centuries seem to have traded freely between such cities as Damascus and the interior of Arabia, the Kibsīs who ran the Kibsī caravan from the Yemen to the Holy Cities. It is a pity that the present is so rapidly overtaking the past that even the memory of so much of it may be forgotten, and such institutions as these may be no more than names, not history that still lives for us.

VII

Sunnah, Qur'ān, ᶜUrf

In this paper I shall treat of the so-called "Constitution of Medina" and certain Qur'ān passages related to it, ᶜUmar's supposed letter to Abū Mūsā al-Ashᶜarī[1] on the office of *qāḍī,* Yemeni customary law codes on *manᶜah,* Bā Ṣabrayn al-Ḥaḍramī's *al-Manāhī al-rabbāniyyah* and other studies, drawing upon my researches completed and not yet completed. The two last named works have not yet been published[2] but I have been working on them for a numbers of years. I shall also refer to Aḥmad Oweidi al-ᶜAbbādī's Cambridge thesis *Bedouin law in Jordan* which Edinburgh University Press has agreed to publish. With Muslim theories on how *sharīᶜah* was formulated I am not directly concerned, but with the history of Arabian law that preceded the *sharīᶜah* and which, termed *ᶜurf* or *ᶜādah,* persists till today, apparently little changed in principle or practice since the pagan Jāhiliyyah age. From this ancient Arabian law branches off the Islamic *sharīᶜah* as a divergent, modifying and adding to it. The theory that Islamic law derives from the Qur'ān supplemented by the Sunnah, then *ijmāᶜ* consensus, and analogical reasoning *(qiyās),* does not reflect the initial historical circumstances of Islam.

First of all the notion of a break, a line separating the Jāhiliyyah from Islam is to be abandoned. Contemporary researches on the south Arabian inscriptions and indeed in Arabic literature itself show ever more clearly how unacceptable it is, and nowhere is this more evident than in the Sunnah. For the purposes of this paper a sunnah in its legal context may be defined as a legal decision taken by an arbiter in a case brought

1 See my The 'Constitution of Medina', *Islamic Quarterly,* London, 1964, VIII, pp. 3-16; 'The *Sunnah Jāmiᶜah,* Pacts with the Yathrib Jews and the *taḥrīm* of Yathrib: Analysis and translation of the documents comprised in the so-called Constitution of Medina', *BSOAS,* London, 1978, XLI, pp. 1-42 (& Variorum reprint, 1981). 'The Caliph ᶜUmar's letters to Abū Mūsā al-Ashᶜarī and Muᶜāwiya' *JSS,* Manchester, 1984, XXIX, pp. 65-79 (& Variorum reprint, 1991). *Cambridge History of Arabic Literature* 'Early Arabic Prose', 1983, pp. 122-151. 'Materials for South Arabian history', *BSOAS,* 1950, XIII, part 2, pp. 589-93.

2 The *manᶜah* codes are in the corpus of Yemenite material collected by the late Ettore Rossi and the Tarīm *Kitāb al-Ādāb wa-'l-lawāzim fī aḥkām al-manᶜah* upon which I am working. Bā Ṣabrayn's *al-Manāhī* in transcript I have begun to translate and annotate. See also E. Rossi, 'Il diritto consuetudinario delle tribù arabe del Yemen', *RSO,* Rome, 1948, XXIII, pp. 1-26.

before him that has become a precedent, a custom. One has to envisage a long series of arbiters before Islam, such an office being hereditary in certain noble houses, as noted in the literature.[3] The Prophet Muḥammad was an arbiter in this continuity of tradition and the theocracy he founded succeeded many others; it has been followed by numerous Islamic sub-theocracies if one may use such a term, within and without the Arabian Peninsula. In fact, so far from regarding Muḥammad as bent upon a policy of innovation, one has to conceive of him as born into a society regulated by a continuous series of sunnahs stretching from a remote past into the Islam of his day, and even beyond his supreme lordship of that theocracy.

A virtue of this system of case law is that a new sunnah may be established to replace an existing sunnah and in a sense the Prophet may be regarded as ratifying some sunnahs and replacing others – the changes were probably relatively few, but of course they are of premier importance. It may be a survival of the possibility of the modification or repeal of an earlier ruling in the practice continuing and inherited from the pagan age that al-Dārimī can cite a Tradition remounting to al-Awzāᶜī[4] (88-157 H.): *Al-sunnah qāḍiyah ᶜala 'l-Qur'ān wa-laysa 'l-Qur'ān qāḍiyah ᶜala 'l-sunnah,* which I understand to mean that in the event of a conflict of law between the Qur'ān and the Sunnah, the latter is decisive. It is to be remarked that the two oldest *madhhabs* (regarded by the Sunnīs as heretical), the Ibāḍī and the Zaydī, make the Sunnah overrule the Qur'ān where there is conflict. Parallel to this, in Jordan of this century tribal law precedents are susceptible to modification, even replacement, by a properly qualified hereditary judge.

The *Fihrist*[5] notes that Hishām b. Muḥammad al-Kalbī (ob.206/821-2) composed a writing/book *(kitāb)* on what the pagan age (al-Jāhiliyyah) used to do and which accords with the judgement *(ḥukm)* of Islam. A

[3] Ibn ᶜAbd Rabbi-hi, *al-ᶜIqd al-farīd,* Cairo, 1359-72/1940-53, I, p.30 states that ᶜAbdullah b. ᶜAbbās wrote to al-Ḥasan b. ᶜAlī when the people made him their ruler after ᶜAlī: *Walli ahl al-buyūtāt tastaṣliḥ bi-him ᶜashā'ira-hum,* Put men of noble houses in charge and through them you will make their tribes well affected (to you).

[4] *Sunan,* Dār Iḥyā' al-Sunnah al-Nabawiyyah, n.d., I, p.144. Al-Awzaᶜī was the Imām of the Syrians especially.

[5] Ibn al-Nadīm, *al-Fihrist,* Cairo, n.d., p.147. Cf.Ibn Ḥabīb, *al-Muḥabbar,* Ḥaydarābād, 1361/1942, p.236.

pre-Islamic poet cited by Ibn Durayd's *Ishtiqāq*[6] as judging in the age of paganism, a judgement consistent with the Sunnah of Islam, is probably quoted from Ibn al-Kalbī's *Kitāb,* not now extant, but drawing no doubt on his father's data. It is of course the other way round – the Islamic Sunnah is inherited from the pre-Islamic era.

The Prophet Muḥammad was the scion of an honourable house, exercising a sort of theocratic control of the Ḥaram of Mecca, but himself of small political consequence. Falling out with his tribe, Quraysh, he found protection with the tribes of Yathrib/Medīnah who sought a neutral arbiter-leader to put an end to their quarrels. At Yathrib he built up a politico-religious ascendancy and in the course of his first year there he arranged two pacts that form part of the document inaptly known in Europe as the "Constitution of Medina". This is the first Islamic document that survives, elements of the Qur'ān apart.

My analysis of it lies before you, and I shall henceforth refer to it as the EIGHT DOCUMENTS of which it consists. The first two of the documents I identify as *al-Sunnah al-Jāmiᶜah,* the two first pacts of Year I which form a united Muslim community, *ummah,* the nucleus around which that community developed. The first document establishes a tribal confederation, basically security arrangements, the second adds supplementary clauses to it. The signatories to them have not been preserved, but since the *mu'minūn* and *muslimūn* of Quraysh and Yathrib are cited in the preamble it can be assumed that they were the Prophet's Quraysh followers from Mecca who had taken protection in Yathrib, and the chiefs, *naqībs* and *sayyids* of the Arab tribes of Yathrib. Even certain Jewish notables may have been included, but the Jews may have been represented by the Arab chiefs to whom they were allied in a secondary capacity as *tābiᶜūn.*

These two documents, the *Sunnah Jāmiᶜah,* are so sophisticated and well drafted that the existence of earlier models may be postulated, and it

6 *Al-Ishtiqāq,* ed. ᶜAbd al-Salām Hārūn, Cairo, 1378/1958, pp. 389, 393. A case in point of a pre-Islamic *sunnah* reported by al-Bukhārī on the authority of ᶜĀ'ishah, is *nikāḥ al-istibḍāᶜ*, a form of marriage which Beeston identifies with a piece in the Sabaic text C. 581, where a surrogate father is involved. This also gives a different aspect to the maxim *al-walad li-'l-firāsh.* The institution of *istibḍāᶜ* by the third Islamic century, would doubtless be condemned by the *fuqahā',* whatever might in practice exist, as inconsistent with the *sunnah* of Islam. See my *'Zinā',* some forms of marriage and allied topics in Western Arabia' in the forthcoming Walter Dostal Festschrift. **See article XII below.**

so happens that Christian Robin and J.-François Breton[7] have discovered a Sabaic inscription at Jabal al-Lawdh in north-east Yemen which they describe as "le pacte de fédération des tribus". While there are uncertainties about the exact rendering of the inscription there can be little doubt about its general import. An approximate rendering into Arabic might be: *"Yawm aqāma kull qawm dh(u/a) Ilah wa-shaym wa dh(u/a) ḥabl wa-ḥumrah"*. When he (the *mukarrib*) organized (?)/joined together(?) every community group (Sabaic *gw*^{m}) of 'Il (God) and (possessed) of honour, and which has a pact and a writing in red. *Shaym* in colloquial Yemeni Arabic means "honour", *wafā, sharaf*[8] etc., and the Zaydī Imāms sprinkle red powder on documents, and the Prophet wrote on the red leather of Khawlān.

While the sense of the inscription is still speculative, the *ḥabl Allāh* (pact of God) of the Qur'ān, iii,103, in the verse *wa-'taṣimū bi-ḥabli 'llāhi jamīᶜan wa-lā tafarraqū wa-'dhkurū niᶜmata 'llāhiᶜalay-kum idh kuntum aᶜdā' wa-allafa bayna qulūbi-kum* is obviously the pact, the *Sunnah Jāmiᶜah,* which put an end to tribal squabbles at Yathrib and founded the *Ummah.* No actual *ḥabl* on the lines of the *Sunnah Jāmiᶜah* has yet come to light from pre-Islamic Arabia but one yet may – just as the rules for the pilgrimage at Itwat have been shown by Maḥmūd al-Ghūl[9] to resemble the *manāsik al-ḥajj.* But the establishment by Muḥammad of a confederation – the *Sunnah Jāmiᶜah,* under theocratic rule was clearly an Arabian practice, well established.

The *Sunnah Jāmiᶜah,* A, rules that each tribal group will deal with the major issue in tribal law, that of the responsibility for blood money (to which it adds ransom) according to *al-maᶜrūf,* recognized custom. In this area of law the Prophet hereby gave positive sanction to *ᶜurf* – indeed his general policy appears to follow existing custom. But the most significant proviso is in B,4. "In whatever thing you are at variance, its reference back is to Allāh, Great and Glorious, and to Muḥammad, Allāh bless and honour him". It is this clause that sets up the theocratic confederation headed by Muḥammad.

Following the Qur'ān verse quoted above, *sūrah* iii, 104, runs: "And let

7 'Le Sanctuaire préislamique du Gabal al-Lawd̲ (Nord-Yemen)', *Comptes-rendus, Académie des Inscriptions et Belles-Lettres,* Paris, 1982, pp. 590-629, especially pp. 616-7.

8 *Shaym* was thus defined to me by Sayyid Aḥmad al-Shāmī.

9 'The Pilgrimage at Itwat', *Proceedings of the Seminar for Arabian Studies,* London, 1984, XIV, pp. 33-41.

there be of you an *Ummah* (confederation) inviting to good and ordering what is customary/recognized *(al-maʿrūf)* and prohibiting what is unrecognized *(munkar)*". The question at once arises – with regard to both verses – did the Qur'ānic injunctions to "have recourse for protection to the pact *(ḥabl)* of Allāh as a collective group" and "let there be of you an *Ummah*" follow or precede the Prophet's concluding of the two pacts which are the *Sunnah Jāmiʿah?* It may be argued either way, but I think the *Sunnah Jāmiʿah*, A, preceded the Qur'ān verses, because the *ḥabl Allāh* as quoted in them appears to be something already in existence and they are giving it sanction.

The injunction to appeal in disputes to the Prophet as ultimate arbiter occurs several times in the Qur'ān, but to the passage containing one of these injunctions that figures in *sūrah* iv,58-60, I did not give full consideration in my original study. This looks to reflect a development following, perhaps quite soon, the conclusion of *Sunnah Jāmiʿah*, B, to which it is related. Omitting redundant phrases perhaps inserted at the Prophet's redaction, the passage runs: "Allāh commands you (plur.) to give back the pledges *(amānāt)*[10] to their owners, and when you judge between the people to judge with justice . . . O those who have trusted/believed *(āmanū)*, obey Allāh and obey the Apostle and those of you in command, and if you dispute over something refer it back to Allāh and the Apostle". The Qur'ān then rebukes those maintaining they have trusted/believed in what was revealed to the Prophet but yet wish to take one another to the *Ṭāghūt* though ordered to disbelieve in him. The *Ṭāghūt*, called *al-kāhin al-Ṭaghūt* by Ibn Ḥabīb[11] is the pagan soothsayer-judge. "Those of you in command" will be the *naqībs* and sayyids of the Aws and Khazraj tribes.

I must digress a little to discuss this passage on pledges on which I hope to write a paper. In the legal procedure known as *munāfarah* or *nifār* the two contending parties each deposited an article with a judge. The loser also lost his pledge to the winner of the case. *Munāfarah* cases as reported

10 Muhammad's Farewell Speech at the Ḥajjat al-Wadāʿ, repeats the injunction of Qur'ān, IV, 58-60: 'With whomsoever there is an *amānah* let him pay it back to him who entrusted him with it'. I regard the Speech as a dramatisation with a chorus, drawing largely on the Qur'ān. This injunction is given a general application, but cf. Qur'ān, ii, 283 which relates to a different situation.

11 Ibn Ḥabīb *al-Munammaq*, Ḥaydarābād, 1384/1964, p. 111.

by Ibn Ḥabīb[12] appear to have an air of fantasy about them till it is realised that they are honour *(sharaf)* cases. Infringement of, or challenge to a tribesman's honour is a serious matter then and now and might even lead to a murder. So a *munāfarah* means much the same as a *muḥākamah.*[13] In Jordan[14] and Beersheba this century the loser's pledge went as a fee to the arbiter. A Yemeni Ms. on tribal law of not later than circa 500 H. which I am editing states: "When two litigants pledge a pledge with a trust worthy party *(thiqah)* and the case *(al-ḥaqq)* goes against one of them, the trustworthy party is allowed to retain the pledge until the party against whom the case has been decided acquits himself of his liability". My *Kitāb al-Ādāb wa-'l-lawāzim fī aḥkām al-manᶜah* (circa 1300 A.D.), of which more below, expatiates on this theme in the same vein. Al-Qurṭubī in *al-Jāmiᶜ li-aḥkām al-Qur'ān*[15] is the only authority consulted by me who seems to interpret the passage correctly. He says the *amānāt* are articles deposited *(wadīᶜah)*, pledges *(rahn)*, etc. with governors *(wulāh)* and they are returned to their owners, the innocent and the guilty.[16]

12 Ibid., p.94 passim. Cf. my 'The White Dune at Abyan: an ancient place of pilgrimage in Southern Arabia', *JSS,* XIV, 1971, pp. 74-83, a case over an accusation of bastardy.

13 The Caliph ᶜUmar uses *muḥākamah* for Zuhayr's *munāfarah.*

14 Ahmad ᶜUwaiḍi/Oweidi al-ᶜAbbādī, *Bedouin justice in Jordan,* Cambridge Ph.D. thesis 1982 (in press) & ᶜĀrif al-ᶜĀrid, *al-Qaḍā' bayn al-badw,* Jerusalem, 1933.

15 Cairo, 1377/1958, V, p.256.

16 I recall hearing in South Arabia that judges with whom litigants have placed a deposit are sometimes reluctant to return them to their owners after the case has been settled. It may have been to avoid this that the Qur'ān, IV, 68-60 was revealed or alternatively it was to abolish an existing custom of the judge taking the loser's pledge as a fee. In an honour case in *al-Munammaq,* p.107, a pledge is deposited with a third party not the *kāhin*-jugde. I found a pledge-holder *(ᶜadalī)* might be a person different from the arbiters ('Two tribal law cases' II, *JRAS;*London, 1951, p.161). *ᶜAdl,* meaning a deposit occurs in Qur'ān, II, 47, 123, the former quoting the *Sunnah Jāmiᶜah,* Doc.B, 3a, the latter also linked with it, as is Qur'ān, VI, 70. These passages might be dated to year 1 og 2. Weapons were used as a pledge in the Prophet's time (Ibn Hishām, *Sīrah,* ed. Saqqā et alii, Cairo, 1375/1955, II, p.55. I have noted, 'The White Dune at Abyan', *JSS,* Manchester, XVI, 1971, in an honour case, 15 muskets and 100 camels pledged before a sort of trial by ordeal. Perhaps honour cases come into Islam as *qadhf* cases. After the trial *lawm* money is paid over.

In an honour case immediately preceding Islam between the Bajīlah and Kalb tribes 'they made arbiter *(ḥakkamū)* al-Aqraᶜ b. Ḥābis and placed pledges *(ruhūn)* in the hands of ᶜUqbah b. Rabīᶜah b. ᶜAbd Shams al-Qurashī among the nobles *(ashrāf)* of Quraysh'. Each party when asked for a guarantor *(kafīl)* of fulfilment (*wafā,* of the judgement?) nominated several pagan gods where recent Ḥaḍramī documents in my hands nomi-

To return to the EIGHT DOCUMENTS – three shorter pacts deal with the client-ally relationships of the Jewish, and probably one Christian, tribes to the Arab Aws and Khazraj. With their disappearance from Yathrib-Medīnah these pacts have only historic interest and are unrelated to subsequent Islamic legislation on the status of the Jews in the Muslum community. Document G of the EIGHT is the treaty of mutual protection concluded before the so called battle of the Trench by the Muslim groups in Yathrib to which the Jews of Aws subscribed. Two documents that define the regulations for creating and regulating the sacred enclave, the Ḥaram, of Yathrib now named *Madīnat al-Nabiyy,* are important and valid, in principle, today.

To sum up, the *Sunnah Jāmiᶜah,* i.e. the EIGHT DOCUMENTS, A and B, are the basis, the founding charter, of the Muslim community, the *Ahl al-Sunnah wa-'l-Jamāᶜah,* laying down the principles for its unity and making it possible for others to join the *Ummah – man tabiᶜa fa-laḥiqa bi-him.* Muhammad is in this the *mujammiᶜ,* the uniter, probably like the *mukarribs* and others in Arabia before him.

It is astonishing that the ulema of the 2nd hijrah century onwards should have relatively neglected it – yet there are two clear quotations from it in the Qur'ān. I think other passages in the Qur'ān, if studied carefully, would be seen to reflect the *Sunnah Jāmiᶜah* and possibly others of the EIGHT DOCUMENTS. For instance *sūrah* II,40-48 I hold as addressed to the Jewish Banū Qurayẓah at the confrontation at al-Khandaq, the Trench, the last verse clearly couched in terms of the *Sunnah Jāmiᶜah* B & A. Phrases from the EIGHT occur in the great Tradition collections. If collected and studied the alterations or accretions to them in the course of transmission would emerge, and what is undeniably genuine would be established. (The EIGHT are patently genuine in themselves and, in contrast to the Qur'ān, show no sign of redaction). This might prove a corrective to what is over-destructive in the work of Goldziher and Schacht.

The *Sunnah Jāmiᶜah* remains a reference of central importance for at least a century and a half. The Prophet's death left the Medinan tribes in

nate Allāh as *kafīl. The Naḳā'iḍ of Jarīr and AlFarazdaḳ,* ed.A.A. Bevan, Leiden, 1905, I, p.140.

I noted from the late Sayyid Ṣāliḥ b. ᶜAlī al-Ḥāmid in Ḥaḍramawt: *Ṭaraḥū 'adā'il bayna-hum fī mā jarā,* They put down pledges between them over what had taken place. I.e. over an incident.

a quandary over his successor. A piece missing from the published text of Ibn Aᶜtham's *Futūḥ,* but discovered by Miklos Muranyi,[17] provides valuable new information about the eventful meeting at the Saqīfah of the Banū Sāᶜidah at which the problem was discussed. Ibn Aᶜtham reports that Thābit b. Qays, orator of the Anṣār before and during the Prophet's time, stated that the Prophet "has gone out of the world without designating a particular man as successor and he entrusted the people to only such of the Qur'ān and the *Sunnah Jāmiᶜah* as Allāh made (His) agent/trustee/guardian *(wakīl)* and Allāh will not unite *(yajmaᶜ)* this *Ummah* on (the basis of) error". One has to consider the possibilities either that this statement was invented to refute the Shīᶜah doctrine that the Prophet made a *naṣṣ* designating ᶜAlī b. Abī Ṭālib as his successor, or that the Shīᶜah historians such as al-Yaᶜqūbī[18] deliberately excised it from their account of the Saqīfah. My own view is that the fundamental position of the *Sunnah Jāmiᶜah* with regard to the *Ummah* meant that it would be in the minds of all present at the Saqīfah meeting. I regard the statement as authentic, and the Prophet's inaction on the issue of succession to himself as deliberate and for good reason – I hope to develop this theme in another paper.

The first major crisis in Islam came with the murder of the third Caliph, ᶜUthmān, the conflict between ᶜAlī b. Abī Ṭālib and Muᶜāwiyah, the relation of ᶜUthmān, their confrontation at Ṣiffīn[19] and the treaty of arbitration concluded between them in 36/656-57. This treaty consists of three brief and distinct agreements concluded at different times. The first rules that the arbitration will be made in accordance with the *Qur'ān alone.* The second adds *"wa-'l-sunnah al-ᶜādilah al-jāmiᶜah ghayr al-mufarriqah",* the just uniting sunnah, not the dividing sunnah, thus contradicting the first agreement. Why? My solution would be that the political leaders on either side would be more directly acquainted with the *Sunnah Jāmiᶜah* with its clear cut provisos, than they would be with the Qur-ān – anyway the *Sunnah Jāmiᶜah* is essentially a tribal confederal agreement though concluded under the aegis of Allāh. Again, following

[17] 'Ein neuer Bericht über die Wahl des ersten Kalifen Abū Bakr', *Arabica,* Leiden, 1978, XXV, pp. 233-60. A slight emendation has to be made (p.239, line 17). The second *inna-mā* should read *ilā mā.*

[18] Al-Yaᶜqūbī, *Tārīkh,* Beirut, 1379/1960, II, p.123, alludes to Thābit b. Qays, the orator but states only that he mentioned the *faḍl* of the Anṣār.
Ṭabarī, *Tārīkh,* II, I, p.508, Year 65, Qur'ān, III, 103, & *Sunnah Jāmiᶜah* B, 2a.

[19] For my discussion of the Ṣiffīn arbitration documents see *CHAL,* I, pp. 142 seq.

the slaying of Ḥusayn, son of ᶜAlī b. Abī Ṭālib, at Karbalā', it is to the *Kitāb Allāh* and the Sunnah of His Prophet that al-Murrī appeals to avenge his death. This can only be the *Sunnah Jāmiᶜah,* not just a vague body of sunnahs. So the *Sunnah Jāmiᶜah* seems to be known variously as the *Sunnat Rasūl Allāh, Sunnat Nabiyyi-hi,* sometimes as the *Ḥabl Allāh.* The poet al-Farazdaq[20] says of the Umayyad Caliph Hishām: "*Ḥabl Allāh ḥablu-ka,* The pact bond of Allāh is your pact bond". By this is to be understood the protection afforded by Allāh's pact, i.e. the *Sunnah Jāmiᶜah.*

The *Sunnah Jāmiᶜah* continued important in Shīᶜah eyes and the Imām Jaᶜfar al-Ṣādiq defines it as consisting of 30 clauses – this exactly fits the length of the first three documents of the EIGHT, but includes document C which establishes the client-ally relation of the Jewish to the Arab tribes of Yathrib.

In the historical writing of the first Islamic century and a half it should be attempted to distinguish when the *sunnat al-Nabiyy/Rasūl* means the *Sunnah Jāmiᶜah,* the sunnah par excellence of the Prophet, and when it comes to mean, early no doubt, Muḥammad's sunnahs in general. In this connection I would draw attention to a study that has not received the attention it merits, M. M. Bravmann's *The Spiritual background of early Islam* (1972), notably the chapter "Sunnah and related concepts"; I concur in his refutation of Schacht's theory on the "Sunnah of the Prophet". Bravmann's discussion of the phrase *sunnat Rasūl Allāh wa-sīratu-hu* suggests to me a possible distinction between the *Sunnah Jāmiᶜah* and decisions made by the Prophet in a relatively routine way – but this requires further study.

It is strange that in the nine major works on Tradition covered by the Wensinck *Concordance et Indices* the term *Sunnah Jāmiᶜah* does not appear at all, although Muslim *(zakāt* 139) does quote: *A-lam ajid-kum ḍullālan . . . wa-mutafarriqīna fa-jamaᶜa-kum Allāh bī?* Dit I not find you in error . . . and split apart, then Allāh brought you together through me? Cf. Qur'ān,iii,103,supra. How could the Traditionists ignore so important a document?

The massive contingents of Arab tribesmen that moved into Syria and the cantonment cities of southern Iraq can hardly have had recourse to other than their existing arbiters and chiefs in legal matters and the

20 A.A. Bevan, *The Naḳā'iḍ of Jarīr and AlFarazdaḳ,* Leiden, 1905-08, II, 1013. The verses are an important indication of the attitude of the time to the sunnah.

inherited tradition of the pagan age. The *Waqʿat Ṣiffīn*[21] indeed says that at the time of the *fitnah* between ʿAlī and Muʿāwiyah: "they were Arabians (*ʿurb*) . . . and in them were the vestiges of (tribal) honour (*ḥamiyyah*)". This looks like an understatement! *ʿUrf* administered by the chiefs no doubt varied from tribe to tribe but it is likely to have been *ʿurf* law, given in time an Islamic tag, that formed the basis of Islamic *sunan*. This is not, of course, to deny that certain sunnahs do remount to the Prophet.

An example of how little Islam might affect tribal customary law even towards the close of the 3rd century appears when the first Zaydī Imām, al-Hādī,[22], arrived in the Jawf of north-east Yemen to find "immoral women" at the Sultan's gate. One of them had received money from a soldier (i.e. a tribesman) with others present, but when she failed to go to him the soldier took the case to the Sultan who punished her and compelled her to go to him.

Let me now turn to the celebrated letter which the Caliph ʿUmar is credited to have sent to Abū Mūsā al-Ashʿarī, his governor in Iraq, which I have examined in detail in the *JSS*, 1984. When reading it with undergraduates I had doubt about its authenticity like earlier scholars. Eventually I happened upon a letter in Ibn Abī Ḥadīd's commentary to the *Nahj al-balāghah* which ʿUmar is stated to have written to Abū Mūsā. Stripped of its obviously much later preamble, it is identical both in content and diction, given minor variations not materially affecting the sense, with a letter ʿUmar sent to Muʿāwiyah, his governor of Syria. Of the genuineness of the letters I am in no doubt. Let me quote the letter to Muʿāwiyah:

> Stick to four practices and your conduct (*dīn*) will be sound and you will attain your most abounding fortune.
> 1. When two opposing parties present themselves, you are responsible (for seeing to the production of) proofs, witnesses of probity and decisive oaths.
> 2. Then admit the man of inferior status(*ḍaʿīf*) so that his tongue may be loosened and his heart emboldened.
> 3. Look after the stranger, for when he is long detained he will abandon his suit and go back to his people.
> 4. Take pains to arrive at conciliation (*ṣulḥ*) so long as judgement is not clear.
> Peace be upon you.

[21] Al-Minqarī, *Waqʿat Ṣiffīn*, Cairo, 1382 (ed. ʿAbd al-Salām Hārūn).

[22] See my 'The Interplay between tribal affinities and religious (Zaydī) authority in the Yemen', *al-Abḥāth*, Beirut, 1982, XXX, pp. 11-50 quoting the *Sīrat al-Hādī*, Beirut, 1392/1972, p.94.

The virtually identical letter to Abū Mūsā al-Ashʿarī I believe to be the basis of the famous letter ascribed to ʿUmar, expanded and "improved" by Abū Mūsā's descendants from the simple concise message neglected by early Islamic scholars. Such evidence as there is would make the "improved" letter not later than the first two decades of the second century of the hijrah. But it was not accepted by all early scholars and the Spanish Ibn Ḥazm rejected the letter as not genuine. I favour Bilāl b. Abī Burdah, Abū Mūsā's grandson, as the likely "improver". The "improved" version inserts instruction for which there is no basis in the original letters and it alters the general purpose of certain clauses in the genuine letter. It opens with the assertion that "Pronouncing judgement *(qaḍā')* is an established practice", which from the scant evidence available seems contrary to ʿUmar's commendation of Zuhayr's statement that the three methods of deciding a case, are oath taking, summoning before a judge *(nifār)* or proof. But the most significant principle fathered on ʿUmar reads: "Pay attention to comprehending what . . . has no Qur'ān or practice *(sunnah)* applicable to it, and become acquainted with similarities and analogies. Then after that compare matters. Then have recourse to that which is most preferable to Allāh and most in conformity of them to justice/right *(ḥaqq)* as you see it". Though not ʿUmar's letter and not to be regarded as reflecting actual practice in the first century, it is a sound basis for an Islamic theory of law.

The formulation of Islamic law as we know it took place in Iraq, the Holy Cities, even Ṣanʿā'. A sampling of the eleven volume *Muṣannaf* however, written by the 2nd century ʿAbd al-Razzāq al-Ṣanʿānī, does not seem to reveal material divergencies from the Iraqīs and Ḥijāzīs. The *fuqahā'* of those countries display a prejudice against a number of aspects of tribal custom. The "improved" letter of ʿUmar very significantly relegates conciliation *(ṣulḥ)* to a secondary place – a subtle change from ʿUmar's ruling. At this point I should like to quote *in extenso* from Colonel Aḥmad Oweidi's interpretation of the bedouin – I would say "tribal" – attitude in Jordan to law. It seems to me to embody the principles lying behind the customary law known as *manʿah* to which I shall come later in this paper, but I think it would also reflect the tribal outlook in 6th and 7th century Arabia. The importance of *ṣulḥ,* conciliation, in the scheme of tribal society, to which in a sense *qaḍā'* emerges as secondary, is plain to see.

> "Justice cannot prevail until any imbalance caused by a violation of the limit of acceptability (Oweidi means by this, the tribal moral feeling) is resolved in such a way as to bring all the parties back within it. Hence the verdicts of a Bedouin judge must satisfy all parties concerned, and restore them to the recognized limit of acceptability – *kull min-hum yarja^c li-ḥadd-uh* – everyone should return to his position within the limit of acceptability. This is so because the most important link binding Bedouin communities together is that of extended kinship and the concept of the limit of acceptability. Conciliation, *ṣulḥ,* and the satisfaction of all parties concerned, is essential to preserve balance and equilibrium. Since the limit of acceptability is flexible, differing according to time, place and the individual community, Bedouin justice varies likewise. A sentence is gradually implemented and modified until the line of equilibrium is once again reached to the satisfaction of all, and only then is it considered that justice has been achieved. A Bedouin judge would sentence a culprit to the most severe punishment. Then mediators beg the injured party for forgiveness – in a series of mediations the judge, the head of the community and the injured party, all gradually mitigate the sentence until the punishment becomes minimal. The process restores both the culprit and the injured party to their previous positions with the limit of acceptability and each *rija^c li-ḥadd-uh.*"

Let me just say that in 1947 a tribesman who had been inciting his son to fire at me, was brought before the Wāḥidī Sultan and the Arab political assistant advised me to plead for mitigation of his sentence, and others did likewise. Though threatening with arms is a serious offence in tribal law the man was let off with perhaps a day's imprisonment.

The *fuqahā'* clearly dislike *qasāmah,* the oath taken by 50 men of the kin of the accused, but which I have shown is standard procedure among the south Arabian tribes today.[23] Yet another issue on which the *fuqahā'* have acted, modifying the milder attitude taken by the Prophet, is the question of *zinā,* fornication – on which I have written a paper (in press). Ṭabarī[24] quotes Ibn ᶜAbbās as saying of the Arabs of the Jāhiliyyah: 'They used to forbid such adultery *(zinā')* as appeared, but to allow what was hidden, saying, 'concerning what appears it is disgrace *(lu'm)* but as for what is hidden, that does not matter'. The entirely different attitude of tribes from what became *sharīᶜah* law on *zinā'* has been discussed in Walter Dostal's excellent paper on *'Sexual hospitality' and the problem of matrilinearity in Southern Arabia.*[25]

[23] 'Dawlah, tribal shaykhs, the Manṣab of the Waliyyah Saᶜīdah, *qasamah* in the Faḍlī Sultanate, South Arabian Federation', *Arabian studies in honour of Mahmoud Ghul,* Wiesbaden, 1989, p.147.

[24] *Tafsīr,* Cairo, 1321, V.14.

[25] *Proceedings of the Seminar for Arabian Studies,* London, 1990, pp. 17-30.

Ibn al-Mujāwir[26] (7th/13th century) reveals the actual law prevailing in western Arabia of his day in a most important statement. "All the ʿArab of these provinces, the mountains along with the Tihāmahs up to the borders *(ḥudūd)* of the Ḥijāz – not one accepts the judgement *(ḥukm)* of the *sharʿ* – and they only assent to the *ḥukm al-manʿah*. There is no doubt that it is the judgement of the Jāhiliyyah to which they used to go with one another to court *(yataḥākamūn)* at the *kāhins*". To judge by Colonel Oweidi's study this is likely to have been the case also in the rest of western Arabia as far, at least, as Jordan.

Manaʿa[27] means – to defend from injustice, tyranny, attack, transgression, and *manʿah* is the verbal noun derived from it. The Prophet was *fī sharaf/ʿizz wa-manʿah,* honoured and protected – i.e. as a member of an arms-bearing tribal house. *Manʿah* is that body of customary law which governs the maintenance of security. It covers a multitude of sides of tribal life but not business or market law, and non-arms-bearers only in their relation as protected persons to tribesmen. There is emphasis on anything touching on tribal honour. *Ṣulḥ* is stated to come before all other judgements *(aḥkām)*.

One of the Mss. I have edited but not yet published is attributed to Ibn Zinbāʿ whose name, but little else, is known to Yemenis. Much of the Ms. is derived from what the illustrious qāḍī al-Ḥusayn b. ʿImrān b. al-Fāḍil (correctly al-Faḍl) al-Yāmī wrote of the book of *al-Manʿ*, comprising all the categories of it and the arbiters of *manʿ* before it. Sayyid Aḥmad al-Shāmī pointed out to me that ʿImrān b. al-Faḍl was a well known supporter of the Ṣulayḥids. The Yāmīs supported the Ḥāfiẓī Daʿwah of the later Fāṭimids, as ʿAbbās al-Hamdānī informs me. Al-Ḥusayn would have composed his treatise ca. 500 H. but drew on earlier arbiters, perhaps, indeed probably, remounting to the age of paganism.[28] *Manʿ* at any rate was followed by al-Ḥusayn and probably his father in Ṣanʿā', where he was governor, but it is not connected with Ismāʿīlism.

Al-Ḥusayn's dictum maintains that 'the judge must judge by the *sharʿ* in its relation to *(min)* the *sharʿ*, and by *manʿ* in that to which *manʿ* pertains. He should also judge by *siyāsah* (shrewdness, diplomacy?) in

26 *Tārīkh al-mustabṣir,* ed. O. Löfgren, Leiden, 1951-54, p.99.

27 *Tāj al-ʿarūs,* Kuwait, 1405/1985, XXII, pp. 218-9, *manʿ* is *al-ḥaylūlah bayna* and *al-ḥimāyah; manaʿa-hu nāsun . . . yamnaʿūna-hu min al-ḍaym wa-'l-taʿaddī ʿalayh* and *wa-maʿa-hu man yamnaʿa-hu min ʿashīrati-hi.*

28 The tribal *sijills,* may have contained Manʿah law. Hamdānī alludes to a pre-islamic *sijill.*

accordance with his ability to make an independent judgement *ʿalā qadr ijtihādi-hi)*'. Like the later Shāfiʿī author of *al-Ādāb . . . fī aḥkām al-manʿah* (supra) he sees no inconsistency between *manʿ* and *sharʿ*. I do not indeed think there is a conflict in principle between the *Sunnah Jāmiʿah* of the Prophet which federates the Yathrib-Medīnah tribes, and *manʿ*, yet I was told that when Imam Yaḥyā came on treatises such as these he would destroy them and execute the possessor.

It will be appreciated that *manʿah* law has only limited applications to urban communities which in any case would fall within the category of protected persons of tribes resident and dominating in a city. Tarīm for example during last century was ruled by three separate groups of Yāfiʿī tribesmen who domineered over the town's artisans and others, whom they despised. ʿAlawī b. Ṭāhir[29] tells of the ʿAmūdī Mashāyikh of his native Dawʿan that Allāh has empowered the tribes over them and they have become *raʿiyyah* to the extent they cannot marry any of their daughters without their permission. They had other humiliating rights *(ḥuqūq)* also.

In tribal customary law, *manʿah* apart, practices diametrically opposed to *sharīʿah* obtain – I do not deny of course that some *manʿ* customs may not conform to Islam. The most commonly cited is that women may not inherit land, etc. In Tarīm I even came across a treatise which allowed a woman to make over to a male relative by *nadhr* the share she should inherit under Islamic law – compliance being thus made with *sharīʿah* while tribal custom was preserved.

Certain of these customs[30] were severely censured by the late 19th century Ḥaḍramī writer Bā Ṣabrayn. 'One of the most horrible things', he says, 'is what is well known of the *bādiyah* (tribesfolk of Dawʿan

[29] *Kitāb al-Shāmil fī tārīkh Ḥaḍramawt,* printed in Singapore in 1940 but not published, p.182.

[30] Many un-Islamic practices existed up to modern times in other parts of Arabia, but the Saʿudis have followed a deliberate policy of suppressing them; other Arab states seem to have followed suit. H.R.P. Dickson reports (1920): 'Ibn Saud assured me that so ignorant had the Bedouin of Nejd been in the past that, until the new revival ninety per cent of them had never heard of religion, marriage had never been solemnized and circumcision had been unknown'. *The Arab Bulletin,* Cairo, 1919, IV, p.110, reprint with notes by Robin Bidwell, Gerrards Cross, 1986. An attack on un-Islamic customs in the Yemeni Tihāmah was made by ʿAbdullah b. Sulaymān b. Ḥamīd al-Najdī, *Naṣīḥat al-Muslimīn ʿan al-bidaʿ . . .* ed. Muḥammad Sālim al-Bayḥānī, fifth printing, Fatāt al-Jazīrah Press, Aden, 1372/1935.

province), that the fornicator *(zānī)* comes to the wife of another man, and such as the husband happens upon the two of them, but does not kill them both, or does not kill him. On the contrary he says to him: *'Artabiṭ ᶜinda-hā fī miyah wa-ᶜishrīn riyāl'*, the sense being I shall not release you until you undertake to pay me that amount (120 *riyāls*) and I shall divorce her, for example – and he does so'. The adulterer, called *al-marbūṭ*, has to pay the injured husband double the *dafᶜ* marriage present, but not the *mahr* dower (which a man does not normally pay over unless he divorces) and double all the marriage expenses, two thirds going to the injured husband and a third to the woman's family *(ahl al-ḥurmah)*.

The *Ādāb wa-lawāzim al-manᶜah* interestingly enough also details regulations governing marriage by capture.

Bā Ṣabrayn attacks many other practises current in Ḥaḍramawt in his day, notably those relating to agriculture and the *zakāt* on crops. He categorically condemns the compromise between customary law and the *sharᶜ* which, I think, had evolved centuries before. 'One of the most disgraceful of forbidden things,' he says, 'is belief that judgement by reason, deriving from the means of cultivation *(asbāb al-ḥirāthah)*, commerce *(tijārah)*, tribalism *(qabwalah)* and the handicrafts *(ḥiraf)*, contrary to the judgement/law of the *sharᶜ*, branches out from *(mufarriᶜ ᶜalā)* the judgement of the *sharᶜ*. What accords with the judgement of the *sharᶜ* is called *ḥukm sharᶜī* or *sharᶜī*, and what conflicts with it is called *ḥukm farᶜī* or *farᶜī* and is recognized because of its being branching out, according to belief about it (?), from *sharᶜī*. The truth and rightness (of the matter) is that what accords with the judgement of Allāh, the Almighty Ruler, is the judgement of the *sharᶜ*; anything contrary to that is the judgement of the false *Ṭāghūt*. Calling falsity truth is forbidden like calling truth falsity. So take heed!' *Ḥukm* is to be understood as 'law', and the *ḥukm farᶜī* is not the Islamic *furūᶜ*. In Jordan Aḥmad ᶜUwayḍī (thesis, 219) has described the *quḍāt al-furūᶜ*, dealing with cases related to particular crafts, trades and professions, e.g. land, cattle, horses. These obviously had no training in *sharīᶜah* law and no doubt followed the custom pervading their bedouin ambience.

So Bā Ṣabrayn condemns 'the *Ṭāghūt* judges *(ḥukkām)* of the Dayyin (federation), the Bā Ḥanḥan', specialising in agricultural disputes, running tribal law courts as they were doing in 1967 and probably do today. The Marāqishah of the Faḍlī sultanate told me in 1964 that 'their own procedure was preferable (to the *sharīᶜ-ah* courts) because it was plea and counter-plea in one day and judgement in one day and payment settlement in one day' because of the interminable delays, etc. of *sharīʿah*.[31] For this and other reasons I think tribesfolk everywhere prefer customary lawcourts or individual judges. Nevertheless I do not think *sharīʿah* law is entirely disregarded in tribal districts and *ṣulḥ* is certainly common procedure in towns – but then as the ancient proverb says: *Al-Ṣulḥ khayr/sayyid al-aḥkām,* Conciliation is the best/lord of judgements.

[31] 'Dawlah, tribal shaykhs . . .', p.142.

VIII

The Fātimī – Taiyibī (Ismāʿīlī) Daʿwah. Ideologies and Community

The Fatīmī-Taīyibī Daʿwah is a quite remarkable sect of Islam, both in regard to its not negligible role in history and its activities today, its small numbers not withstanding. Its ideology contrasts with what we are hearing at the Colloquium today, for it may be said to have neither political objectives or attitudes. Over fourteen centuries of Islam it has moved from Syria to the Maghrib to Arabia and India; today its adherents are widely spread. M. Hanafi has distinguished for us, most persuasively, the two opposing trends in Islamic political thought, the harking back to an (idealized) past, and the trend to concentrate on adjustment to the modern age. The Daʿwah keeps its Islamic tradition very much alive while encouraging its members to equip themselves with all the modern sciences and skills.

Almost by accident I became interested, nearly twenty years ago, in the Dāwūdī Bohrahs when the late Saiyīd-nā Tāhir Saif al-Dīn's daughter, Shehrbanu, came to enter a course of research at Cambridge. Her father was the 51st Dāʿī Mutlaq of the community, its absolute spiritual and temporal head – later one of the sons of the present Dāʿī, Saiyid-nā H.H. Burhān al-Dīn, Prince Badr al-Dīn, also joined us. Our professional acquaintance ripened into personal friendship with the Dāʿī's House which provided me the opportunity to visit Bohrah centres in India.[1] As long ago as 1940 I had met Bohrah leaders in Aden but I was too inexperienced to enquire further into the sect with them and otherwise engaged. Again in 1957 while on a Government mission to examine Muslim education I met Bohrahs in

---

(1) It is my pleasure to express my gratitude and indebtness to Daʿwah members in London, for allowing me to draw on their writings, supplying me verbally with information and for looking through this paper to correct any slips I might have made. I aim to present the Daʿwah as it sees itself, but at the same time I have been under no pressures from the Daʿwah to alter or suppress opinions, of my own or others, and historical assessments.

Tanganyika and Zanzibar. Though I have since read much about the Ismāʿīlīs, to whom the Bohrahs belong, my main interest is in their role in the Yemen, my special field of research, and I cannot claim any specialist knowledge of their philosophy or history which have been well studied by other scholars.(2)

Firstly I must say who the Bohrah or Fāṭimī-Ṭaiyibī Ismāʿīlīs are, as simply as I can, for the story is complicated. Ismāʿīlī doctrine had early found partisans in the Yemen and in the 5th and 6th centuries, the Sulaihī sultans accepted it and adhered to the Fāṭimid Caliphs or Imāms of Egypt. When the Nizārī and Mustaʿlī factions contested the succession to the Fāṭimid Caliphate, the Yemen and India held to al-Mustaʿlī who won recognition as Imām. When the latter's son, al-Āmir was assassinated in 526/1132(3) he left a son, al-Taiyib, two and a half years old. The Regent, appointed to act during the child's minority usurped the office of Imām-Caliph.

Al-Taiyib's fate is unknown but Fāṭimī sources say he went into seclusion. The Sulaihid Queen Arwā of the Yemen, who held the high rank of Hujjah in the Ismāʿīlī Daʿwah, maintained al-Ṭaiyib's right to the Imamate and the Yemeni Ismāʿīlīs became independent of the Fāṭimids of Egypt and are properly described as the Fāṭimī-Taiyibī Daʿwah.

In the absence of the Imām, considered to have retreated into seclusion (*satr*), Queen Arwā appointed to take charge of the Daʿwah and Ismāʿīlī community in the Yemen, on the instructions of Imām al-Âmir(4), a Yemeni, Dhu'aib al-Wādiʿī, who was entrusted with the office of al-Dāʿī al-Mutlaq.

At this juncture it is necessary to understand how the Fāṭimī-Taiyibīs conceive of the Daʿwah and I draw upon the definitions of the term and office as set out by Shehrbanu.

In Islamic usage *daʿwah* is a technical term that means summoning to Allah. To deliver the summons the existence of a person empowered by Allah to do so is essential. In this context Daʿwah becomes synonymous with the term Islam itself-comprising the beliefs and practices of Islam and the Islamic *sharīʿah*. In the context of Islamic history it has acquired a politico-religious sense also. According to Ibn Khaldūn, *daʿwah* is used to denote a doctrine employed as a means toward the overthrow of an existing political régime and its replacement by a new order, which, however, is discarded once that new order is achieved. A case in point, she observes, is the ʿAbbāsid Daʿwah, discarded after the

---

(2) Notably S.M. Stern, Abbas Hamdani, etc.

(3) Zambaur, *Manuel*, Ar. Trans., *Muʿdjam*, Cairo, 1951, 145, gives the date as 526/1130, followed by two years when the office remained vacant. This ignores the existence of al-Taiyib.

(4) So say Fāṭimī sources.

collapse of the Umaiyads, and there were the various ʿAlawī *daʿwahs*, rebellious movements in their turn, against the ʿAbbāsids.

The term al-Daʿwah al-Fātimīyah was used without the same political connotation, for, contrary to those movements the Fātimī imāms continued to promote their Daʿwah with or without *dawlah*, i.e. established political power. Instead they chose to give up *dawlah* so as to preserve the Daʿwah. The main objective of the Fātimī imāms was, in effect, concentrated on promoting and establishing the Daʿwah – not the creation of a *dawlah*. So it is that in Fātimī philosophy and ideology Daʿwah assumes a far more comprehensive sense than a doctrine used to support a political cause.

This then is a Fātimī rationalisation of the sequence of events of their history.

The Fātimī concept of the Daʿwah, as defined by its scholars, is basically founded upon two Qur'ānic verses(5):

Lahu daʿwatu'l-haqq, His is the Daʿwah of the truth.

Udʿu ilā sabīli Rabbi-ka bi-'l-hikmati wa'l-mawʿizati'l-hasanati, Summon to the path of thy Lord with wisdom and kindly warning.

The Daʿwah originates with Allah and the summons is made to Allah. The summons (*daʿwah*) is made by a prophet sent by Allah or His representative on Earth (*khalīfat Allah fi 'l-ard*). This being is present on Earth throughout all time, to perform the Daʿwah and is known as Sāhib al-Daʿwah. Allah's command (*amr*) authorises the Prophet to summon people to Him. He who is commanded to do so is known as Sāhib al-Amr. Muhammad, Apostle of Allah, was the Sāhib al-Amr of his age and the person to whom the Prophet hands over this command is the Sāhib al-Amr of the age in which he lives. Fātimī philosophers hold that among the people of the Earth *must* be one person, be he the Prophet, the Legatee (Wasī), Imām or Dāʿī entrusted with the Daʿwah, summoning to Allah and the Straight Path (*al-Sirāt al-Mustaqīm*) – he is the Sāhib al-Amr.

Fātimīs hold that even before Muhammad the Daʿwah was in continuous existence and will be promoted after him by his descendants and their posterity in an unbroken chain of succession until Judgment Day, each Imām designating his son to succeed him by *nass*. This is a difficult term to translate – testamentary disposition, explicit pronouncement, of a successor. For Fātimī ulema the *sūrah's* term Daʿwat al-Haqq is synonymous with al-Daʿwat al-Fātimīyah. The command and permission (*amr waidhn*) of Allah by which Muhammad the Apostle established the Daʿwah has been maintained by successive imāms without break or change and the Daʿwah today is the original Daʿwah of Muhammad. It is based on Islamic doctrine (*ʿaqīdah*) and *sharīʿah*

(5) *Sūrahs* XIII, 14, XVI, 125, but there are of course many other relevant verses.

law. Those responding to the summons of the Sāhib al-Amr enter the fold of the Daᶜwah and constitute the Ahl al-Daᶜwah, its particular community.

The Fātimī-Taiyibīs consider that after the infant Imām al-Taiyib had gone into seclusion, imāms continued to follow one after another though not of course to manifest themselves, the Daᶜwah being controlled by the Dāᶜī Mutlaq acting as vice-gerent on behalf of the Imām. The imamate has phases of manifestation (*zuhūr*) and seclusion (*satr*). The first *satr*, they say, was planned in advance by the celebrated Imām Djaᶜfar al-Sādiq and this allowed Muhammad b. Ismāᶜīl his grandson to leave Medina without attracting the attention of ᶜAbbāsid agents. This first *satr* is known as al-Hidjāb[6], when the descendants of ᶜAlī and Fātimah had to take to concealment until the first Fātimids were successful in promulgating the Daᶜwah in the Maghrib. The Hidjāb lasted about a century during which it is maintained that the imāmate continued in the posterity of Muhammad b. Ismāᶜīl the seventh Imām, father of the first of the Concealed Imāms[7]. During this phase the Imāms were at great pains to conceal themselves by the assumption of names of others so as to throw their ᶜAbbāsid enemies off the scent – which resulted in confusion over personalities even in Fātimī sources. Probably the characteristic secrecy of the Daᶜwah developed in these difficult times. But we should accept, I think, Ibn Khaldūn's verdict on those historians "who deny [the Fātimid Imāms] their descent from Ismāᶜīl son of Djaᶜfar al-Sādiq", basing themselves on "stories concocted in favour of the weak ᶜAbbāsid Caliphs" and curry favour by accusations against their active opponents. The Fātimīs however were not idle when it came to propaganda, and it is now generally accepted, says ᶜAbbas Hamdānī, that the Epistles of the Brethren of Purity (*Rasā'il Ikhwān al-Safā'*), the famous encyclopaedia, is an Ismāᶜīlī compilation, composed by a group of Fātimī dāᶜīs dedicate to the overthrow of the ᶜAbbāsid Caliphate. The *Epistles* belong to the Hidjāb *satr* period (148-297/765-909) during which there was continuity in the line of the concealed Imāms. The initiator (the Arabic term is *munshī*) of the *Epistles* the Fātimīs hold is the Imām Ahmad b. ᶜAbdullah b. Muhammad b. Ismāᶜīl b. Djaᶜfar[8]. It is an eclectic work, and, the Brethren's aims being revolutionary, to avoid ᶜAbbāsid censorship ambiguities and allusions abound – the names of the authors are also secret. The movement had political ambitions – to establish a new

---

(6) *Hidjāb* does not seem to be a Fātimī term for what Fātimīs would call the first *satr* phase.

(7) The Concealed Imāms are ᶜAbdullah b. Ismāᶜīl (8), his son Ahmad (9) and Husain b. Ahmad (10) – three in all.

(8) The last of the Concealed Imāms.

Caliphate. To an outside observer the emphasis on abandoning temporal power (*dawlah*), of more recent Fātimī ideology, would seem to reflect rationalisation of the move to Indian conditions.

The Daʿwah has in fact evolved a philosophical theory of the Universe – there is the *dawr al-kashf* phase wherein good prevails and the esoteric (*bātin*) is openly promulgated as is the *sharīʿah* but without compulsion to obey it. Then the *dawr al-fatrah* phase follows in which goodness loses its hold over people and religion becomes corrupted – then *dawr al-satr* when, due to adverse circumstances, the imāms go into hiding and the Daʿwah is carried on secretly. The underlying reason for phases of manifestation (*zuhūr*) and seclusion (*satr*) is to preserve the Daʿwah.

When the Imām holds the reins of power his temporal commands apply to all citizens of the state, but, though he would like all Muslims to accept the Fātimī doctrine of Islam, he does not force them to enter the Daʿwah – so other sects co-exist with the Ahl al-Daʿwah, the community of the Daʿwah.

The Fātimī-Taiyibīs maintain that the Fātimid Caliph-Imām al-Âmir actually arranged for his son al-Taiyib to go into seclusion, but ʿAbbās al-Hamdānī presents the situation as the result of the Fātimid court at Cairo trying to exert closer control over Queen Arwā leaving in her heart "a deep distrust of the Fātimid court and a desire for independence from it". The opportunity to gain this independence came with the death of Caliph al-Âmir in 524/1130[9] and the usurpation of the infant Imām Taiyib's rights by the eleventh Fātimid Caliph ʿAbd al-Madjīd al-Hāfiz.

During the reigns of al-Mustansir and al-Âmir the Daʿwah was known as al-Daʿwah al-Mustansirīyah and al-Âmirīyah respectively. But when the Imām choses to live in seclusion he appoints a representative in his place to preserve and propagate the Daʿwah – this is the Dāʿī who is empowered with the full authority of the Imām and is therefore called al-Dāʿī al-Mutlaq, the Absolute Dāʿī. The appointment is made by *nass*, testamentary disposition, and he hands on his office to his successor by *nass*, an so it proceeds, right up to the present day. Shehrbanu states that the rank of Dāʿī Mutlaq was not defined with all its powers in the first *satr* phase of the Hidjāb, because it was of short duration, and the Dāʿīs knew the whereabouts of the Imām, but after the assassination, or as Fātimīs say, the martyrdom, of the Fātimid al-Âmir the *satr* phase was destined to be of long duration. So his powers were specifically defined by the Imām and the Dāʿī became the fountainhead of the Daʿwah.

The Dāʿī Mutlaq is the custodian of the accumulated knowledge

(9) This date, see n.3, is considered incorrect by the Fatimis.

(*ᶜilm*) of the Daᶜwah from the time of the appointment of the first holder of the office, Dhu'aib al-Wādiᶜī. It is believed that the transfer of Ismāᶜīlī books and documents commenced in the time of Caliph al-Mustansir, by the hand of the Sulaihī Qādī the Dāᶜī Lamak who spent some years in Egypt as head of a deputation from the Yemen. Shaykh Shākir of the al-Jāmiᶜah al-Saifīyah College, Surat, has drawn my attention to a statement by Idrīs ᶜImād al-Dīn in volume VII of *ᶜUyūn al-Akhbār* that the Fātimid Imām al-Âmir declared he was going on a long journey and it is thought he transferred Ismaᶜīlī books, documents etc. to the Yemen for safety. It is likely that envoys going to and fro between the Yemen and Egypt brought this literature with them.

The office of Dāᶜī Mutlaq is not hereditary according to Fātimī doctrine but in practice it seems to have remained in one house or another for a number of generations, a son even succeeding his father. The present Dāᶜī is descended from the 45th Dāᶜī Saiyid-nā Taiyib Zain al-Dīn, the house being known as Bait-e Zainī after him, but daᶜīs of other houses seem to have alternated with them. The house of the 51st Dāᶜī, Saiyid-nā Tāhir Saif al-Dīn father of the 52nd Dāᶜī Saiyid-nā Burhān al-Dīn, is known as Qasr-e ᶜAlī. Though this Dāᶜī house is not descended, in the male line, from ᶜAlī b. Abī Tālib the Dāᶜī is treated with ceremonial, reverence and respect much exceeding that I have seen accorded the present Zaidī Imām when received by him in the Yemen and al-Tā'if. Both the Zaidīs and the Fātimī-Taiyibīs can quote Qur'ān XXXIII, 36 for their authority: "And it is not for a believing man or a believing woman, when Allah and His Apostle have decided a matter, that they should have a choice in their matter, and whosoever disobeys Allah and His Apostle, is in manifest error".

Adherents of the Daᶜwah take the oath of allegiance (*ᶜahd*), called also *bayᶜah* or *mīthāq*. It is doubtless traditional that the *ᶜahd* is administered, at least once a year, on the day of Ghadīr Khumm (18 Dhu 'l-Hidjdjah) upon which the Prophet designated ᶜAlī his successor and administered the *ᶜahd* to all present. Only the Dāᶜī, as in the line of succession going back to the Prophet, or a person authorised by him, can administer the *ᶜahd*, bond and oath, and introduce an aspirant to the Daᶜwah. The text of the *ᶜahd* states that the Qur'an alludes to the *ᶜahd* in some seventy places and it defines the doctrine *ᶜaqīdah* which the aspirant must accept. Conventionai practice is that when a child of the Daᶜwah community attains the age of puberty, by permission of the Dāᶜī the *ᶜahd* is administered to him on this special day of Ghadīr al-Khumm.

In 1978 we attended a great assembly on Ghadīr Khumm day in the hall at Saifī Mahall, Bombay. Seated on a throne H.H. the Dāᶜī Burhān al-Dīn spoke of the significance of Ghadīr Khumm in the *lisān al-Daᶜwah*, not a secret language – basically it is Gujerati but with Arabic religious terminology. Relating the tragedy of Karbalā' the Dāᶜī exclaimed an Aah, Aah of distressful grief, and the congregation beat their breasts, exclaiming "Ya Husain, yā ᶜAlī". Some wept. All the community, mostly dressed in white, seemed to attend, and small children were also brought to experience the occasion. The *wathīqah*, bond and oath, was administered and allegiance paid by clasping of the hand (*safaqah*).

The Dāᶜī has a position of great power though this has of course to be exercised with wisdom. In the event of misconduct or flagrant disobedience he may pronounce *barāt* (Arabic *barīah*) disassociation from the community upon an individual member. Even today this is a matter of serious consequence for the member thus "excommunicated".

From its early days of the Hidjāb period the Daᶜwah has evolved an hierarchical structure – it had to attract adherents from all classes of society – and the movement had originally to be secret[10] for political reasons; it bound its members to secrecy as it was necessary to preserve its esoteric philosophical doctrines from charges of heresy. The *ᶜahd* also bound its members to co-operation with one another. The aspirant, *al-akh al-mustadjīb*, to join the Daᶜwah was required to subscribe to the *ᶜahd*. Let me interpolate at this point that the Daᶜwah teachings seem always to be of a strongly ethical nature.

The various ranks or degrees in the Daᶜwah have a rather confused terminology at various stages in its history. Usually the Imām is regarded as having under him twelve *hudjdjahs* (lit. proofs) acting as a Council, each one in charge of a province (*djazīrah*) or sector; each *hudjdjah* in turn had a Council of lesser officers called dāᶜī. Queen Arwā, as seen, in her capacity as a *hudjdjah*, was empowered to appoint the first Dāᶜī Mutlaq, Absolute Dāᶜī. It seems that in the Yemen he had several lesser *daᶜis* under his command, in India he was and is today the sole Dāᶜī. In descending order (which I have somewhat simplified) come the *ma'dhūn*, licentiate, assistant to the Dāᶜī, and the *mukāsir*[11] who has partial authority. In the *satr* phase the *ma'dhūn* and the *mukāsir* are two dignitaries "under the hand" (*zīr dast*) of the Dāᶜī, i.e. subordinate to him. They are responsible for carrying out the duties assigned them by the Dāᶜī. An ordinary initiate to the doctrine is called *al-mu'min al-bāligh* while the aspirant *mustadjīb* and those outside the Daᶜwah are known as *ᶜāmmat al-Muslimīn*, the generality of Muslims. The areas with

---

(10) The *Mīthāq* binds one taking it to "conceal what you heard from the observances of religious deeds or esoteric meaning of the Quran".

(11) From Arabic *kasara*, to break. The *mukāsir* "breaks" the *mustadjīb* by argument and by explaining the doctrines of the Daᶜwah, thus preparing him to accept its ideology.

Bohrah communities in India and elsewhere are divided for administrative purposes into *ᶜilāqahs* (pl. *āt*)[12], each consisting of major and minor centres headed by an *ᶜāmil*; when there is no *ᶜāmil* a *vālī mullā* represents the Dāᶜī. Shibani Roy, upon whose *Dawoodi Bohrahs* I have drawn, says that the *ᶜāmil* represents the Dāᶜī, and presides over marriage, burial, settles disputes, administers the *mīthāq* or *ᶜahd*, looks after the mosques, *jamāt-khānah* (assembly halls), *madrasahs* and collects the taxes. By taxes she appears to mean the *zakāt*. The Bohrah community in Britain has its *ᶜāmil*, my friend Dr Idris Zainuddin.

After the establishment of the Fātimid Caliph-Imāms in Egypt the two major events in Daᶜwah history are its Transfer (*intiqāl*) from Egypt to the Yemen, and thence to India, in the 6th and 10th hidjrī centuries respectively. But in India itself the Dāᶜīs had, from time to time, to move their seat to another centre when persecuted or threatened with persecution. The history of the Transfer to the Yemen I have already briefly outlined. Non-Fātimī historians ascribe the motive for the Transfer to India to the existence there of many more adherents to the Daᶜwah than in the Yemen. But I am inclined to regard it as at least equally significant that, by the 10th century, Fātimī controlled areas had shrunk greatly, the Zaidīs were their bitter and powerful enemies and the invading Ottoman Turks probably ready only to make use of them to counter the Zaidīs. About this time it is suggested also that there was a considerable emigration of Daᶜwah adherents to India.

The Daᶜwah view is that the Transfers in either case were not motivated either by political, economic or other factors; it points indeed to the worsening of conditions later when it met with the persecution of Awrungzīb, the Moghul emperor. Projecting itself back in history, Daᶜwah ideology sees the Prophet's *hidjrah* to Medina as the earliest Transfer of itself in a series – in which follows ᶜAlī's Transfer to Kūfah, the promulgation of the Daᶜwah in the Maghrib and the Fātimid move thence to Egypt. The Fātimī-Taiyibīs insist that, guided by Divine inspiration, the Imāms prepared in the most meticulous detail for each Transfer. Importantly these preparations included the recruitment and training of Men (*Ridjāl*) – the word seems to have an almost technical application – who were either dispatched to, or resided in, the country to which the Transfer was to be made. This of course involved sending missionaries to swear aspirant adherents (*mustadjīb*) into the Daᶜwah and introduce them to that degree of knowledge (*ᶜilm*) appropriate to their stage of initiation,

---

(12) Shibani Roy's statement that in India the Dāᶜī has divided the areas with Bohrah communities into nine *sūbahs* or districts, each under a *wālī*, governor, under whom there are *ᶜāmils*, is stated by the Daᶜwah to be incorrect.

bound, as we have seen, by secrecy. The *Ridjāl* I understand to be those persons qualified by their training in *ʿilm* and personality to promote the Daʿwah.

The mediaeval history of the Daʿwah in the Yemen is still yet to be written though some Fātimī historical and other writings have been printed, but we do not know what unrecorded material the Daʿwah Library in Surat and Bombay may contain. Much Zaidī and Shāfiʿī literature, possibly relevant, remains in Ms. Published non-Fātimī sources are usually hostile and generally not well informed. The tangle of Yemeni tribal affiliations, disputes, changing alliances, complicates the picture even further. However the Fātimī Dāʿīs of Hamdān continued established at Sanʿā' and in control of a line of forts lying just north of it, extending in the east from Dha/Dhū Marmar, Fiddah/Af'idah near the mouth of Wādī Dahr westwards, al-Qalʿah further up the Wādī on its south side, overlooking it, later renamed Taibah by the Zaidīs when they captured it in their southward push in 931/1524-25. This marks the Zaidī Imāms' advance into territory once controlled by the Daʿwah. Several Dāʿīs were buried at Fiddah or Dhū Marmar but when we climbed up this latter now hardly accessible fort in 1972 we found the Fātimī buildings, mosque included, had been deliberately demolished. The same had happened at Taibah but the tombs and other structures there were probably mostly of the Sulaimānī branch of the Daʿwah, of which I shall say more later.

The third Dāʿī, Hātim b. Ibrāhīm, supported by the Yaʿburī tribe of Hamdān, managed to establish himself in the high massif of Harāz between Sanʿā' and the Red Sea coast, in the summit fortresses, Shibām, Djawhab and Hutaib – which latter I visited all too briefly, chancing on a bus-load of Indian pilgrims come to visit the shrine at Hutaib, up the new but not very easy road built at the expense of the present Dāʿī, Saiyīd-nā Burhan al-Dīn b. Tāhir. Dāʿī Hātim who died in 596/1199 is buried in the plain below the fort at Hutaib. In the important Ismāʿīlī book he composed, *Tuhfat al-Qulūb*, he included a description of the hierarchy of the Daʿwah.

Relations of the Daʿwah with the Aiyūbid, Rasūlid and Tāhirid dynasties of the Yemen, Poonawala characterises as "fair", but between the moderate Shīʿah Zaidīs, called sometimes *al-madhhab al-khāmis*, they were not so, partly, I suppose, for ideological reasons, partly because both contested the Yemeni highlands. In the time of the 23rd Dāʿī, Muhammad ʿIzz al-Dīn al-Walid the Zaidīs had captured most of the strongholds in Djabal Harāz. This Dāʿī died in 944/1537-38 at coastal Zabīd to which he had evidently retreated. The Zaidīs destroyed a number of Fātimī-Ismāʿīlī books – one small volume was averred to contain a declaration that marriage of persons within the degrees Allah prohibits, was lawful. Though accusations of sexual liberty made against the Qarmatīs[13] about the close of the 3rd century H. may certainly, I think, have been justified, I cannot believe that this was any part of Daᶜwah doctrine in the 16th century – but the Fātimīs could well have felt alarm about the loss of their books. This last Yemeni Dāᶜī appointed, before his death, by letter of *nass* to the *wālī* in India, an Indian from Sidhpur in Gujerat, Yūsuf b. Sulaimān, and the *wālī* sent to the Daᶜwah officers (*hudūd*) in Ahmadābād to bring Yūsuf there. His appointment marks the Transfer from the Yemen to India.

In conjunction with Hamdān leaders in Sanᶜā', Harāz, Yām, etcetera, the Ismāᶜīlīs set to recover their territory from the Zaidīs, the chief of the tribal soldiery being Muhammad b. Ismāᶜīl al-Dāᶜī, while Yūsuf, Dāᶜī Mutlaq, controlled payment of the *zakāt* and religious affairs. They collaborated with the Ottoman Turks, but the Turks seized Yūsuf and threw him into fetters. He died a prisoner at Taibah[14]. Some of his followers removed to India.

It was the 21st Dāᶜī (died 1572) whose *wālī* chose Ahmadābād as the Daᶜwah centre in India. The Transfer of the Ismāᶜīlī literary corpus to India seems to have taken place in the days of the latter Tāhirids with whom the Yemeni Ismāᶜīlīs were on good terms.

The Indian Dāᶜīs sent and received writings to and from the Yemen via Tāhirid ports and in *Qarātīs al-Yaman* there are indications that the Indian Fātimīs would ask the Yemenis to send them copies of works they did not possess or which were incomplete, with the scholars coming and going between the two countries.

The Daᶜwah regards the Transfer to India as following a predestined plan though the situation there was unpropitious, persecution having scattered the Ahl al-Daᶜwah to other provinces. ᶜAbbās al-Hamdānī attributes the Transfer to the existence of the larger Daᶜwah communities there, but more cogent reasons appear to me to be the extinction of the Daᶜwah's teaching and adverse Yemeni condition, should the Zaidīs remain in control of Harāz. With the Daᶜwah's

---

(13) I have proposed that the notorious poem attributed to a Qarmatī poet, with its rejection of Islam and its moral code, is not an outright forgery, but the expression of a reaction against Islamic restrictions on practices upon which Yemeni tribes took a contrary view. The argument is set forth in my "The interplay between tribal affinities and religious (Zaydi) authority in the Yemen", *al-Abhāth*, Beirut, American University, XXX, 1982, 20 *seq.*

(14) Muhammad b. Ahmad al-Nahrawālī, *al-Barq al-Yamānī fī 'l-fath al-ᶜUthmānī*, ed Hamad al-Djāsir, as *Ghazawāt al-Djarākisah wa'l-Atrāk fī Djanūb al-Djazīrah*, al-Riyād, 1387/1967, 170. The Daᶜwah states that he did not die in prison. Yūsuf is stated by al-Nahrawālī to have come from a tribe (*tā'ifah*) of Lūtīyā, whom he calls *malāhidah*, of Gujerat who used to pay *djizyah*. Mr Zainul b. Idrīs informs me that they were a trading tribe from which early converts came – hence the Bohrah were called Lūtiyā in a general way.

castles lost, and forced himself to retire to Zabīd, no doubt the Dāʿī did prepare for the Transfer by appointing an Indian Dāʿī.

Under the Hindu rajahs of Gujerat Ismāʿīlī missionaries were able to propagate the Daʿwah, but in the 15th and 16th centuries the Bahmanī kings of Gujerat favoured the spread of Sunnism and on occasion the Bohrahs were exposed to severe persecution. There is for example Fitnat Djaʿfar when the apostate, Djaʿfar b. Khwādjā about the middle of the 9th/15th century, turned Sunni and persuaded the dissolute Bahmani ruler at Ahmadābād, where the Daʿwah had an academy (*dars*), to take action against the Bohrahs. The Academy gave preliminary training in the *zāhir (ʿilm al-zawāhir)* but students went on to complete their education in the Yemen where they studied the *bātin* at the Dāʿī's court. The Bohrah were forced to pay *djizyah* like pagan Hindus and wear a black cloth on their shoulders. Hundreds of Daʿwah followers were killed and buried in the cemetery which became known as Choti (Little) Karbalā', a name it bears to this day. Visiting it in 1978 I noticed offerings of rose-petals on the tombs of the martyrs.

Nine Dāʿīs are buried in Ahmadābād and on the other side of the road lies the tomb of Sulaimān b. Hasan the first Dāʿī of the Sulaimānī Bohrahs – it is not venerated by the Dāwūdī Bohrahs, but when we went to look at it we were given a smear of perfume by an old man there.

A curious point of the attack on the Daʿwah by Djaʿfar was directed against its divergence from the Sunnīs, in that, whereas the latter mark the beginning and end of Ramadān by the sighting of the new moon, the Daʿwah does so by reckoning and sighting (*hisāb wa ru'yah*). The Daʿwah's procedure seems more scientific, typical of the intellectual approach of Ismāʿīlīsm, but the matter in itself seems trivial.

During the Moghul period the Dāʿī Dāwūd b. Qutbshāh was recognized by the liberal-minded emperor Akbar as leader of the Ismāʿīlī community but a later emperor, Awrungzīb, turned to persecuting the Bohrahs of Ahmadābād, putting their leader to death with 700 of his followers.

While in 1591 Dāwūd b. Qutbshāh was accepted as Dāʿī by most Bohrahs, a minority favoured the grandson of the grandson of the first Indian Dāʿī, by name Sulaimān b. Hasan, whose tomb I visited, and who had been in charge of the community in the Yemen. This split the Daʿwah into the Dāwūdī Bohrahs and the Sulaimānīs – in India the Sulaimānīs were not very numerous and were located at Ahmadābād. In the Yemen in 1677, the Sulaimānī Dāʿī-ship passed to the Yemeni Makramī (Makārim) family with which it remains till our present time. The 31st (Sulaimānī) Dāʿī, fleeing from Taibah of Wādī Dahr, towards the end of the 17th century, established himself with the support of Yām at Nadjrān. Yām even gained control of Harāz at one time – there are still some Sulaimānīs there today. An officer (*mansūb*) of the Yemeni Sulaimānī Dāʿī resides at Baroda where there is also a library of Daʿwah literature.

The Makramīs played quite a role over more than two centuries of south Arabian history but they have probably been driven underground by Wahhābī, Saʿūdī, disapproval of the sect. Philby in *Highlands of Arabia*(15) provides a valuable if not always entirely accurate account of them. He states that the 47th Dāʿī was not allowed to assume the title by Ibn Saʿūd, but Poonawala names his son as Dāʿī and furthermore supplies the names of two Dāʿīs following him, the latter still living at Nadjrān in 1977. It looks as if the Sulaimānī branch still flourishes in concealment. Crossing from the Yemen into Nadjrān in 1966 with Royalist Yemeni, I was met by a police officer of the Yām tribe whom I tried to question about Ismāʿīlīsm in Yām, but he simply ignored the subject – this evidently was not a safe topic of conversation! During the Zaidī occupation of Nadjrān much deliberate damage was done to the property of the leading Makārimah – this in 1933-34.

In the course of its long history there have been quite a number of breakaways from the Daʿwah, for example the ʿAlīyah now located at Baroda with a succession of 16 *dāʿīs* of their own.

To the British the Bohrah was known as the name of an Islamic sect by the early 17th century. In the 18th century they assisted the Dāʿī when moving from Surat to Poona because of harassment, and some years later they assisted the 43rd Dāʿī also. The 42nd Dāʿī, because he helped in a conflagration at Surat, was authorised by the British Government to use a four horse carriage. When we attended ʿAshūrā ceremonies in Bombay some years ago, the Dāʿī arrived in just such a carriage. When the 47th Dāʿī was recommended by Government for the rank of Sirdar in the Deccan in 1866, the citation says of the Bohrahs: "They are a most orderly set of people, one remarkable feature is the outward absence of poverty among them". They numbered about 80,000 and the Dāʿī's revenue was about a lac of rupees, much of which went in charity to the helpless and infirm and in keeping schools. The Dāʿī spent large sums on public utilities, notably in building an aqueduct at Poona costing a lac of rupees. So respected was he by the British that the Governor of Poona received him with a review of troops in his honour. The Dāʿī in question, ʿAbd al-Qādir Nadjm al-Dīn, the 47th of the line, had had his appointment as Dāʿī Mutlaq contested by some of the community on the grounds that the preceding Dāʿī, to whom ʿAbd al-Qādir was *mukāsir*,

---

(15) 1952, 356-59 passim.

assistant, had died by night without making a *nass jalī* or public designation of his successor. A secret designation (*nass khafī*) is under some circumstances allowable. A commission of four ulema issued a *fatwā* declaring that there had been a *nass*, a ruling accepted apparently by a majority of Bohrahs. Poonawala however calls his office *nāzim*[16] which he renders as "caretaker". The Privy Council in London, over a hundred years later in 1947 ruled in favour of the legitimacy of the appointment. The issue of his succession had been revived in a new series of legal battles commencing in 1917 at the Bombay High Court. These battles took place with a minority group opposing, says Poonawala, "the Dāʿī's claim to undisputable authority" and "demanding social reforms, democratization of local institutions, and financial accountability of all the money collected from the community". They wanted, in short, to strip the Dāʿī of his power and acquire control of the Daʿwah's substantial revenues. They contested the legitimacy of the Dāʿī's powers to excommunicate (*barāt*, Arabic *barā'ah*) which cuts off adherents of the Daʿwah from its blessing of birth and marriage ceremonies and the right of burial in Bohrah cemeteries.

Shibani Roy, a Hindu lady, in her study of the Bohrahs, suggests that the Dāʿī, with his religious status, power, wealth and influence inspired rivalry in some of the Bohrah businessmen who have acquired considerable wealth... and aspired to be looked upon as leading distinguished personalities and expected treatment with deference by Saiyid-nā (the Dāʿī) himself. Disappointed of this they were determined to ruin his good name and the British courts offered the arena for their costly legal battles.

Several wealthy families ruined themselves in this litigation. The tables seem to have been turned when Saiyid-nā himself purchased the house of the once wealthy Sir Adamji Pirbhai's house on the Malabar Hill, Bombay, the magnate who had initiated a well known case against him in 1917. There seems also to have been an intellectual element in the opposition to the Dāʿī, probably prompted by exposure to western democratic ideas. One of those "excommunicated" by the Dāʿī was Faidullāh al-Hamdānī, grandfather of Professor ʿAbbās. The leaders of the opposition are known in the Lisān al-Daʿwah by the Qur'ānic term Tāghūt, pagan judges banned by Muhammad, and their

(16) The Daʿwah people state it is incorrect historically to say the 46th Dāʿī died without appointing his successor.The term *nāzim* was concocted by those who did not believe in the 47th Dāʿī and they introduced it to deny his position as Dāʿī Mutlaq – coining the word to express a theory that in the absence of a Dāʿī Mutlaq, there must be someone to control the affairs and administration of the Daʿwah. Fātimī-Taiyibī ideology rejects this term and the idea lying behind it, of a break in the continuity of the Daʿwah.

followers as al-Mukhālifūn. Shibani Roy calls the Privy Council's reaffirmation of the Dāʿī's rights, confirmed, after Independence, by the Supreme Court of India, "a great damper for the reformists".

At Udaypur in 1973-74 the Bohrah Youth Association, a "reformist" group, resorted to violence against community members loyal to the Dāʿī that resulted in a number of actual criminal cases being brought against them in the courts.

Knowing few persons who might be called "reformists" I can only offer impressions on the dispute. With Shibani Roy I incline to think that the Bohrah community would lose rather than gain if the Dāʿī's powers were devolved to a committee including "reformists". But, as she expresses it, the Dāʿī has "out-manœuvred the reformist youth" by providing funds for modern and technical education – this, after all, is simply following Daʿwah tradition. If, though today unfashionable, the control of the Daʿwah is concentrated in a small group of families, they assiduously practice their religion without making a parade of it. They live, in the reasonable comfort appropriate to their station, quiet sober lives that contrast favourably with the extravagance of some oil nouveaux-riches. A minority but very wealthy sect and community needs strong, wise, diplomatic leadership to meet potential dangers to it in India and in other places in Asia and Africa, from, for instance, those who might seek to take advantage of factions in the community to divert some of this wealth to themselves. As Shibani Roy says however: "the money collected by Saiyid-nā is utilised with thrift for bettering the living conditions, not only of his own followers, but also of non-Bohrahs for whom he makes substantial donations". The Dāʿī, also known as Sultan, Mullahjee, etcetera, takes a close personal interest in his subjects and protects their interests.

The Dāʿī, Saiyid-nā, is conscious of the relevance of Fātimī history to the Daʿwah and, with leading members of the sect, has visited such places connected with that history as Salamīyah in Syria, Mahdīyah in Tunis and many other places. In Cairo the Daʿwah has magnificently restored the Fātimid Mosque of Anwar – the opening in 1982 was attended by the late President Sadat and dignatories from the Azhar. In the Yemen I hear the Hūth Mosque, which I knew only as a ruin, has been restored at the Daʿwah's expense. The Hutaib sanctuary in Djabal Harāz has been re-built by his followers and I travelled up the steep road to it from Manākhah constructed at the Dāʿī's expense.

In Bombay a marble mausoleum known as Rawdah Tāhirah was built by voluntary subscription from Dāwūdī Bohrahs in many parts of the world for the 51st Dāʿī, Saiyid-nā Tāhir Saif al-Dīn, the present Dāʿī's father, and, in his memory, the splendid al-Masdjid al-Fātimī close by, on the pattern of Cairo's Anwar Mosque. The Daʿwah's interest in preserving the tradition of Fātimid art is expressed in the Mosque qiblah which combines the forms of those qiblahs of

Cairo's Jami' Juyūshī and the Fātimī qiblah in Ibn Tūlūn's Mosque. On the marble slab wall of the mosque the entire Qur'ānic text is engraved, picked out in gold and decorated with precious stones.

There are many other places where the Da'wah has founded religious and secular buildings, for example in Karachi and the large religious and community centre complex at Northolt, London.

While the Dā'ī is concerned with preserving the Fātimī past, I must emphasize that he is also most actively concerned with promoting training of members of the community to play their part in the modern present and in the future. Many highly trained professional men are thus to be found among the Bohrahs.

Writing of course of the mediaeval period, Stern[17] has described the Ismā'īlīs as the best-hated sect in Islam. This attitude still persists in places today. So far as my limited knowledge extends, the Da'wah exhibits no sign of sinister aims or doctrines today – it seems eminently a quietist sect. Nor can the actual political activities of the mediaeval *da'is* be seen to differ from those of their contemporaries. The secrecy imposed by circumstances upon the Da'wah in earlier times doubtless gave rise to the extreme prejudice and violent polemics against it.

Nowadays, while not budging from its own *'aqīdah* (doctrines), the Da'wah, from what I have seen of it, seeks brotherly relations with other Muslims. It is evidently accepted by leading Muslims in India, Egypt and elsewhere, participating, for example in the Islamic Council of Europe at the First International Islamic Conference in London in 1976. Both the present Dā'ī and his father received doctorates from al-Azhar, very appropriately since it was found by the Fātimids, and they have close links with Aligarh Muslim University in India.

At a rather different level, may I say that when I visited the tomb of Queen Arwā at al-Djiblah last November the Ismā'īlī attendants, simple enough folk, receiving Indian pilgrims at the shrine, were intent on impressing me that they are Muslims, by way of rejecting, I suppose, any accusations of heresy that are so often made by other Muslims against them.

I should like to conclude with a few remarks about the Library of the Da'wah to which I have made several references. It is kept at Surat and Bombay. Permission has to be granted by the Dā'ī Mutlaq to read the books in it, and it is not conceded to every rank, even in the Dā'ī's own family. A number of the writings in the collection are known in copies elsewhere, notably in the Husain al-Hamdānī collection and with the 'Alīyah (at Baroda?) but the Da'wah maintains that it has the oldest and best copies. The Sulaimanīs in Nadjrān, according to Sir

(17) *Studies...*, 257.

Fuad Hamza[18] maintain the same secrecy about their writings as the Indian Bohrahs.

It is a matter of interest that to conceal information about Daʿwah affairs data relating to some topic or other may be embodied in separate parts in different writings, so that guidance is essential to reconstruct the whole; perhaps secret information may be conveyed in some other guise, the uninstructed reader being unaware of it. Possibly over the last two decades or so there has been a more relaxed attitude to the disclosure of information, especially since others have published Daʿwah literature, but strict control of the Surat Library remains.

(18) "Najran", 638.

Appendix

At the discussion in the Colloquium it was stated that persons coming to Cairo from India, belonging to what, for convenience's sake, I shall call the "opposition" to the Fātimī establishment, claim that the Daʿwah has adopted features of the Indian caste system. This is directly contradicted by Shibani Roy who has plenty to say about the "opposition". "The Bohras till date have no class or caste hierarchy amongst themselves" (p.3). Caste in fact is utterly foreign to Fātimī ideology. Living cheek by jowl with Hindus they do seem to have some quite innocuous customs practised by Hindus, as I think I noticed myself, but these are trivial, and I am sure the same can be said of other Indian Muslim sects.

Poonawala[19] outlines the main lines of the opposition (to which he is sympathetic) to the policy of the 51st Dāʿī, Saiyid-nā Tāhir Saif al-Dīn which aimed at "re-establishing", as he says, the position of the Dāʿī Mutlaq. Poonawala states that the 49th Dāʿī accepted that the Dāʿī's rank was that of a *nāzim*, so it may be that this Dāʿī gave ground on this issue, whereas Saiyid-nā Tāhir re-asserted the policy of his grandfather, the 47th Dāʿī, the *nass* of whose succession was called in question a little over a century ago. Shibani Roy's more objective account of the "opposition" at Udaipur should be taken in conjunction with that of Poonawala.

(19) Poonawala, *Biobibliography*, 237-8.

REFERENCES[20]

Encyclopaedia of Islam (2), arts., Bohorās, Fātimids, etc.

Hamdani, Abbas, "The Dāᶜī Hātim b. Ibrāhīm al-Hāmidī (D. 596 H./1199 A.D) and his book *Tuhfat al-Qulūb*", *Oriens*, Leiden, 1970-71, XXIII-IV, 258.300.

"Evolution of the organizational structure of the Fātimī Daᶜwah: the Yemeni and Persian contribution", *Arabian Studies*, Cambridge-London, 1976, III, 85-114.

"Shades of Shīᶜism in the Tracts of the Brethren of Purity, Traditions in Contact and Change", *Selected Proceedings of the XIVth Congress of the International Association for the History of Religions*, ed. Peter Slat, Donald Wiebe et alii, Ontario, 1980, 447-60.

Hamdani, Husain F., "Some unknown Ismāᶜīlī authors and their works", *Jl. of the Royal Asiatic Society*, London, 1933, 339-78.

Hamza, Fuad, "Najran", *Jl. of the Royal Central Asian Society*, London, Oct., 1935, XXIV, 631-40.

Al-Nahrawālī, Muhammad b. Ahmad, *al-Barq al-Yamānī fi 'l-fath al-ᶜUthmānī*, ed Hamad al-Djāsir, as *Ghanawāt al-Jarākisah wa'l-Atrāk fī Djanūb al-Jazīrah*, al-Riyād, 1387/1967.

Philby, H. St., J.B., *Arabian Highlands*, Ithaca, New York, 1952.

---

(20) Only sources immediately drawn upon for this paper are listed but Poonawala's excellent bibliography shows the extent of Ismāᶜīlī studies. Information from Daᶜwah personalities does not figure above, but I have found most of it also in *Daw' nūr al-haqq al-mubīn* (v. Poonawala, 238) the first volume of the series, *al-Rasā'il al-Ramadānīyah*, composed by Saiyid-nā Tāhir and continued by his son, Saiyid-nā Burhan al-Dīn. The *Daw'* was published at Bombay in 1335/1917. The set presented me by the Daᶜwah numbers some 43 volumes of varying length.

Poonawala, I.K., "Ismāʿīlī sources for the history of south-west Arabia", *Studies in the history of Arabic sources for the history of Arabia*, Riyadh University Press, 1979, I,I, 151-59.

Bibliography of Ismāʿīlī literature, Malibu, California, 1977.

Roy, Shibani, *The Dawoodi Bohras: an anthropological perspective*, Delhi, 1984. (Though with many errors, mainly in presentation, she has much valuable information).

Stern, S.M., *Studies in early Ismāʿīlīsm*, Jerusalem, 1983.

IX

SOCIÉTÉ ET GOUVERNEMENT EN ARABIE DU SUD

JUSQU'À ces dernières années, l'Arabie du Sud a été si isolée, non seulement de l'Occident, mais aussi de pays arabes mieux connus comme l'Égypte, la Syrie et l'Irak, que même les Arabes de ces pays ne connaissaient guère du Yémen et du Ḥaḍramawt que leur nom, et n'avaient très souvent qu'une idée très sommaire de leur position géographique. Et c'est précisément à cause de cet isolement relatif que la société de l'Arabie du Sud n'a pratiquement pas changé de structure et a très peu subi l'influence étrangère depuis la période pré-islamique ou depuis le début de l'Islam, et ressemble encore d'une manière extraordinaire à la société dans laquelle le Prophète Muḥammad vit le jour. Les habitants du Yémen ont évidemment joué un rôle important dans la formulation de l'Islam des premiers jours, et les Ḥaḍramīs ont largement contribué à la création et à la diffusion de l'Islam en Afrique Orientale et en Extrême Orient. Aussi la connaissance de la société de l'Arabie du Sud, évidemment avant les récents bouleversements politiques qui viennent de commencer à la transformer, est indispensable à l'étude de l'histoire du début de l'Islam et de l'évolution de la société islamique.

* * *

Pour essayer de décrire la structure sociale comme je la conçois, je vais commencer par donner une description sommaire de chaque classe sociale, car la société de l'Arabie est aussi stratifiée et aussi peu égalitaire que celle de la plupart des pays européens, mais le passage d'une classe à une autre beaucoup plus difficile.

Les habitants de l'Arabie, on le sait, sont divisés en tribus, mais on ignore en général que la plupart des tribus de l'Arabie du Sud sont en fait sédentaires, vivant dans les villages, et non point nomades. Cependant, par exemple en Ḥaḍramawt, les tribus sont connues sous le nom de *badw* — et je soupçonne que lorsque Ibn

Ḫaldūn parle de « bédouins » en Afrique du Nord, désignant par ce mot la société tribale qui y est installée, il utilise ce mot dans le même sens. Les tribus dans le Sud de l'Arabie sont peut-être plus nombreuses que dans le Nord, et leur culture matérielle traditionnelle est à certains égards supérieure. Les tribus peuvent être considérées comme une sorte d'aristocratie qui a droit au port d'armes, mais, même entre elles, il n'y a pas d'égalité, car il y a souvent des différences de niveau social d'une tribu à l'autre. On reconnaît la position sociale des aristocraties tribales et religieuses — je parlerai de ces dernières par la suite — à ce qu'on les considère comme assez honorables pour marier sa fille à un de leurs membres. Ce principe est consacré dans le droit islamique de *kafā'a*, mais il me semble impossible de ne pas conclure qu'il faisait partie du droit coutumier en vigueur longtemps avant l'avènement de l'Islam. Aucun membre d'une classe inférieure aux tribus n'était évidemment considéré comme un mari possible pour la fille d'un homme de tribu. Certaines tribus de l'antiquité étaient si exclusives que, selon l'écrivain du Xe siècle al-Hamdānī, leur descendance avait fini par s'éteindre.

L'homme de tribu se considère comme possesseur de la qualité appelée *šaraf* ou « honneur », mais l'élément le plus important de cet honneur semble être la tradition consistant à porter les armes, et à être capable de se défendre ainsi que sa famille. Le respect de leur *šaraf* impose aussi aux hommes des tribus un code compliqué de conventions et d'actions, et ce seul fait les rend à différents égards vulnérables même par ceux qui ne possèdent pas le *šaraf*. Les hommes sans *šaraf* sont appelés *nāqiṣ*, c'est-à-dire « faibles » — encore qu'il y ait beaucoup de mots pour exprimer cette idée. Le *šaraf* d'un homme de tribu est « brisé » comme ils disent, par le *'ayb*, mot que l'on ne peut traduire exactement, mais dont « disgrâce » est peut-être l'équivalent le plus proche. Un homme de tribu peut commettre un *'ayb* en agissant d'une manière dégradante pour lui-même — par exemple en tuant une femme ou une personne d'un niveau social inférieur au sien. Ou au contraire, on peut lui infliger un *'ayb* quand, par exemple, un autre homme de tribu tue ou simplement moleste un homme ou une femme sous sa protection, vole son bien, ou traverse son territoire sans son autorisation. L'honneur de l'homme de tribu est souillé, et pour effacer la souillure, le *'ayb* doit être lavé dans le sang, ou la victime doit recevoir une indemnité en espèces, à titre de dommages-intérêts.

Les cheikhs ou sultans, ou les chefs de ces tribus, sont élus par les membres de la tribu, parmi les familles au sein desquelles cette charge est héréditaire. En fait, on peut ajouter que dans toutes les classes les fonctions politiques et religieuses appartiennent d'une manière héréditaire à certaines familles, mais il y a aussi élection en ce sens que celui qui exerce cette fonction est élu parmi les membres de cette famille. Mais les cheikhs tribaux sont imbus d'un tel orgueil qu'ils trouvent impossible d'accepter l'autorité suzeraine de n'importe quel autre cheikh. Même le cheikh supérieur de grandes confédérations comme les Bakīl ou les Ḥāšid du Yémen ne dirigent pas les cheikhs des autres tribus du même groupe qu'eux; en effet, ils semblent avoir très peu d'autorité en dehors de leur propre tribu. Autant que j'aie pu le découvrir, leur rôle est de diriger la confédération tribale en temps de guerre, et de jouer le rôle d'arbitre jusqu'à un certain point, mais pour la plupart ils se rapprochent davantage de présidents de comités que de chefs d'État. La coopération permanente entre les cheikhs est donc difficile, excepté quand d'autres classes interviennent comme nous allons le voir.

Les classes sujettes à la domination tribale sont diverses, mais le pourcentage de la population tenue en sujétion par les chefs de tribus varie considérablement d'une région à une autre.

Au premier rang de l'ordre social on trouve les marchands et les artisans. En Ḥaḍramawt, ils sont connus sous le nom de *miskīn*, terme à rattacher au sens de « sédentaire » que la racine renferme plutôt qu'au sens d'« indigent » — il est curieux de trouver ce mot utilisé dans le même sens au Kurdistān. Le riche marchand inspire naturellement un certain respect parmi les tribus, mais au Yémen par exemple le barbier, connu sous le nom de *muzayyin*, est dédaigné, et le boucher tend à être méprisé. L'une des raisons pour lesquelles le président Sallāl du Yémen ne peut être reconnu par les tribus vient du fait que son père appartenait à cette classe et était, à ce qu'on dit, boucher. Il est aussi intéressant de noter que le vendeur de poireaux est méprisé, si l'on se rappelle que, selon la tradition, le Prophète détestait l'odeur du poireau et de l'oignon dans la mosquée. En Ḥaḍramawt où les lignes de démarcation sociale sont peut-être les plus compliquées et les plus primitives, on trouve une classe inférieure aux *miskīn*, les *ḍuʿafāʾ* (pl. de *ḍaʿīf*), qui m'ont été décrits comme travaillant l'argile, c'est-à-dire les maçons, les potiers et les travailleurs agricoles. Le *ḍaʿīf* est un homme « faible », non pas physiquement, mais simplement du fait qu'il ne porte pas les armes. Un robuste forgeron pourrait être un *ḍaʿīf*, par opposition avec un puissant homme de tribu (*qawī*) ou avec une personne de noble naissance appelée *šarīf*. Le mot arabe *ḍaʿīf* a été utilisé dans ce sens depuis des temps immémoriaux, et j'ai recueilli un grand nombre d'exemples classiques, du moyen âge, et même relativement modernes, qui indiquent clairement qu'il en est ainsi; on trouve même un passage dans le Coran où je crois pouvoir avancer que le mot *ḍaʿīf* possède ce sens.

Les pêcheurs et les marins des boutres arabes appartiennent aussi à ces classes assujetties, bien qu'actuellement, en certains endroits, les membres des tribus se livrent quelquefois à la pêche.

Dans les plaines de la Tihāma, au Yémen, et dans plusieurs régions des protectorats d'Aden, nous trouvons une population noire d'origine africaine qui a manifestement habité ces régions depuis une époque très reculée. Elle semble appartenir à différentes couches d'immigration. J'accepte la thèse traditionnelle selon laquelle les régions du Yémen renferment la population considérée dans l'antiquité comme étant des Abyssins, quel qu'ait pu être le sens de ce nom, et que ces gens sont les descendants des Abyssins de l'antiquité. Mais il me semble que certains de ces non-Arabes sont peut-être des aborigènes antérieurs aux Arabes. De toute façon, au Yémen et en Ḥaḍramawt, ces noirs sont pour la plupart des cultivateurs, mais à Aden, ils travaillent comme balayeurs, ce qui n'est pas loin de faire d'eux une sorte de caste d'intouchables; en raison de leur travail, on ne leur permet pas de prendre leurs repas avec les autres membres de la communauté musulmane, mais ils peuvent prier avec eux dans la mosquée. Les balayeurs sont aussi recrutés parmi les Ǧabartī qui sont des immigrants venant des côtes africaines de la mer Rouge.

Des esclaves ont été introduits dans le Sud de l'Arabie depuis des temps très reculés. Dans certaines régions de l'Arabie du Sud, ils constituaient les armées permanentes des petits sultans, mais ils étaient aussi dans certaines régions utilisés comme cultivateurs et domestiques. Bien que considérés comme *milk*, c'est-à-dire « biens meubles », les esclaves-soldats possédaient leur propre chef en Ḥaḍramawt, et les sultans traitaient avec eux par son intermédiaire. En Ḥaḍramawt autrefois, les esclaves soldats, étant indispensables aux sultans, jouissaient d'une situation plus favorable que beaucoup d'autres classes que je viens de décrire.

Les Juifs en Arabie du Sud formaient un groupe à part, en raison évidemment de leur religion différente, mais ils s'intégraient dans le contexte social comme *ra'iyya*, et semblent, à ce qu'on dit, avoir été efficacement protégés. S'ils se convertissaient à l'Islam, ils devenaient, dans la communauté arabe, membres de la classe sociale à laquelle ils appartenaient du fait de leur métier; mais les convertis depuis plusieurs générations sont appelés non par *muslim*, mais *muslimānī*. Ils ne sont pas tous partis en Israël, car il y a encore des communautés juives dans la région de Ṣa'da, au nord du Yémen, et on m'a montré, au cours de mes récents voyages, bien des villages où ils habitaient autrefois. Dans la région tribale Wāḥidī de la fédération d'Aden, les habitants d'un village se plaignaient même que la communauté juive qui, comme ils le disaient, avait été élevée avec eux, eût été éloignée. Les Juifs étaient pour la plupart des artisans, mais dans le Ḫawlān, j'ai appris qu'ils avaient même employé des cultivateurs arabes pour travailler leurs terres en partageant les récoltes. Ce qui me paraît très intéressant, car cela pourrait expliquer qui étaient les gens connus en arabe sous le nom de *biṭāna*, ou associés des tribus juives de Médine — c'est-à-dire peut-être des cultivateurs arabes travaillant la terre des Juifs. Dans quelques endroits du Yémen, j'ai vu des graffiti en hébreu d'origine assez récente, mais le départ de la plupart des communautés a rendu difficile l'étude de leur rôle dans la société traditionnelle de l'Arabie du Sud. Les hommes adultes juifs payaient naturellement le petit impôt connu sous le nom de *ǧizya*, comme dans les autres États traditionnels islamiques.

A part les Européens, la seule communauté étrangère importante était celle des *Baniyān*, ou commerçants indiens fixés dans les villes le long des côtes et en différents endroits à l'intérieur du pays, depuis le moyen âge au moins.

* * *

Des classes sous la protection tribale, passons maintenant aux communautés ayant une position sociale supérieure aux hommes des tribus. Il serait inexact de considérer les sultans ou chefs de tribus connus sous les noms de *šayḫ*, *muqaddam*, *'āqil* ou *ḥāḏiq* comme supérieurs aux hommes des tribus, car ils sont issus essentiellement de la même souche, et quoiqu'il soit pratiquement impossible d'accéder d'une des classes que j'ai mentionnées à une classe supérieure, la destinée des familles appartenant à la classe dirigeante peut subir bien des variations. J'ai découvert, par exemple, qu'au Yémen les royalistes s'étaient récemment mis d'accord pour déposer le cheikh suprême de la grande confédération des Bakīl, qui avait soutenu la République, et le remplacer par un célèbre cheikh Ḫawlānī qui avait combattu sans répit la République, et avait finalement éliminé cette dernière de ses territoires. Cependant on témoigne quelquefois un certain respect aux sultans: j'ai pu voir dans la région ʿAwḏalī qu'on leur baisait les mains et les genoux, mais je ne puis me rappeler si c'était des hommes de tribu ou des *raʿiyya* qui le faisaient.

Les tribus reconnaissent même certains groupes comme leur étant supérieurs, principalement les *Mašāyiḫ*, les *Sayyid*-s et les *Šarīf*-s. On rencontre principalement les Mašāyiḫ dans les pays annexes d'Aden, mais il se peut qu'on en trouve dans les régions šāfiʿites du bas-Yémen. Faute de meilleur terme, je les décris souvent comme des « familles saintes », c'est-à-dire qu'on les distingue grâce à un certain don héréditaire propre à chaque membre de ces familles. Certaines familles Mašāyiḫ sont spécialisées dans les guérisons, d'autres dans la prospection des sources, d'autres encore viennent au secours des marins en détresse, et ainsi de suite. Les Mašāyiḫ sont presque toujours les descendants d'un saint enterré dans un mausolée à coupole, ou *qubba*, qui est entretenu par une branche de la famille. Les Mašāyiḫ semblent représenter l'ancien système qui existait, tout au moins en Arabie du Sud, et qui consistait en un sacerdoce héréditaire dont les membres étaient en même temps dépositaires du droit coutumier. Quelques familles Mašāyiḫ telles que les Bā ʿAbbād, associés au mausolée du prophète Hūd en Ḥaḍramawt, qui est pré-islamique et qui existe encore, peuvent fort bien remonter à la période pré-islamique, mais il y en a d'autres d'une origine plus récente. Il n'y a aucun doute pour moi que le Prophète Muḥammad lui-même appartenait à une de ces familles, car le généalogiste Ibn Ḥazm décrit son ancêtre Hāšim comme le père de cette branche des Quṣayy qui possédait « la maison » (*al-bayt*), ce qui est synonyme d'*al-šaraf*, ou l'honneur. Muḥammad appartenait donc à la « famille sainte » des Qurayš de la Mekke.

Les Sayyid-s et les Šarīf-s sont les descendants de Muḥammad par ses deux petits-fils Ḥasan et Ḥusayn, et forment l'aristocratie religieuse de l'Islam dans presque tous les pays musulmans, excepté dans quelques pays où des sectes comme les Ibāḍites sont au pouvoir. Mais je dois ajouter ici que tandis que les Šīʿites soulignent plus tard la parenté de ʿAlī avec le Prophète par l'intermédiaire de Fāṭima, fille de Muḥammad, et qu'ils revendiquent cette parenté comme la principale raison pour lui succéder à la tête de la communauté musulmane, son titre le plus important aux yeux de l'adversaire de ʿAlī, Muʿāwiya, est le fait qu'il est le cousin du Prophète. Au Yémen, les Sayyid-s formaient la plus grande partie de l'élite intellectuelle et la majorité de la classe dirigeante officielle, et continuent de l'être même dans la moitié républicaine du pays. En Ḥaḍramawt aussi, les Sayyid-s ont beaucoup d'influence, bien que dans les régions tribales et dans la Fédération d'Aden ils soient peu nombreux. Au Yémen, les grandes familles Sayyid appartiennent à l'école šīʿite modérée des Zaydites, et comptent environ deux à trois cent mille membres, alors qu'au Ḥaḍramawt ce sont des Šāfiʿites orthodoxes. En réalité, cette différence d'obédience n'a aucune influence sur leur prestige dans le Sud de l'Arabie en tant qu'aristocratie religieuse de type théocratique, encore qu'en Ḥaḍramawt ils n'aient jamais joui du pouvoir temporel dont les Sayyid-s zaydites disposent au Yémen encore aujourd'hui.

Il est intéressant de noter qu'alors que les Sayyid-s zaydites portent les armes, et que leur *imām* doit toujours avoir participé à la guerre sainte, en application du principe zaydite qui « recommande ce qui est bien et défend ce qui est mal », les Sayyid-s du Ḥaḍramawt ont abandonné le port des armes et comptent sur leur prestige spirituel pour conserver leur place dans la société, bien que quelques tribus de Sayyid-s portent encore les armes comme elles le faisaient sans doute à l'époque de leur arrivée dans le pays, il y a environ mille ans. Quelques Mašāyiḫ ont aussi renoncé au port d'armes, et il se peut que dans les deux cas leur mobile soit un mélange d'idées ṣūfies et de pression sociale. En raison de leur prétention à être supérieurs, et du fait qu'ils revendiquent un don religieux grâce à leur ancêtre, les Sayyid-s du Ḥaḍramawt se sont, en de nombreux endroits, arrogé les fonctions des Mašāyiḫ et souvent, mais pas toujours, une rivalité acerbe règne entre les deux sortes de familles saintes.

Les Sayyid-s et les Mašāyiḫ sont tous deux traités avec une certaine vénération par les tribus. On leur baise les mains et les genoux et on leur accorde naturellement la place d'honneur dans les réceptions. Cependant, c'est là pour un homme de tribu un mélange d'amour et de haine, car on n'aime pas être en leur pouvoir.

Un proverbe dit: « Un baiser sur la main signifie de la haine ». Dans la classe des Sayyid-s et des Šarīf-s, la règle selon laquelle la fille ne peut épouser un homme d'une classe sociale inférieure est observée d'une manière très stricte; c'est même devenu un problème juridique dans les livres des Šāfi'ites de savoir, au cas où aucun homme du même rang ne se présente, si on peut permettre à une Šarīfa d'épouser quelqu'un qui n'est pas son égal, ou si elle doit rester fille.

Tels sont donc les éléments qui forment la structure de la société de l'Arabie du Sud. Passons à la description du fonctionnement de cette société.

* * *

Il est essentiel en premier lieu de reconnaître que, quelle qu'ait été la forme de gouvernement en Arabie du Sud, les véritables détenteurs du pouvoir sont les grandes tribus qui portent les armes, virtuellement inattaquables en raison de leurs repaires dans les montagnes, et qui possèdent aussi l'autorité dans les villes et les plaines agricoles, ou encore sur les plateaux. Des conquérants tels que les Ayyūbides, les Mamlūk-s, les Turcs Ottomans et aujourd'hui les Égyptiens ont pu s'emparer et occuper pendant un certain temps les plaines, mais leurs efforts pour conquérir les régions montagneuses ont toujours échoué, et les Égyptiens, en abandonnant le Nord du Yémen, n'ont fait que suivre l'exemple classique des autres conquérants. Aussi les tribus ont-elles continué à être les suzerains des cultivateurs, de la population noire de la Tihāma et des communautés de pêcheurs des côtes, soit de droit, soit en tant que troupes tribales des souverains dirigeants. Aden par exemple semble à un certain moment avoir été dirigée par les tribus guerrières que nous appelons maintenant les 'Awlaqī, et à d'autres par les Yāfi', qui autrefois exportaient leurs guerriers en Inde et en Afrique Orientale. Cette tribu de Yāfi' remonte à l'époque préislamique. La prise d'Aden par les Anglais en 1839 libéra le port de la domination tribale qui aurait pu nuire à sa prospérité.

L'homme des tribus a peu de respect pour l'habitant des villes qu'il appelle avec mépris un *sūqī* — ce qui peut se traduire librement par « rat de marché ». Il déteste le langage grossier et souvent obscène des marchés, car l'homme des tribus est très pudique dans son langage. Quand il est assez puissant pour le faire, il tire le maximum du citadin, du paysan et du pêcheur. Avant la pénétration des Anglais, les tribus du Ḥaḍramawt levaient un grand nombre d'impôts différents: il y avait l'impôt pour la protection des palmiers, en théorie 5% mais en fait beaucoup plus; il y avait les impôts sur les prises des pêcheurs, les cadeaux imposés aux classes plus riches à différentes époques de l'année, et ainsi de suite. Les tribus de toute l'Arabie du Sud faisaient payer un droit d'escorte appelé *siyāra*, qui est l'ancienne *ḫafāra* arabe; ils percevaient aussi un impôt pour protéger les marchés ou pour la permission d'occuper une place dans un marché. Ces impôts étaient quelquefois perçus par les hommes des tribus eux-mêmes, quelquefois par leurs chefs ou par leurs sultans. Il est évident que les ports d'Aden, Šiḥr et Ẓufār étaient pour eux une source de revenus, car par leur intermédiaire ils pouvaient lever un impôt sur le commerce avec l'Inde. Quand un puissant gouvernement centralisé s'emparait de ces ports ou des villes de l'intérieur, il touchait à son tour ces droits et redevances, mais dans le pays, même sous un gouvernement centralisé imposé aux tribus, elles continuaient quand même à percevoir de nombreux impôts différents qui leur revenaient selon le droit coutumier quand elles ne dépendaient d'aucun gouvernement.

D'autre part, les tribus reconnaissaient en revanche certaines obligations à l'égard des communautés qui leur étaient assujetties, notamment l'obligation de les protéger des autres tribus, comme je viens de le dire. Le rejet de cette obligation était non seulement préjudiciable à l'honneur de l'homme des tribus, mais encore risquait de porter atteinte à sa source de revenus, car si sa protection était violée impunément, d'autres tribus s'arrogeaient le droit de l'attaquer et de tirer avantage de lui. Aussi, à la moindre violation, même accidentelle, de ses droits, l'homme des tribus est-il prêt à recourir immédiatement aux armes. Cette situation mènerait rapidement à l'anarchie si elle n'était pas contrôlée, et nous devons avouer qu'il y a très souvent des périodes d'anarchie tribale. Mais en plusieurs millénaires de système tribal, des institutions se sont dégagées pour régulariser et freiner même les hommes des tribus dont les chefs ne reconnaissent aucune autorité extérieure. Avoir recours à un tiers pour arbitrer les transactions, même les moins importantes, me semble presque une caractéristique de cette société; ainsi les tribus ont-elles recours d'un côté à l'aristocratie religieuse, ou de l'autre au groupe non-porteur d'armes qui leur est inférieur. Pour communiquer les uns avec les autres, ils se serviront du *dallāl*, ou courtier, qui les reçoit quand ils viennent en ville et vend ou achète pour eux moyennant un pourcentage. Il connaît leurs habitudes et leurs lois, et jouera au besoin le rôle d'arbitre. Je parlerai plus bas du rôle de l'aristocratie religieuse par rapport aux tribus, et je me propose de l'étudier en détail, mais je voudrais tout d'abord dire quelque chose des *raʿiyya*, ou classes assujetties.

En Ḥaḍramawt, et, je pense, à Aden jusqu'à l'arrivée des Anglais, les plus grandes villes étaient divisées en un certain nombre de quartiers qui s'étaient développés d'une manière systématique, chacun jouissant de sa propre organisation, pour diriger ses affaires, et autant que possible protéger ses intérêts contres les empiètements d'autres groupes sociaux. Malheureusement, je n'ai pas de renseignements sur les grandes villes du Yémen. A Tarīm, en Ḥaḍramawt, où l'organisation de quartier apparaît sous la forme la plus compliquée, les quartiers sont dirigés par des chefs (*al-Abu*) sortis de la classe des *miskīn*, c'est-à-dire des artisans, des courtiers, des commerçants, et des *ḍaʿīf*-s, ou travailleurs de l'argile, mais ces derniers ont moins d'influence sur les affaires. Ils sont responsables de toute une série de services au profit de la communauté, du secours en cas d'incendie et d'accident, et étaient même utilisés comme personnel auxiliaire aux mariages et aux enterrements. Ils jouissent de certains privilèges reconnus par les autres groupes sociaux de la ville, Sayyid-s, hommes des tribus et autres. De plus, les organisations artisanales que je n'irai pas jusqu'à appeler corporations pouvaient faire respecter certains règlements qu'ils avaient approuvés. Par exemple, on ne pouvait renvoyer un charpentier de son quartier et en embaucher un autre, ou employer un charpentier d'un autre quartier. Plusieurs organisations artisanales ont aussi leurs salaires fixes, et certaines professions ont des pratiques restrictives comme les syndicats modernes. Les quartiers sont célèbres pour leurs querelles, tout particulièrement en ce qui concerne les limites de chaque quartier, et de même que les tribus, ils doivent généralement avoir recours à un tiers pour régler leurs différends ; l'arbitre sera souvent un Sayyid. Bien que la classe des marchands dans les villes, qui comprend souvent les marchands Sayyid-s, fût exploitée au maximum par les sultans, leurs exactions étaient souvent freinées de peur que les marchands ne trouvassent leur situation trop difficile et n'allassent s'installer ailleurs, comme menaçait de le faire il y a plus d'un siècle un riche marchand de la famille sayyid des Āl Ibn Sahl. La fortune des Āl Ibn Sahl venait du commerce avec Singapour. La classe des travailleurs agricoles est théoriquement libre, mais bien souvent le cultivateur est lié à un homme riche par un contrat qui assure le partage des récoltes avec ce dernier, et il devient pratiquement un serf; la seule manière d'échapper à ses dettes sera de s'enfuir. Même les communautés juives semblent avoir disposé de certains moyens pour se défendre contre les abus. Au Yémen, ils pouvaient avoir recours à l'imām, qui aurait sans doute réglé leurs problèmes.

* * *

Toutes ces classes, groupes et communautés étaient et sont toujours principalement gouvernés par leur propre droit coutumier — c'est-à-dire indépendamment de la *šarīʿa*. La *šarīʿa* est évidemment de toute façon le droit des descendants du Prophète et ils essaient de l'imposer partout, bien qu'il soit loin d'être accepté sans difficulté par les tribus et les autres groupes, dont les lois sont quelquefois en contradiction avec la *šarīʿa*. Le droit coutumier en ce qui concerne le comportement sexuel des Ṣubyān noirs de la côte Sud, par exemple, donne une latitude que la *šarīʿa* ne permettrait jamais. Au Yémen, il y a des régions où, en dépit de l'insistance des imāms zaydites à appliquer à la lettre la *šarīʿa*, les tribus continuent encore de nos jours à appliquer leur propre droit coutumier. Le droit des pêcheurs est naturellement extrêmement spécialisé, et admis exclusivement par les chefs pêcheurs qui appliquent les principes de ce droit non-écrit. Les lois relatives à l'irrigation et aux affaires agricoles qui concernent directement la majorité des habitants de l'Arabie du Sud comportent bien des aspects techniques, mais on trouve des experts locaux dans la communauté même. En principe donc, ces groupes règlent leurs litiges entre eux, mais quand cela leur est impossible, ils ont souvent recours à l'intervention de tiers, bien que cela soit, je suppose, plus courant dans le cas de litiges non-techniques. A l'époque actuelle même, quand un État centralisé est la forme de gouvernement d'un territoire, les fonctionnaires utiliseront les arbitres traditionnels pour régler certains litiges.

Les arbitres traditionnels sont les sultans ou les chefs, les Sayyid-s ou les Šarīf-s, et les Mašāyiḫ. Ces deux types d'aristocratie religieuse sont elles-mêmes organisées en familles, et même en tribus, et elles règlent leur propres litiges entre elles. A une certaine époque, il y avait en Ḥaḍramawt un chef (*naqīb*) des Sayyid-s; la charge était héréditaire dans la famille ʿAydarūs, qui jouait probablement le rôle d'arbitre entre les familles Sayyid.

L'Arabie du Sud semble passer par des périodes de gouvernement centralisé et par des retours à l'anarchie tribale, quand chaque confédération tribale agit indépendamment et est normalement en guerre avec son voisin, ou en trève provisoire. La centralisation me paraît être de deux sortes: la centralisation séculière et la centralisation théocratique. La centralisation séculière, quand elle n'est pas imposée par une puissance étrangère, revient aux groupes tribaux dont le chef est parvenu à une plus grande puissance que les autres, ce qui est extrêmement difficile. Du point de vue historique, cela peut dépendre d'une puissance militaire supérieure, grâce à des armes nouvelles, d'une meilleure organisation, ou d'un soutien extérieur. En raison de mes recherches, je suis persuadé que l'état théocratique est la forme de centralisation qui convient le mieux à l'Arabie du Sud, mais je ne prétends pas que ce soit la formule inévitable de l'avenir. Les conditions sont en train d'évoluer, mais il semble que c'est la forme de gouvernement centralisé logique, tout au moins pour quelques-uns des territoires du sud.

J'ai affirmé que les cheikhs tribaux qui n'acceptent aucun contrôle de la part de leurs pairs étaient les véritables détenteurs du pouvoir politique. La solution à cette impasse fut élaborée avant même l'avènement de l'Islam par la création d'une organisation centrée sur l'enclave sacrée, le *ḥaram*, dirigée par une aristocratie religieuse héréditaire, respectée et protégée par les tribus. Comme la famille sainte à la tête de l'enclave sacrée détient une autorité divine ou surnaturelle, les tribus peuvent accepter ses décisions dans certaines choses sans pour autant s'exposer à perdre leur honneur. J'ai déjà développé cette thèse dans une contribution aux *Mélanges Ṭaha Ḥusayn*, mais je la résumerai brièvement. L'enclave sacrée est un fragment de territoire gouverné par Dieu, par l'intermédiaire de la famille sainte qui assume l'entretien du temple, de la mosquée ou du mausolée qu'elle contient toujours. Les tribus des environs liées par un traité la protègent, la conservent, et contribuent aux frais d'entretien. Le seigneur de l'enclave, un Sayyid ou un cheikh, joue le rôle d'arbitre dans les querelles perpétuelles de ces tribus. Si le seigneur de l'enclave sacrée est un homme à forte personnalité, il peut devenir très puissant en manœuvrant les tribus, art qu'il aura appris en assistant aux assemblées. Si la famille sainte s'agrandit, les branches cadettes émigrent vers d'autres centres et souvent créent de nouvelles enclaves sacrées. Le droit et la religion sont naturellement le métier habituel de ces familles saintes. J'ai pu dresser ce tableau d'après les renseignements que j'ai pu recueillir dans l'Arabie du Sud moderne, mais si l'on étudie les débuts de l'Islam, il devient évident que l'avènement de Muḥammad suit ce modèle politique. Je ne tiens naturellement pas compte ici de ses dons prophétiques.

Dans l'ouvrage intitulé *Dalāʾil al-nubuwwa*, on peut trouver un grand nombre de détails circonstanciels qui ne figurent pas dans les biographies classiques, sur la manière dont Muḥammad alla de tribu en tribu, sollicitant leur protection. Les détails fragmentaires des documents conservés dans sa biographie montrent qu'à Médine la protection fut accordée à Muḥammad. De nos jours, au Yémen, le fait pour un Sayyid de recevoir la protection d'une tribu apporte à cette dernière la *baraka* ou bénédiction, et est connu sous le nom de *hiǧra*; d'autre part, une *hiǧra* semble aussi désigner une centre commun et sûr, où les différentes tribus d'une confédération peuvent se rencontrer. Il se peut que nous soyons amenés à modifier la traduction classique de *hiǧra*, car le mot pourrait bien ne pas désigner la « fuite » du Prophète à Médine, ce qui est l'interprétation habituellement donnée. La dynastie zaydite du Yémen remonte au premier ancêtre qui se réfugia à Ṣaʿda, dans le Nord, et joua le rôle d'arbitre dans les querelles tribales.

* * *

Le régime théocratique comporte certaines faiblesses, car le souverain, ou imām, est tributaire du bon vouloir de ses tribus à combattre pour lui. Il doit pouvoir les manœuvrer de manière à ce qu'elles ne puissent pas se liguer contre lui et qu'elles s'engagent à combattre ses ennemis. Un imām à forte personnalité et ayant un certain génie politique, comme le défunt imām Aḥmad, peut réussir à persuader les tribus de prendre les armes pour lui, comme il le fit en 1948, même sans leur verser de solde. De 1918 à 1962, le Yémen a eu beaucoup de chance avec ses imāms, tout au moins à un certain point de vue si ce n'est à d'autres, car ils ont été capables de manœuvrer les tribus de manière à unifier le pays et à instaurer la paix; mais les actions qu'ils ont crues nécessaires et auxquelles ils ont eu recours pour maintenir le pouvoir centralisé, en diminuant la puissance des importants cheikhs tribaux et de leurs rivaux possibles des familles de Sayyid-s, ont suscité beaucoup d'opposition de la part de ces classes.

Je pense que ʿAlī b. Abī Ṭālib doit avoir été accepté au Yémen de cette manière par les Hamdān — tribu qui a soutenu ses descendants au cours de la guerre actuelle — car il serait absurde de penser qu'il a conquis le Yémen par la force. En tant que membre de la famille sainte de la Mekke, il pouvait être accepté comme arbitre par les tribus du Yémen, dont beaucoup combattirent pour lui à Ṣiffīn. Il est remarquable cependant que lorsqu'un groupe d'hommes de tribus en colère venu d'Égypte assassina ʿUṯmān à Médine, ni lui ni ʿAlī ne disposaient de troupes. Il me semble que les débuts de l'Islam doivent en grande partie être considérés comme l'exercice de manœuvres sur les tribus au profit d'une famille sainte, à laquelle les Umayyades appartenaient aussi, à savoir la famille des ʿAbd Manāf.

Pour en revenir cependant à la société de l'Arabie du Sud, je crois pouvoir y détecter une sorte d'équilibre naturel qui lui est propre, et ces mêmes tribus qui opprimeraient les autres classes de la société ne peuvent dépasser certaines limites. Quand un paysan ou un travailleur est injustement traité, il a recours aux Sayyid-s qui intercèderont pour lui « de par le droit de mon ancêtre », dit-on c'est-à-dire du Prophète. Un homme ou une tribu peut le cas échéant s'adresser à une autre, et sacrifier un animal à sa porte, sacrifice qui porte le nom de *ʿaqīra*, pour le prier de l'aider à obtenir réparation pour le dommage subi. Un cas de *ʿaqīra* intéressant est la prière récemment faite par le président Sallāl, ou Ruʿaynī — j'ai oublié lequel des deux —, lequel envoya cette offrande à certaines grandes tribus zaydites qui avaient soutenu la République, pour demander leur aide contre les forces de l'imām. Mais ces tribus ayant perdu beaucoup d'hommes réunirent le montant du prix des animaux et le remboursèrent, refusant de continuer à combattre.

L'influence des familles saintes ou seigneurs des enclaves diminue également s'ils se contentent simplement de « manger » les revenus du mausolée, ou s'ils ne mènent pas une vie exemplaire.

* * *

Ceci termine ce que j'ai à dire sur la société de l'Arabie du Sud. Pour peu l'on connaisse des pays comme le Maroc, on reconnaîtra, j'en suis sûr, bien des points communs avec l'Arabie du Sud. Il en est de même, en vérité, pour beaucoup d'autres pays islamiques. Il serait intéressant de faire une étude détaillée des rapports entre ces différentes sociétés.

X

THE ZAYDĪ TRIBES OF THE YEMEN: A NEW FIELD STUDY

In a recent work, Paul Dresch [1] gives us an admirable study, hard to praise too highly, well researched, engagingly written, with mercifully little of sociological jargon. His field contact and knowledge of the (Zaydī) tribes of the northern Yemeni Arab Republic is of the kind of experienced political officers in the former Aden Protectorates like the well-known late Major Ian Snell and 'Johnny' Johnson, to which he adds the ability to relate his findings to the Arabian cultural background. Dresch makes use of Arabic documents, printed or MS, and uses the valuable evidence of political verse that I do not recall seeing utilized by other writers on Yemeni society. It is a pleasure to see Arabic correctly vocalized and transliterated, not mangled and distorted. A glossary of the technical terms of tribal law would have been of great value to scholars—many of these are known but more than a few, special to the region, are not. (Can one hope to see these in a further publication?)

Tribal law, the core of Dresch's book, is in principle that upon which I have been working since my acquisition of *al-Ādāb wa-'l-lawāzim fī aḥkām al-man'a* in 1947 (*BSOAS*, XIII, 3, 1950, 589) compiled by a Shāfi'ī, but its ten principles (*al-uṣūl al-'ashara*) are likely to be identical with the Baraṭ *qawā'id* noted by Dresch. It was my intention to illustrate the *aḥkām al-man'a* with tribal comment and cases I had collected, but this and more has in fact been achieved by Dresch who has wide practical experience of how tribal law actually works in our time of more or less modern weaponry and trucking—the latter having replaced the camels and donkeys I rode when first in Imamic/Royalist Yemen in 1964. Since my first visit to the Republic in 1969 a great spate of writing on the Yemen has poured forth, much of it superficial, often inaccurate, but some of high quality like the studies of Martha Mundy, Robert Wilson, Dan Varisco and others. So Dresch has been able to draw also on a wide range of studies, including agricultural and economic surveys as well as Arabic sources that have appeared over the last two decades. In 1964 and 1966 in Royalist Yemen I often had only the vaguest idea of where I was but all this is changed by the excellent Swiss geographical studies on the region.

By way of introduction of tribal law concepts to those unfamiliar with them Dresch defines and explains such basic and known terms as *'ayb*, *wajh*, *rafīq*, *mujawwir*, *sharaf*, *'ayb aswad*, *naqīb 'āqil*, etc. Very important is the concept of *naqā*—I have discussed it in *BSOAS*, XLI, 1, 1978, 21 where I advanced the proposition that *ittaqā* of the *Sunna Jāmi'a* derives from the root *nqy*, not *wqy*, and in actual fact an 'Awdhalī tribesmen once said to me, '*intaqayt*', i.e. 'I absolved myself (from a treacherous act)'. The term *taqwā*, counter-plea, of the Wāḥidīs (*JRAS*, 1951, 37) must be derived from the root *nqy*. *Nqy* figures frequently in my collection of tribal law MSS, including the Rossi MSS, parts of one of which remount to the fifth century A.H. Dresch's ear does not deceive him over the term *'adl* (p. 113) which he renders as 'surety' but which I translate as 'pledge', equivalent to the *rahn* in classical *munāfara* cases and for which the synonym *'arbūn* is often used in my experience. It appears in classical *'adl wa-ṣarf* (= Ḥaḍramī *suqṭān*) of the *Sunna Jāmi'a*, pledge and propitiatory

[1] Paul Dresch, *Tribes, government, and history of Yemen*, Oxford: Clarendon Press, 1989. xxix, 440 pp., 14 plates. £40.

gift. The pledges deposited by the parties proceeding to arbitration must eventually be returned to them and this seems to be what is meant in Qur'ān 4:58 where judges are required to return the *amānāt* to their owners. In Jordan and Beersheba the loser of a case loses his pledge as fee to the arbiter. The *thawr al-hajīn* (p. 50) seems to be this *ṣarf*, propitiatory gift.

It is stated (p. 181) that the tribal world claims that the tribes have always been as they are and that *sinna*/*'urf* is unchanging, not subject to any hierarchy of learning. *'Urf al-jiha* applies to the district rather than the group. But though it may not be subject to any hierarchy of learning, in Faḍlī country for instance new precedents (*sawābil*) are made by all the headmen (*'uqqāl*) of the Marāqisha, the office of headman being hereditary in certain families (see *Arabian studies in honour of Mahmoud Ghul*, (ed.) Moawiyah M. Ibrahim, Wiesbaden-Irbid, 1989, 141). In Jordan, too, Dr. Oweidi's 1982 thesis [2] shows how tribal law there can be modified, even quite drastically. After all, the *sharī'a* itself is based on precedents and *sunna* could hardly be said to be subject to a hierarchy of learning in the first Islamic century so tribal ideology in this respect cannot be accepted. As Dresch says, *ṭāghūt* is sometimes opposed to *sharī'a*, but *man'* law, presumably a part of *ṭāghūt*, is claimed by the MSS in my possession not to be inconsistent with *shar'*, and cases should be judged by which of the two categories covers the individual case. I am inclined to think that the more directly opposed usages to Islamic law are concealed from non-tribal society. For example, the *irtibāṭ* of western Ḥaḍramawt by which an adultery may be compounded for a money payment cannot but have given rise to precedents in tribal law of which no evidence has so far been forthcoming.

The scale of *diya* for woundings of various sorts is cited in a fragment from Sufyān (p. 376), and for other offences (pp. 47 ff.)—this probably corresponds to the treatise *arsh al-jināyāt* which I have transcribed from Yemeni MSS in Rome and Milan (my *The Portuguese off the South Arabian coast*, Oxford 1963, 153) but I have not yet resolved difficulties in them over coinage. I noted in 1947 that the Manṣab of Aṣba'ūn (Wāḥidī sultanate) had a list of such offences and penalties for them. But the list of woundings employing the same technical terms is ancient—it forms part of the Prophet's instructions to 'Amr b. Ḥazm when he sends him as governor to Najrān (Hamidullah, *al-Wathā'iq al-siyāsiyya*, ed. Beirut, 1974, no. 106). Cf. al-Shāfi'ī *al-Umm*, VI, 66–7. It is not without interest that this list should be associated with a province next to the area covered by Dresch's field studies. In 'Awdhalī tribal *shar'*, *al-dam mā*, blood is water, i.e. does not carry a *diya* penalty, but in Sufyān it appears to bring a fine of under 5 *riyāls*. *Bādiyah* (p. 377) should read *bāḍiyah*.

Grain is sold by tribesmen through ' weak ' intermediaries (p. 120) and T. B. Stevenson (p. 122) calls these ' middlemen (*maṣlaḥīn*) ' (incorrectly for *muṣliḥīn*)—how these operate is described in our *Ṣan'ā'* (*Ṣan'ā': an Arabian Islamic city*, (ed.) R. B. Serjeant and R. Lewcock, London, 1983, 163). The *muṣliḥ* is ' weak ', *ḍa'īf*, a term I prefer not to translate, as ' weak ' does not convey the sense of the Arabic. President al-Sallāl was of *ḍa'īf* status though an officer in the army. Dresch speaks of ' a more general distinction within market society between lowly servitors and potentially prosperous traders ', adding that to the tribesman these distinctions are entirely irrelevant. In the *JAOS* (1990, 476) I note that Ibn Hishām distinguished three social groupings in pre-Islamic Mecca, notables with *sharaf* and *man'a*, an intermediate class of merchants (*tājir*), and *ḍa'īfs*. It has impressed itself on me that Arabian cities do have a definite class, that I should like to dub ' burgers ', distinguished by wealth

[2] Ahmad al-Oweidi al-Abbadi, ' Bedouin justice in Jordan ', University of Cambridge.

acquired through business, in certain cases some generations back; they are respected for their wealth but they are not aristocracy. Another observation I have made is that tribesmen living in towns may retain their tribal status for generations, probably as long as they mainly follow the profession of arms, but if they engage in trade they become detribalized and merge with the urban population. Dresch notes (p. 195) that *fuqahā'* is applied to categories of ' weak ' people quite different from the *qāḍīs*. But to think of them as learned men or as ever having been such would be to overestimate their role. In the Yemeni village I have called the *faqīh* the village dominie, rather like the Sudanese fikī, a ' hedge-priest '. In western Ḥaḍramawt the *fuqahā'*, sometimes *fuqarā'*, seem to be quite humble followers of some local ṣūfī.

Some forms of oath are given in an appendix (p. 404) similar to certain of those quoted to me in Dathīna in 1954 (Mahmoud Ghul volume, 150) and see *JRAS*, 1951, 159. The oath is and always has been of major importance from even before Islam (cf. *The Cambridge history of Arabic literature*, I, 123) in tribal law cases, as is indicated by the poet Zuhayr. The Zubayrī oath as taken in the Ṣan'ā' Jāmi' is described and quoted in our *Ṣan'ā'* (p. 317). It goes back to the time of the Caliph Hārūn al-Rashīd and was originally forced upon 'Abdullāh al-Zubayrī by his *wazīr*; it has been preserved almost verbatim in the Yemen from that time (*JRAS*, 1989, 135). It is the strongest of oaths. The oath within the *khaṭṭ Allāh* is described in considerable detail by Landberg (*Arabica*, V, Leyde, 1898, 131 ff.) from Ḥarīb and is doubtless the same as that witnessed by Dresch.

In connexion with the *jidhn* (pp. 95, 128) which Dresch calls ' a scarecrow placed in public to shame defaulters ', I recall a conversation I had with Sharīf Habīlī of Nuqūb in 1964. A man who has committed a shameful offence (*'āyib*), he said, an *'ayb* of the worst sort, will not be allowed to come near the well (*bīr*) of a tribe. A dog will have a nick taken out of its ear and be called after him to disgrace him. A tree (trunk) will be taken and burned and the black stump stuck up on the road and named after him in order to proclaim his disgrace—this of a man who has not cleared/absolved himself (*mā niqī*). If he says: ' *Al-salām 'alayk* ' they will answer ' *Lā ḥalā* ', i.e. *salām-ak marjū'*, ' your (peace) greeting is rejected '. As Dresch says, quoting Rossi, the *radd al-salām* forms a truce in customary law and this is also treated at some length in my *al-Ādāb . . . fī aḥkām al-man'a* (*BSOAS*, XIII, 3 1950, 589). I had not however connected the Bayḥān practice with al-Shawkānī's *jidhn* which should be equivalent to classical and colloquial *jidhr*, the lower part of a tree trunk, the term used by al-Habīlī.

It is not without significance that Jewish *jīrān*, persons protected by the tribes, are called in Upper Yemen, Yahūd Banī Fulān which would support my finding that the Yahūd Bani 'l-Najjār (and other Yathrib Arab tribes) were not Jewish members of the tribe but separate allied groups. Dresch quotes information that around Mārib in 1986 Jews were still or again carrying arms. I had heard about 1964 that there were Jewish groups in the Mashriq who acted in every way like tribes but this was contradicted on a subsequent occasion—it seems my original informant may have been right! In Dathīna in 1953 it was said that Jewish converts to Islam after the 1950 exodus would rank as Muslims according to their profession—which there meant that they would not join the tribal class.

A number of lesser points made by Dresch are of some interest to Arabists. A man identifying himself with his family or tribe on occasion, often as a sort of battle-cry (p. 39), the classical and South Arabian *'azwa*, is ancient usage, as for instance in al-Wāqidī's *al-Maghāzī* (ed. Marsden Jones, London-Oxford, 1966). Too much should not be read into the use of *jāhil* for child, ordinary Aden *gāhil*

(p. 49). A bull that died of itself is given (p. 319) to the *'abīd* to eat—Aḥmad al-Sharjī, *Ṭabaqāt al-khawāṣṣ* (Cairo, 1903), 94 speaks of an extremely low class near Zabīd who eat carrion and drink intoxicants and they are also mentioned in the *Talqīḥ al-ḥukkām* of al-Mi'zābī (my corpus of tribal law documents), and it seems that the *'abīd* mentioned by Dresch also come from the Tihāma. The *bar'a* dance (for which, in Ḥaḍramawt, Yāfi' is specially well known) is so called, according to Landberg, because ' on lève les jambes et les bras ' as in a photograph I have. Adra's suggestion (p. 388) that it derives from the idea of excellence or surpassing skill is merely lexical. The use of *laḥām* (one would have expected *liḥām*, pl. of *laḥm*) by the Shawwāf of Rajūza for tribal sections (p. 209) is ancient. The *Glossaire daṯînois* (2621) discusses the term, quoting also al-Hamdānī, 156, *Luḥūm al-'Arab = buṭūn al-'Arab*. Cf. our *Ṣan'ā'* quoting al-Wāqidī, *aqāribu-nā wa-laḥmu-nā*, the paternal line.

Dresch quotes comparative matter from other Arab countries, even distant Morocco, but strangely Landberg's most relevant material, both linguistic and sociological, does not seem to have been consulted by him. It is ungracious in so fine a study to point to slips but (p. 138) Baḥḥūt should be read Bāhūt, Imām Aḥmad's nickname and spelled thus in his own verses in *Arabian Studies*, v, 1979, 92. The place spelled Harān must, I think, be Hirrān—a Ḥamīd al-Dīn prince had his headquarters in a cave there in which I stayed in 1966.

In a passage I cannot relocate Dresch questions the descent of the Lahej sultans from Yāfi'. Certainly the nineteenth-century *Ḥawliyyāt Yamāniyya* (ed. 'Abdullāh b. Muḥammad al-Ḥabshī/Ḥibshī, Damascus, 1400/1980, 100) maintains that the 'Abdalī house of Lahej comes from north Yemen Arḥab and the Faḍlī house of Shuqra from Ānis and that the eighteenth-century Imām al-Mahdī al-'Abbās appointed them to govern Aden and Shuqrah respectively, but in the seventeenth-century *al-Sīrat al-Mutawakkiliyya* of al-Jarmūzī (photograph of the Mukallā MS in the writer's possession) the Faḍlī figures more as a local chief and nothing is said of any origin from Ānis. In the *Hadiyyat al-zaman* of Aḥmad Faḍl al-'Abdalī (pp. 39, 41) the Āl Muḥsin Sultans of Lahej are descended from Āl Sallām, a *fakhidh* of Kalad of Yāfi'. I think the *Ḥawliyyāt* is inventing a spurious origin for these two houses for political reasons!

That Dresch should assent to the term ' civil war ' for what Yemenis know as the ' *thawra* ' of 1962–68 is regrettable. This young officer coup, sparked off by the Egyptian chargé d'affaires, was welcomed by urban and semi-urban dissidents, supported financially by the merchants and joined by tribal elements resentful of Imām Aḥmad's forceful way of bringing them to heel, but there was much not unwilling acquiescence in Ḥamīd al-Dīn rule. This is evident from a neglected book by a somewhat ingenuous young Irish student, Peter Somerville-Large, *Tribes and tribulations* (London, 1967), who arrived in the first months after the coup, to find the Republican rebel junta nervous of their future, faced by ' Royalist ' opposition, despite the presence of Nasser's troops. Royalist tribes in fact spoke of themselves as fighting ' Pharaonic colonialism (*al-isti'mār al-Fir'awnī*) ' and were contemptuous of Republican levies. Royalist and Republican delegates at the Ḥaraḍ Conference could not achieve agreement because the Egyptians promised to kill the Republicans if they did! Nevertheless, *de facto* peace existed between tribes of both factions in the north in 1966 and, with tribal escort, I was able to cross two tongues of Republican territory (Ḥāshid). In fact throughout the period the two sides remained clandestinely in touch. The final (Royalist) siege of Ṣan'ā' was raised by a mainly NLF column from the south and another from Hodeida—they had Russian air support and a Russian pilot was brought down in Jihāna—I have photographs of his logbook and aircraft. So I prefer to call this period the ' Nasserite occupation ' since there was little fighting between Yemenis, and many Republicans resented strongly the Nasserite intrusion into their country.

I do not believe Dresch's informant who maintained that cutting off the heads of slain enemies is not a Yemeni custom (though between tribes it could bring a heavy punishment for infringing honour). The Imām is said to have forbidden this fairly early in the war but that it happened I can prove from photographs, and I saw an Egyptian hand suspended from a rock and heard of other mutilations. In fact the Āl Quṭayb of the former Western Aden Protectorate cut off the heads of a handful of SAS who had fought an isolated but gallant battle with them until killed.

Sayyids lost by the '*thawra*' (p. 140) it is true, though Sayyids were numbered among the officers of the *coup d'état*, but Ḥamīd al-Dīn policy aimed at weakening their potential rivals, the great Sayyid houses and the *hijras* by which they were protected, while Imām Aḥmad gave prominent offices to the *Qāḍī* class—an aristocracy, I think, like the Mashāyikh families of the Shāfi'ī south. (*Qāḍī* is an hereditary title and such *Qāḍī* houses as al-Akwa' demonstrably medieval.) But even before 1962, young men, Zaydīs themselves too, were exposed to educational influences (especially from Egypt) hostile to Sayyids, and the younger Ḥamīd al-Dīn princes were said to have lost that certainty of faith in the imamate held by Imām Aḥmad.

Dresch shows the contrived nature of the conception of *hijra* formulated by Zaydī authors (p. 160 passim) and his further study of it and *tahjīr* in general is particularly interesting and valuable. Nevertheless, it seems to me that his own linkage of it to the Prophet's *hijra* (taking protection of a tribal group) is so obvious an Arabian pattern as to require no actual historical link to demonstrate it (p. 146). Our *Ṣan'ā'* (p. 42a) proposes that *hjr* in certain pre-Islamic inscriptions means 'protected person', but the *Sabaic dictionary* (A. F. L. Beeston *et al.*, Beyrouth, 1982, 56) plays for safety, describing *hjr* as a collective noun meaning 'townsfolk'!

In today's Yemen Dresch opines (p. 266) that the older association between power and knowledge (*'ilm*) has been severed and, far more so, that between power and birth. This doubtless is how such classes as officials, businessmen, school teachers, etc. would like to see it. Doubtless too, wealthy persons of humble birth may sometimes marry into noble families—as a first-century Arab poet said, *ḥubb al-ḍarāhim* can affect such a fundamental Arabian feeling as that relating to *kafā'a*. But is the change really so great? In the past, learning without personality might bring respect, but would it bring power? Many Sayyids and Quḍā who held power were men of outstanding personality—as indeed were Imāms Yaḥyā and Aḥmad—but al-Badr is not of their calibre. I cannot believe that noble families do not still retain much power in their hands though it might well be less apparent. The Y.A.R. has theoretically abolished social rankings but though, for example, I found recently in Zabīd that my driver at first avoided using the term *khādim* for the socially inferior class known as such, I doubt if in practice their status has changed in any way. Significantly, Dresch points out that 'the army has become immensely important'. In Imamic days the Sāda, and I think others, regarded the soldiery with a certain contempt, and of course they were the direct oppressors of the *ra'iyya*. One hears occasionally of individuals in the army taking advantage of their position and if the Yemen were to suffer an economic set-back one does not know how this might affect the soldiery. The condition of the ordinary Yemeni, however, has vastly improved since Imamic days, but this is due to economic factors not political change.

In a chapter on the tribes and events in the modern world their situation is brought up to date while another chapter 'Tribal and national imagination' presents a selection of the writings of mostly contemporary 'intellectuals' on how they see the tribes. Like their counterparts in sister Arab countries they tend to lack sympathy, often displaying active hostility to tribes and tribalism, but it must be said that the tribes themselves are affected by the winds of change as they were in the Aden Protectorates during the fifties and sixties.

Since Paul Dresch completed his study about three years ago momentous events (for Yemenis) have disturbed the never over-even tenor of Yemeni life. The union of the Y.A.R. with the P.D.R.Y. was rapturously welcomed by the Yemeni media—which naturally take no account of reservations or problems in the attitude of the northern tribes. The expulsion of Yemeni labourers by Saudi Arabia in the wake of the Yemen Government's support for Saddam Husayn cannot but have struck disastrously at the Yemen's frail economy. In this fluid phase of Yemen history one can but express the hope that Paul Dresch may have the opportunity to study the process of events with the care and expertise that he has devoted to the Zaydī tribes of the north.

XI

Wards and quarters of towns in South-West Arabia

On my first visit to Hadramawt in early 1947 I had the unusual experience of living in a very ancient Arabian town, Tarim, the spiritual capital of the Wadi. At this time Tarim was little affected by the outside world, though there were certain superficial influences on it from Malaya and Indonesia since the leading family and others had made their fortunes there, but this had hardly gone deeper than some elements in the decor of its lovely buildings, certain items of dress, and other trifles. Tarim was unknown apart from superficial descriptions of travellers and everything had to be explored—from its traditional Islam learning to the colloquial language, literature, customs, social order, etc. Tarim and other Hadrami cities had greatly influenced the course of Islamic civilisation in East Africa, the western coast of India, and Indonesia, but underneath the culture of this city of mediaeval Islamic learning there lay a sort of municipal organisation formed by other far less sophisticated strata of society than the Hadrami Saiyids who dominated it. This urban organisation represents, I believe, a stage of development of Islamic cities more primitive than that of the great centres of the Arab world, prior of course in both cases to westernisation. For example, at Cambridge we have been studying a series of 18th century documents on the organisation of the artisans of Algiers[1] which already show a much more developed community than that of Tarim, though it is still mediaeval in character. Even the urban artisan community of San'a[2], capital of the Yemen, representes a stage of development considerably beyond that of Tarim.

In 1947 and 1953 I was able to collect and copy a series of documents held by the quarters or wards of Tarim city which I had explained and commented upon to me there, and on my last visit to Hadramawt in late 1964 I was further able to collect data on the coastal town and port al-Shihr and discover how the same type of quarter organisation applies to a maritime town engaged in fishing and trading. Both Tarim and al-Shihr are walled towns but their dependence on agriculture and fishing respectively is reflected by the quite considerable areas of open land enclosed by their walls, for Tarim has fields among its houses, whereas al-Shihr has spaces given over to the drying of fish and beaching of sambooks and canoes. The quarter documents which I have are mainly concerned with disputes within or without the quarter, the settlement of which they record, but the very nature of these disputes reveals much of the everyday life of these communities. Many years of reading in Arabic literature[3] have produced for me evidence that inter-quarter disputes were common in the Islamic cities of the Middle East, but there is not much information about the quarters themselves, and this I think can be reconstructed by inference from the documents at my disposal.

To understand the nature and operation of the quarters in Hadramawt, and, *mutatis mutandis* in the Yemen, one must know something of the social stratification of Southern Arabia, a subject with which I have dealt at greater length in a lecture at the Sorbonne[4] some years ago.

To commence with the lower orders—the quarters of Tarim are inhabited by small shopkeepers, artisans, and workers in clay—builders, potters, cultivators, but the most important group perhaps is the *dallals* or brokers working on a commission basis, who are the intermediaries with the tribesfolk coming in from the country to buy and sell. Al-Shihr closely resembles Tarim except that, instead of cultivators, it has a large class of fishermen or seamen and its *dallals* are much concerned with fishing or port activities. All these classes are regarded by the arms-bearing tribesfolk as of inferior social standing to themselves. It is these lower orders and esclusively they who form the "Children of the Quarter *('Iyal al-Hafah)*.". Tarim is the capital of that celebrated religious aristocracy, the Saiyids of Hadramawt,[5] scholars, but frequently also they are the capitalists who finance the share-cropping agriculture of the country. An older religious aristocracy, the Mashayikh, is also represented by certain families. Though in the Yemen, Saiyids are armed fighting men like the tribes, in Hadramawt they are mostly not armed, and act as mediators in tribal disputes. Many Hadrami Saiyid families are also spiritual lords (*mansabs*) of sacred enclaves in which tribal law does not run and war may not be waged. In Tarim the Saiyids like the lower orders were groups protected by the tribes though they generally respected and sometimes feared them and the Mashayikh. I must emphasize the fact that tribesmen living in towns can do so for generations without losing their tribal fighting qualities unless they abandon arms for the despised occupations of petty trade, artisanship, and agricultural labour. Like the religious classes they do not seem to have had any part in the quarter organisation, though of course the quarters affected the daily lives of all the other groups. Society had a certain balance with tribal capacity to some extent limited by their fear of the Saiyids and their oppression of the lower orders by fear of killing the goose that laid the golden eggs. In Tarim and other Hadrami cities, tribal factions headed by Sultans were in control, and a love-hate relationship existed between them and the Saiyids, both classes being economically reliant on the lower orders.

In the histories we find reference in mediaeval times to the Harat Al Ba Sharif, clearly a special quarter of the Saiyids,[6] to the fort Husn al-Ranad which occupies a pre-Islamic site, and to a quarter of washermen, dobies, where one supposes there would also have been dyers and indigo-beaters. Today the largest quarter is Hafat al-Suq, the Market Quarter, but there are Hafat al-Khilaif, Hafat al-Sahil, the latter a strip of land under the mountain overlooking Tarim, Hafat al-Nuwaidarah,[7] Hafat al-Hawi which is a sacred enclave or *hawtah* of the Haddad family of Saiyids, Hafat al-Rudaimah, Hafat 'Aidid, a suburb outside the walls, Hafat al-Mijaft, the old washermen's quarter, and Hafat al-Siddah, the quarter of the Gate. Only five of these are important, and some lesser quarters "follow", as they say, the bigger quarters. There were several of these sacred enclaves within the city of Tarim and the present day Hawtat Ba 'Alawi is probably the old Harat Al Ba Sharif, but apart from Hafat al-Hawi these enclaves appear to have become absorbed into the ordinary Quarter structure of the town.

The Suq or Market Quarter seems to be mainly run by the brokers (*dallal*) who, apart from their general functions, are the tribesman's agent. The tribesman stays in the broker's house when he comes to town to sell his animals and buy cloth, dates, etc.

The brokers used to treat their goodwill in the tribesmen as a commercial asset, buying and selling among themselves the right to act for certain tribes—I have a number of documents to this effect. In some of the other quarters weavers used to predominate, but there were in Tarim also carpenters, blacksmiths, potters, tinsmiths, masons, and others. I propose to treat of these quarters in respect of their government, duties and offices held within them, their boundaries, religious ceremonial, and hunting.

Each quarter is run by its headmen or fathers—the *abwa/ubwa*, also called *muqaddams* or *aqils*. They conduct the affairs of the quarter and settle disputes between members of it. The weakness of the quarters lies in the fact that they are perpetually quarrelling with each-other, and the Hadrami press of the fifties and sixties has many notices on their differences during which persons were sometimes killed or maimed with sticks —the characteristic weapon of the quarters. The main cause of these disputes lay in the occasions when one quarter, in full ceremonial procession on some religious or secular ground, attempted to cross the boundaries of another quarter—this also seems in the literature of Arabic to have been a common cause of trouble. Such occasions would be when the quarter was going out to the Hunt—a very ancient ritual, as well as a sport, connected in ancient and present times with rain-making, on the pilgrimage to the pre-Islamic prophet Hud[8], and even in several recorded instances, at a funeral. The quarters had then to take their quarrel for settlement to a third party, sometimes to the Saiyids, but sometimes, as in a case in 1911, to the Sultan of the day, Mihsin b. Ghalib al-Kathiri. The penalty for infringing the quarter boundary was beating —the punishment executed by the *Abwa*, or Fathers. One can of course come and go freely in the ordinary way between one quarter and another as a private individual. Last century the town of Tarim was divided into three tribal fiefs under three Yafi i Sultans and at that time the normal procedure in a jugdement in a quarrel of the quarters or other groups was that witnesses should take an oath on a saint's tomb—though recourse was had to the *bish'ah*—trial by ordeal— the tongue being lightly flicked with a red-hot knife—and this in the highly orthodox city of Tarim—though I must suppose that the actual performance of the ordeal did not take place there. Of course the calling in of a third party to mediate always lays it open to that party to stir up mischief between contestants, which he can then turn to his own advantage.

Each craft sought to retain its own particular trade in its own family or families, and so much so is this engrained in the social structure that instead of asking for a mason in Tarim to come and work for you, could ask for Ba Sumbul—the family of masons in which the craft is hereditary, and again for the grave-diggers one would say

Ba Huraish[9] since their name is synonymous with the profession. Such families allowed no other to practice their trade if they were in the position to prevent it, and a craft, for example, like the carpenters has the exclusive right to hand goors. In Tarim you had to employ a carpenter from your own quarter—nor could you dismiss him and take on another carpenter unless you could show that he had defaulted in his work in some way. I heard that in some cases a family with a particular monopoly in a craft could take legal action against persons attempting to infringe it, though this must, I think, have been in customary rather than *shariah iaw*.

In the coastal town of al-Mukalla some trades were even able to impose a fixed fee for certain services. On my first arrival there I challenged the porterage bill as excessive—which it was— only to be visited by the headman of the porters who informed me that I had been charged at the rate standard for locals and foreigners alike—which it was in fact. In Tarim during the economic depression of the thirties the builders came out in strike when the Saiyids attempted to reduce their wage and succeeded not only in winning their point but furthermore managed to increase their rate of pay. Nevertheless I hardly think these trades and crafts can properly be called either guilds or trades-unions, though in the two coastal towns of al-Mukalla and al-Shihr they may be nearer to these types of organisation than in Tarim. It seems to me that they really represent a stage in the development of urban society anterior to the guild structure. The very paucity of references to any institution like a guild or trades-union in Abbasid literature—at the moment I can only remember Jahiz's headman of the sweepers[10]— may indicate that such organisation of the trades as there was resembled what we have in Hadramawt today.

In Hadramawt the artisan class in general is known as *haik* or weaver, a class despised widely in the Arab countries at all periods to the extent that this is even embodied in Islamic *Hadith* or Tradition[11]. Yet, though, from the quarter documents I have, the headmen of the quarters were drawn from various trades, it is clear that the workers in clay, i.e. fieldworkers, builders, potters, the latter sometimes itinerant workers in Hadramawt, were inferior in status to the other artisans and "followed" them.

The quarters in Hadramawt in general organised quite extensive social services and they manage the principal festive and social occasions of the year. I draw mainly on my experience of Tarim. There at least one of the quarters has a house at the Jami mosque, a *waqf*, where the dead are washed, containing basins for this purpose. It is maintained by certain dues collected in the *suq* by the headmen. The quarter pays for the burial of paupers. In Ghail Ba Wazir some years ago one quarter bearing the bier of one of its deceased, attempting to pass through another quarter, was stopped by it, and the bier neglected while they set to fighting. In January 1962 the Kathiri Sultan punished headmen of al-Hawtah quarter by beating for quarrelling over ceremonial at a funeral with another quarter.

At weddings however it is that the quarter appears at its best—it provides the necessary gear for the entertainment such as pots and pans. Men are detailed for the services of fetching firewood, drawing water, slaughtering sheep, and serving the food. At Ghail and doubtless most other places, the Shabwani dance is organised by the headmen for the wedding days, but disputes can arise even over the dance, for in Tarim in 1951, when two persons hailing from a different quarter participated in the Shabwani of al-Nuwaidarah quarter, this gave rise to a fight in which no less that six persons were hurt.

There is a clear-cut division in the duties of the Masakin—the petty shopmen and artisans on the one hand, and the Da'fa/Du'afa or workers in clay —mainly builders and cultivators. The Masakin act at the "mourning", taking turns at carrying the bier of the deceased, and in performing the services at weddings. It may be remarked that the person holding a wedding must invite some of the headmen as guests to ensure that the quarter services are available. The Da'fa on the other hand have functions of their own special to them, and are even distinguished by the dances they perform on ceremonial occasions—the razih dance being peculiar to the Da'fa. To them exclusively belongs the function of dealing with the clearing out (*unatil*) of wells when this is necessary. To have your well dealt with you approach the abu or headman of the Quarter who sends a man down the well to examine it and makes an estimate of what requires to be done. The *abu* then summons the *'Iyal al-Hatab* to do the work, and the well owner pays the *abu* who presumably divides the money out among the men. The Da'fa, immediately a call goes up of fire, flood or the collapse of a house wall, must turn out to deal with the situation and rescue any persons trapped— the nearest man to provide the tackle—buckets if it be a fire, mattocks and baskets for removing earth if a wall or bank has fallen. Again no person from another quarter may intervene to help even though he be closer at hand than the men of the quarter themselves. The technical term for this emergency in Hadramawt is *ghariq hariq wa-bait muhaddam*, i.e. drowing, burning, or house collapse and the amazing thing to my mind is that this phrase is exactly parallel to that quoted by Jahiz[12] some thousand years ago for Iraq—*al-harq wa—'l—Gharq wa-mail ustuwan*, fire, drowning, and falling of a pillar.

In Tarim Quarter dues are collected at "the scale"—*al-Quffan*, in the Suq Quarter which is operated by the *dallals* or brokers. If for instance a load of fish comes in from the Mananli tribe the buyer and the Minhali each pay a percentage to the *dallal* who divides it out—part to the Dawlah, i.e. the Sultans,[13] part to the *dallal*, but there is a share also for the grave-digger, for the porter who carries the fish to house or shop of the purchaser, and a share is laid aside for the bastards. This brings to light a very curious old custom—near al-Qaffan is a little niche in the wall called *Taqat al-Farkh*, the Bastard's Niche, to which a woman who has borne a child out of wedlock will secretly take her baby and lay it down there. When found it is maintained by quarter charity. Another source of revenue was that the skin of every animal slaughtered in the Suq Quarter is paid to the quarter. In 1954, when I collected the bulk of this information, it was remarked to me that there was no money in the Suq Quarter now as the *muqaddams* or headmen had dishonestly "eaten" it all, but the quarters usually maintain a sort of reserve fund for emergencies.

Beside the dances arranged by the quarter—of men only of course, though the women dance in their houses, there are numerous other social occasions—in some parts of South Arabia there is even a sort of All Fools' Day! There are also many religious festivals. Some of these latter are of an antiquity which goes far back into pre-Islamic paganism. There is, to cite a case in point, the Cattlemen's Picnic when the owners of the plough-oxen go out dancing and weaving their long loose hair; they think this picnic is connected with the well-being of their beasts. There is the Hunt of the Ibex on which I recently published a monograph, and it is linked with rain-making and is characterised by a strict ritual of procedure. Ancient indeed also is the pilgrimage to the pre-Islamic prophet Hud who is mentioned in the Koran—I have written on this already and myself made the pilgrimage and later watched the quarters turn out in force to welcome the returning pilgrims. Each quarter has its own patron saint, that of the Suq Quarter being 'Umar al-Mihdar, and all the quarters have their own special cries very often mentioning the name of the saint, as, e.g. 'Umar al-Mihdar, in every matter we shout for assistance to him. And the head of the foe whom we have made up our mind (to attack) we shall bring. One of these saints, of a Mashayikh family, is known as "He of the Ibex", but though there are Mashavikh saints in many places, most saints in Tarim are Saiyids. So life in a Hadrami town is full of turbulant incident, but it is full also of singing, dancing, and the composing of extempore verse, though in Tarim musical instruments are frowned upon by the ulema.

Tarim city is felt to have a personality of its own—just as did Mecca and its sacred enclave in ancient days, perhaps up to this time of ours. For example when there was an attempt to build an air-strip just outside it, some thirty years ago or more, the plan was abandoned, after a plane, crash it is said,—because as my old shaikh told me, the city or the pious ancestors, I cannot remember which, did not want an airfield. Tarim is perhaps to be identified with the city of 'Abdal (Servant of God) mentioned by the geographer Yaqut.[14] The town is full of saints—the dead in their tombs, and the living saints who inhabit Tarim though they may not be known to be saints. Hadramis returning from abroad follow the custom of first visiting the cemeteries and the pious ancestors interred there before even going to their families. Of these cementeries, within the walls there are three, each for a different social class, the Saiyid, the Mashayikh or non-Saiyid religious aristocracy, and the Masakin. There is even the mosque of a pre-Islamic Christian saint, St. Sergius.[15]

Al-Shihr is traditionally the port of Hadramawt and also a mooring place for the India trade-fleets of earlier times, with a long history before Islam, a centre of the fishing industry. It is also the port through which pilgrims passed to perform the pilgrimage to the pre-Islamic prophet Hud of Hadramawt. Nevertheless it is astonishingly little known. Al-Shihr lies along a sandy beach and shipping simply moors in the open roads before it. There are clay mounds along the shore which ought to be examined, but just as no excavations were made in Aden city because it was so easy of access under the British, so nobody has bothered even to cut a trial trench into these mounds. In 1948 I picked up mediaeval glass and Chinese and Persian glazed sherds. Behind the town is a low mountain with a path to the top and vestiges of what may have been some kind of shelter—this I think was a look-out post for reporting the arrival of shipping.

Al-Shihr is divided into two parts by a flood course normally dry, and at one time a large rock stood there and was the focus of local ceremonies on which I am unfortunately not informed since the Qu'aiti Government, considering these superstitious, blew it up.

The entire coast, including al-Shihr port itself, is called al-Mahjab—meaning "The Mooring Place". The town seems to consist of ten quarters—one of these called al-Qaryah, i.e. the village, seems to have been the original nucleus of the town and is to be accounted the oldest part—at one time it contained Suq al-Khan according to the historians, but this name seems not now to be known. The Majraf Quarter can only be so named from the *jarif net* basically a large cylindrical bag with a rope attached to each side; this net is drawn into the shore at the season when the sardine shoals, by two teams of men, sometimes with animals, and the bag emptied on the beach—so this name means something like "The place of the *Jarif*-Net Landing". This net is commonly used on the Hadrami coast and on the Batinah coast of Oman. East of this lies al-Ramlah, The Sand, which can be used for drying nets or fish. These two quarters are wide open spaces with some houses, and numbers of what is called a *hawsh*, fish-curing premises with yards for drying and curing fish and tanks for storing fish-oils. Let me add that the whole coast is divided into separate stretches in each of which local customary maritime law is administered by fisher headmen who may have nothing to do with the town headmen, though they may become headmen in the town also—so a Shihri fisherman knows that the jurisdiction of his headmen runs between fixed eastern and western points on the coast. Some of the quarters have the title *Aql* as in 'Aql Ba 'Uwain, and I am informed that this means a place where Bedouins coming to the town hobbled their beasts—perhaps these quarters originally lay beyond the town, and today there is still al-Mahatt, outside the town to the north-east where there is a camel park. The larger quarters are divided into what is termed a *rub*, literally a quarter, but 'Aql Ba 'Uwain has six of these sub-divisons and the headman is called *muqaddam tamimah*, *tamimah* being a term not heard by me in areas west of this, but common in Oman. There is a quarter called al-Hawtah which would of course, at least at one time, have meant a sacred enclave, but I have no information about it.

Al-Shihr has a great many saints' tombs, and there are ceremonies connected with these of considerable interest. In one I chanced upon two women, one of whom seemed to be busy with the sword of a sword-fish. These swords one sees frequently in South Arabian shrines and I think I have also seen them in little shrines on the east African coast. I have heard though not altogether confirmed that women embrace the sword for fertility reasons. though I have many times enquired why these swords are kept in shrines I have never had a satisfactory answer other than what is perhaps a half-truth, that they are there as a sort of decoration. Hadramis are most reluctant to allude to such superstitions though they are well aware they exist.

Much more unusual however than ordinary enough fertility practices is the *Sawban*. When the sea is bad Shihris will go to the saint Bin Jawban, and, sitting on the ground just as they would in one of their dug-out canoes of Malabar workmanship, they go through the motions of sea-fishing—their *rubban* or captain standing up to cast the net they have brought with them just as if at sea. They sing a refrain:

Sawban sawban,
'Ubaid hannu luh, Henna they've splashed on 'Ubaid.
Sawban sawban,
We-qattatu rujuluh, Patterns on his feet they've made.

As in all cases when a visitation is made to a saint the fishermen bring with them a gift for him. Al-Shihr has a number of markets such as the Shark Market, the Indian Market, the Date Market, and the Shibam Market, called after Shibam the commercial centre of the Wadi Hadramawt.

The headmen of the quarters manage the visitations to the saints, but these are less than in former days because they are expensive—the quarters engage singers for these occasions and have to contribute to the cost of them. They also have the same duties with regard to weddings and funerals as the headmen of Tarim, and for the former cooking pots and a sail are provided, the latter to be used as an awning over the street—I have also seen this in Mombasa in the Arab quarter there. At one time it seems that the Quarters of al-Shihr used to look after their poor, needy and orphans.

A survival of a custom—traces of which I think are still to be found in Arab countries—is the giving of nicknames to towns and villages—as perhaps Tunis (country) is called al-Khadra. Some of these names as in the case of Saiwun are merely descriptive—because it is a long straggling town it is called al-Tawilah, and I have heard camel-men using such phrases as, "We'll reach al-Tawilah in the afternoon." Tarim is called al-Ghanna' or al-Ghunna' a name also recorded in the literature on Hadramawt because it has so many singing birds—but other villages have mocking names reminiscent of the Wise Men of Gotham, and some nicknames have even sexual allusions. One Hadrami village which has no mountain hunting grounds of its own has the nickname, "They planted a (stone) rolling pin." This, it is explained, is so that it would grow into a mountain! An illustration of how strongly people feel about these names is to be found in the story told of Saiwun, which for some reason, has also the nickname, "*Jurr*", a word that should mean "drag" or "draw", the implication of which I never could discover—so perhaps it has some particularly improper sense. The tale is told of a preacher in Saiwun reciting the verse on Moses and Aaron which contains the sentence "*Wa-akhadha bi-ra'si akhini yaiurru-hus*," (Kor. VII, 149) who so disliked even this word reminiscent of the town's nickname that he substituted a synonym for *yajurru* of the sacred text!

From these remarks drawn from a large collection of data on the quarters made over some 25 years and which I hope to publish in detail some time, it will be seen that the townsfolk of Arabia have a rich and vigorous social organisation. Of this the British Residency in Hadramawt during the fifties seems to have been hardly aware, and in Tarim the setting up of a municipality which ignored the quarter organisation of the town had the adverse effect of weakening it and causing a certain social dislocation, for I think it upset the balance of power between the classes there. In many ways the quarter behaves as if it were an Arab tribe, except that of course its members carry no weapon other than a stick, the arm characteristic of the Miskin though he may also carry a knife. The people of the quarters of Arab towns have left[16] little mark on Arabic literature, nor have the quarters as such left much impression on local architecture, for the important buildings are the mosques sponsored by the religious aristocracy and the castles of the tribal lords—very much as in mediaeval Europe, but theirs are the hands that have built them, and they are the human element that makes the pulsating life of the Arab suq so attractive to all.

[1]Ms. no. 1378 of the Bibliothèque Nationale, Algiers. Cf. E. Fagnan, *Cat. général des mss. des bibliothèques publiques de France, Departements, Alger*, Paris, 1893.

[2]Cf. al-Qadi Husain b. Ahmad al-Sayāghi, Qanun san a *Majallat al-makhtutat al-'Arabiyah*, Cairo, 1964, c, I, 273-307.

[3]E.g. al-Maqdisi, *Descriptio imperii Moslemici*, ed. M.J. de Goeje, B.G.A. III, Leiden, 1876, & 1906, 102 for disputes between artisan groups in Aden, Ibn al-Jawzi, *K. al-Muntazam*, Hyderabad, 1359 H. VII, 1494 passim. Cf. A.K.S. Lambton, *Islamic society in Persia*, London 1964, for rioting between different wards of a city etc..

[4]Société et gouvèrnement en Arabie du Sud, *Arabica*, Leiden, 1967, XIV, III, 284-97.

[5]Cf. my *Saiyids of Hadramawt*, London, 1957.

[6]Perhaps this is what is meant by Muh. al-Shilli, *al-Mashra al-rawi*, (Cairo, 1319 H.), I, 140. "What lies between these three mosques, I mean the Masjid Āl Bā 'Alawi, the Masjid al-Saqqaf, and the Masjid al-'Aidarūs, is called al-Hawtah, and it has never ceased to be respected, the Sultan and those below him respecting it, so that the price of land in it has become much and its streets narrow." The author also tells us that if anyone enters the 'Umar al-Mihdar Mosque as a *mustajir*, i.e. seeking protection, no one dares touch him, but they remain watching till he emerges.

[7]*Khilaif, sahil, nuwaidarah*, all are topographical names applied to land, so that they figure in other cities also sometimes as names of Quarters.

[8]Cf. my Hud and other south Arabian prophets, *Le Muséon*, Louvain, 1954, XVII, 121-79.

[9]See my Cemeteries of Tarim, *Le Muséon*, Louvain, 1949, LXII, I-II, 153-60, and in connection with this paper, Building and builders in Hadramawt, *Le Muséon*, 1949, XII, III-IV, 275-84, The Quarters of Tarim and their tansurahs, *Le Muséon*, 1950, LXIII, III-IV, 277-84. A poem by 'Askul my *Prose and Poetry from Hadramawt*, London, 1951, Ar. text 157 seq. contains names of families of artisans.

[10]*K. al-Hayawan*, ed. 'Abd al-Salam Harun, Cairo, 1938-45, III, 13.

[11]This theme is developed in the 10th/16th century author Ibn Tulun, *Daw' al-siraj fi-ma qila fi l-nassaj*, Chester Beatty Ms. 3317, an edition of which I have commenced. For "craftsmen and labourers of low status", see Muhammad Abdul Jabbar Begg, The social history of the labouring classes in 'Iraq under the 'Abbasids, Cambridge Ph.D. thesis, 1971, which has assembled a considerable deal of information on these classes relevant to the study of the Islamic town, and R. Brunschvig, Métiers vils en Islam, *Studia Islamica* Paris, 1962, XVI, 41-60.

[12]*K. al-Bukhala'*, edit. Taha al-Hajiri, (Cairo, 1948), 77.

[13]Market taxes were collected in former times by the *dallals* for the Sultans who protected the *suq*. The doubtless important issue of the *suq* at Medina in the time of the Prophet Muhammad has been examined insofar as the rather scant material allows by K.J. Kister, The market of the Prophet, *Jl. of the Economic and Social History of the Orient*, Leiden, 1965, VIII, III, 272-6. One of the accusations levelled against the Caliph 'Uthman was of introducing a tax on the Medina market, though the Prophet himself had laid down that no tax should be taken on it.

[14]F. Wüstenfeld, *Jacut's geographisches Wörterbuch*, Leipzig, 1866-71, III, 603, but one asks if this is perhaps 'Andal of Ibn Khurdadhbah, *al-Masālik wa, 'l-Mamalik*, edit. M.J. de Goeje, B.G.A., VI, Leiden, 1889, 143.

[15]Cf. *Bulletin of the School of Oriental & African Studies*, London, 1959, XXII, III, 574-5.

[16]It is a pity that we have scarcely a scrap of information about the Quarters of Aden before the British captured it, though from the histories we know it had Quarters such as al-Hubush, and more recently al-Hunud and al-Yahud. The deep impress on Aden life made by the British is apparent in the term Hafat al-Rizmint (Regiment) for Aden Front Bay, though soldiers had long ceased to have barracks there.
I have lists of Quarters for some towns in the Yemen such as al-Shaharah, and information on the Quarters of Mogadiscio, the latter apparently organised in a rather similar fashion to those in Arabia

XII

Zinā, some Forms of Marriage and allied Topics in Western Arabia

For some years I have intended to explore what was meant by zinā, fornication, adultery, in early Islam, and consider it against the background of the customary practices governing the relations between the sexes in western Arabia, particularly the Yemen. These practices are often utterly opposed to what became Islamic orthodoxy and are relatively well documented. Following Walter Dostal's article, "'Sexual hospitality' and the problem of matrilinearity in South Arabia"[1] it seems to me appropriate to offer these reflections on the occasion of his 65th anniversary.

As early as 1905 Landberg had cast a new light on the marital and extra-marital relations customary among the tribes of south western Arabia, basing himself on the data to be found in Ibn al-Mujāwir, Tārīkh al-mustabṣir which he consulted in manuscript, and other literary sources – these he combined with information collected from his fieldwork on the Arabian dialects. His study, embedded in his monumental Daṯînah[2] is scarcely known, even to Arabists. Jacques Ryckmans, in 1983, in an article[3] on matrilineal ancestry in pre-Islamic Arabia has assembled the inscriptional data available up to that year on that subject, particularly in connection with Beeston's study of the inscription CIH. 581. For some centuries before Islam it is clear that Arabian society was predominantly patrilineal, but even earlier it seems to me that there are other explanations possible for the occurrence of women's names in genealogical sequences beside the matrilineal one.

In the pages following the proposition is advanced that the usages reported by Ibn al-Mujāwir have not only continued without interruption to the present day but are inherited from the pre-Islamic age – notwithstanding the efforts of the ulema to "reform" them. From a tribal viewpoint the application of the sharʿ law on zinā is an intrusion on their ancient custom. Their reaction to it is well expressed about the end of the 3rd/9th century in verses of their Zaydī foes:[4]

"They said: 'We cannot do without wines
And sinning [fisq] with the secluded girl of swelling breasts,
You [Zaydīs] prevent folk against their will
From [enjoying] pleasures and desired delights.'"

Evidence of sexual mores in the pre-Islamic age is scant and scattered and Islamic writers ignored what was unpalatable in the data available to them. The Qur'ān aims to regularize the institution of marriage and, given the circumstances of the age, the Prophet, while condemning zinā, took a temperate attitude toward it. That this was made more restrictive and punishment more severe by the fuqahā' of succeding ages is proposed from the evidence of the texts. In general they set about this through "improving" texts by various devices, even going so far as to invent the "stoning verse", supposedly omitted from the Qur'ān. I have shown how for example a simple letter from the Caliph ʿUmar to Abū Mūsā al-Ashʿarī has been "improved" out of its original intent. Incidents presenting the Prophet's Companions in an unfavourable light are toned down and, in still later writings, omitted altogether – the process is understandable.

The conditions imposed by the Prophet on tribes wishing to adhere to Islam seem mostly to have been that they destroy idols and pay zakāt, the former a politico-religious measure, the latter economic – but zinā does not often, if it does, come into the picture though the tribe of Hudhayl[5] is cited as asking the Apostle to make zinā lawful for them – which he refused. At the surrender of Mecca the Prophet said to Hind bint ʿUtbah, wife of Abū Sufyān: "You will not commit adultery [taznīna]". To this she made the proud but slightly equivocal reply: "Apostle of Allāh, does a free woman [ḥurrah] commit adultery [taznī]?"[6]

Again in the 3rd/9th century at Bayt Zūd in north Yemen a sultan judged that a soldier who had given money to a dancing woman who promised to come to him at night but failed to do so, should be compelled to fulfil her agreement.[7] This is directly opposed to the spirit of Qur'ān XXIV, 33: "Do not compel your girls to prostitution". It is to be presumed that the sultan gave judgement following the local ʿurf, customary law.

About this time came the emergence of the Qarmaṭī, 'Alī b. al-Faḍl who rejected the restrictions imposed by Islam on the relations between the sexes. It is understandable that he should find support among the south Arabian tribes, for outside the towns Islam seems to have made little impact on the conduct of the tribes. Ibn al-Mujāwir[8] states that the law followed up to the Ḥijāz borders in both the mountains and the Tihāmahs, the coastal lowlands, was manʿ not sharʿ, and he considers manʿ to be the law of the Jāhiliyyah before Islam.

In northern Arabia, for one reason or another, little is known about pagan sexual practices that may have continued to flourish under the Islamic veneer and the Saʿūdis have been zealous in suppressing paganism, but it is significant that Colonel H. R. P. Dickson[9] was told by Ibn Saʿūd that in Najd before the new revival (of Wahhabism) ninety per cent of the Bedouin in the province had never heard of religion, marriage had never been solemnized and circumcision was unknown!

It is not of course suggested that the concept of zinā was unknown before Islam, but the Qur'ān establishes it as a sin and lays down punishments for it. Perhaps it attached a shame to it that previously was only felt when an adultery was openly known to have taken place. The very fact that the Caliph Muʿāwiyah was able to recognize his father's son, Ziyād b. Abī-hi, by a temporary union, as his half-brother, may indicate that this was not generally considered shameful, though his relations did protest at it.

But first it is necessary to look at the more important passage in the Qur'ān that relates to zinā.[10]

Zinā in Qur'ānic verses

To comprehend the Prophet's attitude towards zinā a brief glance must be cast on what the Qur'ān has to say about it. Sūrah XVII,32 says simply "Do not approach zinā it is an evil path"; sūrah XXV,68 prohibits it and prescribes double punishment for it on the Day of Resurrection. Surah XXXIII,30 adresses the wives of the Prophet and promises them double punishment if they commit a fāḥishah mubayyinah, a clear shaming act, i. e. an open adultery – the punishment may be that in the present world and that in the hereafter.

Sūrah IV,15 states that "Those of your women who commit a fāḥishah, shaming act – produce witnesses against them, four of you, and if they testify [against them] keep them in rooms [al-buyūt][11] until death gathers them to itself or Allāh assigns them a way". It simply seems to mean – do not let them go out of the house. Given the way restrictions are placed on women in traditional society of the Arabian towns this is no tremendous hardship. The verse is supposed to have been revealed after Uḥud.

Sūrah XXIV,2 says: "The zānī and the zāniyah – beat each of them a hundred lashes, and do not let pity for them take hold of you in the religion/law of Allāh if you are mu'mins [believers] in Allāh and the Last Day, and let a party of the mu'minūn attend the punishment of them". The zānī and zāniyah are allowed only to marry one another or a polytheist (mushrik[ah]). Those falsely bringing accusations against chaste women are to be beaten with eighty lashes, and their testimony is to be rejected for ever. There is every reason to accept the tradition that this verse was revealed when

ʻĀ'ishah was suspected of adultery[12] with a young tribesman in what Schacht calls her "notorious adventure" but her own account seems to have the ring of truth, and the motive of her enemies to shame the Prophet and create tension between him and Abū Bakr. Be this as it may, there is no question of stoning the zānī and zāniyah. Sūrah XXXIII,30 quoted above, reveals the strength of feeling against an open adultery by the Prophet's wives. The social restraints on ʻĀ'ishah and the Prophet's unquestioned marital capacities make an infidelity on her part unlikely.

These and other passages not concerned with zinā indicate that the Prophet's attitude to women was far from harsh, even in cases of zinā and the emphasis is on open[13] adultery or fornication which shames. The exception is of course the admonitory punishment of a hundred strokes for the zānī or the zāniyah following the accidental compromising circumstance into which ʻĀ'ishah was thrown, but Qur'ānic punishments for theft are not less severe.

The "stoning verse", i. e. the verse supposed to have been left out of the Qur'ān, declaring the penalty for the zānī and the zāniyah to be stoning to death is a palpable forgery – it simply does not fit. In the tribal society of Medina it cannot be imagined that a tribe would allow one of its members to be put to death in this shameful way for a misdemeanour it would handle differently. In Medina too I suspect that tribal attitudes regarding sexual matters approximated to that of the Yemeni tribes discussed infra. Schacht's[14] dictum that "it is improbable that this verse is genuine, the traditions relating to it and the mention of ʻUmar are clearly tendentious; the stories that the Prophet punished by stoning are also unworthy of credence" will be generally accepted by western scholars, as also Schacht's view that the punishment by stoning came into Islam early, certainly from Jewish law.

The Prophet's adress at the Farewell Pilgrimage

Ibn Isḥāq (85–151 H.)[15] supplies the text of an oration (khuṭbah) on his own authority, delivered to the assembled pilgrims at the farewell pilgrimage (ḥajjat al-wadāʻ). Supplementary pieces on the authority of others place its delivery at ʻArafāt. There is nothing inherently improbable that the Prophet did, in year 10, address the pilgrims there and it is reasonable to suppose that within, say, a century from its delivery it was reliably reported and accepted as authentic. Nor does the fact that certain clauses are based on Qur'ānic āyahs invalidate it. In form the khuṭbah has something of a dramatic quality, with a kind of chorus, wa-qad ballaghtu. The clause important to this study runs:

"You have a right [ḥaqq] over your women and they have a right over you. Your [right] over them is that they should not make one you dislike/detest/find repugnant tread your beds [furūsh][16] and it is their duty not to commit an open shaming act [fāḥishah[17] mubayyinah]. If they do so Allāh permits you to put them away/repudiate them in beds and beat them a beating, not a severely painful one. If they desist they are due their food and clothing in accordance with custom [al-maʿrūf]". Injunctions to treat women kindly follow.

This clause evidently disturbed some fuqahā' and al-Jāḥiẓ gives a deliberately corrupted and "improved" version with which I have dealt in The Cambridge History of Arabic Literature[18]. The Muslim scholar M. Ḥamīdullāh[19] offers al-Jāḥiẓ's dishonest version and Guillaume fudges the plain statement in Ibn Isḥāq's text.

The passage has significant implications for the Prophet's practice and Islamic law. An inescapable corollary to it is that the Prophet does not condemn a husband's sanctioning another man to have intercourse with his wives or slave-women. It will be seen infra that this was a pre-Islamic practice, probably still current in the Prophet's time. Would he then consider it zinā? It is the openness[20] of the fāḥishah that is emphasized in Qur'ānic passages – this is relevant to known attitudes in later times. The treatment of the adultress prescribed is humane – the beating that, in the Prophet's distress over the scandal his opponents fabricated over ʿĀ'ishah, was severe, becomes more of a token punishment. The sentence for calumniators is not reduced. The ruling at the Farewell Pilgrimage is not inconsistent with the Qur'ānic passages on zinā supra and I am inclined to believe it genuinely represents the Prophet's attitude to the question of zinā.

The ruling, though negative in form, would seem to allow a sterile man to invite one more potent to have intercourse with his wife in the hope of producing a male child. From this emerges a new significance to the Tradition that the child belongs to the marriage bed (al-walad li-'l-firāsh) and the alternative interpretation of the maxim li-'l-ʿāhir al-ḥajar/ḥajr,[21] that the fornicator is deprived (ḥajr), i. e., has no claim to the child, makes excellent sense.

In this connection must be considered what Bukhārī[22] has to say on istibḍāʿ. "A man would say to his wife when she was clean of her menses: ›Send to so-and-so and ask him to have intercourse [with you]‹ and her husband would separate from her and never touch her until she clearly was pregnant, and when she was pregnant her husband would take her if he wanted. He would do that only for the sake of having a healthy[23] child. This marriage was called nikāḥ al-istibḍā'". Beeston[24] identifies this nikāḥ with the case in Sabaic text C.581 in which "two childless women, married into the same family, accept to have intercourse with a man – not mentioned by name – and thank the god for the fact that one of them has become pregnant." Beeston objects that the woman's taking the initiative precludes a strict comparison with nikāḥ al-istibḍā', but the initiative clearly lies with the husband who sends her to the intended surrogate father (as he would be termed in contemporary jargon). The reason seems obvious – that it would be distasteful for the husband to approach the other man, confessing his own shortcoming.[25] Bukhārī avers that this is a naw' min nikāḥ al-Jāhiliyyah, a marriage custom of the pre-Islamic age. His statement is vindicated by the evidence of the inscription. In this context nikāḥ is to be understood as sexual relation rather than the conventional rendering as marriage.

Returning by night from a journey

The collections of the Traditions contain, with one wording or another, the Prophet's injunction that on his return from a journey a man should not go to his family at night – nahā 'l-nabiyy an yaṭruqa ahla-hu layl-an. Wāqidī[26] quotes a tradition remounting to Umm 'Umārah who said that the Prophet when he stopped at al-Jurf[27] commanded his followers: "'Do not go by night to women after the 'ishā' prayer' ...and a man of the tribe went and came at night to his family [ahla-hu] and saw what he did not like, but he let [his family] be and did not disturb it for he was too much attached to his wife, had sons by her and loved her. But he disobeyed the Apostle of Allāh and saw what he does not like".[28] The Traditionists, ever intent on toning down or even eliminating what they consider unseemly, try to avoid acknowledging that the Prophet's reason for issuing the prohibition was so that a man's wife (ahl meaning wife, "wife" itself being avoided then as now) should dismiss a lover, if she had one with her. The Tradition as reported by Bukhārī is "improved" in that it alleges that the wife would have time to comb her hair and remove her pubic hair![29] Ibn al-Mujāwir[30] however leaves us in no doubt about the reason behind the injunction.

* The tribes of the Sarw, the Bajīlah, he says, are not governed by a sultan but by mashāyikh of their own. "When one of them goes on a journey the wife goes to the house ['ind] of the mukhlif, replacer,[31] i. e. the lover ['Ashiq] of this [woman] who takes her in his arms till her husband returns. When the traveller draws near his dwelling he shouts at the top of his voice: 'O obtrusive [lajūj] mukhlif, the time has come to get out [khurūj]!'[32] And he en-

Cf. G. Rex Smith, 'Ibn al-Mujāwir's 7th/13th century Arabia - the wonderous and the humerous', in A.K. Irvine, R.B. Serjeant and G. Rex Smith (eds.), *A Miscellany of Middle Eastern Articles - in Memorium Thomas Muir Johnstone...*, Harlow, 1988, 118–19 and note 52.

ters the dwelling abruptly and if he finds him in his dwelling he kills him, but if he has already left Allāh pardons what has happened before. I questioned one of their men in Mecca, saying to him: 'O man, staying [in the Holy City], what does the mukhlif do?' The man questioned [by me] replied:[33] 'He pounds on the water-furrow and kills [= exhausts] the woman'".

When discussing this Tradition which is quoted in the Kitāb al-lawāzim fī aḥkām al-manʿah[34] with tribesmen they said that an 'Awlaqʿi, returning at night to his house in the wadi, would shout from the top of its cliff-like sides that he had come back, announcing his name in the 'Azwah,[35] still some distance away, so that if there is something happening at night which might shame, such as fornication, the lovers could slip away and the qabīlī's honour be preserved!

There is no reason to question that the Prophet actually did try to restrain his followers from surprising their wives by returning at night, but it appears to have been an established custom, not an innovation of his own, in view of its persistence in territories superficially islamized up to our time. If so, he was tacitly admitting to the existence of fāḥishahs among his followers which were not overt (mubayyinah) and therefore not punishable.

There can be no doubt that the practice of mutʿah, "marriage of pleasure", a temporary marriage which is contracted for a fixed period on rewarding the woman (E.I. I)[36], was a custom before Islam at Mecca, a city with temporary pilgrim affluxes and trading. It is specifically sanctioned in the Qur'ān IV,24. "And further you are permitted to seek out wives with your money in decorous conduct but not in fornication [musāfiḥīn]; but give them their wages [ujūr] for what you have enjoyed of them [istamtaʿtum] in keeping with your promise" (Heffening, with slight re-wording). The Prophet availed himself of this custom, Ibn 'Abbās "was an ardent champion" of it and it is recognized by the Shīʿah.[37] It is significant that Ibn 'Abbās had supporters on this issue in Mecca and the Yemen. The "improvers" attribute to the Caliph ʿUmar at the end of his caliphate the prohibition of mutʿah as they do the "stoning verse". But this is not consistent with the story, if it be true, that ʿUmar found a pretext for acquitting the powerful Mughīrah b. Shuʿbah on a charge of an adultery that, in our courts would be judged flagrantly evident.

At Mecca, just over a century ago, Snouck Hurgronje[38] tells us "the mutʿah which the Sunnites denounce in the heretics [he means the Shīʿah] has been smuggled in by the Sunnites themselves". So standardized was it in his time that the woman made out an account of the several payments she should receive, the agreement being almost invariably fulfilled. He comments that the practice of the Sunnites as in many other cases, is so divergent from the tenor of the law, that verbal promises and agreements of all kinds ... are binding.

The likelihood is of course that at Mecca, no less than other places, the pre-Islamic practice of mutʻah, similarly to the other sexual usages discussed here, simply never ceased to be followed, the objections of the fuqahā' being merely bypassed. It would be interesting to see if the Saʻūdis have set about dealing with mutʻah, and, if so, with what success.

Payment to a prostitute for her services was forbidden by the Prophet but, as seen, when the Zaydī Imām al-Hādī ilā 'l-Ḥaqq arrived in north Yemen in 284/897 a sultan forced a woman to fulfil a bargain she had made to provide sexual intercourse and he must have ruled according to customary law, not the sharīʻah.

Provision of a concubine for the guest

An Āl Shihāb Sayyid told me nearly forty years ago (1991) that the Bayt ʻAlī of the Ḥumūm have the custom of providing a girl to spend the night with a stranger to increase the number of the tribe. This was also stated by the late Major Ian ("Jock") Snell who says the Ḥumūm were famous for breeding purposely illegitimates whom they believe to be the toughest men and the best shots. In Tarīm I was told by another informant that a tribe considers it an advantage to have some bastards among them because, in the event of the tribe having to put to death one of its members to expiate a particularly serious crime (not necessarily the person guilty), a bastard can be killed without setting up a blood feud – Sayyid Sir Bū Bakr b. Shaykh told me this is called qatal fī 'l-ṣawwānah. My Āl Shihāb informant said that a girl becoming pregnant says "kasabt", and speaks of her child as kasbī. This is not a custom among the Manāhīl and the ʻAwāmir. Others told me that the Ḥumūmīs extend the hospitality with their women only to qabīlīs, but not to miskīns and ḍaʻīfs[39] – it is also alleged that they would not give their women to Sayyids, which is possible since they call them farth, dung, as opposed to qabīlīs who are dam, blood, but on this point I am not certain. It is said to the girl: "Rūḥī, waddī dihn li-'l-gharīb,[40] Go and put oil on the stranger". So she comes and rubs the tribesman's legs with oil. I have given further particulars on this Ḥumūmī practice from other informants elsewhere.[41]

This custom I mentioned to a senior official in the Yemen Arab Republic quite a few years ago – the official had served under Imām Aḥmad and, if my memory is correct, under Imām Yaḥyā also. This reminded him, he said, of a young qāḍī he knew, when still himself a young man, sent to collect tax in a Zaydī tribal district. The chief of the district was not at home, but his wife and three daughters were. They took his animals (qurāsh) and fed them and fed him. Then the mother said to her daughters something like: "Man yidaffi' li-'l-ḍayf, Who will warm the guest?" One of the girls said she would and got into the sleeping bag Yemenis carry in the mountains because of the cold, with him. The qāḍī told my host that because of the fear of what might be done to him if he went further with the girl, and because she smelt, he left her alone, but remained awake worrying all night! Unfortunately as this was told me over the dinner-table I did not note down the tribe or district mentioned.

The use of the term kasb and verb kasaba has an interest I did not appreciate at the time. Ibn al-Athīr's Nihāyah[42] says that a man's son (walad) is min kasbi-hi, something he has acquired and explains "One makes the son a kasb simply because the genitor wanted him and strove to get him; kasb is ṭalab". Kusayb is the proper name of a man and two persons in Ṭabarī's Tārīkh[43] are so called, but the name does not figure in Ibn Durayd's Ishtiqāq – perhaps because he did not want to discuss the etymology of it – but clearly it could mean something like "a little acquisition" and refer to a male child born in or out of wedlock. There is a hint at this in the Tāj al-ʿarūs[44] commenting on the lines of the poet of the Umayyad period, al-Jarīr:

"O Ibn Kusayb there is no boasting over us.
A round breasted woman reeking of unguents vanquished you;
(Then she came to the Amir's gate crying out for help.)"

The lady in question is said to be Laylā al-Akhyaliyyah who excited (hājat) the poet al-ʿAjjāj b. Ru'bah, whose ancestor Kusayb was. She apparently seduced him and then went crying to the Amīr that she had been raped.[45] It is however the comment of the lexicographer that concerns us. "Qad yakūn Ibn Kusayb walad al-zinā, wa-bi-hi yufassar al-shiʿr al-madhkūr, Ibn Kusayb may be the child of zinā, and the aforementioned verse is explained thus." So the Ḥumūmī girl who spoke of the child she had conceived by a stranger as kasbī would seem to be employing a term for a child born out of wedlock current in the first century of Islam and before that.

The Prophet forbade the kasb al-imā' of a woman who kasabat bi-farjihā, slave women who earned through their farj. Quraysh and the Arabs used to do this in the Ḥijāz and elsewhere.[46] The Kalb tribe at the Dūmat al-Jandal fair used to compel their girls to prostitution (fatayāt-hum ʿalā 'l-bighā'); these do not seem to be slave women, and the reason may have been to increase the numbers of the tribe.[47]

When al-Hādī ilā 'l-Ḥaqq was at Khaywān in north Yemen,[48] he heard that tribes in a district called al-Aʿṣūm, at about a day's distance away, when a guest came to them the owner of the house entertains him. "He brings in his daughter or sister, all dolled-up [wa-qad zayyanahā], and she spends her day or her night, so they say, he touches her stomach [baṭn] and her privy parts [mawḍiʿ al-ʿAwrah], with her father and her mother looking on. It is not said anything immoral takes place between them [...] They consider this lawful [ḥalāl]".

A certain ʿAbdullāh b. Sulaymān b. Ḥamīd al-Najdī, probably a Wahhābī, certainly so in his attitude to Arabian customs Wahhābīs consider un-Islamic, wrote a pamphlet[49] against them which the well known Aden divine Shaykh Muḥammad Sālim al-Bayḥānī edited and published, the fifth edition being printed at Aden in 1935. It may be that al-Najdī came with the Saʿūdī forces to the Yemen in 1934. When in the Tihāmah he came across heresies (bidaʿ) and customs (ʿAwā'id) contrary to the Islamic sharʿ among both the bādiyah and the ḥāḍirah, tribes and villagers. This is the Shāfiʿī Tihāmah ruled by the Zaydī Imām Yaḥyā who appointed governors to the province. The following is a summary of his report.

In these districts a vile custom is the marriage called sitr[50] which is an ʿār, a shaming thing [the word is a strong one] – the marriage of women pregnant through fornication [zinā] when they know the fornicator [zānī] or the woman claims that so-and-so made her pregnant. Her people and the headmen [ʿuqqāl] of the tribe compel him to marry her to "cover her" [li-yastur ʿalay-hā]. When a man asks to be betrothed to a woman [khaṭaba], some people do not disapprove of his entering upon her and passing nights with her. When they see him they vacate the room for him, saying: 'So-and-so and his betrothed [khaṭībah]'. Then, when she becomes pregnant they contract the marriage, often saying: 'This is his child'. Sometimes when a man has married off his daughter already pregnant through fornication, then bearing a child by her husband, the girl's father claims a boy from the husband, saying: 'He is my daughter's son'. The husband cannot keep the child unless he redeems him with something. Al-Najdī adds that some Tihāmah people do not bother to observe the ʿiddah period before a woman remarries, and some ask for a woman's hand during the ʿiddah period. In this case where the girl's father claims his daughter's son for himself the maxim li-l-ʿāhir al-ḥajr[51], taken in the sense that the fornicator is deprived of the child, is of very relevant application.

I have noted[52] that if a boy is claimed by his maternal grandfather and not redeemed by. his father he is known as, say, Ṣāliḥ am-Zanū, among the

Nakha'īs. The choice of to which house a boy belongs is important in questions of blood money etc.

Irtibāṭ

The Ḥaḍramī author Bā Ṣabrayn of the Wadi Daw'ān, fulminating against heathen practices, in a treatise composed in 1294/1877, highly disapproves of "what is well known among the Bādiyah, namely that the adulterer [zānī] comes to the wife of another man, and such as the husband comes upon the two of them but does not kill them and he does not kill him, but on the contrary, he says to him 'artabiṭ 'inda-hā, I withhold myself from her (?) for 120 riyāls', meaning – I shall not leave you until you make me depart for that amount and I shall divorce her, for example, so that you may marry her, and he does so".

Of the Ḥumūm, Jock Snell[53] says (1952): Many still have the custom that if a man is found with another's wife, the husband divorces and the woman marries the miscreant immediately. He then pays the injured husband the original [marriage] settlement plus a third, and any children born within nine months go to the injured husband. If the children are girls he will probably not ask for them.

I was told that the alternative to irtibāṭ is to kill the offending party, the adulterer, who is called al-marbūṭ – the husband yarbuṭuh 'ind al-ḥurmah, ties him up with the woman.

In 1954 I was able to enquire further about irtibāṭ. The adulterer pays double the original daf' (al-daf' marratayn), but the husband must divorce his wife. However the adulterer does not seem responsible for paying the mahr (dower) and of course, in the normal way, a man does not pay his wife the mahr unless he divorces – at this date it was 12 riyāls. The daf' was described as the (girl's) father's right (ḥaqq al-wālid), up to 1,000 or 2,000 shillings, and rashwah[54] connected with the girl, i. e. clothing (thiyāb), silver (fiḍḍah) and what is required for the marriage (ḥājāt al-'urs) – not unnaturally a woman with money receives more than a poor girl. The offender must also pay entertainment money (ḥaqq al-ḍiyāfah), known technically as 'Ashā wa-ḍuḥā, i.e. two meals a day for two to three days – the ḍuḥā must have ghee (samn) with bread and the 'Ashā must have meat with it. In fact the adulterer must pay all the marriage expenses of the man he has wronged; all these charges are paid double (mardūf), two thirds going to the injured husband and one third to the woman's family (ahl al-ḥurmah).

In cases where there is doubt about the commission of the act but good circumstantial evidence, two witnesses are required, each swearing five oaths. There is a judgement/decision in rabaṭ cases to be taken by the headman (ḥaqq fī 'l-rabaṭ 'ind al-muqaddam) as to whether the accuser's plea is valid. If he does not prove his case he may perhaps have to pay six riyāls. This sum looks like half the mahr. If you cannot agree on the irtibāṭ you may resort to the bish'ah,[55] trial by ordeal.

If you kill the adulterer you must produce two witnesses to support your case, but if it took place in a desert (khabt) and of course you have no witnesses, then you must resort to the bish'ah to affirm your case. If the accuser is successful in proving his case the killing gives no rise to blood (dam) and the killer is not due to pay compensation to the slain man's relatives. The adulterer is known in the Bedouin areas as qāfiz al-zarībah, the wolf that jumps over the thorn fence of the fold – instead of entering in the normal way – in Ḥaḍramawt he is known as qāfiz al-firāsh, the jumper into the bed.

This study has drawn, inevitably, on a range of sources varied in time and place. Certain methodological objections may be raised in criticism of this but the indications are that the sexual mores among the tribes and ḥaḍar of western Arabia have continued to preserve the practice of the pre-Islamic era up to the present day. Custom may vary to some extent from one group to another but there appears to be a broad consistency between them. Sharī'ah has been effective in supplanting pre-Islamic custom mostly in the towns and areas under their direct influence. Islamic writers such as al-Najdī speak conventionally in the idiom of innovators (mubtadi'ūn) and innovations/heresies (bida'), as if there had in times past existed all over the country a completely islamized society. It is of course Islamic sharī'ah that is innovatory in the territories that adhere to the traditional sexual mores, and sharī'ah is not infrequently resented by them.

Zinā is primarily seen as possibly touching a man's honour, rather than as "an injury to the rights and property of a fellow tribesman" as Schacht expresses it – though of course this can enter into question.[56] In south Arabia, at any rate outside ulema circles, zinā hardly seems to be a question of morality. With sexual emotions this paper is not concerned.

The Islamic code for sexual conduct has of course penetrated areas where pagan sexual attitudes once prevailed and has been encouraged to do so by the Arabian rulers and ulema, but with the profound change taking place everywhere, the future seems unlikely to be as simple as Islamization rolling back the frontiers of pagan custom.[57]

NOTES

1 "Sexual hospitality" and the problem of matrilinearity in Southern Arabia, Proceedings of the Seminar for Arabian Studies, London, 1990, XX, 17–30.
2 Leiden, 1905–13, 907–73. Only certain of the data it provides are utilized here.
3 A three generations' matrilineal genealogy in a Hasaean inscription: matrilineal ancestry in Pre-Islamic Arabia, Bahrain through the ages: the Archaeology, ed. Shaikha Haya & Michael Rice, London, 1986, 407–17.
4 R. B. Serjeant, The Interplay between tribal affinities and religious (Zaydī) authority in the Yemen, Al-Abḥāth, Beirut, 1982, XXX, 21, Reprint in Customary and Sharī'ah Law in Arabian Society. Great Yarmouth, 1991, III, 21.
5 Al-Mubarrad, al-Kāmil, Cairo, 1355–76/1936–56, II, 444.
6 Ṭabarī, Tārīkh, ed. de Goeje et al., Leiden, 1882–85, II, 1643.
7 'Alī b. Muḥammad b. 'Ubayd Allāh al-'Abbāsī al-'Alawī, Sīrat al-Hādī ilā 'l-Ḥaqq Yaḥyā b. al-Ḥusayn, ed. Suhayl Zakkār, Beirut, 1392/1972, 94.
8 Descriptio Arabiae Meridionalis ... Tārīkh al-Mustabṣir, ed. O. Löfgren, Leiden, 1951–54, 99.
9 The Arab Bulletin, with notes by R. Bidwell, IV, 1919. Reprint, Gerrards Cross, 1986. Notes on the Middle East, 110.
10 I have relied much on Schacht's article zinā in E.I. I.
11 Buyūt of course means "houses" more often than "rooms".
12 Bukhārī, Ṣaḥīḥ, Cairo, 1345, III, 227 (Shahādāt, 15).
13 Mubayyinah (sometimes mubayyanah is read), "to make apparent, manifest, evident, clear, plain, or perspicuous".
14 In E.I. I. R. Bell, A Commentary on the Qur'ān, II, Manchester, 1991, "The verse in its traditional form hardly seems genuine".
15 Sīrah, ed. Saqqā et al., Cairo, 1375/1955, II, 603; Al-Wāqidī, al-Maghāzī, ed. Marsden Jones, London, 1966, III, 103.
16 Sing. firāsh, also "woman" by extension.
17 Fāḥishah in the Qur'ān is always a sexual misdemeanour, though not explicitly so in XLII, 37. Sūrah VI, 151 says: "Do not come near fawāḥish, the open or hidden ones". This I understand as not to put oneself in temptation's way. It is explained as relating to zinā. Sūrah VII, 28 is directed against homosexuality. Sūrah VII, 28 says: "When they commit a fāḥishah they say: 'We found our fathers following it'. But Allāh did not order it. Say – Allāh does not order faḥshā'". Faḥshā' means a grossly immoral act and can mean zinā like fāḥishah. The commentators' assertion that the verse refers to the worship of idols and exposure of the privy parts while circumambulating the Ka'bah naked in the pre-Islamic era, can only be accepted. But could the verse also refer to opposition to more stringent restrictions on sexual conduct introduced by Islam? In fact the same Sūrah, 33, a little further on, refers to fawāḥish in a context which suggests zinā.
18 1983, I, 121.
19 Al-Wathā'iq al-Islāmiyyah, Beirut, 1389/1969, 308. A. Guillaume, The Life of Muhammad, Oxford, 1955, 651.
20 Because it involves a detraction from a man's honour.
21 Discussed in my The "White Dune" at Abyan: an ancient place of pilgrimage in southern Arabia, Journal of Semitic Studies, Manchester, 1971, XVI, 83, in reprint (see note 4, supra).

22 Quoted by Jacques Ryckmans, op. cit., 411 (note 3). Ibtiḍāʿ should be emended to istibḍāʿ. This is distinct from mutʿah both in form and motivation. Ibn al-Athīr, Nihāyah, I, 82, defines istibḍāʿ as taṭlub al-marʿah jimāʿ al-rajul li-tanāl min-hu al-walad.

23 Landberg, Daṯînah, 845, understands najābat al-walad as "avoir un enfant sain" not "noble progeniture" which latter would not concord with the circumstances.

24 Temporary marriage in pre-Islamic South Arabia, Arabian Studies, London–Cambridge, 1978, IV, 21–25.

25 It would also mean a loss of honour. Though not calling in question the two author's views on the higher status of women before Islam than subsequently, the case in question does not seem to support that thesis. Muḥammad b. Ḥabīb, al-Muḥabbar, Ḥaydarābād, 1361/1942, 398, points out that certain women could stay with or leave their husbands "on account of their honour and standing [sharaf & qadr].

26 Al-Maghāzī, II, 712; III, 1115.

27 Al-Jurf is about three miles north of Medina. On another occasion he stopped at al-Muʿarras, six miles from Medina.

28 Ṣaḥīḥ, VII, 51. ʿAbd al-Razzāq al-Ṣanʿānī, al-Muṣannaf, ed. al-Aʿẓamī, Beirut, 1390/1970 (flor. 126–211 H.) reports this Tradition in several forms. Of the two men who entered Medina at night one version runs: "Both found a man with his wife. This was mentioned to the Prophet and he said: 'I had forbidden you to go to the women at night'". The Tradition suggests that the mukhlif was not only known as a Medinan custom but that the Prophet was well aware of it. The "improvers" had not yet got to work on the Tradition in this early collection.

29 Li-kay tamtashiṭa al-shaʿithah wa-tastaḥidda al-mughībatu, the well known custom before intercourse.

30 Descriptio Arabiae Meridionalis ... Tārīkh al-Mustabṣir, ed. O. Löfgren, Leiden, 1951–54, 28.

31 Landberg, Daṯînah, 914, cites Burckhardt, Reisen in Arabien, Weimar, 1830, 682, who says that a man of Banī Yām going on a journey, sends his wife to a friend to replace the husband during his absence. Burckhardt, 675, speaks of the "sexual hospitality" of the Muraqqidah of ʿAsīr, often the wife of the master of the house acting in this capacity.

32 Note the rhyming formula.

33 Daṯînah, 913. Landberg's text is corrected by Löfgren, op. cit., 26, and should read yasḥaq al-khabr wa-yamḥaq al-marʿah. The khabr is the masīl, flood-bed, Lane "place where the water falls, such as the water-course has furrowed". Maḥaqa (al-shay') = aḥraqa-hu wa-ahlaka-hu, burns and makes perish, perhaps here used figuratively. But saḥaqa and maḥaqa seem to be virtually synonymous. Daṯînah, 909, quoting Ibn al-Mujāwir, says of Ḥaly on the ʿAsīr coast, the host says to the nazīl, bus wa-sāḥiq wa-ʿuḍḍ wa-ʿāniq [...] wa-lā tadkhul maʿa-hā [...] fa-idhā dakhalta maʿa-hā adkhalnā maʿaka hādha 'l-khanjar, Kiss, rub, bite, embrace [...] but do not penetrate into her [...] and if you do, I shall make this dagger penetrate into you! The sense of the passage is not then left in doubt.

34 Cf. BSOAS, London, 1950, XIII, 589, Ms. 56a.

35 I. e. declaiming one's name and origin.

36 Article by W. Heffening. Cf. more recently, I. K. A. Howard, Mutʿa marriage reconsidered in the context of the formal procedures for Islamic marriage, Journal of Semitic Studies, Manchester, 1975, XX, 82–92.

37 Quite evidently Meccans accustomed to mutʿah arrangements in a pilgrim city were in favour of it, not only Ibn ʿAbbās but also the ʿAbd Manāf house.

38 Mekka in the latter part of the nineteenth century, transl. J. H. Monahan, Leyde–London, 1931, 194–95. The account presented by the woman was 10 dollars marriage payment, 12 dollars a month subsistence money (including the 3 months ʿiddah payment after termination of the marriage), the whole to be paid in advance – not a bad bargain for the time.

39 For ḍaʿīfs see my The Ḍaʿīf and Mustaḍʿaf and the status accorded them in the Qur'ān, Tyskrif vir Islamkunde, Johannesburg, 1987, 32–47 – reprint in Customary and Sharīʿah Law, op. cit.

40 Daṯînah, 909, Rūḥī akrimī al-ḍayf, said by the husband to his wife (Ibn al-Mujāwir).

41 Yāfiʿ, Zaydīs, Āl Bū Bakr b. Sālim and others: Tribes and Sayyids ..., Arabian Studies in honour of Mahmoud al-Ghul, ed. Muʿāwiyah Ibrāhīm, Wiesbaden, 1989, 95–reprint in Customary and Sharīʿah Law.

42 Walada-hu [al-rajul] min kasbi-hi – innamā jaʿala 'l-walada kasb-an liʿanna 'l-wālida ṭalaba-hu wa-saʿā fī taḥsīli-hi, wa-'l-kasbu 'l-ṭalabu.

43 Ṭabarī, Tārīkh, II, 455, 594, Kusayb al-ʿAnbarī, and Kusayb of the Banū Mālik b. Saʿd.

44 Kuwait, 1382/1968, IV, 147. Verse 3 is from Sharḥ Dīwān Jarīr of Muḥammad al-Ṣāwī, Beirut, n. d., I, 114, with different readings.

45 Ṣarkhah is the cry for help. In this case it would be at an attempted rape. The story itself looks legendary.

46 Bukhārī, Ṣaḥīḥ, Ijārah, 20. Cf. Ibn al-Athīr, Nihāyah, IV, 19.

47 Muḥammad b. Ḥabīb, al-Muḥabbar, Ḥaydarābād, 1361/1942, 340 & 264. I have left aside the Prophet's regulations for slaves and slave women.

48 Sīrat al-Hādī, 125.

49 Naṣīḥat al-Muslimīn ʿan bidaʿ al-mubtadiʿīn wa-ʿAwā'id al-ḍāllīn. ed. & printed by Shaykh Muḥammad Sālim al-Bayḥānī, Fatāt al-Jazīrah Press, Aden, 1372/1935, 43. This is the fifth printing.

50 Landberg, Daṯînah, 846, quoting Ibn Ḥajar al-Asqalānī, on the authority of al-Dāwūdī (al-Sijistānī ?), says that (the Arabians) used to say: "What is hidden is no matter, but what appears is blame (ma 'statara fa-lā ba'sa bi-hi wa-mā ẓahara fa-huwa lawmun). This is in connection with women who take lovers (muttakhidhāt akhdān)".

51 See my The "White Dune" at Abyan, 76. There is a sort of trial by ordeal to determine whether a child is a bastard or not. This is an honour case.

52 See my Materials for South Arabian History, II, BSOAS, London, 1950, XIII, III, 593.

53 Brief notes on the way of life and economic conditions of the different tribes of the Eastern Aden Protectorate (typescript in my possession), 1962.

54 Note the interesting usage of rashwah.

55 Several types of bishʿah are noted in Yāfiʿ, Zaydīs ... (note 41 supra). The Āl ʿAbd al-Wadūd was a well known family of mubashshiʿs on the Ḥaḍramī coast, but when I met them in 1964 they had abandoned bishʿah.

56 See my Two tribal law cases (documents), II, JRAS, London, 1951, 156 (reprint in Customary and Sharīʿah Law) for the case of a runaway wife – the case is centred on clothing and jewellery not paid to the wife and compensation for loss of her services.

57 The Mufaḍḍaliyāt, ed. C. J. Lyall, Oxford, 1921, 102–3, has a tale of the Banū Zanyah, a man of whom came to the Prophet, Mālik b. Mālik b. Thaʿlabah b. Dūdān by name. You are not Banū Zanyah, said the Prophet, but Banū Rashdah. But they declined to have their name altered, saying zinyat al-marʿah, is the last of her children, like ʿijzah and nuḍāḍah.

XIII

The Yemeni Poet Al-Zubayrī and his Polemic against the Zaydī Imāms

Muḥammad Maḥmūd al-Zubayrī is the hero of Yemen Arab Republic ideology, a man of unsullied reputation, a patriot and lover of his country, a figure of high tragedy, a political failure whose career at its apogee was abruptly terminated by his murder, a 'martyr', a poet of outstanding quality, one who inspired personal affection even in his political opponents.

One of the first leaders of the Yemeni Liberals (al-Aḥrār), Zubayrī was also a political pamphleteer, and if the Liberals were not very effective in the sphere of practical politics, their writings played their part in formulating the outlook of the generation discontent with Imāmic rule. Ṣawt al-'Arab and other organs of the massive Nasserite propaganda machine utilised the Liberal leaders or discarded them in accordance with current Nasserite policy.

Zubayrī's *The Imāmate and its menace to Yemen unity*, written about twenty years ago, has an historic interest as formulating and embodying views current in Yemeni Liberal circles in Cairo, Beirut and elsewhere. That the pamphlet is controversial, often even factually incorrect, does not detract from its importance as an expression of the attitudes of the Aḥrār in the hot-house political climate of the Nasserite era.

When staying in Beirut in the summer of 1969 I had the opportunity of discussing Zubayrī's pamphlet both with his life-long friend and closest associate, the veteran politician Aḥmad Nu'mān, and my friend H. E. Sayyid Aḥmad al-Shāmī then still Foreign Minister to the Imām al-Badr but at one time associated with the Aḥrār when they first set up in Aden. I am further indebted to H. E. Ḥusayn al-'Amrī, son of Imām Yaḥyā's *wazīr*, Qāḍī 'Abdullāh, murdered with him in 1948, for comment of clarification on individual points, but he is in no sense responsible for views expressed here.

Muḥammad Maḥmūd al-Zubayrī: perhaps the happiest of all the photographs of him. It was taken in the Yemen and shows him in serene and reflective mood.

Top left, Zubayrī photographed in Aden in 1946 when he was a leader of the Yemenite Liberals with his friend 'al-Ustādh' Aḥmad Nu'mān. Top right, Zubayrī in Cairo during the eventful days of September 1962. Above, 'If only al-Zubayrī were with us now to see what has been accomplished!' Reading from left to right we see 'Agriculture, justice, roads, University, projects, factories' (cartoon from special number of *Al-Thawrah* commemorating al-Zubayrī, 14 Rabī' II, 1397/3.iv.1977).

Politico-Economic background

After World War I, Imām Yaḥyā al-Mutawakkil 'ala 'llāh of the Ḥamīd al-Dīn virtually re-conquered a large part of what now constitutes the Yemen Arab Republic. He clashed with the British on certain areas of the Aden Protectorate over which Britain re-asserted its influence, under already existing treaties, with the willing co-operation of the tribes who preferred *de facto* independence to the paying of taxes to a centralised government in Ṣan'ā'. Most of the Protectorate tribal districts were held for only brief periods by the Zaydī Imāms. The sultans or chiefs had expelled Zaydī garrisons long before the arrival of the British. Yet the Ḥamīd al-Dīn never admitted the British suzerainty over the Protectorates. Had the British, on the other hand, cared to press a forward policy after World War I they might have brought much of the Shāfi'ī south of the Yemen into Protectorate status—but this was emphatically not a British interest. Up to the young officer coup in Ṣan'ā' of 1962, a *modus vivendi* prevailed to the advantage of both sides of the border.

Imām Yaḥyā had headed the movement to liberate the Yemen from the Ottoman Turks. He was greatly respected in the Yemen, and Yemenis, especially the Shāfi'īs, rightly in my view, blamed the corruption of his officials for the various injustices they suffered. Yaḥyā hoarded silver bullion, perhaps as a reserve war-chest against emergencies, and he was excessively parsimonious in Government expenditure. While the Imāmate preserved security and ruled and observed the law—for which it is still praised today—there was criticism of Government shortcomings in the essentially moderate manifesto issued by the Yemeni Liberals in Yaḥyā's latter years.

Yaḥyā attempted to keep the Yemen in isolation. He tried to prevent the Arabic press from entering the country, and he disapproved of even such moderate Egyptian reformers as Muḥammad 'Abduh whom he considered 'contemporary' (*'aṣrī)* which for him meant 'bad'! However, with such numbers of Shāfi'ī Yemenis going from the southern districts to Aden for employment, but returning periodically to their villages, this was clearly an impossibility, for they contrasted conditions there, especially later, in the heyday of Aden's prosperity, with the backward state of their own country. On the intellectual level the disgruntled among the leading administrative families and those educated on traditional Islamic lines, especially those who went on to the Azhar at Cairo, grew increasingly critical of Yaḥyā's rule while meeting no response from him. In 1944 al-Zubayrī, a Zaydī of the Qāḍī class, and Aḥmad Nu'mān of a leading Shāfi'ī family of am-Turbah fled to Aden where they opened a campaign for political reform in the Yemen.

In 1948 Imām Yaḥyā was murdered by a notorious tribal malcontent just south of Ṣan'ā', instigated by a group of conspirators in Ṣan'ā', and the well-known Sayyid 'Abdullāh al-Wazīr was proclaimed Imām there. Crown Prince Aḥmad however managed to raise the Zaydī tribes and crush the rebellion within a matter of weeks, but the tribal sack of Ṣan'ā' left bitter memories. The rebellion was purely a bid for power in which the Liberals in Aden had little or no part and in fact the murder of the Imām made them extremely unpopular with Yemenis in Aden. Aḥmad became Imām assuming the title of al-Nāṣir li-Dīn Allāh. He ruled on traditional lines until his death from natural causes in 1962, though he had to put down two serious attempts on his life.

Yaḥyā and Aḥmad were outstanding personalities firmly handling a naturally turbulent country. The immense volume of propaganda against them has not only obscured their virtues while magnifying their faults, but takes no account of the problems which confronted them; little attempt has been made to assess their successes and failures objectively.

The external policy of the Ḥamīd al-Dīn is relatively well understood, but the internal political situation is very little known.

The Imāms were backed by the Zaydī tribes of the north but had at first no standing army. When a tribe got out of hand it could be brought to heel only by setting other tribes against it. Imām Yaḥyā, with mainly Turkish officers, developed a standing army, but the fateful military mission he despatched to Iraq before World War II produced young officers imbued with subversive sentiments and an Iraqi officer was brought to Ṣan'ā'—described to me as 'the dynamo' of the 1948 Wazīr revolt. A second (educational) mission sent by Yaḥyā to Lebanon, but diverted after his murder to Cairo by Imām Aḥmad, contained 'Abdullāh Juzaylān[1] and others who were to become 'the Officers of the Revolution' (i.e. the military coup of 1962) or officials of the Republic. The army might form a counter-balance to the armed Zaydī tribes but was ineffectual in defence against the Sa'ūdīs in 1934 and for action against the British Protectorates. The leading Sayyid houses, men of both sword and pen, regarded the mere *'askarī* with some contempt—Imām Aḥmad himself used to speak slightingly of Bimbāshī (Major) Jamāl al-Dīn 'Abd al-Nāṣir (Nasser),[2] not to be rated on same level as the Shaykh of the Azhar! Whether by design or through circumstance, the army was maintained at a fairly low level. None of this was to the taste of the young officers trained abroad. Aḥmad's severe measures against recalcitrant tribes engendered grievances against the Ḥamīd al-Dīn in certain tribal leaders. An impression of the times and Aḥmad's tough personality can be formed from the verses exchanged with the notable Khawlānī chief Nājī b. 'Alī al-Ghādir at the time of the unrest in Khawlān when Nājī was parleying with the most outstanding of the Protectorate chiefs, Sharīf Ḥusayn of Bayḥān—this Aḥmad suspected of being aimed against himself. Alluding to the executions of political rebels, Nājī says:[3]

Say I—'Izrā'īl stops in your days, to forego
Dealing out life and death; for him you have outdone.
Extravagently I speak, you say. Tis not so!
By other swords than yours has there died then anyone?

To which Aḥmad makes riposte:

He who's off to Bayḥān no honour has, to trust.
How were [the Sharīf's] terms when *qāt* you chewed, apart?
Bāhūt, the Terrible, confronts you, judging, just!
From the rebellious he plucks out lungs and heart!

Some prominent Sayyid houses, notably those that had provided Imāms in earlier times, would enter into intrigues with tribes and chiefs against the Ḥamīd al-Dīn, so the dynasty has to be on its guard against the possibility of troubles from this quarter also.

The north, especially the Mashriq, required an outlet for the surplus population of a hard country. So to provide a livelihood for their northern Zaydī tribes whose support was essential to them, the Imāms would despatch tribal contingents to the Shāfi'ī districts where they acted as a sort of gendarmerie in support of the Imām's administrative officials. Officials were drawn from the Sayyid and Qāḍī classes. It is alleged that the Qāḍīs felt a sense of grievance against the Sayyids[4]—about this I am dubious, and it may be that political theorists have imposed this facile concept of class rivalry, without adequate justification, on the relationship between the two groups.

Broadly speaking, the tribal Zaydī north was governed by indirect rule with subsidies provided for the chiefs. The Shāfi'ī south was less fortunate in being under direct rule by government officials working in concert with local headmen.

Economically the Yemen was largely self-sufficient in the twenties and possibly the early thirties. The expanding population of the Shāfi'ī districts found good employment in Aden—with a notable rise in wages commencing from the building of the B.P. refinery onwards. In pursuit of higher wages a great exodus of labour to Aden and other countries followed. Propagandists blamed this movement on the Imāms, but a parallel movement had taken place earlier, from Ḥaḍramawt to Sa'ūdī Arabia, to take advantage of the economic opportunity afforded by the exploitation of oil wealth, despite the vigorous aid given to agricultural development by the benevolent British protecting power. During the last two or three years, emigration to Sa'ūdī Arabia from the Yemen Arab Republic is on a scale that menaces agriculture everywhere.[5]

The Imāms drew their revenues mostly from the tithes (*'ushūr*) on crops and the customs duties (*mukūs*), the latter regarded by strictly orthodox *'ulamā'* as breaking Islamic law—so it was essential to collect the full revenue from agriculture. By contrast today only a small part of the revenue of the Republic consists of the tithes on crops, and so the Government can afford to let the *zakāt*, as it is called, be used in part for purely local projects. Under the Imāms many Yemenis lived at subsistence level but the country was independant—today it is economically dependant on other Arab states, mainly Sa'ūdī Arabia, and therefore politically dependant also, with a fantastically high proportion of its menfolk working outside the country—but living standards in general have vastly improved.

It must be obvious that the Yemen lacked the capital to embark on major development projects like the Ṣan'ā'-Hodeidah road, quite apart from possessing none of the technical skills required. Nevertheless from my own experience I can say that the Imāms did pay some attention to building roads and to agricultural development, even if the latter was only for their personal advantage. Of course their modest efforts cannot compare with the major projects of today mainly financed by gifts of foreign capital.

Zubayrī however belongs to the era of the Imāms and is concerned with attacking the existing political situation while economics mean little to him. Today already he appears as belonging to a far by-gone-age.

Biography

Of Zubayrī's career, on which I intend to publish an account, a few relevant details are necessary. Appointed a government official about 1937, in the district (*qaḍā'*) of al-Qa'āmirah with its capital Māwiyah about 50 km. east of Ta'izz, near the Aden Protectorate frontier, he was so disquieted by the unjust practices of officials that he left and went to Egypt in 1357/1938-9, accompanying Sayyid 'Abdullāh b. 'Alī al-Wazīr with whom his father had been a close friend. 'Abdullāh al-Wazīr had looked after Zubayrī when his father died. In Cairo he attached himself to Dār al-'Ulūm as an auditor (*tilmīdh mustami'*) and in the same role he also attended lectures at Fu'ād I University, because of course he possessed no university entrance qualifications. He is said to have returned to the Yemen in 1360/1941 during World War II, and, according to one writer, only to find conditions there worse!

In 1944, as has been seen, he, Aḥmad Nu'mān and Sayyid Zayd b. 'Alī al-Mawshakī (the *nisbah* is to Mawshak, a village outside Dhamār) fled to Aden where they set up a branch of the Liberal Party and ran a newspaper. Zubayrī was on a mission to Sa'ūdī Arabia when the 'Abdullāh al-Wazīr revolt of 1948 was quelled and so escaped imprisonment in Ḥajjah. He spent some years in Pakistan, but went to Egypt after Faruq's deposition and embarked on his long political campaign against the régime in the Yemen. He published polemics in verse, notably *Thawrat al-shi'r* (The Revolution of Poetry, Cairo, 1382/1962) just before the officer coup in Ṣan'ā', and also in prose. An enthusiast at first for the 'Revolution', he soon became disillusioned[6] and, trying to form a break-away party, he was murdered at Rajūzah/Arjūzah of Jabal Baraṭ in 1965. A verse composed in his despair shortly before his death is frequently quoted:

Baḥathtu 'an hibat-in aḥbū-ka yā waṭanī
Fa-lam ajid laka illā qalbiya 'l-dāmī.
Country mine, a gift to give you I sought
Save my heart, bleeding for you, I found nought.

In the spring of 1977 I attended the festival (*mihrajān*) of Zubayrī at Ṣan'ā' University—perhaps it was a sort of triumph.[7]

Anti-Sayyid propaganda: the 'Adnān versus Qaḥṭān motive: Aḥmad al-Shāmī's counter-blasts

Sayyid Aḥmad al-Shāmī who was appointed Yemeni Mutawakkilite Ambassador in London by Imām Aḥmad in 1961, and, after the officer coup in Ṣan'ā' on September 26th, 1962, became Royalist Foreign Minister, a poet and writer, pokes sly fun at the Yemeni Liberal (al-Aḥrār) intellectuals who made the onslaught on the Hāshimites and developed the theme of antagonism in the Yemen between 'Adnān and Qaḥṭān.[8] 'Adnān is the eponymous ancestor of the northern Arabs and *ergo* of the Yemeni Hāshimites/'Alawīs /Sayyids, while Qaḥṭān is the eponym of the southern Arabs. 'In this present age of ours,' he says,[9] 'some men of letters, such as the author Aḥmad b. 'Abd al-Raḥmān al-Mu'allimī[10] and Mr Muḥammad Aḥmad Nu'mān and their followers have attempted to stir up the subject of Qaḥṭānism and 'Adnānism and revive ethnic and sectarian chauvinism, but their propaganda would have won no acceptance but for the "Army action", then the interference with fire and sword on the part of the "Egyptians", on the 26th September, 1962.' Both al-Mu'allimī and Zubayrī, al-Shāmī told me with a naughty chuckle, are 'Adnānī by descent, the Zubayrī family claiming descent from al-Zubayr b. al-'Awwām, a Companion of the Prophet! He also alludes to the scurrilous anti-Hāshimite propaganda of 'Abd al-Raḥmān al-Bayḍānī on the radio, later reproduced in book form![11] Al-Bayḍānī's allegations against Imām Aḥmad which, or so I am told, used to arouse him to fury, are without substantiation—plainly lying invention. Moreover he had been expelled from the Liberals led by al-Zubayrī and the 'Ustādh' 'Aḥmad Nu'mān in Cairo. Though he takes up the anti-Hāshimite ideas of the Liberals about this time, he does not represent them in any way. Indeed 'Abdullāh Juzaylān who directed the officer attack on al-Badr's mansion, Dār al-Bashā'ir, says[12] that 'Dr' 'Abd al-Raḥmān al-Bayḍānī broadcasting from Ṣawt al-'Arab, 'attacked the Hāshimites violently without any justification, not realising that nearly 80 per cent of the officers of the revolution were Hāshimites (as also were a large number in the prisons) as a punishment for their open disobedience and revolt against the Ḥamīd al-Dīn family ruling in Ṣan'ā'.' Juzaylān got in touch with Muḥammad 'Abd al-Wāḥid of the Egyptian Embassy informing him of the highly unfavourable reactions produced by 'Dr' Bayḍānī's 'ignorance of Yemeni society', and Cairo put a stop to his talks.

Zubayrī, though he had a background of the traditional Zaydī learning before going to Cairo, was clearly a poet and in no sense an objective scholarly historian. Insofar as can be judged he was unacquainted with western scholarship, and it is likely that he did not even read very widely. At the time he wrote his attack on the Imāmate he was spokesman of the Yemeni Union (al-Ittiḥād al-Yamanī) in Cairo. Though a good speaker, honest and sincere, regarded with affection and respect, his argument in the pamphlet translated here could, without difficulty, be demolished by the highly intelligent aristocratic *'ulamā'* of the Zaydi Sayyids or Qāḍīs. Since the nominal unity between Egypt and the Yemen, into which Imām Aḥmad had adroitly inveigled Nasser, their agreement had resulted in Nasser's muzzling the Yemeni Liberals in Cairo—so the pamphlet had to be published in Beirut—naturally the Liberals were turned on again when Imām Aḥmad's celebrated anti-'nationalisation' poem brought about the break with Nasser.

Nu'mān *père* ('al-Ustādh' Aḥmad Nu'mān) said that, from the point of view of the Yemeni Liberals, the great advantage of Zubayrī's pamphlet attacking the Imāmate was that it should have been written by a Zaydī and not by a Shāfi'ī like himself. Zubayrī in turn was to influence a much younger man, Muḥsin al-'Aynī (later to become a Premier in Republican Yemen), especially by the views expounded in his *al-Khud'at al-kubrā*[13] where Zubayrī advances the proposition that the populace (*sha'b*) must have sovereignty in the Yemen as the cure for the country's ills. 'In saying this I do not invite the elimination of the Mutawakkilī ruler but I do invite elimination of his divine will which persists in enslaving the populace, negating its humanity and denying its rights, as also it refuses that it should have a government representing it and expressing its will [*irādah*].' These remarks have about them the ring of our own 17th-century attack on the theory of divine right and are with other expressions in fact not part of the native Yemeni vocabulary but are derived from the West.

Muḥsin al-'Aynī, drawn from a different social class from that of Zubayrī, a product of the Orphan School at Ṣan'ā' and a Ba'thist, writing about 1957 speaks in more moderate tones.[14] We want a ruler, he says, who derives his power from us—We the Tribes. (Muḥsin is of tribal descent, it is said of Banī Bahlūl.) We want a ruler stripped of his holiness—we want a ruler called Mus'id, Ṣāliḥ, Sa'īd, 'Alī, Muḥammad, just like you, me and other people. We have tried these (Imāmic titles) al-Mutawakkil 'ala 'llāh, al-Hādī ila 'l-Ḥaqq for 1,096 years, and the result is plain to see. I direct these words to the Sayyids first of all, and say that we are not against the Sayyids as a group among the people, but we do not want the ruler to be a ruler because he is a Sayyid. There is no reason why a Sayyid should not govern the Yemen, but because he is a man, because he is competent, because he is one of the people. Muḥsin points out, that in Cairo, Sayyids do not differentiate between themselves and others. Some Sayyids with whom he has discussed the Yemen have a liberal outlook and attribute the state of affairs there to a ruler who justifies his evil actions behind the names of God! He avers that he is not attacking the Sayyids as such, nor are all the Sayyids to blame for the current situation and the privileges they enjoy. 'On the contrary you tribes and men of the Yemen are those who diligently sought out the Sayyid, looking everywhere for him, according him the place of honour at your meetings, urging him to idleness and seeking good fortune (*barakāt*) through him'. You made the Sayyids a special class, he says, neither cultivating nor labouring, but ruling, judging and living by your efforts. (In point of fact this is not quite true for, in Shahārah, I photographed Sayyids with little picks going to work in their fields) There should be no Zaydism and Shāfi'īsm, no Hāshimism and Qaḥṭānism, no tribes- and towns-men, no turbans and caps, no Tihāmah and Mountain folk, no tribes and peasants (*ra'āyā*), but only Yemenis!

There is much more in similar vein, some coming near to repeating Zubayrī's tract verbatim.

Muḥammad Nu'mān (*fils*) is credited with the development of the 'Adnān-Qaḥṭān rivalry as a pressing political question. It was later to be taken up by 'Abdullāh al-Sallāl. Sayyid Aḥmad al-Shāmī asks with mischievous innocence why the Hāshimite House should be considered foreigners in the Yemen when they have been there for 1,100 years, for the Iryānīs for example would not be called foreigners because they came from Iraq 300 years ago! In the preface to his poem *Dāmighat al-Dawāmigh*[15] Aḥmad al-Shāmī makes a well documented refutation of the attack on the 'Alawīs citing the relevant historical sources and concluding with verses from Zubayrī himself whose inconsistent attitude he underlines.

> *Wa-Banū Hāshim-in 'urūq-un karīmat-un lanā min judhūr-in Ya'rubiyyah.*
> Banū Hāshim are noble stocks belonging to us, from our Ya'rubī roots.

In another counter-attack *The myth of Arabia Felix*[16] which he dedicates 'to those who have distorted/defamed the history of the Imāmate in the Yemen', al-Shāmī points out that, in the major physical or political disasters that have afflicted the Yemen, no Imāms were involved, and he alludes to those who recently have been writing on Hāshimīs and Qaḥṭānīs, and *al-Aṭrāf al-ma'niyyah,* Muḥammad Nu'mān's well-known booklet.[17]

In fact Yemeni literature seems devoid of the anti-Hāshimite motive after the days of Hamdānī and the 6th/12th century Nashwān b. Sa'īd,[18] until pamphlets (*manshūrāt*) on this topic began to appear in the early 1940s. It is said that the sons of Imām Yaḥyā, of whom there were fourteen, were opposed to the Qāḍī class, presumably because of rivalry arising from the appointment of the princes to high government office, and it is implied that this may have given rise, in part at least, to anti-Hāshimite propaganda. Imām Aḥmad however, in his day, made no distinction in this respect between Sayyids and Qāḍīs.

The Nasser regime in Egypt, in its hostility to the Hāshimites and monarchies, against which it campaigned so assiduously, was more than sympathetic to the anti-Imāmic line developed by the Liberals. The context of Zubayrī's polemic is, nevertheless, wholly Yemeni and he did not want the Yemen to rely on any external power—including Egypt—this was the major point of difference with the Egyptian agent al-Bayḍānī.

Many Americans seem to have been susceptible to propaganda prejudicial to the Sayyids. A Foreign Service officer[19] displays this bias markedly in speaking of a dole issued to some Sayyids by the Imām on which they lived, averring of Sayyids in general that 'seldom were they known to engage in gainful activity other than as officials of the Imāmate'. Quite on the contrary, numbers of Sayyids in Ṣan'ā' are engaged in business and even in the manual crafts. In exploring this alleged 'dole' with informed Yemenis the following statements emerged. In Yaḥyā's time a *Daftar al-Ṣadaqah*, also called *Dār al-I'āshāt*, was set up in Ṣan'ā' near al-'Urḍī, the Barracks, which provided needy persons with two baps (*kidmah*) of bread a day, and two *riyāls* per month. It was maintained by the Bayt al-Māl, the Treasury. Many persons had monthly stipends (*murattabāt*), Sayyids, Qāḍīs, and others even if not officials—in some cases at least these seem to have been supporters of Imām Yaḥyā before the departure of the Turks. These came from the Bayt al-Māl or al-Khizānat al-'Āmmah. From the time of Yaḥyā the revenues, whether *zakāt*, aid (*musā'adāt*), *jizyah* (poll-tax on non-Muslims) or other taxes had become mixed together in the Bayt al-Māl, but no distinction was made in stipends (*ma'āshāt*) and gifts from it made by the Imām, between a Sayyid or a member of any other class. M. Wenner's[20] assertion that a worth while result of the 1962 coup was that 'it eliminated most of the influence and power of the Sayyid class, probably the largest stumbling block to reform in the past' is an unwarranted aspersion on a class that produced numbers of able men, whether as administrators, scholars or others. These dicta reveal a fundamental lack of understanding of Yemeni society.

Aḥmad al-Shāmī had commenced on a counterblast to Zubayrī's tract but had abandoned work on it and, in Beirut in 1969, permitted me to copy from his draft.

He points out that the Imāmate is not 'a sectarian factional concept' (cf. para. 4 a *infra*) of the Zaydīs but every Muslim saw it was essential to choose the Imām so as to have a source of reference (*marja'*) and reliance (*amīn*)—on this Shāfi'īs, Zaydīs and all other schools concur, even if they differ as to persons and methods of selection. He avers that Shāfi'īs believe in loyalty and absolute obedience to the Imām more than the Zaydīs. He is unaware of any 'tenets, religious rites, and sectarian laws' (para. 4b) the Imāmate imposes on the Shāfi'īs. He does not deny there have been individual Imāms who have ruled unjustly and acted wrongfully or tyranically like (secular) monarchs, but this is no more the fault of the Imāmate as an institution than a criminal's actions are the fault of the *sharī'ah*.

He justly refutes Zubayrī's absurd assertion (para. 4d) that the Imāmate divided the Yemeni populace into two sections, and points out how it united the country (*waḥḥad kalimat al-sha'b*) against the Mamlūks and Ottomans. He agrees that the Lower Yemen has suffered great injustice and been subjected to armed force (para. 4d) but this is not the fault of the institution of the Imāmate, and the (Zaydī) northern districts in Rasūlid times suffered from their raids.

Zubayrī deceives himself (paras 7e and 7f) and the truth in considering that 'opening the gate of independent judgement' was a trick to introduce the Fifth School. He counsels Zubayrī to consider matters from a scholarly level, to stick to facts, and not to deceive himself. 'Individuals do not endure for ever, nor do families, but the principle endures and circulates with generations (*ajyāl*).'[21]

Translation of al-Zubayrī's attack on the Imāmate

The Yemeni Union
The Committee for Education and Publication[22]

The Imāmate
and its menace to Yemeni Unity

Muḥammad Maḥmūd al-Zubayrī[23]

[3]

1. *In the cause of popular sovereignty and national unity*

(*a*) Today the Yemen is passing through a critical phase of its political history, for political tendencies are contending there with each-other, swaying its future hither and thither in violent fashion.

(*b*) The strongest of the political tendencies in respect of reaction and aggression against the populace[24] is the tendency of that front working to buttress up the Imāmate, adopting the Sayf al-Ḥasan[25] as its leader, spokesman and candidate for the Imāmate in the future.

(*c*) The Yemeni Liberals who have raised the slogan of national unity and popular sovereignty, herein declare their frank opinion on the issue of the Imāmate, so that the Arab populace in the Yemen may become aware of the reality of the unexpected perils lurking in wait for its future behind an administration headed by that doyen of reaction in the Yemen, Sayf al-Islām al-Ḥasan.

(*d*) For this very reason the Committee for Education and Publication of the Yemeni Union presents this comprehensive study on the disastrous[26] Imāmate through which the Yemen has suffered for about a thousand years. The issuing of this treatise is by way of participation only in this battle and to illumine the path, the path of the fighters throughout the whole of the Yemen.

Victory must come.
The country is above all.
Rule belongs to the populace only.

The Committee for Education and Publication

[4]
2. *Popular sovereignty*

(*a*) We wish to liberate our life from every one of the sorts of bondage. political servitude as represented in Colonialism coming to us from without, Despotic rule from within which grips us by the throat, and spiritual bondage as it manifests itself in the false and oppressive prejudices, under the burden of which the spirit of the populace collapses, under which the humanity of the masses is trampled into powder, and because of which the wheel of history and laws of evolution stall, and which, leaving that aside, contain (factors) That threaten to tear the populace apart and shatter its unity, and social bondage concealed within certain of the reactionary traditional usages and discriminatory barriers which[27] differentiate between the classes and groups of the populace in a way that is based on no foundation either of logic or justice.

(*b*) We have already defined how we stand in the sphere of political and social emancipation in publishing our many lectures and declarations opposed to Colonialism, then, *The demands of the populace,*[28] and *The objectives of the Liberals*, and, as time goes on, we shall define our position in other spheres and through various media.

[5]
3. *National unity*

(*a*) The Yemen is a small part of the great Arab home-land, but Colonialism has insisted on partitioning it into two main segments ... the occupied segment, i.e. what is called Aden and the Eastern and Western Protectorates,[29] and the independent segment, i.e. what is called the Mutawakkilite Kingdom.

(*b*) Colonialism has moreover insisted upon dividing what may not be divided,[30] i.e. the segment held under duress, for it has made out of it an unending chain of emirates, sultanates, and shaykhdoms,[31] as too, Despotism, in the ages of darkness and ignorance, has insisted on preposterous fission between the inhabitants of the independent segment, cherishing, through its iniquitous measures, the sectarian and regional division, and discriminating in its dealings between what it calls a Shāfiʿī segment and what it calls a Zaydī segment. It further discriminates between the regional and tribal segments, and between the towns and villages, and it advances him whose spirit glories in descent and family.[32]

(*c*) This, Colonialism and Despotism have done in concert, in order that facility may be accorded the diabolical principle of 'Divide and rule' to tear apart the unity of the populace, and prevent it from uniting *en bloc* against existing circumstances, but the unjust reactionary pacts[33] have failed to a great extent, faced by the awareness, firmness, and temperament of the populace. This is because profound patriotic sentiment and the innate sense of unity[34] are of such stubbornly unbending force that they cannot be smashed into fragments by mere personal pacts between rulers [6] and colonisers that are no more than scraps of paper.

(*d*) Moreover the discontent which is shared by and pervades all classes in the independent part, and is widespread throughout every district, every tribe, town and village, was and remains stronger than all the stratagems to rend asunder and separate. On the contrary indeed it has created a sanctified bond of suffering and has given a unity to the aims, sentiments, and struggle of the populace, more especially once the Liberals assumed the task of propaganda on behalf of popular unity, and drew the attention of the sons of the populace to the diabolical plot[35] which Tyranny and Colonialism are engineering against their national patriotic entity.

(*e*) Local Yemeni unity—we mean by this only that it should be strengthened and pervade all parts of the independent segment as between each other, and that it should be effected in the parts of the occupied segment held under duress, but with the provision that a joint struggle of the sons of the populace in both segments should rise up against Colonialism, Despotism, and partition, to prepare the way for complete political unity between the two principal parts ... although unification between them will not be completed until after liberation from Colonialism.

[7]

4. *The menace of the Imāmate to national unity*

(*a*) From its foundation the Imāmate has been basically a sectarian factional concept, embraced by a half[36] of the sons of the populace from ancient time, namely the Zaydiyyah, the inhabitants of the Upper Yemen only.

(*b*) As for the majority of the populace in the Lower Yemen, Tihāmah, and the whole of the Occupied Yemen, they do not profess adhesion to this Imāmate, nor do they consider it has any right to dominate over them. On the contrary they see in it an authority imposed upon them both politically and spiritually. This Imāmate does not stop at the limits of its political authority but imposes tenets, religious rites[37] and sectarian laws on half of the populace, incompatible with the sect to which it adheres.

(*d*) It is of the nature of this arbitrary rule that it leaves a bitter feeling in the majority of the populace, turning the division into a dark and fearful shadow which envelops the country and perpetually threatens its progress —so too, it makes the Imāmic government in the eyes of this segment like a government alien to it which expresses neither its own will nor its own creed. Even worse than this is that it considers it (the Imāmic government) as a government particular to the Upper Yemen only, as if the inhabitants of the Upper Yemen as a whole constitute a ruling stratum of society maintaining for itself a monopoly of rule, and making a mere *lebensraum* for itself of the Lower Yemen. So it is—while the inhabitants of the Upper Yemen themselves are untouched by this false invention[38] and injustice. Yet, on the contrary, they (the inhabitants of the Upper Yemen) have remained longest in endurance of the bitterness of Imāmic tyranny, and they see [8] in it a rule which has intruded[39] upon them, alien to their life, imposing on them, alongside political authority, spiritual authority which lives in their blood[40] like a terrifying nightmare, stunting their Arabism (*'Urūbah*) and their humanity,[41] isolating them in a darkness of ignorance, deprivation, and starvation,[42] making them swallow the poisonous Imāmic doctrines, then looses them on the other section of their fellow countrymen like rabid wolves.[43]

In this fashion the Imāmate has succeeded in sorting out the populace into two different sections in each of which lies an instrument for one of its objectives. If the Lower Yemeni segment has much to endure in the way of robbery and coercion by armed force, the Upper segment imbibes the spiritual poisons that compel its sons to blind obedience to the Imām without discussion or reckoning and without expectation of reward. When the sky rains one is told, 'These are the Imām's blessings.' When it is a year of dearth one is told, 'This is through an invocation by the Imām against the recalcitrant rebels.'[44] The *zakāt*[45] is given only to the Imām, and certain prayers[46] are only effective if the Imām be present. Prosperity[47] arrives and it is through the grace of the Imām; poverty, misery and death come down and the miserable murdered wretches are transferred to the Imām's pomegranates, grapes and delights in Paradise![48]

One of the terrible Imāmic famines descended on Ṣan'ā', and after eating cats and dogs most of its people died though the Government magazines were full of grain, and people went to ask the Imām Yaḥyā for relief, but he made a contemptuous face at them and delivered his famous maxim, 'He who dies is a martyr—he who lives is delivered.'[49]

The personality of the Yemenis was crushed beneath the shade[50] of the Imāmate, [9] the leadership of their country was prohibited them—even to contemplate it became a crime, at the same time religious and political. Yemeni history was distorted, so that we began to read therein nothing but the names of the saints,[51] the gods of Imāms, their adherents,[52] and partisans.[53] As for the personalities of the populace, no sooner did any hero of their raise his head to renown and honour, but the 'Pure' Imāms would make haste to despatch him accompanied by their curses, to his grave. Then they would allude to him in history only as the oppressor, the enemy of God, the profligate heretic, the denier of the interpretation,[54] as well as other epithets beside these.

In this fashion the operation of crushing the Arabism[55] of the Yemen, its popular personalities, and its struggling revolutions carried on continuously for more than a thousand years.

[10]

5. *Authority[56] derived from Heaven*

No kings and despots on earth throughout history can ascend their thrones without relying on some structure of tribal solidarity or class feeling[57] which they acquire from among their people, making them partners in their gains, and with whom they are obliged to ingratiate themselves through various kinds of favours and reform,[58] even in the darkest eras of history—except the Imāms of the Yemen, for they felt the need of nothing of this sort, but managed to convince the populace that no reward should be expected in return for their support and service, their slogan handed down by tradition being:

'Whosoever loves us, the People of the House (Ahl al-Bayt), let him make ready a cloak against tribulation.'[59]

It is sufficient for one of them to ascend the throne that he should then say to the people: God it was who appointed him ruler. God it was who commanded the people to obey, serve, and revere him, endure and die for the sake of supporting him. His authority is not derived from the populace, nor through the favour of the populace. On the contrary, it is a privilege bestowed by Heaven. He is God's shadow, God's Vicegerent and Caliph.

[11]

6. *The function of the Imām*

In accordance with this psychology[60] the Imām applies himself to the burdens of his office, but these burdens are virtually confined to confiscating the wealth of the populace in the name of the *zakāt*-tax,[61] the suppression of popular tremors in the name of the Holy War,[62] to doing battle with oppressors, and then, to the building of a mosque with the name of the Imām, to the vicinity of which generally is adjoined the dome of this Imām's tomb,[63] to prolong his spiritual influence even when he is in the grave, then to (bequeathing) a generous legacy[64] of land which he leaves to his sons and his grandsons, after stealing it from the populace by any sort of means.

As for the chief message the Imām takes upon himself (to deliver) it is the propagation of the spirit of asceticism, abandoning building a thriving life, along with finding fault in any inclination towards building and construction, apart from Imāmic castles, mosques, and domes of tombs.[65]

Here lies the magic key to the secret locked up in the history of the Yemen for over a thousand years, this era of rigid paralysis. When the human race was still in its cradle, the Yemen had a civilisation, a culture and diverse arts of living, the most important of which were the arts of architecture and engineering of the dams without which the Yemen cannot live, but these long Imāmic era have gone by without a single dam remaining in the whole of Yemen, whereas the barbarous colonising Abyssinians, who stayed no longer than seventy years in the Yemen in the remotest dark ages, [12] were inspired by the natural circumstances of the Yemen and its agricultural requirements to renew the structure of the Dam in Ma'rib after its collapse.

The other preoccupation of any Imām is to consolidate his spiritual position among the tribes under the pretext of belonging to the party of the People of the House, so that it becomes firmly established in the mentality of the populace in the Upper segment ... that the Imām is the shadow of God, his Vicegerent by right, and his standing like that of the Apostle of God,[66] God bless and honour him, whose relation with the people and whose position with regard to them is ordained by Divine legislation in this holy verse:

'It is not for a believing man or a believing woman to have a choice in their affair when God and His Apostle have decided an affair.'[67]

All that comes down concerning obedience to God and His Apostle applies also to the Imām because he is God's Vicegerent and Caliph.

These spiritual teachings are combined in the Upper segment of the Yemen with factional[68] attacks against what they call 'Deniers of Interpretation'[69] who do not hold with the Imāmic doctrine—the majority of the populace.[70] This is to justify the violent plundering[71] forays which inevitably every Imām despatches against the cultivators, the peaceful sons of the populace in the Lower Yemen and Tihāmah.

[13]

7. *The Imāmate and the propagation of learning*

The Yemen, in truth, even under the auspices[72] of the Imāms, was profuse in activity on an extensive scale in (the sphere of) learning, the door of independent judgement (*ijtihād*)[73] was open, the mosques crowded with scholars (*'ulamā'*) and pupils, and production in the field of (literary) composition used to excite astonishment and admiration.[74]

The underlying reason for this is that the Yemeni populace possesses an ancient heritage of civilisation, and inclines by its nature towards learning and knowledge, in quest of which it roves to the remotest parts of the earth. Added to this inclination is the fact that the door of independent judgement (*ijtihād*) lies open, and that the stipulations[75] for the Chosen Imām are that he should have attained the degree of independent judgement (*ijtihād*), for pre-eminence in this freedom with regard to learning is the foundation upon which the Imāmate is essentially based. The Imāms would not have had the right to the development of an entity distinct from the authority of the Islamic Caliphate had they not been able to demolish the traditional framework[76] that used to encompass the populaces of the Arab Islamic Caliphate.

The obstinate rigid notion holding that the Islamic Schools have become restricted to the Four Schools had become spread abroad, and it had become difficult to conceive of creating another school except through a revolutionary venture.

Moreover, since the jurisprudence (*fiqh*), sciences of learning, and Schools of the four Imāms[77] had emerged under the auspices of the Umayyad and 'Abbāsid Caliphs only, and by the very nature [14] of the case the title to the Caliphate of the People of the House was ignored, it was inevitable that any ambitious person of the 'Alawīs wishing to avenge himself, or retaliate, or to found an 'Alawī state on a religious basis, should demand the return of the title to the Caliphate to the People of the House. Before anything else, any ambitious person of this sort must inevitably smash the iron moulds into which the Four Imāms had poured the fundamental bases (*uṣūl*) of jurisprudence (*fiqh*), legislation (*tashrī'*), and the fundamental Islamic principles, one and all, after which they had closed the door of independent judgement (*ijtihād*).

Hence sprang the revolutionary theory of the opening of the gate of independent judgement (*ijtihād*), so that the first Fifth School, namely the Hādī-ite[78] Zaydī School, might enter through it, and so that it would be feasible for him to force a political theory, which the other Imāms (of the four Schools) do not recognise, onto the fundamental principles (*uṣūl*) of the religion, namely that the Caliphate can lie in the 'Alawīs of the sons of Fāṭimah[79] only—as also it introduces a yet more dangerous politico-religious theory, namely the duty of revolting against the unjust.[80] This was so that it would be the easier for him to revolt against the Caliphs, and found a separate state from them and a Caliphate for the 'Alawīs of the People of the House.

Thus the chief aim of the oppressed but ambitious among the 'Alawīs was to revive the right of the 'Alawīs to the Caliphate. This aim it was which was first instrumental in opening the door of independent judgement (*ijtihād*), and which formulated the theory of revolt against the unjust, and then the theory of the aim itself, namely the exclusive right of the 'Alawīs to the Caliphate.[81]

[15]

8. *Freedom of independent judgement* (ijtihād)

(*a*) This is one of the politico-religious theories which the propagandists of the Imāms promulgated.

(*b*) Certainly these are splendid theories, but the real value they have, and the true balance against which history will weight its judgement in favour of these Imāms or against them, lies in the extent alone to which these theories share in practical application to real life.

(*c*) In the matter of independent judgement (*ijtihād*) it must be borne in mind that in fundamental (*uṣūlī*) questions it is prohibited, and therefore nobody has derived any advantage in the fields of controversy around the important issues of Islam. Nor has the propaganda of the Imāms been guiltless of disseminating the spirit of partisanship among the inhabitants of the Upper segment against those of the Lower segment, and among tribal circles against the town-dwellers, and of dubbing those who belong to such Islamic sects as the Ash'arīs,[82] 'Infidels of Interpretation', and of exploiting those theories for political and economic ends.

(*d*) Even in questions of jurisprudence (*fiqh*) possibly touching, closely or remotely, judicial or administrative affairs the opinion[83] of the Imām is what is imposed on the populace in North and South, and any independent judgement (*ijtihād*) running counter to the opinion of the Imām is (accorded) no value.[84] [16]

(*e*) All this apart, the effectiveness of the freedom of independent judgement (*ijtihād*) has, over the years, declined and diminished,[85] and a frightening reality has taken its place, namely that while a formal freedom, from the theoretical aspect only, does exist among the *'ulamā'*, the protagonists of Imāmic thought work in tribal circles, in a reverse direction, spreading the doctrine of sanctification and deification of the Imāmic office, and all that this basic doctrine comprises in the way of theories consequent upon it. All these serve the throne of the Imāms and fashion an ignorant popular partisan support for them out of the tribal element, eliminating any value attached to freedom of independent judgement (*ijtihād*), stifling the breath of the liberal *'ulamā'* and causing them to live throughout their lives under a sort of stranglehold, till, perchance, a moderate Imām who will try to encourage the liberal *'ulamā'* succeeds the partisan Imām. But the ruling class of factionaries[86] around him will manipulate the partisan warrior elements so as to divest the Imām of his might and power and impose the opinion it wishes.

(*f*) Yemeni history tells us that the very learned Sayyid Muḥammad b. Ismā'īl al-Amīr, born in 1099 H. (A.D. 1687-8), a leading personality of the liberal Hāshimite *'ulamā'*, exemplifying the high-minded struggle against the partisan Imāmic attitude, endured[87] numerous afflictions in the time of al-Mutawakkil 'ala 'llāh al-Qāsim b. al-Ḥusayn, then (in that of) al-Ḥusayn b. al-Qāsim and in the days of the Imām al-Mahdī al-'Abbās b. al-Ḥusayn.[88]

(*g*) Al-Manṣūr confided to him the office of preacher in the Great Jāmi '-Mosque of Ṣan'ā'.[89] Then he attempted to drop the mention of the Imāms at the (Friday) address. So the family of the Imām conspired with an alien person called al-Sayyid Yūsuf al-'Ajamī[90]—they conspired to murder Muḥammad b. Ismā'īl at the next Friday (prayer), but al-Manṣūr put them under detention, [17] subsequently expelling al-'Ajamī from the Yemen and releasing the others, but he did not permit al-Amīr (to deliver) the address after that. They had accused al-Amīr of 'hostility[91] to the People of the House', although he was one of them. This was because they were considering him presuming to (exercise) independent judgement in that which is contrary to the general (Zaydī) doctrine[92] in such matters as raising and clasping the hands in the prayer.[93]

(*g*) The very learned al-Shawkānī[94] is of the opinion that the culpability was not that of the people at large, 'for they follow any croaker'. If they are told, 'This is truth', they take sides for it.[95] If they are told, 'This is false', they take sides against it. The culpability is the culpability only of defective jurisprudence (*fiqh*) that accuses of unbelief (*kufr*) anyone wishing to be liberated, to exercise independent judgement (*ijtihād*) and hold independent views.[96]

(*i*) It is curious that the very learned al-Shawkānī, a most scholarly person of penetrating judgement (*ra'y*) considers this partisan attitude is not religious but, on the contrary, temporal, and that it assumes the veil of religion only. This is because a common contrived and hypocritical notion is wide-spread among people that defending and partisanship for the People of the House profits one for the most part, more especially if the partisan is so arrogant as to threaten those liberal *'ulamā'* whose minds entice them into exercising independent judgement on some matter, in opposition to the People of the House.[97]

(*j*) Al-Shawkānī said, It had happened that rumours had spread abroad against the very learned Muḥammad b. Ismā'īl al-Amīr to the effect that he was opposing the People of the House, and persons of ulterior motives disseminated these among some partisan milieux. So they rallied in revolt against the Imām because of his support of Muḥammad b. Ismā'īl al-Amīr. The Imām attempted to convince them but they would not be satisfied until he had assigned them 20,000 *riyāls* per annum.[98]

(*k*) Al-Shawkānī said, 'So they left off rebellion against the Imām since their sole object of desire[99] was (the goods of this) [18] world'.

(*l*) Al-Shawkānī goes on to say,[100] One of the tribulations of this world is that thousands of those partisans come into Ṣan'ā' and threaten anyone who reads the books of the *Sunnah*, but the culpability is not theirs—it is the culpability alone of those who instigate them.

(*m*) Al-Shawkānī then adduced the example of a tragic dissension[101] of this sort during which a bloody battle broke out between certain tribes and the townsfolk of Ṣan'ā' because the promoters of the dissension were instigating the tribes to pick a quarrel with the people of Ṣan'ā' and so terrorize them that none of them would dare disobey the People of the House.

(*n*) These are samples drawn from the history of the Yemen but they contain an effective pointer in support of the view I hold—namely, that freedom of independent judgement (*ijtihād*) is but superficial,[102] divided, or confined within a narrow compass, and that the objectives of the Imāmate are well preserved objectives, to encroach upon which the alleged freedom of independent judgement (*ijtihād*) will not dare.[103]

[19]

9. *The duty to revolt against the unjust*

(*a*) This is another of the resplendent principles which the propagandists of the Imāmate bore along with them. It is a principle, in embracing and believing which, the first of those who bore it to the Yemen were perhaps sincere because, in actual fact, they were in revolt against the 'Abbāsid and Umayyad Caliphates.

(*b*) But is this principle applied against any one of the Imāms?

(*c*) Would one of the sons of the populace have the temerity to revolt against one of the Imāms, then to become a 'heretic', 'oppressor', 'the enemy of God' both in the eyes of the state (*dawlah*) and the subservient[104] *'ulamā'*?

(*d*) When we have perceived that the Imāmate has broken the back of the populace and made two segments out of it, one of them the Zaydī segment and the other the Shāfi'ī segment—there are yet further well established chains of divisions and segmentations, one grasping the throat of the other, emanating, all of them, from this single chronic malady—the divine right to govern mankind.

(*e*) The Shāfi'īs, as I have shown, consider the Imāmate a single authority, and that the Zaydīs as a group are those who govern the Shāfi'īs, ruling over and exploiting them.

(*f*) When, however, we turn to the Zaydīs we do not find they hold this view [20] or put themselves in this position. On the contrary they feel a bitter vehement resentment that it is a particular stratum of Hāshimite families which enjoys the divine right to govern, that is specially favoured with it and passes it, turn about, among the ambitious male members of it, generation after generation, feeling a consciousness of superiority and distinction over the rest of the sons of the populace.

(*g*) Then, when we turn to the Hāshimites, we find poor wretches, unfortunates and deprived persons. These we find pointing their fingers in fear and trembling at a single family of the Hāshimites—the Royal Family that has ruled despotically, exploiting and singling out for itself the benefits of government and attacking the great Hāshimites[105] more than it has attacked any other group.

(*h*) From one angle so it appears, but when, from another angle, we examine the sentiments of the greatest force among the populace, i.e., the tribes, those of them who farm—and those who do not, then indeed we find them harbouring a general sense of bitterness against the inhabitants of the towns as a whole, considering the townsfolk, as they maintain, to be sharing with the Imāms in the benefits and gains of government, and responsible for its outrages and misdeeds.[106]

(*i*) Hence we perceive the distinguishing marks of this ill-omened rupture between Shāfi'īs and Zaydīs, Hāshimīs and Qaḥṭānīs, then between tribes and townsfolk.

(*j*) A sequence of fragmentation! All of it emanating from the feeling of these 'popular' groups as a whole that they have no right to govern themselves and that there is a special chosen group alone that enjoys this right in perpetuity—the right of the sacrosanct Imāmate!

(*k*) In the past the Yemeni populace lived with the conviction that the Imāmate [21] was divinely bestowed upon a particular chosen stock, and only a small number of exceptional individuals was stirred to contest this frightful sacro-sanctity—whom the swords of the Imāms despatched, ridding themselves of them as 'criminals, heretics[107] and enemies of God'.

(*l*) This apart, there was the long bitter struggle between the Imāms themselves in the Upper Yemen, one against another, then between them and the kings and rulers of the other districts.

(*m*) Where the populace was concerned, during most phases of history it was (merely) an onlooker, sizing up the muscles of the contenders for government and domination over it, as if it were heaps of debris and rubble of antique statues quarrelled over by robber hands.

(*n*) Except, today, now that the populace has developed, stood up for itself, revolted, and been stirred up by the bright revolutionary (war)-cry of Arab nationalism (*'Urūbah*), its morrow cannot possibly be like its yesterday, nor its future like its past, and from now onwards its role will not be that of onlooker.

(*o*) It inevitably must define its attitude regarding each problem that concerns it and demand each one of its rights.

(*p*) It would be absurd for it to continue in the belief that, from all eternity, the choice of Heaven has fallen upon a number of families which, age upon age, take their turn of the divine right to rule.

(*q*) The Shāfi'ī majority[108] of the populace will not continue to accept that it be governed by a sectarian military rule expressing neither its will nor its doctrine.

[22]

(*r*) Nor will the Zaydiyyah continue subject and submissive to a 'racist'[109] government that looks down (on them), aspiring to live forever pampered by Heaven and Earth.

(*s*) Nay indeed—the populace will not assent to its morrow being like its yesterday. It must inevitably assume its full role in the contest for this is the way of life—whosoever urges it to the contrary will be bereft of sense and success.[110]

(*t*) The contest will revolve around this major leading issue—that of divine right to govern the populace.

(*u*) Who is to possess this right? Who is better entitled to it?

(*v*) Is there to be a class of mankind chosen by Heaven to rule?

(*w*) Is it to be permitted that there remain in the Yemen a sectarian[111] faction ruling another faction till eternity?

(*x*) This is the major issue of the future—around it will revolve future battles and events, and from it will develop many other issues. The Arab and international powers will exploit these whether we will or no, and the Yemen will be exposed to perils without end.

(*y*) If Yemenis wish to avert all these frightening possibilities from their country, to preserve its independence, sovereignty and unity and keep its name on the map, let them efface this superstition calling itself a sacrosanct right to rule possessed by a specific section of people and let them extend equal opportunities for governing to all sections of the populace.

(*z*) That is the straight clear truth. I do not speak of it from partisanship for one section of Yemenis as apart from another. I speak of it only from desire for the unity, freedom and independence of the populace as a whole.

[23]

10. *A menace also to the Hāshimites*

It may be said, or it may occur to mind at the first glance, that abolition of the sectarian Imāmate would be to the disadvantage and contrary to the interests of the Hāshimites alone.

(*a*) But this is a fallacious theory, for no menace, present or future, threatens the Hāshimites as does the menace of the Imāmate. Each Imām arises in one single Hāshimite family, and to him it seems that his opponents and rivals are the prominent men in the Hāshimite families only. So, from the outset, he tries to rid himself of them before any others. This on one hand—while on another, the entire populace feels that all the Hāshimite families are an arrogant class distinct from the populace and detached from it as if they were not of the populace in any way—on the contrary indeed, as if they were alien to it and intruding on it. Now, if distinctiveness was, in the ages of ignorance, a privilege for specially distinguished stocks, it will, in the future, constitute a great menace to these stocks and rouse the aversion of the populace to them, partisanship in it against them, and (lead) it to stigmatise them as reactionaries.[112]

(*b*) Consequently, as generations go by, they will become isolated from the populace, as if they were a foreign community within it, not an (integral) part of it. After that no power will be found on the face of the earth capable of subjugating the populace to an insignificant minority for ever.

[24]

(*c*) This is the result, inevitably to be expected, of the complications of the menace of the Imāmate and from preserving the Hāshimite families in (their) privilege over the populace.

(*d*) Yet, were the noble Hāshimite families to become aware of these realities, attend to warding off this menace, and their liberals to head the opposition to the Imāmic concept, the cry for a republic and the extension of equal opportunities to all of the sons of the populace to share in the right to govern, they would thereby save the unity of the homeland and spare the country many woes.

(*e*) In Egypt and all the lands of Arabism (*'Urūbah*) and Islam are Hāshimite families preserving their noble lineage and tracing back their descent (to the Prophet) but they do not make means to rule and privilege out of this descent. Through this they have been able to merge with the populace and become a basic constituent (composed) of its noblest constituents, sire-ing among their sons heroes who rise to the highest ranks of society through their personal abilities, not by their descent and noble lineage. On this account these outstanding persons do not come across those who attack their position or attempt to remove them from it.

(*f*) How many great heroes we have known who shot up to the ranks of political or scholarly leadership, enjoying an overwhelming popularity,[113] and when we enquire into their descent we find them to be of pure Prophetic stock, but this descent of theirs was not a reason for their supremacy in society, for they attained dominance through their abilities and valour alone.

(*g*) On the contrary, it is certain that had they clung to the attribute of descent, becoming [25] thereby distinct from populaces, it would have been difficult indeed for them to attain what they did.

(*h*) No-one is unaware that in the Yemen, centuries ago, there were remnants of the Persians[114] and families specially distinct left behind from the era of the Persian occupation. They continued for a number of centuries to maintain their distinctness from Yemeni society. Thus they provoked the resentment[115] of the populace, driving it to league together against them and become estranged from them. Yet foolhardy sons of these families kept boasting at the Arabs and trying to emulate them in their own native Yemeni country until eventually they isolated themselves from the populace and (came to) realise a feeling of loneliness, isolation and constriction.

(*i*) Ultimately they were obliged to abandon their Shah-like Sasanian traditions, to merge with the populace and become part of it.

(*j*) Nowadays we do not find any Yemeni referring to these families or possessing any knowledge[116] of them. Nor do we consider it improbable, when the principle that government is the right of the people is realised, that the day will come when some gifted man (drawn) from these elements merged in the populace may come to head the people's government[117] through application of the principle of equality of opportunity among all citizens.

(*k*) So if this was the case with the remnants of the occupying Persian Abnā' how then will the case be with the Arab Hāshimite families in the era of Arab nationalism (*qawmiyyah*) which is carrying along the Arabs towards complete unity, and, be it sooner or later, to a unitary Arab state?

[26]

11. *No partisanship*[118]

(a) It would be a major error—the very reverse of logic—that those who take up the cry for popular government should be suspected of stirring up sectionalist[119] partisanship.

(*b*) The reality, on the contrary, is that they are taking up the cry for the unity of the populace, a unity safe and sound, based upon guarantees of its permanence in the future without squalls.

(*c*) Those who place their faith in sectionalism are the very persons who defend the barriers and discriminations that divide them from the rest of the groups and classes of the populace, insisting that they be distinct from the populace and set apart from it by political and social rights—as if not disposed to accept that they be numbered among its sons or be on the same human plane as its humanity.[120]

(*d*) This arrogant attitude is the sectionalist attitude and the thing most dangerous to the Hāshimites and their future, whether they live in the Yemen or in any other Arab country.

(*e*) No Arab populace accepts the deification of one family of it, or its being kept distinct from it by any (special) right whatsoever.

(*f*) The Egyptian Revolution is not a sectionalist revolution[121] because the populace of Egypt is, without exception, the furthest removed of populaces from the sectionalism (deriving from difference in) birth. [27] From the outset it rejected the existence in Egypt of a class distinguished from the populace (by privilege) like the Pashas and Feudalists.[122]

(*g*) When it (the Revolution) put its programme into practice it did not eliminate the Pashas in their capacity as Egyptians, but only the barriers and distinctions (of privilege that used to raise them over the level of the populace.

(*h*) It (the Revolution) did, in my view a good turn to the future of these Pashas and warded off the resentments of the populace from them.

(*i*) Nevertheless they did have the possibility of doing themselves a (still) better turn than this had they forestalled the Revolution by demolishing with their own hands, those barriers that used to keep them apart from the populace.

* * * * *

Al-Badr Muḥammad b. Ismā'īl al-Amīr

Zubayrī makes great play with the person of the celebrated twelfth/eighteenth century scholar al-Badr Muḥammad b. Ismā'īl b. Ṣalāḥ al-Amīr al-Khawlānī, then al-Ṣan'ānī, defined by al-Shawkānī an *imām mujaddid,* but he brazenly twists history into anti-Imāmic polemic. This gave certain Republican writers the inspiration to publish a contentious biography, *Ibn al-Amīr and his era: a picture of the struggle of the Yemeni populace.*[123] The main author, it is alleged, was Qāsim Ghālib Aḥmad, now deceased, a Shāfi'ī, a man of poor reputation and a pronounced chip on the shoulder. He is the author of a book on suffering and torture in Ḥajjah prison[124] much of which, other former prisoners there tell me, is fabrication. Al-Amīr's *Dīwān*[125] has been printed, so, with this and other Zaydī biographies, one can easily assess the extent which Qāsim Ghālib and his collaborators have grafted their notions onto the views of al-Amīr—Qāsim Ghālib's biography has a validity only in revealing only the political propaganda of the opponents of the Ḥamīd al-Dīn Imāms.

Al-Amīr was born in Kuḥlān in 1099/1687-8 and died in Ṣan'ā' on the 3 Sha'bān 1182/11 December, 1768. In 1107/1695-6 or a few years later, he moved to Ṣan'ā' with his father, and, as his biographer[126] states, 'made open display of independent judgement, took his stand on proof, shunning *taqlīd*[127] and the spuriousness of those jurisprudent opinions for which no proof exists [*aẓhar al-ijtihād wa-'l-wuqūf ma'a 'l-adillah, wa-nafara min al-taqlīd wa-zayf mā lā dalīl 'alay-hi min al-ārā' al-fiqhiyyah*]'. Al-Amīr taught in Ṣan'ā' and is recognised as an outstanding *mujtahid*.[128] Throughout his life he played an important political role, particularly in his earlier phase as a conciliator between various notables of the Imāmic House. In 1151/1738-9 the Imām al-Manṣūr put him in charge of the (Friday) address (*khuṭbah*) in the Ṣan'ā' Jāmi' Mosque, but in 1154/1741-2 slanderers told the Imām, after an address of his in the Mosque, that he wished to contradict/violate the doctrine of the Family (*mukhālafat madhhab al-Āl*),[129] i.e. the Zaydī 'Alawīs. He managed however to satisfy al-Manṣūr—false representations about him had previously been made to the Imām al-Mutawakkil.

The incident cited by Zubayrī (p. 106) is most fully reported in the *Dīwān*.[130] On the first Friday of Jumādā I, 1166/10 March, 1753 he delivered an address in the Jāmi' Mosque of Ṣan'ā'. 'We have a rule (*qā'idah*) that if the first exhortatory address is prolonged we abbreviate the second address and bless the five Ahl al-Kisā'[131] in detail, then we bless the Family (*Āl*) in general (*jumlatan*)—the fashion has gone on for many years', says Muḥ. b. Muḥ. Zabārah. This was what al-Amīr did. That the preacher (*khaṭīb*) should have omitted the name of their ancestor al-Qāsim and the blessing upon him annoyed the ignorant persons of the House of the Imām al-Qāsim So they collected and went to the notables and chiefs of the Imām's house, such as the Lord, the very learned Muḥammad b. Isḥāq,[132] who told them that what al-Amīr had omitted was not obligatory and did not invalidate the address or the prayer.

They eventually persuaded a senior member of the Imām's house, Muḥammad b. 'Alī b. Ḥusayn b. al-Mahdī, who laid the matter before the Khalīfah (the Imām). The Imām told him it was a simple matter which he knew the preacher would not repeat, but this did not satisfy him and he threatened to kill al-Amīr if he were not put in prison. The common folk (*'āmmah*) became excited and there was much outcry. The Imām brought both parties together in the Qaṣr of Ṣan'ā' and the matter was ventilated, but he decided that al-Amīr should stay in prison (Dār al-Adab) and he seems to have been kept under comfortable house arrest in the Qaṣr with the naqīb Almās, one of the Imām's Emirs, for a month or two. Muḥammad b. 'Alī on the other hand the Imām al-Mahdī threw into prison, confiscating his 14 horses and his *iqṭā'* land in Ḍawrān and Ḥubaysh, and he died there. About thirty other persons of the Imāmic Family were imprisoned at the same time. He also dealt with Yūsuf al-'Ajamī al-Imāmī, an Ithnā'asharī Shī'ī an open 'Rāfiḍī'[133] who had come to Ṣan'ā' in the days of the Imām al-Manṣūr and was a teacher at his court (*mudarris bi-ḥaḍrati-hi*), the chief instigator of the trouble. Al-Mahdī expelled him from the Yemen and quiet was restored. Al-Mahdī, though sympathetic to al-Amīr's views and *ijtihād* in general, appointed a new preacher, but al-Amīr continued his teaching, writing, and giving *Fātwās* (*iftā'*).

The real reason for the attack on al-Amīr, his biographers maintain, was because of his reading (with students of course) the Sunnī books of Tradition (*kutub al-ḥadīth al-ummahāt*), and his preoccupation with al-Sunnat al-Nabawiyyah—i.e., Sunnism, teaching it, disseminating it from the pulpit and the like. There was, says al-Shawkānī, no harm in this, since the Zaydī Imāms used these books in their compilations (*muṣannafāt*) from the time the said books arrived in the Yemen. The ordinary folk accused al-Amīr of *naṣb*, hostility to the 'Alawīs, and people also suspected the Khalīfah, al-Mahdī, of being a Sunnī and sympathising with Sunnīs.[134]

It seems to have been after this incident that the Dhū Muḥammad and Dhū Ḥusayn of Jabal Baraṭ, who were at that time a strong confederation (*jamrah*) which none could withstand, collected tribal armies and threatened to come out against al-Mahdī in support of the (Zaydī) Doctrine/School/Rite (*nuṣrat al-Madhhab*) since the Imām was supporting al-Amīr on his course of destruction of it. As Zubayrī says, they had to be bought off by a bribe of an increase in their stipends of 20,000 *riyāls* per annum.

Al-Amīr, to judge from the histories, does not seem to have been animated by any motive of struggling against the Imāms as Zubayrī avers, nor do the Imāms seem to have been opposed to him. The historians do not suggest that he made a deliberate gesture of dropping their names from the prayer—which in Islam would be tantamount to rebellion. Nor yet can the accusation of his enemies that he was anti-Hāshimī/'Alawī be justified. The *Dīwān* speaks of them in the highest terms as *'uṣbah 'Alawiyyah hum zubdat al-kuramā' wa-'l-ashrāf.*[135] Imām al-Mahdī entrusted him with the

Awqāf of Ṣan'ā' in 1161/1748 an office which he discharged honestly for a few years then resigned from it, but left in his will 100 *qirsh* (*riyāls*) to charity and 100 to the poor of the Banū Hāshim, out of scruples about the *waqf*.[136]

In point of fact al-Amīr clearly sought that the Imāms should enforce a just Islamic administration which it was probably impracticable for them to implement without losing the effective political support of their followers. When al-Manṣūr succeeded to the Imāmate he counselled him in verse[137] to entrust just persons with charge of the peasantry (*al-ra'āyā*) and he points to the tyranny (*jawr*) of the assessor, tax-gatherer and collector of the tithe (*muthammir, qabbāḍ, 'ashshār*). He inveighs against customs and tolls (*mukūs*), as do all Islamic *'ulamā'*, not only those of the Zaydī school, though it is an open question whether any Islamic ruler has ever dispensed with this source of revenue. He makes a strong attack[138] on giving *zakāt* money to the 'turbaned' (*al-mu'ammamūna*) and the House of the Imām—which indeed is prohibited the 'Alawīs by the *sharī'ah*—perhaps the Quḍāh are to be included here with the 'Alawīs? He urged al-Mahdī 'Abbās to send teachers to the remoter villages, towns and country-side (*bawādī*) to remove idolatrous beliefs in trees, stones and domes (*qubab*)—i.e., saint-cults.[139] Al-Mahdī assented to this and his governors took over a great wealth of property devoted to these 'idols'. In short al-Amīr's standpoint was that of Zaydī orthodoxy, certainly not a polemic against the Imāmate as an institution. If one can honestly construe the opposition to al-Amīr over his utilisation of Sunnī collections of Ḥadīth Tradition as an attack on the exercise of independent judgement (*ijtihād*), Imām Aḥmad cannot be accused of ignoring the Sunnī canonical works, for, in making his decisions by *ijtihād*, he had no hesitation in selecting from them when he thought it appropriate to do so.

Al-Badr al-Amīr is buried in the cemetery (*ḥawṭah*) south-west of the minaret of al-Madrasah Mosque.

Al-Shāfi'ī and the Yemen

The Shāfi'ī school of Islam is far from being opposed in principle to the 'Alawīs, Sayyids or Ashrāf, and Ḥaḍramī Sayyids are numbered among the leading divines in the branches of this Sunnī rite in south Arabia and Indonesia. Al-Shāfi'ī himself went to the Yemen during the reign of the 'Abbāsid Caliph al-Rashīd and, according to the author of *Ghāyat al-amānī*,[140] 'he entered Ṣan'ā' and received *'ilm* [learning] from the Qāḍī of Ṣan'ā' who was at the day Hishām b. Yūsuf [the Abnā'ī][141] and from Muṭarrif b.

Mādhān, these two being the most important of the companions of Ibn Jurayj who received *'ilm* from 'Aṭā' b. Abī Rabāḥ. Al-Dhahabī said in *Tārīkh al-Islām* that the governor of Ṣan'ā' wrote to al-Rashīd, "If you wish for obedience [*ṭā'ah*] to last in the Yemen you will send for al-Shāfi'ī, for he is one of the propagandists of the Ṭālibīs [i.e. 'Alawīs]." So al-Rashīd sent for him and he was carried to Baghdad. Al-Rashīd imprisoned him, then set him free, and he went to Egypt where he remained until he died, God rest him.'

Politically al-Shāfi'ī was a Shī'ī—this he avows himself in the verse:

In kāna rafḍ-an ḥubbu Āli Muḥammad-in
Fal-yashhadi 'l-Thaqalāni annī Rāfiḍī
If *rafḍ*-ism be love of the Family of Muḥammad
Let Men and Jinn testify that I am a Rāfiḍī.[142]

Rāfiḍī in this context would be the opposite of Nāṣibī, and mean pro-Sayyid/'Alawī, but it is a sobriquet, usually abusive, for the Shī'ah.

Notes

1. His *al-Tārīkh al-sirrī li-'l-thawrat al-Yamaniyyah*, Beirut, 1977, 17, written in rather uneducated Arabic, is a first-hand account of the attitudes and plottings of the young officer element.
2. Ibid, 26.
3. *Aqūl 'Izrā'īl fī 'aṣr-ak waqaf*
W-intah kafayt-ah fī ḥayāt-ah wa-'l-mamāt.
In qult anā ṣārif fa-mā 'indī ṣaraf!
Man dhāk dhī min ghayr sayf-ak zād māt?

Wa-man nizil Bayḥān mā 'ind-ah sharaf.
Kīf al-qawā'id ḥīn khazzantum bi-qāt?
Quddam-ak al-Bāhūt yaḥkum bi-'l-inṣāf!
Man 'ānad-ah yinza' fu'ād-ah wa-'l-riyāt! (*rajaz* metre)

'Izrā'il is the Angel of Death. Al-Bāhūt (syn. *al-mukhīf*) was Aḥmad's nickname.

4. For example by the late Muḥammad Aḥmad Nu'mān, *al-Aṭrāf al-ma'niyyah fi 'l-Yaman*, Beirut, 1965.
5. For the current situation see my summary in *Middle East Annual Review*, 1978, Saffron Walden, 419-23. No reliance is to be placed upon 'Abd al-Raḥmān al-Bayḍānī, *Iqtiṣād al-Yaman*, Cairo, 1961; and Mohamed Said El Attar, *Le sous-développement économique et social du Yemen*, Alger, 1964, is not very trustworthy either.

6. An unusually informative report of an interview with him appears in the *Observer* of 12 April 1964. The Egyptians did not encourage the *Observer*'s correspondent to see Zubayrī, and little wonder, for he declared that the Royal Family could return as private citizens and take their chance in future elections. The Yemen should not be interfered with by any foreign power. By this he meant Egypt, and he wanted the UAR troops to leave.

7. The bibliography of Zubayrī is now considerable. 'A group of Yemeni writers' has issued a series of useful studies, introduced by 'Abd al-'Azīz al-Maqāliḥ, *Al-Zubayrī, shā'ir-un wa-munāḍil-un*, Beirut, 1977. It is interesting to note that (p.32) Zubayrī attributed the weakness of both the 1948 and 1962 movements to their complete neglect of the *fallāḥ* and the tribesman cultivator (*qabīlī fallāḥ*). Cf. Aḥmad al-Shāmī, *Min al-adab al-Yamanī*, Beirut, 1974, passim.

8. For the genealogy one may consult al-Mubarrad, *Nasab 'Adnān wa-Qaḥṭān*, ed. 'Abd al-'Azīz al-Maymanī, Cairo, 1936; al-Hamdānī, *al-Iklīl I*, ed. Muḥ.al-Akwa', Cairo, 1383/1963, 103 ff., *al-farq bayna Qaḥṭān wa-'Adnān*, etc.

9. *Dāmighat al-Dawāmigh*, London, July 1966, 25.

10. From al-Nādirah, a Shāfi'ī, a relative by marriage of former President al-Iryānī, whom I first met in exile in Nairobi in 1957.

11. *Asrār al-Yaman*, dated Cairo, 20 September 1962. He also wrote a series of articles in *Rūz al-Yūsuf* on the despotism of the Imāmate (sic) about this time.

12. Op. cit., 77.

13. To be dated about 1959, p.86. In *al-Zubayrī shā'ir-un*, 146, Zakī Barakāt states that, after the 1955 attack on Imām Aḥmad, Zubayrī rejected the Imāms entirely.

14. *Ma'ārik wa-mu'āmarāt ḍidd qaḍiyyat al-Yaman*, 143 seq. No date or place of publication are given, but the book is reviewed by a certain 'Alī Muḥammad in the paper *al-Fikr*, Aden, 22 June 1957, as *awwal da'wah ṣarīḥah li-'l-Jumhuriyyah fi 'l-Yaman*.

15. Op. cit., 32.

16. *Usṭūrat al-Yaman al-sa'īdah*, Beirut, 24 March 1966/3rd Dhu 'l-Ḥijjah, 1385 H.

17. Published in Cairo, March 1965; cf. p.24, *al-Shī'ah wa-'l-nawāṣib* etc., reviewed in the Ṣan'ā' weekly *al-Thawrah*, 17 March 1966, by Sufyān al-Baraṭī, with a pointed criticism. Muḥammad Nu'mān nevertheless propounds quite interesting theories on Yemeni politics even if, on analysis, one is not altogether convinced by them.

18. Nevertheless an unknown unidentified MS. exists in the Ambrosiana (E.188, i) by a certain Miḥyā b. 'Ulayf, entitled *al-Qaṣīdat al-farīdah, iftikhār al-'Adnān 'alā Qaḥṭān*, but it may have no relevance here.

19. William R. Brown, 'The Yemeni dilemma', *Middle East Journal*, Washington, 1963, xvii, iv, 349-67.

20. *Modern Yemen*, Baltimore, 1967, 230. Cf. review in *B.S.O.A.S.*, 1970, xxxiii, 211-14.

21. A biased and untrustworthy booklet entitled *al-Shī'ah fi 'l-Yaman*, Cairo, 1970, was put out under what must be a pseudonym, 'Abdullāh al-

Muwaffaq, claiming to represent the 'ulamā' al-Sunnah—i.e. the Shāfi'īs, of Ta'izz, Ṣan'ā', al-Ḥudaydah and Ibb, interesting only as representing the extremists among the Shāfi'īs.

22. The Committee in reality seems to have been the late Muḥammad Aḥmad Nu'mān, as I am informed by Dr Muḥammad An'am Ghālib, and the latter himself, with perhaps occasionally others.

23. The title is Muḥammad Maḥmūd al-Zubayrī, *al-Imāmah wa-khaṭaru-hā 'alā waḥdat al-Yaman*, Dār al-Ṣaḥāfah Press, Beirut, n.d. The likely date of publication is 1959, but it can hardly be published earlier than 1958 and *al-Khud'at al-kubrā* (The great deception) in which Zubayrī attacks the union of the Yemen with the UAR, carries an advertisement for *al-Imāmah* as does the latter for *al-Khud'ah*. The union took place in 1958, and Nu'mān *père* told me it was published *ba'd al-waḥdah*.

The Shāfi'ī Qāsim Ghālib Aḥmad (cf. p.111) printed a re-edition of *al-Imāmah* at Cairo in 1968, with strongly biased comments of his own. He has no scruples about occasionally altering Zubayrī's wording, but the sub-headings he introduces and punctuation improve on Zubayrī's rather erratic presentation. He omits section 1, but adds a not uninformative preface of his own.

The numbering of sections and paragraphs is mine, and I have re-punctuated the translation. Another edition is known, *Dār al-Hanā li-'l-Ṭibā'ah*, Beirut, 1972.

24. *Sha'b*, a politically emotive word, is so rendered throughout for emphasis, but it means 'the people'.

25. Ḥasan, son of Imām Yaḥyā, brother by a different mother to Imām Aḥmad. The Ḥamīd al-Dīn House disapproving of Aḥmad's nomination of his son al-Badr as heir-apparent, tended to support Ḥasan, regarded as highly conservative though with his father's reputation for *bukhl* (close-fistedness), as potential successor to Imām Aḥmad. Aḥmad sent Ḥasan to Washington to keep him out of the way. Ḥasan was supported by the conservative elements, especially in the Mashriq and a plot was certainly afoot at the time of Aḥmad's death to substitute him for Badr. This split in the Family led Badr to rely on the dubious loyalty of the young army officers trained by Nasser's officers—which led to the coup of 26 September 1962.

26. For the refutation of Zubayrī's unjustified strictures on the Imāmate see pp.97-9.

27. These are political jargon. *Al-taqālīd al-raj'iyyah* and *fawāriq al-ṣifāt allatī tumayyiz*. Al-Shāmī said *taqālīd* means *'ādāt* here.

28. *Maṭālib al-sha'b* by Zubayrī and Aḥmad Muḥammad Nu'mān (*père*) Maṭba'at Dār al-Janūb, in 1952, an idealistic if quite reasonable proposal for a democratic state, not attacking the Imāmate as such. Al-Shāmī thinks that *Ahdāf al-Aḥrār* was published in Aden, perhaps about 1945 or 1946. It may be noted that his collected verse, his *Dīwān*, has been published recently at Beirut (1978).

29. The 'Occupied South' at this time, in the face of frontier troubles initiated from the Yemen, had been assigned 3 battalions of British troops, stationed in sensitive border villages such as Ḍāli', Mukayrās and Bayḥān.

Ḥaḍramawt had no British troops at all, only a few RAF personnel at Riyān air-strip, to operate it. Previously the whole of this great area had been policed by Arab troops alone. Al-Maqāliḥ (*al-Zubayrī shā'irun*, op. cit, 28-9) says Zubayrī and the Liberals were not anti-Britain in Aden, considering Britain as 'the Neighbour (al-Jārah)' there.

30. This is a well known Mu'tazilite phrase. The Zaydīs of course believe in such Mu'tazilī doctrines as the intermediate position, known as *manzilah bayna manzilatayn*, between the Believer and Infidel, but the Ash'arīs (below, fn. 82) believe there is no such position and there are only Believers and Infidels.

31. Zubayrī completely misrepresents the situation. See p.90 and fn. 33. His account of segmentation in the Yemen is also far from objective.

32. He means the Yemeni Sayyids. Comment was that this is an expression of animosity (*ḥiqd*) towards them.

33. My informants insisted that *'uhūd* is to be taken in the sense of 'ages' here, but they seem mistaken in view of what follows. The British Colonial policy at this period, so far from being 'Divide and rule', concentrated on setting up a federation!

34. Zubayrī here is drawing on his imagination for as Aḥmad al-Shāmī has pointed out a tribesman, an Arḥabī for instance, is an Arḥabī before he is a Yemeni. There was little sense of unity in those times, though education may today have begun to alter attitudes to some extent.

35. This diabolical plot seems to exist only in Zubayrī's imagination!

36. *Shaṭr* in view of what follows might be better rendered as 'a part'. For al-Shāmī's refutation of this concept of the Imāmate see p.98.

37. *Ṭuqūs*, rites, says al-Shāmī, is not a Zaydī word, but a Christian term. For Zubayrī it would mean the Zaydī *adhān, 'Ḥayya 'alā khayr al-'amal'*. It is true of course that the Zaydīs did impose this on such Shāfi'ī territories as Ḥaḍramawt when they conquered it, but the Turks of the second Ottoman occupation forbade it in Ṣan'ā', and it was not imposed on the Shāfi'ī districts at the time Zubayrī was writing. Al-Shawkānī, *al-Badr al-ṭāli'*, Cairo, 1348 H., ii, 122, tells of a Zaydī Imām's persistence in using this form of *adhān* when the Ṭāhirid 'Āmir b. 'Abd al-Wahhāb had entered Ṣan'ā'.

38. *Ifti'āt* was explained as *al-da 'watal-bāṭilah*, false claim.

39. Zubayrī alludes to the coming of the first Zaydī Imām, al-Hādī, to the Yemen some 1,100 years ago—an 'Adnānī not a Qaḥṭānī! He deliberately ignores the essential need of such an office as the Imāmate among the northern tribes. Cf. my 'South Arabia' in C.A.O. van Nieuwenhuijze, *Commoners, climbers and notables,* Leiden, 1977, 226-47.

40. This alludes to the saying, *Al-waswās yajrī fī Ibn Ādam majra 'l-dam,* 'The devil of evil prompting runs in Man as blood runs (in his veins)'.

41. My informants said *ādamiyyah* means 'humanity'.

42. A standard cliché in the political jargon of the time, a Marxist echo.

43. Zubayrī refers to the Zaydī soldiers and officials who collected taxes from the peasants of the Shāfi'ī districts and to the customs officials known for their illegal exactions. From criticisms in the current Ṣan'ā' press it seems that corrupt practice among customs officials persists! A

A traditional attitude is expressed by al-Mujallī, MS. in the Biblioteca Ambrosiana on the law of the Zaydī Imāms, uncatalogued (the author is unknown to my Zaydī informants and the vocalisation of his name is uncertain) 14a, quoting Qur'ān, xlviii, 4 and 7, *Li-'llāhi junūdu 'l-samā' wa-'l-arḍi,* God's are the troops of the Heavens and Earth, averring that al-Zaydiyyah are the 'troops of the Earth'.

44. The Prophet, himself a rain-maker, withheld rain if the *zakāt*-tax was not paid (*South Arabian hunt*, London, 1976, 36; Al-Balādhurī, *Ansāb al-Ashrāf*, ed. Ḥamīdullāh, Cairo, 1957, i, 82). Imām Aḥmad was particularly famed for bringing rain when he came to a place, but the happy virtue of bringing rain might be attributed to anybody, as they say, '*Filān rijl-ah khaḍrā'*, So and so's foot is moist (*khaḍrā' = mubtallah*)'. If it rains when one arrives somewhere people say half-jokingly, 'Your blessing (*barakah*)'. Cf. M. J. Kister, Extracts from Arabic manuscripts concerning the Jāhiliyyah and early Islamic period, Jerusalem, 1969, 8, *K. al-Manāqib al-Mazīdiyyah* ... of Abu 'l-Baqā' Hibatullāh, 'When they fought the Muslims the Prophet invoked against them (*da'ā 'alay-him*), saying, "O God, tread severely on Muḍar and send down upon them (rainless) years like the years of Joseph". And he prayed (*qanata*) against them forty days, invoking (God) against them at each prayer. In consequence drought over them followed seven successive years until they perished ... Then their delegations came to him saying, "O Muḥammad, your people have perished, so invoke God in their favour"'. Of the first Zaydī Imām of the Yemen the *Sīrat al-Hādī* of al-'Abbāsī, Damascus, 1972, 65, tells us that Banū 'Aqīl said, 'Abu 'l-Ḥusayn has never passed through our country but it rains', while others say, 'Rain has come to us through the *barakah* of Abu 'l-Ḥasan'.

45. The position is defined by al-Mujallī, MS. cit., 16 a. In the time of an Imām disposal/administration (*taṣarruf*) in the tithes, *zakāt*, fifth, treasuries, and *fiṭr* alms (*al-ash'ār wa-'l-zakāt wa-'l-akhmās wa-buyūt al-māl wa-ṣadaqat al-fiṭr*) is only by his permission or order. In discussing *ṣadaqah* (ibid, 17 a) he says, '*Mā kāna ilā Rasūl Allāh ... fa-huwa ila 'l-Imām ba 'da-hu bi-la 'khtilāf*, Whatever is to the Apostle of God pertains to the Imām after him, without dispute'. The Imām al-Manṣūr, says al-Mujallī, stated that if the tithes are paid to some other, without the Imām's permission, he is a *kāfir* (infidel) and his territory/house (*dār*) in the event of resort to arms ((?) *ma'a 'l-shawkah*) becomes Dār Ḥarb. Killing them, taking captive their offspring and plundering their properties is licit, as the Companions did after the Prophet.

The *Sīrat al-Hādī*, op. cit., 174, alludes to the Hāshimīs of the earliest Zaydīs in the Yemen as inheriting the Prophet's position (*maqām*).

46. Sayyid Aḥmad al-Shāmī tells me that only the Ṣalāt al-Jum'ah of the Friday comes into this category. He agrees this is not an early Zaydī tenet but in late books it is laid down that, with the presence of a just ruler (*al-ḥākim al-'ādil = al-imām al-'ādil*), one must attend the Friday prayer.

The Head of the Court of Appeal (*Ra'īs al-isti'nāf*) in Ṣan'ā', Zayd al-Daylamī (ob. 1365/1946), for a number of years during the latter days of Imām Yaḥyā, never attended a Jum'ah prayer, on the grounds that '*Lā tu'qadu shar'ī 'iyyat al-Jum'ah illā ma'a wujūd al-Imām al-'ādil'* (The legality of the Jum'ah-prayer is only concluded with the presence of a just Imām). He meant of course that he did not consider Yaḥyā to be such. Cf. Mohamed Said El Attar, *Le sous-développement*, op. cit., 281; propagandist and utterly inaccurate as it is, it reflects the political attitudes of Zubayrī and the opposition to the Imāms.

47. *Al-rakhā'*. The verb *rakhā* in Dathīnah means 'to rain', and this sense may be included here.

48 He means, sarcastically, that through the Imām they obtain the delights they could not get in life.

49. He is 'delivered' (*'atīq*) because he has escaped the famine. The historians of earlier periods make occasional reference to Imāms distributing grain during the periodic famines, but there may be some truth in Zubayrī's implication that Government grain was withheld during the famine of World War II. Yet the Aden paper, *Fatāt al-Jazīrah*, vi, no.291, of 7 Oct. 1945, in an interview with someone from al-Bayḍā' asks, 'Have you quantities of grain[*ṭa'ām*] in the underground silos and stores [*al-madāfin wa-'l-makhāzin*]?' To this the answer was, 'A little is to be found with the *ra'iyyah*, but most is with the Treasury [Bayt al-Māl] estimated to be from 6,000 to 8,000 *qadaḥs*, the price of the *qadaḥ* at the present time being 7 *riyāls*, and the Government lends it to the *ra'iyyah*.' These loans are made till a time of *khayr*, probably harvest being meant, or prosperity. This price is very high. Letters from Ṣan'ā' in November 1943 stated that prices are increasing daily owing to the lack of imports and the poor rainfall. The tribes are starving and typhus and smallpox are very prevalent. At this period also there was an acute famine in Ḥaḍramawt: it was relieved by British aid.

50. *Ẓill*, shade, has also the senses of protection, patronage, sovereignty.

51. *Qiddīs* is applied to Christian saints, and for this reason is doubtless purposely used by Zubayrī. Zaydīs, as contrasted with Yemeni Shāfi'īs, are opposed to saint cults. Qāsim Ghālib's comment to his edition (p.19) attacks Imām Aḥmad for destroying the tombs of Ibn 'Ujayl and Ibn 'Alwān—for which act Aḥmad was satirised by the poet al-Ḥaḍrānī.

52. Lit., *adhnāb*, tails, a favourite expression of Nasserite propaganda for the supporters of a political opponent.

53. Ar., *ashyā'*. Zubayrī's views on historiography are not to be treated seriously!

54. Muḥ. 'Alī al-Shahārī, *Ṭarīq al-thawrat al-Yamaniyyah*, Cairo, 1966, 54, avers that the régime (*niẓām*) of the imāmate 'not only imposes on Shāfi'īs, Ismā'īlīs and others that they be governed, but considers them deniers of interpretation (*kuffār al-ta'wīl*) and makes spoilation of their property lawful.' *Ta'wīl* in relation to *tafsīr* means exposition of the subject matter of the Qur'ān, not of the philology, grammar etc. Al-Shāmī and Nu'mān said the expression goes back to the Mu'tazilite past—*Hal Allāh khalaqa 'l-ma'siyah*, Did God create sin? It is *ikhtilāf uṣūlī fi 'l-aqīdah*, a basic difference of tenet. Other epithets here figure in Zaydī writing on political theory. Cf. Juḥ. b. Ismā'īl al-Amīr, *Tawḍīḥ al-afkār*, ed. Muḥ. Muḥyī 'l-Dīn 'Abd al-Ḥamīd, Cairo, 1366 H., ii, 213, *aqwāl Ahl*

al-Bayt fī qabūl riwāyāt kuffār al-ta' wīl.

55. *'Urūbah*, Arabism, Arab nationalism, which a particularly well-worn political catchword at this period.

56. It was this very sort of authority or rule (*ḥukm*) of the theocratic type that enabled the Imāms to exert any control over the tribes. Cf. my article in *Commoners, climbers*, op. cit., 244.

57. This is reminiscent of Ibn Khaldūn's *Muqaddimah*, which, prior to 1962, was much read and discussed in learned Yemeni circles. Cf. F. Rosenthal's translation, New York, 1958, i, 313, 'Royal authority and large dynastic power are attained only through a group and group feeling (*al-mulk wa-'l-dawlat al-'āmmah innamā yuḥṣal bi-'l-qabīl wa-'l-'aṣabiyyah*)'. For 'group' (*qabīl*) I prefer to substitute 'tribe'.

58. Both al-Shāmī and Nu'mān considered *iṣlāḥ* (reform) makes no sense here and suggested that *maṣāliḥ*, advantages, was intended.

59. This is a proverbial saying which Zubayrī accuses the Imām of spreading abroad in self-vindication.

60. Arabic *nafsiyyah*, thought, spirit, notion, i.e., the people are to have no reward but have to endure tribulation/distress (*balā'*).

61. On 8, xii, 1961, Muḥammad Aḥmad Nu'mān, published *al-Ta'mīm fi 'l-Yaman*, probably in Cairo as it was issued by the Committee, Lajnat al-thaqāfah wa-'l-nashr, of the Yemeni Unity (al-Ittiḥād al-Yamanī) group, as a riposte to Imām Aḥmad's celebrated poem attacking Nasser and his policy of nationalisation. Nu'mān's lively verses enumerate the various taxes Yemenis had to pay, and he quotes Muḥammad Ismā'īl al-Amīr attacking what he calls *al-aḥkām al-ẓālimah li-'l-a'immat al-Hāshimiyyah*, the unjust laws of the Hāshimite Imāms. In point of fact what al-Amīr attacked seems to have been certain malpractices (for which cf. p.114) but most of these are not specially Imāmic.

62. Al-Mujallī, MS. cit., 15 b, defines the attitude of the Zaydīs on this point. *Lā yuḥāribūn illā mubṭil-an min kāfir-in aw bāgh-in wa-man ashbaha-hu mimman yastabāḥ qatlu-hu shar'-an dūna man ḥaẓarat al-sharī'ah qitāla-hu fa-li-hādhā ju'ila 'l-jihād li-'l-Zaydiyyah li'anna-hum ka-dhālika dūna sā'ir al-firaq illa 'l-qalīl.*

He says (18a) that one is breaking one's allegiance (*nākith li-'l-bay'ah*) if neglecting *jihād* and when the Imām summons those who have paid him allegiance to it (holy war—*wa-'da'a 'l-Imām ... li-man bāya'a-hu ilay-hi*). It makes no difference whether the summons is to fight infidels (*kuffār*) oppressors (*bughāh*) or other wrongdoers. Cf. Aḥ. b. Yaḥyā b. al-Murtaḍā, *al-Baḥr al-zakhkhār*, Cairo, 1947/1366—1949/1368, v, 415, *seq. Bāb qitāl al-bughāh*. 'It is the Imām's duty to fight them (the *bughāh*) in accordance with his power to do so. (*'Ala 'l-Imām jihādu-hum ḥasb al-imkān*).

63. Muḥ. al-Ḥajarī's *Masājid Ṣan'ā'*, Ṣan'ā', 1361/1942, though it says much of repairs and new additions made by Imāms to Ṣan'ā' mosques, only mentions four domes (*qubbah*) of Imāms and three built by non-Yemenis; most of the mosques were not founded by the Imāms and only a few are named after them. There are of course domed tombs of Imāms in various parts of Zaydī Yemen, and I visited those at Ẓafīr Ḥajjah in 1966, but I have not come across superstitious practices connected with them. Zaydīs are opposed to saint cults.

Qāsim Ghālib, commenting on the above, speaks of the large areas of ground around these Imāmic tombs where the rich are buried so that they may be resurrected in company with the Imāms. He accuses the Imāms also of appropriating *awqāf* to themselves.

64. Zubayrī cannot but have been aware that it would be a most uncommon Yemeni, of whatever class, who, given the opportunity, would refrain from acquiring land, nor would all Yemenis be scrupulous as to the means used to acquire it. It is not to be supposed that the Imāms' failings in this respect were greater than those of others before or after 1962.

65. In fact the Imāms have developed irrigation projects, built *samsarahs* (hostelries), stone huts for wayfarers. Imāms Yaḥyā and Aḥmad furthermore constructed quite a number of rough motor roads or masonry mountain ways on which I travelled in 1966.

66. Cf. fn. 45 on this attitude.

67. Qur'ān, xxxiii, 36.

68. By 'factional' he means Zaydī.

69. Cf. fn. 54.

70. Nello Lambardi, 'Divisioni amministrative del Yemen: con notizie economiche e demografiche', *Oriente moderno*, Roma, 1947, xxvii, 143-56, quotes a Yemeni document that claims the Zaydīs are slightly in majority. The Central Planning Organisation's *Socio-economic report 1970-1974*, published in Ṣan'ā', avoids any attempt at a breakdown of population by religion, but other sources seem to indicate a definite Shāfi'ī majority. Lambardi's source, *'Ilm al-buldān, Ṣan'ā', 1360/1941, makes the Zaydīs 55%, the Shāfi'īs 45% of the inhabitants—reckoned at somewhere over 4* millions, with 60-70 thousand Jews and 50,000 Ismā'īlīs (Ṭayyibī Fāṭimīs).

71. Zaydī governors and soldiers from the north were appointed by the Imāms to collect taxes from the agriculturally richer districts of the Shāfi'ī south. In theory the system was fair and not burdensome, but, as managed by corrupt officials and tough soldiery, it pressed hard on the peasant. This was the principal and real grievance of the southern peasant. In the north taxes were collected *bi-'l-amānah*, i.e., by local assessment, not by Imāmic officials, but at least in some southern districts the old system of direct Government taxation had not changed under the Republic as late as 1974.

The Shāfi'īs however suffered from their own leaders to judge by the information given me by a Shāfi'ī. The Government assessors, he said, used to go to the villages and the local headman (*'āqil*) would provide them with food and entertainment. They would look only at the few places he took them to see and in three days they would do what, had they inspected the district properly, would have taken them a month. They would then send back their report, but the central authorities, if a man was to pay 100 *riyāls*, might add, say, another 50 *riyāls* to it—the additional sum being dalled *ḍamm*. As far as I am aware this has no basis in law. Tax-farmers (*multazimīn*) bid for the farming (*iltizām*) of the markets at auctions (*muzāyadah*) and kept watchers (*murāqibīn*) so one could not avoid payment, and there were taxes on everything.

It is this harsh incidence of taxation to which Zubayrī is alluding, but as Muḥ. b. Muḥ. Zabārah, *Nashr al-'arf*, Cairo, 1359-76, i, 560, says, after the Turks were driven out of the Yemen after the first Ottoman occupation, the Imāms said that the lands they had held were lawful (*ḥalāl*—at their disposal) because of the unbelief (*kufr*) of the Turks. When Imām Yaḥyā re-took the Yemen after 1918, he considered the Ismā'īlī (Fāṭimī-Ṭayyibī) areas lawful (*abāḥa-hā*) and turned their lands in the Manākhah district and Ṭaybah into *waqf*.

72. See fn. 50.

73. *Ijtihād* is defined as 'exerting oneself to form an opinion' in a case, or to form a rule of law by applying analogy (*qiyās*) to the Qur'ān and Sunnah. It is opposed to *taqlīd*, 'the adoption of the utterances or actions of another as authoritative in their correctness without investigating his reasons'. (Cf. my 'The Zaidis' in Arberry-Beckingham, *Religion in the Middle East*, Cambridge, 1969, ii, 292). Muḥ. b. 'Alī al-Shawkānī, *al-Qawl al-mufīd fī adillat al-ijtihād wa-'l-taqlīd*, ed. 'Abd al-Raḥmān 'Abd al-Khāliq, Kuwait, 1396/1976, has a chapter on the prohibition of *taqlīd* and against the tenet of *sadd bāb al-ijtihād,* closing of the door of independent judgement which he describes as a foul heresy (*bid'ah shanī'ah*)!

74. An extensive if relatively little known Zaydī literature exists. Imām Aḥmad had a few major writings published in Egypt but now many more are being printed.

75. The fourteen qualifications required of the Imām are set forth in R. Strothmann, *Der Staatsrecht der Zaiditen*, Strasbourg, 1912, 80.

76. He seems to mean the shape given Islam by the four Sunnī schools.

77. I.e. Mālik, Ibn Ḥanbal, Abū Ḥanīfah and al-Shāfi'ī.

78. Al-Hādī was the first Zaydī Imām of the Yemen.

79. This is one of the fourteen qualifications. Muḥammad b. Ismā'īl al-Amīr, *Subul al-salām*, 3rd edn., Muḥ 'Abd al-'Azīz al-Khūlī, Cairo, 1369 H., iii 145, says, 'In the province of the Yemen Fāṭimī women, (i.e. of the Sayyids and Ashrāf) have been prevented from that marriage which God made lawful to them, on account of the doctrine (*qawl*) of some of those following the school of the Hādawiyyah, namely that marriage of a Fāṭimī woman to anyone but a Fāṭimī man is forbidden, without their citing any evidence (*dalīl*) to this effect. It is not a doctrine of the Imām of the school/doctrine (*madhhab*) al-Hādī, on him be peace; on the contrary, he married his daughters to the Ṭabarīs and this doctrine only arose after him in the days of the Imām Aḥmad b. Sulaymān (al-Mutawakkil, 532-66/1138/71) and its (? the Hādawiyyah) leading house followed them and said, in language which speaks for itself, "Their ladies (*sharā'if*) for the Fāṭimīs are forbidden except to those the same as themselves". All this is without knowledge (*'ilm*), guidance or Book.' He asks how many Believing women (*Mu'mināt*) have been deprived of marriage because of the pride and arrogance of their guardians? Marriage within a woman's social group is of course not a practice confined to the Fāṭimī Sayyids.

80. In *Musnad al-Imām Zayd*, Beirut, 1966, 358, 360, E. Griffini edit., 247, no. 873, there is reference to fighting the *ahl al-baghy* and *al-fi'at al-bāghiyah*, but no theory is enunciated.

81. Zubayrī's interpretation of history is tendentious. In the first place *ijtihād* is not specifically 'Alawī. As A. K. Kazi, 'Notes on the development

of Zaidī law', *Abr-Nahrain*, Leiden, 1962, ii, 39, says, 'In their reasoning and critical attitude to traditions the early Zaidī imāms are strikingly similar to the early Ḥanafites. Like the Ḥanafite school too, the Zaidiyyah became less and less critical of traditions and made a restrained use of 'reason'.' Broadly speaking the exercise of the law is hereditary in the Prophet's house both before and after Islam, his ancestors acting as *ḥakams* or arbiters. That they should exercise the right of independent judgement in Islam deriving their authority from Muḥammad seems a natural evolution. The Imām al-Hādī in following only three sources of law, Qur'ān, the collectively reported Traditions of the Prophet and reason, is obviously taking a Mu'tazilī attitude.

An old proverb, *Ahl al-bayt adrā bi-mā fi 'l-bayt* (The people of the house know best what is in the house), was cited to me as expressing the hereditary nature of law reposited in the Prophet's House, but the proverb itself has no special application to it.

82. Perhaps because the famous third/ninth century theologian al-Ash'arī left Mu'tazilism for orthodoxy and followed the Shāfi'ī school.

83. By 'opinion' (*madhhab*) Zubayrī means *ijtihādāt al-Imām Yaḥyā wa-'l-Imām Aḥmad, yastanbiṭū-hā min kutub al-fiqh,* the independent judgement of Imāms Yaḥyā and Aḥmad which the Imāms elicit from the law books. Imām Yaḥyā's views have been published by Qāḍī 'Abdullāh b. 'Abd al-Wahhāb al-Shammāḥī, *Sīrat al-'ārifīn ilā idrāk ikhtiyārāt Amīr al-Mu'minīn*, Ṣan'ā', 1356/1937-8, printed at Maṭba'at al-Ma'ārif.

It is all very well for Zubayrī to make these complaints, but, from a practical viewpoint, when there is a conflict of views, it must be that of the Imām as head of state and the judiciary which prevails.

Qāsim Ghālib notes in his edition, p.26, that judgement is made in accordance with the Imām's opinion alone and it is only read in accordance with the Imām's opinion. He states that Sayyidah Arwā bt. Aḥmad al-Sulayḥī (of the Fātimī Tayyibī group considered heretical by Zaydīs and Shāfi'īs) made many waqfs to students of *'ilm* (religious knowledge) but her waqf deeds did not specify to what school they should belong. He accuses al-Ḥasan (cf para. 3b) of allotting special stipends to those who read *al-madhhab al-Hādawī*, the school (opinions) of al-Hādī only, which he paid from the waqfs not of his own ancestors but established by others.

84. The commonly used lawbook in Mutawakkilite Yemen was *Sharḥ al-Azhār*, a commentary upon which had been printed in Cairo in 1328/1910, but a commentary by Muḥ. al-Shawkānī, *al-Sayl al-Jarrār al-mutadaffiq 'alā Ḥadā'iq, al-azhār*, was printed in Cairo in 1970. Qāḍī Ismā'īl al-Akwa' informs me that this volume upset the Zaydī *'ulamā'* because many views were contrary to theirs. *K. al-Azhār fī fiqh al-A'immat al-Aṭhār,* the basic text of al-Mahdī Aḥmad b. Yaḥyā al-Murtaḍā (9th/14th century) was printed in Beirut in 1972. The *Sharḥ* is described as containing the views of the four Sunnī schools, Shāfi'ī, Mālikī, etc., but also of various Zaydī legal authorities, some of them not necessarily even well known. The Imām as *mujtahid* can select whatever view he thinks appropriate from these because 'basic Zaydism is the fundamentals/roots (*al-Zaydiyyah al-aṣliyyah al-uṣūl*)', and the branches (*furū'*) i.e. the systematic elaboration

of canonical law, can be drawn from the doctors of Islamic law, provided the following five fundamentals (*uṣūl*) are observed: 1. *al-'adl wa-'l-tawḥīd* 2. *al-wa'd wa-'l-wa'īd* 3. *al-amr bi-'l-ma'rūf wa-'l-nahy 'an al-munkar* 4. *al-khurūj 'ala 'l-maẓālim* 5. *ḥaṣr al-khilāfah fī awlād al-baṭnayn*. The last of these fundamentals—the restriction of the Caliphate to the descendants of 'Alī's two sons by the Prophet's daughter Fāṭimah is the stipulation most pertinent to this essay.

85. Cf. fn. 81.

86. Ar. *ashyā'*.

87. The text should read *qad 'ānā*, not *wa-qad*.

88. Al-Mutawakkil al-Qāsim b. al-Ḥusayn, 1128-39/1716-27, Al-Manṣūr al-Ḥusayn b. al-Qāsim, 1139-61/1727-48, Al-Mahdī 'Abbās b. al-Ḥusayn, 1161-89/1748-75.

89. Muḥ. b. Ismā'īl's biography, including this incident, is related by al-Shawkānī, *al-Badr al-ṭāli'*, Cairo, 1348 H., ii, 133-9; *Subul al-salām*, op. cit., i, 6; *Nashr al-'arf*, op. cit., ii, 505, i, 217-9, ii, 77; Ṣiddīq b. Ḥusayn al-Qanawjī, *al-Tāj al-mukallal*, Bombay, 1963, 414 *seq*.; Brockelmann, *Gal., Sup*., ii, 556, 74, 552. The editor of his *Dīwān* quotes other, mainly MS., sources of his biography, *Nafaḥāt al-'anbar, Ṭīb al-samr, Sulāfat al-'aṣr*, all known to Brockelmann.

90. There is a Bayt al-'Ajamī, a house of merchants (*tujjār*) in Ṣan'ā' at the present time, Persian by origin.

91. The technical term for this is *naṣb*, a hostile person being known as *nāṣibī* (pl., *nawāṣib*) = *alladhī yunāṣib ahl al-bayt al-'idā'*. Cf. Sīrat al-Hādī, 152, 172, and the verse of al-Mutanabbī (*al-'Urf al-ṭayyib fī sharḥ Dīwān* ... ed. Nāṣīf al-Yāzijī, Beirut, 1955, ii, 10, on a well 'Alawī in his day, 'When an 'Alawī is not the example of Ṭāhir, he is naught but an argument for the anti-'Alawīs (*li-'l-nawāṣibi*)'. This is adapted by a Zaydī poet, with the substitution of 'like Muḥammad' for 'Ṭāhir' (*Nashr al-'arf*, ii, 165.

The Aden paper al-*Yaqẓah*, 1957, no. 153, also defines *naṣb as hostility* to the Ahl al-Bayt and adds that *nāṣibī* is an injurious sobriquet (*nabz*) 'for anyone who opposes the despotic rulers (*al-ḥukkām al-mustabiddīn*)'. The article in question also calls Sayyid Muḥ. b. Ibrāhīm al-Wazīr (d. 840/1436 in Ṣan'ā') 'one of the propagandists (*du'āt*) for liberation from sectarianism (*madhhabiyyah*) and submission to unjust rulers'. This scholar (cf. al-Shawkānī, op. cit., ii, 89, 93) is famous for his *al-'Awāṣim wa-'l-qawāṣim* and composed an anti-Zaydī tract (*Radd 'ala 'l-Zaydiyyah*) but I do not know how far *al-Yaqẓah*'s description of his political attitude is to be trusted.

On this epithet *nawāṣib* cf. Muḥ. Aḥ. Nu'mān, *al-Aṭrāf al-ma'niyyah*, 24, 37.

As early as the *"Corpus iuris" di Zaid ibn 'Alī*, ed. E. Griffini, Milano, 1919, 74, no. 321, we find the injunction, *'Lā tuṣalli ... 'alā man naṣab li-Āl Muḥammad ḥarb-an'*, i.e., one should not bless anyone who raises war against the Family of Muḥammad.

92. *Al-madhhab al-sā'ir*, which might mean 'current school'.

93. The Shāfi'īs, I am informed, clasp the chest (*yaḍummūn*), at the

beginning of the prayer and raise (*yarfa'ūn*) the hands when saying *Allāhu akbar*. This is a superficial difference from the Zaydī form of prayer—Zaydīs keep the hands by the sides. Al-Shawkānī, op. cit., 134, says that Zayd b. 'Alī himself held that this is lawful. Zaydīs do not say *āmīn* after the *Fātiḥah*, holding that no extraneous word should intervene between one passage and another of the Qur'ān.

94. What follows is a paraphrase of al-Shawkānī's account.

95. Al-Shawkānī does not say 'take sides' but simply 'they say, "this is true"', '"this is false"'.

96. This is not a true summary of what al-Shawkānī says, for his text has nothing about wishing to be liberated and hold independent views. In fact he criticises a group that has read some jurisprudence (*fiqh*) but considered anyone of their contemporaries of the rank of *mujtahid* who (took a view) counter to the *fiqh* books to be heretical (*khārij min al-dīn*)—in spite of the fact that both the great and lesser Imāms take views contrary to what has been preferred by the authors in these books.

97. This whole sentence conveys a false impression of al-Shawkānī's text. He in fact concludes by saying that, so far from defending the doctrine (*madhhab*) of the Imāms, those persons who refuse to acknowledge the independent judgements (*ijtihādāt*) of the great *'ulamā'* which are counter to the school/doctrine (*madhhab*) are taking a contrary (view) to the *madhhab* of the Imāms of the People of the House and departing from (*khārij*) from their (the Imāms') consensus (*ijmā'*) since the Imāms prohibit *taqlīd* (defined in fn. 48), i.e. acceptance of authority, to those persons who have attained the rank of *ijtihād*.

98. See p.113.

99. Ar. *maṭma'*. *Ṭam'* is always used to describe the cupidity of tribes and Bedouin.

100. Al-Shawkānī, op. cit., 136, says that these *Ashrār* (he means the tribes Dhū Muḥammad and Dhū Ḥusayn) come into Ṣan'ā' each year for their stipends (*muqarrarāt*) and go to the mosques where books of Tradition are being read with some *'ālim* and stir up troubles. This, he says, is at the instigation of the *shayāṭīn al-fuqahā'*, the scoundrelly jurisprudents! So far from being religious these 'rough Bedouin (*A'rāb*)' mostly neither pray nor fast, and do not follow any of the obligatory ordinances of Islam 'except the two creeds (*al-shahādatayn*) along with the deviation in their pronouncing of them'. (The two creeds are *Lā ilāha illa 'llāh, wa-Muḥammad Rasūl Allāh*). He points to their un-Islamic practices, such as depriving women of the right to inherit, taking one another to judgement by customary law judges (*al-taḥākum ila 'l-ṭāghūt*) and making free with life and property (*istiḥlāl al-dimā' wa-'l-amwāl*), but cf. Martha Mundy's article, pp. 161-89. A current saying in allusion to the alleged lack of religion among the tribes, quoted to me runs, *'Al-qabīlī mā yuṣallī 'alā Muḥammad illā ba'd yadkum rās-ah*, The tribesman only says "Bless Muḥammad" when he knocks his head [on the lintel]'. *'Ṣallī 'alā Muḥammad'* would be his involuntary ejaculation. The sense is that the tribesman does not give any matter his consideration until brought abruptly face to face with it.

101. Op. cit., 137. This incident throws an interesting light on conditions in Ṣan'ā', but it is not as Zubayrī relates it. Al-Shawkānī says that during the very month he was penning this biography the tribes entered Ṣan'ā' treating the Ṣan'ānīs in their usual contemptuous way and robbing in the streets. When they came to the Imām's Gate a townsman saw a cow of his with them which he attempted to take back but the Bakīl tribesman with it drew his sword on him. The ordinary Ṣan'ānīs at the Imām's Gate were stirred by this to throw stones at them and then they took their camels from them and all their other beasts including those of which they had plundered the Ṣan'ānīs as well as most of their guns and other weapons, killing four more of them. On one group of them they inflicted so much harm that they were forced to flee to the mosques and privies (*maḥallāt qaḍā' al-ḥājah*). If the Khalīfah (Imām) had not restrained the ordinary folk they would not have left any one of them (alive). This brought them into deep humiliation —'may God increase their humiliation and diminish their numbers' adds al-Shawkānī.

102. The Arabic was explained as *laysat jawhariyyah.*

103. Zubayrī's conclusion may have some validity but his historical quotations cannot be said to have proved his point.

104. Or 'enslaved'.

105. A verse by 'Abd al-Raḥmān a poet of the rival house of Sharaf al-Dīn expresses the hostility of this leading family to the Ḥamīd al-Dīn.

Fa-innā Banū 'Adnāna dhuqnā marārat-an
Bi-jawri Banī Yaḥyā sakannā 'l-maqābira
Fa-lā anta Maḥmud-un wa-lā anta Kāmil-un
Wa-lā anta bi-'l-Hādī wa-lā anta Nāṣirun.

We Banū 'Adnān (the Sayyids) have tasted bitterness.
Through the tyranny of the Banū Yaḥyā (Ḥamīd al-Dīn) we are become dwellers of cemeteries.
You are not Maḥmūd (lit. 'praiseworthy', but the name of a young favourite of Imām Aḥmad) nor are you Kāmil (lit. 'perfect' but the name of Maḥmūd's brother).
Nor are you al-Hādī (lit. 'guiding', but the name of the first Zaydī Imām) nor even Nāṣir (lit. 'victorious' but the name assumed by Aḥmad on becoming Imām).

106. Qāsim Ghālib's commentary (p.32) specifies these as *al-iqṭā'iyyāt* and the extension of them, probably meaning 'feudal fiefs', and plundering of peaceful fellow-countrymen tribes (*al-qabā'il al-muwāṭinūn al-āminūn*)! *Iqṭā'ī*, feudal, was part of the political jargon of the Nasserite era, but in Rasūlid Yemen there were actual *iqṭā'* fiefs as part of the administrative system. The Ḥamīd al-Dīn do seem to have acquired some tribal lands, in one case known to me, by the legal method of *iḥyā' al-mawāt* or bringing waste land under cultivation. Lands held by the Imāmic House were an insignificant proportion of the total cultivated area, and I am reliably informed by a Republican official that the Imāms were scrupulous that neither they nor their officials should acquire land by illegal means.

107. Stock phrases in Zaydī writings.

108. Cf. fn. 70.

109. *'Unṣuriyyah*, race, racial, ethnic, elemental. It is said to mean here the 'Alawīs as opposed to non-'Alawīs, but it might be an allusion to the alleged 'Adnān-Qaḥṭān split.

110. Or possibly 'fortune and right guidance'. Though not Qur'ānic the phrase has a Qur'ānic echo.

111. I.e. the Zaydiyyah ruling the Shāfi'iyyah.

112. Lit., 'reaction'.

113. Ar. *sha'biyyah sāḥiqah*, popularity, deriving from *sha'b* populace.

114. The reference is to the Persian Abnā' descendants of the invaders who conquered at least parts of the Yemen before Islam. Qāḍī Ismā'īl al-Akwa' informs me that their descendants are to be found in villages in the Banī Ḥushaysh tribal territory called al-Abnā' and al-Furs; some are also in Banī Shihāb territory. Al-Hamdānī *al-Iklīl*, ed. Muḥ. al-Akwa', 1963-67, i, 380, quotes a verse satirising them as 'created for buying and selling goods, and for sesame-presses, butcheries and tanneries (*ma'āṣir, majāzir, madābigh*) which annoy their neighbours, and for weaving cloaks (*mulā'*)'. Ibid, ii, 152 seq., alludes to a governor in the time of the 'Abbāsid Caliph al-Ma'mūn who forbade the Abnā' to marry Yemenis and was deposed for this act. Ibid., 405-6 *passim*, knows Hishām ... al-Abnāwī, known as Qāḍī Ṣan'ā', also Imām of the Jāmi' Mosque and one of the shaykhs of al-Shāfi'ī, a man of prominence who died in 197/812-3. They seem to have been opposed to the Banū Shihāb, but in the sources at my disposal I have come across nothing to suggest that they behaved in the way Zubayrī describes—in fact as butchers and tanners they would belong to the menial class known today as *ahl al-khums*. For their claims to al-Raḥabah plain north of Ṣan'ā' in the time of the 'Abbāsid al-Saffāḥ, purporting to be granted them by a letter from the Prophet, see 'Abd al-Raḥmān b. al-Dayba', *Qurrat al-'uyūn*, ed. Muḥ. al-Akwa', Cairo, 1977, 120-2.

Cf. al-Rāzī al-Ṣan'ānī, *Tārīkh madīnat Ṣan'ā'*, ed. Ḥusayn al-'Amrī and 'Abd al-Jabbār Zakkār, Damascus, 1974, 465, index, al-Abnāwī.

115. Ar. *ḥafīẓah*. The classical sense—indignation at violence or injury done to something one is bound to honour, respect and defend—was doubtless in Zubayrī's mind.

116. Cf. fn. 114.

117. *Al-ḥukūmat al-sha'biyyah*, popular/populace government.

118. He means for the Sayyids versus the rest.

119. Ar. *'unṣurī*. Partisanship for any single section of the population is intended—'Alawīs, Quḍāh, Qabā'il, etc.

120. Perhaps he means 'as the rest of humanity' (?).

121. Zubayrī conveniently ignores the fact that the Egyptian revolution was engineered by the Army and that under Nasser Army officers were specially privileged.

122. The *Iqṭā'iyyūn*. Cf. fn. 106.

123. *Ibn al-Amīr wa-'aṣru-hu: ṣūrah min kifāḥ sha'b al-Yaman*, Qāsim Ghālib Aḥmad, Ḥusayn Aḥmad al-Sayāghī, Muḥ. b. 'Alī

al-Akwa', 'Abdullāh Mujāhid al-Shamāḥī, Maḥmūd Ibrāhīm Zāyid. No date, place of publication or printing house are mentioned, but it was published not later than 1969, probably in Beirut. I am informed that both al-Sayāghī and al-Shamāḥī deny having had anything to do with this book, stating that their names were added without their knowledge or consent, and that the book was written by Qāsim Ghālib and Muḥ. al-Akwa' only. The fifth name was not known—it is thought he may be an Egyptian Azharī.

124. Aḥmad al-Shāmī has described conditions in jail at Ḥajjah in 'Yemeni literature in Ḥajjah prisons', *Arabian Studies*, 1975, 43 ff.

125. Ed. 'Alī al-Sayyid Ṣabaḥ al-Madanī, Cairo, 1384/1964. Cf. fn. 89 for the biographies.

126. *Subul al-salām*, op. cit., 6.

127. Defined in fn. 73.

128. Among his writings is *Irshād al-nuqqād ilā taysīr al-ijtihād.*

129. *Dīwān*, 381.

130. Ibid., 332 seq., with details from the other biographies.

131. The Prophet, 'Alī, Fāṭimah, Ḥasan, Ḥusayn.

132. Biography in *Nashr al-'arf*, ii, 481, (d. 1167/1753-4).

133. Al-'Ajamī, being an Ithnā'asharī, a group to be regarded from a Sunnī viewpoint as far more extreme than the Zaydī school, could naturally be expected to view any tendency towards Sunnism with considerable disfavour.

134. Al-Amīr himself complains in his *Dīwān*, 386, of the hostility shown him on account of his propagation of the Prophet's Sunnah, the use of Sunnī works of Tradition, the science of Tradition, as one biographer states, being not widely spread in the Yemen at that time.

135. Ibid., 250. He pronounces the conventional blessings on the Prophet and al-Āl al-kirām, the noble House (p.372 passim).

136. *Nashr al-'arf*, ii, 518-9. Al-Shāmī informs me that 'Imām Aḥmad, on leaving the Yemen for treatment in Rome, made a will that all he possesses in the way of property, buildings, furniture and coin should go to the Bayt Māl al-Muslimīn. A number of persons bore witness to the bequest (*waṣiyyah*), including the Qāḍī Muḥammad al-'Amrī who told me that Imām Aḥmad said, "Even this pen with which I am writing is (to) be the property of the Bayt Māl al-Muslimīn". He (Aḥmad) said, "As for my books in Ḥajjah and Ta'izz if my son (*al-walad*) al-Badr wishes to use them he is to have them—otherwise they are to be a waqf to the Library of al-Jāmi' al-Kabīr in Ṣan'ā'". He did not make a waqf of his possessions (*amlāk*), it being as if he wished to absolve himself in respect of what he had taken in the way of disbursements (*ṣarfiyyāt*). My friend (*al-akh*) Aḥmad Bāshā told me that some of the officers and al-Bayḍānī found the bequest/will and smuggled it to Cairo after the 'Revolution' lest people should read it and realise the virtue and honesty (*nazāhah*) of Imām Aḥmad, God rest him. I also know that Sayf al-Islām 'Abdullāh son of Imām Yaḥyā, before he was executed, made a will that all he possesses should go to the Bayt Māl al-Muslimīn in return for what he had taken from the Chest (Ṣundūq) of the Bayt al-Māl when he was governor

of Hodeidah'. Cf. Aḥmad al-Murtaḍā, *al-Baḥr al-zakhkhār*, Cairo, 1947-49, ii, 184, re-iterating that *ṣadaqah* is not lawful for Imāms and Hāshimīs.

137. *Dīwān*, 187.

138. Ibid., 252.

139. Ibid., 9. Al-Amīr took the Zaydī attitude of condemning the 'heresy' of Sufism (p.131), was opposed to Muḥammad 'Abd al-Wahhāb (p.134) and commended holding to the Traditions from the (pious) ancestors (*al-aḥādīth min al-salaf*). He had links with the Yemeni Sunnīs and with the Sunnī Ashrāf of the Hijaz.

140. Yaḥyā b. al-Ḥusayn, *Ghāyat al-amānī*, Cairo, 1968, i, 144-5.

141. For this person see *Tārīkh madīnat Ṣan'ā'*, op. cit., index, 542 and fn. 114.

142. *Dīwān*, ed. Zuhdī Yakan, Beirut, 1962, 117.

XIV

Islam

It will occasion no surprise that in the Islamic countries there appear to be close parallels to almost all the beliefs and practices described in this volume as manifest in other civilisations in past ages or at this present time of ours. Islam is rooted in the ancient culture of Arabia, which partakes with other Semitic cultures in a common heritage, so that much that is Arabian is also to be found in the civilisation of the Hebrews, Mesopotamians and other Semitic communities. In the extensive territories where Islam became the dominant religion – Africa, Persia, parts of the Indian sub-continent, Indonesia, etc. – numerous pre-Islamic religious beliefs and practices survive, and even flourish vigorously, whether adapted into Islam or, not infrequently, without pretence of an Islamic veneer. In the latter case they are condemned by the ulema (doctors of theology) even if they be powerless to eradicate them. It is less well known that many vestiges of pre-Islamic pagan religion are still to be found in the Arabian Peninsula itself. In its formative period Islam developed into the distinctive religious culture, more or less as we now know it, exposed to the influences of the Mediterranean world of Greece and Rome, and of converts to the faith from Christianity, Judaism, Iranian religions and others.

Most of this is common knowledge.

From the wealth of evidence of divination by various methods, omens, even certain forms of oracle – whether these exist at a high intellectual level or belong to the everyday life of ordinary folk – it is only possible here to select some limited examples by way of illustration. For a thorough systematic study the reader is referred to Taufic Fahd's excellent book, *La divination arabe. Études religieuses sociologiques et folkloriques sur le milieu natif de l'Islam* (Leiden, 1966), upon which this chapter has liberally drawn. To distinguish between diviner and prophet is not easy and the distinctive line between divination and magic is uncertain. Islam being an Arabian religion, it is logical to start with divination and oracles known from the preceding pagan age, the *Jāhiliyyah* as the Arabs call it, and trace where these have survived on into Islam, or the Islamic era, itself.

In the Ka'bah of Mecca, an idol, said to have been brought from Hīt in Iraq, and known to the pagan Meccans as Hubal, was set up in front of a well or pit inside the actual building. Before this god Hubal lay seven arrows known by the technical name *qidḥ*, a word also used of the arrows in the gambling game called *maysar*. On each arrow was something written; one arrow had written on it 'blood-money', and when two parties were at variance as to the person who should take the responsibility for paying it, the custodian, known as *sādin*, shuffled the arrows for them; the individual whose lot was to draw this arrow assumed the duty of payment. Another arrow had written on it, 'Yes', and, when they required an answer about some affair, if the arrow marked 'Yes' fell to their lot they acted in accordance with it. Another had 'No' and when they wanted to do something they shuffled it among the arrows, and if it fell to their lot they did not do that thing.

Another arrow had written on it, 'Belongs to you' or, as another version has it, 'Of pure descent', while another had 'Attached', and yet a third had 'Belonging to others, not to yourselves.' This was used to determine paternity in a disputed case. Affiliation is still an important issue among Arab tribes because of the responsibility of relatives for blood-money and blood revenge; furthermore, in parts of Arabia there is a custom current among the tribes of providing a woman concubine for the guest, and of course there is the case of plain fornication. Only some thirty to forty miles from Aden I came across a sort of oracle in 'the Bastard's Rock'. If an accusation of illegitimacy is made, the child of suspect legitimacy – always, I imagine, a boy – is made to crawl under a great square rock poised on stones with a small space between it and the ground, a natural phenomenon. If the child gets through he is legitimate. I was told of a case where a boy stuck under the rock and his mother burst into a fury of rage because he had unjustly impugned her honour! The mediaeval writer Usāmah ibn Munqidh tells of a rock-cleft at Petra which was used in the same way.

Another account of this type of oracle runs as follows:

An arrow had written upon it 'Waters' and when they wanted to dig for water they shuffled the arrows with that one among them, and they acted in accordance with wherever it came out. They used, when they wished to circumcise a lad, to give a woman in marriage, to bury a deceased person, or, if they doubted the ancestry of a person, to take him to Hubal along with 100 dirhams (silver drachmae) and a slaughter-camel which they would give to the man in charge of the arrows who shuffles them. Then they would bring up their man about whom they wished to ascertain – whatever it was. 'O God of ours', they would say, 'this is so and so, about whom we want to know such and such a thing. Produce the truth about him.' They would then say to the man in charge of the arrows, 'Shuffle' (literally, 'Strike!'). If 'Belongs to you' came out, he was a *wasīṭ*, of good quality as far as the tribe was concerned. If 'Belonging to others' came out he was an ally (*ḥalīf*); and if 'Attached' came out he was linked to them because of residing among them, but without any relationship or pact of alliance. If 'No' came out they would postpone an action for that year, until they decided to come for a second time, and they would go on with this affair of theirs until the arrows produced a positive answer. An ancient pre-Islamic verse runs:

Inna 'khtalafnā fa-habi 'ṣ-ṣirāḥā
Thalātat-an yā Hubalu fiṣāḥā
Al-maytu wa-'l-udhratu wa-'n-nikāḥā,
Wa-'l-bur' fi 'l-marḍā wa-'ṣ-ṣiḥāḥā.
In lam taqul-hu fa-muri 'l-qidāḥā.

When we are in dispute, give us rest
In three things, o Hubal, a clear (verdict),
The dead, circumcision and marriage,

Recovery for the sick and sound health.
If you do not utter it [i.e., make a sign] – command the arrows (to do so).

These verses quite evidently represent authentically how and why the pre-Islamic Arabians sought oracles from the gods of paganism, and I am inclined to regard the verses themselves as actually pre-Islamic. The pre-Islamic south Arabian inscriptions confirm the practice, in that in one there is a question (*ms'l*) posed to the god Ilumqah, while another god, Ta'lab, gives an indication of his wish by a sign.

Settling by lot, called *istiqsām* – which of course is what resort to divination by the arrows is – is condemned by the Qur'ān, yet, in affairs more or less mundane, the Prophet himself did sometimes make a decision by lot. In ancient Israel this was also practised and the technical term employed comes from the same root as the Arabic *istiqsām*.

Arab tribesmen today occasionally treat their local saints, whose shrines have taken the place of those of the pre-Islamic gods, to demands couched in somewhat peremptory language. So also did the celebrated prince of ancient Arabian poets, Imru'u 'l-Qays. Sworn to avenge the slaying of his father Ḥujr, he paid a visit to the oracle of Dhu 'l-Khalaṣah, north of Najrān, on the present-day Sa'udi-North Yemen border, and consulted the god in the ordinary way by drawing from three arrows entitled 'The Commanding', 'The Prohibiting' and 'The Waiting'. Drawing the second, he broke the arrows in his anger and dashed them in the face of the idol, exclaiming with a coarse imprecation, 'If *your* father had been slain you would not have hindered me.'

In ancient and contemporary Arabia the most important political function is that of arbitration between two contending parties. One of Muhammad's chief preoccupations indeed at Medina was to enforce compliance with the agreement he had made with the tribes there constituting him the ultimate arbiter in disputes. Until that time one of the several ways of settling a dispute was for the two parties to a quarrel to go to a *kāhin* who settled cases by divinatory or magic procedures. It need hardly be pointed out that *kāhin* is the same word as Hebrew *cohen*, both deriving from the common Semitic civilisation, but *kāhin* perhaps represented the function at a less developed and sophisticated stage than the Biblical *cohen*. The Arabian *kāhins* pronounced their decisions in rhymed prose of lofty style and cryptic oracular diction; this was nevertheless no mere exercise in rhetoric, for their utterances clothed verdicts concluded with professional forensic skill.

An office parallel to that of the *kāhin*, the *Ṭāghūt*, is alluded to in the Qur'ān eight times. The Believers were prohibited from seeking judgment from the *Ṭāghūt*, but must refer their differences to Allah and His Apostle. The term survives in the northern Yemen, meaning the head of a tribe who judges by customary law. I have not heard that the *Ṭāghūt* relies on oracular methods, but in some places, even today, recourse is had to supernatural means to determine a case, as will be mentioned. The ancient *Ṭāghūt* judge was called a *shayṭān* (lit. Satan) or a magician (*sāḥir*) because of his association with a familiar spirit. The Medina Jews seem to have fitted into the system, for the Aslamī *kāhin*, Abū Burdah, was invited by the Jewish Naḍīr and Qurayẓah tribes to judge between them, and the half-Jewish Ka'b ibn al-Ashraf is identified with the *Ṭāghūt*. That the *Ṭāghūt* was associated with ancient Arabian religion is apparent in the description of the *Ṭawāghīt* as 'interpreters of the idols, speaking with the people with their tongues.' 'There was one in every tribe, upon whom the *shayṭāns* were caused to descend.'

North Arabians might repair to a *kāhin* at the north Yemen city of Ṣa'dah. A noble Quraysh lady was accused of adultery by her husband and sent back to her father. To exonerate herself she took the oath that she was innocent and volunteered to go to one of the Yemen *kāhins* to put the matter to test. When, however, she and her father had nearly arrived she began to show some disquiet so he asked her if this was because she had done some unseemly thing. This the lady denied. 'But I know,' she said, 'that you are coming to a human being who both makes errors and hits the mark, and I cannot be sure that he will not mark me with a brand-mark (or, possibly, branding iron) which will be a disgrace until the Day of Judgment.'

This appears a clear allusion to trial by ordeal, known in

Arabia today as *bish'ah*, and the only classical reference to it of which I am aware. It is found in our time at Bir Sheba in southern Palestine, in Jordan, in Ḥaḍramawt and in Yāfiʿī country on the Yemen border. The best known *bish'ah* is to heat a knife red-hot; with this the *mubashshi'* (arbiter) flicks the tip of the tongue of the accused; if it burns his tongue, this proves him guilty. I discussed *bish'ah* with a shaykh of the Āl 'Abd al-Wadūd, the *mubashshi'*-judge of Raydat 'Abd al-Wadūd on the east Ḥaḍramawt coast. He emphasized that the professional *mubashshi'* – the function is hereditary in families – would spend a long time discussing with the litigants, painting a fearful picture of the red-hot knife and trying to bring them to agree to a settlement. An interesting aside is that he kept on saying that he had 'broken' the knife and when I persisted in asking to see even the pieces, someone told me that *kasara*, 'to break', here means 'to leave off.' In the Residency files I found that the local Arab Government had abolished *bish'ah* as a heathen practice contrary to Islamic *sharī'ah* (law), but one Arab official had written a defence of it as highly effective with the tribes. My theory is that while interrogating the parties the *mubashshi'* and his family carry on private investigations as to the guilty party and manipulate the red-hot knife appropriately.

When, in ancient times, contestants selected a *kāhin* to arbitrate between them they first tested his powers by asking him to guess at a certain object they had picked up on their way to him. To this the *kāhin* or *Ṭāghūt* would reply with high-sounding oaths, identifying it. In the case of the Quḍā'ah *kāhin* whose familiar or *shayṭān* was called *'Uzzā* the two parties picked up a dead vulture which they concealed for him to guess. His answer typifies the rhetoric of the *kāhins*.

> You have concealed for me the owner of a wing with a long neck, lengthy of leg, black mixed with white, when it hastens it soars and circles in its flight, when it swoops from the height of the sky it splits (its prey) from end to end, owner of a keen-pointed claw, living until worn out. . . . I swear by the light and the moon, thunder and fate, the winds and the creation, you have concealed for me a

vulture's corpse in a saddle-cloth of hair, with the gallant lad of Banū Naṣr.

This testing of the *kāhin* was authenticated to me in a curious way, for when enquiring about trial by ordeal in Abyan in 1964, my informants told me that two parties repairing to the *mubashshi*ʻ in Upper Yāfiʻ, would ask him to divine the secret thing they had brought with them – for example, they said, *a locust in a leather bag*. In this same year also was published for the first time, in Ḥaydarābād, *Kitāb al-Munammaq* and to my astonishment, when reading through it, I found that two parties going to the *kāhin* of Quḍāʻah some fourteen centuries ago, hid for him to divine and thereby test his confidence, the head of a locust in a water-skin (*ra's jarādah fī khurbat mazādah*).

Muhammad set himself firmly against judgment by divination and seems to have disclaimed for himself power to perform magic. He opposed magic, though on more than one occasion he recognised himself as having been bewitched. Once he was asked by a Bedouin to prove he was the Apostle of Allah, as his Companions maintained, by telling him what was in the belly of his she-camel (in the same way as *kāhins* are tested), the Bedouin meaning that he should tell him whether the foetus was male or female. His request only brought him a coarse rejoinder from the Companions.

Nevertheless Muhammad in his outward manifestations appears to us like the *kāhins*. He was an ecstatic and took omens from his dreams as they did. At the beginning his dreams anticipated real events. However he did not draw revelation from *shayṭāns* but revelations were brought to him by Gabriel. Islamic Tradition has preserved evidently genuine accounts of how revelation came to Muhammad. 'When Muhammad received a revelation . . . this caused him much pain. so that we perceived it.' Even on cold days sweat appeared on his forehead. He would cover his head. He snored as one asleep or rattled like a young camel. The pagan prophet al-ʻAnsī in Ṣanʻā' seems to have groaned or cried out in the travail of receiving revelation as the Arab historians inform us. Ecstatic states in Arabia are associated with intense trembling or shaking and this is also found in popular forms in Sufism. However in the sources consulted it does not seem that Muhammad is recorded as trembling.

The way in which pagan gods manifested a sign may perhaps be understood in the light of an unusual experience I had in 1940 when stationed in the Ṣubayḥī tribal area west of Aden, in a village of the most farouche tribe I have ever encountered. This district had a number of ecstatics, known as *majdhūb* or *mamlūk*, possessed, associated with a saint, al-Qāḍī, and his shrine. When I questioned these ecstatics about this saint one of them stated that he was of Banāt al-'Arsh, the Daughters of the (Heavenly) Throne. I would have asked a great deal more but my more orthodox soldiers shut him up and told him this was nonsense. In fact these 'Islamic' saints function exactly as the ancient pagan tutelary deities.

We engaged some of these *majdhūbs* as tribal auxiliaries and upon an occasion one of them fell into a trance which even our regular soldiers recognised as being effected by the saint. We were at this time holding on behalf of the Lahej sultanate, several hostages from two tribal sub-sections, preparatory to judgment in an abduction case. One morning, the chief of the auxiliaries, himself a *majdhūb*, came to me, visibly distressed and trembling in every limb, with beads of sweat on his brow though it was an exceptionally cool day after the summer rains. The other *majdhūbs* present were also trembling and they knew that other *majdhūbs* with whom they had not been in contact would be trembling also. The fuss arose because our soldiers, though feeding the hostages, refused to provide them with water which was short because it had to be conveyed up the mountainside. The saint had demonstrated his displeasure at the failure to provide for hostages in their or his territory, visiting it on the *majdhūbs* and they had to discover the cause and seek to appease him.

In a northern Arabian context we seem to have a remarkable survival of pre-Islamic religion that enables us to interpret the rather bald statements of Arab genealogists and historians. These writers tell us that in such and such a section of a tribal confederation of the migratory tribes of the north lay the honour (*sharaf*) and the *bayt* – literally 'house', meaning also a 'temple' and, for Bedouin, a leather 'tent'. It is suggested that the *bayt* may have been a sort of portable temple, but I am also inclined to associate with that the family or 'house' which had charge of it. (In southern Arabia where the population is mostly settled the *bayt* would be a building.)

Now the famous scholar Alois Musil, who lived with and studied the migrating Rwalah tribes of Syria before World War I, describes what looks like a sort of camel-litter called Abu 'd-Duhūr, meaning literally 'Father of the Ages', but the name recalls *dahr* or *Manāt*, Fate, the latter being the well-known pre-Islamic goddess. Abu 'd-Duhūr is kept in the tent of the prince and is a sign of the princely authority of its holder. When the tribe goes on warlike manoeuvres, Abu 'd-Duhūr is borne on a white camel at the head of the tribal warriors. The Rwalah believe that Allah gives signs to them through the intermediary of Abu 'd-Duhūr. At times of dead calm, the ostrich feathers with which it is adorned begin to flutter; at other times the litter moves to right or left, but suddenly straightens itself. When the feathers wave, the Rwalah believe that Allah has touched it with his power. From such movements auguries are taken and it may be surmised that the *bayt* of the migrating Bedouin of ancient times had also an oracular function as Abu 'd-Duhūr has or had at any rate in very recent times.

While on the one hand Muhammad rejected the notion that he could perform miracles and denied that he was a *kāhin* (whether or not he actually considered *kāhins* had really the power of divination) it is reported by his biographers that he did pay great attention to the omen, *fa'l*, and to his dreams as has been already mentioned. Sūrat Yūsuf of the Qur'ān approves of Joseph in interpreting dreams, and Islamic Tradition sees Muhammad as an interpreter of dreams like the Prophets preceding him. Historians indeed tell that Muhammad's mission was foretold in the dream of a king of pre-Islamic Yemen – that his country would be occupied by the Abyssinians but liberated by the Yemeni leader Sayf ibn Dhī Yazan with the aid of the Persians, and that there would arrive an Arabian Prophet.

In popular Islam, the beliefs of common folk, the tradition of presage of future events or decisions made by supernatural agency through the medium of dreams seems to be universal. It figures for instance in the hagiologies of Sudanese *fiqihs*, the religious leaders and saints of the countryside, rather unsophisticated in type. The *fiqih* might be in a *khalwah*, i.e. the retreat of an ascetic which would also contain a school for teaching religion, or in the domed tomb, *qubbah*, of a departed saint, and be vouchsafed, when he falls asleep, a dream of guidance for his future actions. The Bān al-Naqā' are hereditary *fiqihs* of the districts north of Khartoum, and 'Abd al-Raḥmān wadd Bān al-Naqā' saw in a dream his grandfather flying between the Heavens and Earth, his own father flying behind him, and himself behind his father. He recounted this vision to Sharīf 'Abdullāh who said to him, 'They have indicated to you that you should occupy yourself with exoteric learning.' Yet another *fiqih* of this same family had the experience, while in a *khalwah*, of his soul departing his body in a dream and penetrating to the Heavens where he met the Prophet Muhammad who assigned Shamharūsh, the cadi of the Jinnīs, to his service, while various deceased Sudanese saints conferred on him the gifts of saintship and 'the fire of the *fiqih* Badawī.' In olden time in the Sudan fires were lighted at night so that the *fiqih* could see to study with his pupils, so that the 'fire of the *fiqih*' comes to mean his teaching circle.

The belief in familiar spirits survives into our own time and in southern Arabia it is, of all people, Muhammad's descendants, the Sayyids, who are credited with having service (*khidmah*) from the Jinnīs by even the orthodox biographical collections, as also with the power to summon (*taḥḍīr*) the Jinnīs and, one assumes, to consult them. We made the acquaintance of a Ḥaḍramī Sayyid, whose Jinnī was called Sharyūt, but his Jinnī, when willing to obey him, only performed simple tricks of white magic. It is however widely believed in the popular Islamic world that if you have a ring with the secret name of God (*khātam al-ism*), the Jinnīs will come and offer you their service.

To revert however to the question of dreams. At an early period in Islam data relating to the interpretation of dreams began to be collected, the great name associated with this activity being that of Ibn Sīrīn, who flourished in the latter part of the first *hijrah* century/7th century AD. This developed into a sort of pseudo-science known in Arabic as *ta'bīr al-ru'yā*. About the beginning of the 4th/10th century AD, the name of Artemidorus of Ephesus, and his work on dreams, starts to figure in Islamic literature, though actually the translation from Greek into Arabic took place about a century earlier. It appears to have exerted some influence on the formulation of the principles of this pseudo-science, which developed into a sort of discipline and gave rise to an extensive literature.

We are told that Ibn Sīrīn, 'When a dream was submitted to him, remained a good part of the day questioning the dreamer about his conditions, his person, his profession, his family and mode of life; in short, he neglected nothing of a kind that would supply the least indication, and he took these replies into account when pronouncing on the dream.' It will be immediately apparent that his method of ascertaining all relevant information closely resembles that of the *mubashshi*' before he puts his client to the test of the red-hot knife.

By way of contrast to Ibn Sīrīn's rather empirical approach to the interpretation of dreams let me quote from the celebrated philosopher of history, Ibn Khaldūn, in his rationalisation of dream visions. He says:

> Dream vision is an awareness on the part of the rational soul in its spiritual essence, of glimpse(s) of the forms of events. While the soul is spiritual, the forms of events have actual existence in it, as is the case with all spiritual essences. The soul becomes spiritual through freeing itself from bodily matters and corporeal perceptions. This happens to the soul (in the form of) glimpse(s) through the agency of sleep. . . . Through (these glimpses) (the soul) gains the knowledge of future events that it desires and by means of which it regains the perceptions that (properly) belong to it. When this process is weak and indistinct, the soul applies to it allegory and imaginary pictures, in order to gain (the desired knowledge). Such allegory, then, necessitates interpretation.[1]

'Incubation' is defined for us as sleeping in the sanctuary with the formal intention of receiving, in a dream, the reply to a question asked of the god, having performed certain prescribed rites beforehand. It appears that incubation was practised in pre-Islamic Arabia since, in two inscriptions, thanksgiving offerings are recorded for visions revealed in the temples of 'Athtar and Awwam', while a third inscription alludes to a vision which is described as 'what he showed him in his slumber.'

Ibn Khaldūn maintains that the dream vision about things one desires may be induced. He says,

> It consists of saying, upon falling asleep, and after obtaining freedom of the inner senses and finding one's way clear (*sc.* for supernatural perception), the following non-Arabic words (apparently meaningless): *Tamāghis ba'dān yaswādda waghdās nawfanā ghādis*. The person should then mention what he wants, and the thing he asks for will be shown him in his sleep. . . . With the help of these words. I have myself had remarkable dream visions, through which I learned things about myself that I wanted to know.

He rationalizes this by saying that 'The dream words produce a preparedness in the soul for a dream vision.'

The Islamic practice known as *istikhārah* is by some considered a survival of incubation. *Istikhārah* is the prayer of a person who has not yet made up his mind, in order to be inspired with a sound decision regarding an enterprise he is about to undertake. In popular practice there are many forms of this *istikhārah* not sanctioned by Tradition, among which is seeking an answer through consulting the Qur'ān. The early nineteenth century Arabist Edward Lane says that in Egypt in his day the procedure was to repeat thrice the *Fātiḥah* of the Qur'ān, the four brief verses of Sūrat al-Ikhlāṣ, and the verse from Sūrat al-An'ām commencing *Wa-'inda-hu mafātīḥ al-ghayb lā ya'lamu-hā illā huwa* (With Him are the keys of the mysterious, no-one knows them but He). 'They let the book fall open, or open it at random, and from the seventh line of the right-hand page draw their answer.' This is forbidden by the Sunnī ulema but is doubtless done everywhere. In Ṣan'ā' of the Yemen in the first half of the 11th/17th century a party of notables at a banquet decided to consult the Holy Book to see whom Allah would chose as Caliph, i.e. Imām of the Yemen, and, after reciting the *Fātiḥah* and praying, the identical passage came up three times, 'Mention in the Book Ismā'īl.' In the event Ismā'īl son of al-Qāsim the Great succeeded in the year 1054/1644, taking the title of al-Mutawakkil.

In Persian speaking circles the Sufi *Mathnawī* of Jalāl al-Dīn Rūmī or the *Dīwān* of the poet Ḥāfiẓ are often used for the same purpose.

The means whereby presage of good or ill fortune was sought that figures perhaps most commonly in the Islamic histories is consultation of the stars. Names of astrologers or astronomers – the Arabic word *munajjim* means both – are preserved even from the pre-Islamic age; moreover a south Arabian inscription has come to light which alludes to a *kawkabān ṣ(i)dqm*, probably meaning 'a true star', in the prayer for male children of good star and fortune.

It is curious that so distinguished a scientist as al-Bīrūnī, who had spent much time and labour in studying Greek and Indian astrology and whose book on *Tanjīm*, composed in 420/1029, deals with both astronomy and astrology, should apparently have believed in the influence of the planets on the sub-lunary world and that he should even have shared the general belief in the efficacy of charms and talismans, whereas his contemporary, Avicenna, contemptuously refutes astrologers.

How general was the credence given this other pseudo-science, astrology, during the early mediaeval period can be seen from the *Qaṣīdah* of Abū Dulaf al-Khazrejī, writing, in the 4th/10th century, of tricksters and beggars, mainly in Iraq and Iran, and using the cant or argot of their professions. One of these he calls

> a band of people who peer into omens (*fa'l*), auguries (*zajr*) and the meaning of the stars. They give money to a group of onlookers on the understanding that these last should come to them and ask them about their lucky stars and about their future circumstances, so that the fortune-tellers may look into their horoscopes. The customers then give back their money to the fortune-tellers. The latter usually keep it, but they may say to another person, 'We won't take your money because your star has not come out as you would like it.'; until the dupe falls into the harvest of victims ready for slaughter.

'Al-Tanbal,' he adds, 'is the simpleton who is the victim of tricks played on him and who is taken in by the fortune-tellers' returning his money to them. So he too lays out his money, fully expecting the fortune-teller to give it back to him; but the latter takes it from him, thus making him look ridiculous.' Readers of the *Arabian Nights* may also remember *The story told by the tailor*, in which the glib barber delays his exasperated victim whilst he finds with his astrolabe the precise moment auspicious for the shaving.

Recourse to astrologers was not restricted to ordinary folk in the sūq. In the fiscal and administrative survey of the Yemen under the brilliant Rasūlid dynasty, compiled at the beginning of the 9th/15th century, is included the item, among a list of other government servants, of

> the calculators of astronomical or astrological observations, experts, philosophers, who have perused the instructive books and have the reputation for sound auspicious astrological judgments and whose prognostications of propitious times to undertake a certain action coincide with auspicious movements (*sc.* of the stars, planets etc.) – what they have laid down having been (proven) sound, be it old or new. They will not leave the Royal Court (al-Bāb al-Sharīf) because of the needs of the sovereign, and the requirement of astrological observations to be made on newly-born children and the selection of (propitious) movements (of stars etc.). Even if they be two, three or four persons they are indispensable.

An accusation levelled against the late Imām Aḥmad of the Yemen who died as recently as 1962 was that he consulted astrologers whom he maintained at his court.

In fact one reads in many of the histories of professional astrologers attached to the courts of Islamic monarchs, and the following is related of the 'Abbāsid period. The philosopher al-Kindī, at the court of the Caliph in early 3rd/9th century Baghdad, evidently practised astrology as part of his duties and equipment as a scholar. On a particular occasion his assertion of his superiority in the field of scholarship was challenged by a prominent '*ālim* or professional scholar who conceded however that he would admit to this if al-Kindī could show himself able to divine something that he, the *'ālim*, would write down on a piece of paper. So they laid a wager – the *'ālim* staked his valuable cloak and al-Kindī his mule with its expensive trappings. The *'ālim* wrote on his piece of paper which was placed under the quilt of the Caliph. Asked to guess what he had written, al-Kindī

> asked for a tray of earth, rose up, took the altitude, ascertained the Ascendant, drew an astrological figure on the tray of earth, determined the positions of the stars and located them in the signs of the Zodiac and fulfilled all the conditions of divination and thought-reading, literally, guessing the nature of a hidden object. He then pronounced that the *'ālim* had written something which was 'first a plant and then an animal'.

The writing turned out to say, 'The rod of Moses' – which of course turned into a snake in front of Pharaoh!

If this story from the Persian *Chahār Maqālah* or *Four Discourses* is to be considered more entertainment than historical fact, it does nevertheless contain certain points of resemblance to the testing of the *kāhin* in an earlier age.

In many countries individuals are credited with the ability to divine or to see a robbery enacted before their eyes and describe it detail by detail to the robbed so that they are able to apprehend the thief. A cynical Aden proverb runs, *Mā fāt 'ala 'l-sāriq shall-uh al-munajjim*, 'What the thief missed the astrologer has carried off.' The astrologer's fee has been so exorbitant that the owner of the stolen goods has nothing left.

The elaborate Chinese compass illustrated on Plate 4 employed in fortune-telling is to some extent to be matched by the *zā'irajah* (fig. 11) attributed to a Moroccan scholar of Csuta about the close of the 6th/12th century. It consists of a large circle enclosing other concentric circles for the spheres, the elements, the created things, the *spiritualia*, as well as other types of beings and sciences. Each circle is divided into sections, the areas of which represent signs of the Zodiac, or the elements, or other things. The lines dividing each section run to the centre, and are called chords. Along each chord there are sets of letters that have a conventional (numerical) value. Some are *zimām* ciphers, the same as those used for numerals by government officials and accountants in the contemporary Maghrib. Others are the ordinary *ghubār*[2] ciphers. Inside the *zā'irajah*, between the circles are found the names of the sciences and topics of the created (world). On the back of the page containing the circles, there is a table with many squares.

One commences by writing down the question to be solved by the *zā'irajah* in unconnected letters and by determining the Ascendant of that day, i.e. one of the signs

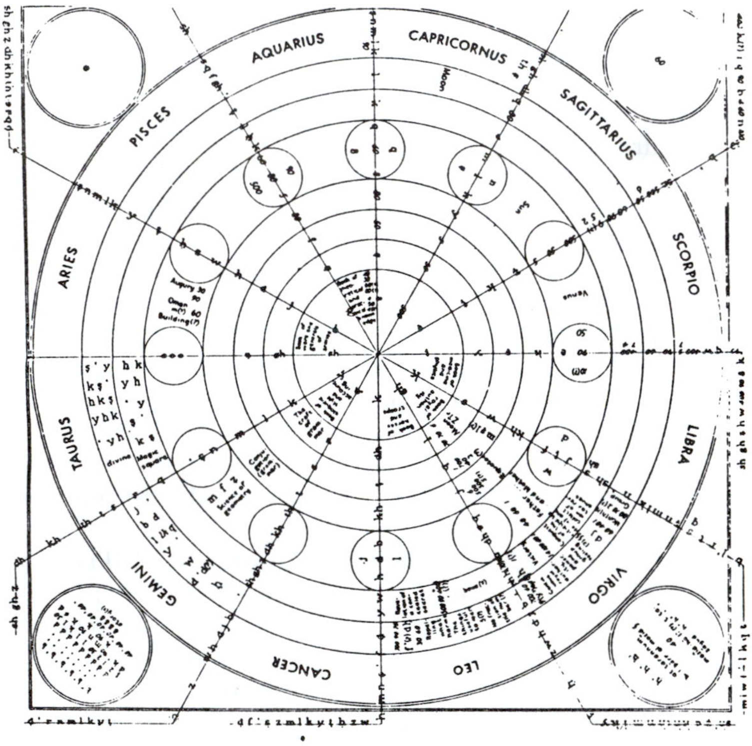

Figure 11. *The Zā'irajah*; from Franz Rosenthal, *Ibn Khaldûn: the Muqaddimah*, Bollingen series, Princeton, 1958. Reprinted by permission of Princeton University Press, and Routledge and Kegan Paul Limited.

of the Zodiac and the degree (of the sign on the horizon), so the particular chord bordering the sign of the Zodiac of that Ascendant is chosen. There then follows a most complicated set of calculations involving the numerical values of the letters of the alphabet. A very simple form of *zā'irajah* from early 19th century Egypt is shown by Edward Lane in his *Manners and Customs of the Modern Egyptians*; this is a square table containing a hundred letters, but it has nothing in common with the Moroccan *zā'irajah* other than the name. It is thought that the word itself derives from the Persian *zā'ichah*, horoscope, astronomical tables.

Augury by the flight of birds (*ṭīrah*) was condemned by the Prophet as pagan superstition, but it has survived vigorously enough among, for example, the northern Rwalah tribe. Musil reports that two ravens flying above a raiding party are a good omen, but a single raven or a vulture is a bad omen. Like the ancient Arabs the Rwalah took auguries from the movements of animals. A Rwalah Bedouin starting on an important task considered the gazelle unlucky and would shout at it, '*Ghazāl ghazāl, wa-sharr-an zāl!*' ('Gazelle, gazelle, let misfortune vanish as well!'). For the ancient Arabs, a gazelle passing from right to left was a bad omen but, in general, the movement from left to right was considered to bring misfortune, though they do not seem to have been consistent over this. The Rwalah carefully observe the fox. If, on catching sight of a Rwalah raiding party, it halts, they know they need expect no mishap but will return with booty. A white mare, ass, camel, are good omens; a black dog is a bad omen.

These then are a few of the forms in which divination is or was practised in Islamic countries or some of them. I have not dealt with geomancy or divination based on drawing lines in sand, and many other ways of telling the future. There is, to take a case in point, the large literature on *jafr*,[3] which is particularly the domain of Shī'ah Muslims, its origin being attributed to 'Alī, the fourth Caliph, himself. It contains predictions, often apocalyptic, and covers all methods of divination based on letters of the alphabet and their numerical values. This category seems sometimes to be called *ḥisbān*, and it is a lasting regret to me that on my two tours of the former Wāḥidī sultanate circumstances prevented me from consulting a manuscript *ḥisbāniyyah* in the hands of the Bā Qādir manṣab of the sanctuary at Ṣa'Īd, but in the Yemen in 1966 I was able to copy a poem attributed to a semi-legendary poet, al-Ḥārith al-Rayyāshī, which was said to foretell the eventual victory of the Imām al-Badr over Nasser and the Republic. The poem was an accretion of individual verses but it looked archaic; the main interest of it however is that at the present day a poet could be held to have divinatory functions just like the ancient Arabian poets with their *hājis*, meaning muse or inspiration, who sometimes acted as oracles.

Notes

1 Franz Rosenthal, trans., *Ibn Khaldûn: the Muqaddimah*, Bollingen Series XLIII, New York, 1958.

2 A form of the Arabic numerals close to that used in the west to-day.

3 Said to be a book written by the sixth Shiʿah Imām containing all that was to happen until the Last Day.

XV

A FORTIFIED TOWER-HOUSE IN WĀDĪ JIRDĀN (WĀḤIDĪ SULTANATE) — I

By Brian Doe and R. B. Serjeant

(PLATES I–VIII)

In September 1964 we were able, after considerable difficulty, to reach the village al-Jinainah (al-Junainah) of Wādī Jirdān (which we had already visited earlier in the year along the spectacular new road from Wādī ʻAmaqīn). In the afternoon of that day and early next morning before leaving to return to ʻAtaq we made a brief survey of the tower known as al-Muqaiyad—the subject of this article. The visit being so hurried and part of the work being carried out after dark, we were not able to record everything in quite the detail we should have wished. We are much indebted to Lt.-Col. Adrian Donaldson, D.S.O., M.B.E., the C.O., and Major S. F. B. Francis, T.D., then of the 5th Battalion, Federal Regular Army, the latter escorting us to the mouth of Wādī Jirdān at ʻAyādh, and for the generous hospitality they gave us at ʻAtaq. We acknowledge with pleasure the courtesy of Shaikh Ruwais b. Miḥsin b. Ḥasan Namārī Hilālī, Federal Councillor, who permitted us to survey the *ḥuṣn* and supplied us with much information on it, as also to his brother Ḥasan b. Miḥsin.

Wādī Jirdān, famed for its honey,[1] is one of the most beautiful valleys in South Arabia, rich in *musht* (*Polypodium crenatum*)[2] and *ʻilb* trees as well as other vegetation, with 12,000 *ḍamds* of arable land, and full of pre-Islamic ruins and inscriptions. It has already been described, on the basis of data supplied by informants, by Landberg,[3] on the whole very accurately. Near its mouth lies ʻAyādh/ʻAyād village and fort, visited by Philby[4] who reports that it is not a very old village, but in this he is mistaken. Certainly it is not mentioned in Hamdānī's *Ṣifat Jazīrat al-ʻArab* under this name, but a MS in possession of the late Qāḍī of Ḥuraiḍah, Saiyid ʻAlī b Sālim al-ʻAṭṭās, entitled *Manāqib al-Shaikh ʻAbdullāh Bā ʻAbbād*, states that this saint (born 616/1219–20) of the celebrated ʻAbbād family, had followers in Jirdān, ʻAyādh, which is described as *qaryah bi-Jirdān*, Shabwah, Rakhyah, and Wādī Ḥaḍramawt. Again, Bal-Faqīh al-Shiḥrī[5] under the annals for the year 956/1549–50, speaks of the flight of Āl ʻĀmir to ʻAyādh when threatened by the advance of the Kathīrī Sulṭān on Shabwah. West of it stands the Salt Mountain, the revenues from which are a perpetual cause of dispute in the district; on our return we visited it also. On

[1] cf. R. B. Serjeant, *Prose and poetry from Ḥaḍramawt*, London, 1951, Engl. pref., 11, Ar. text, 80. The Manṣab of al-Bāridah offered us it like a sort of treacle which we ate by dipping the forefinger in it. The *Tāj al-ʻarūs*, II, 319, quoting the *Takmilah*, places it between wādīs ʻAmaqīn and Ḥabbān, spelling it Jurdān, and adding that it has some castles (*quṣūr*).

[2] C. de Landberg, *Études sur les dialectes de l'Arabie méridionale*, I, *Ḥaḍramoût*, Leiden, 1901, 349, from Forskål.

[3] *Arabica*, V, Leiden, 1898, 235 f.

[4] H. St. J. B. Philby, *Sheba's daughters*, London, 1939, 326.

[5] For these two authors cf. *BSOAS*, XIII, 3, 1950, 589, XXV, 2, 1960, 244, XIII, 2, 1950, 292 f.

both occasions we visited the Manṣab of the Āl ʻAbd al-Ḥaqq, al-Shaikh ʻAbd al-Malik b. ʻAbd al-Malik, in his village at al-Bāridah, who seems to be the *manqad* or appeal-judge meant by Hamilton [6] though his legal functions now appear to be much in abeyance. Al-Bāridah is the *ḥawṭat qabr ʻAbd al-Ḥaqq*, the sacred enclave of ʻAbd al-Ḥaqq's tomb, he being the ancestor of the family which possesses a *musawwadah* copy of his biography.

Al-Jinainah village is situated on the edge of a hill, Ḥaid al-Jibail, which lies just above the point where the Wādī al-ʻAlhānah [7] from the south joins the Wādī Jirdān running in a westerly and slightly northern direction to ʻAyādh. Just below the village is the cultivated land (*ṭīn*), and on the hill-slope beyond it are *zarībahs* for animals with doors of the *shijib* type [8] set in a wooden frame; there are also *zarībahs* for millet-cane called *mashwā ḥaqq al-qaṣab* (plates I and III). Clay bats used as brick are made on the hill-slope above the village, and outside it is carried on the carpentry for the beams. *ʻIlb*-wood is used mostly, but another tree was also mentioned called *wadf* which is *imḍāḍ*, presumably the *muḍāḍ* of Landberg,[9] the *Grewia popolifolia* or *shawḥaṭ*. *ʻIlb*-wood should be cut in the *shitā*' season after *kharīf*.[10]

According to Landberg [11] al-Jinainah, which belongs to the Hal Ḥasan of Namārah, contained in his day, i.e. some 75 years ago, 10 *ḥuṣns* and some houses, but although there are *ḥuṣns* belonging to the Hal Ḥasan in the near vicinity at what would seem to be strategic points, there are only three in the actual village complex, Ḥuṣn Āl Jidʻān on the northern Wādī Jirdān side, al-Muqaiyad, nearest to the Wādī al-ʻAlhānah, and Ḥuṣn Bil-Qār. We noticed two large cisterns (*jābiyah*) in or close by the village excavated out of the ground, the older one (plate IV(*b*)) in the village, lined with local lime, and the very recent one with imported cement. These *ḥuṣns* would, it is to be supposed, be described as *zabīn*, i.e. *manīʻ*, strong, defensible. A *zaban* is defined as a *makān ghair murtafiʻ illā annah qawī*, a place not high, but strong, or a *makān murtafiʻ yatazabbanūn fīhi 'l-nās*, a high place in which people fortify/defend themselves. From the number of storage rooms (*sufūl*) in al-Muqaiyad tower, it is to be deduced that during a siege the defenders would not lack for food, and water would be available from the cistern near-by.

[6] (R.) A. (B.) Hamilton, *The kingdom of Melchior*, London, 1949, 154. His suggestion that this is part of the ancient legal system of Maʻīn is fanciful. Families in which the office of appeal-judge is hereditary exist in other places besides al-Bāridah.

[7] See H. v. Wissmann's map, *Aden Protectorate*, Sheet 1, 1 : 500,000, published by the Royal Geographical Society, London, 1957, co-ordinates 47°1′ × 14°14′. It was only possible partially to check the Arabic of the names of this map and this name supplied by Shaikh Ruwais should be substituted for al-ʻAlh of the map. Additional names of hill features supplied by him are حيد القيمه to the north, جبل با زَرَارَه (for the map's J. Bazarah) to the south, and three names, حيد جُنْدُب ، حيد الحَمْرُورَه ، الحيد الطويل to the west.

[8] cf. E. Rossi, ' Terminologia delle costruzioni nel Yemen ', *A Francesco Gabrieli*, Roma, 1964, 351–7, citing *shujbah*, a little window, and *shij*ʻ, a door.

[9] *Glossaire daṯînois*, Leiden, 1920–42, 2699.

[10] cf. R. B. Serjeant, ' Star-calendars and an almanac from south-west Arabia ', *Anthropos*, XLIX, 3–4, 1954, 456.

[11] *Arabica*, v, 243.

The Namārah tribe of the ancient Banī Hilāl, so famous for its epic of migration to North Africa, inhabits Wādī Jirdān,[12] and is divided into four houses (*diyār*), Āl Ḥasan, al-ʻĀṭif, al-Siraiʻ, and al-Ḍubāb. Other Hilālī tribes in near-by territories are the Khalīfah of al-Ḥāḍinah/Ḥāẓinah, the well-known Nisīyīn of Markhah, traditionally reputed to have acquired this name because they were forgotten or left behind in the great Hilālī migration, and the Āl Māḍī of Wādī ʻAmd in western Ḥaḍramawt.[13] The ancestor of all these Hilālī tribes is Numaiy, one of whose sons, Ṣāliḥ b. Numaiy is described as Ṣāḥib Markhah, the forbear of the Nisīyīn, and Numair b. Numaiy is the ancestor of the Jirdān Namārah. Bil-Qār is the ancestor of the Lamāḍī (Āl Māḍī), some of whom dwell in Jirdān, and Khalīfah b. ʻIlbah, whom they called after his mother (*sammaw-h bi-umm-ah*), is the ancestor of the Khalīfah. The Ilahīn [14] presumably the ʻIlih south of Jibāl al-Nisīyīn, are, they say, a section (*faṣīlah*) of the Banī Hilāl—*Iḥnā ikhwah* ʻ We are brothers'. Numair b. Numaiy was said to be amīr of all the Hilālīs, and today the *ʻāqil* of all the Banī Hilāl and shaikh of the Āl Ḥasan of the Namārah, Ṣāliḥ b. Saʻīd b. Muḥ b. ʻAlī b. Ḥasan, Qā'im al-Qadīmah, lives a little further down the wādī from al-Jinainah at al-Nuqaiyib.

There is much more to be said of the history of the Banī Hilāl in these parts where it remains a living memory, and where poems of the celebrated Hilālī cycle are still known, although no doubt the radio is fast killing the memory of them. As Jirdān lies in a region of ancient Arabian culture the Hilālī tradition is of very considerable interest. Qarn Barīrah,[15] a little eminence at the foot of the cultivation there, is said to be the ruins of a Hilālī village—there are three relatively recent buildings on it.

Nowadays at least, it seems that only in time of war does the family come into al-Muqaiyad tower, described as a *ḥuṣn ḥaqq Āl ʻAlī b. Ṭālib Āl Ḥasan al-Hilālīyīn*, and all live in the same room. *Waqt al-ḥuraibah*, the time of war, is contrasted with *waqt al-ʻāfiyah*, the time of peace (*ṣulḥ*) or security (*amān*), *ʻĀfiyah* seems to have been used in this sense in early Islam,[16] and also by the Ḥaḍramī historian Shanbal [17] in his annals for the year 913/1507–8 in the phrase, *ʻala 'l-ṭīb wa-'l-ʻāfiyah*.

Description of Ḥuṣn al-Muqaiyad (fig. 1)

We approached al-Muqaiyad and its enceinte by way of the perimeter track along the west side of the village, turning up the short lane on the right (plate II), paved with flat stones or rock called *ṣirf/ṣarf*, to the main gate (plate V(*a*)). On the wooden threshold (*mirdam*) of the gateway there was blood—an animal

[12] cf. F. A. Mukhlis, *Studies and comparison of the cycles of the Banū Hilāl romance*, Ph.D. thesis, University of London, 1964.

[13] *Prose and poetry*, 12.

[14] C. de Landberg, *Arabica*, IV, Leiden, 1897, 14 f.

[15] This place, which has been seen in a MS vocalized as Burairah, is discussed by H. von Wissmann, ' Al-Barīra in Ǧirdān ', *Le Muséon*, LXXV, 1–2, 1962, 177–209.

[16] cf. Naṣr b. Muzāḥim al-Minqarī, *Waqʻat Ṣiffīn*, second ed., Cairo, 1382/1962–3, 16, 99, *passim*.

[17] cf. *BSOAS*, XIII, 2, 1950, 291.

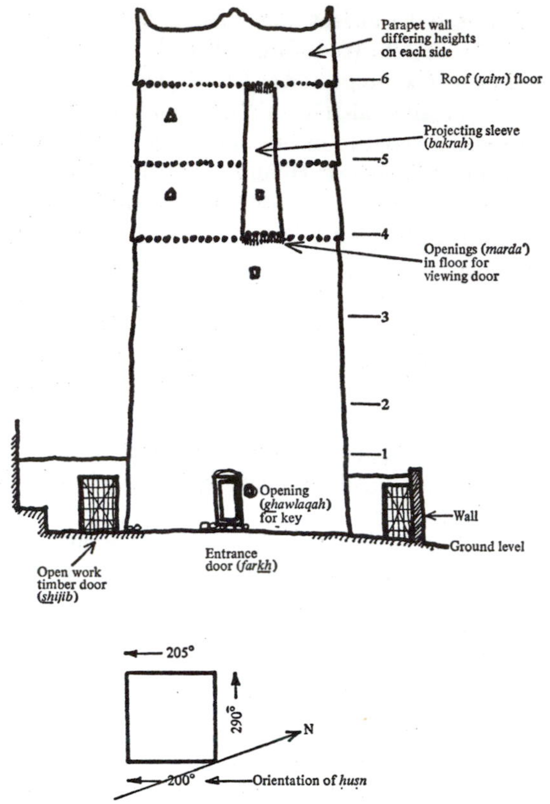

Fig. 1

had been sacrificed for *barakah*, which, for brevity's sake, may be rendered so as to obtain benign influence,[18] because of the *sikin*, household ghosts or *jinn*. A fettered woman, al-Muqaiyadah, they told us, goes up and down the stairs inside the *ḥuṣn*—hence its name—but no tale of why she should be haunting it was forthcoming. This may be one reason why people no longer actually live in it. In deference to this belief we abandoned the idea of spending the night there and bivouacked by the *wādī*-bed.

On the right-hand side of the entrance gate was a little cupboard-like door (*'alaqah*) [19] with some carving on it, set in the mud outer wall. This is opened so that the wooden key (*qilīd*) can be inserted in the wooden lock (*qaishamah*) [20] of a type common in Arabia, and, at one time, in other Arab countries such as

[18] For *barakah* in general cf. E. Westermarck, *Pagan survivals in Mohammedan civilisation*, London, 1933, ch. iv and v.

[19] The Faḍlīs also speak of *'alaqat siddah*, i.e. a wooden door-lock.

[20] cf. Landberg, *Ḥaḍramoût*, 690, *qāshimah*, boîte de la serrure en bois. It was described as, مزلاج صغير طولها تقريبًا شبر ونصف، والعرض أربع بنانين.

Egypt [21] also, up to fairly modern times. The lock which is sketched as it appears from the *inner* side of the entrance gate (fig. 2) consists of a sliding bolt (*milsin*),[22] shown here in the open position; when it is pushed home to the right, wooden teeth fall into holes on its upper surface and hold it in position. The bolt can be released and drawn to the left, when a jaw-bone shaped key is inserted, via the opening at the end-block of the *milsin*, under the holes, the pegs on the upper surface of the key then pushing up the teeth which have engaged in the

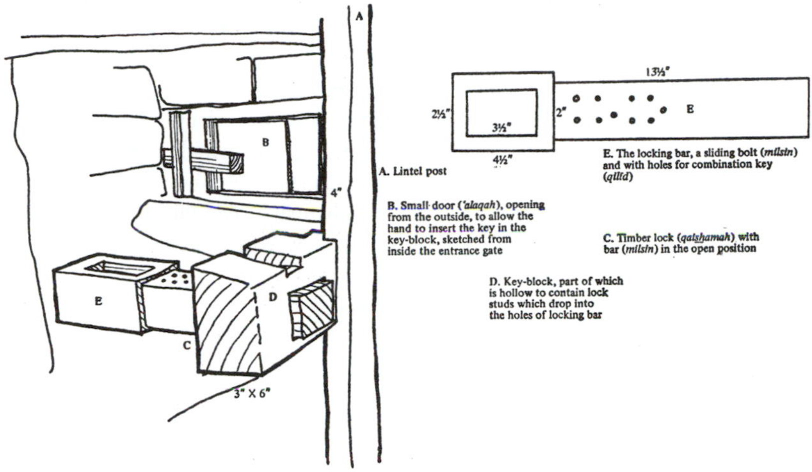

FIG. 2. Drawing of lock at gate of al-Muqaiyad enceinte

holes, thus allowing the *milsin*-bolt to run freely back. Arabs may often be seen with the wooden key stuck in the belt, behind the dagger perhaps, if they are armed.

Almost everywhere in south-west Arabia one finds the metal padlock made in the Yemen, the G͟hut͟haimī lock.[23] In the northern Yemen one sees actual locks of local manufacture with a very long key, and people still seem indeed to make these nowadays.

To revert now to the entrance gate to al-Muqaiyad enceinte, it may be perceived that into the clay of the wall over the gate, as also over other gates external or internal, thorns have been set—this is called *taḥbīr*. One assumes

[21] E. W. Lane, *Manners and customs of the modern Egyptians*, London, 1895, 38.

[22] Perhaps equivalent to *malsan* of *Gloss. daṯ.*, 2629, ' boucle '.

[23] cf. *Arabica*, v, 89. Writing over 75 years ago, Landberg says the G͟hut͟haim make these locks in Ṣan'ā'; this is not so now, nor are they made at Ṣa'dah. He says they used to be made in Wādī 'Ain in Baiḥān al-Asfal, and that traditionally there was an iron industry in Baiḥān and Ḥarīb, and suggests this is an ancient pre-Islamic industry. Cf. also R. B. Serjeant, ' A metal padlock and keys from South Arabia ', *Man*, LIX, 1959, no. 65, p. 49. Regulations for the manufacture of wooden locks may be found in R. Levy (ed.), *The Ma'ālim al-qurba . . . of . . . Ibn al-Ukhuwwa* (' Gibb Memorial ' Series, NS, XII), London, 1938, Ar. text, 237 (288), Engl. abstract, 95.

these thorns are intended as protection against wild animals. The wooden gate (*siddah*) consists of perpendicular planks bound by horizontal cross-pieces known as *al-zawāfir ḥaqq al-siddah*, and by decorated iron flanges. The knocker (*ḥilqah*) has a clapper (*mismār al-ḥilqah*). A *suqqāṭah* is a bolt on the top of the gate.

The precincts of the *ḥuṣn* are a complex of yards, stables, and other domestic buildings, but, while the photographic mosaics give a general impression of the layout, we had too short a time to ascertain precisely how much of this constitutes the appurtenances of al-Muqaiyad, and to what extent and why there is intercommunication with other properties.

Passing through the entrance gate to enter the yard, one is confronted by a heap of night-soil from the lavatory, showing as a projection in the wall of the *ḥuṣn* in the front of plate II, along with the gutter which carried off liquid separately to spill on to the open yard. The stones lying about this part of the yard may possibly have been employed for cleansing, though, in Ḥaḍramawt, clods of hard earth (*fuqsh*) from the field usually serve for this purpose.

To the right of the entrance gate is a court (*ḥawsh*, pl. *ḥawaish*) for sheep and goats (*ghanam*), with a stair leading to a roofed stable (*sirih*) also for *ghanam*. Inside the stable is a *mīfā* oven (plate V(*b*)) for making *khubz*, Arab bread, and a fire-place (*mawqid*); there are recesses (*ṭāqah*) in the walls for shelves, wooden pegs (*watad*) set in the walls for hanging things, and, in both the *ḥuṣn* and outbuildings, poles (*miṭwāḥ*) [24] running from wall to wall, upon which they hung carpet-bedding (*firāsh*), etc. The pillars of wood in these buildings to hold up cross-beams are called *rakīzah* (pl. *rakāyiz*) and the capital (*kabsh*) [25] is called here *rās al-rakīzah*.[26] Rue (*ḥarmal*) [27] and *qaraḍ* (*Euphorbia garad.*) are pounded in here on a stone, the latter, or perhaps both, used in tanning (*lidmān*).[28] Upon the smooth clay walls were smears of *qaraḍ* where the tanners had wiped their hands to clean up after the process of tanning. Either in this stable or one of the other large rooms next to it were some very large jars for storage purposes, and a large cauldron (*burmah*) of an unusual squarish shape. Bundles of millet-cane (*qaṣab*), mainly used for animal fodder, lie pitched down in the court. In this district camels were formerly used for transport, as is still the case to a more limited extent, but they had no horses. Horses are in any case rare in south-west Arabia, and were only used for riding.

[24] Abū Bakr b. Aḥmad b. ʿAbdullāh al-Khaṭīb al-Anṣārī al-Tarīmī (ob. 1352/1933–4), *al-Fatāwā al-nāfiʿah fī masāʾil al-aḥwāl al-wāqiʿah*, Cairo, 1960, 104, writes, متاوح, if this be the same word ?

[25] For *kabsh* in this sense, cf. Ibn Ṭūlūn, *Mufākahat al-khillān fī ḥawādith al-zamān*, Cairo, 1962–4, II, 117.

[26] cf. R. B. Serjeant, ' Building and builders in Ḥaḍramawt ', *Le Muséon*, LXII, 3–4, 1949, 281, 283, where the *rakīzah* has the shape of a formalized palm-tree.

[27] The medical uses of *ḥarmal* are described by Yūsuf b. ʿUmar . . . b. Rasūl al-Ghassānī, *al-Muʿtamad fī 'l-adwiyat al-mufradah*, second ed., Cairo, 1951, 92. The author, writing towards the close of the seventh/thirteenth century, does not, however, mention that it is used in tanning.

[28] *Damān* in this sense does not appear to be reported elsewhere and its ordinary sense is ' dung ', which is used in tanning in, at least, parts of South Arabia.

PLATE I

FOR DESCRIPTION, SEE P. 23

XV

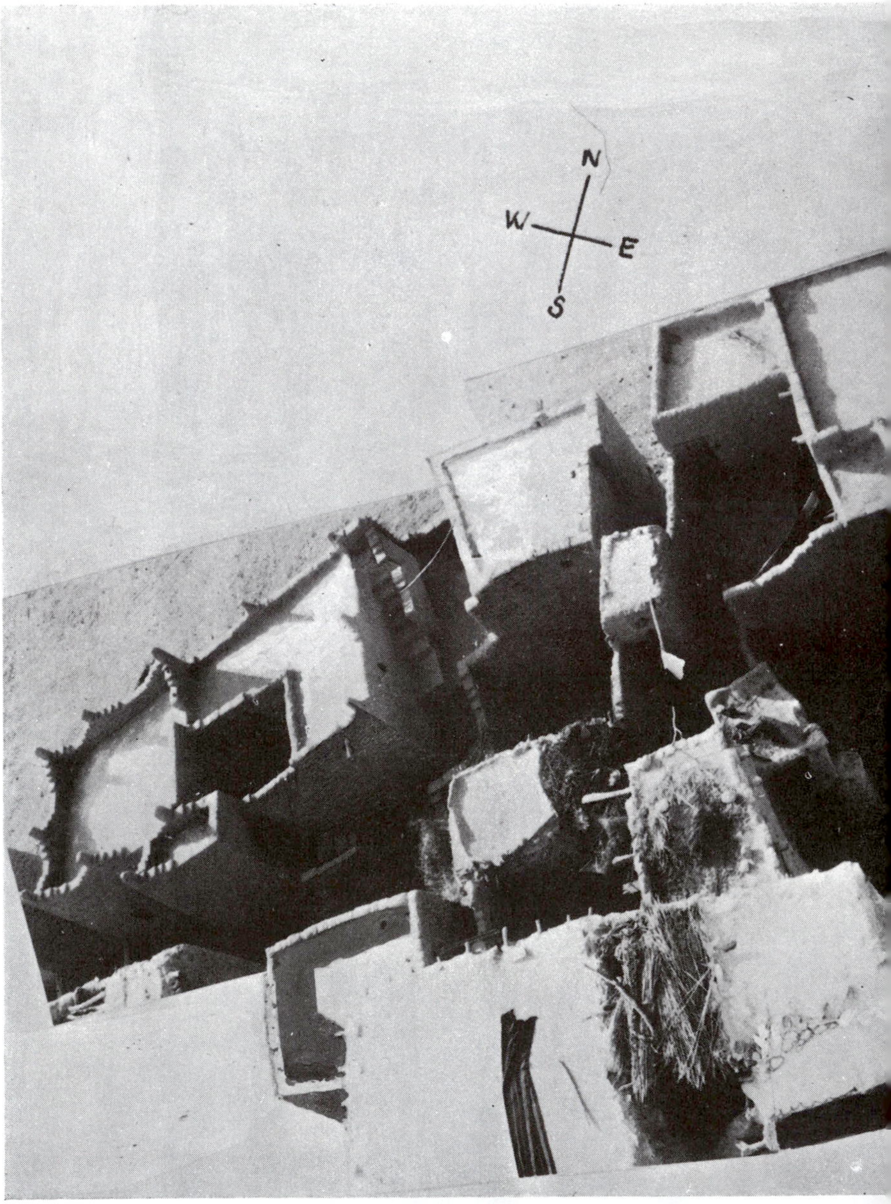

FOR DESCRIPTI

PLATE II

p. 23

XV

For descripti

Plate III

E P. 23

(a)

FOR DESCRIPTI

(b)

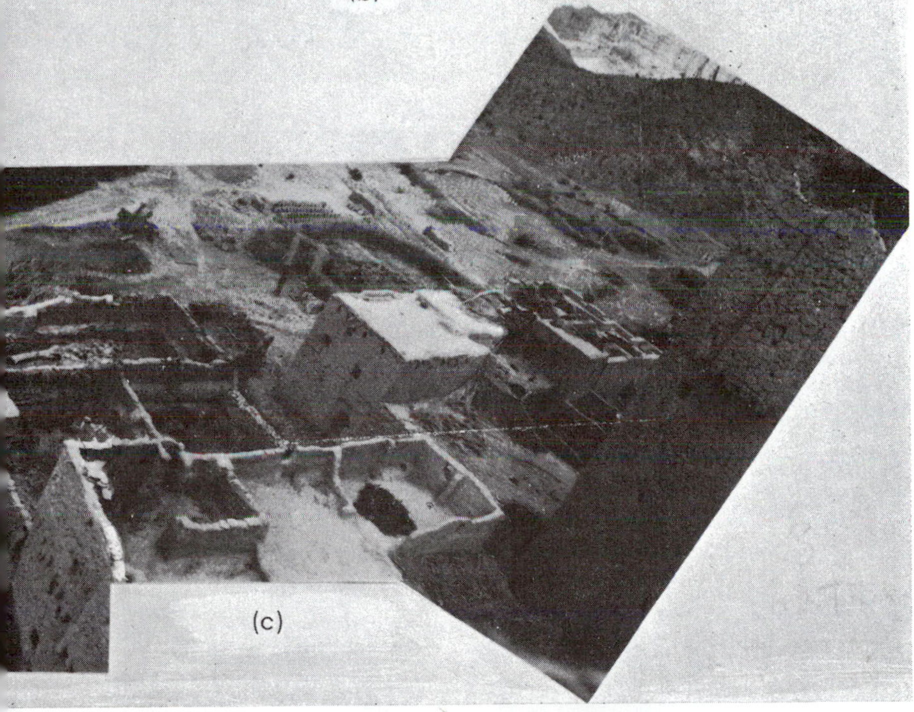

(c)

ᴇᴇ P. 23

XV

PLATE V

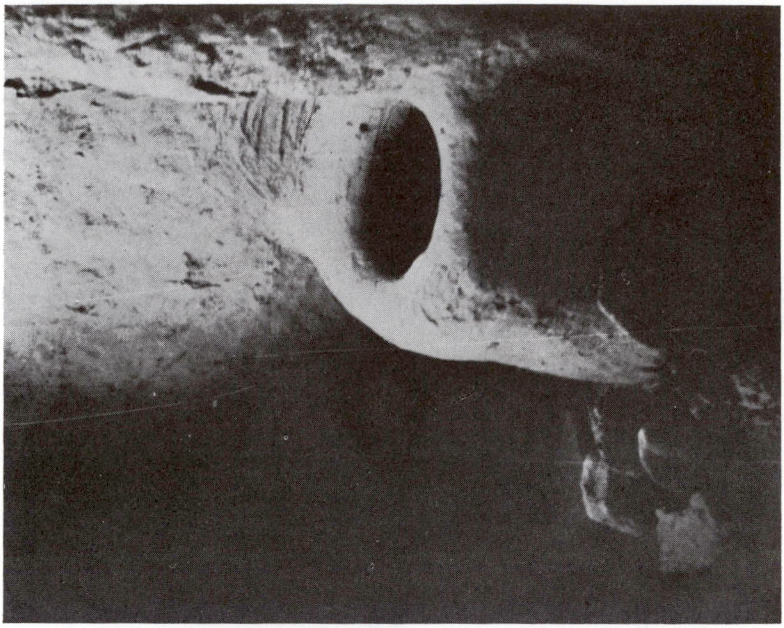

(b)

(a)

FOR DESCRIPTION, SEE P. 23

Agricultural instruments we saw in various places in the outbuildings included a sort of mallet (*mifjāḥ*) to break up clods of earth (*jaḥal*) in the fields, a wooden pitch-fork (*mis̲h̲ʿabah*) fig. 3, made of *ʿilb* to carry fodder, an axe-head (*fās*) fig. 4, a small well-pulley wheel (*dirjah*).

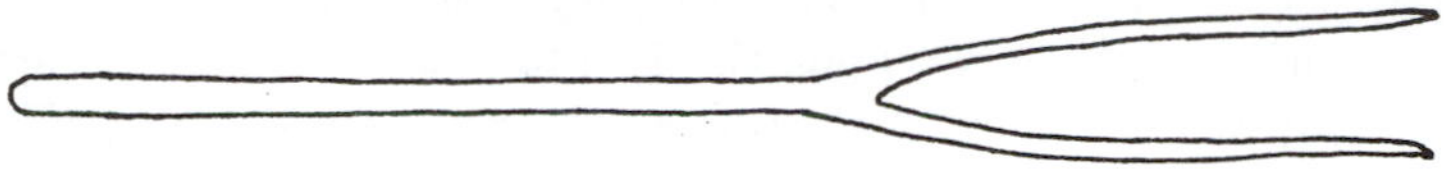

Fig. 3. Pitch-fork (*mis̲h̲ʿabah*) of *ʿilb*-wood

Fig. 4. Axe-head (*fās*)

On the roof of an adjacent building (plate II) is lying a heavy rug (*farīqah*); these are mostly of black goat-wool, but other natural colours are used here also. Woollen balls are lying about, obviously for weaving carpets of this type which, with local variations, are to be seen all up the eastern side of the Yemen, in K̲h̲awlān, ʿAyāl Siraiḥ, etc. In Baiḥān these are called *farīq*, but, in some other parts of the country, *ḥanābil*. In Baiḥān, according to a fairly recent press notice, black goat-hair is dearer than sheep's wool, and it takes a whole day to make one *ḥanbal*, working from dawn to dusk. Baiḥān is also famous for making *ḥabawāt* (sing. *ḥabwah*), the bands of cloth the tribesmen loop round the knees and small of the back when sitting on their haunches, but coloured bands are now imported, probably from Japan, as well.

In the second court on the right, a covered doorway leads off to a dwelling-house which has, on the left of the entrance to its yard, a privy, the spoil of which would be removed by way of the short re-entrant from the perimeter track. Just before the covered door-way there is a small covered stable with a wooden *kalb* (fig. 5) set in the wall to which a donkey can be tethered; this has a

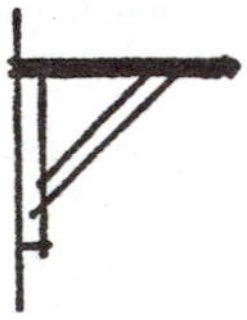

Fig. 5. Wooden *kalb* for tethering donkey

barred or slatted door of the type known as *shijib*, the side-posts being called *bakarah*. A *shijib* can be seen in plate I, the slats mostly made of palm-*jarīds*.

The stone foundation plinths of the *ḥuṣn* and its outbuildings are known as *sās* and the clay wall above is called *jadar*. These walls are constructed of sun-dried clay bats (*libnah*) measuring approximately 19 in. × 12 in. × 3 in. thick, the corresponding size in 'Ayādh being 17–18 in. × 12 in. × 2½ in. The bats are made of mud (*khulb*) [29] mixed with straw of the millet known as *ṭahaf/ṭuhuf* (*Eragrostis abyssinica*) [30] to form a mixture known as *ḍiyād*. The spaces in the rough clay bat wall of dry *libn* bricks are filled in with soft *khulb* puddled for this purpose into a paste, and smoothed over. The interior wall surfaces after being plastered with mud are often, in the case of living and reception rooms, whitewashed with *nūrah*, though not in this *ḥuṣn*. The action of applying the smooth surface to the wall is called *maḥaḍ*, the wall then being described as constructed of *libn mamḥūḍah*; this finish is carried about half-way up the *ḥuṣn*. Signs of weathering seem to show on the walls of the upper storeys of the *ḥuṣn* which is, after all, to judge by the dated lintel, over two and a quarter centuries old, but in Saiwūn of Ḥaḍramawt, one or two mud houses are reckoned to have stood for no less than five centuries.

In all three towers the ends of the beams supporting the floors of the three top storeys project a few inches outside the walls. A narrow wooden shelf has been run along the top of each row of beam-ends in order to throw the rain off the walls beneath; we registered no name for these shelves. Flat stones (*ṣalīl*) defined as *lā ḥajar wa-lā ṭīn*, neither stone nor clay, Landberg's [31] ' dalles plates ', are used to proof the parapets against rain with which, then it seems, Jirdān must be well favoured. We cannot ever recollect seeing in this district the elaborate thick polished plaster-work of the larger towns in Wādī Ḥaḍramawt, and even the roof of the *ḥuṣn* was of mud over the retaining flat *ṣalīl* stone. Nor in al-Jinainah do we remember seeing windows and other apertures picked out in whitewash as is so common in other districts of the Federation and the Yemen. Where the neighbouring Upper 'Awlaqī territory is concerned, Mubārak 'Abdullāh al-Ṭawṣalī stated that it was only on such festive occasions as a marriage that this whitewash was applied. The windows are small and set low down, quite near the floor—upon which people sit on rugs or palm-leaf mats, reclining on cushions. Windows consist of a simple frame with a central mullion, and are fitted, on the outside, with small wooden shutters.

[29] Defined by *Gloss. daṯ.*, 628, as ' terre mélée d'eau, boue compacte et visqueuse produite par la pluie ou le sel '. A Yemeni informant described *khulab* [*sic*] as *al-turāb al-ma'jūn bi 'l-mā'*, in words similar to *al-Jawhar al-shaffāf* of 'Abd al-Raḥmān al-Khaṭīb. SOAS photocopy, tale, 432. *Bughl* is a Mukallā word for a mixture of clay and dung.

[30] cf. G.B. Naval Intelligence Division, *Western Arabia and the Red Sea*, London, 1946, 482, 595.

[31] *Arabica*, v, 239. This appears to be an ancient word if the suggestion of Professor A. F. L. Beeston, ' The ritual hunt ', *Le Muséon*, LXI, 3–4, 1948, 190, regarding inscription Philby 84, be accepted. It is Yemeni colloquial Arabic. Cf. al-Ānisī, *Tarjī' al-aṭyār*, ed. 'Abd al-Raḥmān al-Iryānī and 'Abdullāh . . . al-Aghbarī al-Fā'ishī, Cairo, 1369/1949–50, 312: الصلال جمع صلالة — حجرة التى يصل بها القبر — اى يبلط.

In an earlier article (see p. 6, n. 26) attention has already been drawn to the wooden columns carved to represent a formalized palm-tree, degenerating in Ḥaḍramawt often into so abstract a form as not to be recognizable as such. On the external mud and plaster decoration of some of the older houses, that of the late Saiyid Ṣāliḥ b. ʻAlī al-Ḥāmidī for example, palm motives in shallow relief were used. The window of traditional type, however, is yet more obviously a representation of the two plants most essential to the Ḥaḍramī, the palm and *dhurah* millet. In the typical windows (plate VI) photographed in 1964 in Saiyid ʻAlī b. ʻAqīl's house in Saiwūn, the mullion unquestionably represents a palm trunk, the rough patterned surface being rendered into a neat fretted design, while the fretting of the lower half of the window is a stylized representation of a millet field, the larger lozenges being the heads of millet. The cross-bar is less easily explainable, unless it be the top of a more distant field of millet indicated in a sort of primitive perspective! In northern Yemen a constantly recurring motive, especially in external plaster-work, and notably on mosques and their domes, seems to be the young *dhurah* plant. Perhaps these motives had some religious significance in pre-Islamic Arabia if one may assume they were used on ancient buildings. In al-Muqaiyad, however, the windows are of simple rectangular shape and uncarved.

A projecting sleeve (*bakrah*) shows on the east flank of the *ḥuṣn* over its only door, at the lower end of which is a machicolation for defence so that the doorway can be commanded by firearms, while a second *bakrah* on the west flank forms part of the garde-robe. The main construction of the *ḥuṣn* is entirely of mud with, of course, wooden rafters and frames for doors and windows.

The *ḥuṣn* has a single door centred in the east side (plate VII and fig. 6) with a few steps leading up to it. The clay sill underneath the door-frame is called *maqwā* [32] and the wooden base of the frame *musāʻid al-lānah*, the jambs or side-posts *lānah*, and the top *mirdam*. The door, known as *farkh*,[33] four feet high, is constructed of thick *ʻilb*-wood like the entrance gate, i.e. with vertical planks held together by carved cross-bars and strengthened with decorated iron flanges or mountings. The cross-bars are fastened to the door with the large round-headed nails [34] (often coated with shiny tin) commonly used in Ḥaḍramawt. The door and the planks above it are carved, the latter with an inscription in the archaic native script of the country which one sees along with other pre-Islamic, graffiti in numerous places on rocks or masonry, as well as in the handwriting of older men today, though it is unfortunately disappearing owing to the teaching of *ruqʻah* in the new schools, with, perhaps, the erroneous notion that it is somehow superior. The Arabic, which was deciphered with the aid of Ruwais b. Miḥsin al-Raiyis—as far as was possible, runs as follows.

[32] From our notes it is regrettably not quite certain that the *maqwā* is the clay under the wooden sill, and the vocalization of *musāʻid* is also dubious.

[33] *Farkh* commonly means a bastard, as well as a chicken.

[34] The Museum of Ethnology, Cambridge, has an example of this kind of nail.

سنة خمس واربعين بعد مايه والف
ومن كان مع الله كان الله معه وغفر له

الحمد لله وحده بسلـــخ   محمد الفقير الى الله صالح
شهر رجب تاريـــخ . . .   بن طاهر . . . غفر الله له

'Year 1145 A.H. [1732 A.D.]. Whosoever is with God, God is with him and pardons him. Praise to God alone. The end of the month of Rajab, date . . . [part broken off]. Muḥammad the faqīr ilā Allāh, Ṣāliḥ b. Ṭāhir . . . [illegible to us]—God pardon him'.

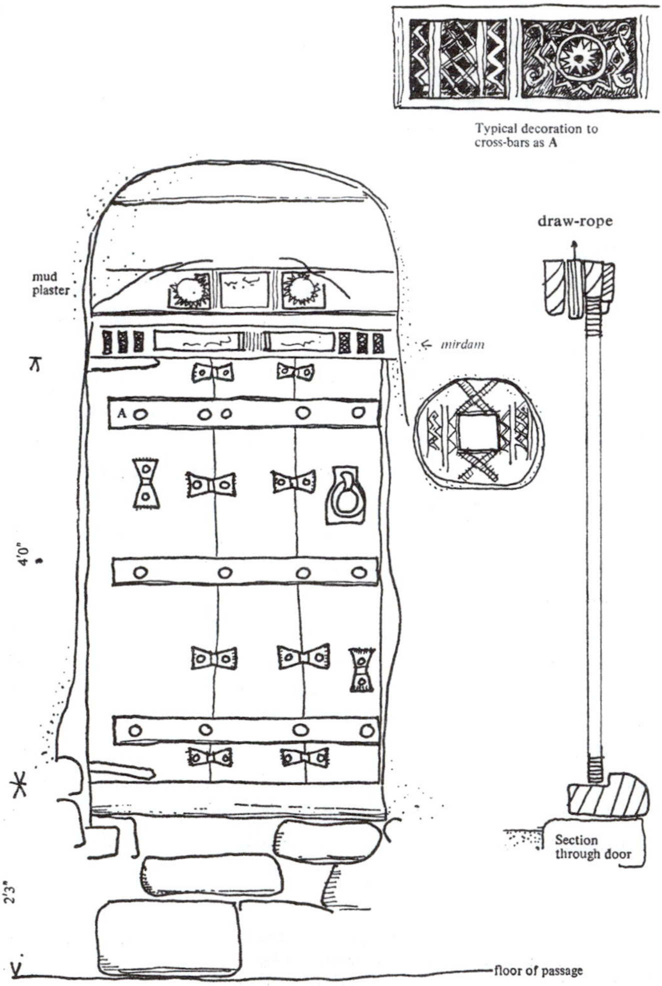

FIG. 6

This Muḥammad b. Ṣāliḥ was not known to Ruwais, so it would seem that the very memory of him has perished unless his name be found still preserved in some local book of genealogies—which is not impossible.

The small hole to the right of the door into which the hand is inserted to place the key in the lock was called *ghawlaqah* ; it is similar to the larger hole at the entrance gate in all respects. On the inside of the door are three locks or bolts, the *qaishamah* which was also described as *iqlīd*, the *marfaḍah*-bolt, and the bolt at the top side of the door termed *ghalq*. A draw-rope is attached to the door so that it can be opened from an upper room, and as we recorded no special name for it, the Ḥaḍramī term *majarr* was probably used.

The interior of al-Muqaiyad

Al-Muqaiyad consists of a ground-floor (*al-siddah*), above which are five storeys (*qaṣr*) as well as a roof floor called here and in Ḥaḍramawt *raim*, an ancient word found in a pre-Islamic inscription from Baiḥān.[35] Upon this *raim* is set a little square turret, in a ruinous state in al-Muqaiyad but still perfectly preserved in the other two towers.

1. The ground floor (*al-siddah*) (fig. 7)

A passage, called *al-siddah* runs straight from the door to the stairs at the back of the *ḥuṣn*, thus dividing the ground floor into two halves. The area at the foot of the stairs is called *bāb al-siddah*. Abū 'Ubaid al-Qāsim b. Sallām al-Harawī (d. 224/838) [36] defines *al-suddah* as *al-saqīfah fawq bāb al-dār*, and again he says it means *al-bāb nafsu-hu*. This sense appears to apply here, though one assumes that the ground floor is called *al-siddah* because it contains the door, or more usually the gate, to the house. The floor is, as in the rest of the house, made of mud.

On the right, as one enters the door, is a quern (*maṭḥan*) for grinding grain and, in Wāḥidī country, the guest on the upper floors, while he is yet drinking *qishr*-coffee and eating dates, will hear stone ringing on stone as the *dhurah* is ground to make the good coarse meal bread to entertain him. The sheep selected for his meal by his host is brought into the reception room for him to approve, feeling its belly for fatness, before it is slaughtered outside. As the family, were al-Muqaiyad inhabited, sleeps on the ground floor during the winter cold, all their household gear (*mā'ūn*) is kept here in the *sifl* rooms, such as the *minḥāz* or mortar for pounding the coffee bean and spices, and their bedding (*firāsh*), though this latter is generally hung on the pole (*miṭwāḥ*) running above, behind, and parallel with the door, across the passage from one wall to the other.

On each side of the main passage are two doors leading into the four rooms (*sifl*, pl. *sufūl*) of the ground floor, the *sifl* under the stair on the left having a very small low door. A *khalfah* is a little recess or *ṭāqah* in a *sifl*, but there is

[35] cf. R. LeBaron Bowen and F. P. Albright, *Archaeological discoveries in South Arabia* (Publications of the American Foundation for the Study of Man, II), Baltimore, 1958, 143–4 (Jamme 405). Cf. *al-Fatāwā al-nāfi'ah*, 269, where *raim* means *saṭḥ*, roof.

[36] *K al-ajnās*, ed. Imtiyāz 'Alī 'Arshī, Bombay, 1938, 28.

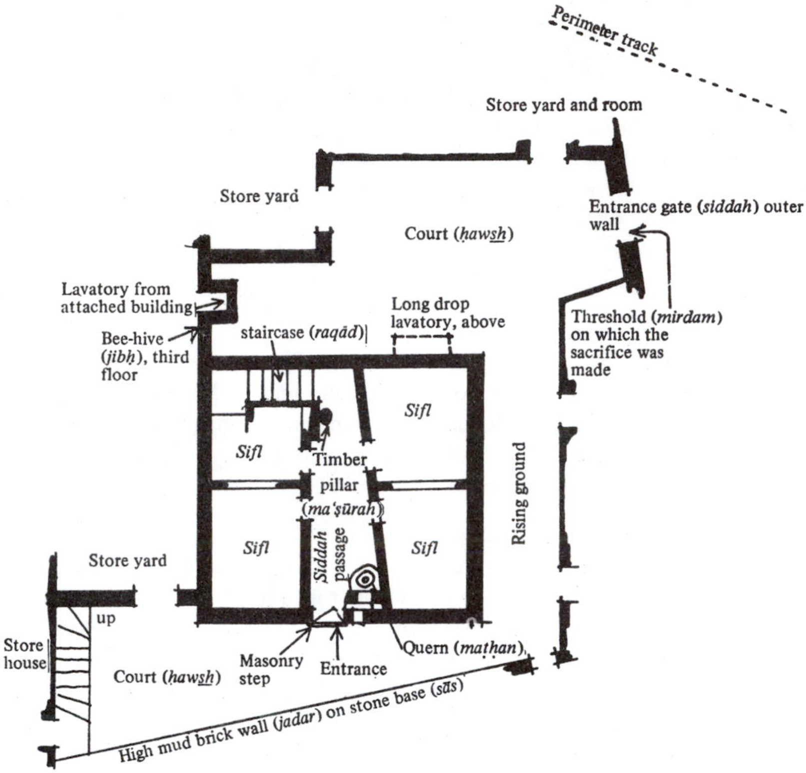

FIG. 7. Ground floor plan with outer gate and gates to storage yards

nowhere on the ground floor a window or aperture, for security reasons obviously, and this would also keep the floor warm in the winter. In the *sifl* grain (*ḥabb*, *ṭa'ām*) and other things would be stored. Animals do not come inside the *sufūl* of houses here as they do in some of the bigger domestic buildings of northern Yemen and in parts of the Federal sultanates, but remain outside in the courts (*aḥwāsh*) around the house.

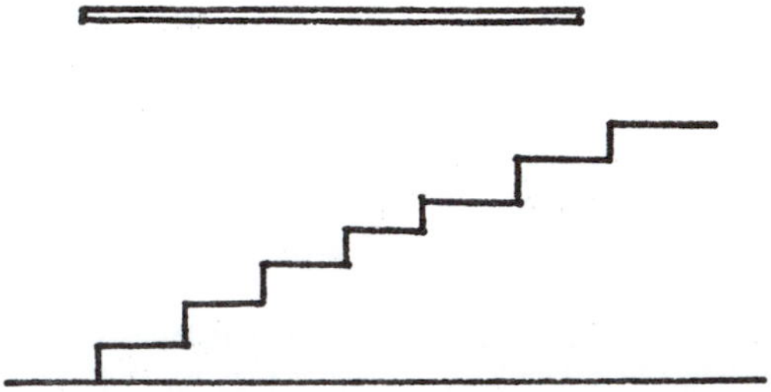

FIG. 8. Stairs (*dirij/diraj* or *raqād*) leading from the ground floor passage (*siddah*) with a shelf (*siff*) running along the stair-wall

The stairs (*diraj* or *raqād*, fig. 8) are set round a sort of pier or column (*ma'ṣūrah*) in the south-west corner of the house which runs up through all the floors to the roof. A sort of shelf (*siff*) is, in places, run along a side-wall of the staircase, parallel with the floor. *Ṣarḥ* is the name of the transverse wooden support of short thin split logs or branches which holds the mud steps of the stair.

2. *The first floor* (fig. 9)

This comprises four small and very dark *sufūl* rooms with low doors, used for the storage of grain or goods, and kept locked. There are no windows or apertures on this floor either, and the darkness, were an enemy to enter the *ḥuṣn* in daytime, would operate in favour of the inmates who can see their way about, while a person entering from the glare outside has to grope his way.

3. *The second floor* (fig. 10)

There are three *sufūl* rooms on this storey, and apertures only, for light, called *mishwāf* (pl. *mashāwīf*) [37] to admit light or to act as loop-holes. In the passage outside the rooms which were locked, was a heap of fine dust (*turāb*)—they bury grain in this dust so that it will not go bad. The types of grain which would be stored in this way would be millet (*dhurah*), *musaibilī* (*Setaria italica*), *dukhn* or bulrush millet, and *ṭahaf*.

4. *The third floor* (fig. 11)

This floor contains two *sufūl*,[38] one of which is the lavatory (*ṭahārah*, fig. 12), called, in some parts of Ḥaḍramawt at least, *makhwāl* (pl. *makhāwīl*).[39] There is a little antechamber which might be used to house the large water jars (*zīr*) of fired clay, the water being employed for general domestic purposes, though to obtain cool water for drinking, a goatskin will be hung up in a current of air. This is separated by a partition-screen (which, though we recorded no specific name for it, might be called *mūfir*), from the actual garde-robe. As remarked earlier the garde-robe projects over the entrance-court—the technical term *bakrah*,[40] applied to this projection, seems properly to apply to any piece of the

[37] Muḥ. b. Hāshim, *Tārīkh al-dawlat al-Kathīrīyah*, Cairo, 1948, 160, calls the *mishwāf*, كوّة صغيرة أو ثقب نافذ فى الجدار يوضع فيه عنق البندقيّة ويطلق منه الرصاص.

[38] The slight discrepancy between our notes and the plan here, the latter showing three rooms, arises from our being unable to enter the locked rooms but on the basis of the doors two are assumed.

[39] Saif al-Qu'aiṭī, *al-Amthāl wa 'l-aqwāl al-Ḥaḍramīyah*, MS in Ḥaidarābād, India, 106, reports a proverb, ومن ساير الدجاج دخلن به المخاويل 'one who accompanies poultry will be taken by them into lavatories'. Hens are always to be seen in Ḥaḍramawt pecking around the foot of the 'long drop'. This may be why tribal people often regard them as unfit for eating. The sense of the proverb is presumably that if one keeps bad or worthless company it will bring one into trouble. Al-Qu'aiṭī calls the *makhwāl* '*bait al-ṭahārah*'. The word is used in Tarīm.

[40] A question sent to Saiyid 'Alawī b. 'Abdullāh . . . Āl al-Shaikh Bū Bakr in Aden produced the reply that *bakrah* was where the beam was placed to build the *saqf*, ceiling, which is a possible sense from other comparative material, but it is difficult to accept this here. He also considers *marda'* to be an error for *m r d m* which he defines as a hole in the *bakrah*, but this is also difficult to accept.

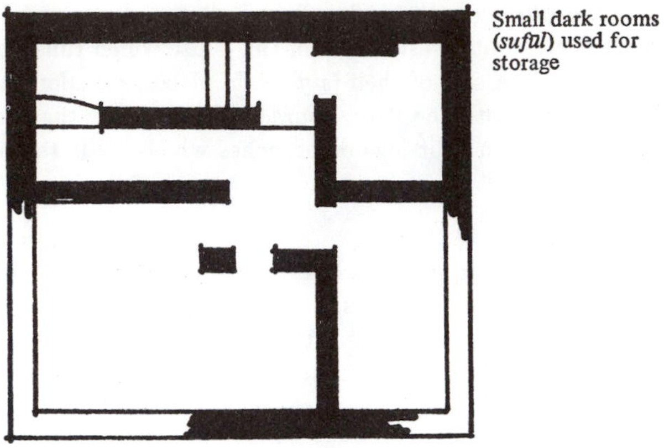

Fig. 9.
First floor

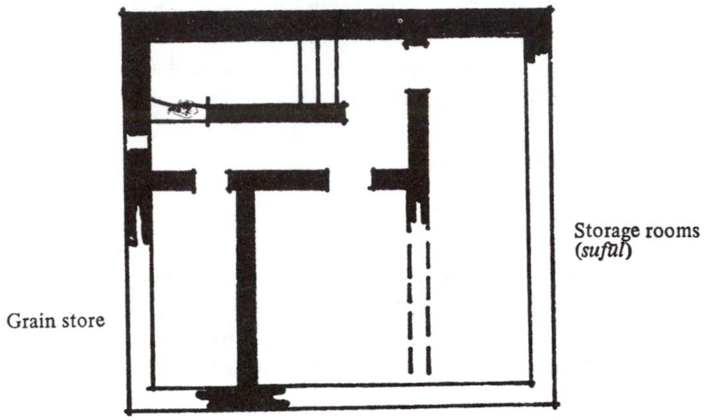

Fig. 10.
Second floor

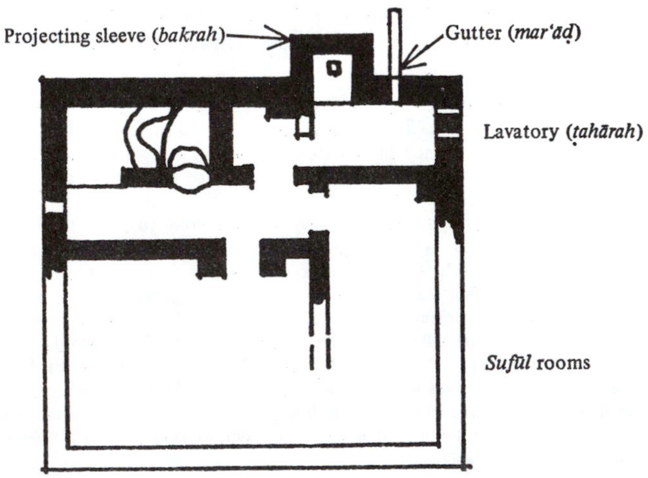

Fig. 11.
Third floor

building that sticks out beyond the side of the house-wall, such as, for instance, the small projections that may be perceived on the battlements of some of these *ḥuṣns*.

The lavatory is of course of the Asiatic type, a small platform, the hole in which is called *marda'*,[40] while the pipe or gutter to the side of it, conveying urine and ablution-water outside and clear of the mud wall of the *ḥuṣn*, is called *mar'āḍ*.[41] This section of the room has also a triangular shelf (*riff*) in one corner and *maṭāwiḥ* for hanging clothes. Were it in actual use there would also be here water-*zīrs* and a scoop for ablution, clods of earth or perhaps pebbles in a receptacle, and most likely an incense-burner with charcoal and *lubān*-frankincense. While incense is burned as an air-sweetener it is to be remembered that the *ṭahārah* is a favourite haunt of the jinn, so that fumigation with incense may have a second aim, i.e. that of appeasing these spirits. In Ḥaḍramawt the dry spoil of the *ṭahārah* is carried in donkey panniers to spread on the fields and it

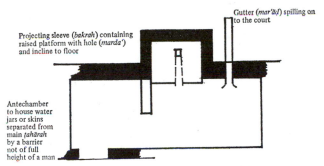

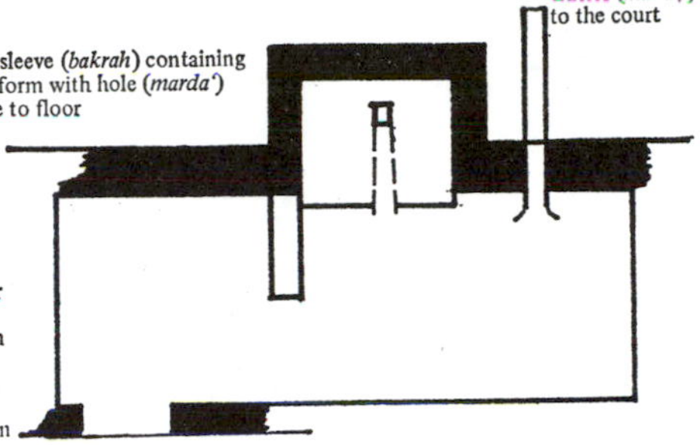

FIG. 12. Plan of lavatory (*ṭahārah*) on third floor

has a market value, though small—during the second World War when there was a shortage, the Kathīrī government even put a control on the price of this commodity in some of the towns of the state. We cannot say whether it is used here for manuring the fields, for it might be that the floods bring down sufficient silt bearing organic matter which, combined with animal manure from the *ḥawsh* would make the Jirdān people less reliant on human manure. The efficiency of this type of *ṭahārah* and lack of offensiveness may be contrasted with the custom in some of the otherwise highly civilized villages of northern Yemen where the roof is used for this purpose. Curiously enough too a British official inspecting the Jewish quarter in Aden some time in the 1920's found this was the custom there at least in some houses.[42]

The wall bee-hive

Near the *ṭahārah*, set in the western external wall is a hole which is the

[41] L. W. C. van den Berg, *Le Ḥadhramout et les colonies arabes dans l'Archipel indien*, Batavia, 1886, 67, *mur'āḍ*. An alternative spelling is *mir'āḍ*, *BSOAS*, XXVII, 1, 1964, 47.

[42] One hears of tribesmen seeking blood-revenge, lying in wait outside the *ḥuṣn* of their enemy to shoot him in the *ṭahārah*.

entrance to a hive (*jibḥ*) [43] for bees (*nūb*) [44]—this seems a feature of other *ḥuṣns* also. We do not know why the hive should be sited here nor with which room it is linked on the inside. In Wādī Yas͟hbum of Upper 'Awlaqī country the practice is to build a hollowed-out log into the clay wall of the *ḥuṣn*, running in parallel with the course of the wall. An entrance-hole to the outside surface of the wall is made in the middle of the log so that the bees have free passage to and fro. The two ends of the log, which are accessible from the room inside, are stopped up with clay; the bees store their honey in the right and left arms of the shallow T-shaped hive thus formed. By simply breaking open the clay stopping of one of the arms inside the house the rich round honeycomb can be extracted. In the Wāḥidī village al-K͟habr in the summer of 1954 two kinds of honey were available, *baghīyah*, the top and choice part at a *raṭl* and a *rub'* for a *riyāl*, but *k͟hulfī* the honey at the bottom only fetched a *riyāl* for two *raṭls*. At al-Qārah of north

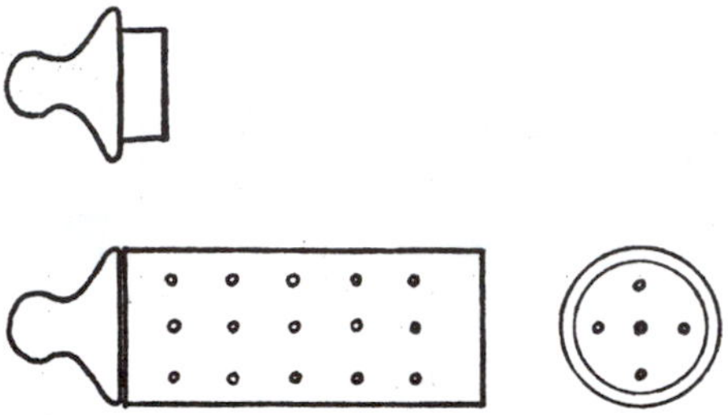

FIG. 13. Round wooden box (*k͟hais͟hah*) with stopper and perforations for holding a queen bee, approximately quarter-size. The base-plate is also perforated

Yemen the first honey season was stated to be in *al-k͟hāmis* when bees eat of the *ḍubb* tree (unknown) and the second in *al-sābi'* when they eat of the flowers of *qāt*, *bunn* (coffee), *'ilb*, and all sweet flowering trees and shrubs.

In Abyan of the Faḍlī sultanate near Aden, Mr. Stephen Day, then of the Aden Political Service, purchased a container, called *k͟hais͟hah* (fig. 13) for the queen bee. It is circular, of turned wood, and perforated with small holes; the base-plate, also perforated, is a circular piece fitted into the *k͟hais͟hah*, and the top is closed with a wooden stopper. The queen bee is fed by the bees through the holes and, as anyway they say, water is brought on the bees' wings to the queen, and *t͟hamar*, which ought to mean fruit but must obviously refer to what the bees collect from flowers. The South Arabians think the queen bee is a male

[43] 'Alawī b. Ṭāhir, *K al-s͟hāmil*, Singapore, 1359/1940, 203, says that *jubūḥ* (plur.) are round hollow pottery (*k͟hazaf*) which when joined end to end are used as pipes, the joins sealed with *nūrah*, i.e. lime beaten up with cotton and oil. Cf. Aḥ. b. 'Alī al-Maqrīzī, *Naḥl 'ibar al-naḥl*, ed. Jamāl al-Dīn al-S͟haiyāl, Cairo, 1365/1946, 20, 25, *jibḥ*, and 70, on differences in *zakāt al-'asal*.

[44] For verses on bees see *BSOAS*, XXVII, 1, 1964, 64; *Prose and poetry*, Engl. pref., 21. Ibn Mājid (G. Ferrand, *Instructions nautiques . . .*, Paris, 1921–8, I, 83a) alludes to *nawb al-'asal al-musammā 'inda-nā al-d nī*. Al-Subkī, *Ṭabaqāt al-S͟hāfi'īyah*, Cairo, 1964–7, II, 202–3, has *nūb*. The anonymous *al-Ḥayāt al-sa'īdah fī Ḥaḍramawt*, Singapore, 1953, 7, has the phrase النوب الحدّار وعسل فى كلّ صمار 'Many bees and honey in every hive'. *Ṣumār* = *jibḥ*.

and regard it as a kind of Arab chief. If the Shaikh (queen bee) dies, the owner selects a new one and puts it in the *khaishah*-box. Each day a different contingent (*firqah*) of bees goes out collecting while the others rest, but the Amīr remains where he is, not going out with them (*al-mīr gālis, mā yarūḥ*). They appear to entertain ideas about the bees as censors of morals, for, said a Faḍlī tribesman, if one does not pray (*mā yuṣallī*) the bees do not stay !

The Islamic jurists, as Yaḥyā b. Ādam [45] points out, are at some variance with regard to the taxation of honey. Mu'ādh b. Jabal, the Companion of the Prophet sent by him to the Yemen, did not collect a tax on it, while Qudāmah b. Ja'far [46] states that the Prophet collected a tax of one skin of honey [47] in ten. In medieval Rasūlid Yemen the revenue on honey was an important enough item to figure in the fiscal schedules, being paid in kind. So Muḥammad Aḥmad Nu'mān when he complains of the tithes on honey in his *al-Ta'mīm fī 'l-Yaman*,[48] a riposte to Imām Aḥmad's celebrated poem attacking Jamāl 'Abd al-Nāṣir and nationalization, cannot find support in either the Prophet's practice or the custom of Yemenite rulers !

5. *The fourth floor* (fig. 14)

Between the third and fourth floors is a square window (*mashla'*), something like a *mishwāf* or loop-hole, and on the stairs above this are other such windows. An *'ukrah*, of which there are quite a few in the walls of the upper floors at strategic points commanding what lies below, is a loop-hole for the *bunduq*, musket or rifle. We bought in the village muskets with silver mountings, one with a number of teeth of the *wabar* (hyrax) set in beeswax stuck on to it, iron powder-horns plated with brass and silver, and brass horns for the primer—one of the muskets still had a length of the wick/match-thread (*fatīlah*) attached to it.[49]

[45] A. Ben Shemesh, *Taxation in Islam*, I, Leiden, 1958, 34. Al-Balādhurī, trans. P. K. Hitti, *The origins of the Islamic state*, Columbia, Beirut, 1966, 87, cites the case where Thaqīf of al-Ṭā'if had failed to pay one skin of honey in ten—as they used to do to the Prophet. The Caliph 'Umar ordered them to do so or their valley would not be protected, i.e. probably not remain a *ḥimā*.

[46] A. Ben Shemesh, *Taxation in Islam*, II, Leiden, 1965, 39–40. Cf. al-Shāfi'ī, *al-Umm*, Cairo, 1321/1903–4—1326/1908–9, II, 33. Abū 'Ubaid, *K al-amwāl*, Cairo, n.d., 496–7, says that a *qirbah* of middling size is taken on every ten as *'ushr*. Another source says a tenth is taken on honey from the plain but a fifth from mountain honey. Others say no *ṣadaqah* is payable on it at all.

[47] *Ziqq* is given the usual sense of 'wineskin' by Ben Shemesh, and is called, inaccurately, a 'vase' by Hitti, but the term is not restricted to wineskins. South Arabians now store their honey in bottles or tins, but as late as 1954 in Ḍāli' they used to keep it in gourds with a tiny window cut out in the side, and the piece used as a stopper. In Daw'an tins of a circular shape are made from old kerosene tins by local tinsmiths to hold the circular comb.

[48] Published on 8 December 1961, probably in Cairo. There is an amusing play on the word *ta'mīm* which can be understood as 'nationalization' or as 'imāmization'.

[49] A certain Shaikh Ḥusain b. Muḥ. b. al-Ḥusain Ibrīq al-Ḥaḍramī al-Ḥabbānī composed in 1216/1801–2 *Taḥrīḍ al-ikhwān al-kirām wa-badhl al-naṣīḥah fī 'l-taḥarruz min Yām al-li'ām wa-af'āli-him al-qabīḥah*; the original is in Tarīm, but a photocopy is in the possession of R. B. Serjeant. Though this book is concerned with the north Yemen tribe of Yām, Makramīs, the author hails from the Wāḥidī capital, and his book has much to say of the musket, its parts, and its employment.

FIG. 14.
Fourth floor

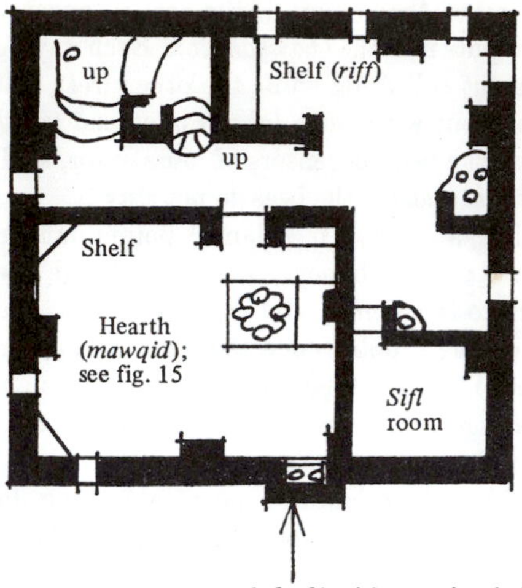

On the right as you ascend the stairs is a reception room (*maḥḍarah*) for men. on the north side of which is a *bakrah* projecting beyond the wall of the *ḥuṣn*. In the floor of the *bakrah*, which looks over and commands the doorway, is a *marda'* of two holes through which one could fire on persons trying to enter below.

The reception room has a hearth (*mawqid*), also called *maifā* with four stones called *marākid* (sing. *markad*) [50] *ḥaqq al-mawqid* (fig. 15) for supporting a kettle. The hearth would be used for brewing coffee, and the man preparing it would sit on the slightly raised platform (*maq'ad*) between the hearth and the wall. To his left is a trough for holding firewood, and on his right a shelf (*riff*) in the wall

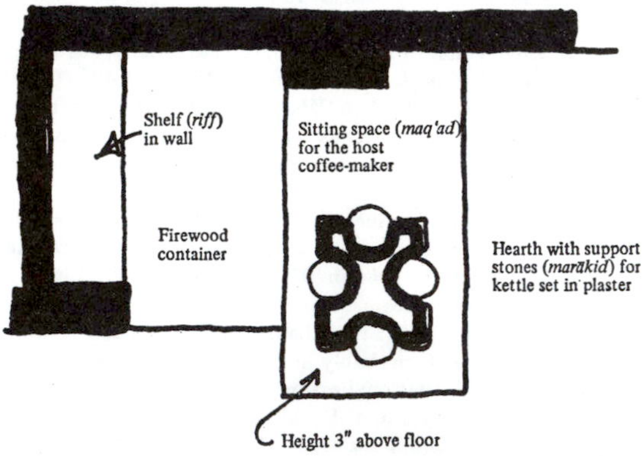

FIG. 15. Details of coffee-hearth (*mawqid*) on fourth floor

[50] *Gloss. daṯ.*, 1393, *markadah* ' pierre de l'âtre '.

where probably coffee-cups and other gear were kept. Many ruined sites and villages still inhabited have sherds of blue and white Chinese tea or coffee bowls, which show how widespread their use was. These are not very old and whole cups can still be bought occasionally. We found a cache of these in Holkat (Ḥuqqāt) Bay in Aden, perhaps damaged pieces from a shop. Nowadays Japanese bowls are universally used. Inside this room and in other rooms where there happens to be a hearth, the rafters are blackened by smoke. Here in Wādī Jirdān people used to drink *bunn Yāfiʿī* which is justly prized; then it was not to be had, so they drank the infusion of coffee-husk (*qis͟hr*); but nowadays (1964) again they drink either Yāfiʿī or Ḥabas͟hī *bunn*—it seems a little strange to import coffee from Ethiopia into southern Arabia the land of the coffee-bean!

There is another large room, probably also a reception room, on this floor, with a coffee-hearth (*maifā*), on the lower side of which is a windowless *sifl* for grain (*ḥabb*). The windows, which are provided with shutters (*lahj*, plur. *luhūj*), have a horizontal flap of wood on the external wall above them to ward off rain.

In rooms such as these two reception rooms the honoured guest would be set in the corner between the two windows where he would have the benefit of the cool breeze on both sides, and the notable guests would sit beside him.

6. *The fifth floor* (fig. 16, p. 20)

This floor consists of only a single large room with a coffee-hearth and platform (*maqʿad*) for the coffee-maker behind it, a trough (*mag͟hwaz*) for firewood to the left, and a hole for coffee-cups to the right behind the sitter (fig. 17). As is often the case in the Wāḥidī sultanate with public rooms, it is entered obliquely from the stair-head [51]—this seems to be a defence measure, though if this is so it is surprising to find this arrangement at the top of the house where the women usually are, so perhaps it may be to allow the men of the household to speak to their womenfolk from the top of the stairs when women visitors happen to be present. The roof-top would also belong to the women, and the preparation of food would take place there—this would generally be limited to the *qurṣ* of bread and perhaps a stew of vegetables or shark to make a savoury to eat with it, but apart from fears about the haunting of the *ḥuṣn*, the owners may have found it more convenient, in those more peaceful days especially, to

[51] An interesting usage is that the ʿAwlaqīs apply the word *bait* to that part of the room shown in fig. 18 as shaded. In Ḥaḍramawt the corresponding term for this part of the room is *dār*.

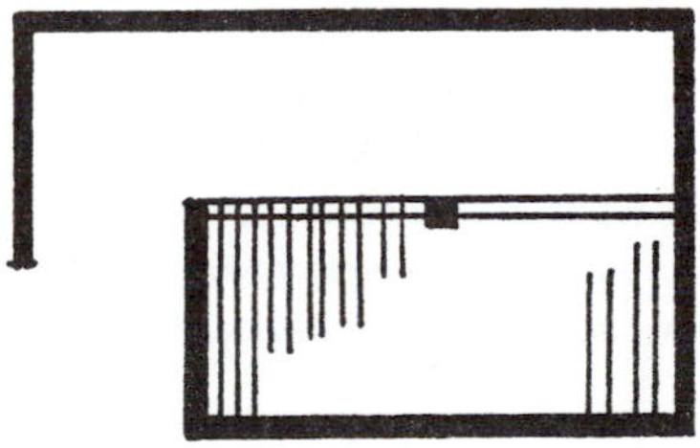

FIG. 18

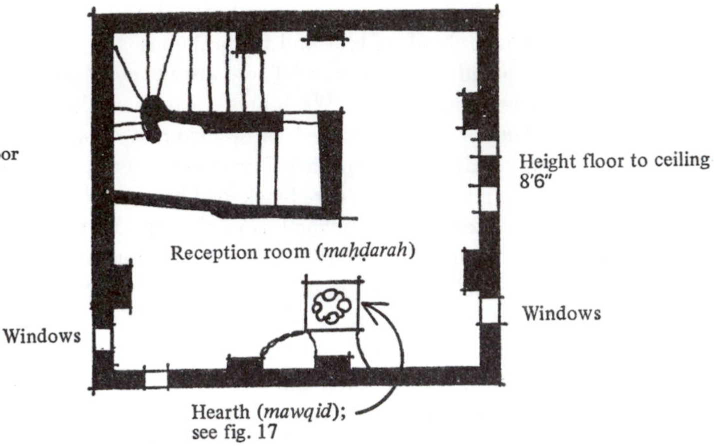

FIG. 16.
Fifth floor

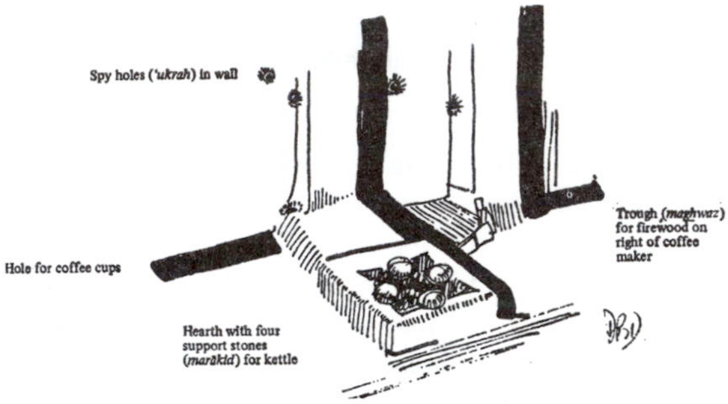

FIG. 17. Details of coffee-hearth (*mawqid*) on fifth floor

move into the buildings of one or two storeys only within the enceinte of the tower. For about 20 years, from 1947 to 1967, the Wāḥidī sultanate, after Sulṭān Nāṣir's effective succession, enjoyed unprecedented peace, security, and prosperity, marred only occasionally by violent incidents such as the assassination of the State Secretary Muḥammad b. Sa'īd [52] when a bomb was planted in his plane in 1966. The general security (in 1964) may have led the villagers to relax their security precautions somewhat while still maintaining the *ḥuṣn*, and to build without so much attention to defence.

The windows on this and the floor below have an oblong lower part (*khalfah*) above which is a blind triangular recess (*ṭāqah*) with a shelf (fig. 19). In the fine houses of the learned in Ḥaḍramawt books are kept on these shelves laid flat on their sides with the ends showing in traditional style going back to the 'Abbāsid period, but there are few books in the Wāḥidī sultanate or any of the surrounding tribal districts.

[52] cf. *JRAS*, 1951, 1–2, p. 39.

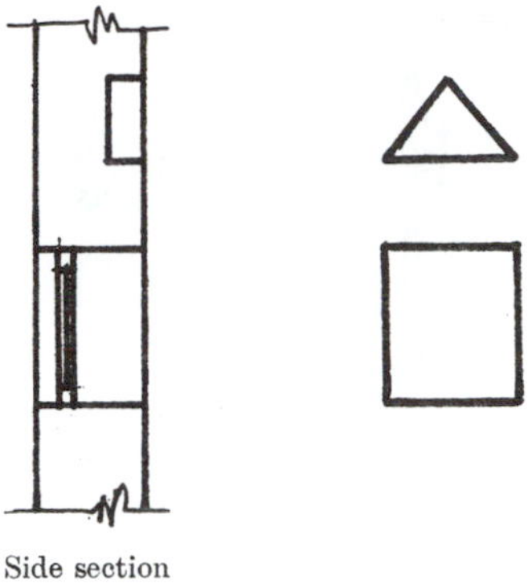

FIG. 19. Fifth-floor window (*khalfah*) above which is a blind triangular recess (*ṭāqah*) with a shelf. The side section shows also the shutters (*lahj*, pl. *luhūj*) to the window

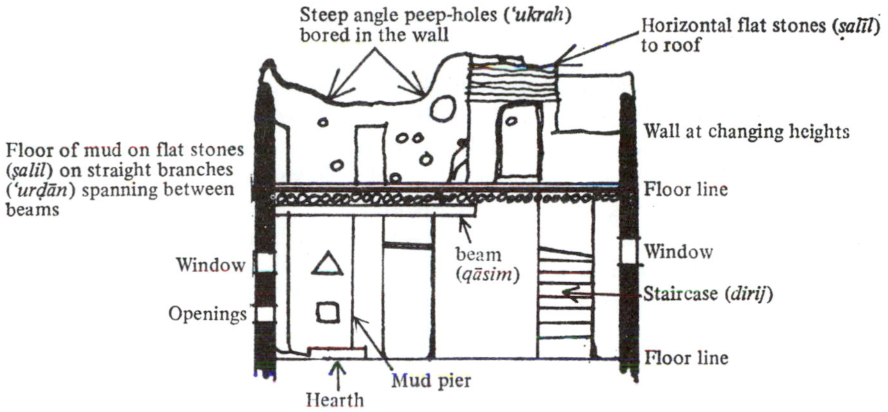

FIG. 20. Section through fifth floor and roof terrace showing inner face of south parapet

7. *The roof* (*raim*) (fig. 21)

From the fifth storey a stairway leads up to the *raim* or roof-floor. Over the main cross-beams (*qāsim*, plur. *qawāsim*) of the roof are the small transverse beams (*'āriḍ*, plur. *'urḍān*), and upon the *'urḍān* are placed the *ṣalīl* stones, Landberg's [53] ' dalles plates ', to retain the clay covering of the roof above them, this clay roof forming the floor of the open *raim*.

The doorless entrance at the stair-head (*rās al-diraj/dirij*) is called *fanā*, and the clay threshold step at the top of the stairs is also called *maqwā*. In front of it is a clay wall (*mūfir*), described as a barrier (*ḥājī*), the purpose of which is not quite certain, unless it be to keep out bad weather. On top of the roofed part of the stair-head is set a *muṣabbaḥ*, a little square turret (plate VIII), ruined in al-Muqaiyad, but visible in the other two *ḥuṣns* of Bil-Qār and Āl Jid'ān; it has a drainage-gutter called *al-mīzāb ḥaqq al-muṣabbaḥ*. In summer people sleep on the *raim*.

[53] *Arabica*, v, 239.

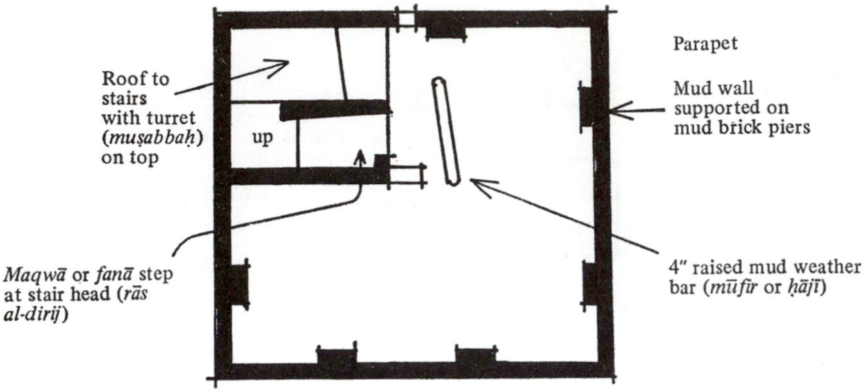

FIG. 21. Roof terrace (*raim*) (see also figs. 20, 22–3)

The ordinary triangular projections of the battlement wall of the *raim* are known as *sharaf*, and the slightly more elaborate corners are *bāshūrah* (plur. *bawāshīr*) (figs. 22–3). In the outside wall of the *raim*, near the top, are set small stones to form little crevices for nesting birds. To keep off the rain and prevent bullets from entering the walls, so we were told, are added *ṣalīl wa-madar*, flat stones and mud. The mud wall is reckoned thick enough, it seems, to stop bullets, though of course the *ḥuṣn* was built at a time when muskets were in use. The walls of the *ḥuṣn* would not be proof against bazooka shells, a weapon become unpleasantly common in South Arabia.

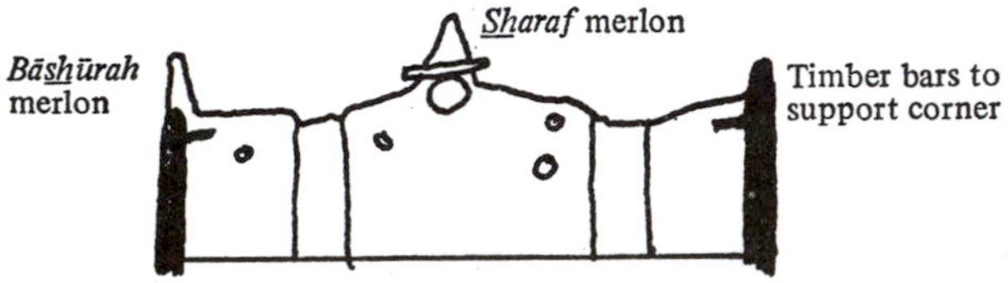

FIG. 22. Inner face of north parapet wall showing the peep-holes

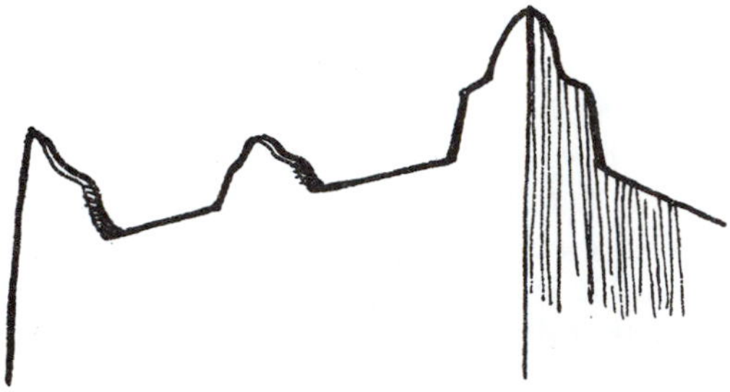

FIG. 23. Battlements of the roof terrace (*raim*) with the corner merlons (*bāshūrah*) and centre merlon (*sharaf*)

DESCRIPTIONS OF PLATES

Plate I. The fortified tower houses (*ḥuṣn*) at al-Jinainah from the perimeter track, from left to right—Ḥuṣn Āl Jid'ān, Ḥuṣn Āl Bil-Qār, only a corner of which shows, and al-Muqaiyad. A *zarībah* with a *shijib* door beside which are some clay brick-bats can be seen in the foreground to the left, and another with a stone wall on the right; in front of the latter is a sawyer's trestle with beams of *'ilb*-wood. The alley by which entrance is made to al-Muqaiyad is round the corner to the right.

Plate II. The view northwards from al-Muqaiyad to the perimeter track and field with sheep returning to the village in the evening. On the right is the alley paved with *ṣirf/ṣarf* stones and marked with a white arrow leading from the track to the main gate of the al-Muqaiyad enceinte, the gate being ajar. The top of the gate and that of the gate opposite it to the right has a *taḥbīr* or cover of thorns set in the clay to keep out intruders. The gate leads into a courtyard where stones and spoil from the privy can be seen lying on the ground below the projecting *bakrah* and gutter-drain of the privy itself on the third floor (bottom right). To the other side of the courtyard are yards and outbuildings attached to al-Muqaiyad with *dhurah* (millet) cane for fodder. On a roof to the left is more *dhurah* cane and a black and white goat-wool rug (*farīqah*). To the extreme left is a small mosque on the roof of which the prayer is presumably performed in hot weather. The buildings appear to intercommunicate—a useful device should the village be assailed from outside.

Plate III. The view westwards from al-Muqaiyad. Ḥuṣn Āl Bil-Qār stands on the left; some structures to the right of it are in a ruinous state though there is new building outside the village cluster. *Zarībahs*, including the kind known as *mashwā ḥaqq al-qaṣab* to contain millet cane, and threshing floors (*waṣar*) can be seen at the top, and, beyond them, the Wādī al-'Alhānah flowing (from the top left) to join the Wādī Jirdān. A heap of dry dung lies between the two front *zarībahs*.

Plate IV(*a*). Part of al-Jinainah showing the new *karīf*-cistern built alongside the perimeter track, using concrete, in the prosperous days of the early 1960's.

Plate IV(*b*). Part of al-Jinainah showing the traditional type of cistern (*jābiyah*) for storing water.

Plate IV(*c*). View from al-Muqaiyad looking to the north-east (the oblong building, bottom left, is identical with that in plate II, top right), showing yards for storing millet cane and other purposes, *zarībahs*, and Ḥuṣn Āl Jid'ān with its approach alley on the right.

Plate V(*a*). Gateway to Ḥuṣn al-Muqaiyad at the end of the alley paved with *ṣirf/ṣarf* stone. The door or gate (*siddah*) is bound by iron flanges and horizontal cross-bars (*zawāfir*) and has a knocker (*ḥilqah*). The cross-pieces are carved and nailed on to the door planks. To the right is a carved cupboard-like door (*'alaqah*) inside which is a wooden lock (*qaishamah*) (see fig. 2). The top of the gate has a crown of thorns (*taḥbīr*). On the wooden threshold of the gate is a splash of blood from an animal sacrificed to the household ghosts or jinn. (R. B. S.)

Plate V(*b*). Oven (*mīfā*) for making bread (*khubz*) in the roofed stable (*sirih*) on the right-hand side of the passage leading from the gate to the *ḥuṣn*.

Plate VI. Windows in Saiwūn, the mullion representing a palm trunk, and the arches palm fronds with formalized date clusters above them. The fretting of the lower half of the windows seems to be a formalized representation of a field of millet, with larger lozenges as millet heads. Window (*a*) has wooden shutters to its upper but not lower half whereas (*b*) has shutters for the whole window. (*a*) has, as it were, only one row of palm heads whereas (*b*) has two. In (*a*), the hole in the middle of the sill is for water to drain away. (R. B. S.)

Plate VII. The *'ilb*-wood door (*farkh*) of al-Muqaiyad of similar construction to the gate of the enceinte, and with a lock-cupboard (*ghawlaqah*) to the right also. The wooden base of the door-frame is called *musā'id al-lānah*, the posts *lānah*, and the lintel *mirdam*; the inscription is carved on the *mirdam*.

Plate VIII. Small square turret (*muṣabbaḥ*) of *ṣalīl* stone on top of the staircase to the roof terrace (*raim*), in semi-ruined state. The entrance to the stairs can be seen underneath the turret.

PLATE VI

(a)

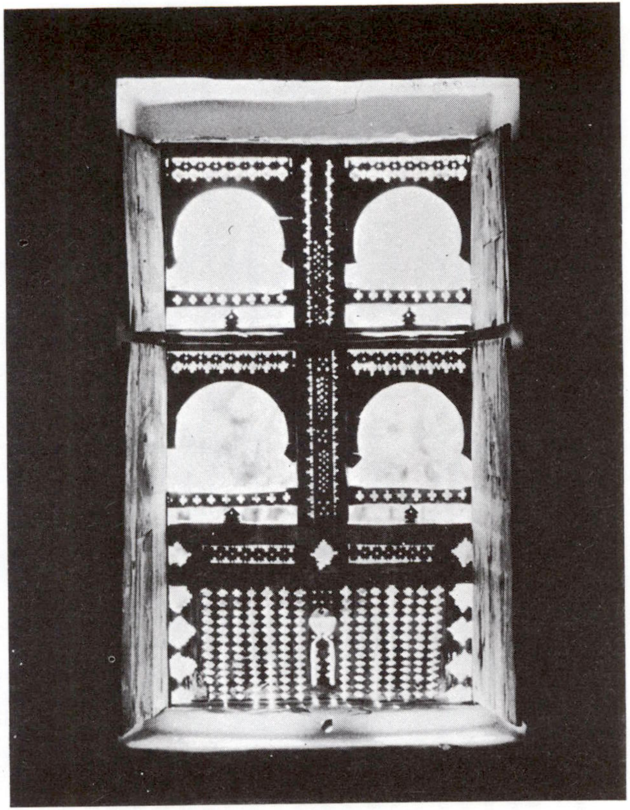

(b)

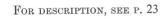

FOR DESCRIPTION, SEE P. 23

Plate VII

For description, see p. 23

PLATE VIII

FOR DESCRIPTION, SEE P. 23

A FORTIFIED TOWER-HOUSE IN WĀDĪ JIRDĀN (WĀḤIDĪ SULTANATE)—II

By Brian Doe and R. B. Serjeant

(PLATES I–IV)

Building sacrifices

Sacrifices of animals at the various stages in the construction of a house are already reported from the country of the Ṣubbaiḥah, Daw'an, and Tarīm.[1] Ibn al-Mujāwir [2] even records in the Middle Ages that when a road was being built between Mafālīs and Ta'izz, about 425/1033–4 up a mountain pass (*naqīl*) with 360 bends (*malwīy*), a head of cattle (*rās baqar*) was slaughtered at each bend as a sacrifice (*fidyah*); he calls a bend *f rkah*. Wheat also somehow formed part of the sacrifice, but Ibn al-Mujāwir is not explicit about this. At each bend there was a *masjid* and a *siqāyah*, just as so often one finds in the mountains of northern Yemen at certain points in a *naqīl* a little stone shelter-hut (*daimah*, pl. *diyām*) with a cistern (*birkah*)—these are pious foundations in many cases, and sometimes have a *waqf* to maintain them. Rossi calls the *daimah* a kitchen. Ibn al-Mujāwir's *fidyah*, though he does not say so, must undoubtedly have been intended to propitiate the Jinn. For example Saif al-Qu'aiṭī [3] records a proverb, *Al-siknī fidā-h baiḍah* ' The *siknī* (spirit) is propitiated with an egg '. He comments on this proverb, *Al-shayāṭīn tufaddā bi-'l-baiḍ 'āmmat-an.* The allusion is to the common Ḥaḍramī practice of breaking eggs in places supposedly frequented by the Jinn,[4] and a place so haunted would be said to be *maskūn*.

In al-Jinainah the *fidū* is slaughtered on the *sūs* or stone plinth at the western corner (*al-rukn al-qiblī*) on its reaching completion, and the blood flows for the *Jānn*. The next *fidū* belongs to the second storey and it is also invariably slaughtered on *al-rub'* (i.e. *al-rukn*) *al-qiblī*, and so on, each storey (*qaṣr*) having its own *fidū*. On the *raim* the *fidū* was stated to be slaughtered *'a 'l-mawfir/mūfir ḥaqq al-jadar* this being the parapet wall, but the term *mawfir* is fully explained in the list of technical building terms below (p. 293). They said that they slaughter over the *jadar* for feasts (*la'yād*)—in this case perhaps the blood runs down the outside wall, a sign of *karam*, and a kind of ostentation.

The salt-mine at 'Ayādh

The Mukallā Secretariat files at the Residency state that 'Ayādh at the mouth of Wādī Jirdān is inhabited by the Qarāmīsh who are hereditary *'askar al-Wāḥidī*, soldiers of the Wāḥidī sulṭāns, and have brothers further to the east

[1] cf. ' Building and builders in Ḥaḍramawt ', *Le Muséon*, LXII, 3–4, 1949, 277.

[2] *Descriptio Arabiae meridionalis . . . Ta'rīkh al-mustabṣir, ed.* O. Löfgren, Leiden, 1951–4, 150.

[3] *Al-Amthāl wa-'l-aqwāl al-Ḥaḍramīyah*, MS in Ḥaidarābād, India, 66.

[4] This practice has already been discussed. Cf. ' Building and builders ', 278.

in Wādī Rakhyah, but the 'Awlaqīs have an old right to a dollar a load on salt, exactly as do the Kurab at Shabwah. Though Landberg calls the Qarāmīsh an independent tribe,[5] Philby [6] says that they claimed to be of the Banī Jabr. The Banī Jabr are a tribe of the Yemeni Khawlān al-Ṭiyāl district, and von Wissmann [7] has even marked a district Qarāmīsh west of Ṣirwāḥ which would be Banī Jabr country. We stopped at Ḥuṣn al-Qarāmīsh called Rakhmān. Philby says that the salt-mines belong to the Qarāmīsh, and this appears to be correct.

Wādī Jirdān seems to lose itself in the steppe somewhere west of 'Ayādh, the area about the Salt Mountain or Ḥaid al-Milḥ, being described as *mitnah*, which is smooth flat bottom (*qā'*), good for transport to run upon, as indeed it was. One arrives through a re-entrant at the mine in the middle of a small mass of low mountain in the plain surrounded by low hills, to find a small entrance leading into an enormous cavern rather like the inside of a cathedral in size. The salt has been hacked away for generation after generation, the interior being scored everywhere with marks of the tools used by the salt-workers, and yet this mine is not known to al-Hamdānī's geography. The bottom of the mine is reached by a steep slippery narrow path coming up which one meets the salt-workers carrying up the salt in baskets. They empty these on to separate piles, each with the owner's distinguishing mark upon it, a strand of palm leaf, and as it is bagged the salt is loaded on to camels couched close at hand (plate I).

There are five houses (*khams diyār*) of the Qarāmīsh in 'Ayādh, each of which has a share marked out in the Salt Mountain. Our information is that, to the Qurmūsh, 2 shillings are paid on each load (*ḥiml*), the *ḥiml* consisting of two bags (*gawānī*), the total weight of the *ḥiml* being 14 *farāsilahs*, each *farāsilah* of 28 *raṭls*. The camel-load would therefore amount to 392 *raṭls*, assuming a *raṭl* is 16 ounces and not 12 as in older times in certain parts of South Arabia. One can judge what a man earns for he can work two loads a day, and in 'Ataq the load sells for 20 shillings.

Philby, writing of his 1936 journey,[8] says of Ḥaid al-Milḥ that ' the *Mijba* or dues exacted by these folk amount to one Riyal on three camel-loads, in addition to which the salt merchants pay a *Masra*, or fee of a quarter Riyal on each camel to the owners—the people of Husn Juwaibiya '.[9] The last-named seems to be a *ḥuṣn* on the edge of the cultivation at 'Ayādh, so they would be

[5] *Arabica*, v, 245.

[6] *Sheba's daughters*, London, 1939, 326, 328.

[7] ' Das vorislamische Südarabien ', map in H. von Wissmann and Maria Höfner, *Beiträge zur historischen Geographie des vorislamischen Südarabien*, Mainz and Wiesbaden, 1952.

[8] op. cit., 330.

[9] *Mijba* is no doubt equivalent to the *majbā* ' octroi ' of *Gloss. daṯ.*, 261, and Landberg, loc. cit., speaks of *muṣrā 'alā kull wiqrah/wuqrah* ' un *muṣrā* sur chaque charge lourde '. The *muṣrā* varies, but the Qu'aiṭī Weights and Measures Decree of 26 January 1943, fixed the *muṣrā* there at 3½ lb. But might it not be *masraḥ*, in the sense of a payment for being allowed to depart? Cf. *Arabica*, v, 100, the Amīr of Ḥarīb in Landberg's day, taking a *migbā* of an eighth of a *riyāl* on every camel entering Ḥarīb except from those of the inhabitants of the town itself.

For pictures of the mouth of the mine taken on our trip there see D. B. Doe, *Southern Arabia*, London, 1970, figs. 99 and 100.

Qarāmīsh. The officer at 'Ayādh, Muḥammad Qāsim Yāfi'ī, told us that the salt extracted here is distinguishable from Shabawī salt which one finds sold widely in Ḥaḍramawt, and for example, in 1954 anyway, in Lawdar *sūq* of the 'Awdhalī sultanate. From Jabal al-Milḥ at 'Ayādh salt in quantity goes to the Yemen.

Salt mines are found in several places of this eastern Yemen area, the most celebrated of all being that of Ma'rib, for Abyaḍ b. Ḥammāl al-Ma'ribī asked the Prophet for the salt which is at Ma'rib as a fief (*istaqṭa'a al-Nabī al-milḥ alladhī bi-Ma'rib*). This the Prophet granted him, but later he revoked the grant because he was subsequently informed that he had not, as he supposed, granted him dead land to bring into cultivation, but land, as al-Hamdānī [10] describes it, with wells and spring water, unequalled and clear like crystal. The Egyptian journalist Muḥammad Muḥammad 'Abd al-Raḥmān [11] reports that the 'Abīdah tribe specializes in the transport of salt at Ma'rib, and the Ashrāf tribe sells it—presumably he means the Ashrāf of al-Jawf, some houses, he adds, being filled to the roof with salt. The salt mountain of Sāfir, one stage from Ma'rib is already well known.[12] Ṣan'ānīs still use *milḥ Māribī* today.

Of the rock-salt of Baiḥān, 'Abd al-Raḥmān Girgirah [13] says that the Bal-Ḥārith have the right to trade in it, and another source informs us that this tribe is considered to be the owners of the mine. One passes by their camels in Wādī 'Ubailāt laden with the black woollen sacks of salt. The correct name of the mine seems to be Ayādīm.[14]

A little-known letter [15] of the Prophet to the Aqwāl/Aqyāl of Shabwah guarantees the security of their salt (mines) and interdicted pastures (*maḥjar*)—which does give some indication that salt has been worked in this district for centuries.

Building and house law in Ḥaḍramawt

On our all too brief visits to the Wādī Jirdān we had no time to investigate customary or *sharī'ah* law relating to either building or property rights, which in any case would undoubtedly be of considerable complexity, involving many

[10] D. H. Müller, *Al-Hamdânî's Geographie der arabischen Halbinsel*, Leiden, 1884–91, I, 201. Cf. Ibn al-Athīr, *Usd al-ghābah*, Cairo, 1285–6/1868–9, I, 45; Qāsim b. Sallām, *Kitāb al-amwāl*, Cairo, n.d., 275, no. 683 where al-Māzinī is incorrectly read for al-Ma'ribī; al-Ṣūlī, *Adab al-kuttāb*, Cairo, 1341/1922–3, 311, to be corrected by the above; A. Ben Shemesh, *Taxation in Islam*, I, 76 (Yaḥyā b. Ādam), II, 35 (Qudāmah b. Ja'far); al-Balādhurī, trans. P. K. Hitti, *The origins of the Islamic state*, Beirut, 1966, 111.

[11] *Arḍ al-buṭūlāt wa 'l-amjād*, Cairo, 1964.

[12] C. F. Beckingham and R. B. Serjeant, 'A journey by two Jesuits from Dhufār to San'ā in 1590', *Geographical Journal*, CXV, 4–6, 1950, 206; *Arabica*, V, 100.

[13] 'Abd al-Raḥmān Gargarah [*sic*], *Arḍu-nā al-ṭaiyibah, hādha 'l-Janūb*, Beirut, 1967, 21.

[14] This is the form of the name as given in R. LeBaron Bowen and F. P. Albright, *Archaeological discoveries in South Arabia*, Baltimore, 1958, 35–6, but Philby calls it Aiyadin and Girgirah al-Abāyim.

[15] M. Ḥamīdullāh, *Majmū'at al-wathā'iq al-siyāsīyah*, third ed., Beirut, 1969, 204, from various texts in MS.

new local technical terms, since such abound even in the printed legal treatises of the Sh̲āfiʿī *ʿulamāʾ* who do not even always bother to explain them. In the types of contract compiled by Ḥaḍramī authors from Baḥraq [16] to those of the present day [17] one perceives from the texts something of the issues at stake. A familiar sort of case, also found in early *sh̲arīʿah* law, can be consulted in the *Fatāwā* of Bā Makh̲ramah [18] (907/1501–2–972/1564–5), a younger contemporary of Baḥraq, relating to the disposal of the water draining from the *mīzāb* or water-spout/gutter, of a house.[19] Again [20] the making of an aperture or apertures in the upper part of his house (*fatḥ kuwwah* [21] *aw kuwwāt fī aʿlā baiti-hi*) in such a way that the person concerned can see out of them, if it is detrimental to the privacy of other persons, is prohibited. The right to construct another storey on one's house has in some districts to be specifically entered in a deed.[22] In Tarīm a dispute over the right to build in the *ḥaram* (Class. *ḥarīm*), the immediate environs of two houses, and lying between them, was settled by allowing either to build (1233/1817–18),[23] though the settlement seems to be questionable in *sh̲arīʿah* law.

A quite common legal question in the sources is whether the appurtenances of a house through which there may be access to the house or not, actually form part of the house, as in the case where the famous *qāḍī* of al-Sh̲iḥr, Abū Makh̲ramah,[24] was asked:

مسألة :— باع داراً فيها بيت داخل فى تربيعها ، لكنّه غير نافذ إليها ، كالمخازن فى ديار الجهة. فهل تدخل فى مطلق بيعها أم لا ؟

'Question: (A person) sold a house within which is a room [25] entering into

[16] R. B. Serjeant, ' Forms of plea, a Šāfiʿī manual from al-Šiḥr ', *Rivista degli Studi Orientali*, xxx, 1–2, 1955, 9.

[17] Notably Muḥ. b. al-Sh̲aikh̲ ʿAbdullāh b. Aḥmad Bā Sawdān, *Taḥṣīl al-maqṣūd fī mā ṭuliba min taʿrīf ṣiyag̲h̲ al-ʿuqūd*, photocopy of Tarīm MS in R. B. Serjeant's possession, 8. (This well-known scholar, a Dawʿanī from al-Kh̲uraibah, flourished from 1206/1791–2 to 1281/1864–5, cf. ʿAbdullāh . . . b. Ḥāmid al-Saqqāf, *Tārīkh̲ al-sh̲uʿarāʾ al-Ḥaḍramīyīn*, Cairo, 1353/1934–5— , iii, 196, which omits *Taḥṣīl* from the afore-going title, while Abū Bakr b. Aḥmad b. ʿAbdullāh al-Kh̲aṭīb al-Anṣārī al-Tarīmī, *al-Fatāwā al-nāfiʿah fī masāʾil al-aḥwāl al-wāqiʿah*, Cairo, 1960, 48, merely entitles it *Ṣiyag̲h̲ al-ʿuqūd*.) Saiyid Muḥsin b. Jaʿfar b. ʿAlawī Bū Numaiy, *Tashīl al-daʿāwī fī rafʿ al-sh̲akāwī*, al-Mukallā, 1954.

[18] For this author see R. B. Serjeant, *The Portuguese off the South Arabian coast*, Oxford, 1963, 28. The cases discussed are taken from a photocopy of the Mukallā MS of his *al-Fatāwā al-ʿAdanīyah*, fols. 215a, 218b.

[19] cf. *al-Fatāwā al-nāfiʿah*, 99, and Bū Numaiy, op. cit., 12.

[20] See n. 18, above.

[21] A *kuwwah* can also be an aperture above a door or window.

[22] cf. R. B. Serjeant, ' A Judeo-Arab house-deed from Ḥabbān '. *Journal of the Royal Asiatic Society*, 1953, 3–4, p. 127. Cf. Bū Numaiy, op. cit., 13.

[23] *Al-Fatāwā al-nāfiʿah*, 95.

[24] op. cit., 187b.

[25] cf. pt. i of this article, *BSOAS*, xxxviii, 1, 1975, p. 19, n. 51. In Tarīm *manzil* seemed the ordinary word for a room.

(i.e. inside) the area enclosed by its four (foundation [26]) walls (*tarbī‘*), but without access to it (i.e. the main house), like *makhāzin* in the houses of the district. Do these enter into the general (act of) sale, or not ? '

To this the reply was in the affirmative in the case of these *makhāzin*, which would mean ' stores ' or ' shops ' [27] or the courtyards (reading *durū‘* for *rū‘*), and the walls (*al-ḥajāyā* [28]) connected with the house, if considered part of it, and with or without access to it, even if they have a door to the outside.

Another similar problem is concerned with the appurtenances of the house (*marāfiq al-bait*) which lie *outside* its four walls, and this figures also in Bā Makhramah's *Fatāwā* [29]

وقد سئل العلّامة عبد الله بَلْحَاجّ بما لفظه: الصّور [30] والاصوار المتّصلة بالدّيار عندنا - هل تدخل فى بيعها ؟ أجاب: — الّذى يظهر أنّها لا تدخل إلّا إن كان لها باب إلى الدّار .فإن كان لها باب إلى الدّار فهذا يظهر أنّه كحجرة متّصلة بالدّار ، فلا يدخل، وفى حضرموت مثل ذلك إلّا أنّها تسمّى دُروعاً، ولكن لا تبنى إلّا للدّار ، وفيها ما يحتاج إليه الدّار من حطب وغيره. فما أشكّ أنّه جزء من الدّار فهذا ما ظهر لى (انتهى). قلتُ : وما ذكر من أنّ لها أبواب [كذا] وباب آخر خارجها أنّها «كحجرة متّصلة بالدّار، فلا يدخل» — هذا إذا كان الدِرْع أو الوَصَر لا يُعدّ من توابع الدّار ومرافقها. فأمّا إذا كان يُعدّ من ذلك فلا يظهر به إلّا الدّخول — وإن كان له باب آخر إلى خارج . . .

An opinion is offered that the threshing floors or yards do not enter into the sale unless they have a door into the house which makes them like a room in the house. The comparison is made with *durū‘*, courtyards, which are built only for the (use of) the house and contain firewood, etc., required by the house. Bā Makhramah disagrees with Bal-Ḥājj (a Ḥaḍramī) on the issue as to whether they are part of the house or not, and says it is really a matter of whether the *dir‘* or threshing-floor (*waṣar*) is considered to be an appurtenance of the house or not that counts, even if it has a second door to the outside of the house. Bū Numaiy,[31] our near contemporary today, certainly takes these arguments into account in drafting his pleas of a contract of purchase—when he gives an

[26] So rendered after a phrase in the Judaeo-Arab house-deed.

[27] Landberg, *Ḥaḍramoût*, renders *makhzan* as *magasin*.

[28] This is assumed, though without authority of an informant, to be the plural of the Jirdān word *ḥājī* ' barrier ' ; see pt. I of this article, p. 21.

[29] op. cit., fol. 188a. The *marāfiq* of a dwelling fit to be provided for a wife comprise a roof (*saṭḥ*), lavatory (*ṭahārah*), stairs (*dirij*), and kitchen (*maṭbakh*) (op. cit., 170).

[30] This word seems unknown, and Bā Maṭraf suggests reading *wuṣūr*, plur. of *waṣar* (another plur. being *āṣār* which he calls a yard (*sāḥah*) for harvesting grain crops.

[31] op. cit., 7.

example of a plea that a house has been purchased without ' its eastern or western store/shop (*al-makhzan al-sharqī aw al-qiblī*) '.[32]

Abū Bakr . . . al-Khaṭīb [33] produces yet another variation of the problem where a man makes a bequest (*nadhr*) of a house with all that pertains to it in *shar*' and '*urf* in the way of:

أحرام وممرّات وحجاو ودروع وبئر ومصلّى وجابية . . . وجميع ما فى الدار المعروف المذكور أعلا من ماعون وفرش ونحاس وأثاث.

The question arising is—does the furniture, etc., which is mentioned also include what is in the *murabba'āt* (detached) rooms and courts (*ḥajāw* [34]) which are outside the house?

The Ṣan'ānī Jews had workshops or premises that normally had no door leading to the living quarters, these former establishments being approached from the outside by their owners. Goitein [35] thinks that this was because it was not deemed safe that the interior of a house should be accessible from the street except through the main entrance. As, however, to judge by the query on stores/shops which do not communicate with the house, *supra*, it was custom commonly enough among the Arab population also, Goitein's suggestion is not entirely convincing—it might equally well be that the arrangement in Ṣan'ā', and I am sure many other towns, was made for other reasons of convenience or privacy.

In Jirdān, which 'Alawī b. Ṭāhir considers only partly to lie in Ḥaḍramawt, decisions in property cases would most likely be made by '*urf* or custom, but the *fatwās* of Bā Makhramah and other jurists do in some degree, reflect what that '*urf* was.

A conflict between property owners and the sulṭān, in one of the Ḥaḍramī towns, probably Tarīm or Saiwūn, is embodied in a *fatwā* which Abū Bakr . . . al-Khaṭīb (a Tarīmī) [36] pronounced, supporting the property owners, though

[32] In Ḥaḍramawt north and south are *najdī* and *baḥrī* respectively, in Yemen (cf. *Tarjī' al-aṭyār*, 46) *qiblah* and '*Adan*. Cf. Bā Sawdān, op. cit., 8, defining a property; as parts of a house to be sold with it he adds, علوها وسفلها وأوصارها.

[33] *Al-Fatāwā al-nāfi'ah*, 245.

[34] *Ḥajāw* is presumably the plural of *ḥijwah*, reported also by Landberg, *Ḥaḍramoût*, 360, as *ḥujwah/ḥajwah*. At Tarīm it was described as *dir'*, equivalent to *dawr* and *dāyir* (though the two latter appear to be the name of the wall applied to the enclosure as a whole), and to the *waṣar* of Daw'an, the common word for a threshing-floor, but perhaps in Daw'an it may sometimes be enclosed by a wall (?). Cf. *al-Fatāwā al-nāfi'ah*, 95, *khushm al-ḥijwah*, the corner of the court, 254, where *ḥijwah* is defined as *al-fanā' al-amāmī al-muḥawwaṭ al-tābi' li 'l-bait*, and 257 for a brief reference to *dir'*. Cf. 'Alawī b. Ṭāhir, *al-Shāmil*, Singapore, 1359/1940, 190, الطاق منزل أرضيّ يجعل أمامه فسحة لتجفيف التمر وغيره، وهو معروف بالجرن ويسمّيه أهد أسفل الوادى حيوه. *Ḥiywah/ḥaywah* would be Ḥaḍramī pronunciation for *ḥijwah* and *jurn* or *jarīn* is a threshing-floor.

[35] Carl Rathjens and S. D. Goitein, *Jewish domestic architecture in San'a, Yemen* (Oriental Notes and Studies, No. 7), Israel Oriental Society, 1957, 6. This is, of course, a very different type of dwelling from our *ḥuṣn*, but it might have affinities with non-tribal domestic buildings in such places as Mocha or al-Shiḥr were these to be studied.

[36] *Al-Fatāwā al-nāfi'ah*, 101.

unfortunately all names are suppressed. The point raised, in brief, is that the sulṭān had given orders to build in a wide street running between ancient houses and courtyards (*ḥawsh*)—can the owners claim between their properties and the new building the right to which the *sharī'ah* entitles them, of a space of 8 *dhirā'*, or, in customary usage (*ma'rūf*), 10 *dhirā'* in the streets and lanes (? *maṭāriq wa-maḍāyīq*), in order to preserve the amenities of ventilation and sun and daylight, and to stop his walls from coming up to their walls? A supplementary question inquires whether, in the case of a market-place (*sāḥat sūq*) bounded on all sides by houses and courtyards, the owners can pierce entrances (*mafāqir*), or build shops (*makhāzin*), or make openings (*kuwwāt*) on to this market-place. The owners consider that the sulṭān should return to the law of God (*ḥukm Allāh*) which they regard him as having transgressed—one can scarcely doubt that they must have mostly been saiyids!

Miscellaneous notes on builders, tools, materials

Outside al-Jinainah village we spoke with a builder called 'Umar b. Ḥasan al-Ḥaddād. From what he said it was apparent that there is no stigma attaching to building work—this in Ḥaḍramawt would be a craft in which none but the class of *ḍa'īfs* should employ themselves.[37] Here builders may belong to any of the groups like *mashāyikh*, *qabā'il*, *ḍu'fā*, though saiyids were not mentioned, but in these districts their numbers are very small. Early Islamic history seems to indicate that the aristocratic Umaiyad 'Uthmān b. 'Affān [38] would not take part with the Prophet and his Companions in handling the clay bats (*libnah*) to build the first mosque, while on the other hand the man of humble birth 'Ammār b. Yāsir fell to with a will—'Ammār, of course, in the Yemen, means a builder.[39]

The hereditary builders of Tarīm, the Bā Ḥuraish,[40] build in clay and stone, and work *nūrah*, plaster, and whitewash. 'All stone is the specialty of Bā Ḥuraish' (*Kull ḥajar khāṣṣ bi-Bā Ḥuraish*). Their religious attachment was described as to the Manṣab of al-Ramlah, al-'Aidarūs, of the well-known saiyid family. The *mu'allim*,[41] masterbuilder, is paid more than the rest, and in 1953 he received about 7 shillings per diem; it is probably he who gives the estimate (*qāwal*). The men are paid daily. Local architects in Tarīm made the plans, simple ground-plans without elevations. Estimates for building by 1953 were made in terms of a price per thousand *madrahs* or clay bats, and for work on upper storeys a higher rate was paid than for the ground floor. The Bā Ḥuraish also constructed dams/barrages (*sudūd*).

[37] cf. R. B. Serjeant, 'The cemeteries of Tarīm', *Le Muséon*, LXII, 1–2, 1949, 151.

[38] A. Guillaume (tr.), *The life of Muhammad*, London, 1955, 229.

[39] Al-Balādhurī, *Ansāb al-ashrāf*, ed. Muḥammad Ḥamīdullāh, Cairo, 1959– , I, 168.

[40] cf. R. B. Serjeant, 'Some irrigation systems in Ḥaḍramawt', *BSOAS*, XXVII, 1, 1964, 54.

[41] In the Yemen a skilled craftsman in building or carpentry is called *usṭā* (*Tarjī' al-aṭyār*, 300). According to Syed Hamood Hason, *Arabic simplified*, [India ?], 1919, 397, 582, in Aden a mason is *usṭah/wusṭāh* (*asaṭīyah*).

FIG. 1. Wooden pin (*rifqah*) for sewing palm-leaf matting on to the roof beams, forming a surface upon which to lay roof-clay (*ṭīn*). The *rifqah* is rounded and the cord is attached by winding it round the narrow part below the handle

A cord (*khaiṭ*) is employed to ensure the correct alignment of a wall as in plate II. In Tarīm a wooden pin (*rifqah*) (fig. 1) is used for sewing cord round beams. A stretcher, in Shibām called *ri'ih* is used there for carrying the clay bats. A curious passage in *al-Fawā'id al-sanīyah* [42] seems to refer to a sledge or a bullock-cart:

وقيل إنّه بُنى من طين أموالهم فى بيت جُبَيْر—كانوا ينقلون اللّبن على الحَرَاديم، وهى آلة الهند، وتجرّه البقر. وكذلك الطين يطرح فى الجبول ويوضع عليها، وتجرّه أيضاً. وبنى أسفله بالآجر . . . وعاد بقى من عمارته الدّايِر ودعايم الصّفّ الأوّل، وصفتهن حِصِى صُبَّ فى مِثَال.

'It is said that it (a mosque) was built of the clay from their properties in Bait Jubair (a little south of Tarīm)—they used to transport the clay bats on the *ḥarādīm*,[43] the Indian apparatus, which cattle used to draw. Clay was also put into ass-panniers and placed on them, and they would draw that too. The lower part was constructed in baked brick . . . , and the wall [44] of the building and columns of the first row still remain, consisting of small pebbles (mixed with lime (*nūrah*) and) cast in a mould.'

At the present time burnt brick construction in the districts east of Abyan is extremely rare, nor does one see traces of burnt brick in ruins. A brick-built mosque in Niṣāb is stated to have been constructed by a Yemeni, and this some hundreds of years ago. Brick burned red is commonly used in the cities of the southern Yemenite Tihāmah. It might be observed that in at least the last two decades of British rule in Aden the building workers were seemingly all Yemenis. In the Dathīnah district in the 1950's the builders were said to be mainly Yāfi'īs.

The making of the mixture of clay and straw for the clay bats (plate III (*a*)) is *tamdīr*,[45] and the clay or lime (*nūrah*) between them is known by the Classical Arabic term *milāṭ*.[46] 'Alawī b. Ṭāhir [47] states that in his home valley of Daw'an, 'The custom was in our village (*balad*, i.e. Qaidūn) that they should help someone who wished to build by carrying clay bats (*libin*) on their beasts to the

[42] Aḥmad b. Ḥasan . . . al-Ḥaddād, *al-Fawā'id* . . . , fols. 103b–104a, MS described in *BSOAS*, XIII, 2, 1950, 296–7.

[43] This word does not figure in the Arabic lexicons consulted.

[44] *Dāyir*, a wall, synonyms *ḥāyil* and *sitrah*, for which last see *al-Fatāwā al-nāfi'ah*, 257, and glossary, below. *Tarjī' al-aṭyār*, 424, gives a plural, *dawā'ir*.

[45] 'Alawī b. Ṭāhir, *al-Shāmil*, 227.

[46] ibid., 96.

[47] ibid., 213.

place of building if this were requested of them'. As a piece of good-neighbourliness without payment, he apparently means, they did this. Again,[48] the earth/clay (*ṭīn*) for the clay brick (*madar*) was taken from the arable fields (*jurūb al-ḥarth*), either against payment, or as a gift. Where flood silt has from time to time to be removed to keep the level of the field constant for irrigation purposes this operation would have to be undertaken anyway—in fact the problem often is in certain places where to put the silt. From the language in which this is couched one would understand that these voluntary services were extended to everyone, but one wonders if the learned saiyid does not perhaps mean that they were extended to saiyids, not necessarily to others, since saiyid Manṣabs in some districts in Ḥaḍramawt, perhaps only in such *ḥawṭahs* as al-Ḥāwī in Tarīm, did, to some extent, receive voluntary services from craftsmen on occasion.

Once more a *fatwā* question illustrates how the Ḥaḍramīs dealt over these matters with one another. The following question was put to Abū Bakr al-Khaṭīb [49]:

'So-and-so asked us to give him permission for a *j rūrat yawm* (a day's drawing ? [50]) from the clay of the ruin (*ṭīn al-kharābah*) at al-Muḥaiḍarah [51] in Tarīm, belonging to the (our) grandfather So-and-so (presumably now deceased) in which a number of people have shares, there being absentee (*aghyāb*) brothers and the paternal uncle So-and-so, and children of paternal uncle So-and-so; and it cost us a *lakk*. We are afraid of committing a sin meriting punishment (*ḥarj*)'.

Clearly he means that if those present in Tarīm, owners of shares in this ruin, dispose of them in the absence of the others (and so many Ḥaḍramīs were abroad in those days and now), he will have transgressed the law. The *muftī*'s reply was very sensible. Most of al-Muḥaiḍarah, he said, which is in ruins, is of clay one part of which is indistinguishable from another, and so the questioner has a right to take his share of it even in the absence of the other owners. In fact al-Muḥaiḍarah was much developed after the second World War, especially in the early 1950's, though the *fatwā* cannot be later than the first decade after the first World War. The absentees would almost certainly be those Ḥaḍramīs who had emigrated to Indonesia or Malaya.

A wooden lock

A wooden lock specially made by 'Awaḍ Bā Ḥashwān,[52] a Tarīm carpenter, in 1947, is now in the Museum of Archaeology and Ethnology in Cambridge

[48] ibid., 227.

[49] *Al-Fatāwā al-nāfi'ah*, 274.

[50] This word is not known to us, but the sense appears to be so.

[51] We lived in al-Muḥaiḍarah in 1947 (R. B. S.).

[52] cf. R. B. Serjeant, *Prose and poetry from Ḥaḍramawt*, London, 1951, 8. Since this article was written Werner Diem's wide-ranging and instructive article 'Untersuchungen zu Technik u. Terminologie der arabisch-islamischen Türschlösser', *Der Islam*, L, 1, 1973, 98–156, with drawings of locks, has appeared.

(plate IV). It is called *qūlidih ḥimr*, i.e. a lock (*qūlidah*, pl. *qawālid*) of *ḥimr* which is *ʿilb*-wood (*Zizyphus spina-Christi*). This particular specimen is a *qūlidah ḥaqq mirwāḥ ʿarūs*, a lock for a bride's room. In Ḥaḍramawt a *mirwāḥ* is a room on the third floor in which the bride and groom sleep on the bridal-night. On the inside of the door of the bridal chamber there is a small wooden bolt called *ṣumbaʿah*.[53] Convention demands that when the last attendant, the *kūbarah*,[54] or women's hairdresser, tire-woman, leaves the bride, the groom must then immediately jump up and shoot the inside bolt home, in order to show how lively and active he is. Convention, on the other hand, requires that when he takes off the silver ornaments with which the bride is laden, he must do so with care, and lay them out neatly. The richly ornamented external lock, however, is mounted on the outside only to show honour, but it is not locked, except by the bride or groom when they leave the room next day.

The component parts of the Tarīm lock are differently named from those of the Jirdān locks. The upright part of the lock is known as *qūshimah* (pl. *qawāshim*),[55] and the bar or bolt as *mijarrah*. The teeth in the lock above the bolt are *ḥandhūlah* (pl. *ḥanādhīl*), and the holes in the *mijarrah* which receive them are called *khadar al-aḍrās*, though, as the pegs on the key (*iqlīd*) are known as *ḍurūs* or *aḍrās*, they are really named ' the peg-holes ' after them. In Ḥaḍramawt the name of the house is sometimes carved on the lock.

A Tarīm proverb says, *Mā ḥad misik qūshimat bābak*, lit. ' No one has grasped the front of your lock ', i.e. No one has knocked at your door, meaning that nobody has bothered you. Saif b. Ḥusain al-Quʿaiṭī [56] reports another proverb, *Mā kull ʿūd iqlīd* ' Not every stick is a key '. Landberg, however, quotes a proverb with a sense diametrically opposite ! [57]

Round towers in the Zaidī highlands of the Yemen

On Jabal Wishḥah, near al-Qārah, Imām al-Badr's headquarters during much of the Egyptian occupation of the Yemen, may be seen round towers of several storeys, as also in the Ṣarārah district of Jabal ʿAyāl Yazīd north of Ṣanʿā', and in other places. These are really fortified dwellings, built in stone, quite different from the mud towers of north-eastern Yemen and Najrān,[58] sometimes round, sometimes square. Al-Ānisī [59] says of a powerful Zaidī Imām who brought the Jabal and other districts to heel,

كم قَصِيب وكم دوائر وكم حصن حَصِينْ
صيّرتْهُن جيوشِهْ خَرابَهْ

[53] cf. Landberg, *Ḥaḍramoût*, 635, ' verrou en bois '.

[54] cf. R. B. Serjeant, ' Recent marriage legislation from al-Mukallā with notes on marriage customs ', *BSOAS*, XXV, 3, 1962, 487.

[55] cf. part I of this article, *BSOAS*, XXXVIII, 1, 1975, p. 4, n. 20.

[56] *Al-Amthāl wa 'l-aqwāl al-Ḥaḍramīyah*, 145.

[57] *Ḥaḍramoût*, 350. Any wood is suitable for making a key.

[58] The distinctive style of northern mud architecture can be perceived in Khalil Abou el-Nasr's ' Architecture in Asir ', *Middle East Forum* (Beirut), April 1962, 29–32.

[59] *Tarjīʿ al-aṭyār*, 424 ; a *qaṣabah* is a *nawbah mudawwarah*.

'How many (round) towers, how many walls, how many a strong fort
Have his armies made a ruin!'

The tower seen in Ṣarārah was called *qaṣabah* (plur. *qaṣīb*) and was constructed with four internal arches (*'uqūd*) springing from a central column (fig. 2) within the circle formed by the walls of the tower.

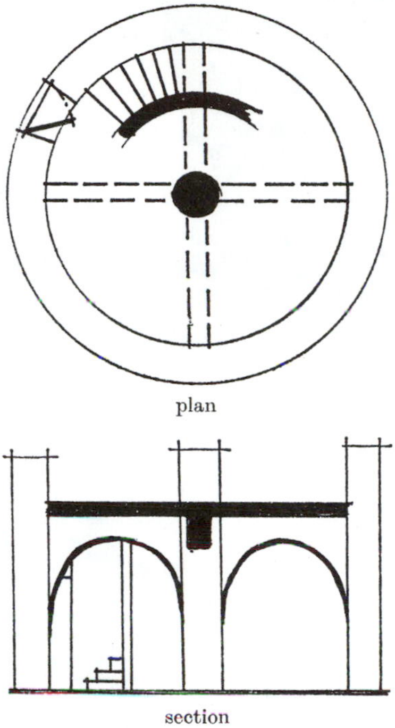

FIG. 2. Round tower (*qaṣabah*) at Ṣarārah of Jabal 'Ayāl Yazīd (Yemen) constructed on four arches (*'uqūd*) springing from a central column

The single door to the tower called *'adan* has on the left and immediately inside the building a stairway running round the inside of the circular wall. A *makhṭā* is a passage on the ground floor. The men's room is known as *dīwān*, and the *suqwaf* is the part allotted to the womenfolk. The *jibā/jubā* is the roof which is *mushawshawafah* provided with a battlemented wall (*al-tishwāf al-ḥarbī*); under the *jibā* [60] is stored the grain (*ṭa'ām*). A *mawshaq* (plur. *mawāshiq*) is a loophole [61] for firing through at attackers, and a *ṭāqah* (plur. *ṭiyāq*) is a window. The place where the animals are kept is called *al-ḥarr*, probably outside the tower itself.

A square tower here (*hānā*, here, as they pronounce it), would be *bait murabba' 'alā arba'ah arkān*.

[60] Hayyim Habshush, *Travels in the Yemen*, ed. S. D. Goitein, Jerusalem, 1941, 83, writes it *juba'*.

[61] cf. Sayed Hamood Hason, op. cit., 578.

XV

PLATE I

FOR DESCRIPTION, SEE P. 295

PLATE II

FOR DESCRIPTION, SEE P. 295

Plate III

(*a*)

(*b*)

For descriptions, see p. 295

Plate IV

[*Courtesy Museum of Archaeology and Ethnology, Cambridge*

Ḥaḍramī lock with key in position

Though basically this is an account of a field study, it has seemed appropriate while writing it up, to include data collected on various occasions, including lists of technical building terms from several districts, or culled from Arabic works unlikely to be at the disposal of most readers. On the other hand no attempt has been made to ransack systematically such well-known publications as Hayyim Habshush's account of his journey to Najrān in 1870.[62] The systematic study of Yemenite architecture, the excellent little Rathjens-Goitein volume apart, is still to be made, and it is a field rich in promise. Of course the architecture these two authors describe is not distinctively Jewish in the main, but properly only traditional Yemeni architecture. Habshush's own house survives and is pointed out to visitors to Ṣan'ā'. Let it be said that the description of Abrahah's church in Ṣan'ā' with its courses of different coloured stone and triangular patterns is very like that of present-day Yemen.[63] When the technical terms here are compared with Landberg's account [64] of the operations in building, the dialect of Jirdān in this respect is similar to that of settled Ḥadramawt of the interior. On the other hand the terms used by Muḥ. b. Aḥ. al-Ḥajarī, *Masājid Ṣan'ā'*, Ṣan'ā', 1361/1942, or Ettore Rossi in his publications, differ greatly from those of Ḥadramawt.

Additionally to those persons who made it possible for us to execute our

[62] Data in R. B. Serjeant, ' Building and builders ', are not repeated though complementary to this study. A more general article, D. B. Doe, ' Home is a husn ', *The Architect and Building News*, VI, 3, 1970, 26–32, may also be consulted, but we were unable to see R. Kasdorff, *Haus und Hauswesen im alten Arabien (bis zur Zeit des Chalifen Othman)*, Halle, 1914, apparently a dissertation of 71 pp.

[63] cf. al-Azraqī, *Akhbār Makkah*, in F. Wüstenfeld, *Geschichte und Beschreibung der Stadt Mekka*, Leipzig, 1858, 88–9. The church wall built by Abrahah al-Ḥabashī in Ṣan'ā' was square in plan (*murabba' mustawī al-tarbī'*) whereas the site, called Ghurqat al-Qalīs, of the ancient church in the old town shown today is a shallow circular pit (*ghurqah*). Abrahah's church was 60 *dhirā'* high. Its raised area (*kibs*, lit. ' earth placed on an area to level it ', etc.) inside was 10 *dhirā'* high, and it was approached by marble steps. There was a wall surrounding the church, presumably forming an enceinte, 100 *dhirā'* from it. This description reminds one of the circular wall at the Ma'rib temple. The wall was constructed of stones called in the Yemen *jurūb*, carved/painted (? *manqūshah*) fitted into each other (*muṭābaqah*) so that a needle could not enter between them, stuck close together (*muṭabbaqah*), 20 *dhirā'* in height. Between (the courses of ?) *jurūb* stones he put triangular stones like a camel's hump (*sharaf*), entering into each other, of red, white, yellow, and black stone, and *sāsam* wood between each course (*sāf*), round of head (*rās*), thick of timber, like a man's side, protruding from the building. The *jurūb* appear to have had the shape (fig. 3 (*a*)), and the courses of coloured stone seem to have the shape (fig. 3 (*b*)). Over this a marble frieze was placed, carved, and projecting a *dhirā'* beyond the building, and 2 *dhirā'* in height. Over this was set shining black stone from Nuqum mountain, then shining yellow stone, and on top of all, white stone (perhaps that called *balaq*). These and many other details correspond closely to north Yemenite architecture as seen today.

(*a*)

(*b*)

FIG. 3. Recent examination of the Ghurqat al-Qalīs site shows that its dimensions are not inconsistent at least with a dome set on a base 30 *dhirā'* square at the east end of the nave

[64] *Ḥadramoût*, 394 f. Cf. L. W. C. van den Berg, *Le Hadhramout et les colonies arabes*, Batavia, 1886, or 1969 reprint, 62 f.

work in Jirdān we are indebted to Dr. ʻAbdullāh Maqṭarī, Shaikh Muḥ. ʻAbd al-Qādir Bā Maṭraf, Saiyid ʻAlawī b. ʻAbdullāh, and Dr. M. A. Ghanem for answering our queries, as also to Dr. G. Bushnell of the Museum of Archaeology and Ethnology, Cambridge, for permission to reproduce photographs of the locks there. All drawings and photographs are by Brian Doe unless stated to the contrary.

General list of terms connected with building

إخْتِطاط Yem., *Tarjīʻ al-aṭyār*, 74, defined as *al-shurūʻ fī ʼl-bināʼ wa-waḍʻ ʻalāmāt*, marking out a building. Class. Arabic.

با جَناح Tarīm, precise meaning uncertain, but as *janāḥ* means a fourth storey room, it is probably a building with such a room.

با دَرْف Tarīm, door with a single leaf.

باب أمْلَس Tarīm, door with no horizontal bars on the back of it for strength.

باب مُزَفَّر Tarīm, a door with horizontal bars (*zūfar*) on it.

بَرْحَه (pl. ات) Ḥaḍramawt, courtyard for sitting in the evening in front of the house. Cf. *rawḥah*.

بُونَي Tarīm, Saiwūn, door. e.g. بوني الرقاد a door on the stairs, or, more precisely, leading off the stairs.

تَجْوَاب Yem., the wall round the roof of a house for privacy, and/or to prevent women seeing over it. Cf. Rossi, *Terminologia*, 353.

تَقْدُومَه Ḥaḍramawt (al-Shiḥr), façade of a building.

تَنْوِير Aden, etc., whitewashing. S. H. Hason, 671. Cf. *rushūsh*.

تَيْرُومَه (pl. تَيَارِم) Ḥaḍramawt, roof of upper rooms, not surrounded by a wall; or roof (*saqf*) of the stairs leading to the roof-top (*saṭḥ*).

تَيْسُورَه Tarīm, a syn. of *ʻarūs al-riqād* (q.v.).

ثُرَيَّا Yem., a type of window with tracery.

جَذْوَه Ṣanʻā', the *dakkah* or platform around the Jāmiʻ mosque at the place of the *sail*-flood which used to wash against it. See *sājil*.

جَهْوَه (pl. جِهِي) Jīzān, Saudi Arabia, stone hut.

حُجْرَة (pl. حجر, ات) Yem., *Tarjīʻ al-aṭyār*, 120, and Goitein and Rathjens, 77, the latter calling it *ḥijrah*, an inner open court, but the former a central place between two rooms like a passage. Cf. Rossi, *Terminologia*, *ḥajrah* ʻ portico ʼ.

حزام Ṣanʻā', course of decoration between two storeys.

خُشْم (pl. أَخْشام) syn. ربع (q.v.) Tarīm, the outside or external corner (*rukn*) of a house. Cf. *al-Fatāwā al-nāfi'ah*, 257.

خُلُص Tarīm etc., hole in the middle of a window-shelf to which the shelf itself slopes to allow water to drain to the outside of the house if it should fall on the shelf.

خَيْش Ḥaḍramawt of the coast. Clay bats or stones set on the top of a wall, leaning against each other to form an open zigzag pattern (fig. 4). Khaish can also mean a metal grille.

FIG. 4

دَرْب N. Yem., Kuhlān district, a tower-fort, syn. *nawbah*.

دَفاه Tarīm, round cover, with handle to cover the *tannūr/tinnār* bread-oven made of clay pottery.

دَكّة platform outside a building. For data upon, cf. Ibn Ḥajar al-Haitamī, *al-Fatāwā al-kubrā al-fiqhīyah*, Cairo, 1938; and *al-Fatāwā al-nāfi'ah*, 101.

دَيْل (pl. دُيول), Yem., course, row of stones.

رَبْع Tarīm, outside corner of a house. syn. khushm (q.v.).

رَدَّه Tarīm, passage on top of a house.

رُشُوش Tarīm, Aden, etc., whitewashing. Cf. Landberg, *Ḥaḍramoût*, 406 *passim*. S. H. Hason, 671, syn. *tanwīr*.

رِفْقَه Tarīm, a peg or pin (see fig. 1).

رُقْدَه Ḥaḍramawt, *ruqdat al-qahwah*, coffee-hearth, with slightly raised dais on which coffee-maker sits.

رِكْبَه (pl. رِكَب) a column of clay, opposed to a *sahm*, column of wood. One says, 'A reception room with such and such a number of columns' (مَحْضَره على كَم رِكَب).

رَوْحَه Tarīm, court for sitting in the evening situated in front of the house.

رَوْضَه Tarim, corner inside house, or room thereof.

رُوَيْجَعَه Tarīm, small store (*makhzan*), under the inside or outside stair of a house.

زَقْطُوط (pl. زَقاطِيط) Aden, lane. S. H. Hason, 573.

زُوفَر Tarīm, also زافر (pl. زوافر), horizontal bar on the back of a door or shutter.

زَوْق Tarīm, projecting cornice between storeys.

ساجِل Ṣan'ā' and district, flat rain-water drainage course running directly off the roof down the wall, constructed of *qaḍāḍ*, a sort of mortar composition containing small stones. A *qaḍāḍ* course can last 500 years. See *jad͟hwah*.

ساس has a plural also سِيسان, S. H. Hason, 555.

سَبِخَة الحِيطان Ḥaḍramawt. Of a house (*dār*), containing salt in the clay of which it is constructed, salty walls, a fault. Muḥsin Bū Numaiy, *Tashīl al-da'āwī*, 13.

سَتْرَه/سُتْرَه (pl. سَتَر) Ḥaḍramawt, wall. Cf. Rossi, *Terminologia*, 357.

سَحْسُوح (pl. سَحَاسِيح) Ḥaḍramawt, a place usually behind the *dār* on to which waste water from the kitchens or lavatories pours; it may be inside the dwelling. Another source calls it a lavatory or washing place also.

سَرْع Ṣan'ā', a course of stones.

سِقَالَه (pl. سَقَايِل) Aden, scaffold. S. H. Hason 630, from Greek σχάλα.

سِيرِى Ta'izz, a wooden tripod with cross-bars, forming a type of ladder, used in mosques.

شَمْشَه/شُمْسِه Tarīm, an open place in the middle of a house, فى مِثْنات البيت, the latter phrase explained as *fī wasṭ al-dār*.

شَمْسِيَّه (pl. شَمَاسِى) Yem., Ta'izz, etc., open part of the open court of a mosque.

ضِبْر (ه) Tarīm, Mukallā, the inside corner in a house, e.g. of a room, contrasted with *k͟hus͟hm*, etc. Syn. *zāwiyah*. *Gloss. daṯ.*, 2165. Cf. Rossi, *Terminologia*, 354, *dubr*, with *dāl*.

ضَيْقَه (pl. ضِيَق) Ḥaḍramawt, narrow passage on ground floor of a house from main door (*siddah*).

طَارُوط Upper Yem., covered way above a street connecting one house with another. Cf. Rossi, *Terminologia*, 354, *ṭārūd*. 'portico della moschea.'

طَرَّاحَه Jīzān, Saudi Arabia, mud floor of *tukul* type huts ornamented in whorls of clay, made by women.

طَرْحَه Upper Yem., storey of a house. Cf. Rossi, *Terminologia*, 356, *ṭarḥah* 'pieno di casa'.

عارِض (pl. عُرْضان) al-S͟hiḥr, a small beam. Cf. *'arrāḍī*.

عَتَبَة الخَلْفه (pl. ات) Ḥaḍramawt, MS *Manāqib Bā 'Abbād* (possession of the late Saiyid Ṣāliḥ b. 'Alī al-Ḥāmidī), lower strake of wood of window lintel. Cf. Rossi, *Terminologia*, 352.

عَرَّاضِي (pl. ات) Aden, rafter. S. H. Hason, 617.

عَروس الرِقاد Tarīm, the plastered panel, sometimes with decoration, approximately three feet in height which runs up the wall of a staircase, above the stairs.

عِضاده e.g. عضادة الباب Ḥaḍramawt, MS Bā Makhramah, *Fatāwā*, collected works, a single volume of which was seen in Dathīnah, wooden side part of a door.

عُكْرَه (pl. عُكَر) Tarīm, a small circular window set over an ordinary rectangular window.

علالى Yemen, *Tarjī' al-aṭyār*, 158, 363, described as شرفات الدور.

غَيْله Tarīm, first storey room, e.g. غيله على ثلاثه سَوَاقِط مُقبِّل a first storey room on (with ?) three beams, facing north. غيله على شِرْقَتَيْن a first storey room on (with ?) two beams running from wall to wall.

فاضِلة Ḥaḍramawt, Ṣāliḥ b. Ghālib al-Qu'aiṭī, *al-Riḥlat al-sulṭānīyah*, Cheribon, 1370/1950–1, a *majlis* like a reception room (*maḥḍarah*). Cf. Landberg, *Ḥaḍramoût*, 398, 'chambre'. Cf. Rossi, *Terminologia*, 357, *fawāḍil* 'il piano'.

قُبَع (pl. قَنَابِع) Al-Shiḥr, crenellations of a mosque. Muḥ. b. 'Abd al-Qādir Bā Maṭraf quoted the following saying, من شاف القنابع والخيش ظن ان عندنا من المال فيش والواقع ان ما عندنا الّا قناعه فى العيش.

قرقاعه Ḥaḍramawt, circular brass or iron door-knocker.

كابه (pl. ات) Yem., wall buttress. *Gloss. daṯ.* gives parallel senses. S. H. Hason, 603, calls it 'pillar'.

كَشَارِى Tarīm, pillars (no singular), supporting an arch (*'akf*).

كَفَاه Tarīm, lintel.

كَلَّاب (pl. كَلاليب) Ḥaḍramawt, hook, for hanging clothes, etc., upon.

كَيْد Upper Yem., flat roof of a house. Syn. *jubā*.

لِهِى Ḥaḍramī pronunciation of لهج, the shutter of a window (*khalfah*). Cf. Rossi, *Terminologia*, 356, window.

مَاد (pl. مَوَاد) e.g. ماد الرَّيْم a little passage or entry into a room (fig. 5, p. 292).

مِثْناه (pl. ات) Tarīm, Saiwūn, open place in middle of a house. Bā Maṭraf says *al-mathnāh* is the interior of anything, not the same as *shumsih*, an open court in the middle of a house.

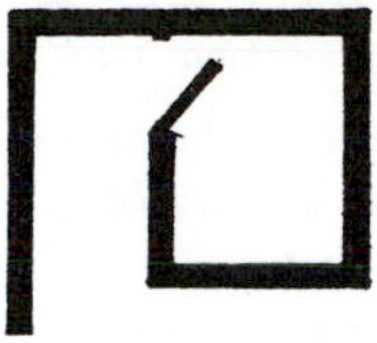

Fig. 5

مِحْراب ‘Awlaqī. Seen in Ma‘nī shaikhdom, a *miḥrāb* moulded in the mortar-like plaster of the floor in flat relief, the pointed end showing the direction of Mecca.

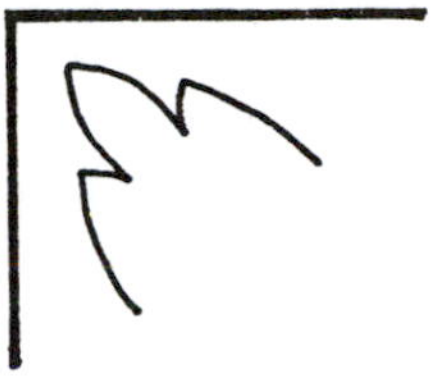

Fig. 6

مِحْمَر (pl. مَحَامِر) Aden, rafter. S. H. Hason, 617.

مُدَرَّج Yem., as نَقِيل مدرّج, a pass in the mountains upon which a stone stairway has been constructed.

مُرَبَّعَه Tarīm, ground floor room, syn. *maisamah*. *Al-Fatāwā al-nāfi‘ah*, 269, calls it a room on the first (ground) or second floor.

مَرْبوع الرِّقاد Tārīm, the square quarter-landing between two flights of steps at right angles to each other.

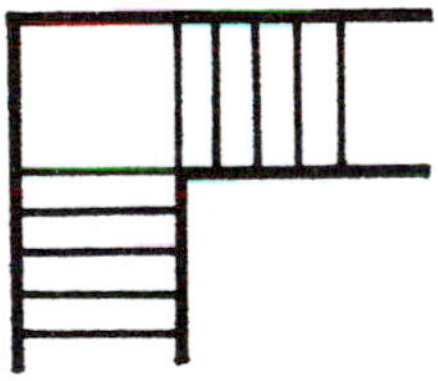

Fig. 7

مَرْصوص تمام properly built, of stone and mortar, Cf. Landberg, *Ḥaḍramoût*, 590, *raṣṣ* ‘ ordonner l’une chose sur l’autre ’.

مَرُو Jīzān, Saudi Arabia, a white marble-like stone sometimes used for decoration (*zīnah*) in a *jahwah* (q.v.).

مَرْوَة Yem., a place in a house for animal fodder, agricultural implements. Cf. al-Hamdānī, *Iklīl*, II, ed. Muḥ. . . . al-Akwa‘, Cairo, 1967, 5. Stone shed for animals (Ṣan‘ā’ district).

مَسْروقه Tarīm, a small room between two larger rooms, or a cupboard (*khazānah*), storeroom, made from the area of one of the larger rooms. It was described as bigger than a *murabba'ah* but smaller than a *maḥḍarah*, reception room.

مسقط Ṣan'ā' region, syn. of *maṭal* and *manṭal*. Cf. Rossi, *Terminologia*, 357, from Wuṣāb district.

مَصْلُوله Yem., Jiblah, paved—of the lane into the town. Cf. Rossi, *Terminologia*, 353.

مِصْناع (pl. مَصَانيع) Ḥaḍramawt, small cupboard for keeping things arranged inside the wall.

مَضْرَب Ḥaḍramawt, place where building lime (*nūrah*) is beaten out, or millet. The pole with which it is beaten has the same name, and *maḍrab* is also the name of the pole used to measure or survey land.

مَطْروق بالنُّوره Ḥaḍramawt. Cf. Landberg, *Ḥaḍramoût*, 645.

مَطَل Ṣan'ā' area, oblong machicolated masonry box projecting over the main door of a house for throwing or shooting at would-be hostile entry. Cf. *masqaṭ* and *manṭal*.

مَعْزُوب Dathīnah, a kind of hut of clay (*ṭīn*) and millet stalk (*qaṣab*), etc.

مُعَقَّد Tarīm, with arches.

مَغْسَى (pl. مَغَاسِي) Ḥaḍramawt, two parallel poles fixed from wall to wall of a room at a suitable height to hang the folded bedding of the household to preserve it.

مغْواس Tarīm, a lane.

مَقْصوره Tarīm, passage over the street from one house to another. It is also explained (with a pl. *maqāṣīr*) as the place specially allocated at the lowest part of the house for the kitchen and other purposes such as the place for grinding and pounding of wheat. Another Ḥaḍramī explanation is that it is a room looking out on to the street, in Aden called *manẓarah*.

منطل Ṣan'ā', syn. of *maṭal* and *masqaṭ* (q.v.).

مَهْ Ḥaḍramawt, Bā Makhramah, op. cit., states that in the colloquial usage (*'urf*) of the district *al-mah* means *'iḍādat al-bāb*.

مَوْثَر Yem., stated to be the same as the Ḥaḍramī *sās*, stone foundation of a house. Cf. al-Hamdānī, *Iklīl*, II, ed. Muḥ. al-Akwa', 8.

مَوْفَر (pl. مَوَافِر) Ḥaḍramawt. When a wall is being built in stages, each two *dhirā'* (approx. three feet) high is called *mawfar*. Another source says—ten or more clay bats (*libnah*) high of a wall.

مَيْسَمَه Tarīm, synonymous almost with *murabba'ah* (q.v.). *Al-Fatāwā al-nāfi'ah*, 269, has an interesting description of a *maisamah* and *murabba'ah*, رَيم حقّ مَيْسَمَه ملاصِقه لمُسْلِف مُشاع ومُربّعه للغير ، وللرّيم المذكور مفقر مؤسّس قبل القسمة وممرّه من رَقاد المربّعه حقّ الغير . An enclosed roof belonging to a ground-floor room adjoining a side/back door held in common, and a first floor room belonging to a second party, the afore-mentioned enclosed roof having an access set up before the division (of the whole house), the way to which (access) is the stair of the first floor room belonging to the second party.

وَضيع Tarīm, a little store-room. syn. *khazānah*.

يَالِي Al-Ḥāmī, Ḥaḍramī coast, perpendicular wooden lattice of window.

Some Baiḥān architectural terms

The following words were given by Amīr Ṣāliḥ of Baiḥān as applying to a room in the old *ḥuṣn* at Nuqūb.

مِرْدَم top part of door-frame. Landberg, *Ḥaḍramoût*, 587, 'seuil', and *Gloss. daṯ*.

لَالَه posts of frame of door. Cf. Rossi, *Terminologia*, 354, لوالى 'stipiti della porta'.

مِعْقَم base of wooden frame of door. Landberg, *Ḥaḍramoût*, 660, 'seuil de la porte', and *Gloss. daṯ*. Cf. Rossi, *Terminologia*, 354, ground under the door.

كَوَّه a small square hole in a door through which the hand is inserted to open it.

لَهَج Aden مِشْكَه, a wooden window shutter. Cf. *Gloss. daṯ*.

مَرْكَب, pl. مَرَاكِب, the main beams of a ceiling.

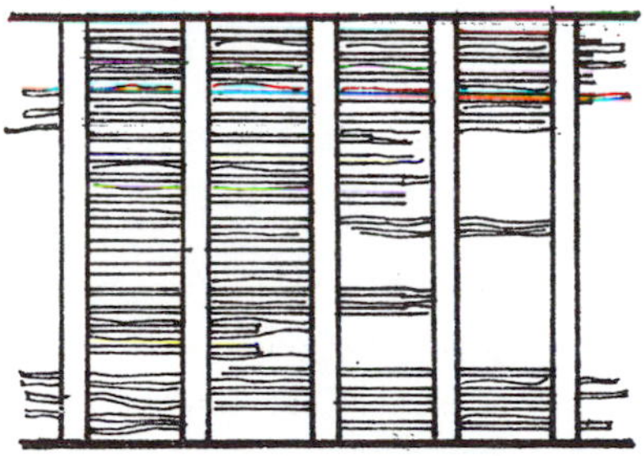

FIG. 8. Ceiling in the old *ḥuṣn* at Nuqūb (Baiḥān) showing the main beams (*marākib*) with small sticks (*qīr*) above them

قِير small sticks running over the *marākib*, and at right angles to them, to form a base for the clay roof above them. Cf. Rossi, *Terminologia*, 357.

هدَح the clay bench in Baiḥān houses.

سيَاع a pole across the end of a room. Cf. Rossi, *Terminologia*, 355, مِسْوَاع (pl. مَسَاوِع), ' legni trasversali appoggiati sulle travi '.

زَفِيف clay and sticks running between the *siyā'* and the wall, so that the whole forms a clay shelf.

خَلَال a wall peg. *Gloss. daṯ.*, *khilāl.*

مِسْرِيب probably the same as *mizrāb*, gutter, but sense not noted.

Descriptions of plates

Plate I. Salt mine at 'Ayādh. The entrance to the mine is by the black area to the right. Salt poured into heaps is being bagged for transport on the couched camel, each heap belonging to an individual owner and distinguished by his own mark, a piece of palm leaf. (R. B. S.)

Plate II. Building a wall using the cord (*khaiṭ*) probably in Dathīnah. (Information Office, Aden, 1957.)

Plate III (*a*). Puddling mud and straw to make clay brick-bats at Baiḥān in 1958 using a *misḥāh*, basket (*maḥfarah*) of chopped straw, and *tanak* of water. (R. B. S.)

Plate III (*b*). Beating out lime (*nūrah*) for use in building in Wādī Yashbum, the action being called *ṣabāṭah*. The workers flail the lime in unison—to the rhythm of verses sung to this work. (R. B. S.)

XVI

Tihāmah Notes

To my old friend and colleague Freddie Beeston I offer these observations made on a number of visits, generally very brief, to the Tihāmah between 1969 and 1986, but with longer stays in Jīzān, Zabīd, and the Wādīs Rimaʿ and Mawr.

From my four reports on irrigation and allied matters I hope and intend to publish certain extracts, but in the course of moving about the country one naturally happens on things of more general interest. These have been recorded, so far as circumstances permitted, in my fieldbooks, though other obligations did not allow me to pursue all the enquiries I might have made. These field observations have since been correlated with certain relevant Arabic literary works, and it is hoped that they may form a basis for further research.

Parading of slaughter beasts at Zabīd

One Wednesday in January 1986, while standing outside the new *sūq* on the north side of Zabīd, I heard a great commotion inside, and going to the gate, I was confronted by a young fully grown camel being driven out of the *sūq*, roaring and so agitated that its owner, leading it by its muzzle-cord, could scarcely control it. They were followed by an excited crowd of young men and boys who were shouting, clapping and singing. When I asked what all this was about, the bystanders told me that it was a camel to be slaughtered for meat and that it was being escorted by *akhdām* playing on the drums called *marāfiʿ* and *ṭubūl*. The *akhdām* are normally employed in such jobs as porterage, loading trucks, sweepers, *etc.*, but they do come together for such an occasion. Their role is to attract a crowd (*ʿalā shān yijammiʿ al-nās*). First they go round to the house of the butcher (*jazzār*) and spend the siesta up till 4 p.m. (*yiqayyilū ilā ghāyat al-sāʿah arbaʿah*) and light a fire to heat the drums (*li-tiḥmā al-marāfiʿ*) and tighten the skins. Then from 4 p.m. to sunset (*maghrib*) they parade round the town with the slaughter camel. The owner of the camel cries his wares (*ṣāḥib al-jamal yinādī*), praising it for a fine beast (*jamal malīḥ*), free of disease, and so on. Often the camel is decorated with flowers — *full*, Arabian jasmine, which grows much about Zabīd — on the ears, neck (*raqabah*), and hump (though this had not been done when I saw it leave the *sūq*). Sometimes they henna the animal. Cattle are also treated in the same way, and, for instance, a calf (*ʿijl*) will be henna-ed. All this is done as a publicity and sales gimmick and seems to have no religious significance.

At *Niṣf Sha'bān*, called in Zabīd *al-Bahjah* (joy, beauty), or at *al-Mi'rāj*, Muḥammad's ascension, or on *Mawlid al-Nabiyy*, 12 Rabīʻ I, they decorate the beast with bells (*galāgil*) and flowers (*wurūd*) grown at al-Maghras, a place known to Ibn al-Daybaʻ, and white jasmine in the ears and on the neck. Cattle are treated in the same way. Dostal[1] has described a bull to be slaughtered at the *'īd* in Jabal 'Iyāl Yazīd, decorated very much in this way, the horn 'with a braid of fragrant plants and flowers'. The forehead is adorned with a 'bunch of plants' (*mashqūr*);[2] and he shows clearly that this bunch of flowers is represented in the many carved alabaster heads of bulls that have survived from pre-Islamic times, in the conventional form of a triangle with some sort of cross-hatching. But I must add to this that *Shaqr* is an epithet of the Qatabanian moon-god — I suppose it might equally well be vocalized *Shuqr*. So here we have linked the horns so often symbolic of the crescent moon and the name of the moon-god himself. Yet nowadays in Zabīd, as my informants insisted at least, the beasts are so adorned in order to attract people to buy the meat. The beast is slaughtered on the day following the parade, *i.e.* on Thursday, and the meat will be ready for Friday.

A camel is slaughtered in the same manner as in Tarīm, by plunging a long dagger (*khanjar*)[3] into its throat. Before slaughtering, they make the head face the *qiblah* (*yuwajjihu 'l-ras qiblah*), and the formula pronounced at the act is *Bismillāh al-Raḥmān al-Raḥīm, Allāh akbar*, or simply *Bismillāh, Allāh akbar, ḥalāl*. They slaughter it (*yinḥarū-h*) at 5 a.m. (*fajran*) in the abattoir outside the town (*wasṭ al-mijzarah barrā*). Most slaughtering is on the north side. Selling carries on until about 8 a.m. when the butcher will have sold half his meat. The other half he takes into the town. Slaughtering took place inside the town in the 7th/13th century (and doubtless much later also), for al-Khazrajī speaks of Sūq al-Minḥārah, (near) al-Sūq al-Kabīr.[4] On a Friday, about 7.30 a.m., I saw outside al-Tuḥaytā village, west of Zabīd, butchers cutting up meat from carcases suspended from a structure rather like football posts and skinning it (*yiḥillū al-gild minn-uh*).

The butcher families of Zabīd at the present time are the Banī Baṣal of Ḥārat (or Rubʻ) al-Mujanbal in the neighbourhood of the celebrated Masjid al-Ashāʻir. In the Rubʻ al-Jāmiʻ were the Banī Najm, Muḥammad Ismāʻīl and Muḥammad 'Abduh Najm. Formerly there was a butcher family the Banī Zayd. A butcher Aḥmad al-Dubdubī, now deceased, was also mentioned, as was an Aḥmad Darsī. Some may have migrated or abandoned the trade.

Sālim al-Jarhazī, our driver, himself a Zabīdī by origin, took me to a gate-man at the Tihāmah Development Authority camp at Zabīd, Sālim 'Alī al-Shinaynī, formerly a butcher of the Rub' al-Jāmi' quarter of Zabīd, from whom I took down some calls current at these occasions, while the *akhdām* beat the drum (*yimarfa'ū*) all the time, to much shouting, singing and handclapping:

Yā Baṣal baṣṣil yā wālidtāh 'O Onions (a pun on the name of the butcher family), onion it, mother.' [*i.e.* add onions to the meat]

hab luh qandūrah, 'Abdullāh 'Alī al-Dubdubī al-jazzār 'Give him a piece of the hump,[5] 'Abdullāh 'Alī al-Dubdubī the butcher!'

mā 'l-kabshah yirda' kubāshatī 'There's no ram will butt my ram.' [*i.e.* 'No animal can match mine.'] The call does not refer to sheep and goats,[6] for which no such ceremony takes place, but is confined, apart from camels, to the bull or fat cow (*al-thawr aw al-baqarah al-samīnah*).

Wōōh, hab luh al-sublah 'Wooh, give him the tail!'.

Yā Zawqaliyyah, ḥabbah qiliyyah 'O Zawqalī girl, just one bean!' Perhaps there is a *double entente* here.

They will repeat these cries three or four times, praising the butcher for his fine meat (*yimdaḥū-h 'ind-uh laḥm malīḥah*).

When I described my happening on this parade of the slaughter-camel to a visitor from Ta'izz, he commented that this custom was also current in Ta'izz. It may be, therefore, possibly general to Yemeni cities, though I have not come across it in Ṣan'ā'. In Wādī Rima' meat is dealt with *bi'l-sahm*, by the share, *i.e.* a number of persons agree to take certain portions of the animal. Though gas is now widely used for cooking in this area, at a popular/folk restaurant (*maṭ'am sha'bī*) — some years ago they would have called it a *miqhāyah* — quite near the main road, a *mawfā*, a sort of round clay oven in the ground, was still in use. Branches were burned in it, and when they turned to hot coals, meat wrapped in banana leaf parcels was heaped in on top of these. Over them was placed a mat which was covered with puddled mud, and the opening to the fire at the bottom was stopped up in the same way.

The quarters of present-day Zabīd

When I asked Sālim al-Jarhazī about the various quarters or wards of the city, he said there were four: Ḥārat al-'Ilī, Ḥārat al-Mujanbal, Rub' al-Jāmi' and al-Jiz'.[7] Each quarter had a gate. Until the 1970s the town was surrounded by a wall (*jawlah* = *sawr*) that I remember well. This has since been demolished, and only the gates are left. al-Mujanbal is clearly to be identified with al-Janābidh, constructed by the Ismā'īlī *dā'ī* in the Yemen, 'Alī b. Muḥammad al-Ṣulayḥī (d. 459/1067),[8] on the west side of

Zabīd, as shown on the plan of Zabīd by Ibn al-Mujāwir.[9] al-Janābidh (Persian *junbadh/gunbad* 'dome') appears to have been a row of three domed structures of burnt brick[10] and gypsum plaster, each only four *dhirā'* 'cubits' apart. Bā Makhramah calls them 'the three well-known domes'.[11] In a number of places in the Tihāmah one sees religious buildings consisting of a row of three domes, but forming of course a single construction. The only known trace of al-Janābidh nowadays is the name of the quarter where they once stood.

Each quarter had till recently its own headman (*'āqil*), but by 1986 there was only one to serve all four. Their duties were more or less the same as described in *Ṣan'ā'*[12] and elsewhere, dealing with quarrels (*miḍrāb*) and thieving. In past times there were the usual inter-quarter squabbles. Each quarter had its boundary (*kull rub' lah ḥadd*), and one could not encroach on another (*mā ḥad yiqdir ya'tadī 'alā thānī*). That this was ancient custom seems supported by the account by Ibn al-Dayba'[13] of a body of people of Rub' al-Mujanbadh who made a visitation to the tomb of shaykh 'Īsā al-Hattār[14] at al-Turaybah village in Wādī Zabīd. Returning in the evening of the same day, they alighted at Rub' al-Ma'āṣir, the Quarter of the Sesame-oil-presses, when another group emerged from al-Ḥawzah[15] and started rioting with them. In this a lad of al-Mujanbadh folk struck one of the people of al-Ma'āṣir who died. It looks as if the pilgrims to the shaykh's tomb were regarded as attempting to use an official occasion to cross the boundaries of the other quarter.

That to-day Zabīd has only one *'āqil*, where once there were four, is evidence that the traditional quarter organization is breaking down, probably in part under pressure from the generation in the Republic seeking for social change. In Ḥaḍramawt I found hostility to the quarter organization in certain sections of society thirty or more years ago.

In line also with current ideology that has officially abolished social and caste distinctions, al-Jarhazī did not at first use the term *akhdām* for this well-known so-called 'pariah' group of southern Arabia, numbers of whom live in Zabīd, partly in the quarter of al-Jiz' and partly in that of al-Mujanbal.[16] Chelhod calls them 'anciens Abyssins';[17] and indeed one often hears this identification wherever there are *akhdām* or *ṣubyān* communities in the Yemen, but I think this merely reading back into history, without substantiation.

A Ḥāfat al-Dāmūṭ (Damot is in the Ogaden province of Abyssinia) is mentioned by Ibn al-Dayba'[18] as a place where, in 886/1481, a fire broke out that extended to the Fawfalah[19] mosque and also burned many vines. Thus it was most likely to have been a village of brushwood huts in the country outside the Zabīd walls. Qāḍī Baḥraq (869-930/1465-1524)[20] refers in several places to a black Dāmūṭī slave or a yellow (*ṣafrā'*)

Dāmūṭī slave-girl. The Damot slaves may have been prisoners taken in the wars of the Christian with the Muslim Abyssinians of the time, but they are not to be identified with the *akhdām*.

Mirbā' is a general word for a livestock market (*sūq al-mawāshī*), and Ibn al-Dayba' remarks on the outbreak of a fire from west of Sūq al-Mirbā' to al-Suwayqah 'the little market' at Zabīd in 786/1384, in which some *dawābb* (usually 'donkeys') perished. In 799/1396 there was another fire that extended from al-Mirbā' to Fawfalah.[21]

'Abd al-Raḥmān al-Ḥaḍramī, the well-known scholar of Zabīd, pointed out to me the *Muṣallā* of Zabīd, which lies just east of the main modern road and at the north side of the junction of the track to the reputed tomb of Uways al-Qaranī. This *Muṣallā* outside the town walls would be where the prayer at the two *'īd*s is performed, as at the very large *Muṣallā*, called also al-Jabbānah, formerly outside Ṣan'ā', but now engulfed in its massive expansion. al-Sharjī alludes to a mosque in the Ḥāfat al-Muṣallā —one is there still—about the end of the 6th/12th century.[22] Ibn al-Dayba' also records that in 793/1391 the Ḥāfat al-Muṣallā was burned down. Thus it is likely there were brushwood *'arīsh* huts there. It is improbable that the site has shifted over the centuries.

The *khān* and *qaysāriyah* of Zabīd

In the course of preparing a paper on Yemeni merchants,[23] I noted the existence of a *qaysāriyah* in medieval Zabīd; and when I asked al-Jarhazī whether such a building still existed in the city, he took me to an ancient structure, now in a very dilapidated state, quite near to the Masjid al-Ashā'ir.

The *qaysāriyah* is approached by an arched gateway, the two springs of the arch being connected by a wooden beam not apparently of recent origin, above which is an infill of several courses of brick. Above each rib of the arch is a six-pointed star, also in brick, composed of two interlacing triangles. On the wall to the right of the gateway is an ornament in brick, most simply described as a kind of formalized hour-glass shape, possibly an heraldic device, the blazon of Sultan al-Mujāhid, its founder. From the gateway a kind of barrel vault containing two or three massive brick arches leads to an open court. The gateway is approximately eight feet wide. al-Jarhazī remembers that when he was a boy (forty years ago?), loaded camels would enter the *qaysāriyah* through this gateway, but this would be impossible now — but whether this is because the ground level has risen or because the introduction of the beam has lowered the entrance I cannot say. The *qaysāriyah* was at one time used as a school.

On the left of the passage is a door to what would probably have been the supervisor's room, and there is a room on the right, beyond which is a large pair of scales, like the scales one may see in Ṣan'ā' in Samsarat al-Mīzān. On the far side of the court as one enters is a row of store-chambers with somewhat makeshift doors. In the area to the left of the entrance passage there are said to have been more chambers, now demolished.

On the left of the gateway are four shops (*dukkān*), opening on to the lane. The right external side of the court is also flanked by shops, all these belonging to the *qaysāriyah*, which is itself *waqf* property (*al-qaysāriyah tābi'ah li-Wizārat al-Awqāf*). Opposite the *qaysāriyah* on the other side of the lane is a bakery (*mikhbāzah*).

The sketch ground plan of the *qaysāriyah* in my diary is a very rough approximation, the measurements of which I did not even pace out, but it may be very similar in area to the medieval Samsarat al-Mīzān of Ṣan'ā'. It does not seem a large building for an entrepôt city. By my reasoning it would have been founded about the second quarter of the 8th/14th century or a decade later.

Qaysāriyah, khān and, I think, *samsarah* appear to be terms more or less synonymous and interchangeable. This gives rise to a problem, for historians of Zabīd speak of a *qaysāriyah* and a *khān*.

al-Khazrajī alludes to the Masjid al-Jabartī 'which is in[side] the town of Zabīd at the new Mujāhidī *khān*'.[24] The Rasūlid Sultan al-Mujāhid ruled from 721/1321 to 764/1362. In 795/1393 a great fire broke out 'starting north (*qiblī*) of the Jāmi', and it reached the *khān*, then Sūq al-Ma'āṣir'. Again in 890/1485, an earthquake caused people to leave the Zabīd Sūq al-Khān in such haste that they rushed out barefoot and without their shoulder-cloths (*ardiyah*). Ibn al-Dayba' records that in 912/1507 a certain Ibn Jallād cut through (*shaqqa*) the *sūq*s of Zabīd to the *khān* and put a seal (*khatama*) on the store-rooms (*khazā'in*) of his slave, Jawhar. This evidence shows that this *khān* was inside the town.

Another series of notices refers to a *qaysāriyah* in a place, al-Mimlāḥ, the Salt Market, and further to complicate the situation, there were two Mimlāḥs at Zabīd. al-Khazrajī records that in 788/1386 the village of al-Mimlāḥ al-Asfal, Lower Mimlāḥ, was destroyed by fire, with the loss of much dead and live stock. There must therefore have been an Upper Mimlāḥ, but I have come across no reference specfically to it.

Both al-Khazrajī and Ibn al-Dayba' state that in 786/1374 al-Malik al-Ashraf Ismā'īl 'ordered the construction of the *qaysāriyah* in al-Mimlāḥ village, so that the troops stationed there, and others, might provision themselves at it [the *qaysāriyah*]'.

A *mimlāḥ*, from this account, was evidently not only a stock market, but a place where comestibles in general were sold — Ṣan'ā' has a Sūq al-Milḥ and so has Ta'izz.[25]

Ibn al-Dayba‘ states that a small mosque was built in al-Mimlāḥ in the time of Sultan al-Mujāhid (*i.e.* before 764/1362). al-Malik al-Ashraf founded the Jāmi‘ mosque of al-Mimlāḥ *outside* the town of Zabīd, and it was marked out in 790/1388.[26]

An innovation, no doubt of some importance, was the commencement of the building of the *Matjar* at Zabīd at the hands of the Qāḍī Sirāj al-Dīn on the orders of al-Malik al-Ashraf in 798/1396. The *Matjar* was the Sultan's trading establishment,[27] and its employees were state officials. This, however, is to look ahead, for a significant political event intervenes.

In 791/1389, in face of the advance of the forces of the Zaydī Imām on Zabīd, the Rasūlid Sultan al-Malik al-Ashraf Ismā‘īl ordered the people of al-Nuwaydirah, a village lying north-west of the Zabīd wall, to move out of their village because of its proximity to the town wall and gate.[28] This they duly did, and indeed both the people of al-Nuwaydirah and al-Mimlāḥ later moved into Zabīd.[27] In order to prevent the Imām's soldiers from taking up quarters in the villages on the outskirts of Zabīd, the Sultan's *amīr*s and officers (*maqādimah*) set fire to al-Nuwaydirah, the two Mimlāḥs, al-Msrḥ,[29] and Ḥāfat al-Widn,[30] but a strong wind fanned the flames, and the city burned from the Bāb Sihām, on the north side, to the Bāb al-Shabārīq, on the north-east. The Imām's troops assaulted the west gate because of the *makhālīl* (openings in the wall?) there, from which the rain-water finds its exit. This gate must be the Bāb al-Nakhl at the south-west of Zabīd, where there was a hollow/stagnant pool (*qullah*)—al-Sharjī even mentions the Ḥāfat al-Sā'ilah, the Quarter of the Flood-course, near the Bāb al-Nakhl, inside Zabīd.[31]

When the Imām's troops were repulsed, they set fire to al-Nuwaydirah, Qaryat al-Msrḥ, Ḥāfat al-Widn, the two Mimlāḥs and the round towers (*dawrah*) of the Sultan outside the town. Bā Makhramah, citing al-Khazrajī, refers to the Jāmi‘ mosque of al-Mimlāḥ at the Zabīd gate (*‘alā Bāb Zabīd*).[32] The puzzle is which gate is intended, Sihām or al-Nakhl.

In 843/1439 the Qurashiyyūn of Wādī Rima‘ attacked al-Mimlāḥ village outside (*fī ẓāhir*) Zabīd and plundered the *qaysāriyah*.

Ibn al-Dayba‘ records yet another conflagration at Zabīd in 918/1512 when ‘Ḥāfat al-Misrāḥ of Rub‘ al-A‘lā was burned'.[33] al-Rub‘ al-A‘lā ‘the highest quarter' must surely be identified with Rub‘ al-‘Ilī, which lies to the east. Only three months later the Indian Quarter, Ḥāfat al-Hunūd, was burned down in a conflagration that commenced west of the *khān* and proceeded in a northerly direction.

In the Ṭāhirid period, as probably also under the Rasūlids, the *qaysāriyah* was farmed out, for Ibn al-Dayba‘ notes that in 905/1500 the farmer (*ḍāmin*), Muḥammad b. Nūḥ, was dismissed and replaced by a cousin of his.[34] The *qaysāriyah* (al-Mimlāḥ[?]) also figures in a *fatwā* of Ibn Ja'mān (d. 1034/1624), in circumstances not very explicit, though it may be deduced from the text that cloth was taxed there, in some way, by an inspector.[35]

In conclusion, it appears that al-Mujāhid set up the *khān* inside the city in the quarter known as al-'Ilī, and al-Malik al-Ashraf had the *qaysāriyah* built in the village al-Mimlāḥ outside the walls. The building originally known as the *khān* is known now to al-Jarhazī as the *qaysāriyah*—or might it be an alternative name for it?

al-Jarhazī confirmed that the present day *qaysāriyah* is in Sūq Ḥārat al-'Ilī. All commodities from abroad or from other parts of the Yemen were brought to it and weighed on the scales there. They included ghee (*saman*), indigo (*nīl*), grain (*ḥabb*), etc., and they were presumably sold there, for the commission agents (*dalāyil*) received their fee from both parties (*akhadhū ḥaqqa-hum min al-ṭarafayn*), vendor and purchaser.

al-Ḥawṭah (Ḥawṭat al-Salāmah)

Seeing al-Ḥawṭah marked on the map of the lower Wādī Rima' area, I took the opportunity of visiting it in January 1986, it being the only place in the locality with this title — though I know many *ḥawṭah*s in Ḥaḍramawt and the former Western Aden Protectorate.[36] There are two nice old brick reception rooms or halls, with plaster decoration like the other buildings around, intended for the use of guests on a visitation (*ziyārah*) to the shrine. One of these is now disused, but in the other we met the *Manṣūb*,[37] a pleasant, gentle old man, a little henna-ed about the beard, sitting comfortably with the villagers on charpoys, holding a *qāt* session. They made al-Jarhazī and me welcome and gave us tea. al-Jarhazī explained my rather unfamiliar Arabic to him, but the *Manṣūb* seemed to understand me without difficulty. The villagers said that no foreigner had ever visited them.

The *Manṣūb* said that this *ḥawṭah*, called Ḥawṭat al-Salāmah, the Salāmah being a tribe of the Ash'arīs[38] of Wādī Rima', is the *ḥawṭah* of al-Khayyīr al-Mizjājī. On consulting the hagiographies, I discovered that the Banū 'l-Mizjājī were numerous in the 9th/15th century, mostly of the open country (*al-bādiyah*) and originally from a village al-Hazmah, whence they moved to al-Mizjāj. However, there was no mention of al-Khayyīr, which may only be a title disguising a personage known to the hagiographers by another name. The *Manṣūb* was of course his lineal descendant.

The *Manṣūb* said that al-Khayyīr was of the Ṣawfah, which al-Jarhazī insisted was not to be identified with Ṣūfīs. This interested me considerably, because in 1940, when stationed at am-Fajarah in Ṣubayḥī country, I met one of the Ṣawfah riding a camel. He had come from the Yemen and seemed to be held in great veneration by the Ṣubayḥīs. These Ṣawfah merit further enquiry.

The *Manṣūb* took me to see the mosque, which has two squinch domes in typical Tihāmah style and plan, with its *minbar* recessed into the wall on the right of the *miḥrāb*. We then went to the *ḥawṭah*, an area enclosed by an old brick wall with a kind of crenellated top, within which were tombs,[39] including that of the ancestor of the *Manṣūb*, at whose tomb he said a prayer and the *Fātiḥah*. It has an ornamental pillar almost at the top end of it containing a recess for burning incense — one is reminded of the pillar tombs of East Africa.[40] It was not unlike those seen in the Aden protectorates, but with more ornament in plaster. The tombs had around them a low brick and plaster wall, about a foot in height, all in a state of decay. The *Manṣūb* drew water from a *misqāyah* (= Ḥaḍramī *siqāyah*), giving it to us to drink for *barakah*; and, for *barakah* too, an old woman present also drank of it.

At the *ziyārah*, animals used to be slaughtered for the entertainment of guests, but, for sanitary reasons, away from the village. This no longer takes place, and all the panache ceremonies of the *ziyārah* are now abandoned. This took place about six years after the '*thawrah*' of 1962, because money is no longer available and because of the general falling off in the belief of local people in the saints. No doubt there is also discouragement from such groups as the Muslim Brothers and others.

The sight of this *ḥawṭah* did suggest to me how the highly developed institution of the *ḥawṭah* in the Ḥaḍramawt may have evolved. This *ḥawṭah*, like *ḥawṭah*s in other parts of the Yemen, is a cemetery. I did not discover that it was regarded as affording protection in the same way as a Ḥaḍramī *ḥawṭah*, though it may be so regarded. The medieval texts have numerous instances of persons taking refuge (*istajāra*) with a living saint or *faqīh*, perhaps of course the descendant of a dead saint, even from a ruler as powerful as a Rasūlid sultan. So perhaps from a simple cemetery enclosed by a wall, the *ḥawṭah* became in time an inviolable sanctuary.

The Bayt al-Muḥibb Sayyids

Near al-Mitaynah/Mutaynah, described by al-Sharjī[41] as *qaryah ākhir Wādī Zabīd*, at the end of Wādī Zabīd, and in any case near the coast, we came upon a square reception room, at the right side of which is a little shelter covering a heap of dust mixed with sweet basil (*rayḥān*) and possibly other substances. To this place come those desiring to be cured of syphilis (*al-ṭayr*), from all parts, including Sa'udi Arabia. The patients rub this dust over the body, then go and wash in the sea, after which, presumably, they are considered cured. *al-Ṭayr* was describe to me as 'a disease of the sea'. It is probably therefore acquired by sailors, travellers and others frequenting the ports, but Zabīd at times, according to the reports of Ibn al-Dayba', was noted for its depravity. Unfortunately, the *Manṣūb* in charge of the cure was absent, and I was unable to obtain further details, including any formulae that might be used; but he is al-Amīn Ḥasan al-Muḥibb, and I have already noted that this house of Sayyids, or a branch of it, near Mocha, has the peculiar virtue of curing venereal disease.[42] The maps show a Bayt al-Maḥibb (probably Muḥibb) a little north-west of al-Ḥawṭah. On the north bank of Wādī Rima' are marked a Bayt Maḥibb and a *maḥjar*[43] al-Maḥābīb, just north of al-Ḥusayniyyah. I should think all are branches to the Muḥibb house.

Some other saints and tombs

In January 1986 I visited at al-Tuḥaytā the tomb of al-Shaykh Abkar b. Ḥassān (d. 802/1399-1400).[44] The domed tomb of this saint (*waliyy*), which is obviously very old, is perhaps some ten to fifteen feet below the level of the ground around it. In the wall opposite the entrance, and behind the tomb, is a writing in the old southern style of Arabic calligraphy that was common in the former Aden Protectorates before the *ruq'ah* introduced by the schools began to replace it; it is heavily covered with plaster that would have to be removed to read it. The mosque near the tomb is also old, though the *miḥrāb* has two dates, one 1275/1858-59 and another earlier date, probably both relating to repairs. It had a well, now closed up, and a pool (*birkah*) for bathing, but this is half full of rubble and other rubbish. It has lovely brick and plaster decoration, with a design pattern which, I think, suggests *dhurah* stalk, but different from the Yemen highlands. The *minbar* is set in the wall, its edge flush with it, a fairly common feature in the region. Both buildings have many arched wall niches. The annual *ziyārah* visitation to Abkar is the first Jum'ah of Sha'bān, there being a day for the men, and one for the women who visit on al-Khamīs before the men.

The whole Zabīd area has many *misqāyah*s. In fact, there seems to have been an elaborate network of them on the older roads. They are now no longer maintained and falling into ruin, though I suppose there must be *waqf*s for the latter purpose.

Three years earlier I had visited the supposed tomb of Uways al-Qaranī,[45] a second-generation Muslim of the first century of Islam. This is at al-Ḥimā on the track road a little east of Zabīd. In the dome over the tomb there is an interesting but not seemingly very old decoration. On the west side of it is an oblong *maqṣūrah* with clay benches all round it, used for teaching. The actual tomb has been dressed with covers etc. by the Pakistanis of the Khān Construction Co. On top of it there are some five *riyāl* notes, to which I added. Outside is a very deep well, heavily plastered with *nūrah*. Near by is the tomb of Bin

Qāsim (about whom I have no information), which looks old and has old inscriptions, archaic in type, heavily plastered over, the calligraphy looking a little floriated. The tomb itself has local medieval potsherds on the surface and roughly octagonal stones set in the ground of the graveyard. The mosque is set high up on a mound, and has remains of old plastered decoration on the dome and roundels with Quranic quotations in an excellent old script on the east side. It looks interesting enough achitecturally to merit further study. The children here come and demand a *ziyārah*, *i.e.* a present from the visitant.

al-Ḥimā 'an interdicted area, prohibited pasture' is an interesting name in itself, and when we passed by it in 1986 'Abd al-Raḥmān al-Ḥaḍramī said it was so called because protected by an ancient hero, a legend of whom he related at some length. It appears to be an historic site of some cultic significance and might reward investigation.

On the right bank of the Wādī Zabīd, above the area of the new barrages and channels established to control the valley waters, stands the mosque of Mu'ādh b. Jabal, famous companion of the Prophet and its reputed builder,[46] this and the mosque of al-Fāzzah being *mubārak*, *i.e.* where one's prayers are answered. al-Sharjī says that it is visited by the ordinary folk (*'awāmm*) of Zabīd in Rajab. It has a chamber (*maqṣūrah*) for Qur'ān reading at the side overlooking the Wādī.

The *madabb*, tunnels in the packed clay

In 1983 I paid quite a number of visits to Bāsāt to study documents with Shaykh Abkar, and in the course of conversation the villagers told me that besides the ordinary cemetery there is a sort of tunnel underground, a *madabb*,[47] somehow associated the the local saint of unknown name, *waliyy al-balad*, access to it being through a hole in its roof. They take the corpse down into the *madabb* and place it on a sort of square bench, working by the light of an oil lamp. They spoke of pots or pieces of pot lying in the *madabb*, but there was nothing very definite about its contents. One old shaykh, seeing the interest I showed in it, asked me if I would like them to reserve a place there! It seems that there are no particular restrictions as to whom they bury in it. This recalled to me the Sabaean bee-hive tomb which I cleared at Bīr Aḥmad airfield near Aden in 1941, cut in the heavy alluvial clay and with a hole in the top of the dome covered by a heavy stone.

In Zabīd itself there is said to be a subterranean tunnel (*nafaq*) in the middle of the *sūq* near Masjid al-Ashā'ir; and it is averred that in graveyards at Zabīd they sometimes come across underground springs (*'ayn*).

In January 1986 I revisited al-Fāzzah. On the *qiblah* side of the three-domed mosque is buried the saint al-Fāzz. His standard (*bayraq*) was lying in the place where the tomb is, and the tomb itself has what I would call a *shāhid* 'tomb pillar', with a recess for an incense burner in it. The saint al-Fāzz is said to have married from Mu'ādh b. Jabal and Mu'ādh from him, *i.e.* each took a girl in marriage from the house of the other.

Water is said to come to al-Fāzzah by a *madabb* from the mosque of Mu'ādh b. Jabal, or, as stated by others, simply from Zabīd. Just north of the mosque is an inlet, now rather shallow. It was originally deeper but has become filled with sand and earth. The *madabb* came out on to the beach, and water used to flow from it into the inlet, but some two years before our visit it became stopped up by sand. To me it seems obvious that the great increase in the use of motor pumps must have so lowered the water table that this spring no longer flows. Just above the former exit of the spring into the inlet is buried a saint, al-Ḥunduj/Ḥundug, in an oblong tomb — he has a *manṣab* in the village a hundred or two yards behind the sea-coast. An Abū Bakr b. Ḥunduj (d. 821/1419) is buried at Sharjat Ḥays, and other members of the house are known to al-Sharjī.[48] The maps show a Bayt al-Ḥunduj between Bāsāt and Madan.[49]

The old port of al-Fāzzah is said to be on the north side (*qiblah*) of the three-domed mosque. Beyond the inlet there is said to be an old pier (*dakkah*) about a fathom (*qāmah*) under the surface of the sea to the west, but I had no means of investigating this. Perhaps al-Fāzzah had some minor importance as a haven where fresh water could be obtained, called in some pilot books *mamzar*, and it would be useful at least to small craft. We saw fishing rafts (*ramas*, pl. *armās*) lying on the beach. If there are ruins there, they must be covered with sand. To the south of the mosque is a brick and plaster (*nūrah*) building destroyed or fallen into ruin only about six years ago.[50]

Dhubāb

In December 1973 Paolo Costa and I visited the little port of Dhubāb, local pronunciation Dubāb, which lies about forty kilometres south of Mocha, passing a large rock, fortified and used as checkpoint. It is a fishing port that exports fish, and, as al-Waysī[51] says, it is an important strategic place on the Red Sea. No doubt for this reason foreigners have not been permitted to visit it for a number of years. It is situated on an eminence, and behind it is a fort separate from the main village. Though this fort is probably modern, there are signs of older walls along its sides. During their occupation of the Yemen the UAR forces did not apparently fortify Dhubāb and other little coastal ports, but only Bāb al-Mandab. The houses in the village were constructed from the wood of packing cases, flotsam and jetsam from shipping passing up and down the Red Sea, in neat chalet style, like other small coastal villages I have passed through along the coast between Bāb al-Mandab and Aden. One house had a refrigerator and sold cool drinks!

On the promontory, to the south or left of which is the summer (*shimāl*) anchorage, lies the tomb, said to be very old, of al-Shaykh Maknūn. On it were scattered a pear-shaped water jar, red clay incense burners and pieces of wood, as we saw on a tomb at Mocha. Some ships were beached on the south bay, where there were beds of coral or shell surrounded by an edge of stones, upon which to dry fish — though there were no fish on them. They were similar to those I had seen at Shuqrah to the east of Aden in earlier years. The north bay, used in the Azyab monsoon, had several vessels in it, some of them bigger than, say, a Mukallā sambook. It is a good anchorage. In fact, it seems the best anchorage on the coast, Mocha excepted. Camels were to be seen on the beach, perhaps to take the fish to the interior. There were also Barbarī sheep, about, but these are imported only for the *'īd* and not at any other time.[52]

A *khaddām*, perhaps here an intendant, like the *khādim* of the saint's tomb at am-Nighdah in the 'Awdhalī country, holds the key to the Shādhilī[53] tomb here. At Dhubāb also I photographed the tomb of a child (*nūnū*) on top of which lay an incense burner, a water vessel, three palm fronds and pieces of wood.

Near by a village south of Mocha, Wāḥigah/Wāḥijah[54], said to be of the *qabīlah* of the shaykh Muḥammad Zāyid, we saw the tomb of a saint of that strange category of holy men, a Ṣawfī, already mentioned.

Salt-pans

At the coastal village of Yakhtul there is what was called *dār al-milḥ* 'the place of salt'. Here salt-pans called *dārah* are cut out of the hard ground and the soil heaped up on the sides to form bunds (*zabīr al-dārah*). In the hard bed of the salt-pans are hollowed out rows of shallow holes about one *dhirā'* in diameter and a little less in depth, called *ḥawf* (sing. and pl.), into which sea-water is led by opening a channel (*sāqiyah*). The evaporation takes six months, followed by another six months, perhaps after the salt has been taken out of the *ḥawf* and piled into heaps called *kawm al-milḥ* or *'arīsh al-milḥ*. A good *ḥawf* of salt at that time (1973) would fetch two to three or more *riyāl*s. It is taken to Ta'izz, Assab, Mocha[55] and Mawza'.[56] A *dārah* may have a single owner, or several *dārah*s may be owned by one person. My informant had a piece of bone of the *zuqrah* fish, about 3 by 9 inches, like a scraper, called *muqshaṭah ḥaqq al-milḥ*, for removing the salt.

Fish-traps

At a place north of Mocha, where one turns inland from the coastal road to Zabīd, I noticed the only fish-traps I have seen in southern Arabia — and this includes the whole of the southern coast from Perim to al-Muṣayna'ah. They looked to be made of palm *jarīd*s and wire, and were on the flat coastal beach at this part of the coast, but we were unable to examine them. A man told us that they are called *baytah.* They are very much inferior in their construction to the *ḥaḍrah*s of Bahrain and other parts of the Gulf. Fishermen on the coast here complained of their wretched lot (1973), but perhaps their conditions have since altered.

NOTES

1. Walter Dostal, 'Some remarks on the ritual significance of the bull in pre-Islamic South Arabia', in R.L. Bidwell and G.R. Smith (eds.), *Arabian and Islamic studies: articles presented to R.B. Serjeant,* London 1987, pp.196-213.
2. Reading *mashqūr* for the clearly incorrect *mashkūr*. Dostal's *sharikah ḥaqq al-'īd* means 'a piece of meat (read *shirkah*) for the feast' not a 'festival company'., *shuqr* being sweet basil (*ocimum basilicum*). *Mashqūr* would be 'ornamented with sweet basil'.
3. In Tarīm of Ḥaḍramawt a *jambiyyah*, curved dagger, is used.
4. al-Khazrajī, *al-'Uqūd al-lu'lu'iyyah*, ed. 'Asal, GMS, 1, 174.
5. *Qandūrah* = *waṣlah min al-sanam* a piece of the hump. I have not found this word in the usual sources in this sense.
6. My notes say that when a *kabsh* is sold, a sort of tax of 1½ *riyāl*s, called *tamwīn*, is paid to the *shurṭah*, police. The fee of a *dallāl*, commission agent for selling animals, was 5‡.
7. Muḥammad 'Alī Luqmān and his son Fārūq, *Qiṣṣat al-thawrah al-Yamaniyyah*, Aden, n.d. (1963 or 1964?), 101, allude to the existence of five quarters of Zabīd, and seem to indicate the existence of more. Ḥārat Abū l-Khayr was not mentioned to me when I listed the four quarters in 1973. Like the Luqmāns, I heard 'Mujanbadh' at that time. Al-'Ilī is on the east, al-Jāmi' on the north, al-Jiz' to the west, and al-Mujanbadh to the south. The gates I noted as Bāb al-Shabāriq on the east, Bāb Sihām/Sahām on the north, Bāb al-Nakhl on the west, Bāb al-Qurtub on the south. The fort has, facing the mountain, a Turkish gate, Bāb al-Naṣr. The Luqmāns mention the prominent families living in the various quarters: in al-'Ilī, Bayt al-Sālimī, Bayt al-Abhārī, Bayt al-Ahdal (Sayyids); in al-Jāmi', merchants of Bayt al-Wāqidī and Banī Hārūn; in al-Jiz' and Abū l-Khayr, Bayt Fayṣal, Bayt Aḥmad 'Umar Ismā'īl Bayt Isḥāq, Bayt Maṭṭah(?), Bayt B.lū(?). In al-Jiz' quarter they specially mention the Bayt al-Wajīh, in whose house we stayed in 1974.
8. See Ismail K. Poonawala, *Biobibliography of Ismā'īlī Literature*, Malibu 1977, 103.
9. O. Löfgren (ed.), *Descriptio Arabiae Meridionalis* (*Ta'rīkh al-mustabṣir*), Leiden 1951–4, 1, 77.
10. *Ibid.*, 75. *al-ājurr al-maḥkūk wa-l-jiṣṣ*—possibly Ibn al-Mujāwir may have incorrectly heard *maḥkūk* 'rubbed' for *maḥrūq* 'burned, fired'; but *al-Faḍl al-mazīd*, 101, records that Zabīd was walled (*darraba*) in 771/1370 with *ājurr*, when previously it had been walled with clay brick (*libn*).
11. O. Löfgren (ed.), *Arabische Texte zur Kenntnis der Stadt Aden im Mittelalter*, Uppsala 1936-50, 1, 70: *al-thalāth al-qubab al-ma'rūfah*.
12. Serjeant and Lewcock (eds.), *Ṣan'ā'*, London 1983, *passim*. *Cf.* my 'Social stratification in Arabia' in R.B. Serjeant (ed.) *The Islamic city: selected papers from the colloquium held at the*

Middle East Centre, Cambridge, 1976, UNESCO, Paris 1980, 126-47, espec. 135, 139ff.

13. Ibn al-Dayba', *al-Faḍl al-mazīd 'alā Bughyat al-mustafīd fī akhbār madīnat Zabīd*, ed. Yūsuf Shulḥūd, Beirut and Ṣan'ā' 1983, 311.
14. al-Sharjī, *Ṭabaqāt al-khawāṣṣ*, Cairo 1321/1903, 109ff. Al-Hattār (d. 606/1209-10) was an ecstatic (*majdhūb*).
15. *Ḥawzah*, lit. a place surrounded by walls or a bank.
16. In al-Ḥudaydah the *akhdām* used to live in al-Duhmiyyah quarter in *qushāsh* = *'ushash*, the circular huts of the Tihāmah, among which fires often started. See YAR, *Tourist Map of al-Ḥudaydah*, Survey Authority, Ṣan'ā', 1983. Cf. Aḥmad 'Uthmān Muṭayr, *al-Durrat al-farīda fī ta'rīkh madīnat al-Ḥudaydah*, n.d. but post-1983.
17. 'Introduction à l'histoire sociale et urbaine de Zabīd', *Arabica* 25, I [1978], 67. For discussion of the *akhdām* and *ṣubyān*, see my 'South Arabia and Ethiopia—African elements in the South Arabian population', *Proceedings of the third international conference of Ethiopian studies*, Addis Ababa 1966, 25-34.
18. Ibn al-Dayba', *Bughyat al-mustafīd fī akhbār madīnat Zabīd*, ed. 'Abdullāh al-Ḥabshī, Ṣan'ā' 1979, 169: Damūt [*sic*]; *al-Faḍl al-mazīd*, 161.
19. *Fawfal, areca*, is noted by Ibn al-Dayba', *Bughyah*, 101, as being transplanted to a new garden about the end of the 8th/14th century.
20. See my 'Forms of plea, a Šāfi'ī manual from al-Šiḥr', *RSO* 30, 1-2 [1955], 6, 13, *passim*.
21. *al-Faḍl al-mazīd*, 159; al-Khazrajī, *op. cit.*, 2, 289.
22. al-Sharjī, *Ṭabaqāt al-khawāṣṣ*, Cairo 1321/1903, 154; *al-Faḍl al-mazīd*, 151.
23. 'Yemeni and Ḥaḍramī merchants' at the colloquium 'Les milieux marchands asiatiques de l'Océan Indien et de la Mer de Chine', Paris 1985.
24. al-Khazrajī, *op.cit.*, 1, 363; 2, 202; and, for places *infra*, I, 293, 2, 180, 188, 244; *al-Faḍl al-mazīd*, 161, 165, 599; *Bughyah*, 94, 100; Yajima Hikoichi, *A chronicle of the Rasūlid dynasty of the Yemen*, Tokio 1974, 46.
25. Abū Makhramah, *Descriptio*, 1, 69, defines a *mimlāḥ* as a place where salt is dried out (*yujmad*). The *mif'āl* form for places is common in the area, e.g. *miḥnāṭ* 'corn market', *mi'qāb* 'grain store', *mijlāb* 'sheep-and-goats market, etc.; also *mishnāqah* 'gallows'.
26. Abū Makhramah, in *Descriptio*, 2, 21.
27. al-Khazrajī, *op. cit.*, 2, 205-7.
28. Al-Sharjī, 138, says that al-Nuwaydirah is a *qaryah 'alā Bāb Sahām*, and Ibn al-Mujāwir's plan of Zabīd shows it on the north-west side of the town. *Nādirah* should mean 'projecting, sticking out', and al-Nuwaydirah is a not uncommon name for a town ward or quarter in southern Arabia. It is shown as protruding from the circular wall of the city.
29. Yajima, *op. cit.*, 48. I have not found this place in the other sources, and I wonder if it is the Ḥāfat al-Misrāḥ mentioned elsewhere.
30. Ibn al-Mujāwir's plan shows Ḥāfat al-Widn outside the walls on the south-east side. *Al-Faḍl al-mazīd*, 164, places it 'outside Bāb al-Qurtub'. Cf. *Bughyah*, 172.
31. al-Khazrajī, *op. cit.*, 2, 193.
32. in Löfgren, *op. cit.*, 21.
33. Ibn al-Dayba', *al-Faḍl al-mazīd*, 336; see also *Bughyah*, 113, and *Qurrat al-'Uyūn*, ed. Muḥammad al-Akwa', Cairo 1977, 2, 137.
34. Ibn al-Dayba', *al-Faḍl al-mazīd*, p.253.
35. See my 'Yemeni merchants' (see note 23 above).
36. As in 'Ḥaram and ḥawṭah, the sacred enclave in Arabia', in 'Abd al-Raḥmān Badawī (ed.), Mélanges Ṭāhā Ḥusain, Cairo 1962, reprinted in my *Studies in Arabian history and civilization*, London 1981.
37. *al-Faḍl al-mazīd*, 319, for *manṣab uses manṣūb*, as is usual in this corner of the Yemen; it clearly means 'installed in office', i.e. as *dhū manṣab* holder of office at a shrine or *ḥawṭah*. In 1940 I had to do with the *manṣūb* of Qaryat al-Qāḍī in Wādī Ma'ādin of Ṣubayḥī country. The

Luqmāns, *Qiṣṣah*, 104, talk of a lady al-Manṣūbah 'one of Allah's saints (*awliyā'*) in Bayt Dab' (? vocalization), a *sharīfah* of al-Hulaybī. al-Sharjī, 194, says that the Hulaybīs are Ashrāf from the Ḥijāz who used to sell hashish (in the Yemen) and are now known as Banū l-Ḥashshāsh. In 850/1456 a group of *'abīd* took refuge in the house of the *manāṣib* of Zabīd. In 897/1492 the Sultan ordered the date crop outside Zabīd to be cut, even the dates of the *dhawī l-manāṣib*.

38. Wādī Wakī', according to 'Abd al-Raḥmān al-Ḥaḍramī, has 'Akk tribes to the north of it and Ashā'ir like the Sawādah and Salāmah to the south of it. Wakī', he said, is a pre-Islamic personage.

39. Yajima, *op. cit.*, 169, alludes to an emir buried in the cemetery (*majannah*) of Zabīd in the *ḥiyāṭ Farḥāniyyah*. *Ḥiyāṭ* is the plural of *ḥā'iṭ* 'wall', synonymous with *ḥawṭah*, so special enclosures were presumably found in cemeteries there.

40. J.S. Kirkman, 'The great pillars of Malindi and Mambrui', *Oriental Art*, IV, 2, 55-68.

41. *op. cit.*, 183; *Bughyah*, *passim*.

42. 'Notices on the "Frankish chancre" (syphilis) in Yemen, Egypt and Persia', *JSS* 10, 2 [1965], 241-252. The Luqmāns, *op. cit.*, 104, speak of the people's faith (*'aqā'id*) in the Banū l-Sirājī of Mocha, to whom they repair for all such diseases.

43. A *maḥjar* is an interdicted pasture. The map also shows al-Maḥjar of Wādī Dawba'ah near the road.

44. According to al-Sharjī, *Ṭabaqāt* 176, Abū Bakr b. Muḥammad b. Ḥassān al-Muḍarī.

45. al-Sharjī, 41ff, states that he died in Damascus; al-Balādhurī categorically places his tomb at Kūfah. He is said to have been killed at Ṣiffīn. Uways was of the Murād tribe in the Mashriq of the Yemen, remote from Zabīd. al-Sharjī, himself a Zabīdī, could scarcely *not* have mentioned his tomb at al-Ḥimā. In a tablet newly attached to the building by the Pakistanis Uways has become al-Karnī.

46. Cf. al-Sharjī, 6; al-Burayhī, 280. For his building activities, see P.M. Costa, 'The Mosque of al-Janad', in Bidwell and Smith, *op. cit.*, 43, and Serjeant and Lewcock, *Ṣan'ā'*, *passim*.

47. Cf. *Gloss. daṯ.*, *dabbāb* 'passage souterrain'. *Bughyah*, 178, refers to a place al-Madabb near Jāzān.

48. al-Sharjī, *op. cit.*, 182.

49. YAR 50 1443 C2, approximately lat. 14° 20′ N., long. 43°24′ E. In 1983 I noted that at this latter village, the market day of which is Monday, bananas were being sold by the *rub'*, quarter, of a hundred.

50. See also 'Supplementary note' to John Baldry, 'Early History of al-Ḥudaydah', *Arabian Studies*, 7 [1985], 35.

51. *Al-Yaman al-kubrā*, Cairo 1962, 28.

52. Sheep and riding camels (the *baḥrī* camel of medieval writers) are imported to Mocha and al-Khawkhah from Africa, as are livestock from the Danqalī coast.

53. There is a village al-Shādhiliyyah marked on the map south east of Bāsāt, for the Shādhilī family of Mocha seems to have spread over the country. Cf. al-Mahādilah, the Ahdalī Sayyid house, whose name also figures on the maps. This house has extended into East Africa.

54. Al-Sharjī, 167, Wāḥijah.

55. Bā Makhramah, *Arabische Texte*, I, 20, has a passage which seems to suggest that the Wāḥijah salt-pans were farmed out (*ḍamān*) as in the case of Aden al-Mimlāḥ. The Luqmāns, *Qiṣṣah*, 104, allude to Mocha salt-pans as well-known.

56. I actually wrote down in my diary at the time 'Mūzā' [*sic*], which was evidently how I heard it pronounced — very interesting in view of the spelling of the *Periplus*, but I cannot think of any other place today to which salt would be sent that has a name resembling Mūzā.

XVII

The Coastal Population of Socotra

INTRODUCTION

My brief sojourn on the lovely island of Socotra, with its blue sea, long beaches and palm groves and a background of the misty blue Haggier mountains, came as a delightful and romantic interlude after my travels in the then Royalist Yemen.

My interest in Socotra was mostly confined to the coastal communities (which are either Arabic speaking or have some, often very imperfect, knowledge of Arabic as a second language) – of necessity since I do not know Socotri, a tongue in which my late colleague Tom Johnstone soon made himself remarkably competent. This was also by way of complementing my studies of the maritime activities on the coast of Hadramawt. My ignorance of Socotri imposed limitations on my enquiries and as our stay was short it was not possible to check findings as one could in Arabia, or explore them to the extent one could wish.

The coastal population, permanent or floating, consisted of Arabs, descendants of black imported slaves, independent Somalis and a scattering of other races. The Socotrans proper are referred to as Bedu and seem a simple unsophisticated people who do not bear arms – they are said to have been disarmed and only the Sultan's soldiers bear arms.

The coastal community – the Arabs – though mainly hailing from Ḥaḍramawt and with many distinctively Ḥaḍramī institutions and dialect words, also includes the Muscat and Gulf Arabs and even Gulf Indians. Seamen from Dubai have an historic association with the island and have married here for several generations. The Sultanic house is of Mahrah, which tribe speaks a dialect akin to Socotri, not Arabic. Thus there are Gulf Arabic terms used by the communities, and links with the Gulf as well as with the Ḥaḍramī coast. Links with east Africa are also important, perhaps for economic rather than cultural reasons.

An excellent (but unpublished) report was written by G.H.H. Brown on 16 July 1966, *Social and economic conditions and possible development of Socotra*. There is archival material in the Aden Records at the India Office Library, but – apart from Brown's report to a limited extent – I have not drawn on the material. Socotra was little known to the Arabs and thus does not figure much in Arabic literature, and then only in brief scattered references that afford the researcher no coherent account of its history. Moreover, the island was probably not economically attractive enough to merit permanent conquest by the Arabs – and the consequent fighting in defendable mountains – when such profit as there was could probably be obtained more easily on the northern coast, which was accessible to mariners for seven months in the year.

This contribution discusses the coastal population of Socotra, mainly Arabic speaking, not the Socotri-speaking Bedu of the interior. It gives an outline account of their social organization and something of their maritime activities, fishing and navigation. There is a detailed account of the organization of the port of Qalansiyyah and the interesting star calendar in use on the island, which has not been published before. Such historical material as is to be found in the Arabic authors is from the early tenth century (al-Hamdānī) up to the pilot books of Ibn Mājid and Sulaymān al-Mahrī of about AD 1500, as well as some information drawn from *The Portuguese off the South Arabian coast.*

DESCRIPTION: THE TRADE AND CROPS

The south side of Socotra island is called *al-ẓahr,* the back, and the north side would be called *al-baṭn,* the belly. In the Gulf the north side would be the *ẓahr* and the south the *baṭn,* as of course in Oman we find the *Ẓāhirah* and *Bāṭinah.* In the Gulf these names are given because the wind is generally strong in the north and shipping would shelter on the south side. Ibn Mājid mentions sailing in the *ẓahr* of Socotra, in one of his sailing directions. Sulaymān al-Māhri, writing about 917 AH/ AD 1511 speaks of its three capes from west to east, Rās al-Sha'b, Rās Māmi, and south-west Shar'ayn (perhaps the map's Rās Katanan) and its two bandars or ports; al-Sūq, the bandar for the district (*balad*); and al-Sha'b, which is the bander of Qalansiyyah. According to a report given during World War II to the Residency at al-Mukallā, the Sultan of the island at that time, when questioned about territorial waters, said it was customary for Socotrans to consider that the boundaries reach as far as the eye can see from the shore.

The well known Kuwaiti dhow-master of our times, the late 'Īsā al-Quṭāmī, names the places to him on the north side, with some errors into which it is all too easy to fall. From east to west these are Rās Mūmī (his incorrect Mu'min); Bandar Nakam – probably correctly Kām a wadi above Ḥawlaf: Rās Karmah; Qalansiyyah; Badū (Bādōh) – written Baduwa on the map; Rās al-Sha'b. He mentions the islands lying to the west by a name unknown elsewhere, to the best of my knowledge, al-Ṣābūniyyāt, 'the Soapy Ones', which he calls *ṣayyal* (a small mountain in the sea); Darzī; Samḥā and Qarāqir Fir'awn (Pharaoh's Boats). (The last is called Ki'āl Fir'awn, Pharaoh's Balls, by the pilot Bā Ṭāyi' in a poem composed in 1217 AH/ AD 1802, so al-Quṭāmī seems either to have misheard or glossed over the name.)

The Portuguese fort was al al-Sūq, and on a spur to the east of it was a look-out post like the lookouts at Jabal al-Manẓar of Aden and one we found on the mountain east of al-Shiḥr. I was told that at al-Sūq, ships once anchored where now there are palms growing and that there used to be a *khawr* or lagoon there. This local tradition is not at all impossible as the beaches shift during heavy storms in the summer. It might also explain why were was a movement of population from al-Sūq to Ḥadībūh, the latter also known to some western reports as Tamarida.

There is no special *sūq* day in Ḥadībūh as there is nothing special to sell. It is only when the seasonal shipping (*mūsim*) puts in, as from the Sawāḥil (east African coastal ports) in or about the end of April; or when vessels begin to arrive about the time of the Opening (*Futūḥ*) of the sea, the end of September.

The 1966 report categorizes the three important exports of the island as labour, dried fish and ghee. There is a small export of salt from pans owned by the Mahrī group Bayt Kalshat on its south side – salt comes from Nayr. The Socotrans salt fish down and when enough has accumulated it is sent to Zanzibar; the maize is brought from east Africa, which takes much of the dried fish and ghee. Imports are almost entirely confined to cloth, grain and some sugar, or were so in times past. Other exports include Dragon's blood, a commodity I noticed mentioned in a list of imports at Ragusa in 1458 and Socotran aloes at Marseilles in 1227 and Florence on a list dated 1310-40, but doubtless they were coming to the west long before these dates. Rugs, pearls and shells are also exported.

Again and again writers on Socotra maintain that the island produced no grain. The *Periplus of the Erythraean Sea* says that it has no vines or grain, Marco Polo notes they only have rice (which must mean imported rice). Yet we saw in the hills behind Ḥadībūh many signs of irrigation channels, fields not now used, walls for palm groves and other agricultural purposes. 'Abd al-Razzāq al-Khālidī, writing in 1959, alludes to millet of the *dukhn* variety, white sorghum and a little wheat, and Brown's report does state that grain – except for the small *bāmbe* (Eleusine) millet grown on irrigated terraces in some parts of the Haggier (mountains) – is used by Bedu only as famine food. It is a 55/60-day crop.

AL-SŪQ: SOME INDUSTRIES

In the wadi at al-Sūq, water can be reached about four feet below ground level; and there we find small dry masonry-lined wells for irrigating the palms. I was told that palms on the seashore are irrigated from the spray of high seas, which at times pound on the beach and send up the spray. Palms are known to like salty ground. Some of the palms are enclosed by fences to protect them from sheep and goats attempting to eat the fallen dates. There is also a larger type of enclosure called by the Yemeni term *maḥḍarah* – a plot enclosed by a fence of palm ribs (*jarīds*), where onions and tobacco are grown, though sometimes the tobacco is grown separately in its own plots. Melons (*baṭṭīkh* and *ḥabḥab*, the latter with red flesh and black pips), tomatoes (*ṭamāṭim*, potatoes, pumpkin (*dibbā*), are grown. In Ḥadībūh a little *bāmiyā*, (ladies' fingers) and *fijil*, (white radish) are also grown. No doubt there are fuller details in Government reports. Red peppers were produced for us in al-Sūq.

In the channels round each plant goat or sheep droppings are placed as fertilizers. In one small palm plantation the trees, about 3-4ft high, were being watered, each palm by hand, with water brought in a bucket from a well – there were four such waterings a week. The wall of a palm plantation is called by the Arabic word *darb*. The Sultan has palms in al-Sūq and also a plot near the camp. Land belongs to individuals, and boundaries are marked by whitewashed stones, while individual palms are marked with an owner's sign – one, two or three horizontal lines. I also saw a cross, but no particular significance should be attached to this. The date crop (*kharīf*) ripens in the Kaws season – I noted *jiljil* (plural *jalājil)*, as meaning a date cluster.

I recorded as best I could, since the names seem to be Socotri, a list of names of different kinds of date native to the island, but I cannot guarantee that the spelling is correct, *Baynī, Drīmaḥaytin Dī Haḍhul, Dī qul uskut* (the two latter words mean in Arabic, 'say, be quiet!'), *Farīṭaṭ, Ḥimhir, Ḥawkām*, a red variety said to be the same as the Gulf *Khinayzī, Ḥabashiyyah* (Abyssinian), *Libānaynuh* (cf. Ḥaḍramī *Lubānī*, _ 'like incense'), *Maqṭanah/Maqṭānah, Niqāḍah, Qilā'ānah, Qabāhan, Shawqhāyub, Ṣimhiyyah* (there is a Hadrami term *ṣim*, dates stoned and pounded), *Zarafān*.

The Suquṭrāwī palm also grows in some parts of Ḥaḍramawt. Dates used to come from Basrah to Socotra as indeed to all south Arabian ports and east Africa, but they now come from Qaṭīf. We saw some bananas growing in Ḥadībūh, but they are mostly said to be imported from Zanzibar.

Another industry is lime-burning, carried out in circular pits lined with dry masonry. One sees heaps of white stone, on top of two or three of which marks of ownership are palm ribs. Palm logs are used as fuel and the pits are called *maḥrīkah (maḥārīk)*, corresponding to the Yemeni *miḥrāq*.

First a layer of firewood is put down, then the limestone or whatever it is, then another layer of wood, then limestone again and so on until they have filled the pit and no wood shows. The lime *(nūrah)* has nothing else added to it but is of course slaked with water when it is being used.

POTTERY

In a village in the hills behind and above Ḥadībūh we found pottery being made. Women only are engaged in making these pots, the men having no part in the work. The strange thing is that they have no kiln but an open fire upon which they fire the pots, a score at a time. No wheel is in use and the pots are built up in coils on a base and are very symmetrical. There are pots with a rim made of a sort of yellowish clay. We also saw in a village a kind of platter with a tongue on the rim. Two types of shell are used to smooth the outside and mouth of the pot. We bought a pottery animal – a children's toy no doubt – but so crude that it was impossible to guess what it represented! It was coloured with Dragon's blood which was also used to decorate the pots. We saw no local glazed wares.

BEADS

There are many strange beads to be seen on Socotra, some of which look as if they may be of some antiquity. At Qaḍb (Qaḍub) we saw pear-shaped onyx beads closely similar to those we bought at Shibām of Wadi Ḥaḍramawt in 1947; these are probably pre-Islamic. Others of various shapes were purchased in Ḥadībūh or perhaps at al-Sūq.

Black beads with white spots on them called *gāzi'*, Arabic *jaz'*, onyx, but made of glass, are used by the hill Bedu against the insect identified by Marion as probably the Bott fly, common in parts of Africa, but not Arabia, that appears at certain times of the year and tries to enter the nose or mouth to lay eggs. This fly appears about the star al-Ḥūt, i.e. mid-October. These beads are sold in Ḥadībūh and are said to come from Bombay via Aden.

At Ghubbah an old man came to us wearing large yellow beads round his neck – we did not find out why!

HISTORICAL DATA

(including visitors' and travellers' descriptions)

The celebrated geographer and traveller al-Mas'ūdī (died about 345 AH/AD 956) who would have passed by Socotra, even if he may not actually have visited it, on his voyage to Zanzibar, has left an account of it part of which is repeated in the geographical dictionary of Yāqūt some centuries later. Al-Mas'ūdī has evidently drawn on literary sources for his information; there are certain discrepancies in the various editions of the text. After preliminary remarks about Socotran aloes (*ṣabir*

Suquṭrī): *found nowhere else but on it and brought only from it,* he says:

Aristotle had written to Alexander son of Philip when he set out for India/Syria, about this island, counselling him to send a body of Greeks (Yūnāniyyūn, Ionians) there, to settle them there because of the aloes which come in purgatives etc. Alexander did send Greek people to this island, most of them coming from Asṭāghār[ā] (Stagirus), Aristotle's own town, in vessels with their families, by way of Baḥr Qulzum [the Red Sea]. They conquered those [of the kings of India] in it and took possession of the island. The Indians had a large idol in it and this idol was transferred [to India] according to tales too lengthy to relate. Those Greeks on the island multiplied, Alexander passed away, the Masīh [son of Mary] appeared and those on it became Christians [and remained so] up to this time. Nor is there any place in the world, and God knows best, where a people of the Greeks (Yūnāniyyūn) preserve their lineage without [any] Rūm or others mixing with them in their lineage. At this time Indian ships (bawārij al-Hind) *who waylay the Muslims in these ships [to rob them] resort to them [the Socotrans] in these* bawārij, *i.e. vessels [waylaying] any who voyage to China and India etc. From the island of Socotra are brought aloes and other simples. There are marvellous tales about this island and the plants and simples special to it of many of which we have given a complete account in our earlier books.*

It is a curious coincidence that, though it is agreed that the name Socotra is derived from Sanskrit *dyīpa sukhadhara*, the radical letters of Aristotle's birthplace Stagirus/Asṭāghārā, *s ṭ gh r*, allowing for a simple metathesis and the very common interchange of the letters *gh*/ *q* in Arabic, are the same as those of Socotra/Suquṭrā. Al-Mas'ūdī's story of a Greek population, however, does not tally with the statement of the anonymous author of the *Periplus*, about the late third century AD, that . . . *they are a mixed people consisting of Arabs and Indians, and a few Greeks who have sailed out* [there] *for trade*. This agrees with a situation depicted in early Arabic sources of a cyclical movement from Dumah, of merchants to the Persian Gulf and round Arabia via al-Shihr of the Mahrah and up the Red Sea, in which both Indian and Greek merchants took part; this would be before the seventh century but could have been a pattern remounting also to a much earlier period. *Bārijah* (plural *bawārij)* is an Indian word, Hindustani *bīzah* from *bīrah* current in Arabic at that time. Yāqūt in the thirteenth century AD glosses al-Mas'ūdī's note on the Indian pirates by saying this no longer happened in his day and he maintains that the Socotrans are mostly Christian Arabs (Naṣārā 'Arab).

Ships called *Bawārij* are mentioned by Ṭabarī the historian as entering the Tigris via Basrah in 251 AH/865 AD during March.

Roughly contemporary with al-Mas'ūdī is the celebrated geographer of the Arabian Peninsula, al-Hamdānī, (died, 334/945) who quotes from an apparently unknown earlier writer called Abū Rāshid. As the account of Socotra he gives in *Iklīl I* differs in some respects from that in his *Description (Ṣifah) of the Arabian Peninsula*, both passages are given.

He said, 'On the island of Socotra are (people) from all of the tribes of Mahrah. It is an island, as he maintains, eighty parasangs in length, with Socotran aloes and many palms in it. Ambergris ('anbar} *is cast up to it and Dragon's Blood* (Dam al-Akhawayn) *is (found) in it. If a Mahrī is addressed as "Yā Suquṭrī" he gets angry.' He said, 'Socotra is of the Greeks* (al-Rūm) *only who were there, (descendants) of the sons of the Greeks: they entered into the lineage* [i.e. intermarried with] *al-*

Qamar [tribe] *of Mahrah and are (well) known.' He said, 'There are 10,000 fighting men in it and there were Christians – that is to say they mention that Chosroes settled a people from the land of the Greeks there and there they lived until Mahrah crossed over to them and conquered them and the island . . .' He said, 'They sometimes say that there were no Greeks in it but monks* [lit. monkery, rahbāniyyah] *following the Greek religion of Christianity. The warriors* (shurāt) *of Mahrah entered (Socotra) and Ḥaḍramawt and killed those who were there.'*

The *Shurāt* are those who are ready to sell their lives for the faith and this term is regularly used in the Omani chronicles for Ibādī warriors and al-Hamdānī simply seems to have adopted it, so he means those adherents of the Ibāḍī sect who arrived in Ḥaḍramawt in the second quarter of the 2nd century of the hijrah and according to al-Mas'ūdī still had the adherence of most of Ḥaḍramawt in his day.

In his *Description* al-Hamdānī says: *Socotra island – Socotran aloes is called after it. It and the island of Barbarā are part of (the area) that intervenes between Aden and the land of the Negroes (Zinj), situated on the route (to it). A person putting to sea from Aden to the land of the Zinj starts out as if making for Oman and Socotra island runs along with him on his right until it ends and he turns in the direction of the Zinj Sea. The length of this island is eighty parasangs and in it are* [people] *from all the tribes of Mahrah. Among them are about 10,000 fighting men, they being Christians. They say that Chosroes settled a people from the land of the Greeks there. Then tribes of Mahrah came down to them, dwelt alongside them and some of them turned Christian* (tanaṣṣar) *with them. It has many palms, ambergris is cast up to it by the sea, in it is (found) Dam al-Akhawayn which is al-Ayda', and much aloes. The Aden people however say that no Greeks (Rūm) entered it but it had monks (monkery) then they passed away, Mahrah settled in it and people of the warriors* (shurāt). *The call to Islam appeared there, the extremists multiplied and attacked the Muslims there, killing them all but ten persons. There is a mosque there in a place called al-Sūq.* This *ayda'*, Dragon's Blood, a red varnish is mentioned by a Hijaz poet early in the seventh century.

The historian of Oman, al-Sālimī, writing in 1912, reproduces an account from some source not mentioned by him, of a naval expedition from his country, in the third century AH/ninth AD, to re-assert Omani control over Socotra. In this century, as John Wilkinson says, the Azdī Imāms of the Ibādī sect . . . *had led a more or less unified Imāmate, the frontiers of which extended from the borderlands of al-Baḥrayn towards those of the Yemen and whose maritime trade was of ever growing importance.* To the source from which al-Sālimī derives his account there had already been accretions of highly dubious historicity, yet there is no cause to doubt that an expedition did take place to restore Omani overlordship of, say, the little ports of Socotra's northern coast.

The Imām al-Ṣalt (b. Mālik al-Kharūṣī) is said to have reigned in Oman from 237 AH/AD 857-8 until deposed in 273 AH/AD 886. In the political crises in the country at the end of that time it is to be supposed that authority over Socotra would slip from the hands of the Imāms. The expedition is thus likely to have taken place in the earlier part of his reign.

In his (al-ṣalt's) days the Christians (Naṣārā) behaved treacherously, breaking the pact between them and the Muslims. They made an assault on Socotra, killing the Imām's governor and young men (?) [sic] *along with him, robbing, plundering, seizing the country and possessing themselves of it by force.*

Socotra is an island eighty parasangs long containing aloes and many palms. Ambergris is thrown up on it and it has Dragon's Blood. It is to the south of Oman, the Baḥr al-Ḥabashah lying between it and Oman.

A woman of the Socotra people called al-Zahrā' wrote a poem to the Imām (al-Ṣalt) in which she reminded him of what had happened in Socotra through the Christians, complaining to him of their injustice and seeking his support against them.

Al-Zahrā' addresses the Imām, praising the nobility of his house and goes on to make her plea, from which I have selected the following verses:

Socotra is now become destitute of Islam

Where once were sharī'ah *laws, revelation* (al-Furqān) *and books* [Qur'ān?]

Where once a tribe, having settled, had become envied for its well-being under the shade of their ruler with property and esteem.

. . .

Instead of guidance they were brought unbelief and sin, and instead of the call to prayer (the sound) of wooden clappers [nawaqis, *used by oriental Christians to summon prayer].*

. . .

What ails Ṣalt that he can sleep of nights at ease,

While in Socotra there are women left ruined from plundering?

So the Imām mustered armies and fitted out vessels over which he gave the command to Muḥammed b. 'Ashīrah and Sa'īd b. Shimlāl, so that, should something happen to one of them, he who was left should take the place of his comrade. Should something happen to them both, Ḥāzim b. Humām, 'Abd al-Wahhāb b. Yazīd and 'Umar b. Tamīm were to take their place. He wrote them a letter in which he made plain what they should do and what they should leave.

The number of vessels assembled for this raid was a hundred vessels and a vessel. They went to them and God supported them against them. So they took the country and routed the enemy, returning in triumph.

The Imām's letter which seems entirely apocryphal, does, none the less, contain some interesting instruction to his officers: *Strictly insist that the ships' captains* (rubbāniyyah) *do not scatter and that any one of them should out-sail the other, and whoever does get ahead let him hold back for his mates by whatever amount there is to allow one to hear the hail of the other.* This is obviously the sea law of convoy, known as *sinjār,* which still holds today.

You must know that none of the Muslims are permitted to marry Christian women of the Socotra people, nor the people of the covenant of them, nor the women of those at war (with the Muslims), except the women of those people of the covenant who read the Gospel (Injīl). The reference is to the covenant with Muḥammad of Jews and Christians. The poll tax *(jizyah)* is to be imposed on these people and there is a definite order to send the returns from this tax back to the Imām. The bulk of this extremely lengthy letter is concerned with the Islamic precepts the members of the expedition are to observe. Instructions are also given to remove any Socotrans 'of the people of the prayer', men, women and children, who wish to go, until they reach Muslim territory, as also any children of the Ibāḍī warriors *(shurāt)* and those who assisted the Muslims, since Socotra is no longer a place for them after the fighting between them. So whether this was an original part of the Imām's orders or not, the

Omanis evidently did not stay on in Socotra. The number of vessels stated to have been engaged in the expedition seems of course fantastically exaggerated.

* The traveller, Ibn al-Mujāwir who died in 690 AH/AD 1291 has a chapter 'Account of the island of Socotra' which draws upon some sources unknown, and he visited it as appears below when a young men, no less than sixty three years earlier. Unfortunately there are many corrupt passages in the manuscripts of his book and more than a few of these it has been so far impossible to restore to their correct form. Sometimes his expression is also rather vague:

It is said that in ancient times all these places [he appears to mean the coastal villages of Ḥaḍramawt] *were land* [text, 'sea'], *nought else, Socotra lying between the sea and the land. When God open up the mouth from opposite the mountain (of Socotra) the sea submerged up to Bāb al-Mandab (which lies) between Aden and Zabīd and the water stopped there. When Bāb al-Mandab was opened it* [the water] *stopped at the end of the regions of the Red Sea (Baḥr al-Qulzum) and the mountain of Socotra now became an island in the depths of the sea.*

The correct circumference of the island is forty parasangs and somewhat more . . . Al-Hammāmī said. Its true circumference is eighty parasangs and somewhat more. [Its all-over length as the crow flies is in fact about 78 miles.]

Nor, in all these seas, is there a larger or pleasanter island, for it has palms, gardens, millet (sorghum) and wheat crops; there are on it camels, cattle and thousands upon thousands of sheep. In it are waters flowing on the surface of the earth, sweet, Euphrates sweet. It is a large gulf the beginning of which starts from the mountains, long and broad. [From the map this seems to describe the area from Rās Ḥawlaf to Rās Qadāmā]. *The sea with its fishes dominates over the rest of it (?)* [sic]. *From it sprouts the Socotran aloe plant and Dragon's Blood, while on its coasts much ambergris is found. Its inhabitants are Christian people, magicians* (saḥarah). *One instance of their magic is that Sayf al-Islām, but the correcter version is Sayf al-Dīn Sunqur, the client* (mawlā) *of Ismā'īl b. Ṭughtakīn* [the Ayyūbid 593-8 AH/AD 1197-1202], *despatched an expeditionary forced of five galleys* (shawānī) *to take the island. When the troops* (qawm) *drew near the island it vanished before their eyes and they set to going up and down, to and fro, day and night, for* [many] *days and nights, without finding a sound of the island, nor happening upon any news of it, so they were sent back* [whence they came]. *In the books of the accursed Greeks* (al-Rūm) *it is said to be written of the island, 'The preserved isle in the land of the Arabs.'*

Account of the Seven Birds (al-sab'ah al-ṭuyūr):

The author of the Routier (Rahnāmaj) *book has remarked that when a voyager in this sea perceives seven birds on the high seas he knows that he is opposite the island of Socotra and everyone who has passed and passes through this sea and traverses the island of Socotra sees the Seven Birds by night and by day, in the morning and evening. From whatever direction vessels approach, the Birds come to meet him but none of those leaving it in his wake comes across them. This is constant, no one ever supposing eight, nine or six birds, but only seven all told. This is of the sum of marvels – how much learned men have pondered over them* [the Seven Birds] *without any of them arriving at the underlying reason for them, nor yet what manner of tale theirs is or what their nature is. Ibn al-Mujāwir said, 'I voyaged from Daybul* [an ancient port of Sind the precise location of which is not

* Cf. G. Rex Smith, 'Ibn al-Mujawir on Dhofar and Socotra', *PSAS* 15 (1985), 85 ff., and review of Doe's book, *JSS* 39/1 (1994), 137–8.

now known] *in the vessel of the* nākhūdhā, *Khawājah Najīb al-Dīn Maḥmūd b. Abi 'l-Qāsim al-Baghawi, īn company with the shaykh 'Abd al-Ghaniyy b. Abi 'l-Faraj al-Baghdādī at the close* [February] *of the year 618/1222 and I saw the Seven Birds in the deep sea and when morning came we saw the island.*

In response to my inquiries about the Seven Birds it was said to me that there is a bird here called Daḥamilhān, a sea bird which one sees remote from the coast; it is white-breasted with a black back, but it does not dive. Mariners look out for this bird and no other and when they see it they know they are near Socotra, but they know nothing of the number seven in connection with it. Ibn Mājid, in his sailing directions of the late fifteenth century, occasionally remarks that the presence of certain birds at sea indicates an imminent landfall at some coastal port. Sulayman al-Mahrī, in his sailing directions, written about 917 AH/AD 1511, states that three species of birds are a sign of the proximity of the coasts to the south side *(ẓahr)* of Socotra up to al-Sawāḥil, the east African coast, and elsewhere he makes a brief reference to the birds of Suhaylī Suquṭrā, seemingly the south side and the islands of Samḥā and Darzā.

According to Ibn al-Mujāwir: *There are four large towns on the island of which are al-Sūq, Fātik* (Fatk = Qalansiyyah), *Mūrī and of the villages around it* (Socotra?) *is Qaryah Mā shā' Allāh.* I can only suggest that Qaryah (lit. village) is the Bandar Garrieh of the British map, but I suspect that the text at this point is corrupt. One would hardly call any of these 'places' towns and it is unlikely any were notably larger then than now.

It is an island with the Mountain running round it, the peak of the Mountain rising up on the horizon. In the Mountain live tribal mountain folk (qawm jibāliyyah) *opposed to the people of the low-lying country. It has sown fields, cultivated inhabited lands, towns and villages some of which have no knowledge of the others. Everyone wears a cross suspended from his neck, each person according to his means. At the extremities of the island are many flat coastal strips* (sawāḥil) *like Bandar Mūsā* [not marked on our map but said still to be known, east of Qalansiyyah] *and Rās Māmī* [making this correction to the text, = Rās Mūmī] *of Socotra. Most of the livelihood of the inhabitants of these coastal strips is with the corsairs, because the corsairs land at their (settlements) and stay with them for a six month period, selling to them what they have taken, eating, drinking and having intercourse with their women. They are crafty* [? malevolent] *folk, pimps, their old hags being more pimpish than their menfolk. Among their menfolk are those who are more pimpish* [lit. more leading] *than a black* [man] *at the head of a rutting camel. As the poet says:*

An old hag who, if tossed to the sea floor,
Leading a whale would [safely] *come to shore.*
Mules a thousand she would through guile have led,
Dragged along by a rope of spider thread.

Ibn al-Mujāwir supplies a diagram of Socotra but it is too crude to identify with the 1960 map, and the caption is corrupt.

Witchcraft then is a long tradition in Socotra. I was told of a case of a suspected witch who had five *raṭls* weight tied on to her chest and five more on to her back. Her arms were tied above the elbow and her legs above the knees. She was then thrown into the sea. If she swam it would seem she was a witch. They told me that this poor woman was able to swim thus proving the case against herself. I was also told that a man was executed a few years before our visit to the island for killing a woman he believed to be a witch.

Sulaymān al-Mahrī remarks, apropos of nothing in particular, that Socotra is evil fortune/ill luck to anyone who rules it (*shu'm 'alā man malaka-hā*). He gives no reason. There is however said to be much 'envy' (hasad) and evil eye (*'ayn*) in Socotra, but magic (*siḥr*) is to be found only with the Bedu and the Blacks, not with the Whites of the coast. When one admires something therefore one adds the usual Islamic *Mā shā' Allāh*, or *Ṣallī 'ala 'l-Nabiyy* to avert the eye.

In our own time al-Khālidī tells of a woman suspected by her son of responsibility for the death of sheep carried off by a fatal pestilence; so the son exiled her to outside the island.

Although Marco Polo, on his return journey from China about the last decade of the thirteenth century, gives some description of Socotra and the ports of Arabia's southern coast, it is thought unlikely that the fleet in which he sailed ever touched there, and that he drew on the tales of pilots. They would have apprised him of its reputation for he says: *Many pirates resort to this island with the goods they have captured, and which the natives purchase of them without scruple, justifying themselves on the ground of their being plundered from idolaters and Saracens.* From his account Socotra was an independent Christian island and the idolaters would be Hindu Indians. The situation he describes appears not to have changed in the following century to judge from the incident that follows.

Although the native Socotrans do not seem to have been a warlike race they evidently had their own ways of hitting back at bad treatment. *If any vessel belonging to a pirate should injure one of theirs,* says Marco Polo, *they do not fail to lay him under a spell, so that he cannot proceed on his cruise until he has made satisfaction for the damage; and even although he should have a fair and leading wind, they have the power of causing it to change, and thereby obliging him to return to the island. They can in like manner cause the sea to become calm, and at their will can raise tempests, occasion shipwrecks, and produce many other extraordinary effects.*

By the time of Sir Thomas Roe the said Sīdī Hāshim had acquired something of these powers: *They impute the violence of the wyndes to his walking, and have him in wonderfull reference . . . He apperes to them, and warnes them of dangers to ensue.*

The Rasūlid monarchs of the Yemen at Ta'izz and Zabīd from the 7th AH/13th AD to the mid 9th/15th centuries usually controlled the coastal ports of southern Arabia as far as Ẓafār al-Ḥabūḍī (now in Oman), drawing substantial revenue from taxation on the shipping plying the Indian trade route. They even maintained a fleet of guard ships, galleys (*shawānī*), against pirates, at various points, to maintain which a tax called *shawānī* had been introduced by their predecessors the Ayyūbids. There is little known historically of these coastal ports but, in my as-yet-unpublished edition of the chronicles of the Ḥaḍramī writer Shanbal, comes an entry under the year 756 AH/AD 1355 to which I have added details culled from other Ḥaḍramī manuscripts.

In the days of the Amīr Dāwūd b. Khalīl al-Hakkārī the Indian prisoners [incorrectly, Indian Magians] *came out in their fetters and swam to a vessel in al-Shiḥr bandar containing goods belonging to the (Rasūlid) Sultan. So* [the Amīr] *dispatched after them vessels the officer* (muqaddam) *in charge of which was*

Aḥmad b. 'Abdullāh Abā Dujānah. They recovered the vessel from them at Socotra and plundered much property from the island, returning with the vessel to al-Shiḥr on the first of the month of Dhu'l-Ḥijjah (December 7th).

Another Ḥaḍramī chronicler, Bā Sharāḥīl, says the abducted vessel was laden with cargo and bound for Aden but little of this was lost. Abā Dujānah 'plundered the islands' – if more than one island, perhaps the islets of 'Abd al-Kūrī and others are intended – and he imposed the poll tax on them, returning with his soldiers to al-Shiḥr.

In the following year, 757 AH/AD 1356: *the Indians besieged Ẓafār, seizing vessels from its bandar and they stopped at sea, seizing any coming from India, until the Ẓafār people paid them much money and they went away.*

Though the chroniclers do not say who these Indians were it may be assumed they were pirates (Bā Sharāḥīl merely called them 'robbers'), probably like the Indians whose vessels used to intercept merchants on their voyages in the early period as mentioned by al-Mas'ūdī. The Amīr is probably a Rasūlid official. Bā Dujānah is a well known Ḥaḍramī family and the Rasūlid Sultan would be al-Mujāhid.

The Indian pirates – we are not told how they came to be prisoners – would doubtless have only leg fetters as is still customary with hostages – and perhaps were allowed to move about in al-Shiḥr without being held in custody. A vessel anchored in al-Shiḥr roads would not lie far from the shore, but to swim in irons is still a feat. It cannot be imagined that men in irons could carry out the strenuous work needed to man a sailing vessel and the irons must surely have been struck off at sea. I have seen this done in north-east Yemen when the fetter was a simple iron ring, the two ends knocked together on a stone, and the ring opened by prising it apart with two iron bars.

It may have been because the northern coast of Socotra was so often a haunt of pirates that we learn from Ibn Mājid that . . . *at the beginning of the Kārim, the Turk dynasty* (dawlah) *and the Banū Ghassān dynasty, they* (i.e. shipping) *used to leave Socotra to the north in going and coming* (to and from India), *and now they* (continue to) *leave it in going and coming. In coming from India it* (Socotra) *used to be confused by them with the mountain of al-Shihr and what lies next to it. So they recorded an estimate/reckoning (?) for it in their old pilot-books* (rahmānajāt) and said: 'When you see the mountain, half of it emerging from the water, cast the lead (*buld*) *and if it* (comes up) *clean it is Socotra, and if it does not* (come up) *clean then it is the land of al-Shiḥr and neighbouring areas.*' I was told in 1964 that fat (*shaḥm*) is rubbed on to the *buld* so that it can bring up some of the soil or sand from the sea bottom. Rās Māmī (present day Mūmī) was the landfall for vessels coming from Malabar.

The Kārim was a kind of international organization of merchants and bankers, which seems to have maintained a regular shipping line from Egypt to India, seemingly from the Fāṭimid period but well established in the twelfth century AD and frequently calling at Aden. *By the beginning of the thirteenth century,* says Goitein, *the powerful association of the so-called Kārimīs made it difficult for individual merchants with limited means to participate in the ventures of the India trade.* What Ibn Mājid means by *the Turk dynasty* is most likely the Ayyūbids, whose troops are always called Ghuzz by the Ḥaḍramī chroniclers – Turkmen who conquered Ḥaḍramawt for the Rasūlids of Ta'izz and Ẓabīd. The Banū Ghassān are the Rāsulids whose dynasty collapsed about the mid-fifteenth century AD.

Vasco da Gama's pilot, Aḥmad b. Mājid has written in his pilot books on Socotra, (which he says was inhabited by Christian barbarians – *Ahmāj: In our time,* he says *'Amr b. 'Afrār and the Banū 'Abd al-Nabiyy al-Salaymānī* (sic) *al-Ḥimyarī, both of the Mashāyikh of the Mahrah built a fort there, and governed over some of its inhabitants, imposing unpaid labour on them, taking from each man a maund of ghee, and from each woman a rug* (shamlah) *of the weave of the country.'* These rugs, of distinctive manufacture, are still woven, and I possess several. They are known as Suquṭrāwī and consist of several strips about 7in. wide and over 6ft in length, sewn together. The colours are usually blacks and browns. Ibn Mājid continues:

In the time of the 'Abbāsids a man of the 'Ajam [the people of the Horn of Africa, known as Barr al-'Ajam] *had taken possession of it, but the people of it* [Socotra] *devised a ruse against him – they made him and his comrades drunk and murdered them. They had killed Aḥmad b. Muḥammad b. 'Afrār who ruled over them after the death of his father. So his paternal uncles and tribe came, and took revenge for him, brought then under constraint, and set Ibn 'Abd al-Nabiyy to rule over them. Consequently they say that it (*Socotra) *is bad luck to him who rules it. They are native people who, when a stranger comes to them, set before him water and provisions, and they set before him their cloth and their women. Ruling over them is a woman, and as for marriage among them, it is in the hands of the priests* (qasīs) *of the Christians who dwell in the churches; they manage them according to the advice of that woman, but in our time her power has ended and become weak.*

Ibn Mājid wrote this towards the end of the 9th AH/15th century AD – he continues: *The Mahrah only took possession of it because they want it for the consequence of their affair* [as a last resort?], *to rally in it when they are weak and in danger from the* [Kathīrī] *Sultans of Ḥaḍramawt and others. Muḥammad b. 'Alī b. 'Amr had sought advice of me for years, years ago, but I did not comply with him over that. Then when he became lord of the Mahrah he expended money and took possession of it, so when he died and his tribe remained they stayed on it for years, and Sha'āwith* [?], *the kings of the al-Shiḥr people, were kept out of it for a period of thirty years. Their maternal uncles the Mahrah aided them against al-Shiḥr and they took it and Sa'd b. Mubārak b. Faris became lord over them after he had besieged it for three entire months and they were starving. So he expelled them from the fort of al-Shiḥr to their country Ḥaḍramawt* [he means, of the interior] *which* [i.e. al-Shiḥr] *at that time was under Badr b. Muḥammad al-Kathīrī. They were driven out, but they gave him* [Badr] *and those with him safe conduct in the year 894/1489, at this date the island of Socotra belonged to the Mahrah, Bani Salaymān and Banī 'Afrār, they being one of the Mahrah septs* (batn), *Bani Ziyād.*

Unfortunately Ibn Mājid is somewhat ambiguous in this account, but evidently Socotra had been under the control of the Mahrah families he mentions, notably the Bāni 'Afrār, about the latter half of the 9th AH/AD 15th century.

The arrival of the Portuguese in the Indian Ocean was to upset a long established trade pattern and result in many political changes in the countries of its littoral, but it affected Socotra very little. I have dealt with Portuguese action from the Arab chronicles in *The Portuguese off the South Arabian Coast* and their relations with the island are well covered by José Pareira da Costa, *Socotorá e o Dominio Portugués no Oriente,* Coimbra, 1973, and by Charles Beckingham. Beckingham

remarks that so far as we know the first Portuguese to report on the island was Diego Fernandes Pereira who, after taking a number of prizes off the African coast, went to spend the season there when the south-west monsoon rendered navigation dangerous, i.e. from late May till early August, 1505.

The Portuguese say that in AD 1480/885-6 AH the nephew of the Sultan of Qishn (which they call the Kingdom of Fartaque), with a force of ten ships, had taken Socotra: *The Socotrans had withdrawn to the mountains, where they could not be pursued, and to keep control the Arabs had built a fort at 'Soco'* (al-Sūq), *which was where trading ships called. A garrison of a hundred men was usually stationed there and tribute was imposed.*

The Arab chroniclers briefly record that short Portuguese incursion into the Island.

Year 912 AH/AD 1506-7

In this year the infidel Franks took Socotra, killing there the son of Ṭaw'arī al-Zuwaydī along with fifty of the Muslims, and built there a fort (Shanbal). Beckingham mentions the commander Shaykh Ibrāhīm, son of the Sultan of Qishn, who was killed along with about fifty Arabs. I have not as yet found his name in Arab writings.

Year 913 AH/AD 1507-8

In this year the Franks, may God abandon them, gained control over the island of Socotra and the island of Hurmūz, granting security to those merchants therein. They built a tower-fort there, imposing a stipulated contribution each year on what is liable to be tithed and on the pearl-fishery (al-Shiḥrī). It is unclear whether the taxes were collected from Socotra or Hurmūz, but they might well have been levied at Socotra. The actual attack on the island by Albuquerque and Tristão da Cunha took place in April 1507 (late 912 AH).

Year 916/1510-11

In this year Khamīs and 'Amr, the sons of Sa'd b. al-Zuwaydī made an expedition against Socotra, it being at that time with the Frank. They entered the town/country (*bilād*) *and made truce with them, but the Franks sallied forth against the Muslims and fought with them. About ten of the infidels were slain, the Muslims prevailing over them, and they looted some property* (Shanbal). Bā Sanjalah, under the year 942 AH/AD 1535-6, refers to this family; the name of the individual at that time being Shaykh al-Mahrah Bayt Ziyād, he being Muḥammad b. Ṭaw'arī b. 'Amr b. 'Ifrār al-Zuwaydī.

Year 917 AH/AD 1511-12

In this year the Franks removed from Socotra and Mahrah built a fort there (Shanbal). The Portuguese finally left Socotra in May 917 AH/AD 1511. The Portuguese fort, which was simply the Mahrah fort they had taken over, was built on level ground about a crossbow shot from the sea, with a mountain on its eastern side. The ruins on the hill which the Expedition found in 1967 must have been a look-out station for observing the movement of vessels; it would, of course, lie east of the site of the fort.

In 1082 AH/AD 1671 the Yemeni history called *Ṭabaq al-ḥalwā* reports that the Franks, presumably the Portuguese, entered Socotra of the land of the Mahrah and (the Mahrah?) made a truce with them through inability to fight them and they settled in a place called Qishn – a wadi on Socotra south of al-Sūq, not Qishn of the Arabian mainland.

In the second half of the 11th AH/17th AD century the Yemen and Oman under vigorous Imāms were expanding their territories by conquest and clashed over Ẓafār province on the Arabian mainland, but the strength of the Omanis lay in their sea-power whereas the Yemeni Imāms were highlanders with no naval tradition. The Omanis were able to raid as far as Mocha in the Red Sea and in 1079 AH/AD 1669 on their return voyage thence to Oman . . . *they laid waste the island of Socotra, robbed it, seized its shaykh, brought their sharp swords to drink of his head and returned, may God disfigure them, to their country.* So says the Yemeni historian ʻAbdullāh ʻAlī al-Wazīr.

The Omani attack on Socotra seems to have been quite unprovoked but, not unnaturally, its ruler sought to maker common cause with the Zaydī Imām of the Yemen against a common foe. In 1084 AH/AD 1673-4 letters arrived from the Mahrī, Lord of the island of Socotra and the Ḥaḍramī coast lying between al-Shiḥr and Ẓafār appealing for the Imamʻs regard and (stating) that he had already resolved upon taking him as Imām and that his reason for this seeking of a link with him was that, in the past, some of those men of the Omani who had come to the coast of Socotra islands had plundered it. He had fled to the coast of al-Shiḥr . . . *and the Amīr of the Omani had entered his country but not managed to get hold of what he had hoped since he* [the Socotri] *had taken with him what he had and those with him.* He laid all that pertained to him before the Imām. But the Imām was advised to deal with more important matters . . . *for the Mahrī has only made proposals to you in order to cure this ache!* The Zaydī Imām had plenty of troubles of his own in the Yemen itself and ignored the request. News came to the Imām in Muḥarram 1085 AH/early April 1674 AD that: *the Omaniʻs men had newly acquired Socotra island this year, killing a group of its inhabitants in cold blood.*

Sir Thomas Roe tells that in AD 1615/1024 AH, Socotra . . . *is governed by Sultan called Amar-ben-Seid, borne in the Island, the sonne of the King of Fartaque* [i.e. the Mahrī Sultan of Qishn] *in Arabia Foelix, called Sultan Seid-ben-Seid, who was Sultan of Socotra in the tyme of his grandfather, as this shalbe king after his father of Fartacque, and his son left at Socatra.* The system of succession that this suggests may be comparable to the co-regencies that appear to have been practised in ancient pre-Islamic south Arabia.

It is not easy to determine who this Sultan was. Beckingham gives a spelling Mulliamer Benzaid (Mawlā-ī ʻAmr b. Saʻīd?) and refers also to a letter from Amer ben Said to James I/VI dated 1032 AH/AD 1622. Seid might represent Arabic Saʻīd or Saʻd – and it may be remarked incidentally that al-Khalidi maintains that Socotri names tend to be Saʻd, Saʻūd, Saʻīd, Masʻūd, all of which should mean fortunate – and it will be recalled that Socotra is bad luck (*shu'm*) to him who rules it. The chroniclers mention so many Mahrīs of the Sultanic house in the 10th AH/16th AD century with similar names that I have so far been unable to identify Seid-ben-Seid. But Thomas Roe talks of a . . . *Petty King about Dofar with whom he dare not meddle, being in the Grandsignior's protection.* This King of Dofar must in 1615 have been the Kathīrī Badr b. ʻUmar, or perhaps one of his relatives acting nominally as his governor. The Mahris were often in conflict with the Kathīrīs.

The Sultan of Socotra at the time of the 1967 Expedition was ʻĪsā b. ʻAlī b. Sālim b. Saʻd al-Ṭawʻarī Al ʻIfrayr. Sultan Saʻd b. ʻAli the eldest surviving brother acts as regent in the absence of Sultan ʻĪsā – he was the first choice of the Nāyib of al-Ghayḍah on the mainland. Sultan ʻAbdullāh b. ʻAlī is little known on the island but the Khawr Garrieh people share-crop his date groves there. All members of the family have the title Sultan. A report to the Mukallā Residency maintains that the Āl Saʻd of ʻAfrār have possession of Socotra as of ancient right. Certainly the Ḥaḍramī chronicler Bā Sanjalah alludes frequently to the ʻAfrār (= ʻIfrayr) house and what appears to be the Ṭawʻarī branch of it, but this is mostly with reference to their capital Qishn on the mainland during the 10th AH/16th AD century, the Kingdom of Fartak as the Portuguese called it. To construct a genealogical tree of the Sultanic House would be difficult. I have a note that the father of ʻĪsā b. Aḥmad al-Ṭawāʻirī, a member of the State Council, was Sultan, but I cannot recollect who exactly this person was. In Qishn the Sultan of Socotra has no representative but a Mahrī, Bal-Rabīʻ, represents him at Sayḥūt.

On Socotra the Sultan has a State Council of five members and his wazīr, Ibrāhīm b. Khālid is his close friend – he calls himself al-Thuqalī but his real name is, they say, al-Nūbī, the Nubian, which implies slave descent. The Sultan's eight soldiers were said to be the only persons armed with rifles on the island; they receive East African shillings 100 shillings per month, plus 35 shillings ration money and a grain issue of 30 lb. – it was said to have been reduced to 100 shillings plus 14lb. of grain. The soldiers could only go on leave if they produced a replacement for their absence. The *muqaddam* at al-Sūq, Sayyid ʻĪsā b. ʻAlī, told me that the Sultan was his maternal uncle (*khāl*), i.e. his father had married the Sultan's sister.

Roe tells us of the Sultan of his day, that: *He Raignes soe absolutely that noe man can sell any thing but him selfe. His People sitt aboute him with great respect; his officers standing by who take account of trade, and receive and pay . . . He hath a handsome Gally and Junk of Suratt, with Mariners that serue him to transport his goodes for wages by the yeare.*

This is not very different from the state of affairs described in the 1954 report, that the only dhow on the island, which is owned jointly by the Sultan, is sailed round to Ḥadībūh from its anchorage at Stīmū and the tribesmen from the eastern area from the star Ṭarfah (which I calculate would be 12-14 February) bring in their ghee, mats, skins and Dragon's Blood. These and pearl shell are loaded and the dhow goes to Qaḍb (Haybaq) and Qalansiyyah where the same arrangements stand. The dhow then goes on to Mombasa with the representatives of each town and merchant to sell the exports and arrange the imports. The one *ʻabrī*, shark dhow on the island accompanies the dhow. Meanwhile all the other *ʻabrīs* which have been fishing off Socotra proceed to Zanzibar to sell the season's catch. The Sultanic dhow fires a gun on entering port, and prior to sailing there is lively dancing.

The Sultan in Socotra judges in cases between the Mahri groups, but they have a *Qāḍī* in Qishn of the Āl Bā ʻAbduh for *sharīʻah* cases. In the village of Qaḍb/Qaḍub also called Haybaq, lying close under the mountain range, lives the teacher (*muʻallim*) ʻAlī b. Aḥmad b. ʻAlī b. Salmān Suquṭrī who is the public (*ʻāmm*) *qāḍī* in the court of Socotra. He acquired his learning in Ḥaḍramawt and from books. His father, now deceased was a *qāḍī* who acquired his learning in the revered city of Tarīm, the capital of the Ḥaḍramī Sayyids, famous for its Ribāṭ, or theological college. His father died in the lifetime of the late Sultan Ahmad b. ʻAbdullāh b. ʻĪsā b. ʻIfrayr some time before 1947. The general statement was made that a *qāḍī* receives a fee for filing a case and a second fee for determining it. In Qalansiyyah

I was told that they judge by *sharī'ah* and according to custom, the *qāḍī* dealing with *sharī'ah* matters, the local *qā'im* judging by custom (*'ādah*). *Bish'ah,* trial by ordeal, practised in south-western Arabia in some places until at least fairly recent time, was said only to be used in the mountains, but the trial of witches by ducking them is of course a form of ordeal also.

'Abd al-Razzāq al-Khālidī, writing in 1959, has recorded that: *If a dispute arises between two individuals which they cannot settle themselves the plaintiff demands of his opponent that they go to the Sultan. Should the opponent refuse, the plaintiff demands that he do so in the name of the Sultan before witnesses whom he produces to testify that the man had disobeyed the Sultan's will. If he persists in his refusal to appear before the Sultan the latter sends for him. He fines him 50* riyāls *for his disobedience, then the settles the case between them. If a man has to be restrained or imprisoned for a short time they put him in a compound for animals or else he is ordered to remain in the mosque.*

The same writer reports that some years earlier, at the time of a famine, there was much theft of animals and therefore the hands of thieves were cut off – so that one day no less than eight were amputated, all of these hands suspended in the streets for a long time. This of course is an Islamic penalty for persistent theft but I do not know if it is also a part of the customary law of the native Socotrans.

INHABITANTS AND SOCIAL ORDER

The native Socotris speak of the Sahriyah and the Joboliyah, the people of the plains and those of the hills, but they also call themselves Bedu, which. as in Ḥaḍramawt, is applied to country dwellers often living in stone houses, as well as to the migratory tribes. The Socotran Bedu are not nomadic, though there is a local seasonal transhumance a mile or two up and downhill; they are, as Brown says, stockmen. The Bedu give the impression of being a 'pure' race, whereas the coastal population is mixed. A report in the Mukallā Residency files estimates that some 85% of the Bedu are Socotrans and the remainder Mahrah tribal sections settled in the island. The inhabitants of the towns and villages of the coast are largely 'foreigners'. There are, however. Socotran groups in Quṣay'ar of the Ḥaḍrami coast living in huts to the west of the village known as Ṣaqāṭirah and in other villages. Those in Quṣay'ar come from the islands of 'Abd al-Kūrī and Samḥā, perhaps also from Qalansiyyah, and there are marriage ties between these islands and the mainland.

At Quṣay'ar when we were there in 1964, probably about late February, there was a Dubai *jālibūt* which brings the shaykh from Socotra to Quṣay'ar and takes salt from Socotra to it. The salt is sold by the *gūniyah* bag and would cost about 15 to 16 shillings. It had taken twelve days to Socotra, fishing for shark there, some of which is landed at Quṣay'ar. At Quṣay'ar there are about nine *'abrīs*, only *'abarī kibār*, large shark fishing boats, which go to Socotra from the star al-Dalū (in al-Shiḥr, October 1st to 13th) to fish. After about five months' fishing there, they go to al-Sawāḥil, taking the fish with them. These boats return thence during the stars Simāk and Ghawfar (April 28th-May 10th). Then follows the beaching at the beginning of Kharīf, commencing at al-Shiḥr on July 2nd. They told me that if they are *'ūmah*, sardine, in the sea the Socotrans will not let them use the *kan'ad* (seer-fish or 'Indian salmon') (*Cybium guttatum*) net.

The Ṣaqāṭirah on the Ḥaḍramī coast and the Bayt Yazīd there eat turtle but at al-Muṣayna'ah they neither eat nor catch it. On Socotra we were told that about the end of April the turtle (*ḥams*) come in large numbers to the beach at Abilḥan and lay their eggs there.

The Ḥaḍramī Sayyids descended from the Prophet Muḥammad have, over the centuries, migrated to settle in Indonesia, Gujerat, east Africa and many other places. It is not surprising to find certain famous Sayyid houses settled on the coastal strip of Socotra. Qaḍb, not far from Ḥadībūh to the west, is described as a Sayyid village. The families of Āl Ḥāmid (of which there is at least one branch in Mahrah territory), Āl al-Shaykh Bū Bakr (with its main centre in 'Īnāt of the Wādī Ḥaḍramawt), Āl-Jifrī and Āl Bā 'Alawī are all represented there. Elsewhere only the Āl Ḥāmid are said to be found as at Qidahah, but there are Ḥaḍramīs of other classes elsewhere. Āl Bā Ḥārith from al-Ghurfah (which has an airport) are settled in Hadībūh, where there are also Āl Qaṭāyib (?) of the Jumahī Ḥumūmī tribe engaged in trading, Āl Maḥārīs from Dīs al-Ḥāmī, and Āl Bā Shanjal said to be Saybān from the coastal port of the Wāḥidī Sultanate Bal-Ḥāf who act as *qāḍīs*, the present *qāḍī* being Khamīs. The Āl Bin Maḥāmīd (?) are Mahrah tribesmen from Arabia now settled in al-Sūq as traders and fisherman.

As Oman has for centuries had close connections with Socotra, naturally enough one finds such families as Āl Salmān who are stated to now own most of the property in Ḥadībūh, and Āl Hadhanam (?) from Muscat as also Āl Falaithi (?) and Āl Ba'ali (?), all traders in Ḥadībūh and even the first generation of a family of Muscat Indians, Āl Ja'far. Their name suggests they may be Shī'ah.

There are some Somalis along the Ghubbah bay where there is the village known as Ghubbah, who have come from the pearl fishing; a Residency report says there are a few Somali fishermen on the island. Somalis consider their own fishermen and sailors to be of inferior social status.

This list cannot claim to be exhaustive of the 'foreign' elements in the coastal population. Europeans, incidentally, are still known as Franjī.

In Ḥaḍramawt there is a strict order of social precedence in descending order, headed by the Sayyids, then the Mashāyikh, both forming a certain religious aristocracy, then the free, arms-bearing tribes, then the protected townsfolk and peasants. In Ḥaḍramī society a man may only marry within his class or take a girl from a lower class. The Sayyids in particular will not allow their girls to marry outside the Sayyid class and this has given rise to bitter disputes not only in Arabia but in every country where they have settled. A Residency report notes that in 1953 the Sultan issued an edict that as there were too many unmarried Sayyid girls (*sharīfāt*) they must marry with other classes. Twelve were subsequently married to merchants and tribesmen. Sayyid women, it seems, then might marry Sultans. However as stated to me, it was said that Sultans marry sultans – for the title sultan is given to any male of the ruling house – so they give their women in marriage to each other outside the Islamic prohibited degrees, of course. This, my informant said, is also the case with Sayyids, except where there should be some cause for marrying outside the group. A girl might be married outside it if something prohibited (*ḥarām*) was feared on her account if she were not married, or in case of need, or as he put it, of hunger (*jū'*).

Apart from this there seems to be no feeling on the island against intermarriage with different races or even colours – except that slaves (*khaddām*) in places like

Ḥadībūh (still actually slaves in the sense of being a possession and unable, for instance, to leave the island without the consent of their masters), do not marry outside their own class. They are looked after by their master, who they call *'amm*, uncle, who arranges for them to be married with their own kind. Brown reports that many Bedu women go out as concubines to township dwellers at £5 to £15 plus their keep and the odd bit of cloth. This is not marriage, he says, nor is there any form of divorce, and the lady can walk out whenever she pleases. I was told, however, by Sa'd 'Alī Bā Ḥārith that the Bedu can and do intermarry with the blacks. Among the blacks a woman of thirty may have married six or seven men – they divorce for trivial reasons. In general in Socotra they say (and it does not apply to Blacks only or Whites only), 'A woman is only sandals on a man's feet (*Al-Ḥurmah illā ni'āl fī rijl al-rajjāl*)'. Al-Khālidī (1959) names Rupees 100 as a young girl's dowry, without specifying to what group this applies.

In the Ḥadībūh area, said Bā Ḥārith there are two groups, the Whites and the Blacks (*Firqat al-Bīḍ wa-firqat al-Sūd*). The Whites, of course, are those of (mainly) Arab descent and the Blacks are former slaves brought from Zanzibar or the African coast. The Whites here may number 60 (males) and the Blacks 200 to 250 (males). In the whole island there are perhaps altogether 500 Blacks. They have a headman (*muqaddam*) chosen for them by the Sultan , but the Whites have no official *muqaddam*. Bā Ḥārith stated that the Whites do not want to be separate from the Blacks but the Blacks do not want the Whites in their organization.

The 1954 Residency report avers that before the Mahrah, Sayyids from Ḥaḍramawt, mainly Āl Ḥāmid and 'Aydarūs became domiciled in Socotra but they have no influence now except that they form the *muqaddam* class, acting as agents between the Bedu and the visiting dhow *nākhudhās*, and they carry out the limited garden cultivation on the island. The Mahrah however have been on Socotra for some centuries and it is more likely that the Sayyid houses came there under Mahrah aegis than otherwise. In fact at the present time the Arab *muqaddam* said, the Sayyids work with the Government. The notables, whether Ashrāf (Sayyids) or other classes, buy or rent from the Sultan various sorts of monopoly: to deal in pearls; the import of grain; export of ghee; transport. We found that a Sayyid had the monopoly of arranging the hire of camels and a private camel-owner pays the agent one day's hire out of five, i.e. 20% of his earnings. Flogging and fines are inflicted on persons who infringe these rights.

The capitalists, it was commented, control affairs in the ports and also in the State Council – my notes record that this consisted, at our meeting with it, of four members and the Sultan (I have recorded no Sayyid names among them). There is no opening for an able man apart from this group. The Sultan, his servants and the merchants are well off but not the rest of the Arab group.

Greetings to the Ashrāf, according to Al-Khālidī, commence with kissing the knee (a sign of respect also in South Arabia) then rubbing noses, then shaking hands – this is a somewhat prolonged proceeding! At Ghubbah we saw women kissing the knees of an older man out of respect. This, they said, is a custom (*ṣil'ah = 'ādah*), adding that 'the young person with us bows down to the old! (*Al-ṣaghīr 'inda-nā yitkī 'ala 'l-shāyib*)'.

ḤADĪBŪH

The palm groves in Ḥadībūh belong to the Whites (*al-Bīḍ*) and the Blacks (*Al-*

Sūd) work on the palms, receiving a fifth of the crop (*maḥsūl*) of dates. Brown thinks that between a quarter and a third of all the palms on the island belong to the Sultanic family. In Ḥadībūh it is at once evident that the large property owners, who sometimes are also merchants, have a strong hold on the place. The Blacks do not have property but engage in manual work, in fishing, etc.

The Khawr or lagoon at Ḥadībūh belongs to the Sultan, and the dam (*sidd*) at the mouth of the lagoon is broken down by the sea four and five times each year and has to be rebuilt. Earlier floods of high seas had destroyed the entrance to the Khawr and if it were left in such a state the area planted with palms would be destroyed by the seas entering and eroding it. To get such work as repairs to the Khawr carried out the Sultan speaks with the *Muqaddam* and he summons to a designated time of meeting or assembly and sees in general to the matter of the repair. On April 10th the Blacks came in procession, followed by the women singing and dancing to drums just as is done in Ḥaḍramawt, the men dancing in ranks of three, four or five. Sultan 'Īsā b. 'Alī does not pay for services of this type, nor is a meal provided for the men. The workmen are summoned to work and the penalty for not turning up is sixty lashes with the rib of a palm frond. I have, however, noted that a *qullah* in Socotra is the term for a *qawṣarah* or basketful of dates paid to the men who mend the Khawr dam – I think, by the Sultan. This I assume to be the Gulf measure, *qallah,* of 37.5 lb. If the Blacks work for the Arab owner (*mawwāl*) of palm groves they demand a wage and refuse to work without it, so they do receive something in return for their labour for private persons.

Bearing in mind the elaborate organization of the quarters or wards of the Ḥaḍramī towns that I have described elsewhere, I made inquiries to see how municipal services operated in Ḥadībūh. There is only a single ward or quarter here and the arrangement for services provided at marriages and funerals (*janāzah*) seems to be similar to those in Ḥaḍramawt. This is of course not surprising in view of the prominent Ḥaḍramī element in the coastal settlements, but it is likely to be much simpler and there is some indication that they also survived in such east African cities as Mogadishu; it would be interesting to see if they also exist in Oman. All through the night of April 8th till the morning of the 9th a marriage was being celebrated in Ḥadībūh with drums and processions, and women were out on the roofs in the morning to see the spectacle. I noticed a squad of men running and chanting with a ship's sail to use as an awning somewhere, just as they do in al-Mukallā and Mombassa.

Most of the foregoing information was provided by Sa'd b. 'Ali Ba Ḥarith, whose ancestors came from Ghurfat Bā 'Abbād of Ḥaḍramawt.

As in Ḥaḍramawt, boys below puberty are distinguished by wearing a sort of pig-tail type of lock allowed to grow on the back of the head the remainder of which is shaved (to the best of my memory anyway); this lock is called *qarhan,* Arabic *qurūn,* horns.

MOSQUES AND CEMETERIES AT ḤADĪBŪH

Even in the coastal townlets and villages one gets the impression that Islam has penetrated only superficially into the lives of the inhabitants – this is in strong contrast to the cities of Ḥaḍramawt where it is all-pervading. 'Abd al-Razzāq al-Khālidī, writing in 1959 speaks about the general ignorance of religion and *sharī'ah* law and gives as an example a decree by the *qāḍī* that one of the Sultan's slaves (*'abīd*) could marry his wife's sister, but an Omani *qādī* on the island stopped any such proceeding. The Sayyids, of some individuals have had a religious education, can be expected to promote the *sharī'ah* where possible.

In Ḥadībūh there are actually four mosques: the Jāmi' Mosque for the Friday Prayer, Masjid al-Rawḍah, also called Masjid Bā Ḥārith, opposite the house of the *Muqadam* who was the Expedition's main local contact; Masjid al-Nūr near the Sultan's mansion; Masjid 'Abd al-Raḥīm fairly close to the shore. Masjid al-Nūr is on the site of the old Ḥukūmah or Government. There are said to have been about four old muzzle-loading guns in Ḥadībūh, one of which lies near this mosque – the others were probably built into its foundations when it was constructed. Probably the remaining gun stood on Ḥukūmah roof.

Somewhat similar to the fashion in Tarīm of Wādī Ḥaḍramawt the several constituent groups of the population are buried separately. The Whites, the Arabs, Sayyids, Sultans, are buried in the cemetery east of Ḥadībūh. It has a strange domed building with nothing inside it. The tombstones of coral rag are inscribed in a curious archaic script difficult to read; dates deciphered often seem to be of the 11th AH/17th AD century. Some show turban forms at the top and some are coloured, or were so in the past. One sees tombstones with carved turbans in Kamaran island in the Red Sea under Ottoman influence. In Socotra they are rather unexpected. Here the Bin Ṭaw'arī 'Ifrayr Sultans are buried, some quite recent sultans, and there was a woman's grave of the Sultanic house. In this and other cemeteries aloes seem to have been deliberately planted. I seem to recall their growing on cemeteries in Somaliland.

The Blacks are buried in a cemetery near the Sīf or shore, and the Bedu (that is the mountain Bedu domiciled in Ḥadībūh) are buried in a cemetery by themselves west of Ḥadībūh. Whereas in Tarīm the three cemeteries are for different social groups, in Ḥadībūh the distinction is ethnic.

At one time, I was told, people used to pay about 70 shillings for a plot near a Waliyy or Saint, but as a Waliyy would be an Arab, or at any rate not of the Bedu or Blacks, this would apply to a cemetery of the Whites.

The other cemeteries in Ḥadībūh, such as that about the Jāmi' Mosque are now disused – one tombstone bore the date 1053 AH/AD 1643-4. The east cemetery, inland a little and east of the Khawr lagoon has a well and one or two *siqāyahs,* little domed receptacles for drinking water of a type so common in Ḥaḍramawt. A *siqāyah* on the waterfront in Ḥadībūh, of a somewhat different pattern, contained water-pots that are filled as necessary by a woman. This is a *waqf* but is not associated with a cemetery. 'Anything can be a *waqf,*' remarked my informant, 'even a slave!'

At al-Sūq may be seen tombstones of the same type in coral rag with inscriptions in archaic Arabic script. A saint, Sayyid Hāshim b. 'Alī, thought to have lived about a century ago, is buried east of our camp there and in this cemetery, near and to the south of his tomb a well has been excavated in the rock. The water, which is salt, is used to sprinkle on the graves so as to keep the soil over them in place – this I can only suppose must be during the violent winds of the Kaws season. Roe comments: *They burye their dead all in Tombes and haue in great reuerence the Monuments of their Saints, whereof there haue been many, But of most account Seidy-Hachim buried at Tamara, who being slaine 100 years since by the Portugalls once inhabiting here, apperes to them, and warnes them of dangers to ensue.* I have not found this saint in the Arabic sources.

In the Jāmi' Mosque at Qaḍb we noticed octagon-shaped pillars, a form one frequently comes across in the pre-Islamic columns re-used in mosques in the Yemen. Outside there is a *jābiyah* or cistern for ablution. There was also a brass candlestick – this is mentioned because there is so little furniture of any kind whatsoever on Socotra.

QALANSIYYAH

Arabic sources consulted seem unaware of this name for Socotra's western port before its mention in the pilot-book composed by Sulaymān al-Mahrī in the early 16th century AD. Ibn al-Mujāwir calling in at the island in AD 1222 alludes to Fatk as one of its four towns. Now the word *fatk* has the sense of a small opening between two mountains (*fatḥah bayn jabalayn*) and this is exactly the situation of Qalansiyyah. Samrān is the name of the low hill lying east of Qalansiyyah (which Brian Doe visited) and to the west of it is Rās al-Sha'b known to both Arab pilots Ibn Majīd and Sulaymān al-Mahrī and identified as bandar Qalansiyyah. Qalansiyyah Bay is formed by the two capes between which it lies. There is a fort on the east side.

When we sailed into the bay from Ḥadībōh on 26th March there were anchored in the port four *'abrīs* (plural *'abārī*) from Quṣay'ar of the Ḥaḍramī coast, come here to catch shark (*lukham*) and other fish – they operate at night (*yukhadmūn fi 'l-layl*) – as well as one *būm* and two *jālibūts,* Gulf vessels like our own *sambūk,* which come from Dubai. On the beach were many canoes (*hūrī*). A dhow, which came into the harbour while we were there, fired off gunshots as a salute – a practice traditional in south Arabian waters, perhaps in the Indian Ocean as a whole. Nowadays Qalansiyyah is reckoned the most important of Socotra's ports, especially for its fish. I noted that the nets (they use the Gulf word *luyūkh* for these) at Qalansiyyah's two capes are prohibited from being set on account of the shipping using the port.

A feature of Qalansiyyah is the lagoon, called in Arabic al-'Ayqah, in which the local people bathe themselves, women as well as men, though the sexes are separated. The water it seemed, in fact rather foul! There were cormorants on the 'Ayqah, and the clump of palms by it at which we camped was infested with land-crabs.

Local industries include lime-burning on the shore and the manufacture of shark-oil. There were also piles of firewood. Salt is brought from the area of Rās al-Sha'b cape and lies on the shore in bags. Fish is salted here and disposed of locally or sold to the vessels arriving in the port. There is some pearl fishing. The rugs known as *shamlah* are woven in Qalansiyyah, some cotton being grown on the island for use in weaving them and for making fishing lines. These rugs, composed of a number of narrow strips of goat hair with cotton woven into them as decoration, were exported to the Yemen over a thousand years ago, for they are mentioned by the Yemeni geographer al-Hamdānī.

We visited a house in the town and think that the building technique is African in nature, the walls being of lumps of coral rag with red clay to cement them. This is the same as in Ḥadībūh houses, where stones are stuck in plaster for the floors at the entrance, and in the plaster of the inside walls. The inside wall of the Qalansiyyah house reception room was plastered and cemented for about four feet up from the ground. The floor was composed of small pebbles of more or less uniform size – which corresponds to the bed of loose small shells one sees in ruined houses in old Bahrain and it is interesting to note that in the earliest mosques in Iraq of the Islamic period the same type of flooring with small pebbles seems also to have been employed. The roof was constructed of beams covered with short sticks, on top of which was laid palm leaf matting of the kind known as *hidmah* (plural, *hidam*). On this foundation can be spread clay and plaster, which are used universally in south Arabia. The windows started flush with the ground and were provided with wooden shutters (*ṭāqah*). Qalansiyyah is very clean and each person with a house sweeps round his precincts and keeps the area clean, but there does not seem to be any local organization to ensure this is done. As the owner of the house said, *Kull wāḥid yinaẓẓim ḥarām dār-uh.*

Qalansiyyah, Socotra's western port, exhibits for its small size, a certain complexity of organization, but in this it probably follows the pattern of Arab ports in the Gulf of Aden and pre-colonial east Africa before the major changes commencing in the nineteenth century.

Qalansiyyah is governed by a *qāyim*, 'Alī b. Muḥammad. There is also a head of customs (*ra'īs al-gumruk*), 'Abdullāh Jam'ān b. Maḥāmīd. These two presumably represent the central government of the Sultan, but there is also a local headman (*muqaddam al-balad*), who settles cases between the people before they go as far as the *qāyim (yisidd-hum qabl al-qayim)*. This headman makes the arrangements for funerals, weddings and all other festivities, which would include the Muslim feasts. I have assumed that as in Ḥaḍramawt he details persons to help in bringing in firewood, cooking and serving, as I have described elsewhere.

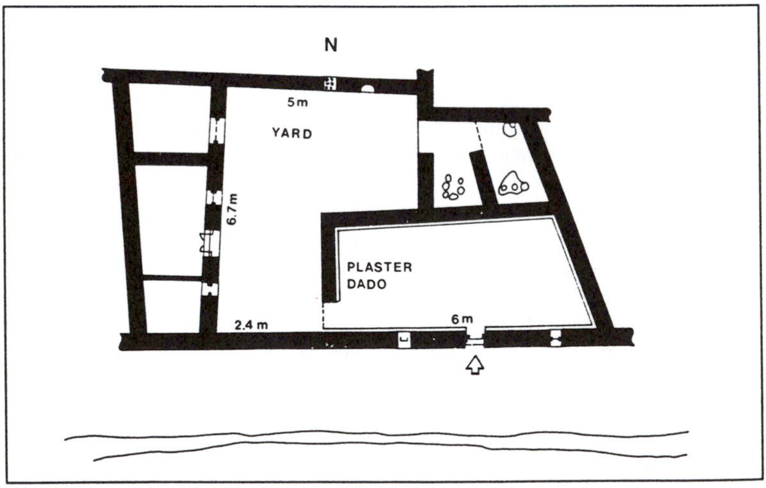

Fig. 49 Qalansiyyah, house near lagoon.

Another office, to be found also in the ports of Arabia, is that of the Amīr al-Baḥr, literally Emir of the Sea, held by a Socotri, Ṭālib b. Umbārak al-Nūbī (i.e. the Nubian, his family no doubt hailing originally from the Sudan coast, and probably of slave descent like the Nūbah of Ḥaḍramawt). He is located at the Customs Office on the shore. His duties are to go out to the dhow captains (*nawkhudhā*) and receive the manifest (*al-gūl*). He returns to the Customs Office with the *nawkhudhā*, bringing back the information about the goods the latter has on board and what he wishes to buy and sell in the port.

The Chief of Customs takes the *gūl* and sends the *nākhudhā* to the *Qāyim*. The *Qāyim* calls in the broker, *dallāl,* who goes round the village and arranges for the supplies of fish he wishes to buy and/or other commodities. The *nākhudhā* cannot leave the port until he has a clearance authorized by the Customs.

The Headman of the Sea (*Muqaddam al-Baḥr*) arranges for lighterage of cargoes (*yuṭalli' al-māl*) to the shore (*sīf*), i.e. the port (*furḍah*), in canoes and for conveying goods from the port to the *sambūks*. He attends to any dispute arising between the sea-captains or the canoes (*ḥādith mā bayn al-nawākhīdh al-baḥriyyah aw al-hawārī*). If a case is too difficult for him to settle he takes it to the *qāyim* to deal with it.

On land the Headman of the Porters (*Muqaddam al-Hammāliyyah*) transports (*yuḥammil*) goods from the port to the houses and brings down (*yunazzil*) goods for shipping from the houses to the port. This Headman, Sha'bān b. Faraj, has a team of porters carrying to and from the port (*al-Minī*).

The Sea Headman only deals with lighterage to and from the ships to the port and the Porter Headman with the transport to and fro on land. The Government (*Ḥukūmah*) of the Sultan has a law (*qānūn*) that decides the charges paid for each of these services. There are two *hūrīs*, dug-out canoes, for bringing goods to the shore, both the property of the broker (*dallāl*), but only Government *hūrīs* can be used for lighterage even when the vessel itself possesses a *hūrī,* so I presume that though privately owned they are regarded as officially licensed. The Headman of the *hūrīs,* also described as *Muqaddam Sambūkī,* is Sa'd Imbrūk.

An institution long established in the ports of Arabia and east Africa such as Mogadishu, is the profession of *dallāl*, who acts as an intermediary and commission agent for the dhow captains in trading and finding cargoes and passengers. In Qalansiyyah there is only one *dallāl,* 'Abbūd b. 'Alī Shāwī, a Socotran who holds an official chit (*waraqah rasmiyyah*) from the Government: he is also holder of the office of Headman of the Sea (*Muqadam al-Baḥr*). At present he is in al-Sawāḥil, the east Africa coast, but Mubārak b. 'Alī is deputizing for him. The *dallāl* has a permanent licence, a paper appointing him *dallāl,* granted him by the Sultan. When he wishes to absent himself he must produce a substitute or deputy who must be a competent person acceptable to the Government. One may assume that a payment is made for this licence, given the Sultan's practice in other cases noted by Brown, but I did not inquire about this.

By way of customs duties the Government takes *'ushūr,* literally tithes, or ten per cent. In Qalansiyyah these tithes used to be charged on what was imported or exported by foreigners, but now they are charged also on exports by locals who formerly were not taxed on what they exported. The tithe is taken even on firewood (*ḥaṭab*) and *shanā*.

One-third of the income from lighterage goes to the canoe owners (*thulth min mahsūl al-tanzīl wa' l-taṭlīʻ li-aṣḥāb al-hawārī*) while two-thirds go to the Muqaddam Sambūkī and his sailors (*baḥḥārah*). When grain comes from east Africa the charge for lighterage(*tanzīl*)from the vessel to the shore is two *kaylah*-measures, a *kaylah* being about 9 *raṭls* or pounds, on each bag of maize (*kīs ṭaʻām mhindī*), and another two from the shore to the house or shop, making four *kaylahs* in all. The bag of maize is 210 *raṭls*, equivalent to 190 *qurṣ* approximately. I noted in 1967 that the lighterage on a bag of grain would cost about two shillings East African.

Each fisherman in Qalansiyyah works for himself, but many of them have a *ṭabīn* (plural *ṭibān*), this last a term familiar in Ḥadramawt for the patron who finances the peasant share-cropper: some fishermen of course work without recourse to *ṭibānah*. The *ṭabīn* would be a merchant (*tājir bayyāʻ-mushtarī*) who will provide the fishermen with clothing (*yiksī-h*), food etc. This no doubt will mostly take place in the Kaws season, 14 April to 11 September, the period of the Closure of the Sea when there is no fishing work (*khidmah*) – though possibly there may be work done on shore in which the fisherman (*baḥrī*) could engage. The fisherman sells his fish to the merchant and the merchant sells to the dhows etc., though if the *ṭabīn* for some reason does not want the fish or the fisherman has discharged his debts to him, he can sell without the intermediary of the *ṭabīn*.

It is not permitted to sell or buy goods for export or import without the intermediary of the *dallāl* and anyone who sells without an order from the Customs Officer (*ṣāḥib al-Gumruk*) will receive punishment from the Government. The *dallāl* informs the Customs of the price and quality of the goods sold for export and the Chief of Customs sees to the collection of the duty of the sale. The *dallāl* receives from the locals whose goods he sells to the outside world 1% (*fi 'l-miyah sh ilin*); on goods imported he receives from the vendor 2.5%.

STAR CALENDARS ON SOCOTRA

As on the Arabian mainland the islanders rely on the 28-star calendar to time all seasonal activities such as navigation, fishing and, no doubt, stock rearing and agriculture. I have already published the Ḥaḍramī version of this calendar known as *ḥisāb al-Shibāmī* along with the agricultural stars of the Yemen. The Ḥaḍramī calendar commences with the star al-Hanʻah on January 1st. Since a comparative table of the Ḥaḍramī and Socotri star-names appears in the Memorial Volume for our late friend and colleague Professor Tom Johnstone in which it is discussed in detail, only the Socotri calendar is given here. Like the Shiḥrī/Sḥerī speakers of Ẓafār of Oman, the native Socotri speakers of the island are dependent for much of their livelihood on raising cattle. It is therefore highly significant that the stars Qānī d-'ilhah, Di'dī, Ṣafáqhon, Karbāloh, mean respectively the two horns of the cow, the cow's front legs, its hind quarters, and its tail-hair.

The Season of Rabīʻ (Spring)

Maʻōdīf	January	4th
Fanzak		17th
Hafānī/Ḥanśiyyoh		30th
Miḍbah	February	12th
Qānī d-'ilhah		25th

Di'dī	March	10th
Ṣafáqhon		23rd
The Season of Sayf (Summer)		
Karbāloh/Midayrakah	April	6th
Midrak/Mudawrik		18th
Shibēloh/Shiballuh	May	1st
Ber Sūd`		14th
Sūd		27th
Ji'ish	June	9th
Qadāham		22nd
The Season of Kharīf (Autumn)		
Fanzak	July	5th
Ḥafānī		18th
Qānī d-'ilhoh/'ilhah		31st
Dā'idī	August	13th
Ṣafáqhon		26th
Karbāloh/Midayraykah	September	8th
Midrak		21st
The Season of Shitā' (Winter)/Ṣayrab		
Shibēloh/Shiballuh	October	4th
Ber Sūd/Sūd al-Ṣaghīr		17th
Sūd/Sūd al-Kabīr		30th (14 days)
Qadāham	November	13th
Shīmah		26th
Māqad	December	9th
Ma 'ōdīf		22nd

Each star period is thirteen days except Sūd/Sūd al-Kabīr which is fourteen. In a leap year a day is added to one of the star periods in Ḥaḍramawt, Han'ah or Haq'ah, but I do not know what is done in Socotra.

Azyab, the north-east monsoon, commences about Shibēloh, early October and continues till Karbāloh, early April, being reckoned as lasting seven months, and Kaws, the south-west monsoon, commences after that and weakens in early September about Karbāloh/Mudayraykah, being reckoned to last about five months. The closure of the sea, *qufāl* was said to commence in Mudawrik about 18 April. *'Abrī* is the north wind, *Maydih* the south, *Ṣarbī* the east and *Ma 'ribuh* the west wind.

The *Kaws* wind my diary records as blowing on 25 and 26 March (1967), which people said was unusual and on 31 March we had a great wind and rainstorm from the north-east which made it difficult to prevent the tents from blowing away. During *Kaws* the people move out, if possible, into the palm gardens from places like Ḥadibuh and they build *'arīsh* huts, which they batten down firmly with ropes and so on. They cannot put to sea for the sea is boiling and the wind raises clouds of sand on the beach. They stay indoors and at this season they get no fish. In the *Kharīf* season when the dates ripen they have no rain.

Socotra is one of several places regarded as perilous by dhow sailors, at which they make what they call a *fawlah:* the word means 'safety, deliverance from danger'. Today this is a festivity with drums, at which the sailors get themselves up in a sort of fancy dress and engage in dancing and horseplay to the sound of drums and singing. The captain gives them presents and if there are passengers they also collect money and present it to the sailors. This is described by the traveller Ibn al-Mujāwir as taking place at Socotra in his day – he does not mention the festival but he notes than an earthen pot is taken and a sail, rudder and ship's gear set upon it, and food is placed on it – a little coconut, salt and ashes, and it is thrown into the sea. Ḥaḍramīs told me that food is today placed in a box and thrown into the sea at Guardafui and other places to ransom themselves from the wrath of the Jinn who inhabit the mountains there. Ashes are commonly put down in places by Ḥaḍramīs when they wish to drive away or exclude the Jinn.

In the Indian Ocean today, as in the age of the 9th AH/AD 15th century Arab pilot Ibn Mājid, sailors have a navigational calendar commencing from Nayrūz (a Persian word), literally New Year, and they date events by the particular day in the 365 days of Nayrūz on which they happen to fall. Historically speaking, Nayrūz has gradually shifted backwards to an earlier date, but for Ibn Mājid it fell in late November. Gerald Tibbetts has supplied me with a summary of his information relating to the seasons for sailing to Socotra from various ports of South Arabia at that time.

Aden – Socotra	As for the normal season for sailing to Gujerat.
Al-Shiḥr – Socotra	Closed on 310-320 of Nayrūz, (September 28th-December 12th) Best about 360 of Nayrūz (November 17th)
Ḥayrīj – Socotra	350 of Nayrūz (November 7th)
Fartak – Socotra	140-150 of Nayrūz (April 1st-11th)
Oman – Socotra	Commencing at the end of the Ṣabā wind (October-April)
Socotra – al-Shiḥr – Ḥayrīj	100 of Nayrūz (March 2nd)
Fartak	110-160 of Nayrūz, (March 12th-May 1st)
Ẓafār	120-170 of Nayrūz (March 22nd-May 11th)
Hurmuz & Gujerat	As for the seasons for sailing from Aden to India

William Barret, in 1584, talking of the Monsoon from Secutra for Ormuz (Hurmuz) notes: *The ships depart about the tenth of August for Ormuz: albeit Secutra is an Islande and hath but few ships which depart as above said.*

In Qalansiyyah Nayrūz is calculated according to the *Ḥisbat Dīs al Sharq*, the reckoning of the village of Dīs which lies east of al-Ḥāmī on the Ḥaḍramī coast. March 28th was *Thalāthīn Nayrūz*, the 30th; so according to this, Nayrūz would fall on 27 February. On 1 April it was told us that in the Gulf it was day 240 in Nayrūz – which would mean that there Nayrūz falls on 5 August – this is practically identical with the date of Nayrūz in Ḥaḍramawt which I have noted as falling on 6 August. In the Nayrūz calendar cited below Nayrūz would fall on 22 November. Arab time is used on Socotra, which means that the day starts at our 6 p.m.

Reckoning from the star Suhayl and the *darr* system (which I found at Ḥallāniyyah of the Kuria Muria islands as well as in the old pilot books), was not used in Socotra.

FISHING

Fishing is an important activity on the island coast both for local consumption and for export to east Africa in dried form, in return for which maize is imported to the island. All local fishing is from *hūrīs*, which themselves are imported from India via al-Mukallā. The Sultan owns nets there operated by his slaves and he sells the fish and/or sends it to the Sawāḥil. He also has *hawārī*. In Bīr ʻAlī a port of the Wāḥidī Sultanate on the mainland, the Sultan's relatives own shops and give advances to the fishermen, who then sell their fish to them. I expect that the arrangements will be practically identical with those described in my 'Customary law among the fishermen of al-Shiḥr.' (The late Sultan ʻAlawī is also said to have dealt in fish.)

This system, as practised in Qalansiyyah, has already been described and there seem to be both fishermen bound by debt – as is probably universally the case on the Arabian coasts – and those who operate on their own account. Brown states that nearly every resident on the north coast has at least a share in a *hūrī. A* hūrī *costs between 550 and 800 shillings, landed in the island, according to size. Being of Calicut teak and carefully looked after they last a long time, and can be amortised or bought by instalments, within the narrow limits of the income of fishing.*

Sardines, called *ʻayd/ʻaydah* in Ḥadībūh, the Ḥaḍramī term for them, are also called by the Gulf and Muscat word *ʻūm*, arrive off the coast from the beginning of the opening of the sea (*awwal al-Futūḥ*), usually early April, and last for about six months. The opening or *Futūḥ*, according to the Gulf system of reckoning, begins with Sihayl/Suhayl; the sea becomes cool but with the appearance of the star known in the Gulf as al-Ḥaymar the sardine no longer remains. Bā Sanjalah speaks of storms at Ḥaymar that wreck vessels when it 'strikes'. This calendar may be consulted in my *Fisherfolk and fish traps in al-Baḥrain*. In Socotra as already seen the *Futūḥ* starts in October or a little earlier and Sihayl/Suhayl falls in August, the *Kaws* season.

The net called by the Gulf term *līkh* from the star Midrak (about 8 September at the earliest according to the calendar) up to the star Midawrak, in which I was told this year we were on 1 April, is used only in the late afternoon until early morning (*al-līkh fi 'l-ʻaṣr ila 'l-ṣabāḥ*). However, according to the calendar Midawrak would be another term for Karbāloh which I have calculated as commencing on 5 April. Sardines are sold locally and for export, but they do not extract oil from them or make *wuzif*. The sardine seine net, the *jarīf*, operated by some forty men, which is so widely used on the coasts of Ḥaḍramawt, has no place in Socotra. At Qaḍb we saw cleared spaces of sand among the stones for the drying of sardines, but this was already over at the time of our visit and had taken place about Ramaḍān, i.e. January of 1967.

At Ḥadībūh shark oil (*al-ṣīfah ḥaqq al-lukham*) is extracted on the beach. It sells by the *tankah*, the petrol can, or by the barrel (*barmīl*) equivalent to 12 *dabbahs*. The Arabs call a shark line *shakkah* (plural *shakkāt*) and the *mīdār* is a hook (*quṭb*) for catching shark, a brutal looking instrument. The harpoon is also used as in Marco Polo's time. Lengthwise slashes (*maṭābiʻ*), five per side, are made in the flesh of the shark at Qalansiyyah, and smaller fish cut open have one or two slashes down the side also lengthwise. At Qaḍb where shark fishing goes on, there were shark sun-drying on the beach, also scored lengthwise; salting of shark and other fish was proceeding. Brown says 'Shark dried is sold by the score pieces – for small pieces of less than 18in. length at up to 20 shillings the score. Pieces over 18in. are graded according to size and make from 25-30 shillings the score.' The prices quoted by him are at Qalansiyyah.

I have noted that fish are sold by the *ṭawbah*, a string of five or six fishes (*ṣaydāt*), but this is for local consumption. Brown found that dried kingfish and whitefish were sold by the *khūt*, a measure of length from the left shoulder to the right fingertips (about 3ft. 6in.).

A Residency reports states that traps and pots are used to catch smaller fish; harpoons (as on the Ḥaḍramī coast) and nets for sharks. The only type of net the Socotri islanders use is the *ṣabb*, which is set up in a straight line; the top of the net has a double horizontal cord in Ḥaḍramawt, it seems, and a cord at the foot. But in Socotra there is no cord at the foot, only stones attached to weight the net down. Aden fishermen use the *tarkīn* type of net with four corners (*rukn*) with anchors (*bāwarah*) at each corner and when there is a wall (*dawwā*) leading to the opening it is made of *'atīr* cord with a wide mesh.

The Socotris are opposed to the use of the *tarkīn* which can catch more fish. I discussed this with a *nākhudhā* captain from Ṣūr of Oman who spends six months at the island and six in Ṣūr, and has two dhows (*sawā'ī, singular, sā'ī*) and a *lansh* or launch. He works on the fishing in Socotra and takes fish to al-Mukallā and Ṣūr, where he sells it. His name is Khamīs b. Rāshid al-Mukhannī and his tribe belongs to the Ghāfiriyyah. There is much *ḥasad* (enviousness) and evil eye, he said, in Socotra. They do not like strangers to catch more fish than they do, and it is for this reason they dislike the *tarkīn* method, but the fish he said is God's providence (*rizq Allāh*) and this is what counts. This Ṣūrī *nākhudhā* obtained a letter from the Sultan to the Muqaddam al-Baḥr at Qalansiyyah granting him permission to use the *tarkīn* net there. Nevertheless the Muqaddam refused to let him do so, so the *nākhudha* appealed to the Sultan and ultimately, through his intervention, he was allowed to use the *tarkīn* there.

It was only this year (1967) I was told, that they had started to use nylon for their fishing lines, though it had been used on the Ḥaḍramī coast for some years.

All over the Socotra coast men henna the palms of their hands as it helps them while working.

The World War II report says it is unusual for Bedouin to eat fish and then it would normally be fresh fish.

As in Ḥaḍramawt, each fishing area has it own rules (*qawānīn*) or customary laws. In ordinary small fishery cases there are lesser persons that 'Alī bin Sālimīn (of whom more below) of Diḥam who make the judgements by this local custom – probably as with the headmen (*'uqqāl*) of the mainland, cases only come up to 'Alī if not settled at a lower level.

We sailed to Qalansiyyah in a *sambūk*, al-Ḥurriyyah (Freedom) with a very young *nākhūdhah* Ḥamad/Aḥmad Sa'īd.

PEARLING

The celebrated geographical and scientific writer al-Bīrūnī, who flourished in the first half of the 5th AH/11th AD century notes that in the Lujjat Barbar, the Deep

Sea of Berberah (?), opposite (?) Aden on the Abyssinian side is 'a pearl bank (*maghāṣ*) of theirs'. He probably means the Somali coast, and he goes on to quote al-Kindī who died in AD 870 as speaking of pearl-banks at Usqūṭar (Socotra) and praising the pearls of Barbar for whiteness, size and beauty. Pearling in a quite small way still goes on at the present time.

The pearling (*maghāṣ*) season commences from the star Sūd i.e. about the last ten days of October, and ends with *Kaws*, i.e. late May – or they leave off pearling at the time of the high waves (*mawjah*). They may temporarily abandon the *ghawṣ* diving in the *Shitā* season (October to December) in such cases. They go pearling from 11 o'clock to 1 o'clock Arab time, i.e. 5 a.m. to 7 p.m. On 28 March the pearlers at Daḥim were back about 4.30 p.m. Each day on which conditions make it possible diving goes on. On Friday it is permissible to operate until 4 o'clock Arab time, i.e. 10 a.m., but then work stops because all must attend the Friday Prayer. Fishing is also prohibited after that hour. This law is also observed in al-Mukallā and probably everywhere else. At the Feast there is no work at sea for two days (*Yawm al-'Īd yawmayn mā shī baḥr*).

A pearl bank is known by the Gulf term *hayr* (*ḥaqq al-ghawṣ*) and the depth varies from about five to fifteen or sixteen fathoms (*abwā'*). *'Irq* is a place of pearl diving and one of these places has the proper name Sha'rah. In Ḥadībūh I noticed a nose-clip (*fiṭām*) of cowhorn suspended from a man's neck – this would be used during the *ghawṣ*. Brown notes that 'the usual method is to search the shingle beds offshore from a canoe, using a glass-bottomed box as viewer: when a cluster of oysters is located, the fisher goes over for them. This would not serve in over three fathoms, and one to two fathoms is the more usual.' At Ghubbah village the *maghāṣ* is near the shore and the Somalis working it there told us they were forbidden to use the glass-faced mask or they would clean out whole beds of oysters. In conversation with us these Somalis claimed that 'Abd al-Kūrī island belong to the Somalis and that if the British occupied it, they would themselves occupy it!

The pearling seems to be free to all comers but the right to deal in pearls is sold by the Sultan. The pearl merchant, called by the Gulf word *ṭawwāsh*, comes from the Gulf to purchase pearls and he gets in touch with the Sultan. The older Residency reports on Socotra state that the Persian Gulf seems to control the pearl industry. Whether there is any tax on the export of pearls I do not know. A man belonging to the Mashāyikh family of Bā Ḥumayd, and coming from Raydat Āl 'Abd al-Wadūd of the Ḥaḍramī mainland, used to offer us pearls for sale. I did not check if he had purchased from the Sultan the right to deal in them. He had, incidentally, three facial scars, made on each upper cheek when he was still a child. This was supposed to be beneficial to his eyesight – I had come across the same practice in the Wāḥidī Sultanate some twenty years previously. It seems that most pearls go to the Gulf for marketing to the external world.

Pearl shell, says Brown, *provides a small but fairly consistent subsistence to the fisherman. It can be bartered for grain at about three-quarters of its own weight in rice – at Socotri rice prices, equivalent to about 80 cents per lb. Of course, the dealer actually paid half the re-sale price for the rice, so is in fact buying at about 40 cents per lb.* I was told that only Somalis export pearl shell (*ṣadif*) or any other shell, on which an export tax is taken of 15 shillings (per *farāsilah?*).

Jawḥāf Shell

A shell, here called *jawḥāf,* is exported to al-Mukallā where a *raṭl* of it sells for about 4 shillings. It was said that it is called *ẓufur* in south Arabia, but if this is the same as *ẓufrī,* which I saw at Khawr 'Umayrah in 1940, it is part of the flesh of a shell-fish of an entirely different shape. It also goes to Aden where it is thought to be ground and used as a sort of perfume. In fact the Arabic translator of Dioscorides knows *aẓfār* as a perfume made from the shards of shells found in an island off the Sea of India. In Socotra it seems this shell is burnt, ground, and put into something (oil?) which women use on their hair.

SOCOTRI WEIGHTS AND MEASURES

Weights and measures in southern Arabia are bewildering in their variety, even as between one small town and the next, so that part of the expertise of the broker, *dallāl,* and commission agent lies in his knowledge of those particular to each place and his ability quickly to quote the price of a commodity according to one set of measures and another. On the mainland the ounce (*ūqiyyah/waqiyyah*) is, to the best of my knowledge, everywhere fixed as the weight of a Maria Theresa dollar and has been so for centuries, but from at least mediaeval times, even in Abyssinia, the pound, *raṭl,* was reckoned to be twelve ounces or thereabouts. The British Resident in al-Mukallā fixed the *raṭl* at 16 ounces to conform with the British pound. In 1967 I was told that the *raṭl* in Socotra is also 16 ounces and the *farāsilah* is 20 *raṭls* which differs from the Aden *farāsilah* – called there a *mann*, but the term *mann* seems to be variously applied. The following list of weights and measures, based on a report to the Residency during World War II, was checked on the island in 1967.

Cereals

Rice and grain are sold by the sack, gunny-bag (*gūniyah*) and the *qurṣ*. The *qurṣ* in Arabic basically means a flat round of unleavened bread but the Ḥaḍramīs use it to measure the honey-comb which in Daw'an and other places has a similar shape. To give an example of how measures vary from place to place, let it be said that the *qurṣ* is used in the Ḥaḍramī coastal districts. 1.5 Shiḥrī *qurṣ* = 2 Ḥāmī *qurṣ*. Two persons eat a Hāmī *qurs* but three can eat a Shiḥrī one! The *qurṣ* of al-Dīs = half a Hāmī *qurṣ*. In al-Ḥāmī both the Shiḥrī and Ḥāmī measures are in current use. The top of a measure is smoothed across with an iron bar (in some places it is left heaped), but this seems to be a fairly modern innovation.

1 *qurṣ* =1 *raṭl* (lb) and a little more.
18 *riyāl Frānṣah*/Maria Theresa dollars/ounces

Rice and millet are sold as follows:

1 *kaylah* measure = 8 *qurṣ*
9 *raṭls*
1 *mann*

Sugar (*sukkar*) is also sold by this *mann*/maund or by the *raṭl*. The maund is a centuries old term but, like the *farāsilah,* it represents a different weight according to the particular commodity to which it is applied.

The bag of maize (*kīs ṭa 'ām mhindī*); c.f. Arabic *hind*. It comes from al-Sawāḥil.

1 *gūniyah* = 190 *qurṣ*
210 *raṭls*

Millet, sorghum (*dhirah/ṭa‘ām*) comes from the south Arabian coast, al-Mukallā and other places. It is reckoned expensive (1967), costing 90 shillings the bag (*kīs*) of 200-205 *raṭls*.

Grain and shells are sold also by the *waznah*.

1 *waznah* = 50 *raṭls*
3 *wazanāt* = 5 *mann*/maunds

Pearl shell (*sadif*) is sold by the *farāsilah* also.

1 *farāsilah* = 28 *raṭls*

Ghee (*saman*) and also oil (*salīṭ*) are sold by the cup (*finjān*), usually half a coconut shell, and the *ṣāj/sāg (plural* ṣiyāj). The World War II report spells this word *sayq*, equivalent to *mikyāl*, but it was stated to me that they were not known to be sold by the *mikyāl*.

1 *finjān* = .5 lb (*nuṣṣ raṭl*)
10 *finjāns* = 1 ṣāj
1 ṣāj = 5 raṭls
1 *farāsilah* = 70 *finjāns*
7 ṣāj = 35 *raṭls* (figure arrived at by calculation, not quoted)

The figure of 36 *raṭls* to the *farāsilah* was what was actually quoted to me; this might be correct in practice because, for example, *Qānūn Ṣan‘ā’* lays down the rule that in San ‘a’ Market, purveyors of ghee should add a little extra to their measure to allow for wastage caused by its sticking to the sides of containers. The World War II report states that *sayq* is equivalent to 1/8th of a Zanzibar maund, i.e. 4 lb. 8 oz.

Ghee is brought into the villages/towns in skins (*qirab*) and is poured into a special large pot called *kibhān* of a hard stone-ware quality, believed to be imported from the Persian Gulf. In this pot the ghee lasts for a year but after that time it begins to have a not very pleasant smell.

Dragon's blood (*dam al-akhawayn*, called in Arabic dictionaries *al-qāṭir al-Makkī*), Socotran aloes (*ṣabir* or *ḥibaylah*), cloves and coffee are sold by the *raṭl* of 16 ounces or by fractions of it.

Ambergris is sold by the *tawlah* (*tola*, one rupee weight). A strange export from the island is *shanā/shinā abyaḍ (Pettigera* Sp.?) there appears to be a black (*sawdā*) variety as well as a white sort – as far as I know this word is not found in the Arabic dictionaries. It seems to be a sort of lichen collected by scraping it off the rocks after rain. In Socotri two types are distinguished *s‘anghir* and *dī ḥānah*. It is sold by the *gūniyah* but we purchased some in a plastic bag. My recollection is that it goes to Aden where it is used for a flavouring, but of this I am uncertain.

Cloth measures were given as follows:

30 *Wār* (yards) = 1 *ṭāqah* or bolt
40 *ṭāqahs* = 1 *bandalah* or bale; e.g. *bandalah Maraykān*, a bale of cotton (lit. American) cloth.
12 *dirā‘* (*sic*, for *dhirā‘*) = 1 *khalaq* or thawb, a woman's dress-length.

Rope is sold by the *bā‘*, fathom, about 6 feet, and *dhirā‘*, cubit. A *bandalah* of rope is 14 *raṭls* weight. *Ṭawiyyāt* are coils of rope. A *tanakah* or tin which is the measure used for dealing in shark oil (*ṣīfah*) is 2.5 *raṭls*. It may also be sold by the *barmīl* (barrel) of 12 *dabbahs* – I have not recorded what the Socotran *dabbah* comprises.

My wife noted in the shop belonging to the father of the Nākhudhā who took us to Qalansiyyah – he came from Dubai – *fūṭahs* from Malaysia sold at 4 shillings, from India they sold at from 10 to 15 shillings or more. Perfume, strong orange wine and blue cotton cloth for girls' dresses, shirts, sugar, ginger root, *qishr* coffee-husk, biscuits in packets, Lifebuoy soap, detergent in packets, silver earrings in tins, belts (either woollen webbing at 15 shillings or plastic at 8 shillings), tins of pineapples at 2 shillings, small onions at 1 shilling 50 the lb, tins of tomato puree, aspirin. I doubt if the shop had much else.

XVIII

TWO SIXTEENTH-CENTURY ARABIAN GEOGRAPHICAL WORKS

DURING the course of my 1953–4 tour in Arabia, I was able to see a great many new MSS, mostly of specifically South Arabian content, amongst which for example was a rare early copy of Ibn Samurah's *Ṭabaḳāt*, the same MS also containing what appears to be an unknown treatise on the grammatical scholars of Baṣrah and Kūfah. A photocopy of this MS is now in the Library of the School, and a brief description is in the *Madjallat al-Makhṭūṭāt al-ʻArabīyah*, II, 2, p. 341. Fu'ād Saiyid of the Dār al-Kutub has recently published an edition of the said *Ṭabaḳāt*.

Some MSS I was able to purchase, the most important of these being a copy of the Chronicle of Bal-Faḳīh al-Shiḥrī, a history which has already been described in the *Bulletin*, and the *Fatāwā* of b. Dja'mān. Other MSS were photographed and are available at the School; in certain cases I was able to make extracts of unrecorded works in MS, but not infrequently I had to content myself with merely recording the existence of previously unknown works. In Rome I was able, through the kindness of Professor G. Levi della Vida, to extract the Yemenite material from his card-index copy of Griffini's check-list of the uncatalogued portion of the Ambrosiana, but this material has subsequently been worked upon by Professor O. Löfgren, and quite recently by Dr. Munajjed on behalf of the Arab League. The Arab League has undertaken the task of cataloguing this most interesting South Arabian collection.

With the new material now at my disposal it is intended to supplement, and in places to correct my previous articles on South Arabian MSS published some years ago in the *Bulletin*, but as this is proving a lengthy task it seemed worth while to publish a notice and some extracts from the two geographical MSS I examined in Tarīm and Dathīnah, for both treatises can contribute fresh information on the historical geography of Arabia.

I

Muḥammad, called Djār Allāh b. ʻAbd al-ʻAzīz (Brockelmann adds b. ʻUmar b. Muḥ.) b. Fahd al-Hāshimī.

Ḥusn al-ḳirā fī awidyat Umm al-Ḳurā

Loc.: Āl Sahl Library, Tarīm (described in *BSOAS*, XIII, 2, 1950, 286). Photocopies at the SOAS Library through the good offices of Saiyids Ḥusain b. ʻAbd al-Ḳādir and Ḥamzah Āl Yaḥyā.

Refs.: Brockelmann, *GAL*, II, 393, *Sup.*, II, 538, for the author only.

Descr. of MS: 25 folios inclusive of the title-page, but one or two end pages are missing, 23 lines to the page, clear naskh hand. The MS is furnished with many marginal notes.

Begins: يقول فقير رحمة ربه . . . اما بعد فهذا تاليف لطيف . . .

Sources: The author quotes from many standard works such as Ibn Khurdādbih, Ibn Djubair, Yāḳūt's *Mushtarik*, Abū Isḥāḳ's *al-Muhadhdhab* (Brockelmann, *Sup.*, II, 669), Ibn al-Athīr's *Nihāyah*, al-Nawawī's *Rawḍah*, al-Sakhāwī's *al-Ḍaw' al-lāmi'*, al-Azraḳī, al-Fākihī, al-Fāsī's *Shifā'* (Brockelmann, *GAL*, II, 172–3, *Sup.*, II, 221) from which he copies very frequently. Another source seems to be Muḥibb al-Dīn Aḥmad b. 'Abdullāh al-Ṭabarī (ob. 694 H. (A.D. 1295)) (cited on fol. 8a), a work of whose entitled *al-Ḳirā li-ḳāṣid Umm al-Ḳurā* figures in P. Voorhoeve's *Handlist of Arabic manuscripts* (Leiden, 1957), p. 274, and has been printed in Cairo (1948); cf. Brockelmann, *GAL*, I, 361. The author states that the only person to compile a work similar to his own in previous times was al-Fāsī from whom he copies, adding material of his own on Mecca, the Wādi 'l-Ṭā'if, and Jedda (all before fol. 13a).

Sources available to the author were the work of his grandfather 'Umar b. Fahd al-Makkī in the '*musawwadat buldānīyāti-hi*', a copy of which has not been remarked so far, evidently some kind of topographical work (cited on 8a, etc.), and *al-Durr al-kamīn bi-Dhail al-'Iḳd al-thamīn* (*al-'Iḳd* being al-Fāsī's history, printed in Cairo and Mecca) (cited on 12b). Other works of his own cited are *al-Farā'id al-bahīyāt fī fawā'id al-buldānīyāt* (cited on 9b) which seems to contain information on trade at Jedda, though a separate work of his on Jedda, under a different title, exists in two copies in Europe according to Brockelmann, and *al-Itti'āẓ li-mā warada fī Sūḳ 'Ukāẓ* (cited on fol. 25b) on the putative site of 'Ukāẓ. A book he mentions but had not seen was *Tanassum al-zahr al-ma'nūs 'an thaghr Djuddah al-maḥrūs* of Muḥ. b. Ya'ḳūb al-Mālikī (cited on 9a), perhaps a treatise on customs-duties, etc., at Jedda though it does not seem to be extant to-day. He also refers to al-Maiyūrḳī's *Bahdjat al-muhadj fi ba'ḍ faḍā'il al-Ṭā'if* (fol. 10b) known to Brockelmann (*Sup.*, II, 635).

Date of composition: After a short description of the contents the title-page has the date *sanat* 947 (A.D. 1540–1) which it would be reasonable to assume is the date when the first draft of the composition was completed. The author died in 954 H. (A.D. 1547). It is suggested that this MS is the autograph of Djār Allāh with marginal notes which he intended to incorporate in the text, but that he never completed this part of his task.

Contents:
- 1b. Preface and introduction.
- 2b. Description of Mecca.
- 4a. The Wādīs of Mecca (Wādi 'l-Ṭā'if, Wādī Mabrad, Wādī Nakhlah).
- 7b. Description of Jedda.
- 10a. Description of al-Ṭā'if.
- 13a. Alphabetical list of villages.

The list of place-names given in the note on the title-page does not correspond with the actual place-names in the text itself, nor does the title-page list amount to the 37–39 names which it variously states are to be found in the text. In other respects the title-page note is inaccurate. By the author's own enumeration the names in the text end at no. 33, al-Hurmuzīyah ; beyond this the title-page only mentions Wāsiṭ al-Haddah and Wāsiṭ Banī Aḥmad, but it also mentions Haddāt Banī D̲jābir which would come before al-Hurmuzīyah—were it in the text. All this confusion indicates, of course, that the work was never completed, and that the author had the intention of giving it a thorough revision.

The list that follows is extracted from the actual text, but additions from the title-page where relevant are given though other problems are left to the editor, Mr. P. Forand, to solve.

13a		ارض حسان
14a		ارض خالد
15a		ارض فراس
15a		ابو عروه
15b		ام العيال
15b		البحرين
15b		بُجَيْر
15b		البردان
16a		البَرَابر
16b		البُرْقة
17a	(Title-page, (?) تنضب المصيف)	تَنْضُب
17a		تنضب الرِقاعى
17a		الجديد
17b		الجُمُوم
20a	(Title-page, الخازنه ويقال لهـا الباركه)	الجميزه
20a	(Title-page, الجديده الحميّمه)	الحادته (*sic*) والحميمه
20b		حدّه
21a		الحُمَيْمه
21b		الخضراء
21b		الخِفْج
21b	(Title-page, correctly خيف)	خَفيف (*sic*) بنى شَديد
22a		الدَكْنَا
22b		الرُكانى

23a	الروضه
23a	الرَيَّان
23b	الزيمه
23b	سَوْلَه
23b	سَرْوَعَه
24a	القَصير
24a	الكدايا
24b	المبارك
24b	نخلة الشامية
25b	الهُرْمُزيّة
(Title-page only)	هداة بنى جابر
(Title-page only)	واسط الهدّه
(Title-page only)	واسط بنى احمد

The author notes that Saiyid Aḥmad b. ʿAdjlān (G. de Gaury, *Rulers of Mecca* (London, 1951), 102, *flor.* A.D. 1360–86) used to rule over six more places which he also describes :

12a	الاصيفر
12a	البَثْنى
12a	بَسَرَه
12b	البقاع
12b	جيف بنى عُمَيْر
12b	الفتح

Notes

Djār Allāh's treatise is dedicated to Abū Numaiy Muḥammad the Sharīfian ruler of Mecca (A.D. 1524–84), whose genealogy he gives, tracing it right back to the Prophet. The treatise is a source of many little pieces of information on the history and activities of the Meccan Sharīfs as well as of geographical interest. Frequent references are made to the working of the irrigation systems in the villages, which Mr. P. Forand has been working out with the assistance in part of the late Ettore Rossi's 'Note sull' irrigazione . . . nel Yemen', *Oriente Moderno*, XXXIII, 8–9, 1953, 349–61. The detailed accounts of the water available in the wādīs may be compared with Ibn Ḥadjar, *al-Fatāwā ad-kubrā al-fikhīyah* (Cairo, 1938), especially vol. II, 147, 158, 189, where the term *wadjbah* is used in the sense of a share of water, p. 158 for instance referring to the sale of a *wadjbah min ʿAin al-Salāmah*. It is noteworthy that the Persians are reputed to have built no fewer than 68 cisterns (*ṣahrīdj*) at Jedda (8b), for they are credited with similar work at Aden. The measurements and description of the Egyptian fortifications at Jedda are given (9a) according to the *dhirā‘ al-‘amal* ‘ used nowadays ’ which is equivalent to one and a third of the Egyptian iron *dhirā‘*. The appearance of the Franks in 922 H. (A.D. 1516) is also mentioned (9b) and details of how the fortifications stood up to their attack. There are also brief notes on the taxes and duties called *lawāzim wa-mukūs* paid at Jedda to the Egyptians in the time of the author's grandfather (8b). At the time of the Mūsim Hindī certain arrangements were made at the port for the collection of duties, and at this time the Friday prayer was held in a third mosque at the gate of the harbour (8a).

II

(al-Ḳāḍī Djamāl al-Dīn) Abū Muḥammad al-Ṭaiyib b. ‘Abdullāh b. ‘Umar Makhramah.

al-Nisbah ila ’l-mawāḍi‘ wa-’l-buldān

Loc. : Copy with the Ḳāḍī of Mūdiyah in 1954, Saiyid Muḥammad b. Dja‘far al-Saḳḳāf, said to be based on an older copy with the Djifrī family in Lahej ; cf. Khalīl Yaḥyā Nāmī, *al-Bi‘that al-miṣrīyah li-taṣwīr al-makhṭūṭāt al-‘arabīyah fī bilād al-Yaman, taḳrīr* . . . (Cairo, 1952), p. 37, photo no. 167. This latter MS is described as a *Muntakhab* or compendium from the above work.

Refs. : ‘ Materials for South Arabian history [I] ’, *BSOAS*, XIII, 2, 1950, 301, where the author is wrongly named perhaps, on the authority of ‘Alawī b. Ṭāhir's *al-Shāmil* (photocopies in SOAS Library, p. 6) which cites him as Abū Muḥ. al-Ṭaiyib b. ‘Abdullāh b. Aḥmad. The title Djamāl al-Dīn would show that his name is in fact Muḥammad, for al-Shardjī (*Ṭabaḳāt al-khawāṣṣ* (Cairo, 1903), p. 26) indicates that the Yemenis call one named Muḥammad, Djamāl al-Dīn, and one named Aḥmad, Shihāb al-Dīn, though of course this practice is universal ; cf. *al-Nūr al-sāfir*, p. 228.

Begins : الحمد لله رب العالمين حمدا يوافى نعمه ويكافى مزيده

Descr. of MS : Copy transcribed in 1353 H. (1935–6), a large two-volume work of 35 lines to the page, in a very legible hand. The work appears to have been composed in 928 H. (A.D. 1521–2), *vide* entry al-Khanfarī, *infra*.

Sources : The author derived much from Ibn Khallikān, though he had no complete text of his biographical dictionary, but only separate parts. Other sources upon which he relied were *Ṭabaḳāt al-Subkī al-kubrā*, *Tārīkh al-Fāsī*, *Tārīkh al-Djanadī*, all well-known authorities, but he then adds,

ثم إنى رأيت ذلك قليل الجدوى والمنفع فضممت اليـه من ينسب الى تلك البلده من المحدثين المشهورين.

For this purpose he relied upon ‘*kitāb mā ittafaḳa lafẓ-an wa-’khtalafa waḍ‘-an*’ of al-Dhahabī, and *K. Tabṣirat al-muntabih bi-taḥrīr al-mushtabih* (Brockelmann, *GAL*, II, 68, gives the British Museum copy the title *Tabṣīr*) of Abu ’l-Faḍl b.

Ḥadjar. He relied especially upon the latter, for his text of al-Dhahabī was very faulty. This he tried to rectify by recourse to al-Shīrāzī's *Ḳāmūs*, and the *Takmilat al-Ṣiḥāḥ* of al-Ṣan'ānī (*sic* for al-Ṣāghānī). Then he found a *musawwadah* or draft of the Ḳāḍī Mas'ūd b. Sa'd b. Aḥmad Abī Shukail al-Anṣārī al-Khazradjī,

ذكر فيها جمله من البلدان مقتصراً على ذكر البلد وصفتها وبعض من ينسب اليها من العلماء والرؤسا المشهورين بل وصل فيها الى اخر باب الرا ثم ذكر بعد ذلك فى حروف متفرقة من كل حرف بلدة او بلدتين فاهمت باتمامه وتبييضه ففقدت النسخه المذكوره مده طويله ولم اظفر بها فشرعت فى جمع شى من ذلك حاذياً حذوه فى الضبط والتبيين.

Some of this material he added to his book, and indeed, from our point of view, this is the most valuable part of it, as the rest of the material is already available in the printed works of the authors themselves. Notes on Ḳāḍī Mas'ūd are given by 'Alawī b. Ṭāhir in '*Uḳūd al-almās* (Singapore, 1949–50), II, 65. Shakīb Arslān (Appendices to *Ḥāḍir al-'ālam al-Islāmī*, of Lothrop Stoddart, trans. Muḥ. b. . . . Shihāb (Cairo, 1352 H.)), mentions a *Tārīkh Abī Shukail al-Mas'ūdī* of which he states, there is a copy in *Ṣan'ā'*. The author might conceivably be the Ḳāḍī Mas'ūd. Shanbal's *Tārīkh* gives his date of birth as 759 H. (A.D. 1357–8), or more likely 760 H. (A.D. 1358–9). He died in 838 H. (A.D. 1434–5).

The author adds that when he introduces information by the phrase, '*Ḳāla 'l-Ḥāfiẓ*', then it is derived from the '*Zawā'id*' of Aḥmad b. 'Alī al-'Asḳalānī (Ibn Ḥadjar) to the '*Tabṣirah 'alā kitāb al-Dhahabī*'.

During my stay in Mūdiyah I was able to avail myself of the Ḳāḍī's kindness to copy out the entries relating to Southern Arabia; with these I have included some entries relating to Africa and India with which it has close connexions. These entries are not complete for I did not copy out material I knew to exist in other sources, and I did not always copy out the lists of scholars, unless there seemed to be some importance in doing so. Some of the geographical material is not yet to my knowledge available anywhere else. I have made little attempt to correct the text, though I have added occasional notes with my initials to some of the contents summarized in English. These were notes taken in the field, and I have been inconsistent, sometimes copying the *nisbah*, sometimes the name of the place itself.

(1) *Entries relating to Southern Arabia*

Yemenite Ibb.	الإبّى
Lahej district (al-Hamdānī, p. 98, بنو أبّه).	ابّه
A *nisbah* to the Persian Abnā'.	الابنائى

الابينى . . . شرقها احور وغربها لحج وشمالها جبل يافع . . . مدنها المشهورة خنفر والمحل وكان فيها من قديم قرى ومدن خربت وبقيت بلا ساكن.

Abyan is described as less than two *marḥalahs* from Aden. Near the sea the author mentions Ribāṭ al-Faḳīh Sālim not far from the place of visitation al-Kat͟hīb al-Abyaḍ (mentioned in other Arab authors, and known to this day : R. B. S.).

الأحورى . . . قال القاضى مسعود كانت فى القديم سلاطينها من كندة يسمّون شجوه (شبحوه) والآن قد سارت فى حكم ال يحيى من بنى ابراهيم يسمون الجحافل وفيها بندر ترسى فيه الخواطف من الشحر وبربره وعدن وغيرهم وهى ذات فروع تتسقى بما المطر وفيها قبر مشهور بالبركة يقال له الشيخ عمر بن ميمون.

الاحقافى — Most of the entry consists of the usual legendary material.

الاَخَبى نسبة الى أخَبه . . . ذكرها القاضى مسعود وقال ان يشرب آل عدن منها قبل Lacuna

It had a *sūḳ* and fields and was inhabited by الاهدوب but destroyed by the two Āl Ṭāhir s͟haik͟hs, ʿAlī and ʿĀmir, as a highwayman's nest, and is described by the author as now ruined.

ارم ذات العماد — This entry contains much legend connected with the plains north of Aden, probably all drawn from known sources.

الاسرارى . . . اسرار قرية من اعمال ريده المشقاص بنواحى الشحر.

A village two days' journey from al-S͟hiḥr. A poet ʿAbdullāh b. Ḥasan b. Muḥ. b. ʿAlī died there.

الاسقطرى — Near Ḥaḍramawt, west of al-S͟hiḥr, lying two days from Dawʿān. (This place is not known to me. R. B. S.)

Here is found الصيد المعروف بصيد اسقط

(Read صبر for صيد. R. B. S.)

أفيق — Near D͟hamār (al-Hamdānī, 104).

الاهواب — On the Yemen coast.

بارق — Yemen (al-Hamdānī, index).

البراشى — *Nisbah* to Mt. براش of Ṣanʿā'.

برع — حصن بذمار

البَروى — كانت بلدة قديمة من اعمال فوه يجلب اليها الصبر السقطرى وكان بها قلعة تسمى عُرْنَه.

The water here is bad. The inhabitants of Barūm are mostly fishermen (as to-day: R. B. S.).

البطان Yemen (al-Hamdānī, 184).

بَعْدانه Mountain near Ta'izz, with many villages, fields, gardens, and forts.

البَوْر — منها آل كثير من بنى ظنّه من آل حرام.

البُوَيْشى — بويش غياض بقرب الشحر . . . وحولها موضعان على البحر احدهما يسمى المكنّى وتسميه العامة المكلّى والثانية روكب وبالمكلا قبر رجل صالح غريب يسمى يعقوب وهو مزار عند مسجده معروف بكرامته ومن نجا الى قبره نجا.

(Extract from Ḳāḍī Mas'ūd).

البياض — حصن باليمن وارض بنجد لبنى عامر.

البيحانى سميت باسم بيحان ابو قبيلة والى القبيلة تنسب الابل البيحانية.

البين — موضع قرب نجران (cf. al-Hamdānī, 82.)

تباله On the road from al-Shiḥr to Ḥaḍramawt, with *nardjīl* (coconut palms), and hot springs.

تباله Of the Yemen. Notes on the Yemenite Ka'bah there and ذو الخلصه.

ترن Yemen.

التُرَيْبى *Nisbah* to a village east of Zabīd where 'Āmir b. 'Abd al-Wahhāb was defeated.

التريمى . . . يقال ان اول من عمرها تريم بن حضرموت بن سبا الاصغر وقد خرج منها علماء فقهاء فضلاء ومشايخ اجلاّ منهم الفقيه يحيى بن سالم اكدر بلج والفقيه على بن احمد بكير وتوفيا معاً سنة سبع وسبعين وخمسمايه . . . واظنهما قتلا فى تلك السنه فى فتنه عثمن الزنجيلى كان بعدن فلما علم بوصول السلطان طغتكين بن ايوب من مصر واستيلائه على زبيد واعمالها خرج خوفاً منه الى حضرموت فقتل بها جمعاً من العلما والفضلا قال القاضى مسعود ومنهم الفقيه سالم با فضل صاحب الذيل على تفسير القشيرى والفقيه شرف الدين احمد بن محمد بن ضَمْعَج والد السبتى صاحب شرح التنبيه والفقيه احمد بن فضل والفقيه الصالح الزاهد على بن محمد بن على بن يحيى بن حاتم والفقيه على بن احمد با مروان والفقيه الشيخ جمال الدين محمد بن على با علوى والفقيه عبد الله بن عبد الرحمن با عبيد صاحب الاكمال لما وقع فى التنبيه من الاشكال والفقيه محمد بن احمد ابى الحب توفى سنة اثنتى عشره وستمائة وفى تريم علماء وعبّاد

وزهاد لا تحصون ومقبرتها مشهورة البركة ومدفون فى جبانه تريم اربعون من اهل بدر انتهى كلام القاضى مسعود وفيها جمع الساده [والاشراف] ال با علوى كالشيخ عبد الرحمن واولاده وحفدته وغيرهم خلق لا يحصون ولما رأ الشيخ على بن عبد الرحمن بن عبد الله بن اسعد مشايخ اليمن ووصل الى حضرموت وأ (أر؟) ما فيها من الصالحين الاحيا والاموات وانشد

مررت بوادى حضرموت مسلما
فالفيته بالبشر متسماً رحبا
والفيت فيه من جهابدة العلى
أئمة لا يلقون شرقا ولا غربا

وممن ينسب اليها من فضلاء المتاخرين اماما وقتنا وبهجة وقتنا شيخى الامام جمال الدين محمد بن احمد فضل التريمى وتلميذه شيخى الامام عفيف الدين عبد الله بن عبد الرحمن با فضل التريمى.

التريسى . . . قرية شرقى محلة المشايخ آل با عبّاد المعروفة بالغرفة.

التعزى . . . دمشق اليمن فى الثمار والانهار والازهار والنزهه يقال انه لم يكن فيها شى من ذلك حتى ملك اليمن توران شاه بن ايوب من قبل اخيه السلطان صلاح الدين بن ايوب . . .

فارسل اليه اخوه صلاح الدين من الشام بجملة انواع من الفواكه فغرسها بتعز. وكانت بها ثعبات نزهة الدنيا وتعز كما قال القايل.

تعز كرسى اليمن
خراجها من عدن
احسب تجد حروفها
جاد اويس القرن

التعكر — Famous place half a stage from al-Djanad, contains a village called العنبره, and Yāfiʿī *faḳīhs* called al-Yaḥyawīyūn.

التنعى . . . تِنْعة قرية قرب حضرموت سميت بتنعة بن هانىء ينسب اليها عياض بن عياض.

Reference by author to the *Ḳāmūs*. This village still exists (R. B. S.).

XVIII

التهامى

التويتّى

ثات . . . ومنه ذو ثات الحميرى قيلٌ من اقيالهـــا.

ثبَاج — Mountain of the Yemen (al-Hamdānī, index).

ثروق (؟) قرية عظيمة لدوس.

الثوبانى — *Nisbah* to a place two *marḥalahs* east of al-Shiḥr.

ثلاء — Well-known place in the Yemen. Wheat and barley are grown here.

الجباى جَبَا . . . قرية بجبل صبر فوق تعز . . . فيه زروع وسكر.

Long description given by author (al-Hamdānī, index).

الجبْلى — Called after a Jew who used to sell pottery (*fakhkhār*) in it.

الجُبَنى جُبَن . . . هى بلدة السلاطين آل طاهر . . . وبها قبورهم.

الجُحَافى — جحاف جبل باليمن مشتمل على قرى وحصون.

الجرْتى

الجَرْدانى — وادى بين عمقين ووادى جيان.

Text Djyān, but probably Ḥabbān should be read.

The author gives the names of scholars from this remote valley.

الجرْفى

الجليلى — جبل الجليل باليمن.

الجندى

الجوفى

الجوّهى — الجوُّه — One stage from al-Djanad (al-Hamdānī, index).

الحاسكى — From Ḥāsik the village near Ẓufār al-Ḥabūẓī.

It has a tomb, said to be that of Ṣāliḥ min awlād al-Nabī Hūd, to which visitations are made. From it is brought Shiḥrī *lubān* and *ṣabir*.

الحبّان — ومدينتها المصنعة.

The following scholars are mentioned here—Abū 'Abdullāh b. Muḥ. b. 'Umar al-Mālikī, 'Alī b. Muḥ. b. 'Umar of al-Raḥbah (? pointing, or al-Zaḥbah), Abū الذبيح Isma'īl b. Muḥ. b. 'Umar, and Isrā'īl b. Muḥ. b. 'Umar, author of a celebrated collection of *Fatāwā*.

الحُجْرى . . . قرية بالجند.

الحَجْرى

A *nisbah* to two places in the Yemen, one being Ḥaḏjar ʻAlwān (pointing added), the other being Ḥaḏjar b. Daghghār al-Kindī (Ḥaḍramawt, R. B. S.) which the author describes, adding :

وعندها اسقطرى الذى يضاف اليه الصبر السقطرى.

الحُدَيْدى — Ḥudaidah.

الحَرَازى — A known mountain of the Yemen where Zaidīs, Shāfiʻīs, and Ismaʻīlīs live.

الحرث — A place near al-Shiḥr and east of Ghail Bā Wazīr.

الحِرْدى — (al-Hamdānī, index, الحِرْدَة).

الحَرَضى (الحَرَض) — Yemen.

الحُرَيْضى — Ḥuraiḍah opp. ʻAndal.

الحزيزى — Yemen (cf. al-Hamdānī, etc.).

الحَصْوَيْلى — Ḥaṣwail in the Mishkāṣ area, with wells and crops.

الحضرمى — The tribes سيبان تميم بنو عكبر الصيعر الاحموم مَهرَه are mentioned as in Ḥaḍramawt.

الحضنى – حَضَن — In Tihāmah.

الحَطيبى

Described as a place near Yashbum of the ʻAwāliḳ. This is probably the Wādī Ḥaṭīb, and the entry evidence of the existence of the tribal name ʻAwāliḳ at this time (R. B. S.) (al-Hamdānī, 89).

الحورى . . . سكان القلعة ال الملكى وسكان اسفل القلعة آل با وزير المتصوفة.

Ḥawrā (Ḥawrah) in Ḥaḍramawt has a *ḳalʻah ḥaṣīnah* (a strong fortress). The Bā Wazīr shaikhs buried there include Abū Bakr and Saʻīd, sons of Muḥ. b. Sālim.

الحيْرِجى . . . بلدة مشهورة على ساحل البحر بحر الظفار وهى ام المشقاص ومحمد الحشريت وشيوخهم الاشعثيون من كنده من ذرية الاشعث بن قيس بن معدى كرب الحضرمى. وفى حيرج بندر يقصده اهل الهند ومقدشوه ويتوسمه اهل الشحر وحضرموت ويحمل منه الكندر والصينه الى عدن وبربره وجده والى كل جهة ذكرها القاضى مسعود.

(For الصيبه the word الصيفه ʻ fish-oil ʼ should probably be read. R. B. S.)

الحيسى

الخاشيمى . . . خاشيم . . . قرية من قرى ريده المشقاص قرب البحر . . . يسكنها بنو مُحَرَّم خدّام لآل با عبّاد الحضرمى.

خبر — من نواحى بلاد حمير قريب الى حوزه الساحل كانت عامره ولم يبق اليوم منها ، سوى الاثار وينسب اليها ملوك حمير يسمّون اليوم الخُمَيْخِميُّون.

الخبّرى (Text الخيّرى)

الخراشى الخرشه برا مهمله وفتحتين ثم الف ثم شين معجمه مكسوره ثم تحتيه مخففه مفتوحه ثم ها.

A village of Lahej on the road from Aden, of the ʻAbādil (ʻAbdalīs: R. B. S.). It is now a *ḥawṭah* of الشيخ احمد بالحفار الاحورى.

الخريبه . . . مدينة بوادى دوعان الايمن ولما استولى الفقيه الصالح الورع الزاهد العالم عفيف الدين عبد الله بن محمد بن عثمان بن محمد بن عثمان العمودى النوخى على وادى دوعان سكن راس الخريبه واقام لهم الشريعه واحيا السنه واطفا البدعه لكن لم يوافق ذلك هواهم فحاربوه واخرجوه وانتقل الى ذمار وتوفى بها فى سنة اربعين وثمانماة كذا وجد فى خط بعض الفضلاء.

الخَلّى — خَلَّة قرية باليمن قرب حَجْر. حَيَاز.

Famous scholars from this village are ابو المذيح اسمعيل بن احمد بن على (ob 724 H.), بن محمد بن سليمان المسلى ابن الزنبول., al-Imām Abu ʼl-Ḥasan ʻAlī b. Aḥmad al-Aṣbaḥī, and Ṣāliḥ b. ʻUmar al-Buraihī.

الخميلى . . . الخميله . . . قريه على وادى عمد بها فقرا صالحون يطعمون الطعام يعرفون بآل يزيد تتصل خرقتهم الى ابى مدين المغربى ذكر ذلك القاضى مسعود.

الخنفرى — خنفر من مدن ابين وهى قاعدة ابين وحاكم ابين يسكنها وبها جامع كبير حسن البنا.

A pious man who lived here was called الشَحْبَلـِي. In the middle of the town are *ḳawm mutaṣawwifah* called البركاتيون of whom he says:

يدهم للشيخ مور بن عمر بن الزغب وهولا البركانيون يسافرون بركب اليمن من الشحر واحور وابين والجبل جميعه وتهامه جميعها . . .

This is, according to the Ḳāḍī Masʻūd,

على ما كان فى زمنه واما اليوم فهى خراب استولى عليها البدو مثل الهيائم والطوالق وال ايوب وغيرهم من داعية الفساد وانتقل البركانيون الذين كانوا بها الى وادى لحج فى عصرنا هذا وهو سنة ثمان وعشرين وتسعمائة تطرق فساد البدو المذكورين الى وادى لحج وخرب اكثرها وغالب قراها وذلك بسبب التفات الدوله الى جمع الحطام الفانى وعدم اعتنائهم بمصالح المسلمين.

الخوارى . . . نسبة الى خوار بن الصَّدف من حمير.

الدَّبَـرى (دبره). *Nisbah* to a place near Ṣan‘ā’ (al-Hamdānī, index).

الدثينى نسبة الى دثينه بالفتح وكسر المثلثه وسكون التحتانية ثم نون مفتوحة ثم ها صقع معروف باليمن بناحية ابين من الشمال وتهامة ورداع الحوامل تحت الكور من الشرق وهى بلاد متسعه فى كل بقعة منها قبيله منقطعة لا تطيع غيرها والعداوه بينهم قائمه والصلح قد يقع بينهم فى بعض الازمان وقاعدتها قرية كبيره تسمى الحافة وسلاطينها الهيائم وكان مقدمهم ال قاحل بالقاف والحا المهمله واليوم المتقدم فيهم حيدره بن مسعود وولده محمد لا اسعدهما الله ابادوا الناس شراً طغوا فى البلاد واكثروا فيها الفساد وعجل الله الانتقام منهم بحوله وقوته قال القاضى مسعود وزعم المنجمون ان طالعها العقرب والمريخ صاحبها فلهذا كان الشر وضد الصلاح غالباً عليهم ويقال انها من المحرومات الاربع فى اليمن وهى تعز والمعافر وصعده ودثينه والمقدسات الاربع الجند والكثيب الابيض وزبيد وصنعا انتهى ما ذكر القاضى مسعود وينسب اليها جماعة من اهل اليمن قال الحافظ ولعله عروه بن غربه الدثينى بزيادة تحتانية بين المثلثه والنون منهم روى عن الضحاك بن فيروز ذكره سيف فى الفتوح انتهى.

(One of the present-day Faṭḥānī tribes is called Al Ḳāḥil. R. B. S.)

الدَّلالى — دلال In the Yemenite district of Ba‘dān in Mi<u>kh</u>lāf <u>D</u>ja‘far (cf. al-Hamdānī pp. 75, 100).

الدوعانى According to a marginal note properly Daw‘an. (The spelling with the long a is not infrequent in medieval MSS. R. B. S.)

In the Wādī Aysar is الدوقه and in al-Ayman, <u>Kh</u>uraibah.

الدَوْمى Wādi ’l-Dawm (pointing added, cf. al-Hamdānī, index) of Lahej. There are *ḥara<u>th</u>* cultivators here. (Full notice in MS.)

الدهلكى . . . وكان بنو اميّه اذا غضبوا على احد من اهل الحجاز نفوه الى دهلك.

Some scholars from this island are mentioned.

الذُبَابه موضع بأجار وموضع بعدن ابين.

الذُبْحَانى جهة المغافر (كذا) فى حكم الدُمْلُوه يسكنها صوفيون يعرفون ببنى المَسَن . . . تجلب منها الاطعمة والسمن والعسل والحلبه الى عدن.

Of the later scholars are mentioned Sa'īd b. Aḥmad al-Dhubḥānī—Ḳara'a 'alā Isma'īl al-Muḳrī, muṣannif al-Irshād (ob. Aden 888 H.), Muḥ. b. Sa'īd b. Aḥmad al-Dhubḥānī of whom a biography is given, the author adding:

وللفواه (كذا) فيه اعتقاد خصوصاً يافع والهنود.

الذِمَارى . . . سميت بفيل (كذا) من اقيال حمير . . . ومن ذمار الابنا اولاد الفرس.

ذمرمر — حصن من اعمال صنعا قيل انها اسم مدينه صنعا وصنعا قصر غمدان الذى بناه التتابعه (كذا)

ذَهْبَان

ذى اصبح — Belongs to Āl Abī 'Abbād, in Ḥaḍramawt. (These are the Mashāyikh connected with the Tomb of Hūd. R. B. S.)

ذى عُدَيْنه — A *sūḳ* and place of *tudjdjār*.

ذى عُقَيْب — قرية بالجنديه.

الرحابى — *Nisbah* to a village in Daw'an (cf. al-Hamdānī). It had scholars, amongst whom was al-Faḳīh Aḥmad b. Sālim Bā Naḳīb.

الرجبى . . . بالجيم من رجبه حى همدان والثانى موضع باليمن بقرب قريه محضن المعروف بحصن المخازم الكنديين قرية يقال لها الرحبه ايضا انشاها الفقيه . . . على بن . . . محمد بن عمر المالكى.

The father of the last-named was from Abyan, and settled in al-Khabar min bilād Ḥimyar (in the Wāḥidī Sultanate: R. B. S.), married there and settled at al-Maṣna'ah Ḥabbān (MS wrong Dj bān). Here the Faḳīh 'Alī was born, and the Faḳīhs, Isma'īl, Isrā'īl, Ibrāhīm, and Bū Bakr. This R dj bah (for which رحبه should be read: R. B. S.) was uncultivated land (*mawāt*) so he asked for it from the people of the district and built a mosque. He was the father of pious sons who يطعمون الطعام, and he died in 882 H. (This is doubtless the ancestor of the famous families of Mashāyikh of the Wāḥidī Sultanate. R. B. S.)

الرخيبى . . . رَخْيَه . . . جهة عريضه ذات مزارع على مطر جبليه واشجارها علوب وفيها بعض نخيل.

(Ḳāḍī Mas'ūd.) Its inhabitants are :

آل بالعُبَيْد آل شحبل وبعض من كنـــده.

الرداعى

There are two districts, one is : رداع الحـَرَامل وهى قرية فوق عقبة دثينـه وفى وسط العقبـه ناس يسمون البركانيون ورداع المذكوره متصله بحصى وهى بلاد اغنام وزرع وفيهم نجده وباس واهلها شافعيه.

The other is رداع العـَرْش of بلاد رديان which has much burr and grapes. (رديان looks incorrect, and الحوامل should probably be read. R. B. S.)

الردمانى This place Radmān has a fort called المـعـْسـال and a village, called Ḳaran, after which اوَيْس القرنى is named.

الرُسغنى Yemenite (?). (al-Hamdānī mentions (p. 99) رسعان.)

الرَّعْرَعِى الرعارع قريه من قرا لحج.

الرَّنْبُولى . . . قال القاضى مسعود . . . هذه النسبه ليست الى بلاد ولا الى قبيله والظاهر انه لقب لبعض اجداد الفقها بنى الرنبول ومنهم شرف الدين احمد بن ابى بكر بن ابراهيم الرنبولى المخزمى نسبه الى قبيله باسفل ميفعه يقال لهم المخازمه من كنده كان عالماً صالحاً صوفيّاً مجاب الدعوه قرا على الفقيه اسمعيل الحضرمى . . . وعنه اخذ القاضيان جمال الدين محمد بن سعد با شكيل وصنوه القاضى شهاب الدين احمد بن سعد با شكيل.

This scholar al-Ranbūlī, mentioned in several hagiologies, died in an Abyan village in 724 H.

الرَوَاحى A village in Ḥarāz.

Reference to the strong tribe of the Banū Ma'n in Aden during Ṣulaiḥid times, and to بنى الكرندى بالمعافر.

الريدى

(Volume II)

الزبرانى Zabarān is a village of al-Djanad (cf. al-Hamdānī, 115).

الزبيدى

الزواحى (حا مهملة) A village of Mikhlāf Dja'far (al-Hamdānī, index).

السآءتى قريه معروفه فى جبل بنى سيف (مشايخ).

السكسكى

السودى (سَوْدة) Yemen, al-Djanad district.

السِيَرى (سِيَر) East of al-Djanad. From it came the celebrated scholar al-Imām Yaḥyā b. Abi 'l-Khair al-'Imrānī, author of البيان والزوايد [*sic*] and other works (cf. al-Hamdānī, 103).

الشَبْوى شبوه . . . بلد ما بين مارب وحضرموت بين جردان وبيحان وبالقرب منها معدن الملح.

الشحرى . . . سميت بذلك لان سكانها كانوا جيلاً من المهره يسمون الشحرات بالفتح وسكون الحا المهمله وفتح الرا المهمله ثم الف فحذفوا الالف وكسروا الشين ومنهم من لا يكسرها والكسر اكثر وتسمى الاشحار ايضا كالجمع وتسمى الاشغا بفتح الهمزه وسكون الشين وفتح الغين المعجمتين ثم الف لانها كان بها واد يسمى الاشغا وكان كثير الشجر وكان فيه ابار ونخيل وكانت البلاد حوله من الجانب الشرقى والمقبره القديمه فى جانبه الغربى ويسمى ايضا سَمْعون . . . لانّ بها واديا يسمى سمعون والمدينه حوله من الشرق والغرب وشرب اهلها من ابار فى سمعون وتسمى الاحقاف ايضا والاحقاف الرمال واحدها حقف والشحر كثير الرمال . . . ذكر هذه الاسما النقيب ابوحنيفه واسمه احمد كان من اولاد تجار عدن ثم صار نقيباً لفقرا زاوية الشيخ جوهر ثم عزم الشحر وامتدح سلطانها عبد الرحمن بن رشد (كذا) باشعار كثير معظمها على البال بال . . .

At this point the margin says that six senseless verses are purposely omitted. They are ضعيفه ملحونه غير موزونه.

(The term *balbāl* is quite ancient and occurs in various Yemenite authors. R. B. S.)

. . . وخرج من الشحر جماعة من العلماء الفضلا كال شكيل وال السبتى وال بن حاتم وغيرهم واليها ينسب خلق كثير منهم محمد بن معاذ الشحرى سمع من ابى عبد الله الغزارى والجمال محمد بن عمر الاصفر الشحرى الشاعر.

الشرجى . . . شَرْجه. North Yemen.

الشَرْعَبى

الشَرْعى آخر قرية باليمن (al-Hamdānī, index.)

الشروانى من نواحى زبيد . . . محمد بن عشير بن معروف ابوبكر الشروانى.
This scholar died in 539 H.

/18/

الشعبى

شُقُره مرسى ببحر اليمن بين احور وابين.

الشَمْهُونى . . . نسبه الى شمهون قريه من اعمال طفار ينسب اليها محمد بن عثمان الشمهونى.

This person is mentioned also in *al-Djawhar al-shaffāf* (microfilm of vol. II in SOAS Library).

الصَبِرى Mount Ṣabir near Ta'izz.

الصدفى

الصَرْدفى Village east of al-Djanad beside a mountain called سورَق. Khazradjī says it is deserted. (al-Hamdānī, index.)

الصعدى

الصليحى

الصهبانى Ṣuhbān near Dhū Djibilah (? pointing). A saint Daḥmal, of this village, was prominent in resisting Tughtakīn's land reforms.

الضبّه . . . قرية بتهامة.

الضحى (كغنى) Yemenite.

الضحيان . . . موضع فى طريق حضرموت الى مكة. (al-Hamdānī, 124.)

الضِراسى *Nisbah* to a Yemenite village.

ضُرَاس . . . جبل بعدن . . . من جهة حُقّات وفى مرسى السفن ولا ساكن به.

ضراس . . . بلد مشهور بجبال اليمن.

طَنُب . . . موضع بين ماوية وذات العُشر.

الظاهرى . . . ظاهر موضع شرقى الشحر على ساحل البحر الهندى وفيه عيون جاريه ويزرع عليها الحبوب الذره والرفه [كذا] والدخن الاصغر كذا ذكر القاضى مسعود والظاهرى نسبه الى الظاهر بحذف الهـا صقع باليمن فوق دثينه يجلب منه الحنطه وغيرها الى عدن وغيره.

الظَفَارى Quotations from Yāḳūt, little original.

ظَفْر Ẓafr is said to be near Zabīd.

العشرى . . . عَشْر . . . جزيره من بحر اليمن سميت باسم مدينه تقابلها فى البر فى راس المخلاف السليمانى بين حَلْى وحرض وقد خربت منذ زمن.

(al-Hamdānī, index.)

العجله — Yemenite village.

العدنى . . . كانت قديما تعرف بعدن ابين لان ابين بن زهير بن الهميسع بن حمير اقام بها لانها كانت من اعمال ابين وتمييزاً بينهما وبين عدن لاعه قريه باليمن ايضا قرب صنعا . . .

سميت عدناً وهى الاقامة لانّ تبعاً كان يحبس بها اصحاب الجرايم.

طول جامع عدن من الباب الشرقى الى الباب الغربى مائة وخمسة وثلاثون ذراعاً باليد وعرضه من الباب القبلى الى الباب الحقانى ماة وسبعة اذرع يد هكذا وجد بخط القاضى جمال الدين ابى شكيل.

(Perhaps one should read al-bāb al-Ḥuḳḳātī. R. B. S.)
The *Ḳāmūs*, says the author, says Aden is an island.

العُدَيْنى

العرجى — (al-Hamdānī, index.)

العيَانى — 'Ayān is a village in the Yemen (cf. al-Hamdānī, index).

الغرفى . . . الغُرْفَه ذات نخيل ومزارع بها فقرا صالحون يعرفون بال ابى عباد ومن مشايخهم الكبار . . . عبد الله بن محمد بن عبد الرحمن با عباد وهو اول من اشتهر بالتصوف بحضرموت . . . ودفن بشبام وتربته من الترب المشهورة المقصودة بالزيارة من الاماكن الشاسعة ومنهم من اعلا مناصب حضرموت.

غُرْق بلاد باليمن — (al-Hamdānī, index.)

الفايشى . . . نسبه الى القيل ذى الفايش الحميرى.

فرسان — Red Sea island.

فرغان — Yemen.

فِلق — Yemenite village.

قبرِين — Place in the Tihāmah.

القرينان جبل بساحر [كذا] بحر الهند من جهة اليمن.

قشن

غب القمر . . . موضع بين ظفار والشحر . . . هو معروف اليوم بعثة [كذا] القمر وهو موضع خطر اذا سقطت اليه السفن قل ان تسلم.

272

قُنُبه — Yemenite village.

قنِي — Village in Maifa‘.

القيدونى   قيدون . . . بوادى دوعن . . . بها فقرا صالحون يعرفون بأل العمودى وبها مشهد الشيخ البكير . . . ابى مدين المغربى وله فى تلك الناحيه ذريه صالحون.

كوكبان

كَيْخار — Place in the Yemen.

اللحجى

المأربى — قصر مارب قصر مشيد باليمن.

Ma’rib is said to be three days’ journey from Ṣan‘ā’.

المَدَرى نسبه الى مدرات كجمع مدره قريه على نصف مرحلة من الجند ناحية القبله.

المُدَيْجِرى المديجره . . . مدينه بمخلاف ريمه.

The margin, unquestionably correctly, suggests المذيخرة.

المعافرى

مَعْبَر — قريه كبيرة فى بلاد الاشعوب. (cf. al-Hamdānī, index.)

المَعْقِر (cf. al-Hamdānī, index.)

مُعِين Yemen (cf. al-Hamdānī, index).

المغزبى . . . نسبه الى المعازبه طائفة كبيرة بقرى زبيد منهم شجعان وعلما وزهاد ولا يزالون يخرجون على السلطان.

ملحان

مُلُص — A village between Ṣan‘ā’ and Dhamār.

فيها معدن العقيق ويقال ان فيه حجراً يقال يشم اخضر الى السواد.

المَنْدَجى . . . المندجه — Village of Lahej.

المِنْكَثى . . . منكث — Yemen (cf. al-Hamdānī, 55, 101).

الناشرى   ناشر حى من المعافر.

Various scholars mentioned who bear this *nisbah*.

النافعى — نافع مخلاف اليمن. Various scholars with this *nisbah* are quoted. (Al-Ṣāghānī quoted in *Tādj al-‘arūs*.)

النجدى النجد قبيل تهامة

النجرانى

نَسَفان مخلاف بقرب ذمار.

النظارى نسبة الى قريه فى جبل بعدان يقال لهــا النظارى.

Ibrāhīm al-Wazīrī of this village ob. 779 H.

نوب Village of Ṣan'ā'.

اليهرى نسبة الى ذى يهر الاكبر الحميرى.

الوسفى الوسف من اعمال همدان.

الوصابى

الهجرى Wādī Daw'an (Ḥaḍramawt), consisting of two villages حَيْداون [sic] and Dammūn. Even in those days it was known as al-Hadjarain. Reference to the *Ḳāmūs*.

هجرة البحبح Near Ṣan'ā'.

هجرة ذى غبب In Dhamār.

هَدَالة Yemenite village.

(*Tādj* من قرى عثّر جهة القبلة R. B. S.)

الهمدانى

الهويب A place at Zabīd.

اليافعى Reference to the *Ḳāmūs* (Ru'ain and Yāfi'). A number of Yāfi'ī scholars are mentioned.

يبوس Reference to the *Ḳāmūs*. Village of Shabwah.

يَفاعى Village of al-Ma'āfir. Al-Fāsī says

من معشار تعز . . . فى واد يقال له القصيبه.

From it comes Zaid b. 'Abdullāh b. Dja'far b. Ibrāhīm, Ṣāḥib al-Bayān.

اليمنى

(2) *Entries relating to Africa*

الباورى . . . من اعمال منفسه . . . بساحل الزنج

This is said to be the *nisbah* of a place باورى, in which there is the Ribāṭ of al-faḳīh Mūsā b. Mūsā.

البراوى (بَرَاوَه) على ساحل جزيره من اعمـال مقدشوه بها مرسى يقصد الخواطف من الهند والسواحل من كل بلده . . . (القاضى مسعود).

البربری ایضـــا نسبة الى بربره . . . بلاد واسعة من مقدشوه الى اول بلاد الحبشه ساكنه امه عظيمه وهى اعجام وغير اعجـام وجميعهم مسلمون وفيهم سرعة العَدْو وقيل لم يغتذوا بشى سوا اللبن واللحم وفيهم الطيشه كذا نقلته من كتاب القاضى مسعود.

البَيْلُولى . . . مدينه بساحل بحر الحبشه عند المعبر الى اليمن وبينها وبين زبيد ثلاثه ايام ومن هذا المكان عبرته (كذا) الحبشه الى المراكب حتى ملكوا اليمن ايـام اصحاب الاخدود وهو اضيق مكان فى البحر ويقال لهـــا فى الزمان الاول اولافقه ومالكها اليوم المديكلى كذا فى كتاب القاضى مسعود.

الجبرتى — Various scholars with this *nisbah* are mentioned.

الجِذَاءى . . . جذا من ارض الحبشه منها محمد بن ابى بكر بن على الجذاى من فضلاء اليمنيين مات سنة ٧٢٣ . . . وكان شخص بعدن مقدم زاوية الجبرت يسمى جِذَايه . . . فسالته عن تسميتـه بذلك فقال انا من بلاد بالحبشه يسمى جذايه.

الحبشه — Al-Ḥabashah is located in the following way. To the north of it is al-Khalīdj al-Barbarī, to the south al-Barbar, to the east al-Zindj, and to the west of it the sea. (The two latter directions must be simply a mistake. R. B. S.) It is opposite Yemen and Dahlak. The Abyssinians are :

قوم سود يرجع نسبهم الى حام بن نوح.

The Nadjāshī of the Prophet's time was called اَصْحَمَه (*sic*, incorrectly).
The Muslims came to him via Dahlak Is.

شرخه . . . بلد بالحبشه يجلب منها الزباد والعاج وغير ذلك.

الفندونى — Fandūn is said to be a village in al-Ḥabashah.

قُمر (or قُمره) . . . موضع ورا بلاد الزنج يجلب منـه الورق القمارى ولا يقال القمرى وهو خرّيف طيب الطعم . . . اما عبد الرحمن بن محمد بن منصور الحضرمى القَمَرى قال السلَفى . . .

Some geographical information on Africa is to be found in the Sharīf 'Aidarūs b. 'Alī al-'Aidarūs al-Nuḍairī, *Bughyat al-āmāl fī Tārīkh al-Ṣawmāl* (Mogadisho, 1955) which claims to draw on Arabic MSS sources.

(3) *Entries relating to India*

با سرور — Ḳāḍī Mas‘ūd says this is an Indian *qaryah* with much rice.

البَيْلَمَانى — Said to be a *nisbah* to some place in the Yemen, Hind, or Sind, famous for swords.

بيله—قريه بالسند.

الجُوجَى (من جزرات) — A city in India.

السُّرتِى . . . نسبة الى سرة كسرة الانسان بلد بالهند وتسمى سرة منيّر.

(This is how the name appears in most South Arabian MSS. R. B. S.)

نَغَر — A place in India.

INDEX

The definite article al- and am- and the usual abbreviation for ibn, b., are ignored in this index – though not the word ibn itself. Where spellings of the same word differ because of the different transliteration systems used in the articles, the main heading follows the spelling of the word as it is found first in the volume and cross references to this main heading are employed, or later variants are placed with the original entry after an oblique stroke.